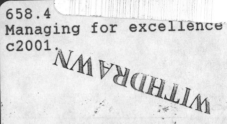

DK MANAGING FOR
EXCELLENCE

DK MANAGING FOR EXCELLENCE

MOI ALI, STEPHEN BROOKSON, ANDY BRUCE,
JOHN EATON, ROBERT HELLER,
ROY JOHNSON, KEN LANGDON,
STEVE SLEIGHT

LONDON, NEW YORK, SYDNEY, DELHI, PARIS
MUNICH, & JOHANNESBURG

Project Editor Claire Ellerton
US Editors Gary Werner and
Margaret Parrish
Senior Art Editor Tracy Miles
DTP Designer Julian Dams
Production Controller Michelle Thomas

Managing Editor Adèle Hayward
Senior Managing Art Editor Nigel Duffield

Published in the United States by
DK Publishing, Inc.
95 Madison Avenue
New York, New York 10016

First American Edition, 2001

01 02 03 04 05 10 9 8 7 6 5 4 3 2 1

Library of Congress Cataloging in Publication Data:
A catalog record for this book is available

ISBN 0-7894-8027-1

Reproduced by Colourpath, London
Printed in Slovakia by TBB

See our complete catalog at
www.dk.com

CONTENTS

INTRODUCTION
ROBERT HELLER

STRIVING FOR EXCELLENCE

Good is no longer good enough. The twenty-first-century manager must continually strive to achieve excellence. That goal applies to all management activities, from selling to managing people, from using financial statistics to the vital necessity of effective leadership. These activities are among the twelve presented in this book, which expresses a single basic truth:

Whatever you are doing, no matter how well
you are doing it, can be done better still.

Great artists, scientists, and other creative people have always known this truth and have spent their lives pursuing perfection. Great managers have the same ambition. They understand that the pursuit of excellence in all areas of life is endless, and that each advance sets the stage for the next.

IMPROVING CONTINUALLY

In management, the principle of continuous, marked improvement operates in a simple technique known as "Half-Way to the Wall." You take any activity and apply a relevant measure, such as time or cost. The wall is zero cost or zero time – obviously impossible. Your feasible target, though, is to halve the gap between present performance and the wall. You then repeat the process the following year, and the next, and so on.

The wall will never be reached, not just because progressively smaller improvements can always be made, but because the playing field will change, through new technology, radical reform or elimination of processes, and/or the success of competitors. However, the essence of the pursuit of excellence remains the same: to strive ceaselessly for both continuous improvement and radical change, and to measure the resulting benefits both in absolute terms and relatively – against the competition.

THE THREE ARENAS

This manual is an indispensable guide to achieving excellence for competitive managers. Such a goal involves working to win in three distinct areas: your own individual performance, the collective performance of your unit, department, or organization, and the external marketplace. These three areas are interlinked and interdependent. By being an excellent manager, you enable and achieve organizational excellence, which constantly measures itself against the best and surpasses that benchmark to set new standards.

Excellence is never easy. Its difficulty explains why Total Quality Management (TQM), which is built around the principles described above, has not been widely accepted and has sometimes been called a failure. The stumbling block is that TQM involves all business activities and all personnel all of the time. You cannot apply total quality to part of the operation and some of the personnel for a limited period. Excellence of quality is either all-embracing, or it is not excellent.

However, TQM has won one battle hands-down. Products were once manufactured to an "acceptable" level of quality– that is, the minimum standard that customers would tolerate. Today the only acceptable standard is zero defects, or as near as makes no matter. Anything less excellent risks rapid defeat in the marketplace. The same lesson now dominates management. There is no acceptable managerial standard short of excellence. Anything less endangers the company and the individual career.

ALL-AROUND EXCELLENCE

Managerial excellence must be all-around. The management tools and techniques covered in this manual range widely but apply in the narrowest specialties. Traditionally, business activities such as financial accounting and managing people have been kept far apart. But that tradition has been exploded. For example, managers are now expected – and compelled – to understand accounting and how to write budgets, while also mastering the arts and crafts of getting top performance from others. Excellent specialists must be excellent generalists.

LEADING OTHERS

The most universal management skill is leadership. Leaders used to be regarded as heroes who single-handedly led their organizations to success (or failure). This was, and still is, a dangerous myth. Leaders depend, and always have, on the contributions of others. Mobilizing those contributions is the task of leaders at all levels. In the excellent organization, the person at the very top is a leader of leaders – and that means everybody who plays a part in its success.

The broader the numbers contributing positively to achieving excellence, the higher the standard of performance and the longer it lasts. Durability is a crucial issue. The excellent manager knows that peaks are followed by troughs unless you constantly renew the pursuit of the best. Excellence fades when the organization and its managers start to believe in their own excellence and forget that its critical achievement lies in the future, not the past.

USING THIS BOOK

The manual begins with the general principles and specific practice of Achieving Excellence. This involves identifying your potential and working out how you can make the most of it. This will require working well through other staff, which leads into the next three sections: Leading Effectively, Managing People, and Coaching Successfully.

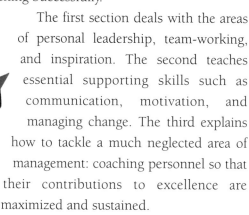

The first section deals with the areas of personal leadership, team-working, and inspiration. The second teaches essential supporting skills such as communication, motivation, and managing change. The third explains how to tackle a much neglected area of management: coaching personnel so that their contributions to excellence are maximized and sustained.

Excellence also depends on mastering technical skills. These are discussed in Managing Projects, Thinking Strategically, Managing Budgets, and Understanding

Accounts. Every manager needs these skills, often on a daily or weekly basis.

The above four sections are all directed inwardly, toward the organization itself. But any internal activity only wins value through its impact in the outside world. Selling Successfully and Marketing Effectively cover a wide range of skills. Once the fear of selling has been overcome, the techniques of effective salesmanship can be easily mastered. However, salespeople can only operate well within a context of effective marketing – using a host of ways to give the customers what they want at a profitable price which they are happy to pay.

Management today is affected both internally and externally by the continuing IT revolution, which revolves increasingly around e-business and the internet. It has been said that all businesses will be e-businesses before long. So it is vital to master what can be done over the web, learning how to use its expanding powers to your best advantage.

Whether the information and advice in this book are familiar or new, excellence will follow from understanding the facts, absorbing the precepts and applying them. Effective management is defined as excellence in every respect and in every action.

ACHIEVING EXCELLENCE

INTRODUCTION

Excellence in today's highly competitive workplace demands more than a thorough knowledge of your specialist field. People skills – such as the ability to inspire others, foster a sense of cooperation, and delegate effectively – are of critical importance. Equally vital is the mastery of a range of practical skills – from effective communicating to time management – and a confident, determined attitude toward your career. A balanced mix of all these elements is what differentiates a competent manager from an outstanding one. Achieving Excellence *provides you with a comprehensive grounding in all these areas. The practical advice is supplemented by 101 indispensable tips and a revealing self-assessment exercise that will highlight your strengths and weaknesses, guiding you to improve your performance and attain excellence.*

DEVELOPING YOUR POTENTIAL

To achieve excellence, you must work to fulfill your own potential. Learn to build on your strengths and to develop the personal qualities that are the keys to performing well.

BUILDING KEY ATTRIBUTES

Human beings have many talents that can be turned into engines of success. Yet the best performance requires more than mere talent: it involves developing a number of important personal strengths, including determination, vision, and confidence.

1 Identify your weaknesses as the first step to rectifying them.

2 Do things the easy way – play to your strengths.

3 Accept critical comments and act to remedy faults.

ASSESSING YOURSELF

You know what comes easily to you, and these strengths can be developed fairly rapidly. Yet your natural powers may not be enough. To reach your full potential, you need to develop all the key attributes. For example, a lack of confidence is a general barrier to advancing in business management. If you are someone who has feelings of low self-esteem, or you lack the courage of your convictions, you will have to work hard to maximize your self-confidence. Begin your self-development by looking objectively at your abilities and where they most need to be improved.

EVALUATING YOUR KEY ATTRIBUTES

ATTRIBUTE	HOW TO ASSESS YOURSELF
AMBITION	Have you written down high and stretching targets and planned how you are going to achieve them?
VISION	Have you formed a clear idea of where you want to be and what you want to be doing in five years' time?
CONFIDENCE	Do you feel able to do anything that is needed now, do it well, and master new abilities and tasks as required?
ABILITY TO TAKE RISKS	Do you believe in your own ability to judge a risk as worth taking and to take your chances effectively?
DRIVE AND ENERGY	Can you bring full mental powers to bear on an issue, to decide on the right action, and see it through?
COMPETITIVE SPIRIT	Are you never satisfied until you have clearly won all the prizes against the best competition around?
SELF-CRITICISM	Are you a relentless perfectionist who constantly seeks to improve and to get others to do the same?
LEADERSHIP	Can you mobilize others to achieve group ambitions, as well as develop other leaders and bring them forward?

ASKING OTHERS

If you are unsure how you rate in a particular area, such as your ability to lead, get objective feedback from somebody else. Once you have all the facts, you can create a vision of where you want to be in the future. Draw up a mission plan of how to get there.

Trusted colleague provides objective feedback

GETTING FEEDBACK ▶
Ask a mentor, colleague, or friend to check whether you have exaggerated your strengths or underplayed your weaknesses.

TAKE CONTROL
Lead your own team or take greater responsibility.

GAIN EXPERIENCE
Seek to develop and expand your leadership skills.

SEEK MORE RESPONSIBILITY
Ensure that you are given responsibility for others.

BROADEN SKILLS
Take a position that will widen your knowledge.

FIND POSITION
Get a job that will give you the experience you need.

GET QUALIFICATIONS
Study for a further qualification that will assist you in reaching your goal.

CREATING A VISION

Once you have assessed yourself and have a realistic understanding of your abilities, you need to form a vision of significant but attainable aims. The great men and women of history all had a sense of vision and mission. They knew where they were going, what they wanted to achieve, and had the power of direction to help take them to their destination. You can mobilize the same power. Ask yourself where you want to be at the end of each decade that lies ahead. Compare that future vision with where you are now. That shows the gap that must be crossed to realize the vision. The next step is to make closing that gap your overriding mission.

◀ ACHIEVING YOUR VISION

Your mission should be broken down into a feasible operating plan that will enable you to take concrete, achievable steps toward realizing your ultimate goals. Keep both vision and mission firmly before your eyes, with revision as and when required, and direct your actions toward attaining them.

IDENTIFYING YOUR MISSION

Now write a hard-headed plan, setting out what you must achieve to realize your vision. The plan must be timed and translated into numbers or hard facts. For example, if your vision is to move into management, your mission might be to acquire the necessary knowledge in year one, join a task force and gain general experience in year two, and obtain a management appointment, inside or outside the company, in year three.

4 Form long-term ambitions to help you notice chances to move forward.

Moving Forward

To help you on the path to achieving your vision, you may find it useful to employ the Japanese techniques of *kaizen* and *kaikaku,* or continuous improvement and radical change. *Kaizen* involves constantly looking for ways to improve any element of your performance, like athletes do when they seek to raise their Personal Best (PB). *Kaikaku* takes place less often. It could be going into business for yourself, moving to a new job in a new industry or new company, or both. Look out for opportunities for radical change, and use them.

5 Take responsibility at the earliest opportunity.

6 Have targets for both achievement and career moves.

7 Never be afraid to learn and use the lessons of your failures.

Looking Ahead

It is far more useful to concentrate on goals achieved and future opportunities than on missed chances. If you miss an opportunity, do not waste time on regrets, but examine why it was ignored or rejected. For example, if you conclude that you lacked the confidence to take a risk, you must develop the confidence to act swiftly next time.

Comparing Visions at Different Career Stages

Senior Manager
At this level, your vision for yourself goes hand-in-hand with a vision of what your organization can become. You see the road from where the organization is now to this future goal, and you envisage yourself playing a key part, maybe the leading one, in the journey.

Unit Manager
You have a clear vision for the success of your unit and an ambitious idea of your own position five years on after achieving that vision.

First Line Manager
You now have responsibility for others and envisage developing your people skills and building the business experience that will take you upward.

First Job Employee
Your vision is personal. You envisage yourself acquiring the knowledge, experience, and skills needed for advancement in the shortest possible time.

DEVELOPING CONFIDENCE

*C*onfidence in yourself and in your abilities is an essential attribute. You can develop self-confidence through experience and training, just as you can learn to use your self-assurance to "sell yourself" when seeking to impress others.

8 Always expect to outdo others at whatever task you undertake.

GETTING FEEDBACK

ASK YOUR SUPERIOR
How well am I doing my job? Am I developing abilities that will earn promotion?

Manager

ASK YOUR PEER
Do I help you to do your job better? Am I an effective member of the team?

Colleague

ASK YOUR SUBORDINATE
Do I give you the support you need? Can I do anything different?

Employee

DOING YOUR BEST

You can strengthen your confidence by dwelling on what you do well. Do not compare yourself unfavorably with others, or suppose that others are judging you adversely. If you do feel inadequate in any area, train to improve your skills. Take pride in what you have done well, and approach your tasks like a professional athlete: train to improve strengths and eliminate weaknesses, but recognize that doing as well as you can, and constantly raising that level, is the most that you (and others) can expect.

SEEKING ADVICE

People continually observe and frequently judge what you are doing and how – think of yourself as an advertisement that is always "on air." Being scrutinized by others may feel uncomfortable, but your confidence will improve if you know that the observations are positive. Do not be afraid to seek feedback from customers, employers, superiors, colleagues, and suppliers. Having received the feedback, act on what you have learned. This is not the same as seeking the approval of others. You are using their informed and critical advice to improve your performance and thus to feel better about yourself. Take criticisms on board – but do not allow others to damage your self-esteem.

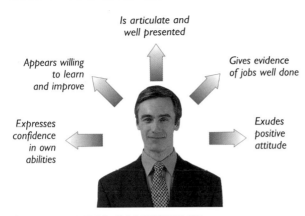

Is articulate and well presented

Appears willing to learn and improve

Gives evidence of jobs well done

Expresses confidence in own abilities

Exudes positive attitude

9 Keep answers in interviews crisp and to the point.

10 Remember to give yourself credit when you know you deserve it.

▲ APPEARING CONFIDENT

When you are being interviewed, or assessed in your current job, those judging you will be looking for signs of a confident attitude. Have faith in your own ability, and others will recognize it.

HANDLING INTERVIEWS

You want to make a confident impression at interviews, whichever side of the table you occupy. For example, whether interviewing an applicant for a job, or applying yourself, you should be neatly attired. Where possible, prepare for the meeting as you would for a speech. Read background information, compile a list of the questions you want to cover, even rehearse especially important points. Seek to end the interview with a definitive summary.

MAKING A GOOD IMPRESSION ▶

It is easier to look confident if you are confident. You should be, provided that you know your subject and are aware of your abilities. Feeling nervous does not mean that you have no confidence; a total lack of anxiety indicates overconfidence.

Direct eye contact shows confidence

Leaning forward indicates eagerness

Hand movements are free and expressive

11 Mentally rehearse how you want an interview to go, and compare that with what does happen.

MASTERING RISK-TAKING

To make significant gains, you must take risks. Confidence and courage are required, as is the ability to look in all directions before you leap. But those who can learn to think, act, and build businesses like entrepreneurs have golden futures.

12 Back yourself – the only risk is that your judgment may not be correct.

HAVING COURAGE

Being entrepreneurial means believing in your own ability and being brave enough to risk being wrong. When dealing with risk, try to think like an entrepreneur: calculate whether a risk is worthwhile, and if it is, have the courage and self-confidence to take it. You can take advice all along the line. But the ultimate "go/no-go" decision is yours alone. If you can take it confidently, then you are being an entrepreneurial manager.

13 Never let an opportunity pass, but think twice before acting.

BEING POSITIVE

Any decision, from starting an enterprise to accepting a new job, has an upside and a potential downside. When facing any risk, adopt the best mental attitude and concentrate on the positive potential, the upside. But be aware that there is always a downside. Even the most gung-ho person considers, even if subconsciously, what will happen if the worst comes to the worst. If the downside is personally unacceptable, look for ways of limiting the risk – ideally a fail-safe position.

▲ ACCEPTING THE DOWNSIDE
Before taking a risk, such as relocating to a new job, decide whether you can accept the downside. If the downside is unacceptable, for example you cannot face selling your family home, look at all the feasible ways of limiting that risk.

CALCULATING RISK

Do not be misled by the old investment maxim that says "the higher the return, the greater the risk." In fact, the upside on a relatively safe move, such as changing jobs, can be very great. However, you must always calculate the risk before taking it, by doing a few simple yet effective calculations. Remember, too, that doing nothing may involve a hidden risk. If you do not make a decision, you might fail to make a breakthrough, either in your career, financially, or in business. If you fail to spot this concealed risk, you will suffer the consequences.

14 Use lists of pros and cons to test your feelings.

15 Do your research, and avoid taking action before you have all the facts.

▼ **RISKING A JOB MOVE**
Work out the likelihood of getting what you want if you move. Next, rate the likelihood of realizing your hopes in your present job. If moving gains a higher total score, the risk is justified.

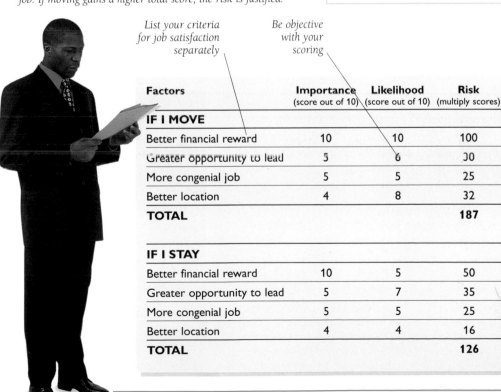

List your criteria for job satisfaction separately

Be objective with your scoring

Factors	Importance (score out of 10)	Likelihood (score out of 10)	Risk (multiply scores)
IF I MOVE			
Better financial reward	10	10	100
Greater opportunity to lead	5	6	30
More congenial job	5	5	25
Better location	4	8	32
TOTAL			**187**
IF I STAY			
Better financial reward	10	5	50
Greater opportunity to lead	5	7	35
More congenial job	5	5	25
Better location	4	4	16
TOTAL			**126**

DEVELOPING DRIVE

You need physical energy to do any job well. But the energy that makes the difference between success and failure is in the mind. You can generate drive by determinedly and persistently channeling your energy toward a chosen purpose.

16 Put ambitions on paper so that you can view them as practical plans.

BEING DETERMINED

It is only human to have grand ideas that you never turn into reality, yet ambitious plans are often perfectly viable. What is lacking is the willpower to activate them. Keep ideas alive by planning action – having the right mind-set will help to draw your attention to valuable observations that you might otherwise miss. Only abandon your plans because analysis has revealed their faults, not because mental laziness or fear have stopped you in your tracks.

17 Make it a rule never to give up easily, but to keep on trying.

MASTERING MIND-SET

Drive and energy suggest physical attributes. It is true that, just as some people are born with greater physical powers, so certain psychological gifts are innate. But there is a critical similarity between the physical and the mental. Everybody can choose and reach a target for personal success. By concentrating on that objective, you will generate drive toward achieving the end. You can multiply your energy by channeling it toward the purpose on which your mind is set.

SETTING A TARGET ▶

Everybody can set themselves a target for, say, running faster, which can be reached by training. Even though most people will never even approach the speed of real athletes, their performance can still improve markedly.

SEEING IT THROUGH

There are times when giving up is the right policy. But it can work like a self-fulfilling prophecy. Because you are willing to stop, the activity stops, whether it is learning a new language or starting a new business. Many people stop short of their full potential by abandoning a project before reaching their original goal. It may still be within reach, in which case you should carry on. On the other hand, everybody knows examples of people fruitlessly chasing impossible targets. Before deciding to give up, analyze the possible outcomes. If the upside still greatly exceeds the downside, mobilize your drive and energy to pursue the desired conclusion.

18 When one goal is achieved, set a new, higher one.

19 Imitate somebody with drive and energy to develop those qualities.

ASSESSING YOUR DRIVE QUOTIENT

Read through the statements below to see which describe you best. If you agree with most statements on the left, your driving ambition is very high. The more statements you agree with on the right, the harder you need to work on developing your drive.

- You see yourself as a younger person.
- You are stable, calm, adventurous, socially bold, confident, and self-assured.
- You have a high need for achievement.
- You welcome change as positive.
- You have a sense of freedom and feel that you are going somewhere.
- You enjoy taking calculated risks.
- You spend a lot of time with superiors.
- Your career has proved more successful than you originally hoped.
- You are willing to move.
- You are rarely ill or absent from work.
- Stress and tension do not affect you.
- You do not smoke and you get exercise.

- You see yourself as an older person.
- You are emotional, shy, restrained, apprehensive, and worry too much.
- You have a low need for achievement.
- You do not like change.
- You feel as though you are locked in, stagnating, and going nowhere.
- You always play it safe.
- You spend no time with superiors.
- Your career has proved less successful than you originally hoped.
- You are unwilling to move.
- You are often ill or absent from work.
- You often feel stressed and tense.
- You smoke and you do not get exercise.

LEADING EFFECTIVELY

The ability to lead others is a prime attribute. To fulfill your leadership potential, learn how to get people to work with you and for you productively, using their initiative for better results. You also need to develop leaders among your staff.

20 Avoid asking others to do anything you would not do yourself.

21 Always seize an opportunity to delegate tasks.

ENCOURAGING PARTICIPATION ▼

Bringing competent employees to the fore is a leader's prime task. Allow others to take the initiative whenever possible, encouraging them to contribute their own suggestions and ideas.

MANAGING OTHERS

To get the best from people who are working for you, it is essential to set a credible example yourself. Employees will excel themselves for somebody in whose strength and wisdom they truly believe. They also expect professional competence, part of which includes delegating tasks in order to increase staff members' self-management and participation. Ascertain where your employees' strengths and weaknesses lie, then delegate responsibilities that will both exploit these strengths and meet the organization's needs.

Employee feels encouraged to use own initiative

Colleague feels free to put forward ideas

Team member feels involved and motivated

Manager takes a back seat during meeting

WINNING COOPERATION

Cooperation between a manager and his or her staff requires commitment from both sides. If you expect cooperation, you must also give it, while still remaining in overall control. Two key questions to ask your staff are: "What do I do that stops you from doing a better job?" and "What can I do to help you perform better?" If you co-operate by acting on their answers, for example by investing in new tools or training if requested, you can bring about major improvements in performance. Not acting on that feedback will have an adverse effect. Your main objective as leader is to help staff to help themselves.

22 Actively seek feedback on your own effectiveness.

23 Always remember that leaders are only as good as those they lead.

QUESTIONS TO ASK YOURSELF

Q Do I give others the chance to speak, rather than invariably put forward my own ideas?

Q Am I loyal to my staff when representing them, both inside and outside the organization?

Q Do I avoid getting involved in office politics?

Q Do I strive to achieve a positive atmosphere, in which people compete with ideas?

DEVELOPING LEADERS

As a manager, you must ensure that you receive the requisite training to develop prioritizing, progress-chasing, delegation, and motivating skills. Make these an integral part of your personal development plan, and ensure that staff members – especially your deputies – also develop their own leadership skills. Listening carefully, criticizing constructively, being tolerant of error while correcting mistakes, and retaining objectivity are all vital leadership qualities. In seeking to develop your own potential, you should also be helping others to develop theirs.

BUILDING LEADERSHIP SKILLS

All leaders need strong personality traits to assert influence and function. They must also have the ability to facilitate and inspire. To lead others well, you must:

- Ensure that everyone is working toward agreed, shared objectives;
- Criticize constructively, praising merit as well as finding fault;
- Encourage the generation of new ideas;
- Insist on the highest standards;
- Develop individual and team skills and strengthen them by training.

STAYING IN SHAPE

*F**itness has many dimensions. It is unfair to yourself to expect peak performance at work when your mind and body are in poor shape. Your lifestyle and the amount of exercise you get will affect both your potential and your achievement.***

24 Measure your fitness and get exercise to raise that level.

MAINTAINING HEALTH

The majority of people need to make only minimal adjustments to their lifestyle to improve their fitness and maintain the good health that is essential for effective performance. Getting adequate rest, eating a balanced diet, and getting regular exercise are all wise policies, and beneficial in themselves. By leading a balanced lifestyle and looking after your physical wellbeing, you will find that you have a great deal more stamina and energy to achieve your potential at work.

◀ IMPROVING FITNESS
Cycling is a great form of exercise; but to improve your level of fitness you need to set yourself targets. Aim to increase your speed over a known distance, and you will soon feel the benefits.

EXERCISING THE BODY

Any fitness program should give you a measured standard of fitness. The best standard is aerobic fitness, which measures the efficiency of the heart and lungs. Some sports, such as rowing, require a high level of aerobic fitness. Others, such as cycling and running, can be used to build up your aerobic fitness gradually, by slowly increasing your speed over a set distance. Choose a sport that you enjoy and set yourself targets for improvement. You will soon feel the benefits, both physically and mentally.

25 Find a fitness regime you enjoy and that makes you feel good.

ACHIEVING FITNESS

SPORT	RECOMMENDED FREQUENCY	AEROBIC VALUE
CYCLING	30–45 minutes, three times a week.	Very high
ROWING	3 hours, once a week.	Very high
RUNNING	30–45 minutes, three times a week.	Very high
SWIMMING	45 minutes, three times a week.	Very high
SOCCER	1–2 hours, twice a week.	High
WALKING	45 minutes, three times a week.	High
SQUASH	1 hour, twice a week.	Medium
TENNIS	1–2 hours, twice a week.	Medium
VOLLEYBALL	1–2 hours, twice a week.	Medium
GOLF	36 holes, once a week.	Low

26 Combine aerobic value with ways of exercising all the key muscles.

27 Do not patiently tolerate pain, but obtain advice about its cause and cure.

STAYING NIMBLE

Aerobic fitness is by no means the only standard. Balance, flexibility, and strength are other, often neglected aspects of fitness. You can improve these by working out in a gym. But you can help yourself a great deal by simply walking briskly, bending, stretching, sitting and standing straight, and so on. Spending 10 minutes a day on suitable stretching exercises, including yoga and t'ai chi, is highly beneficial. If you still end up with aches and pains, they may be work-related – for example, if you slouch at your desk, you may well be straining your back. In such cases, osteopathy and similar therapies can produce miraculous results.

EATING FOR FITNESS

Your food gives you vital nutrients for health and calories for energy. Business life offers many temptations that work against eating sensibly, and the snatched sandwich at the desk, lunchtime drinking, and expense account feasts can all have bad effects on the concentration, the digestion, and the waistline. Have a target weight, keep to it by controling your calories, and take a vitamin supplement as insurance against missing nutrients.

▲ **EATING HEALTHILY**
No matter how busy you are, make time for breakfast. Cereals or bread and fresh fruit or juices give you the energy you need to start the day.

28 Retain your energy levels by eating small, regular meals.

29 Never ignore any symptom of stress – get treatment.

SEEKING HELP

The stresses and strains of working life can trigger breakdowns, ranging from minor depression to total collapse. The solution is the same as for any physical symptoms: if you feel that your mental fitness is being significantly impaired, get advice. Simply talking to a friend or to your doctor may provide enough help. Pharmaceutical drugs can help, while alternative therapies, such as meditation, have their place, too. But suffering in silence will reduce your performance and may eventually devastate your ability to work.

AVOIDING DEPRESSION

The more you agree with these statements, the more likely it is your mental health is good. The more you disagree, the more likely you are to be suffering mild depression or worse:

● I do not feel at all unhappy.
● I am optimistic about the future.
● I do not feel a failure.
● I am fairly satisfied with life.
● I do not feel particularly guilty.

● I have no thoughts of harming myself.
● I am not disappointed with myself.
● I am interested in other people.
● I make decisions as well as ever.
● I look as good as I used to.
● I can work as well as ever.
● I do not get more tired than usual.
● My appetite is as good as ever.
● I do not overindulge.

▲ GETTING AWAY

Vacationing with your family or friends allows you to get away from the pressures of your daily routine and work-related stress. A number of short breaks can be more refreshing than rare, longer vacations. Take every opportunity, including staying extra days or combining business trips with a day or so of relaxation.

TAKING BREAKS

Some people who have built exceptional careers work "all the hours in the day," sometimes in the belief that this gives them a winning edge over those who put in fewer hours. Success, though, depends on the strength of ideas and their execution, neither of which has much to do with the time expended. Overwork, on the other hand, can adversely affect both thinking and performance. Try to avoid taking work home (or going into the office) on weekends. To perform well, you must lead a well-balanced life and schedule time off.

SLEEPING WELL

Sleep is indispensable to good performance. While the hours needed vary from person to person, everybody requires a minimum dose. The requirement can be deliberately reduced. By cutting down sleeping time gradually over a long period, you can reach the probable minimum of four hours, freeing that time for other activities. If you lose sleep without training, though, the results will be cumulative and counterproductive, especially if you do not take catnaps during the day.

POINTS TO REMEMBER

- Arranging flexible working hours may help you to avoid traveling to work during busy, peak times.

- Cycling or walking to work a few times a week will improve fitness.

- Eating small meals at regular intervals is better than indulging in one enormous dinner.

- Relaxing before going to bed by reading, watching television, or listening to music will improve the quality of your sleep.

- Making sure that people at work are aware of your commitments to your family will help to generate understanding when you need to take time off, such as for your child's sports day.

30 If you are feeling tired, try to take a short catnap – it will prove highly restorative.

PURSUING EXCELLENCE

There is no good alternative to the goal of perfectionism – seeking top performance in yourself, and being constantly dissatisfied at less-than-perfect results. Be your own best critic, drawing attention to your faults, and going in search of excellence.

31 Seek excellence, and do not stop at "good" – it is not good enough.

QUESTIONS TO ASK YOURSELF

Q Do I rate the quality of my performance every day?

Q Am I working on a method that will improve results?

Q Do I take criticism from others and react well to it?

Q Do I meet the standards that I demand from others?

Q Do I remind myself of what I did well in the past?

SEEKING PERFECTION

The pursuit of the highest possible standards automatically points you toward achieving excellence. If you achieve perfection in any activity, you must be the best, which is the proper objective in any context. Even momentary perfection is extremely hard to achieve, if not impossible. In practice, aiming for excellence will mean performing significantly better than your present standards, which are always imperfect. Remember that refusal to tolerate imperfection is a powerful force for success.

BEING THE BEST

Just like runners, managers and organizations need opponents, or at least pacesetters, to produce their best performance. The process known as "benchmarking" measures comparable performance to set targets that the company seeks to exceed. The defect in this approach is that the benchmarks may themselves be too low. You want to be the best at what you do. That means looking at the performance of others to see not just what they do well, but how it could be dramatically improved. Being the best means setting new standards, very likely by adopting new methods. This drive for reform can be very demanding, but also highly rewarding.

32 Assume that you can always find a better way to use your abilities.

33 Aim at perfection, even if that seems impossibly out of reach.

34 Welcome new tasks as tests that you will pass.

35 On completing any work, rank your performance out of 100 – strictly.

BEING SELF-CRITICAL

There is a crucial difference between self-criticism and low self-esteem. You need a high personal opinion of your aptitudes and the way that you apply them. But you first earn that high personal regard by subjecting your actions and output to rigorous judgment. By acting as your own most severe critic, you avoid complacency and substitute the pursuit of excellence. Just as with others, it is important to make constructive, rather than negative criticisms, and then take positive action to improve areas of weakness. Beware if you find nothing to criticize, however. That is usually a sign of trouble ahead.

RAISING YOUR STANDARDS

However good you are at something, you can always improve. Similarly, however high the standards you have set for yourself and others, they can always be raised higher. Apply the total quality principle of continuous improvement to everything that you do. When starting a new job, you may feel daunted by new demands and doubt your ability to tackle the tasks successfully. Yet your past experience will confirm that after a few weeks in the new role, you will be performing well and without difficulty. People tend to underestimate their powers, which achieves the opposite of maximizing potential. It is better to overshoot and miss than never to try for the best of which you are capable.

▼ **IMPROVING STANDARDS**
Seek constantly to improve your performance by consistently setting yourself new and higher personal targets, and by taking every possible opportunity to learn and practice new skills.

Increase your skills by taking advantage of one-on-one training courses, where possible

ACCEPTING CHALLENGES

You may be happy doing the same work in the same role for years. However, that is extremely unlikely to represent your full potential. Restlessness is a good sign and a valuable quality. Once a task has been successfully completed, you look for new pastures and challenges. Be biased in favor of accepting these challenges when offered. You have a limited number of years in your career, and it makes sense to move onward and preferably upward whenever you can. This kind of restlessness has nothing to do with dissatisfaction or "itchy feet." It is simply the desire to test your powers in new situations – an angle that should always be followed.

---

36 Do not become a hard taskmaster, but do be a demanding one who helps others to work well.

WELCOMING COMPETITION

You should always welcome competition because it has a positive effect. Lack of competition tends to stultify. Conversely, the urge to outdo the opposition by fair and square means will powerfully stimulate drive and energy, in individuals and organizations alike. Foster that urge, in yourself and your team, by all available means. Choose the best "enemy" you can and make them the one to beat, and their standards the ones to exceed. But keep the aggression under careful, directed control.

INSPIRING EXCELLENCE

Seeking perfection for yourself entitles you to make similar demands of others. Part of your own drive for excellence aims to achieve maximum potential in others. Harness their innate desire to be committed, to excel, to seek responsibility, and to use their mental powers by setting an excellent example yourself. Spur people on to seek excellence by encouraging and rewarding them when they produce outstanding results.

▲ HELPING OTHERS TO EXCEL
Help people to reach the high standards you set by giving them the coaching they need to perform to their best ability. Ensure that you reward and encourage people when they do excel.

PURSUING EXCELLENCE IN THE KEY ATTRIBUTES

ATTRIBUTES	HOW TO ACHIEVE EXCELLENCE
AMBITION Willingness to take initiatives to reach high targets.	● Aim for the "impossible" – it has often been achieved. ● Translate your ambitions into concrete time-scales. ● Regard financial reward as a result of achieving worthwhile, major ambitions, not as an end in itself.
VISION Keeping long-term, future success as a constant guide.	● Never allow the problems of the present to make you forget that there is a future for which to plan. ● Share your vision with others and seek their support. ● Review the vision periodically and revise as needed.
CONFIDENCE The conviction that you can achieve what you want to do.	● If you feel inadequate for a particular task, take immediate steps to obtain any training, etc. you need. ● Do not hesitate to ask for advice from others. ● Do not allow criticism to damage your self-esteem.
ABILITY TO TAKE RISKS Readiness to take chances rather than play safe.	● Consider the downside and upside of any decision. ● Never gamble, but make the best judgment you can of the probabilities: aim for highest return at lowest risk. ● Test your hunches, but do not be afraid to back them.
DRIVE AND ENERGY The ability to concentrate mental and physical powers.	● Be determined and persevere in reaching your goals. ● Devote your drive and energy to planning as well as action, and take steps to maintain the momentum. ● React forcefully to failure and reinforce success.
COMPETITIVE SPIRIT Relentless perfectionism in seeking to be the best.	● Identify your main competition and make it a target. ● Never be content with second best – strive for first. ● Combine constant small improvements in performance with periodic leaps forward through major change.
SELF-CRITICISM Facing up to mistakes and failures, and learning from them.	● Avoid blaming others for anything that goes wrong. ● Make a habit of conducting a calm postmortem to analyze the reasons for error and remove causes. ● If things go really well, rejoice in your success.
LEADERSHIP The ability to mobilize others to achieve group ambitions.	● Remember that bringing other leaders to the fore is a prime task of leadership and a highway to success. ● Lead from the front, but not by doing others' jobs. ● Show strength by consultation and taking advice.

IMPROVING YOUR SKILLS

Whatever stage you have reached in your career, it is vital to keep learning. By widening and applying your knowledge, you can dramatically improve your performance.

INCREASING LEARNING

You are never too old to learn, and the need for learning increases, rather than decreases, as your career advances and jobs become more complex and important. Time for study may be hard to find, but it always pays off.

37 If you feel you need to have more training, ask for what you require.

38 Learn new skills that are not linked to work demands.

39 Never think that training is now all behind you.

EDUCATING YOURSELF

Many people promoted to a new, senior position think that they can learn on the job, without any need for education in the new tasks. Yet, if you wanted to indulge in a new hobby, for example wind-surfing, you would expect to take lessons. The same principle applies to taking up a new position or moving to a new company. Your natural ability needs reinforcement by learning, in both general and specific ways, how to do the work. Many companies fail to insist on this reinforcement. If the employer will not provide the learning, take steps to get it yourself.

LEARNING A LANGUAGE

Mastering other tongues makes a difference in negotiations and business relationships. It is also a valuable exercise for the mind. Cassettes and videos are effective learning tools – but the best learning is interactive. You can sign up for classes or use interactive media. Then, take every chance to use your new skill. It will impress everybody, including your foreign business contacts.

Manager uses cassettes to master a new language

APPLYING YOURSELF ▶

Set aside regular study periods and find a quiet environment where you can concentrate on learning without being distracted.

MASTERING COMPUTERS

However you obtain access to computing power, it is an indispensable extension of your own brain and capabilities. You must quickly master a word-processing program, email, and a spreadsheet. Productivity aids like engagement calendars and personal databases, too, are worth their weight in gold and cost little (in some cases, nothing). Apart from the personal benefits they bring, computers in many organizations now provide essential access to company files, colleagues, messages, customers, suppliers, collaborative working, and the Internet (which will be, and in many cases already is, the conduit to these contacts).

▲ REAPING THE BENEFITS

Computer programs may take time and effort to master, but the investment will be returned many times over. It is important to make that investment.

USING YOUR KNOWLEDGE

Make sure that any courses you plan to attend are relevant to your work. Then do all you can to apply what you have learned. Do not be deterred by less enlightened colleagues who may pour scorn on what you have been taught. You can only discover whether those lessons have real value by putting them into practice in your day-to-day work. Pass on your new knowledge to colleagues, and make them your allies.

40 Insist on getting training you can use, and then insist on using it.

EFFECTIVE THINKING

The most important mental discipline – thinking – is the one least taught in schools or in organizations. You can improve your thinking by using logic and by adopting proven techniques that will lead to better understanding, ideas, and execution.

41 Acquire all the information you need before you draw conclusions.

Assess all the facts before planning action

▲ **PLANNING LOGICALLY**

Write down what is likely to happen and the potential ramifications; then you can plan how to deal with each eventuality.

USING YOUR LOGIC

Logic means correct reasoning. Use your logic and you will reach the ideal stage where the compelling force of the facts eliminates all alternatives except one. This cannot happen all the time, because there will be too many unknowns. But the rational manager starts by seeking factual certainty, from which he or she can proceed to firm conclusions. Logic is no less invaluable in uncertain conditions. You can list possible events and logically establish what consequences will follow if they occur. You can then produce sensible plans for coping with each possibility, and also work out the relative likelihoods. Logic also teaches that the best-laid plans may go wrong, so cover this contingency in your thinking.

THINKING LATERALLY

Lateral thinking, as taught by Edward de Bono, uses various techniques to make you challenge received ideas and arrive at new, improved solutions and suggestions. One such technique is provocation, when you put forward outlandish notions to see what practical ideas are stimulated as a result. Another approach is to seek analogies from other fields. If you are told that something is impossible or will never work, redouble your efforts to see if the idea is, in fact, valuable.

42 Do not confuse wild, far-out, impractical ideas with creativity.

BACKING YOUR INTUITION

Hunch or gut feeling sound far less impressive than logic, lateral thinking, and reasoning. But intuitive thought-processes are as intellectual as any other. Intuition may take into account factors that your consciousness wants to repress, which is why some indefinable doubt may prevent you from making a decision. Never ignore such messages from the interior. But treat intuitive thoughts as analytically as logical plans. Check the intuition against the facts. You may not always establish a complete case for backing your instincts. Going with it in these circumstances may well be the best course – so long as you can stand the consequences of being wrong.

---

43 Encourage people in thinking sessions to give full rein to their intuition as well as their logic.

QUESTIONS TO ASK YOURSELF

Q Have I gathered all the facts I need to help me arrive at the correct solution?

Q Have I considered all possible alternatives before settling on my decision?

Q Have I gone out of my way to find new methods of tackling this situation?

Q Did I collect contributions from everybody who has an interest in the matter?

Q Have I used the best possible thinking process in reaching my conclusion?

Q What do I feel about the matter – am I convinced emotionally as well as intellectually?

Q Have I thought of contingency plans in case my ideas do not work out as intended?

TACKLING ▶ ISSUES LOGICALLY

When you apply reasoning to a situation, the result can be counterintuitive – that is, not what you would expect. In this case, David's intuition was to cut prices to stimulate sales performance. But his boss wanted to probe deeper. His logical analysis showed that the firm would be far worse off as the result of cutting prices. The sales chief's intuitive proposal was not a good one.

CASE STUDY

David, sales chief of a large organization, was concerned about sales trends. He approached his managing director, John, with a proposal to cut prices by 20 percent to stimulate sales. He told John that sales would fall steeply if the price cut did not go through, but would rise sharply if it did. John figured out how much sales would have to rise to cover the lost profit. The answer was fivefold! He then went on to calculate how much sales would have to fall if prices rose by 20 percent, before profits were affected. The figure worked out at 44 percent. He put the analysis before David and asked, "Do you really believe that a 20-percent price differential will raise sales by 400 percent?". Reluctantly, David said no.

IMPROVING MEMORY

A good memory is a great asset, and one that can always be developed. Even the most amazing memory experts rely on acquired techniques to perform their feats. Follow similar approaches, and you will never forget what you need to remember.

44 Always check your memory – it often recalls vividly, but inaccurately.

45 Take training in how to recall if your memory is letting you down.

TESTING MEMORY

People often complain that their memory is failing, but recall is affected by factors, including stress and fatigue, that do not reflect intellectual capability. Try a simple test. Can you, for example, remember a list of ten items in the correct order after one read-through? If you cannot, do not despair. A little training will show that your memory power can accomplish this and many more complex tasks.

REMEMBERING LISTS AND NUMBERS

To help you remember a list, try composing a story that includes all the items. The more outlandish it is, the better. For example: "A man needs **aspirin** for a bad headache after drinking too much **wine** which cost too much **money**. He makes a **note** in his **pad** never to do it again, and starts eating **oranges** as a cure. One of the oranges **flowers** and turns into a tree, which is pulped to make a **book**. The book contains a recipe for cooking cold **sausages** with **soap powder** to make **pet food**." You will now remember the list perfectly.

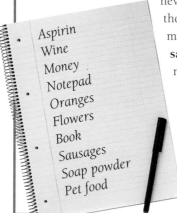

Aspirin
Wine
Money
Notepad
Oranges
Flowers
Book
Sausages
Soap powder
Pet food

If you find it difficult to remember numbers, try substituting word associations for the digits, for example using simple rhymes: 1= Sun, 2= Shoe, 3= Tree, and so on. In this way, you can compose your own numerical associations. Any list of objects, ideas, people, points in a speech, or numbers can be fixed in the memory by association with your ten "number words."

46 Develop a good filing system for items you read and want to keep.

USING ASSOCIATION

Being able to remember what you want or need is very valuable. You do not have to leave it to your natural powers. Association is the key to effective memorizing, and by using it deliberately you can easily accomplish feats you would have thought beyond you, such as delivering a 30-minute speech without notes. Association involves linking what you are trying to remember with other things, such as rhymes. Mnemonics are also a form of association, such as "Columbus sailed the ocean blue in fourteen hundred and ninety two."

AIDING YOUR MEMORY

There is no reason to burden your head with searching your memory when a computer, filing system, or notebook can do the job perfectly well. You should also keep a large number of reference sites, either on the Internet or your bookshelves. The computer makes all these tasks much easier. But it is up to you to take practical steps to record these "memories."

▼ **STORING INFORMATION**
Devise a filing system to suit your needs and make sure that it is efficient – you should be able to locate items easily whenever you need to recall them.

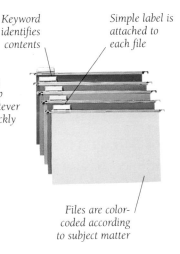

Keyword identifies contents

Simple label is attached to each file

Files are color-coded according to subject matter

Devise an efficient filing system to help you find whatever you want quickly and easily

◀ **KEEPING RECORDS**
Write down as soon as possible your notes on an interview, something you have read, the name of a new contact, or information you have been given, and file it away.

IMPROVING READING

Reading is fundamentally important for efficiency. The faster you read, and the more you understand, the better. The view that comprehension suffers with speed is wrong. Learn to read faster, and you will find that understanding also improves.

> **47** Read for useful tips from other businesses and other countries.

Book is flat on desk

Comfortable posture aids concentration

▲ SKIM-READING
Practice skim-reading from paragraph to paragraph. Read in bursts of about 20 minutes, eliminating distractions.

READING MORE QUICKLY

Few managers know a vital personal statistic. How fast do you read now? The average is somewhere between 250 and 300 words per minute (wpm), but you can train yourself, or be trained, to read much faster. The first tip is only to read what you need to read. Survey the material first, eliminate the superfluous, and read only what is essential. Do not go back over words and sentences that you have already read. Keep the eyes moving forwards between groups of words, taking in as many words as possible in each group. By following such easy tips, you can speed up by 30 percent, saving two hours in reading a book of normal length.

UNDERSTANDING FASTER

In the mistaken belief that reading faster means understanding less, people often reread passages and sentences many times. In fact, their strategy is flawed. Tests show that comprehension rises with increased speed. The trained reader not only manages double the normal speed or more, but also has a higher degree of comprehension. The same methods that raise speed also concentrate the mind more effectively on what is being read. Get into the habit of taking notes. The process of selecting key points itself aids understanding.

> **48** Set time targets for your reading and make sure you stick to them.

THINGS TO DO

1. Test your reading speed and set a faster target.
2. Test your comprehension, reading slowly and fast.
3. Set time aside every day for your reading.
4. Scan books first to see which parts interest you.
5. Have a reading list for books useful in business and for general culture.

CHOOSING A SUBJECT

You probably have plenty to read simply in the course of your job. But that job will be better done if you read much more widely. Set yourself a weekly or monthly reading plan and try to stick to it. You could set a target of at least one good newspaper a day, one relevant magazine a week, and one serious book a month. The book need not be about business management, although excellent works on all its aspects appear every year. Every such book contains valuable lessons, information, and ideas. So do newspapers and magazines. One pizza multimillionaire in the US has the world's biggest library of self-help books. Whether or not these tomes contributed to his success, the principle is powerful. There is much to be gained from reading for self-education. But do not forget to read for relaxation, too – the more you enjoy reading, the less of a chore it becomes.

RETAINING YOUR READING

Study for one hour → Read material thoroughly

Review after 6 minutes → Skim-read again to improve recall

Review after 10 hours → Skim-read a second time

Review after 40 hours → Test recall and review again if necessary

49 Memorize a few facts and figures from everything that you read.

50 Clear out your files from time to time to keep them manageable.

WRITING AND SPEAKING MORE FLUENTLY

Most managers, like most people, find speaking in public and writing well difficult. Obey simple rules and your performance on paper will pass any normal tests, while you also have the potential to be an effective public speaker for any audience.

51 Get a respected friend to read and criticize your writing.

WRITING TEXT

Always choose short words over long ones, and active verbs rather than passive ones, when you are producing text. Keep sentences short and to the point. Do not use self-important devices, like capital letters for words that are not proper names, or management jargon. Avoid archaisms like "albeit" or "notwithstanding." Shun clichés like "on-going" or "at this point in time." In addition, seek a smooth flow, with logical transitions from thought to thought and paragraph to paragraph. Never write more words than you need. If you shorten any piece of writing, you will probably improve its quality. It helps throughout to visualize your audience, and to aim your words at that target.

52 Read all writing aloud or silently to check quality.

Use symbols for common words, such as th for the, k for thousand

Drop all vowels unless they begin a word

Words are still easy to recognize when they are spelled without vowels

Use numerals for numbers

In th sm wy tht spdwrtg ncrss th spd at whch y wrt nts wth a pn or pncl, y cn gtly incrs the spd at whch y mk nts usg a wrd prcssr or typwrtr, if tht is hw y prfr t wrk.

Whn y spdwrt, th shp of th wrds is unffctd by th dltd vwls, & y hv an entrly smpl & prctcl systm.

Y my fnd tht evn whn y ar sklld at spdwrtg, it is snsbl t spll unusual or dffclt wrds in fll. Als, if yr spdwrttn wrd cld b mstkn for 1 or 2 othr wrds, thn it is a gd pln t wrt th wrd in fll.

◄ TAKING NOTES

Space your notes in short paragraphs and concentrate on picking out the main points, facts, and phrases. Try an easy speedwriting system, which can double your speed, by eliminating vowels and using symbols for common words.

▲ **DICTATING TEXT**
You will be able to dictate faster if you plan the document beforehand and have all notes and reference material ready. Allocate the time required and keep on to the end before revising your material.

DICTATING PROSE

Writing takes considerable time. Only experts can write good prose at 20 words a minute or more. Speaking at 160 words per minute (wpm) is comfortable for you and the listener, so it follows that dictation is the fastest form of writing. You will not reach 160 wpm, of course. But you can easily double or triple your current speed. You will need somebody to take the dictation or transcribe the tape, however, and will also have to find time for revision and rewriting. Computer programs can take dictation, too, but they are not yet perfect.

53 Practice giving a talk without referring to your notes or using a watch to check elapsed time.

SPEAKING CLEARLY

Nearly everybody speaks perfectly well in ordinary life. There are extraordinary orators, but you are not competing in their league. In your everyday conversation, you make your meaning clear, have an easy flow, and cover all the necessary ground without being long-winded. That is all that is required in speaking for your professional purposes. Imagine that you are speaking to a group of friends who, like you, are deeply interested in what you have to say, and whom you do not have to impress with wordiness.

Look directly at audience and maintain open stance

Refer to notes only when necessary

◀ **BEING NATURAL**
If you are familiar with your notes, you will appear more natural and will be better able to establish a good rapport with the audience.

OVERCOMING NERVES

Even professional broadcasters, who look thoroughly at ease on camera, admit to nervousness before a program starts. Even prize-winning authors doubt the quality of their latest writing. Such nervousness reflects a desirable stimulus, setting the adrenaline flowing as you gird yourself for the fight. If you suffer very seriously from nerves, relieve them by using relaxation techniques, going for a short walk, or going over your material. Above all, remember that your audiences and associates generally want you to succeed. They are rarely hostile. They want to be pleased as much as you want to please them.

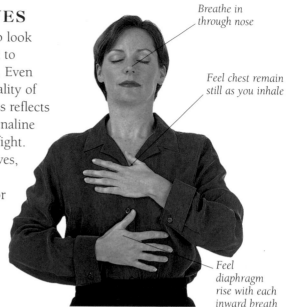

Breathe in through nose

Feel chest remain still as you inhale

Feel diaphragm rise with each inward breath

▲ REDUCING LAST-MINUTE NERVES
Try this breathing exercise to calm your thoughts and dispel tension. Close your eyes. Place one hand on your upper chest, the other on your diaphragm. Breathe in, feeling your diaphragm rise, then breathe out slowly. Repeat several times.

54 Pick a point in the audience some two-thirds back for eye contact.

55 Use professional slides presented via a computer for best effect.

STRUCTURING YOUR TALK

Any talk consists of three Ms: Message, Material, and Manner. What do you want to communicate? Have one overarching, big message you will leave with the audience. Follow the basic sequence of telling the audience what you are going to say (the big message), saying it, and finally repeating what you have said. Within the overall message, write down the key points (as few as possible) in bullet form, and allow about three minutes per point. What will you use to support the message? Write down against each key point the slides, statistics, other facts and stories that you will use. The ideal length is between 20 and 40 minutes. Above that, audiences tend to lose concentration.

PRESENTING YOUR TALK

How will the message and material be presented? You have a wide choice of styles: roaming the stage or room, delivering from a fixed point, using notes, reading a script (which is rarely advisable), formal or informal, participative or lecturing, and so on. Suit the choice to your own personality and preference, but above all to the audience. Learn as much as you can about what each particular audience expects and likes. Maintain eye contact so that you can judge the impact of your talk and adjust if necessary. Use audio-visual aids if at all possible. Videos, slides, and overheads make the message much more effective and memorable than words alone can achieve.

▼ PRESENTING EFFECTIVELY

Make use of visuals wherever possible, since they are powerful aids; but remember to maintain that all-important eye contact by looking at the audience rather than the screen. Try to inject some humor into the presentation as a means of winning over your audience, and always end on a strong, emphatic note.

CULTURAL DIFFERENCES

Americans are fond of moving around while speaking and of trying to become part of the audience. The British are much more likely to use a lectern and to rely quite heavily on audio-visual material. The Japanese can surprise their European or American audiences by giving extremely witty and informal presentations. The Germans, too, can speak humorously, although their humor may be more apparent to German audiences than to other nationalities. The French may be very fluent – even in English.

BECOMING MORE EFFECTIVE

There are a number of tools and techniques that can be used to raise performance. With a little know-how, you can ensure that you are making maximum use of your personal resources.

BOOSTING CREATIVITY

Most people think that creativity is best left to a talented few. They are wrong. Everybody has creative powers and can learn to use them. By opening your mind and changing your approach, you will discover that ideas come easily.

56 Expect everybody to have ideas and to express them with no inhibitions.

57 Look for innovative ideas that can change things for the better.

BEING INVENTIVE

Many organizations fall into the trap of believing that time-honored ways cannot be bettered, or else they lag behind because they always follow the market leader. Individuals also repeat what has worked in the past, and copy others who have been successful. But to be creative, you have to adopt a different approach. Ask yourself what would happen if you turned existing practices upside down. Or search for something that is not being done at all. People will say "If it was a good idea, somebody else would have done it." Take that as a trigger for investigating further.

CHANGING APPROACH

In creating your personal and business strategies, do not merely imitate the competition. It may help you to know that from the time of the ancient Greeks to World War II, out of all the major conflicts and numerous campaigns, only six decisive victories followed from head-on assaults. All the other victors launched flanking attacks – they went around the side. Learn from these historical lessons, and look for an idea that will give a clear differentiation. You can then hope to win without the massive advantage in strength needed for head-on success. In this way, small armies have been able to defeat military giants three times their size. Moreover, in doing the same thing, you may do it worse. Be different and set your own standards.

POINTS TO REMEMBER

- Conventional thinking should not be rejected simply because it is conventional.

- New ideas are as valuable as any others, but should not be adopted simply because they are new.

- Many ideas that seem foolish initially can actually lead to sensible solutions.

- Ideas should never be dismissed out of hand, since this is disheartening and hinders the flow of creativity.

- Disorganization helps in the generation of ideas; organization is vital when developing them.

FINDING IDEAS

Ideas can be found almost anywhere – in other countries, other companies, and other industries. To discover them, you must make reading and observation your tools, and then give full rein to your creative urge to experiment. If you discover a new method or product, you may be able to try it out for a trial period, or in a test market, which allows you to make sure before commitment. "Stolen" ideas are also very valuable, not only in original form but as analogies. By observing or reading, you may find an idea that can be applied successfully in a completely different context.

Cut out interesting items and refer to them when you need inspiration

◀ COLLECTING CLIPPINGS

Magazines, books, and newspapers are invaluable sources of inspiration. Read through them and keep any items of interest so that you build up your own reference library of ideas.

USING TIME EFFICIENTLY

Time is your most valuable asset, and how well you use it has a key bearing on how you perform. By analyzing how you spend your time, you can begin to make changes that will ensure you get the most from your working day.

58 Check how well you have used your time at the end of every day.

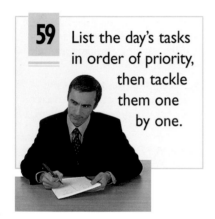

59 List the day's tasks in order of priority, then tackle them one by one.

ANALYZING USE OF TIME

You might think that most of your time is spent doing useful things, but if you were to keep a detailed time-log, you would probably be surprised at the number of superfluous activities. It is easy to spend too much time on routine matters, such as reading mail, at the expense of high-priority, productive tasks. Look at how you divide your day at the moment. Do you prioritize your work so that you tackle important, urgent projects first? Or do you complete enjoyable tasks first? Do you waste a lot of time?

ALLOCATING TIME

The majority of your tasks can be divided into three groups: routine tasks (for example, writing a regular report), one-off tasks (for example, organizing a meeting), and planning and development tasks (for example, making new contacts). To be most effective in your job, you should be spending about 60 percent of your time on the most important Group 3 tasks, 25 percent on Group 2 tasks, and only 15 percent on Group 1 needs. If, like most people, you allocate your time in exactly the opposite proportions, try to reorganize your working day so that you are able to work more consistently and efficiently, and achieve more.

QUESTIONS TO ASK YOURSELF

Q Am I devoting enough time and resources to strategic planning and overall monitoring?

Q Is my desk overflowing with uncompleted tasks?

Q Do I leave enough time to be creative and innovative?

Q Am I delegating routine but necessary tasks to staff?

Q Do I allocate sufficient time to sourcing new contacts?

Q Am I spending too much time in meetings?

DELEGATING WORK

By delegating aspects of your work to others, you give yourself time to complete the most important elements of your job successfully. Divide your necessary tasks into three groups: those that do not need to be done at all – by you or anyone else; those that you could and should delegate; and those that you are not able to delegate and must do yourself. Use this breakdown as a basis for reducing any unnecessary activities, delegating more tasks, and concentrating on tasks that only you can complete.

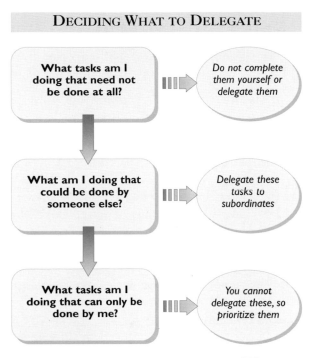

DECIDING WHAT TO DELEGATE

What tasks am I doing that need not be done at all? → Do not complete them yourself or delegate them

What am I doing that could be done by someone else? → Delegate these tasks to subordinates

What tasks am I doing that can only be done by me? → You cannot delegate these, so prioritize them

▲ USING MOMENTS
Make the most of a long journey by writing a report, studying a document, or reading a book or article. Portable computers have made this "stolen" time still more usable.

FILLING IN TIME

Long periods of idleness, such as when traveling or waiting for meetings, are wasteful. Always have work available for filling in these times. If you have a long drive to work, why not take the chance to listen to recorded material? If you travel to work by train, use the time to read or plan your day ahead. Advances in communications mean that we can contact the office or talk to colleagues, wherever we are in the world. Make sure you are equipped with the know-how and the tools to take advantage of new technologies.

BEING MORE PRODUCTIVE

H*aving efficiently allocated your time, you must ensure that you are being as productive as possible within those time restraints. Find ways of measuring your personal performance, set higher targets, and improve processes to close the gap.*

60 Be assured that whatever you do can be executed more effectively.

MEASURING OUTPUT

You can always find measures of output and effectiveness. How quickly do you answer your phone? How punctual are you? Do you clear your desk every night? Once you have chosen measures that fit your working pattern, look at the processes you use to see if you can cut out or speed up any stages. People often develop working habits without questioning their effectiveness – if you can change these habits for the better, do so.

61 Get colleagues to help you sustain improvements in your productivity.

Manager passes on report, confident of the quality

ENSURING QUALITY

Quality is essential. High output at low standards is not productive. For example, responding to letters promptly is worth much less if the letters are badly written, unclear, and inaccurate. The same obvious truth applies to all your work. Take time before beginning any task to decide on the best approach and the objectives – both what you want to achieve and how the work will be presented. It may be wise to put problems on one side, rather than delay the whole work, returning to the difficult areas when the task is broadly finished.

◀ **DOING YOUR BEST**
Before handing over your work, make sure that you are truly satisfied that it has been well done. Be your own strictest inspector, and always allow enough time for review and revision.

MAKING IMPROVEMENTS

One simple way of improving productivity is to concentrate on activities that you control personally, rather than on those that are outside your control. Set yourself new, higher, productivity targets – for example, if you tend to turn up late for meetings, resolve to be punctual every time. Look at the way in which you structure your day in terms of your own productivity. If you know that your energy levels tend to flag during the middle of the afternoon, scheduling an arduous, complicated task for this time of day would not be productive. You might achieve far more by tackling such a complex job early in the morning.

QUESTIONS TO ASK YOURSELF

Q What are the key measures that relate to my effectiveness?

Q Have I set targets for self-improvement?

Q Am I maximizing my output but limiting my input?

Q Do I keep my desk clear and my papers organized?

Q Am I certain that I am improving performance in measurable ways?

62 Insist on people making quality a prime target.

▼ **IMPROVING PRODUCTIVITY**
A clear, well-organized desk and the ability to focus on the task at hand indicate high levels of productivity. Review your working practices regularly, and keep setting yourself new targets to ensure that those high standards are not allowed to slip.

Employee concentrates on task at hand

Paperwork is filed neatly

Reports are produced swiftly, without compromising quality

In-tray is cleared regularly

CHOOSING PRIORITIES

E*ffective time management involves prioritizing. You cannot handle all the tasks that come your way at the same time. Working to a list of priorities is vital. It is also important to give priority to developing your expertise in a chosen area of specialty.*

63 Put what can wait indefinitely into a file, then throw away the contents.

64 Try to finish one task before you start on another.

COMPARING PRIORITIES ▼
Look at the way you prioritize carefully. The good prioritizer puts the future ahead of the past and tackles difficult jobs first. The bad prioritizer puts the past before the future and postpones demanding tasks.

ASSESSING IMPORTANCE

Tasks fall into four categories: very important, important, useful, and unimportant. They also have time horizons: urgent (to be done as soon as possible), fairly urgent (to be done by a near deadline), not urgent (can wait for a while), and optional (no time pressure). The categories and time horizons determine what you can put at the bottom of the pile, and what must go to the top. Estimate the time each task will take, then plan your days and weeks around achieving the top priority tasks, fitting in the others around them.

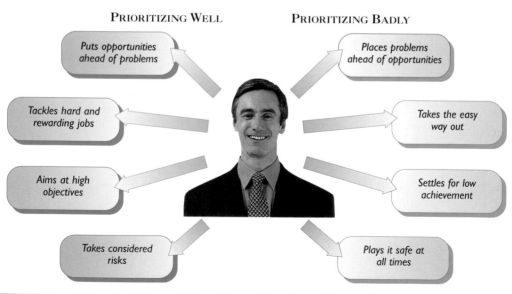

PRIORITIZING WELL — PRIORITIZING BADLY

Puts opportunities ahead of problems

Places problems ahead of opportunities

Tackles hard and rewarding jobs

Takes the easy way out

Aims at high objectives

Settles for low achievement

Takes considered risks

Plays it safe at all times

DEALING WITH DEADLINES

Avoid the practice of most journalists, whose work is ruled by deadlines, but who usually leave everything until the last minute. When you name or accept a deadline, be sure that the chosen completion date is really necessary. Once a date is agreed, missing the deadline is not acceptable: keeping it becomes a key priority. Work back from the deadline for the main task to see which sub tasks have to be completed by what time. If possible, build in some room for slippage. You will probably have reason to be grateful for this contingency. If all else fails, though, be prepared to ask for an extension as early as possible. Do not spring any last-minute surprises on anybody.

◀ **AVOIDING A LAST-MINUTE RUSH**
Set yourself interim deadlines to help you meet a final deadline date. In this way you can work toward achieving your final target in stages, rather than rushing a job at the last minute.

PICKING A SPECIALTY

Making the right choices on priorities also applies to improving areas of personal performance. General ability opens the greatest number of doors, but it also pays to give priority to one area in which you can become expert. First, you stand out from the crowd as the person who knows all about the subject. That knowledge could give you a key position in important projects and discussions. Second, the experience of mastering a subject in depth and having total command in your special area bolsters confidence and builds mindpower. Do not choose a specialization that will rarely, if ever, be used. Rather, seek mainstream areas that are vital to the business of the organization, such as organizing market research or setting up new operations.

> **65** Make a point of finishing work by the time that you have agreed to.

> **66** Do not rely on seniority: rather, win the authority of true expertise.

UNDERSTANDING MONEY

The ability to manage money is crucial to any manager. Accounting is not a natural talent for most people, but it is much easier to master than many suppose. The key to becoming a numerate manager is to practice using numbers all the time.

67 Use your personal financial affairs to develop your numeracy skills.

68 Express plans in words before you go into numbers.

DEFINING THE KEY ▼ NUMERACY SKILLS
This manager has a wide range of aptitudes that make it easier to do his job with full knowledge of the financial consequences and needs.

BECOMING NUMERATE

To master basic numeracy skills, you will need to learn from books or in a classroom. Once you understand the principles, there is no substitute for actually drawing up budgets, writing business plans, doing management accounts, and studying financial reports. At first this may be slow and grinding work, but you will become faster and better with experience. Do not let yourself be blinded with science. The simpler, the better is an excellent guide to managing finances.

Uses spreadsheets

Reads balance sheets

Writes business plans

Understands cash flow

Understands management accounts

Optimizes financial returns

UNDERSTANDING CASH FLOW

You can go bankrupt while still making a profit. The key is cash flow. If bills and wages are paid before customers honor their debts, cash will flow out of the company, possibly in lethal amounts. Effective cash management means speeding the collection of money due, matching your own settlement of accounts to the inward flow, and making good use of the cash balances by investing them for the highest return. When looking at potential profit, always look at the cash flow consequences. Otherwise, you could be crippled by taking on more business than you can finance.

69 Always have your calculations checked by somebody else.

70 If you cannot grasp a concept, admit it frankly.

QUESTIONS TO ASK YOURSELF

Q Is there any financial issue I do not follow?

Q Am I planning to learn about such matters?

Q Can I forecast results with confidence that they will materialize?

Q Do I know with fair accuracy how well or poorly my unit will have performed when the period ends?

LEARNING ACCOUNTING

Every manager should know the principles of double-entry bookkeeping, profit and loss accounts, and balance sheets. But leave applying those principles to professional accountants. As a manager, you are concerned with management accounts, which seek to reflect actual events as closely as possible in financial terms. Training courses will tell you all you need to know about the relationship between income, direct costs, and contribution. You can then concentrate on raising revenue and lowering costs simultaneously – a simple formula, but always effective.

WRITING AN EFFECTIVE BUSINESS PLAN

Start your plan with a statement that sets down, in words, rather than in numbers, the outcome you hope to achieve. Use a spreadsheet to work out the figures that will result if the targets are met. Be as realistic as possible, and make sure that you tone down any extravagant figures – they will not impress readers. List your assumptions in full, and also note anything that could possibly go wrong. Finally, you should include your reasoned analysis of the cost of losing the opportunity.

REDUCING STRESS

Stress in itself is not harmful, but it can seriously affect those who react badly to it. To improve your effectiveness as a manager, you must be able to recognize your limits and take action to reduce stress when it threatens your performance.

71 Work more effectively, rather than for longer hours.

Stressed manager is unable to concentrate on task at hand

RECOGNIZING THE SIGNS

Everyone reacts to stress differently, but it may manifest itself in physical symptoms, such as skin complaints or digestive troubles. You may feel irritable and run-down. Work can become obsessive, and nervous problems can result in depression, anxiety, or other psychological disorders. Look out for warning signs and tackle stress before it becomes debilitating.

◀ **COPING WITH STRESS**
Deal with stress positively by seeking support from superiors, close friends, and colleagues, and prioritizing your workload.

ANALYZING PERSONALITY

Research has shown that certain types of people are more prone to stress and its by-products, such as heart disease. If you are an ambitious manager who is extremely competitive, fast in thought, speech, and action, committed, impatient, and pressed for time, you are likely to be a Type A personality – at risk from stress. If you are more placid, you are less at risk and classed as Type B. Type A managers may also be tense egotists who lack self-control and are quick to anger. If you fit the Type A pattern, modify your behavior to reduce the chances and incidence of stress.

72 Discuss personal problems with a wise listener.

73 Defuse anxieties by listing possible future events, good and bad.

HANDLING ANXIETY

Being anxious is an unpleasant experience. It can have a perfectly understandable cause. A merger or reorganization, for instance, may threaten your job or your powers. Threats produce anxiety. But what action can you take to remove the threat? In the above examples, almost certainly none. However, you should try to calm your anxiety. Avoid listening to rumor and think positively. After all, the threat may not even materialize, in which case, you have made yourself feel awful for nothing. Whatever the cause of the anxiety, identify that cause, develop a plan for removing the cause, if possible, and/or form a contingency plan to cope. Occupying yourself with this three-part formula will lessen anxiety anyway, and could make it wholly unnecessary.

 74 Analyze reasons for procrastination and face them squarely. Then set yourself a deadline for action.

TACKLING DIFFICULTIES

It is easy to procrastinate, but this habit (which is all but universal) can increase your stress in two ways. First, you may feel guilty about leaving the task undone. Second, you are building up stressful time pressure for the future. Procrastination is itself a symptom of stress. For example, a decision may involve taking a risk, or a necessary action (say, firing somebody) may loom ahead. Your reaction to these stresses may be to delay the evil hour. That is bad stress management. You will still have to grab the bull by the horns, and will pass more stressful hours or days before you do so. Do it now.

IDENTIFYING YOUR PERSONALITY TYPE

Read through the following questions. The more "yes" answers you give, the closer you are to the Type A personality. You can reduce your stress levels by adopting the opposite, or Type B, behavior. For example, if you walk and eat rapidly, make a conscious effort to slow down. Do you:

- Feel a constant pressure to get things done?
- Often compete against the clock?
- Always hurry?
- Make decisions quickly?
- Get restless and impatient with being idle?
- Speak fast?
- Always arrive on time?
- Think about and do several things at the same time?
- Move, walk, and eat rapidly?
- Often get impatient?
- See yourself as very ambitious?
- In conversation, display brisk and impatient body movements; taut facial muscles; fist-clenching; explosive and hurried speech patterns; or a lack of bodily relaxation?

USING STRESS POSITIVELY

A crisis can descend out of the blue, or build up over months. It can affect everyone in an organization, or may be entirely personal, but it is important not to allow yourself to slump into despair. In fact, you can turn the stress of a crisis to your advantage. Because stress raises your levels of adrenaline, you can harness that extra energy to resolve the emergency successfully, if that is feasible. Begin by assessing what can actually be done and whether the crisis can be cured. Then start on a no-holds-barred effort to recover from the disaster. You will benefit from the healthy stress of constructive achievement under pressure.

75 Get excited about challenges in a positive manner.

76 Find relaxation methods that suit you and use them.

▼ HANDLING CONFRONTATION

In confrontational situations, it is vital to control your own stress levels. The higher those levels rise, the less likely you are to be able to control the discussion. Slow down your breathing, calm down the situation, and concentrate on what you want to achieve.

Manager controls stress, and resolves disagreement with employee

Stressed manager is approached by angry employee

Manager is unable to control stress levels, and situation deteriorates

LEARNING TO RELAX

The more effectively you rest, the better you use your energies. Few people, however, make positive use of daytime rests, even though that is one of the best means of controlling stress. Make time during the day to get rid of superfluous and stressful emotions, and to substitute relaxed calm. Many techniques are available, from deep breathing to yoga. What they have in common is mental concentration on non-stressful thoughts, and assertion of self control over your emotions and body. The most useful techniques are those that can be applied any time and anywhere, such as the relaxation exercise shown right.

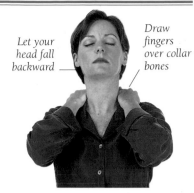

Let your head fall backward

Draw fingers over collar bones

▲ EASING TENSION

Place your hands over your shoulders, exhale, let your head fall backward, and slowly draw your fingers over your collar bones. Repeat several times.

RELAXING AT HOME

Relaxation is a technique that can easily be learned. Take time out to enjoy a regular period of relaxation in your busy daily routine. Find a quiet spot in the house, place a rug or mat on the floor, with a cushion, then lie down and begin the exercise.

1. After having a good stretch, sit or lie in a comfortable position, eyes closed.
2. Concentrate your inner attention on a fixed image or point – try the point between and above your eyebrows.
3. Deeply relax your muscles one by one. Start with the feet and work up the legs to the abdomen, chest, shoulders, neck, and face; let your jaw muscles hang loose.
4. Concentrate on your breath passing deeply, easily, and naturally through the nose, silently repeating the word "one" (or a mantra if you have one) every time you breathe out.
5. Allow yourself to relax completely.
6. If music helps, have it playing softly. Conjure up images of warm climates, and try to imagine your body becoming warmer and heavier.
7. Continue for 10 to 20 minutes; if you fall asleep or doze, it doesn't matter, you are still relaxing.

RELAXING THE BODY ▶

Lie in a comfortable position, supporting your head with a cushion or pillow, and relax your entire body.

Breathe through nose

Relax from feet upward

ASSESSING PROGRESS

Frequent and accurate assessment of progress is essential to improving effectiveness. That requires facts, and managers must find ways to measure their standards effectively in order to set new targets for performing even better in future.

> **77** Remember to test all "facts" to ensure that they are accurate.

▲ **MEASURING YOUR STANDARDS**
Factual targets help you to gauge your performance. For example, if you set yourself a target of answering the telephone within five rings, you are setting a standard that is easily measured.

SEEKING FACTS

How will you know if you have succeeded in a particular activity? Feeling good is pleasant but inadequate. It is far better to target an activity in a meaningful way by applying total quality management principles to your work. This means finding key activities where you can set and measure your standards. For example, an item on your list could be arriving at meetings on time, for which you set a standard of 100 percent. By setting factual targets, you give yourself defined objectives whose achievement nobody can dispute. Tell colleagues about your aims so that they can point out whenever you fail to perform to standard.

> **78** If you set high standards for yourself, be sure to keep to them.

DO'S AND DON'TS

✔ Do be a hard judge of yourself.	✗ Don't congratulate yourself on what other people did.
✔ Do have a good idea of what you want to achieve and why.	✗ Don't get carried away by success.
✔ Do share the credit for achievement.	✗ Don't be boastful.
✔ Do admit failings.	✗ Don't be misled by past comparisons.

ANALYZING SUCCESS

Success can be your enemy. If you have enjoyed a period of great prosperity and are well ahead of your competitors, the temptation is to count the money, lie back, and rest on your laurels. That is the moment when slackness begins to creep in. It is important to analyze success as carefully as failure. What special circumstances, outside your control, contributed to the excellent results? After allowing for these, how well did you really do? What could have been done better, with still better results? Most important, what are you going to do for an encore? The objective is to make success a platform for further advance. What matters most is the new target, not the past.

REVIEWING YOUR PERFORMANCE

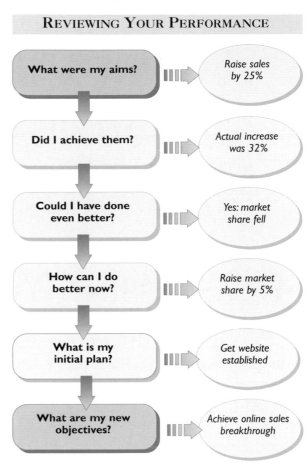

What were my aims?	Raise sales by 25%
Did I achieve them?	Actual increase was 32%
Could I have done even better?	Yes: market share fell
How can I do better now?	Raise market share by 5%
What is my initial plan?	Get website established
What are my new objectives?	Achieve online sales breakthrough

USING COMPARISONS

Comparing one set of results with another is the basis of management accounting. But such comparisons can be misleading. If sales growth slumps from 20 percent to 5 percent, then rises again to 15 percent, that figure is triple the previous year's outcome, but still a quarter below the achievement two years ago. Before hailing today's figures, check that the basis for comparison neither exaggerates nor depreciates your success. For accuracy, compare the past 12 months against the preceding 12 at the end of each quarter.

79 Analyze data with great care to get an understanding of the realities.

ACHIEVING SUCCESS

Success hinges on the ability to manage your career well.
Take every opportunity to advance yourself, and enlist
help from others to further your progress.

REASSESSING YOUR GOALS

*D*ispassionate and methodical analysis of
goals is essential to the success of your
vision. But situations can change. You must
be prepared constantly to reassess and adapt
your ideas as necessary. Use this assessment
process to find ways to take decisive action.

80 Probe deeply into questions to get answers – obvious ones can be wrong.

81 Take objections seriously until proven mistaken.

82 Train everybody in sound methods of investigation.

ASKING QUESTIONS

When assessing future goals, always analyze
them carefully. Never take anything for granted.
In other words, always ask questions until you
are satisfied that, as far as possible, you know the
whole truth. The vital word in your vocabulary is
"Why?" Then you need other short words:
"What?", "How?", "Who?", and "When?" The
analytical "Why?" questions lead on to: What can
be done? How can that be achieved? Who will
carry out the implementation? When will the action
be taken? At all stages, further questions will arise.
Do not leave the answers dangling in the air.

USING THE ANSWERS

The phrase "paralysis by analysis" refers to organizations that spend months on number-crunching and reports and then do nothing. Once you have decided on your goals, if you find it difficult to take action, ask yourself why. Perhaps the effort required is itself inhibiting. Or you may be concerned that once you have moved, it will be hard, maybe impossible, to turn back. So the fear of being wrong, with awful consequences, can paralyze you. By all means try for a "fail-safe" position, so that, if the worst comes to the worst, the situation will be tolerable. But if you have obtained the answers on the "What?" and "How?", make sure you act on them to pursue your goals.

83 Be biased in favor of taking action as soon as possible.

84 Set a time limit on discussion, but be flexible if it proves inadequate.

TAKING ACTION

On taking action to reach your goals, you have two options. One is to follow your chosen path regardless of events. The other is to observe all the outcomes, and to adapt your plan, radically if need be, to improve the chances of success. The first course sometimes works, but equally can lead to disaster. The second course contains the risk that, by pulling back in the face of adversity, you will miss the initial objective when it could have been reached. The correct approach uses elements of both options. Provided the objective still makes sense, concentrate your drive on reaching that goal.

Manager revises goal after hearing comments

Team member supports colleague's view

Colleague makes an important point

CHANGING COURSE ▶
Listen to the opinions of associates. You may learn something that will prompt you to adapt your actions and improve the chances of success.

FINDING MENTORS

Everybody can think of other people who have had a profound influence on their life and work. Learning from mentors, whose experience is more varied and greater than your own, is a key to improving your performance and achieving success.

85 Keep in touch with people who have previously advised you well.

86 Learn from books on and by great managers.

LEARNING FROM OTHERS

A mentor may be a parent, teacher, university lecturer, boss, or close friend. The principle is always the same. Your performance is improved by listening to and learning from knowledgeable minds. You can choose mentors from the past, and indeed many successful businessmen have borrowed ideas from dead business heroes. However, bygone inspirations are no substitute for living advisers, who can listen to your problems and hopes and react as circumstances demand.

ASSESSING A ▼ MENTOR'S QUALITIES
There are several important qualities you should look for in a mentor. He or she will be listening to your problems and hopes and reacting to them, so trust is vital.

Possesses high integrity, honesty, and credibility

Insists on getting things done

Insists on the highest standards

Demonstrates the ability to envisage the future

Sets an inspirational example

Shows deep concern for others' performance

FINDING ALLIES

Selecting the right mentor is an important step toward optimizing your performance. He or she does not necessarily have to be an equal or a superior. They could be a key subordinate, or a colleague of different status. The vital role is to provide talents and resources that you lack. In a career, you may have many different mentors; or one may be at your side for the whole journey, or most of it. Always look for a suitable ally you feel you can work with closely, and whose judgment you will respect.

Mentor rejects ideas out of hand

Partner distrusts mentor's opinion

POOR CHOICE

Mentor gives dispassionate advice

Partner respects mentor's views

GOOD CHOICE

CHOOSING A MENTOR ▶
You need to work closely with someone who knows you and your weaknesses well and on whom you can rely for dispassionate advice.

USING THE BOSS

A good boss is an excellent mentor, whose example and teaching can guide you for a whole career. Even an able leader who spares no time for deliberate coaching can provide information and inspiration. Watch what these exemplars do, and borrow what seems to work best. Much of what they teach will have to do with style and instinct, but these imponderables can make all the difference. Use the boss not only as a source of "lessons and war stories" (which other senior people can also provide), but as a sounding board for your own ideas and ambitions.

87 Look out for the partner who adds to your powers.

88 Do not be shy about approaching others for help in managing.

MAKING CONTACTS

It is not only what you know, but who you know that often makes the difference between success and failure. Your address book is one of the most valuable tools in your possession, and one that will improve greatly in value over time.

89 Make an effort to meet friends working in other companies.

90 Meet frequently with contacts for non-business talks.

91 Back up face-to-face contacts with the telephone and email.

REMEMBERING CONTACTS

A contact whom you forget has lost his or her value. Try to memorize a new contact's name. Get all their details and put these facts on the record (computer programs are ideal). Take every contact seriously. You never know when or in what valuable context you may meet people again.

KEEPING A RECORD

Effective careerists write down the names of every useful or potentially useful contact they make, and periodically update the names, addresses, and contact numbers. It does not matter whether you keep the list in a book or a computer program, although updating and back-up are much easier with the latter. Back-up is important, since losing an uncopied organizer or address book can have disastrous consequences. Cross-reference names, businesses, and areas of expertise wherever possible.

Manager meets new contact and exchanges business cards

▲ **MEETING NEW CONTACTS**

When you meet somebody, use their name as often as possible in the conversation to help you remember it. Get a business card, and ask about their job and where they live. A new contact may have skills or contacts that will assist you or your colleagues.

92 Try to help when contacts ask you for assistance.

Colleague returns favor by helping manager out of a difficult situation

Manager recommends contact to a colleague who is looking for help

STAYING IN TOUCH

Some of your best contacts will be made at work, especially when working in teams. Teams can operate inside departments, or across both departments and functions, and may well involve others outside the company. You can learn much from fellow members, whether as a team member or leader. At close quarters, you learn the strengths and weaknesses of fellow members. To make the relationship successful and lasting, put the team's collective success before your own. To earn their respect, ask for other people's opinion of your contribution, and act on their constructive criticism. Do not be afraid to speak out yourself. Finally, be frank with criticism, but generous with praise, and keep in touch with the colleagues you value.

93 Treat the team as a band of closely knit colleagues, and keep up the relationship later on.

KEEPING THE ▶ TEAM TOGETHER

Charles knew that, collectively, his team possessed many strengths, and that there was still a great deal that could be achieved together. Using business contacts he had made in the industry, he was able to lead their move en masse to a new employer. This benefited the team as a whole, helped the new employer, and enhanced Charles' reputation as a successful team leader.

CASE STUDY
Charles had the good fortune early in his career to take charge of a team of bright young managers who formed a highly skilled staff group, specializing in statistical analysis of tough problems. A change in management meant that the team's future was uncertain. The members were ready to set about finding futures independently. But Charles realized that he was unlikely ever to find such an exceptional group again. He persuaded his colleagues to sell themselves as one package to one employer. The most promising choice was a major manufacturer that was in deep trouble. Charles led the team over to this second employer, where they helped in a big turnround. Charles and two team colleagues then left to start their own firm in another, rising industry. They made a large fortune.

TAKING THE LEAD

T*he more you can show and exercise the attributes of leadership, the more likely you are to succeed. Take the initiative and seek out every opportunity to develop your leadership skills. Your experience will stand you in good stead for the future.*

94 Choose the moment to lead, and then be decisive.

95 Get other people to follow as you start to lead.

96 Turn down a role unless you have the means to master it properly.

SEEKING OPPORTUNITIES

You do not have to wait for an appointment to a leadership position to lead. The chances are that you will be involved in a task force or similar group, or you may be singled out for a particular project. Either event provides an opportunity to push yourself forward by proposing a new idea or by taking up a strong position and becoming its powerful advocate. Be prepared to implement what you have proposed.

▼ **TAKING THE INITIATIVE**
Get into the habit of volunteering to lead or take on extra responsibility – you will gain invaluable experience. He, or she, who hesitates, or shows no interest, will gain nothing.

Manager asks for volunteer to run project

Eager colleague is quick to volunteer

Colleague shows interest but hesitates

Employee is bored and disinterested

SPEAKING OUT

If you have a good idea, have the courage of your convictions, and use your conviction to carry the plan through to acceptance, completion, and success. Reluctance to "stick my neck out" holds back careers – and organizations. The worst you can experience is a refusal. For the best chance of success, be prudent in choosing when to make proposals, and be careful to test them by analysis or by asking close and trusted colleagues.

97 Avoid changing your opinions to match those of the majority.

FINDING ROLES TO BUILD LEADERSHIP SKILLS

WAYS TO LEAD	SKILLS TO BE GAINED
JOIN A TASK FORCE These are usually formed to tackle specific issues.	● Provides excellent experience in directing teams and meeting deadlines. ● Involves start-to-finish identification with task.
JOIN A PROJECT TEAM These bring multi-skilled individuals together to accomplish major plans.	● Usually provides exposure to other disciplines and functions. ● Develops a wider range of personal abilities.
APPLY FOR PROMOTION An appointment to a higher post may involve leading others.	● Offers the chance to bring fresh vision to a job. ● Provides the opportunity to understand a new role and experience processes from a different perspective.
PROPOSE CHANGE Suggest ways of making individual and team improvements.	● Any change initiative brings chances of proposing and leading specific projects. ● Engages initiative and powers of persuasion.
LEAD A SUB-UNIT Take on responsibility for delivering personal profits.	● Brings challenge of meeting self-set targets. ● Given adequate scope, allows leadership to be shown in a highly visible way.
RESOLVE A CRISIS SITUATION Take a lead in any demanding emergency action.	● Pressure of necessity removes barriers to asserting personal authority. ● Encourages capacity for fast, decisive action.

INFLUENCING OTHERS

Convincing others to accept your point of view, ideas, and action plans is essential to success. In debates, negotiations, and confrontations, you cannot expect your view to prevail every time. But you can usually work toward an acceptable compromise.

> **98** Put your position over clearly, but keep in mind that of the other party.

CULTURAL DIFFERENCES

Japanese negotiators may come in a large team and retire for group discussions before giving their response. Americans like to have lawyers present and are very concerned with contractual obligations. Germans value business relationships highly and expect the other side to show equal respect for promises given.

CONVINCING PEOPLE

The first requisite in any debate is to convince yourself. Have a closely reasoned, fact-based case that you have thoroughly examined. Second, while emotions such as enthusiasm are highly desirable in argument, do not allow yourself to become emotional in the sense of losing control. You need control to guide the debate toward the end you want. If others become overly emotional, try to calm the discussion. Never lose sight of your objective, but be prepared to concede some points where facts or diplomacy demand. Above all, seek to persuade the others that your decision or choice is also theirs.

NEGOTIATING TO WIN

Always go into negotiations with a clear idea of the highest outcome you want, what you expect will result, and the lowest acceptable result. You may find that all three ideas change during the course of talks, especially if they are protracted. It helps if you can get the other side to name their proposals first. Then you have a straightforward choice between accepting or asking for more. If you have to play your cards first, do not tone down your proposition to what you think the other side will accept. Never say "no" for somebody else. They will say it themselves soon enough.

POINTS TO REMEMBER

- You should be prepared to change your tactics in order to win agreement.
- The other side should be regarded as partners and not as enemies to be defeated.
- Avoid saying or doing anything rash – you may want to deal with the other side again.
- Keep something in reserve that can be placed on the table should the necessity arise.

DEALING WITH DIFFERENT TYPES OF NEGOTIATION

TYPE OF NEGOTIATION	HANDLING METHODS
RESOLVING DISPUTES Meeting to troubleshoot.	● Seek to obtain the trust of both sides to the dispute. ● Start by establishing an agreed description of the facts. ● Do not allow proceedings to become heated or abusive.
BECOMING PARTNERS Setting up a working relationship.	● Cover essential items clearly in any exchange of letters. ● Resort to full legal agreements only if you have to. ● Allow escape clauses for either side on fair terms.
AGREEING CONTRACTS Formalizing commercial relationships.	● Avoid loading the other side with demanding commitments. ● Watch out carefully for unintended or intended traps. ● Make sure both sides are negotiating in good faith.
SETTLING PRICES Making one-time deals, not installed payment.	● If you are in the stronger position, do not abuse it. ● Try to establish the highest price the deal will bear. ● Leave room for both sides to make adequate profits.
INDIVIDUAL PACKAGES Discussing an employee's rewards.	● Prepare your preferred package before the meeting. ● Expect comparisons with other employees and organizations. ● Be prepared to listen to reasonable demands.
COLLECTIVE BARGAINING Meeting workers' representatives to discuss pay and other issues.	● Cut through inherent animosity or distrust. ● Be firm but sympathetic and willing to compromise. ● Remember that workers rarely strike on non-pay issues.

99 Call a recess if discussions become overheated and tempers rise.

ACCEPTING COMPROMISE

If two propositions are far apart, look for other areas where you can readily agree, and either reach that agreement before returning to the main subject or save it for use as a bargaining counter. Resist the temptation to "defeat" the other side. The best outcome is when both sides are fully satisfied that the result is both in their best interests and the best they could have achieved. Try for that.

PLANNING AHEAD

People who plan their careers mostly outperform those who leave their progress to chance. The plan will probably include changing employers, which has become highly acceptable, as has breaking away to develop an independent career.

100 Plan to achieve more than you expect – you may well get there.

LOOKING TO THE FUTURE

Results for individuals, as for companies, are almost invariably improved by thinking ahead. The natural planning period is the year. By working out a detailed 12-month program and putting it down on paper, you effectively concentrate the mind on what you want to achieve. You also provide yourself with a touchstone for your subsequent decisions. Will they advance you toward these annual goals? If not, you should think again.

This Year's Goals
- Master colloquial French
- Achieve promotion to job with profit responsibility
- Prepare ground for future role inside Single Market
- Join a key corporate task force
- Form club of ambitious young executives
- Become expert in use of ecommerce

◀ **LISTING YOUR GOALS**
An excellent habit is to write down, each year, what goals you want to achieve over the next 12 months. This exercise forces you to think about your real aims and possibilities.

CHANGING JOBS

The most important steps in your progress will almost certainly involve changing jobs, probably companies, and possibly countries. Job-hopping was once a potential liability, but may now even be an asset. Changes usually involve extra money and other benefits. While this matters very much, never make it the only reason for changing. The interest and challenge of the job itself are paramount. If you are changing organizations, research carefully the nature and prospects of the new employer before you make your move.

101 If you miss a career target, name a new one and start again.

AIMING FOR THE TOP

The summit of a management career is reaching the rank of chief executive of a major company. Obviously, only a minority ever reach the peak, but ambitious executives expect to be among those few and prepare themselves accordingly. A career presents other opportunities of taking charge and showing that you are capable of controlling and directing an operation toward your chosen goal. Above all, you need people skills. Practice getting people to work with you and for you productively throughout your ascent. Harness those skills to confidence and vision – a clear sense of the future you want to achieve – and you have a good chance of scaling the summit.

QUESTIONS TO ASK YOURSELF

Q Is it time for me to start thinking of a new career move?

Q What is the ideal position to provide greater experience and challenge?

Q Realistically, is there any reason why I cannot reach the top?

Q Can I do anything to remove the blockage and rise higher?

Q Where do I want to be at intervals of five years from now?

Q What must be done to reach those destinations?

BECOMING INDEPENDENT

Sometimes leaving the corporate world for independent work is forced through redundancy. Those organizations that downsize or become virtual may well "outsource" activities, often employing former executives and experts as freelancers. In other cases, people resign to exploit business opportunities, sometimes ones they have spotted during their employment. It is advisable to keep the possibility of breaking away in mind, so long as you recognize that the skills needed for independent success are quite different, and that life is likely to be less comfortable, more solitary, and more uncertain outside the security of the corporate fold.

▲ SETTING UP ON YOUR OWN

Being your own boss can be challenging and exciting. With the advent of email and the Internet, many more people are now taking the opportunity to work from home.

ASSESSING YOUR ABILITY

*W*orking towards excellence presents a lifelong challenge and opportunity. The following questionnaire will help you to evaluate your strengths and weaknesses and decide where to place the most effort to achieve still more. If your answer is "never", mark Option 1; if it is "always", mark Option 4; and so on. Add your scores together, and refer to the Analysis to see how you scored. Answering as honestly as you can is a good start towards self-improvement.

OPTIONS

1 Never

2 Occasionally

3 Frequently

4 Always

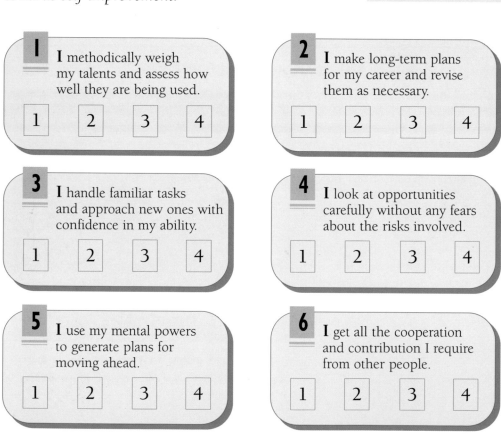

1 I methodically weigh my talents and assess how well they are being used.

1   2   3   4

2 I make long-term plans for my career and revise them as necessary.

1   2   3   4

3 I handle familiar tasks and approach new ones with confidence in my ability.

1   2   3   4

4 I look at opportunities carefully without any fears about the risks involved.

1   2   3   4

5 I use my mental powers to generate plans for moving ahead.

1   2   3   4

6 I get all the cooperation and contribution I require from other people.

1   2   3   4

7 I exercise to maintain fitness standards and keep close to my ideal weight.

| 1 | 2 | 3 | 4 |

8 I eat and sleep well and am careful to avoid working excessive hours.

| 1 | 2 | 3 | 4 |

9 I aim to achieve excellence, and work on areas where I fall short.

| 1 | 2 | 3 | 4 |

10 I strive to win by outdoing the competition on every important aspect.

| 1 | 2 | 3 | 4 |

11 I set aside time to master new and useful training and education.

| 1 | 2 | 3 | 4 |

12 I apply organized mental techniques to help me think more effectively.

| 1 | 2 | 3 | 4 |

13 I recall everything I need to remember readily and without difficulty.

| 1 | 2 | 3 | 4 |

14 I work to improve my reading speed without loss of comprehension.

| 1 | 2 | 3 | 4 |

15 I seek feedback about my writing and speaking, and act on any criticisms.

| 1 | 2 | 3 | 4 |

16 I enjoy giving talks and welcome opportunities to appear before an audience.

| 1 | 2 | 3 | 4 |

17 I look for new ideas from others and seek to develop new ideas myself.

1   2   3   4

18 I systematically manage my time and act to eliminate any waste.

1   2   3   4

19 I have, and apply, meaningful measures of my personal productivity.

1   2   3   4

20 I compile a list of priorities and organize my work accordingly.

1   2   3   4

21 I apply competent numeracy and financial know-how to my activities.

1   2   3   4

22 I act to cope with negative states like anxiety, guilt, and undue stress.

1   2   3   4

23 I find ways of achieving relaxation and I use those methods effectively.

1   2   3   4

24 I regard success as the stepping-stone to further, greater achievement.

1   2   3   4

25 I take care to analyze issues thoroughly, but I also act decisively.

1   2   3   4

26 I turn to valued advisers to help me with personal and business issues.

1   2   3   4

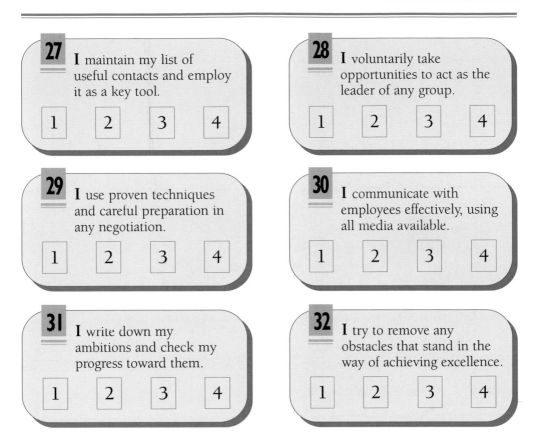

27 I maintain my list of useful contacts and employ it as a key tool.
1   2   3   4

28 I voluntarily take opportunities to act as the leader of any group.
1   2   3   4

29 I use proven techniques and careful preparation in any negotiation.
1   2   3   4

30 I communicate with employees effectively, using all media available.
1   2   3   4

31 I write down my ambitions and check my progress toward them.
1   2   3   4

32 I try to remove any obstacles that stand in the way of achieving excellence.
1   2   3   4

ANALYSIS

Now you have completed the self-assessment, add up the scores and check your performance by referring to the corresponding evaluations:

32–63: You are falling far short of achieving excellence. Forget the excuses and face up to the realities of your working life. You can do better. The only thing that is missing is the will to act. Find that will, and improvement will come.

64–95: You have advanced a fair way toward using your powers to the full. Now take stock, using the questionnaire, to choose the areas where you can most valuably boost your achievement. The payoff should be very quick.

96–128: You have a full and highly effective working life. But you can still achieve much more. You know that, which is one reason why you are doing so well. Keep it up.

LEADING EFFECTIVELY

Introduction

T he key to truly effective leadership lies in mastering a wide range of skills, from implementing and administrating processes to inspiring others to achieve excellence. Leading Effectively shows you how to make the most of opportunities to learn to lead, whether by observing others, through formal training, or through careful evaluation of practical experience. It provides a thorough grounding in the essential skills, and shows you how to put them into action in a variety of situations. With invaluable information on the key leadership skills, including communication, coaching, using authority, learning to delegate, and developing individuals and teams, as well as 101 practical tips, this book helps you to become an inspirational and confident leader, capable of heading an effective team. Two self-assessment exercises help you to assess and improve your leadership ability.

LEARNING TO LEAD

Excellent leaders are made as well as born. To be the best, learn the essential skills of leadership through formal training courses and on-the-job experience.

FOCUSING ON QUALITY

The aim of leadership is to help others to achieve their personal best. This involves setting high but realistic performance goals for yourself and your staff, finding ways to improve operations and procedures, and striving for total quality in all areas.

 Always strive to preach quality and practice improvement.

APPLYING STANDARDS ▼

Work closely with subordinates to set measurable quality standards that they can seek to achieve or exceed.

Leader discusses possible areas for improvement in standards of work

SETTING STANDARDS

Before you or your staff can achieve quality goals, you need to be very clear about your own expectations regarding how things should be done and the standards of performance that must be reached. Once you have defined these expectations you can communicate them clearly to staff, emphasizing your own commitment and the fact that achieving excellence is everyone's responsibility.

RAISING STANDARDS

| **2** | Ensure that you involve all staff members in quality-improving programs. |

Maintaining and exceeding standards is an on-going process involving everyone. Encourage staff to analyze problem areas and to work together to find solutions. Involve them in looking for ways to improve products, processes, and performance, and, if extra skills are needed, arrange the necessary training. This approach not only generates ideas and innovation, but creates an atmosphere of participation and increased motivation, which in turn results in raised quality standards.

IMPROVING STANDARDS OF QUALITY

TARGET STANDARDS	HOW TO ACHIEVE QUALITY
LEADERSHIP Lead your team toward total quality by constantly improving every process and product.	● Ensure that all staff drive toward continuous improvement on all aspects of performance. ● Recognize and appreciate individuals and teams for the success of their efforts.
STRATEGY Seek to uphold and develop the organization's vision, mission, values, and direction.	● Determine all objectives with the aim of reaching the highest quality standards. ● Communicate strategic aims clearly to everybody, and review and update them regularly.
PEOPLE Ensure that staff are motivated, well-managed, and empowered to improve continuously.	● Train all staff in the skills and capabilities they need to meet their quality targets. ● Practice two-way communication, top-down and bottom-up, through all available media.
RESOURCES Aim to use financial and other resources efficiently to achieve the organization's objectives.	● Ensure money is managed efficiently and everyone understands what is happening financially and why. ● Use the best technology available and consistently update it to state-of-the-art levels.
PROCESSES Ensure that all vital processes, including management, are consistently highly effective.	● Develop performance measures and feedback to maintain the improvement momentum. ● Stimulate people to formulate innovative and creative ideas for improving processes.

LEARNING FROM OTHERS

*E*very successful singer has a singing coach, and top singers often give masterclasses. The principle is just the same for leaders. You learn better leadership skills by being coached, and you develop those skills further by coaching others.

> **3** Always be on the lookout for chances to learn valuable lessons.

IMPROVING SKILLS

Leaders must continually assess their performance and look for ways to improve and extend their skills. A great deal can be learned by simply observing others whose behavior appears to get results. A mentor will provide informal guidance where needed, or you may choose a more formal avenue of learning, such as a training program.

> **4** Take a refresher course if you feel you need to brush up on rusty skills.

Personnel director explains new trends

USING FORMAL TRAINING

Even leaders with years of on-the-job experience can benefit from some formal training from time to time. Outside training gives you an opportunity to get away from day-to-day activities, and provides a fresh perspective. Use training to keep abreast of current trends and to brush up on or acquire specific skills. Do not wait to be asked – assess your strengths and weaknesses and put yourself forward for courses that match your needs.

Leader gains an insight into how trends may affect the organization

◀ WIDENING KNOWLEDGE
Take advantage of colleagues' expertise in specific areas to broaden your own skills. You can learn a great deal from people with an in-depth knowledge of their field.

COACHING OTHERS

Training others provides a valuable source of education in the skills needed to become an effective leader, such as communicating clearly, giving instructions, getting feedback, delegating, motivating, and developing people. Always ask for feedback from those you are coaching – they can provide useful insights into your own performance. Share your experience and expertise with other people to help you to clarify your own attitudes, beliefs, and priorities, and to analyze your own performance. Use any time spent coaching your staff to discover their needs, what motivates them, and how they respond to your leadership style. Develop skills in other people to enable you to delegate some of your tasks, leaving more time available for you to spend on activities that will improve your own skills as a leader.

5 Use coaching sessions to learn as well as teach.

6 Set an example to your staff by being trained yourself.

▼ RAISING STANDARDS
Learn new skills, develop existing ones, and use your knowledge and experience to benefit colleagues. In this way, you will improve all-around performance.

| Learn | → | Coach | → | Raise performance |

BEING A ▶ GOOD COACH

Taking over the task that he had assigned to Jean seemed the easy option to Gordon. But he learned from this experience that he had avoided the important issue. He was looking at the problem in the short term, rather than focusing on helping Jean to improve her skills and perform better in future. He realized that training people was far more productive than doing everything himself.

CASE STUDY

Gordon asked Jean, one of his second-level managers, to produce a report that involved a degree of financial knowledge. He took it for granted that she understood the basics of management accounting, and was unpleasantly surprised to find that Jean had made many errors through ignorance. Since time was pressing, and since this was work that came easily to him, Gordon rewrote the report and passed it on. Jean asked for an interview. She was angry, and Gordon assumed that this was because he had taken over writing the report. But Jean was cross for a different reason. As she said, "How do you expect me to learn if you don't tell me what I've done wrong?". Gordon realized that he had failed Jean. He set aside time to coach her in management accounting, and also sent her on a course in finance.

Gaining Experience

Promotion to leadership positions used to depend on rising up the company hierarchy. Now, vital work is increasingly carried out by temporary teams working on specific projects, which provide ideal opportunities for learning leadership skills.

7 Use projects as a way of learning more about other disciplines.

Joining Project Teams

Widen your knowledge and learn new skills by joining a project team. These are usually set up to work on new projects within an existing organization. Such teams can become permanent if the project takes off, and are independent of the vertical hierarchy. The longer the project lasts, the more likely it is that team membership and roles will change during the project's life. This means you can join a project in a subordinate position, but with the hope of finding a leadership role later. The larger the team, and the wider its responsibilities, the greater the chance to change roles or be promoted within the team. Gaining experience on projects led by other people is also an invaluable education in leading your own project.

Subordinate is promoted to lead own team

Subordinate gains experience in leadership skills working as part of a team.

◀ **LEARNING SKILLS ON PROJECT TEAMS**
Working on a project team can provide you with all the necessary experience to run your own team. Show your initiative and make the most of any opportunities that arise.

LEARNING FLEXIBILITY

The leadership of a project is often passed to different people at different stages. For example, it could move from the design department to the production staff to the marketing people, each passing on the baton in turn. This gives you the opportunity to learn crucial lessons in how to organize and collaborate with different functions and departments, from finance to sales, engineering to purchasing. Although the baton changes hands, everyone still works as part of a harmonious team at all times. The abilities to be flexible and to understand how other departments work are essential in leadership.

> **8** Make friends with people in different departments, and get to know how they operate.

BROADENING KNOWLEDGE

Use your experience in multidisciplinary project teams to broaden your general business skills. It is too easy to become and stay a specialist. The Japanese, for instance, believe that every manager should be a complete businessman or woman, able to lead any part of the business successfully. So a personnel head can move easily into sales, or a finance expert into marketing. Get to understand the principles of business and what part each component skill plays in achieving sales and profits. Broaden your knowledge by reading, and by establishing and nurturing contacts in different departments – such efforts will pay great dividends later.

LEARNING NEW SKILLS ON A PROJECT

- How to approach the project
- How to communicate its objectives
- Where to acquire resources
- How to put resources to best use
- How to liaise with other departments
- How to negotiate
- How to monitor performance
- How to troubleshoot
- How to achieve project goals

MASTERING ROLES

*L*eadership is a multidimensional function, requiring knowledge and understanding of many organizational needs. As a leader, you must master the various roles that are required to handle different people and circumstances with skill and efficiency.

9 Think carefully about the best way to behave in every situation.

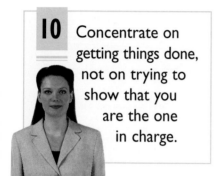

10 Concentrate on getting things done, not on trying to show that you are the one in charge.

TAKING THE OVERVIEW

A leader's role differs materially from that of a manager. While a manager must focus on implementing specific tasks, the leader must act as a grandmaster, a strategist, directing the game as a whole, and organizing the players. All leaders have different talents, and may be stronger in some skills than in others. To be successful you must be able to fill a number of roles, using a range of skills and leadership styles according to the task, the situation, and the people involved.

BEING AN ADMINISTRATOR

Administration is a key role of the leader, and nowadays there is much more to the role than simply "sailing a tight ship" on a predetermined course. The modern administrator is expected to be creative, devising processes and streamlining activities, not only to ensure the smooth-running of procedures, but also to increase efficiency. To get the best from your team, set aside time to organize systems that will minimize time-wasting and improve productivity. Look for ways to reduce paperwork – direct communication is usually more effective. Liaise with other departments to ensure that everyone knows what is expected of them, and keep an open team diary for instant checks on current tasks and deadlines.

QUESTIONS TO ASK YOURSELF

Q Do I communicate directly with my team and also with other departments?

Q Am I sure that every member of the team understands his or her role fully?

Q Am I setting sufficiently ambitious goals?

Q Do I have procedures in place that allow me to check on team progress instantly?

Q Am I constantly looking for new ways to improve efficiency and productivity?

COMPARING LEADERS AND MANAGERS

LEADERS	MANAGERS
Administer	Implement
Originate	Copy
Develop	Maintain
Inspire trust	Control
Think long term	Think short term
Ask what and why	Ask how and when
Watch the horizon	Watch bottom line
Challenge status quo	Accept status quo
Are their own people	Are good soldiers
Do the right thing	Do things right

BECOMING A STRATEGIST

As a leader you need to focus on the wider issues that may affect your team's effectiveness, as well as the day-to-day business of getting things done. With your team, plan what you want to achieve in a given time, and break this down into attainable goals and objectives, ensuring that everyone is aware of their responsibilities. Unexpected problems may require adjustments to elements of the plan, so always leave plenty of room for revision.

11 Keep a checklist of key leadership duties and ensure that you do them.

Promoter of change
Administrator
Communicator
Expert
Strategist

12 Always look beyond the detail and consider the bigger picture.

◄ **FULFILLING KEY ROLES**
A leader must be a good communicator who cares for staff; an expert who is knowledgeable in his or her field; a strategist who looks to the future; an administrator who gets things done; and a proponent of change.

PROMOTING CHANGE

Change is vital for success in the future. By seeking to lead change, you are helping your organization to remain competitive and grow, and creating opportunities for individuals to enrich their careers and personal lives. Dare to be different – if everyone in your industry is stuck in the same pattern, search for changes that will be welcomed by customers and that will enable you to stand out. Encourage staff to generate ideas for change, and involve your team in the planning and implementation of change programs.

13 If you are resisting change, ask yourself why.

▼ INSTIGATING CHANGE

To ensure minimum disruption, communicate every aspect of a change to those concerned as soon as possible. Stress the positive aspects of the change, and gain commitment from others through your own dedication to the project.

| Communicate | Reassure | Stand firm |

FOCUSING ON PEOPLE

Leader suggests a training course to help team members improve skills

The effective management of others is paramount to success. As a leader you must be, and be seen to be, a people person who has the best interests of staff, as well as the organization, at heart. Seek to develop a climate of openness in which people are not afraid to express their opinions and share their ideas with you. Constantly encourage them to adopt the values and behavior that help the team and the organization to reach its goals. Above all, ensure that your people get the training they need to achieve their maximum potential.

◀ BEING AN EXPERT

As leader, you should possess an in-depth knowledge of your chosen field. Ensure that your staff have all the technical skills needed to enable them to perform effectively.

EVALUATING KEY LEADERSHIP ROLES

KEY ROLES	HOW TO FULFILL THEM

EXPERT
Has in-depth understanding of his/her field.

● Strive for the best possible performance, and increase your knowledge in your specific field.
● Use your expertise to improve technical performance and technological strength in key areas.

ADMINISTRATOR
Ensures the smooth running of operations.

● Cut down on paperwork, and devise progressive systems to increase efficiency.
● Set rules, systems, boundaries, and values in order to ensure effective control.

PEOPLE PERSON
Makes staff and their training a top priority.

● Believe and act on the principle that success flows from the effective management of others.
● Seek to develop a climate of openness, and work with, and for, everybody equally.

STRATEGIST
Thinks long term and looks to the future.

● Always ensure that you plan ahead, devising strategies and goals for future success.
● Concentrate systematically on where the organization needs to go and how it will get there.

CHANGE AGENT
Uses change as a key to progress and advancement.

● Be adventurous, and endeavor to focus on enterprise and initiative rather than control.
● Seek to lead change, and actively encourage the generation of new ideas in others.

USING DIFFERENT STYLES

There are many different leadership styles, and to be truly effective in any given situation, you should not only be aware of them all, but be able to use elements of each simultaneously. For example, while managing and developing people, you still need to keep your eye on the strategic future at all times. If you are implementing a major change program, do not neglect your administrative duties or you run the risk of being unable to implement the changes effectively.

14 The greater your expertise, the more authority you will have.

DEVELOPING STRENGTHS

All the attributes that you will require as a leader can be developed – even drive and energy. Self-confidence and self-determination, combined with an ability to manage people and money, will make you a strong leader able to attain your targets.

15 Always work on and build upon your own strengths.

SETTING HIGH GOALS

You cannot hope to achieve without the self-confidence to take risks, which should be carefully calculated, on paper, to ensure that they are acceptable. This will enhance your ability to form high but realistic and achievable goals. Evaluation on paper helps put you in control of your own destiny, and will aid long-term vision of your own future and that of the business.

16 Put all your ambitions down on paper to help you realize them.

ELIMINATING WEAKNESSES

Facing up to your own mistakes and weaknesses is the first step toward eliminating them and raising your leadership ability. You may need help from a mentor, as well as feedback from your people. List aspects of your people management that are unsatisfactory, and determine how to improve them. Ultimate success means getting others to work with you and for you productively.

17 Understand what you are doing in order to achieve your aims.

MASTERING FIGURES

Some leaders are uncomfortable with money. If this applies to you, make sure you take a course. No sensible employer will refuse to pay for this education. There is no substitute, though, for sitting down and working out the figures of a real business, and seeing in real life how reality is reflected and portrayed by the numbers.

18 Never accept any weakness as one that you cannot correct and cure.

BUILDING PERSONAL STRENGTHS

STRENGTHS	HOW TO DEVELOP THEM
DRIVE AND ENERGY The ability to put maximum mental and physical effort behind reaching objectives and to keep going until the aims are achieved.	● Keep physically fit. Join a gym or take up a competitive sport. ● Constantly work through lists of tasks and ensure their completion.
SELF-CONFIDENCE A belief in your ability to carry out self-appointed and other tasks to your satisfaction and that of colleagues.	● Learn to calculate and accept moderate risks. ● Review your work at frequent intervals, comparing plans with outcomes.
MONEY MANAGEMENT Knowing how to read balance sheets, draw up budgets and management accounts, and track paths to higher profits.	● Acquire good training in financial basics – attend a course if necessary. ● Always work out financial consequences of plans and decisions in detail.
MANAGING PEOPLE Understanding how to get the best from your staff, and encouraging them to use their initiative to achieve better results.	● Ask regularly for feedback from your superiors, peers, and subordinates. ● Learn to look at situations through other people's eyes.
GOAL-SETTING Knowing how to set targets that are high enough to stimulate exceptional effort, but are still within achievement range.	● "Benchmark" organizations in your own and other industries to see where and what improvements can be made. ● List your goals and keep reassessing them.
SELF-DETERMINATION The belief that your destiny and that of the business are in your hands, not subject to others or outside forces.	● Form long-range aims for yourself and the organization. ● Put your aims down on paper, complete with plans for implementation.
SELF-EVALUATION The ability to recognize and learn from mistakes and failures, while also analyzing the lessons of success.	● Conduct regular, honest examinations of recent decisions and actions. ● If you discover any weaknesses, draw up plans for rectifying them.
COMPETITIVENESS The will to win, and to take defeat as a challenge, not a disaster, coupled with the pursuit of high personal standards.	● Take every opportunity to study winners, corporate and individual. ● Adopt, adapt, and apply the techniques or qualities that make winners successful.

ASSESSING YOUR LEADERSHIP POTENTIAL

*E*valuate how well you measure up as a prospective leader by responding to the following statements, and mark the options closest to your experience. If your answer is "never," mark Option 1; if it is "always," mark Option 4; and so on. Add your scores together, and refer to the Analysis to see how well you fared. Use your answers to identify the areas that most need improvement.

OPTIONS	
1	Never
2	Occasionally
3	Frequently
4	Always

1 I take the lead in meetings to clarify objectives and agendas.

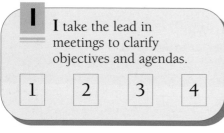

2 I focus strongly on achieving results from the tasks I undertake.

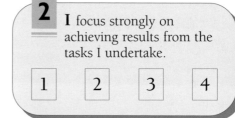

3 I propose original ideas for discussion in meetings.

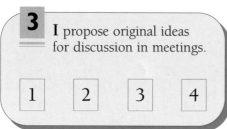

4 I make friends easily and have many useful outside contacts.

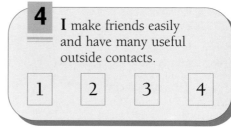

5 I find and tell the objective truth, even if people don't like to hear it.

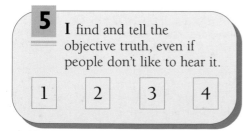

6 I maintain friendly relations with everyone on the team.

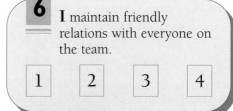

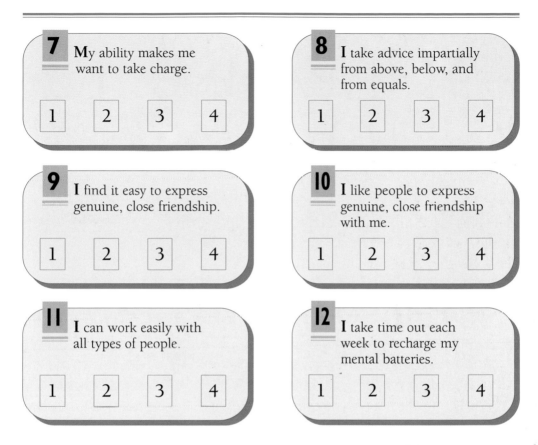

7 My ability makes me want to take charge.

1   2   3   4

8 I take advice impartially from above, below, and from equals.

1   2   3   4

9 I find it easy to express genuine, close friendship.

1   2   3   4

10 I like people to express genuine, close friendship with me.

1   2   3   4

11 I can work easily with all types of people.

1   2   3   4

12 I take time out each week to recharge my mental batteries.

1   2   3   4

ANALYSIS

Now that you have completed the self-assessment, add up your total score, and check your ability by reading the corresponding evaluation. However great your potential as a leader may be, remember that there is always room for improvement. Identify your weakest areas, and refer to the relevant sections in this book, where you will find practical advice and tips to help you understand what it takes to lead others and improve your leadership skills.

12–24: You are potentially competent, but you need to do a lot of work before you can excel in a leadership role.

25–36: Although you have the makings of a good leader, some areas still need to be improved. Identify and work on them.

37–48: Your leadership promise is high, but do not become complacent. Strive to realize it.

LEADING OTHERS

How well you lead others is the prime factor in your team's success. To be an effective leader, you must facilitate, inspire, and implement, rather than control.

PREPARING TO LEAD

Leading others is a stimulating challenge for any leader. Get to know the people who are working for you, establish a framework in which everyone can operate comfortably, and set challenging goals that will motivate and inspire.

> **19** Take time to get your bearings in a new job – but do not take too long.

QUESTIONS TO ASK YOURSELF

Q What are we trying to achieve?

Q In what ways are we trying to achieve it?

Q What major issues do we face?

Q What do others think of the organization – good and bad?

Q Are we properly organized to achieve what we want in the way we want?

GATHERING INFORMATION

Your first priority as a leader, especially if you happen to be taking over a new situation, is to find out what you have, in terms of people, policies, problems, and opportunities. An excellent approach is to go around either all the people, or (in a larger organization) the key ones, and find out their views by asking questions. Discover what they think about the organization and what they are trying to achieve. Not only will you learn a great deal about your new responsibility, but the response to your questions will also teach you a great deal about the people concerned.

ESTABLISHING A FRAMEWORK

Every leader must think about the framework in which the leader and the led can operate effectively and comfortably, both as individuals and as part of a team. Ensure that there are systems in place that enable good, open communication between you and your staff. Be clear about the roles of each team member, and make sure that everyone is aware of their responsibilities.

20 Actively seek the views of your team members.

DO'S AND DON'TS

✔ Do use all means to communicate with your staff.

✔ Do strive to regard your associates as competent people.

✔ Do try to create a positive atmosphere, free from rigidity.

✔ Do show your staff loyalty and support.

✔ Do set challenging, ambitious goals.

✘ Don't ask people to do things that you wouldn't do yourself.

✘ Don't forget that trust is a two-way process that can take time and effort to establish.

✘ Don't take sides or show any favoritism.

✘ Don't dissuade staff from speaking out.

✘ Don't be vague about team members' roles.

ESTABLISHING OBJECTIVES

A leader must always be aware of the ultimate goals of the organization, and know how their own objectives fit in with them. Once these goals have been established, you must ensure that your team understands the direction in which they are heading and why, and the purpose of their own activities within the overall plan. The ultimate objective should be broken down into attainable, yet challenging goals that ideally will be inspiring and motivating for the whole team. Aims should also relate directly to the specific skills of each individual within the team. Working together toward a shared goal gives people a sense of ownership and responsibility, and builds an atmosphere of team spirit.

Leader meets with colleague personally to obtain feedback

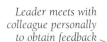

◀ **TALKING TO STAFF**
The leader should talk to colleagues personally in order to discover their views. This results in useful feedback that will help the team to work more effectively.

FORMING A TEAM

Establishing a team or appointing new team members is the responsibility of the leader. Find the best candidates to form a balanced and dynamic team, either through internal promotion or external recruitment, and help them to feel part of the team.

21 Avoid appointing a candidate simply because you are short-staffed.

22 When recruiting team members, look for their growth potential.

▼ RECRUITING STAFF
There are many channels for recruiting people, and all of them should be explored. However, personal contacts are most likely to succeed.

FINDING CANDIDATES

Cast the widest possible net, and spend as much time as needed on the selection process. Draw up a list of criteria, essential characteristics, and skills that the appointee must have. Make sure that the criteria are relevant. A common mistake is to insist on "industry experience", when research shows that it bears little relationship to success in the job. Candidates who fulfill all your criteria will be rare, so be prepared to be flexible at the selection stage.

Advertise in relevant press for applicants

Recruit from within your organization

Approach local colleges for new recruits

Ask friends and colleagues for suggestions

Recruit from government training schemes

Commission an agency to find best candidates

PROMOTING INSIDERS

Internal promotion is not only cheaper, but tells everybody that they have the opportunity to rise, which is the most satisfying form of reward. Leaders should constantly be on the lookout for abilities that can be exploited in higher-level teams. When recruiting internally, give consideration to the morale of other staff, who may feel that they have been passed over. Explain clearly to all concerned why the person that you selected is right for this assignment, and emphasize that there will be other opportunities. Then allow your candidate to prove you right.

BALANCING SKILLS

For any team to function effectively, there must be a balance of technical, problem-solving, decision-making, and interpersonal skills among its members. The ideal group will be creative yet disciplined, able to generate new ideas and find solutions to difficulties, and, at the same time, organized enough to plan and implement a task within a given period.

MAKING AN INTERNAL ▶
APPOINTMENT
Announce the appointment to staff and ensure that they understand your reasons for selecting the candidate.

23 Take into account the feelings of staff when promoting internally.

Leader announces that staff member has been promoted

Newly promoted member of team seeks colleague's support

Employee congratulates colleague on appointment

24 When a referee has reservations, always probe more deeply.

25 Ask candidates what they did really well in their previous jobs.

26 Ensure there are no interruptions during interviews.

CONDUCTING INTERVIEWS

Allow 45 minutes for an interview, preferably with one colleague, or at most, two, joining in. Keep your own talking to a minimum. You want the candidate to say as much as possible about their understanding of the job, your company, their past performance. What did they do best? You are interested in their strengths first, weaknesses second. Observe them carefully, taking into account body language and appearance.

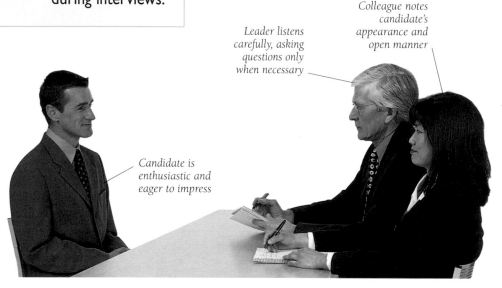

Colleague notes candidate's appearance and open manner

Leader listens carefully, asking questions only when necessary

Candidate is enthusiastic and eager to impress

JUDGING SUITABILITY

Psychometric tests and handwriting analysis (graphology) are sometimes used to evaluate candidates' suitability. But these methods are no substitute for personal judgment, reinforced by the person's track record and references, and by any appropriate skill tests. Conflicts and rivalry within groups are counterproductive, so avoid candidates who display a degree of personal assertiveness that may fracture the team spirit.

▲ ASSESSING A CANDIDATE

Observe the candidate carefully. Keep your checklist of attributes and skills in front of you, and make sure that you address them all. Above all, do not ignore your intuition or your personal reaction – it is very important that you actually like the candidate. Ask yourself whether the candidate seems "nice" and if he or she will fit in.

LEARNING FROM RECRUITS

A leader can learn a great deal from new recruits by exploiting their knowledge of other organizations, methods, or ideas. They have the advantage of an outsider's eye, before being assimilated into your company's ways. Make time for conversations with recruits, asking them for their first impressions. Acting on their suggestions is an important way of promoting their confidence.

27 See that new recruits are welcomed and fully supported.

Leader asks recruit for her impressions of the company

Colleague sits in on meeting

◀ EASING IN RECRUITS
Help new employees to learn about their new environment and master the work by appointing a suitable colleague to act as "nursemaid" while they settle in.

QUESTIONS TO ASK YOURSELF

Q What did I do wrong – did I recruit poorly?

Q Did the person lack the necessary support?

Q Have circumstances changed so that the person no longer fits the original job?

Q Is there another job in which they could succeed?

HANDLING MISFITS

Recruitment failures will inevitably occur, however much care has been taken. Whenever you contemplate dismissing somebody, always ask yourself "why has this happened?". Learn from your analysis, and if the person can be "saved" by making changes, make them. If not, do not allow the person to stay after you have, consciously or subconsciously, decided against it. Explain your reasons fully to the individual, and be as generous as possible in negotiating severance. Also, ensure that coworkers know what has happened and why.

EXERCISING AUTHORITY

The role of a leader is to ensure that everyone understands instructions and carries them out effectively. Since it is rare for everything to go according to plan, put into place reporting systems that enable you to deal with any deviations swiftly.

28 Make sure that any instructions you give are clear and concise.

29 Encourage people to approach you if things go wrong.

30 Act quickly when you learn of any real problems.

GIVING INSTRUCTIONS

The method of giving instructions matters far less than the quality of their content. If a decision has been reached in concert with the team, the leader has no need to win acceptance. But having to say "This is an order" is a sign of malfunction on one side or the other. Before you issue instructions, be absolutely clear in your own mind what your requirements are. This will be reflected in your tone of voice and body language and will reinforce your message. Ask people if they have any reservations about what you have asked of them, so that problems can be cleared up at the outset.

MANAGING BY EXCEPTION

Leaders often spend too much time double-checking everything to ensure conformance with instructions and procedures. The better approach is to manage by exception, which involves concentrating on what is going awry rather than what is not. You should not expect to hear about actions that proceed as planned, but staff or delegates should inform you immediately if there is a serious deviation from the plan. For example, if a sales executive is asked to handle key accounts, and sales targets or profit margins are being missed, he or she must report the problem to you at once.

Marketing director reports that the month's sales of an important product have fallen substantially

BEING CONSISTENT

Since leadership is about getting other people to do what you want, it is essential to maintain the cooperation and respect of your staff. Be consistent in the way you exercise authority, so that people can trust you and know that you mean what you say. This avoids ambiguity, and the danger of ill-feeling or resentment developing is reduced. Being consistent does not mean being overindulgent toward staff – as long as you are always honest, direct, and fair in your dealings with other people, they will respond positively to your authority, even under difficult or stressful circumstances.

31 Insist that staff tell you all the news, good or bad.

32 Use crises as an opportunity to develop people.

Leader asks production boss to report capacity bottlenecks in future

A plan is devised to divert unused capacity for another product, and to raise output to meet the unsatisfied demand

Leader is told that shortfall is caused by lack of capacity

Leader discovers that production is down. He calls in production boss

▲ ORGANIZING CONTROLS
By putting into place a new reporting system, the leader ensures that, in future, he will be aware of any production problems before they affect sales.

DELEGATING TASKS

As leader, you should concentrate your time on activities that nobody else can do. Delegation is a form of time management. It is a way of exercising control and meeting your own responsibilities more effectively, while developing the skills of your staff.

33 Remember that delegation boosts morale and builds confidence.

34 Never keep work simply because you do it better.

35 Set high targets in agreement with your delegates.

INCREASING YOUR TIME

Managers often claim that the demands of operational and routine duties leave them little time to concentrate on important, long-term matters, such as strategic planning and training. To create more time for yourself, it is essential to hand down more routine tasks by delegation. Even if you, the leader, are better and faster at a task than anybody else in the team, the golden rule is that you should not, and cannot, do everything yourself. Leadership involves handing over the task to others, and then helping them to match or exceed your standards.

BRIEFING DELEGATES

Give the delegate a clear, written brief, developed in consultation, that sets out the objectives, the resources available, the constraints, and the time schedule, if relevant. Supplement the written brief with an interview to ensure mutual understanding. If the circumstances change, alter the brief to suit – do not stick to it slavishly.

EXPLAINING THE BRIEF ▶
Make sure that the delegate fully understands the assignment by asking relevant questions at a face-to-face meeting. Invite the delegate to do the same.

Delegate seeks clarification on unclear points

Leader asks delegate to summarize key points of brief

SUPERVISING EFFECTIVELY

Allow the delegate to develop and execute his or her plans, subject only to keeping you fully informed. Constant interference, countermanding decisions and actions taken by the delegate, and checking up continually all add up to poor leadership. By intervening heavily, you will also frustrate the delegate and deny him or her the chance to learn new skills and gain experience. Monitor the progress of the work with a system of written reports and face-to-face meetings with the delegate, and by observing performance.

36 If time pressure increases, ask if you are delegating enough to others.

37 Check regularly and informally on progress of delegated tasks.

REINFORCING A DELEGATE'S ROLE ▼

Always introduce a new delegate to existing team members, as this will help him or her to feel part of the team. It is also important to inform any customers or suppliers who need to know what specific responsibilities the new delegate will have.

New delegate is made to feel welcome

Leader introduces new delegate and clearly states her responsibilities

Team member understands new delegate's role within team

RETAINING TASKS

There are some responsibilities that a leader cannot delegate. These include key areas, such as controlling overall performance, meeting strategic objectives, and confidential human resources matters – how people are rewarded, appraised, promoted, informed, disciplined, coached, and counseled. You may also need to supervise dealings with important customers if delegating ultimate responsibility for these contacts would endanger the relationship.

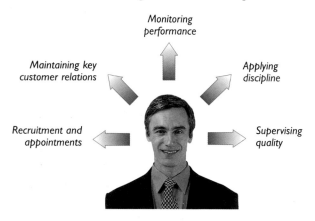

Monitoring performance

Maintaining key customer relations

Applying discipline

Recruitment and appointments

Supervising quality

◀ **KEEPING KEY TASKS**
As a leader, you must keep charge of sensitive matters, such as applying discipline and making appointments, and retain control of important areas, including finance and strategy.

---

38 Keep an open door for all your delegates.

39 Intervene fast when the delegate cannot cope.

PROVIDING SUPPORT

An open-door policy aids effective delegation. The delegate should be able to approach the delegator at any time for advice, information, or revision. The delegator should also be able to approach the delegate, whenever necessary, for an informal, encouraging discussion on how the task is going. If the delegator visits too often, either this is bad delegation, or the delegation is going badly. If delegates come through the door too often, they are either insecure or inadequate. If you are confident in their ability, give them a clear message: "I am confident that you can manage."

CHECKING PROGRESS WITH DELEGATES

When discussing progress with delegates, use positive questions, such as those below, that will encourage delegates to suggest their own solutions to problems. Avoid questions that may discourage or demoralize the delegate.

Is there anything you want to bring to my notice?

We failed to meet that target. Any suggestions as to how that might have happened?

I see that costs are over-running. What steps are you taking to bring them back in line?

How do you think we can avoid making this mistake again?

DEVELOPING DELEGATES

40 Make sure that everybody knows what must always be left to you.

Look out for signs that the delegate is taking too much on his or her own shoulders, and not allowing people who work for them to show initiative and tackle their own tasks without interference. "Getting out of the way" is the key to getting the best from others, and applies to the delegate too. Encourage delegates to think issues through and come up with answers to problems before bringing them to you. The most important lesson for the delegate is that of being accountable for results, with no opportunity for excuses.

◀ ENCOURAGING SOLUTIONS
Being a good delegator, the leader in this case did not want his people to become dependent on him and his decisions. So he forced them to make up their own minds. The boss was still prepared to discuss the issue, but his insistence helped this subordinate to be a real leader.

CASE HISTORY
John was working for a new boss in a new company and a new country. He was given the task of organizing a new project team, complete with an excellent brief. But problems arose. With existing resources, there was no hope of meeting the production targets from internal supply, as ordered. He went back to his American boss, Chuck, with the problem – and was disconcerted by the response.

"I don't want people bringing me problems without solutions," said Chuck. "I want two solutions every time, with your recommendation on which one to take. If you ever bust in here without the two solutions, you'll leave the office a damn sight faster than you came in." John went away and returned with two solutions: subcontract some of the work, or ask for more finance and people. He preferred the first, and so did Chuck.

COMMUNICATING CLEARLY

T*he ability to communicate with staff is essential in leadership. To ensure that messages are received and understood all the way down, flatten the hierarchy of your team structure. To keep communication two-way, invite feedback from your staff.*

41 Talk honestly with your staff and you will get honest answers in return.

COMMUNICATING DIRECTLY

The leader at the apex of the hierarchy passes down information and instructions, level by level, throughout the team. The trouble with this top-down management style is that you cannot always be sure that your message has gone through, or how it has been received, since there is little feedback from the lower levels. Wherever possible, deliver your message in person to ensure that it has been clearly understood by the recipient.

42 Take steps to get accurate reports of team opinions.

▼ **FLATTENING THE HIERARCHY**
You need only three levels of hierarchy and four types of staff. Leaders work in concert with managers, while staff take charge of their own output. All three levels are assisted by experts, such as information technology specialists.

ENTERPRISE MANAGERS
Responsible for strategic direction and overall success of the organization

PEOPLE MANAGERS
Responsible for implementation and the rest of the employees

STAFF
Responsible for quality and quantity of own output

EXPERTS
Responsible for specific areas, such as finance, technologies, etc.

COMMUNICATING ON ALL LEVELS

To ensure that the right message has been received and the right action taken, the top-down process needs to be checked by bottom-up communication. Spend as much time as possible with all levels of staff, and make it clear that you appreciate feedback and are willing to listen and respond. Remember that excellent ideas can come from anywhere, and are not just confined to leaders. Make use of the fact that other people know their own area of work, and can make an invaluable contribution to related issues.

COMMUNICATION

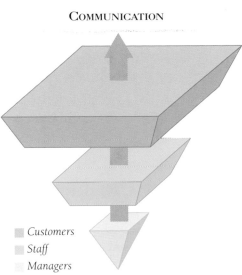

■ *Customers*
■ *Staff*
■ *Managers*

43 If all feedback is positive, you may not have been told the whole truth.

44 Be prepared for misunderstanding of what you are trying to achieve.

▲ INVERTING THE PYRAMID

Some leaders mentally balance the pyramid on its point to reverse the direction of the flow of information. Customers and their needs are put on top, followed by the employees, then the managers.

LISTENING TO STAFF

Encourage people to be open and honest with you by showing that you value their opinions and are willing to listen to them. The best way to do this is through informal conversations, either one-on-one or with groups of staff. Make it clear that even negative feedback is viewed as a positive opportunity for improvement. You must ensure that staff are not intimidated by fear of any repercussions when they express criticisms. Do not always wait for staff to come to you – solicit feedback from them by asking for their comments on issues that affect them. If you want to gain a broad picture of staff attitudes, you will have to use a more formal approach. Many techniques are available, such as surveys, sample polling, suggestion boxes, or focus groups.

DYNAMIZING GROUPS

To dynamize a group, you must give it strong purpose, strong membership, and strong leadership. Use "hot groups" for special operations, choosing the ablest and most motivated candidates for the group. Encourage innovation and creativity.

> **45** Encourage groups to achieve by setting high but realistic targets.

IMPARTING PURPOSE

A group of people striving toward a common goal should be highly motivated, with a strong sense of excitement and anticipation. The way that you, as leader, convey the purpose of the task to your group can help to instill this positive attitude. Emphasize the fact that the group has been put together for a specific purpose, and that the particular skills of each individual member are fundamental to the success of the project. This helps people to identify with the organization's goals, and empowers them to use their creativity.

ROUSING THE TROOPS

Talking to a group as a unit provides an essential test of leadership quality. Be positive and enthusiastic – your energy will inspire confidence and encourage your group to follow your example. While it is important to put across your personality, policies, and objectives, you should also reinforce group identity by providing plenty of opportunities for discussion and debate. Be firm about your expectations, but remember that enjoyment is a key motivator.

Colleague takes opportunity to state his opinion

Team member enjoys being part of dynamic group

STAYING FOCUSED ▶
Hold regular meetings to inform everyone of what has been achieved and how much more needs to be done. Use these times to reinforce motivation and purpose.

FORMING HOT GROUPS

Nothing is more exciting in management than leading a "hot group," a team assembled for a special operation, such as a new product launch. Success requires finding the ablest people and placing them under highly motivated, effective leadership (which encourages sub-leadership). The group continues to recruit talent as a key activity, concentrating on people who are right for each job and can share a powerful vision. It helps to detach the group from all other operations, and to focus change on a chosen rival: "the enemy."

Team member is encouraged by leader's positive approach

Leader encourages constructive debate

BRIEFING
HOT GROUPS

Introduce the subject (and yourself, if appropriate)

Announce the objective

Express confidence in the people present

Emphasize group/team working

Look forward, not backward

Put across your authority

Express confidence in the group's ability

Banish doubt and doubters

Emphasize that efforts will be fully supported

COLLEGIATE LEADERSHIP

*A*re you a "man on horseback" or a first
among equals? The first kind of leader is
the military model; the second is the collegiate
model. The collegiate style is increasingly
winning, since it promotes a sense of unity
and motivation within a company.

46 Always be ready
to allow others
to take the lead
when appropriate.

47 Remember that
everyone in a
team thinks in a
different way.

MEETING AS EQUALS ▼
*Working with genuine colleagues
demands the same behavior whether or
not you are the leader. Respect goes to
expertise, not to rank or seniority.
Do not engage in internal politics, but
focus on what will achieve the group's
objectives, in the knowledge that
everybody benefits from a job well done.*

LEADING AS AN EQUAL

The first-among-equals model is formalized in
German business, where the chief executive is
called the "spokesman" of the management board.
The reason why this approach is spreading is
because many minds are more powerful than one.
Create a pool of shared talent and an environment
of total communication, and consult all team
members before an important decision is made.
Even in small organizations, the range of expertise
required has expanded greatly, probably beyond
the reach of one individual. At particular stages,
moreover, one of your experts should have the
decisive voice by virtue of his or her expertise.

*Expert gives technical
assessment of issue*

*Colleague evaluates
specialist information*

*Leader invites expert
to give her opinion*

Team member checks anger and lowers his voice

Leader calms down both parties

Colleague begins to feel less distressed

HANDLING ▶ DISPUTES

When colleagues seriously disagree, you should intervene to discover what is at issue. No matter what the provocation, never lose your temper. Anger is a bad adviser.

RESOLVING DIFFICULTIES

Even successful partnerships can develop disagreements. When resolving an issue, whether involving yourself or between colleagues, try to analyze the situation calmly. Start with the team's objective. Is it shared by the combatants? If so, what factual points are at issue? If they can be resolved, what are the emotional problems that are preventing agreement? You may conclude that one of the parties, or perhaps both, is intransigent and has lost sight of the aims. If you cannot persuade them to alter their attitude, they will have to leave the team.

48 Seek to defuse emotion before tackling issues.

49 Treating everyone equally will avoid causing resentment.

SEEKING THE ▶ BEST OUTCOME

The leader in this case faced a real conflict between valued members of staff. It was important not to take sides, and to see that the best solution for the company was found. Involving another member of the team got to the real issue, and the leader was able to bring this out into the open and make a clear decision.

CASE STUDY

Roger, in charge of distribution, and Ann, customer services manager, put forward two rival plans for reorganizing the marketing department. Neither would accept the other's arguments. Their boss, Barry, asked Norman, manager of new product development and an excellent analyst, to examine the two plans. The report came down strongly in favor of Ann's ideas. Confronted with the choice, Roger still refused to agree: the reorganization would mean that he reported to Ann, and he did not want to work for a woman. Barry confronted him with this blockage and gave him a choice: accept or leave. Roger argued that his plan had been unfairly treated. Barry brought Norman into the meeting and asked him to give his reasons. Reluctantly, Roger accepted the logic and stayed.

IMPROVING YOUR EFFECTIVENESS

The best leaders seek constantly to improve and develop their skills. For the greatest success and impact, it is essential to work on upgrading and extending the basic techniques.

MAKING DECISIONS

*A*ll decisions involve a series of other decisions, notably when to settle the issue, who else to involve in the decision-making process, and what alternatives to consider. Get these decisions right and you will be poised to make the correct move.

50 If you can safely make a decision quickly, always do so.

TIMING DECISIONS

What kind of decision do you face? Time is the starting point. Does your decision have to be made immediately, by a later deadline, or at your discretion? Making no decision is a decision in itself, and possibly a fateful one. If you take no action, the time may come when an urgent decision is demanded, but it may be too late to undo the damage caused by inaction. Usually, the sooner a decision is made, the better. Even if you do not know what to do, always avoid procrastination. Seek guidance from a trusted colleague or superior, then decide on the best course of action.

Colleague expresses his opinions

CONSIDERING ALL OPTIONS

Some decisions make themselves. Other decisions have either/or choices. Others have multiple options. For decisions with two or more alternatives, be systematic in your approach. Take time to list all the available options and assess their validity and likely consequences – if necessary, involve others to generate ideas and gather relevant information. Only when you have fully researched all the options are you in a good position to select a course of action.

> **51** If you ask for advice from a coworker, expect to act on it.

SEEKING CONSENSUS

Involving others in the decision-making process requires method. The normal Western system is to debate the issue and to argue about the pros and cons of the alternatives. The Eastern way is for each participant to state his or her opinion in turn, without debate. Either way, encourage people to speak their minds. Then summarize the options and seek whatever degree of consensus is possible. Above all, finally decide yourself.

▼ SHARING DECISIONS
Discussing a problem with colleagues and analyzing the alternatives together is often the best way to move toward a decision.

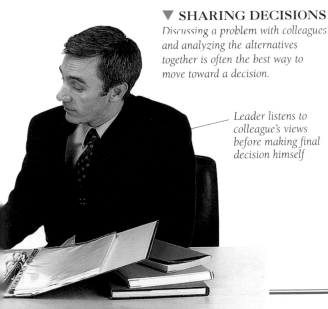

Leader listens to colleague's views before making final decision himself

SEEING DECISIONS THROUGH

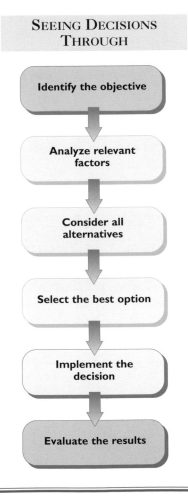

Identify the objective

Analyze relevant factors

Consider all alternatives

Select the best option

Implement the decision

Evaluate the results

SETTING GOALS

Goals are the essence of planning, whether for the long, medium, or short terms. They should be ambitious but achievable. Set stretching, hard-headed, but feasible sub-goals to help your team attain their ultimate goal.

> **52** Seek to turn the impossible into a target that you can achieve.

TESTING CRITERIA FOR GOALS

- Are they clear, hard, and measurable?
- Are they approved by the implementers?
- Can they realistically be achieved?
- Do they have a clear, sensible timeframe?
- Have they been translated into full plans?
- Will they be revised as events dictate?
- Will reaching them advance our strategy?
- Will they generate rewards for people?
- Do they translate into individual goals?

BEING AMBITIOUS

The degree of ambition in setting goals is important because people respond to the promise of high achievement, in sports and business alike. A leader who thinks big can prove that what seemed unrealistic and impossible to achieve is actually within everyone's grasp. Set goals whose accomplishment will fill team members with pride and observers with admiration.

AIMING FOR THE MOON ▶
Every leader needs to seek the equivalent of President Kennedy's commitment of America to "go to the moon". If you think small, you will probably not achieve big results, even by accident.

SELECTING OBJECTIVES

OBJECTIVES	TARGETS	ULTIMATE GOAL

SETTING OBJECTIVES

Goals are seldom met without having to overcome unexpected difficulties, disappointments, and even disasters. Achieving your aims despite such setbacks is a crucial test of leadership. First, do not panic or blame. Neither will help to get the plan back on track, if that still remains feasible. You should take immediate action to deal swiftly and surely with the negative event and its consequences. Remember that a positive state of mind is crucial in reaching goals, so try to instill this in your team.

REVISING GOALS

If you suffer a setback, reassess the viability of the goal as soon as possible. Does it need serious revision? Must more time and/or money be allowed? You may have to abandon the goal – but take this step only if dispassionate analysis shows it to be the only practical alternative. Try to use the setback as a trigger to stimulate renewed effort by being positive and decisive yourself.

▲ **ACHIEVING ENDGOALS**
By selecting your objectives, individuals and teams can be given targets and timescales that, if achieved, will come together to meet the ultimate goal.

53 Expect setbacks, and always have contingency plans fully prepared.

54 Cut your losses fast if failure is truly inevitable.

DEVELOPING TEAMWORK

*F*or a team to work well, several roles must be played – not independently, but collectively. The leader's role is to develop a team that thinks and acts together, with individual and team interests aligned.

> **55** Ensure that team members share the same goals.

ASSIGNING ROLES

The efficient team consists of people who can play several key roles (including coordinator, critic, ideas person, implementer, external contact, inspector, and team builder) in addition to the skills they bring to the basic tasks of the team. As leader, ensure that all these roles are played, sometimes with people combining roles. When organizing the team, fit the roles to the talents available, and provide training if necessary.

KEY TEAM ROLES

COORDINATOR
Pulls together the work of the team as a whole.

CRITIC
Guardian and analyst of the team's effectiveness.

IDEAS PERSON
Encourages the team's innovative vitality.

IMPLEMENTER
Ensures smooth running of the team's actions.

EXTERNAL CONTACT
Looks after the team's external contacts.

INSPECTOR
Ensures that high standards are maintained.

TEAM BUILDER
Develops the team spirit.

DEVELOPING TEAM LEADERSHIP SKILLS

To be an effective team leader, you must:
- Ensure that everyone on the team is working toward agreed, shared objectives;
- Criticize constructively, and make sure that you praise good work as well as find fault;
- Monitor the team members' activities continuously by obtaining effective feedback;
- Constantly encourage and organize the generation of new ideas within the team;
- Always insist on the highest standards of execution from team members;
- Develop the individual and collective skills of the team, and seek to strengthen them by training and recruitment.

MULTITASKING

Teams can function well in a situation where each member has a specific task and does nothing else. But in many cases you need more flexibility, which is when multitasking becomes important. Teams function better when people understand each other's jobs. Allocate time for your team members to work with others on the team. For example, encourage a production worker to accompany a salesperson to see a customer, or sit a marketing person next to an engineer. This broadens perceptions as well as skills, and promotes cooperation.

56 Encourage competition between ideas, not individuals.

POINTS TO REMEMBER

- Roles should be matched to personality rather than the personality pushed into the role.
- If a team has only a few members, roles can be doubled or tripled up to ensure that the team's needs are covered.
- Once roles have been allocated, consult the team members to get their agreement on what needs to be done and how.
- Specific tasks should be allocated to each team member, complete with time scales and reporting responsibilities.
- Performance must be monitored at team meetings.
- It is important to concentrate on collective achievement.
- Individual contributions should be dealt with in a team context.

▲ BUILDING A STRONGER TEAM

Provide the training that enables people to master more than one task, and then your multiskilled team members can be used as understudies and as coworkers when help is needed.

57 Boost a team's effectiveness by training members in new skills.

EMPOWERING TEAMS

Empower team members by giving them whole tasks and allowing them to find the best way of performing them, but make any suggestions you feel necessary for improvement. In this way you are enabling them to use their talents more fully. Let everybody exercise the right to think and contribute their intelligence to the team.

▲ **TAKING A BACK SEAT**

As leader, step back and let team members take the lead when appropriate. You do not have to chair every meeting or make every decision. The more you encourage the team to develop and use leadership skills, the stronger your own leadership will be.

58 Ask people if they have enough responsibility.

59 Do not accept the opinions of others on team abilities.

INHERITED TEAMS

If you inherit a team, or have its membership decided for you, do not jump to conclusions about the members until you have got to know them reasonably well and have understood their present capabilities. Set aside time to talk to each team member, one-on-one, about their individual tasks, their ideas, and their views of their own performance. This will give you a clear insight into their characters and abilities. You can then decide what roles and tasks are appropriate, and whether any training is needed.

UNDERSTANDING REWARDS

Rewards for good performance can take several forms, including pay raises, bonuses, profit-sharing programs, stock options, and recognition such as vacations or prizes. The object of a reward program is to motivate teams and individuals to perform even better. Good leadership also recognizes that team members deserve to share financially in the success that they have created. The best idea is to let employees help to decide how bonus payments should be made.

60 Allow new people and teams to prove how good they are.

61 Reward real merit openly, but never appear to play any favorites.

REWARDING INDIVIDUALS

There is a conflict between the interests of the team and those of the individual. For example, if an individual asks for a pay raise and you meet their demand, you must expect the team to learn what has happened. If they feel the raise is unfair, that might disrupt teamworking. You cannot be unfair to an individual because of the perceptions of other team members. Be frank, explain your decision fully, and stand by it.

CHOOSING A REWARD SYSTEM

REWARD	IMPLEMENTATION	ADVANTAGES
SALARY INCREASES Increases in basic rate of pay, not directly related to performance.	Requires management to decide on overall salary scale and placing of particular jobs within the scale.	● Individuals know exactly where they stand financially. ● Can reduce element of competition within teams.
BONUSES One-time payments linked to performance or financial targets.	Can take several forms, such as sharing financial savings, but payments must be based on meaningful measures.	● Increases motivation and job satisfaction. ● Gives staff incentive for cost-cutting and quality drives.
PROFIT-SHARING An allocated share of the profits is split between employees.	Management must find a fair method of profit distribution, either on a corporate or divisional basis.	● Is an excellent motivator of individuals. ● Gives teams a sense of working toward common aim.
STOCK OWNERSHIP Gift of stocks or chance to buy them on preferential terms.	Any rewards are directly linked to corporate success, and are moving down from top levels in many corporations.	● Encourages long-term loyalty and a sense of involvement. ● Helps staff identify with overall group results.
RECOGNITION REWARDS Many options, including prizes, vacations, parties.	Care should be taken to avoid implying that performing to the highest standards is the exception rather than the rule.	● Can reward teams or individuals. ● Staff are highly motivated by recognition, even if only verbal.
COMPOSITE REWARDS Rewards allocated for individual, team, and company results.	Allows management to combine individual with company-wide rewards, with elements tied to teamwork.	● Varying the reward packages keeps interest fresh. ● Recognition of teamwork elements boosts team spirit.

LEADING DISCUSSIONS

Whether they are formal or casual, involve groups of people, or are conducted on a one-on-one basis, discussions allow people to share ideas or concerns freely. By playing a leading role, you can keep discussions productive and purposeful.

62 Give people a time for meetings and always keep the appointment.

TALKING TO YOUR TEAM

As a leader, you should call your team together on a regular basis to collect feedback, generate ideas, and make decisions. Even when holding small, informal discussions it is important to keep the purpose and a time limit in mind. Give people time to prepare, and make sure that everyone involved is given an opportunity to air their views. Encourage open conversation but discourage digressions and keep the subject matter moving forward toward an action agenda.

QUESTIONS TO ASK YOURSELF

Q Am I seeking to give people information or instructions, or am I merely making an announcement?

Q Am I holding a discussion with the aim of making a decision or decisions?

Q Is the purpose to obtain feedback on progress?

Q Is it a negotiation or a disciplinary meeting?

Q Do I want to discuss long-term strategy?

Q Am I dealing with a short-term matter, perhaps a crisis?

Q Am I only trying to find the facts?

Member feels free to speak openly

▲ **MEETING INFORMALLY**
Informal one-on-one meetings provide opportunities to discuss issues frankly and reach decisions quickly. They also enable leaders to forge stronger relationships with individual members of staff.

63 Keep discussions informal whenever possible to ease staff relationships.

ENCOURAGING DISCUSSION

Facilitate personal contacts by organizing office space to give staff the chance to meet and exchange information. Extra-wide corridors encourage casual discussions, as does sitting staff at round tables in open-plan offices. One company has elevators that stop at only one floor so that people must meet in them. Intranets and other networks achieve the same result electronically. This type of office contact is vital for sharing ideas and information, and for developing friendships.

▲ GETTING TOGETHER SOCIALLY

Events such as lunches, celebrations, and parties are important to foster easy exchanges of information and ideas. Socializing outside the office also helps to strike up friendships and smooth working relations between team members. As leader, you should be at the center of these circles, participating in them fully.

Meeting area is easily accessible

Informal desk layout promotes easy contact

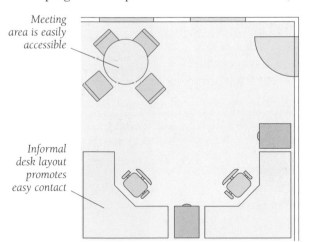

▲ FOSTERING COMMUNICATION

An open-plan office is far more conducive to good communication than an enclosed, square-table office. In a more relaxed and informal setting, round tables are set aside for meetings in quieter areas away from desks. The important factor is to strike a balance between easy contact and efficiency.

CULTURAL DIFFERENCES

In order to facilitate discussion, some top bosses in the United States have abandoned executive suites for open-plan floors. The same can happen in Japan. Although individual offices hinder the flow of information, Germans and Britons still prefer them for reasons of prestige.

64 Never hide behind the closed doors of private offices.

USING MEETINGS

Organizations breed meetings, but often they lack any clear purpose. Ensure that meetings have valid goals – there is no point in bringing people together to rubber-stamp decisions that have already been made – and that they are time-effective.

> **65** Use meetings to take decisions as fast as possible, not to delay them.

> **66** Ask only relevant people to meetings to keep the numbers down.

> **67** Allow staff to stay away if they feel they have nothing to contribute.

MINIMIZING MEETINGS

Most leaders feel pressured by the amount of time that they are expected to spend in meetings. But how many meetings really serve a useful purpose? As leader, always consider the validity of a meeting before arranging it. Is it worth your own and others' time? For example, if you hold a weekly team meeting, does it serve a purpose or are you doing it purely out of habit?

QUESTIONING MEETINGS

To help you decide whether to call a meeting, assume that it is unnecessary unless it can pass the following triple test. Does the meeting have:
● A clearly defined purpose?
● Measurable outcomes?
● An entirely functional membership?
Used unwisely, meetings can reduce the opportunity for leadership because, instead of making decisions, meetings postpone them and dilute responsibility. Never use a meeting when individuals could do the same work.

RUNNING MEETINGS

Go into every meeting with a plan for what you want accomplished, while accepting that this may mean changing your own ideas. Except in emergencies, ensure that all documentation is distributed well before the meeting. In taking the chair, your role is to run an orderly discussion and to ensure that everybody who has something to say says it. End the meeting with a summary that includes an action plan, with deadlines and personal responsibilities for every action.

68 If you are in the chair, do not use the position to be dictatorial.

Leader keeps team standing to ensure meeting is brief

AVOIDING DELAYS

It is important that fixed meetings do not gum up the works. Learn from the example of a store chain that allows one manager to make decisions on a supplier's proposed price change on his own. A rival sends all these decisions to a pricing committee that meets every Monday. The result can be a seven-day delay, which could result in serious competitive loss. Leave similar authorizations to individuals wherever possible.

◀ **STANDING MEETINGS**
Follow the principle used by General Gus Pagonis, supply chief in the Gulf War. His morning meetings were literally standing. Since nobody was allowed to sit down, meetings were brief and to the point.

69 Keep meetings to the shortest time needed to cover a brief agenda.

ANALYZING PROBLEMS

The word problem means "something that is difficult to solve," "a puzzle," "something perplexing." By being positive and using analysis of the issue, you can overcome any obstacles and replace the problem with a solution.

70 Keep it simple and look first for the easy solution.

71 Regard problems as opportunities for team learning.

72 Consider an issue from every possible angle.

THINKING POSITIVELY

One leader found the word "problem" so negative that he banned its use. Instead of problems, managers were told to talk about opportunities. His attitude was right. The word problem really describes the need to choose between alternatives. If you are baffled, that is usually because you are unclear about what you want to accomplish, or because you are unwilling to accept the right alternative, even when analysis makes the best choice obvious. Recognizing the emotional blockage often helps the problem disappear.

EXAMINING THE FACTS

The issue could be isolated, such as whether to build a Web site. Or it may be recurrent, like how to control expenditure. In all cases, ask: What questions do I wish to answer? Why is there an issue? In pursuing the control issue, for example, you will want to know answers to the following questions: How much are the present controls costing? What benefits will result from change? What systems do others use? Who will supervise and who will devise the controls? What are the difficulties? What are the alternatives? Keep going until the questions run out. The answers will provide the essential facts, without which you cannot hope to generate the best solution.

73 Look for the positive side of any negative situation.

74 Ensure you have all the facts before taking action.

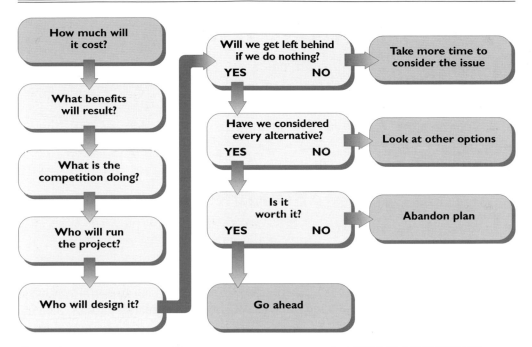

OVERCOMING OBSTACLES

Many issues tend to revolve around gaps. This means that there is a distance between where you are and where you want to be. The question is how to get from A to B. There may be a number of obstacles in your path, such as a shortage of resources (people or money, for example), powerful competitors, planning regulations, or many other snags. You can either explore ways of overcoming the obstacles or compromise on the objective. However, it is important that you do devise a plan for reaching your goal: only weak leaders, having identified the gap, take no action to close it.

▲ ASKING QUESTIONS
When attempting to resolve a problem, it is essential to ask yourself all the relevant questions. Once you have the answers available, the solution will follow.

▼ TAKING ACTION
Management writer Peter Drucker defines management as: "Knowing what to do; knowing how to do it, and doing it." The first two steps (Analysis and Planning) are useless without the third (Action).

GIVING SUPPORT

Trust can be difficult to build, but it is easy to lose. This is partly because people start with a distrustful mind-set. As a leader, you need to work hard at earning trust, fostering that trust by showing loyalty, and supporting your team fully.

> **75** Find ways of showing people that you trust them to act effectively.

POINTS TO REMEMBER

- If promises are made, they should always be kept.
- Going behind people's backs is not permissible.
- People should be kept fully informed of anything that might directly affect them.
- Performance should be judged and rewarded fairly.

BUILDING TRUST

Leaders have to prove themselves trustworthy by word and deed, and then prove themselves all over again. Even then, a few people will continue to believe that you have a hidden agenda, however many assurances and reassurances they have received. Start from the assumption that you are trustworthy and will be trusted. Then, if you are honest, keep your promises, and play fair with people, trust will generally follow.

LOOKING AFTER PEOPLE

Taking care of people is your prime duty as their leader. In the workplace, that involves seeing that working conditions are as pleasant as possible and that sensible requests for changes or improvements are dealt with sensitively. With individuals, it often means working as chief welfare officer. Be prepared to make exceptions to help people in trouble, and do not hesitate if you suspect problems. It is important not to allow situations to worsen. Ask if something is wrong and, if it is, act.

> **76** Never refuse a request without careful thought.

◄ **SHOWING SYMPATHY**
People bring their personal difficulties to a good leader. Whether or not the problems are affecting their work, a prompt and sympathetic response is required.

IMPARTING CONFIDENCE

Achievement builds confidence. People may doubt their ability to achieve a difficult target. When the target is met or surpassed, their feelings about themselves will improve. Reinforce these feelings by celebrating individual and team contributions, using presentations or other media. If mistakes occur, point them out, but do not undermine the person. Conscientious workers will be hard enough on themselves.

77 Reward success with praise as well as material recognition.

78 Always be loyal to your people in any public situation.

79 If you have to criticize someone, do so in private.

PROVIDING BACKUP

The most important support is psychological and costs nothing: loyalty. If you expect loyalty, give it. In confrontations with outsiders, support your colleagues so far as the facts will allow. Any reprimand or disciplinary action takes place in private, between leader and staff member, and not in front of third parties. Material backup is also vital. Giving people the equipment and other resources they need to perform an excellent job is no less than they deserve. Being seen to fight for resources on their behalf, moreover, will strengthen trust and loyalty.

CASE STUDY

Harry managed an important unit in which errors had reached unacceptable levels and staff morale was low. The relationship between Harry and his immediate superior, Lynn, had deteriorated to the point of non-communication. When a new functional director, George, was appointed, Lynn said that his first job was to fire Harry. But George insisted on making his own decision. He

arranged a meeting at which Lynn and Harry aired their differences. They hinged around minor grievances that Lynn had failed to handle, because she took them as symptoms of Harry's general unworthiness. George dealt with the grievances, insisted that Harry and Lynn should meet only in his presence, and gave Harry his confidence. The unit's performance was transformed as Harry proved himself an excellent leader.

◄ INSTILLING FAITH

In this case, an important unit was performing very badly. Its leader had lost his confidence, since his immediate superior seemed to have no faith in his ability. Once the leader's confidence was restored, and his feelings about himself improved, morale and performance within his unit were quickly transformed.

ASSESSING YOUR LEADERSHIP SKILLS

Gauge your ability as an effective leader by responding to the following statements, and mark the options closest to your experience. Be as honest as you can: if your answer is "never," mark Option 1; if it is "always," mark Option 4; and so on. Add your scores together, and refer to the Analysis to see how you scored. Use your answers to identify the areas that need improving.

OPTIONS
1 Never
2 Occasionally
3 Frequency
4 Always

1 I ignore employees' small mistakes and focus on more important matters.

1　2　3　4

2 I am able to accept criticism and always react to it well.

1　2　3　4

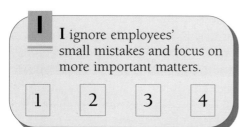

3 I am relaxed at work and keep calm when dealing with others.

1　2　3　4

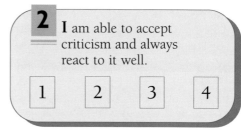

4 I am extremely secure and confident in what I undertake.

1　2　3　4

5 I keep professional and personal relationships separate.

1　2　3　4

6 I give credit to the team as a whole when high levels of productivity are achieved.

1　2　3　4

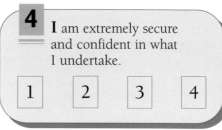

7 I am seen as a fair and just person who never takes sides.

1   2   3   4

8 I convey feelings of security and tranquillity to my team.

1   2   3   4

9 I convey a sense of friendliness and concern for the problems of others.

1   2   3   4

10 I treat people in inferior positions with respect when dealing with them.

1   2   3   4

11 I treat my subordinates in exactly the same way as my superiors.

1   2   3   4

12 I avoid making a point of being the boss, and treat others as equals.

1   2   3   4

13 I show that I am an excellent communicator and can motivate my team.

1   2   3   4

14 I participate with vigor to help my team achieve a specific goal.

1   2   3   4

15 I feel that I am well-respected and held in good opinion by my team.

1   2   3   4

16 I show impartiality in respect of color, religion, nationality, or gender.

1   2   3   4

17 I accept the opinions of others, even when they differ from my own.

1 2 3 4

18 I am just and impartial when awarding prizes and promotions.

1 2 3 4

19 I endeavor to help the group stick together during a crisis.

1 2 3 4

20 I choose between speed and perfection, depending on the situation.

1 2 3 4

21 I involve myself in situations only when my intervention is required.

1 2 3 4

22 I demonstrate deep knowledge of my area of expertise.

1 2 3 4

23 I perform better than my staff if I have to replace someone temporarily.

1 2 3 4

24 I clearly distinguish between what is urgent and what is important.

1 2 3 4

25 I concentrate less on small details and give more time to important matters.

1 2 3 4

26 I show that I am a creative person who is always change-orientated.

1 2 3 4

27 I promote creativity and innovation so that people feel free to suggest ideas.

| 1 | 2 | 3 | 4 |

28 I choose the right people as far as my team is concerned.

| 1 | 2 | 3 | 4 |

29 I make excellent use of the financial resources at my disposal.

| 1 | 2 | 3 | 4 |

30 I make sure that training and related matters are properly done.

| 1 | 2 | 3 | 4 |

31 I perform my tasks well and prove myself to be trustworthy.

| 1 | 2 | 3 | 4 |

32 I represent the company well, encouraging other people to trust it.

| 1 | 2 | 3 | 4 |

ANALYSIS

Now that you have completed the self-assessment, add up your total score, and check your performance by reading the corresponding evaluation. Whatever level of success you have achieved in leading people, it is important to remember that there is always room for improvement. Identify your weakest areas and refer to the relevant chapters to find practical advice to help you develop and refine your leadership skills.

32–64: You may be losing the authority to lead. Use this opportunity to learn from your mistakes and improve your performance, using this book to help you.
65–95: Your leadership skills are generally sound but could improve. Develop those areas where you scored poorly.
96–128: You are a fine leader. Now work to improve further.

INSPIRING EXCELLENCE

The difference between leadership and management lies in the leader's ability to inspire the will to excel. Spur people on to achieve their best through motivation and example.

MOTIVATING OTHERS

People are capable of remarkable achievement if they are given the right motivational leadership. To mobilize a team's inner drive, enthusiasm, and vigor effectively, you need to be a credible leader who sets an inspiring example.

80 Never seek to get results by bullying people beneath you.

81 Use discipline sparingly, but make it swift and effective.

82 Keep the "carrot" visible but the "stick" in hiding.

SHARING A PURPOSE

The key to motivation is to communicate a strong sense of shared purpose. That can only be developed, of course, by sharing the purpose, involving everybody in plans, reviews, and getting results. Organize regular meetings to ensure that staff are up to date on the progress of the company. This knowledge makes team members more aware of their roles. As a result, they feel that their efforts make a difference to achieving common goals. Create the desire to succeed, not only for personal gratification, but also out of a sense of identification with the team objective.

SETTING AN EXAMPLE

A decisive leader who welcomes change and shows personal drive develops similar qualities in others. People will strive to excel for a leader in whose strength and wisdom they truly believe. Your own standards are therefore crucial. On top of that foundation, a high level of energy and purposeful activity is vital.

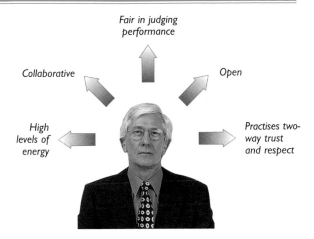

Fair in judging performance

Collaborative

Open

High levels of energy

Practises two-way trust and respect

▲ EVALUATING THE INSPIRATIONAL LEADER

A leader must be fair, open, trustworthy, and wise to inspire others. He or she also needs boundless energy and enthusiasm. Without these qualities, the basis for credibility will not exist.

TESTING YOUR CREDIBILITY

If you can agree with the statements below, you are a credible leader who is able to inspire others.

- I perform to the highest level of competence.
- I take initiatives and risks.
- I adapt to change.
- I make decisions promptly.
- I work cooperatively as a team member.
- I am open, especially with information and knowledge.
- I trust and am trustworthy.
- I respect others and myself.
- I answer for my actions and accept responsibility.
- I judge and am judged, reward and am rewarded, on the basis of performance.

KEEPING MOTIVATION HIGH

When problems or failures occur, a good leader confronts them squarely and seeks to understand their causes before using them as springboards for success. After a careful analysis of the reasons behind failure, be prepared to take responsibility for your own errors. Making honest mistakes once is common and is forgivable in a motivating, no-blame culture. But to keep motivation high, you cannot allow mistakes to be repeated time and again. Discuss with your staff what can be learned from these expensive lessons, and ensure that they are equipped to do better next time.

83 Share responsibility for mistakes and failures, and analyze errors so you can prevent them next time.

ESTABLISHING A VISION

Human beings find it easier to look back rather than forward. But effective and inspirational leadership begins with the long view. Establish a vision of where you want to be in the long term, and your visionary zeal will inspire others to look to the future.

> **84** Write down your ambitions, and revise them periodically.

> **85** If your vision seems unattainable, simply intensify your efforts.

DEVELOPING A VISION

A vision is an aim for the future – at any level, from team, to department, to organization. To develop a vision, define what you are aiming to achieve in the future, and compare it with where you are now. Map out what you will need to bridge the gap, from extra staff or training to purchasing new technology. As leader, you must consider all the necessary steps to achieve the vision.

RECOGNIZING ATTITUDES

VISIONARY
Can see the benefits of change, and has the courage to carry out change despite obstacles.

PRAGMATIST
Will accept innovation, but only after it has been proved to work by somebody else.

CONSERVATIVE
Resists change and is creative only in inventing excuses for rejecting the new.

CREATING VISIONARIES

Any organization can be broken down into visionaries, pragmatists, and conservatives. The last group leads the opposition to change, while pragmatists are followers rather than leaders. You need the pragmatist's interest in proof, facts, and figures and the conservative's attachment to abiding values and accumulated experience. But both need to be animated by the visionary's strong leadership. Involving pragmatists and conservatives in plans for change may, over time, make them more ready to share visions.

EXPRESSING A VISION

Visions need to be expressed as statements to communicate a clear understanding of the long-term aim and the principles underlying it. When creating such a statement, ask yourself if anybody reading it would be able to extract a practical understanding of the business you are in, where your leadership is going, and how it is getting there. That requires a triple focus: on the customers, on the people who serve the customers, and on the constantly improved performance that makes that service excellent. Ensure that you apply that focus in ways that are different to and better than the competition. That is unlikely to be the case if your statement reads much like everybody else's. Become the strongest critic of your own vision.

86 Keep vision and mission wording brief, clear, and prescriptive.

87 Give statements to others to check before you finalize them.

STRENGTHENING VISION STATEMENTS

WEAK STATEMENTS	QUESTIONS RAISED	STRONG STATEMENTS
"We have a strong people orientation and demonstrate care for every employee in the company."	● What does "people orientation" mean in practice? ● What kind of "care?"	"We will lead local suppliers in share, product/service quality, value, customer satisfaction, and good conduct by being different and measurably better."
"We sustain a strong results orientation coupled with a prudent approach to business."	● What does "results orientation" mean in practice? ● What is "prudence" about?	"Strategies, policies, and implementation are designed for and by our people, who ally with suppliers to achieve high customer ratings."
"Our aim is to be the biggest and best in our market."	● What do "biggest and best" actually mean? ● On what criteria are they applied?	"We invest and innovate to double real revenues every three years, while raising operating profits, cash flow, giving added value, and sharing the rewards."

GENERATING IDEAS

T he leader does not have to be the most inventive person on the team. But as leader, you need to release the potential for generating ideas that exists in all individuals and teams. This will help in both achieving a vision and resolving day-to-day issues.

88 Make people see that it is everyone's job to generate ideas.

PROMOTING CREATIVITY

Actively promote creativity by example, encouragement, rewards, training, procedures, budgeting processes, and promotion. Lower any creative barriers by tolerating failure and eccentricity, flattening organizational structures and removing blockages, and refusing to tolerate concepts such as "Not invented here," "It will never work," "If it was any good somebody else would have done it," and their equivalents. Also, recognize that consensus can be the enemy of creativity, and do not allow the pursuit of agreement to kill creative initiatives. If a creative idea is proposed to you, always consider it.

89 Try to implement suggestions, as long as they will cause no harm.

STIMULATING IDEAS

If you wait for ideas to come, they probably will not. A few rare people spout ideas all the time. But most of those attending an ideas meeting will be relatively quiet participants. To stop that from happening, insist on two rules. First, everybody must come to the meeting with two or three genuinely new ideas, which can be as far-fetched as they like. Second, nobody is allowed to "shoot ideas down in flames" – trashing proposals without discussion. The important needs are to get ideas on the table and to encourage everybody to believe in their own powers of idea generation.

Challenger visualizes an idea

Dreamer conceptualizes the idea

BRAINSTORMING

Getting people together to generate ideas, or brainstorming, has sent many groups down the wrong path to creativity. Badly practiced, it encourages the belief that throwing ideas into the pot is itself creative. Organized creativity is far more effective. A simple procedure is to start by analyzing the situation and to end with a shortlist of strong ideas. At each stage of this process there should be a challenging session, in which people can challenge assumptions. Often what is taken for granted should not be.

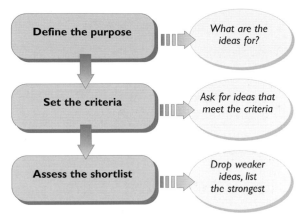

Define the purpose	▸	What are the ideas for?
Set the criteria	▸	Ask for ideas that meet the criteria
Assess the shortlist	▸	Drop weaker ideas, list the strongest

▲ IDENTIFYING THE BEST IDEAS

Organized creativity can be extremely productive. A brainstorming meeting should be divided into three main stages, enabling the group to agree on a shortlist of strong ideas.

Explorer analyzes the idea

Map maker mobilizes troops and resources

Path cutter realizes the idea and makes it happen

90 Make sure ideas are challenged with respect and not with contempt.

◀ UNDERSTANDING INNOVATION

A good creative team comprises individuals who can take an idea from conception to fruition. The first stage is to come up with a concept. Next, the team must assess whether the concept will work, evaluate the practical implications, and decide how the idea will be implemented. Finally, the plan has to be followed through. Each stage fits and needs different personalities.

MANAGING OPENLY

Sharing information has a positive effect on performance. Withholding it has the opposite effect. By trusting your staff with information and by being open and honest with them, you will help and inspire them to perform better.

91 If unsure about whether or not you should pass on information, do so.

COMMUNICATING FULLY

As the leader of a multinational company said, "However much you communicate, it is never enough." Information is the lifeblood of an organization, and communication its main artery. Make sure that the channels of communication are always open in all directions. Keeping staff up-to-date with the latest developments generates goodwill toward the company. Use every means available to ensure that whatever you know, your staff know, and as soon as possible.

Leader openly discusses facts and figures with team member

SECRETIVE MANAGEMENT

Employee acts deceptively to gain information

AVOIDING SECRECY ▲
Unnecessary secrecy demoralizes people and diminishes their potential. Conversely, their performance is enhanced, often greatly, by fuller knowledge. Financial information, for instance, is often on the secret list. But if people are given figures that reflect the performance of their part of the company, they will understand the financial results of their actions.

OPEN MANAGEMENT

CHOOSING COMMUNICATION TOOLS

EMAIL
This prime means of communication is fast, effective, and user-friendly.

MEETINGS
Face-to-face meetings build relationships and trust, and promote instant feedback.

JOURNALISM
In-house newsletters and magazines are a good way of keeping people informed.

INTERNAL MARKETING
Colorful marketing is a good way of "selling" change using consumer techniques.

NOTICEBOARDS
Bulletin boards are a basic means of giving information that can also be used by staff.

TELEPHONE
The telephone is vital for one-on-one communication, but not for lengthy talks.

92 Ensure that your messages reach all members of staff.

93 Make sure that you encourage staff to participate in decision-making.

SHARING INFORMATION

Open management involves regular exchanges of information between leaders and team members. Problems and tactics are discussed openly, and everybody is invited to make suggestions. Open management favors the creation of a positive, motivational atmosphere in the workplace: staff feel that they are part of the decision process and that their opinions are valued. Leaders also benefit: they can keep a finger on the pulse and learn of potential problems at an early stage. Make sure that you are visible and approachable: staying behind closed doors makes you remote and inaccessible. Be available for discussion and, if you can, facilitate collaboration among team members by having open-plan layouts.

BOOSTING ACHIEVEMENT

A *good leader insists on positive outcomes for both short-term goals and for the long-term vision. Make sure that team members know what your desired result is, and monitor their performance as individuals and as a team in terms of output.*

94 Always keep your mind firmly on the outcome that you are seeking.

95 Encourage people to seek clarification if they are unsure about any of their objectives.

CHOOSING A MONITORING SYSTEM

SYSTEM	RESULT
WRITTEN REPORTS Staff provide written summary of actions, results, and figures.	Encourages staff to organize their thoughts and review their actions clearly.
PERSONAL REPORTS Regular meetings are held with each team member to assess progress.	Allows for informal updates and facilitates early airings of potential problems.
OPEN-DOOR POLICY Individuals are encouraged to discuss day-to-day problems at any time.	Shows strong support, but may prevent team members from using their initiative.
APPRAISAL Formal interviews are held to assess performance and set improvement targets.	Appraisal produces improved results if practiced continuously and informally.

MONITORING PROGRESS

It is essential to keep an eye on how plans are progressing so that you can spot problems early. If all is going well, you may want to raise targets to exploit the opportunity. The key is to make progress measurable. For example, build in key dates and quality targets, and compare budgets with actual expenditure. Regular checks should help you and your staff to adjust targets, budgets, and so on, while keeping teams on course to achieve the desired outcome. As a leader, you are in a good position to see the overall picture – if several aspects are going awry, drastic action may be needed.

96 Make the outcome measurable if at all possible.

JUDGING OUTPUT

Are your staff contributing enough toward the overall desired outcome? If the answer is "Yes," your leadership has passed the first and most important test. If the reply is "No," you have two options. Either tell subordinates precisely what you want from them and how you want it achieved, or be clear about the outcome and leave the choice of route and methods to them.

97 Get staff fully involved in achieving the ultimate objective.

98 Let your staff know exactly what you expect from them.

99 Use appraisals to develop your staff, not as ends in themselves.

RAISING OUTPUT

Annual appraisals provide an opportunity for a leader to discuss performance and output with staff and to set targets for improvement. However, you will find the process far easier if you practice continuous appraisal, talking to everyone about their jobs. This informal contact helps to keep people focused on desired outcomes, as well as keeping you up to date with their progress. Provide feedback to ensure that staff feel a sense of direction and achievement; ask for and act on their input; and provide support and training readily when necessary. Continuous involvement should help to boost morale and raise output.

HELPING PEOPLE TO IMPROVE OUTPUT

It is important to talk to people regularly about their jobs and how you and they think performance could be improved. Remember to include your own role in the discussion. Always use positive questions, such as the following:

Is there anything you think could be done better?

What am I doing that is stopping you from performing your job better?

Can I do something that would help you to excel?

Is there any way in which we could change the project to achieve better results?

BEING COMPETITIVE

*E*ntrepreneurs, people who spot and
take a new business opportunity, are
inspirational leaders who know that it is
vital to accept the risk of failure to achieve
anything worthwhile. Emulate such people
by seeing risks and threats as opportunities.

> **100** Do not gamble,
> but back your own
> best judgment in
> going for results.

IDENTIFYING OPPORTUNITIES

Taking charge of a project may not in itself be
entrepreneurial, but you still need to identify
and express the objective, form and activate
an effective team, and realize the ultimate goal
by executing an excellent plan. The more you
behave like an entrepreneur, the more successful
your leadership is likely to be. What opportunities
exist – not only in the marketplace, but internally
– that could bring higher profits and greater
customer satisfaction? What new, higher
ambitions will transform the unit's prospects?

TAKING RISKS

Leaders realize that every opportunity involves
two risks: first, that the perceived opportunity
may not exist; second, if it does, that poor
execution may lose you the perceived chance.
Either way, the resulting failure can cause loss and
humiliation. But the key to risk-taking is certainty:
you must have complete confidence in your ability
to win. You should also take every care (using
analytical and intuitive skills) to ensure that you do
not lose. Do this by listing the possible consequences
of the risk, and assess how likely each is to occur.
Be clear-sighted, and seek to minimize negative
consequences and maximize positive ones.

*The chance of
making gains
is small*

*The risk of
large losses
is great*

▲ WEIGHING UP THE RISK

*It makes no sense to risk large losses
(the downside) in order to make small
gains (the upside). Always compare the
downside risk with the upside potential
to make sure that the risk is really
worthwhile. If not, you need to look at
ways of substantially reducing the risk
or increasing the gains.*

TACKLING COMPETITION

All leaders want to outdo the competition. As well as a spirit of determination, this takes careful thought and forward planning. Do not base your actions or reactions on the belief that a rival business is bound to fail or does not know what it is doing. Instead, assume that the competition will succeed unless you mount a vigorous response. Never ignore signs that customers prefer other, competitive offerings. The true competitor must outperform rivals on every aspect that matters to the customer.

POINTS TO REMEMBER

- Reports and rumors of errors by opponents should never lead you to lower your guard.
- Reports of opponents' successes should not be discounted either.
- All angles and alternatives should be considered before reacting.
- Respond to a threat with a better strategy that turns the tables on the competition.

 101 Keep up-to-date on the progress of competitors.

COVERING EVERY ANGLE

Leaders must always be on the lookout for potential threats. The main questions to ask are:

COMPETITION AND THE MARKET
- Could newcomers create damaging competition?
- Is there an existing powerful force in the market that could muscle into your territory?
- Does a competitor have a stronger hold on your biggest customers?
- Is the market developing in ways that favor competitors more than you?
- Is there a growing market segment where you are being left behind?

CUSTOMERS
- Are you aware of the latest customer feedback?
- Could your customers take away major sources of revenue?

OUTSIDE THREATS
- Is there a rival technology or other development that could generate a major difference?
- Could an unsuspected challenge arrive from outside the existing industry?

PLAYING TO WIN

Running scared is much healthier than being overly complacent. To avoid complacency, always analyze your strengths, weaknesses, opportunities, and threats, and those of the competition. Keep abreast of changes and developments in your field, and spend time analyzing trends. Some threats can be predicted, but unpredictable threats increasingly arise. With a flexible attitude, you will be ready to treat each one on its merits.

MANAGING PEOPLE

INTRODUCTION

Today's fast-moving business environment demands that the effective manager be both a well-organized administrator and highly adept in understanding people's basic needs and behavior in the workplace. Gaining commitment, nurturing talent, and ensuring that people are motivated and productive requires open communication and trust between managers and staff. Managing People will help you to master the fundamentals of successful management techniques that will enable you to get the best out of the people who work for you. It also demonstrates how, by identifying and avoiding common problems, managers can turn potential failure into success for their organization. A wealth of practical advice is supplemented by 101 useful tips and a comprehensive self-assessment exercise.

DEVELOPING BASIC PEOPLE SKILLS

Knowing why people behave as they do is the key to gaining their commitment. Aim to understand people's needs in order to motivate them and thus meet the demands of the organization.

UNDERSTANDING BEHAVIOR

Natural, instinctive behavior is not always appropriate in the workplace. Make an effort to produce behavioral patterns that lead to productive and effective teamwork in your employees.

BEHAVING NATURALLY

People at work naturally tend to adopt instinctive modes of behavior that are self-protective rather than open and collaborative. This explains why emotion is a strong force in the workplace, and why management often reacts fiercely to criticism and usually seeks to control rather than take risks. People also tend to leap to conclusions and fragment into small, often warring, groups. Companies exhibiting "natural" behavior like this are highly political and emphasize status and hierarchy. They are less pleasant to work for and generally at odds with the needs of people and the marketplace.

▲ **ENCOURAGING CONSTRUCTIVENESS**
You can encourage constructive attitudes in people most effectively by example and reward, and by always approving of their good conduct and positive contributions.

BEHAVING APPROPRIATELY

Natural behavior is based on subjective responses that can often lead not only to negative feelings (such as insecurity), but also to mistaken perceptions concerning the intentions of other staff members. More constructive behavioral attributes will encourage cooperation, openness, and self-confidence. Some readily recognizable traits of people with appropriate behavioral skills include a proven facility to communicate positively and confidently with colleagues at all levels; the swift and generous recognition of the achievements of others; the ability to learn from mistakes and failures; and a general approach that is based on collaboration with fellow workers rather than competition.

1 Try to influence behavior rather than to change personalities.

2 Encourage and reward constructive behavior.

REPLACING NEGATIVE CHARACTERISTICS

NATURAL BEHAVIOR

- Reacting emotionally when information is received.
- Avoiding risks through fear or insecurity.
- Fighting fiercely and defensively when under threat.
- Making snap judgments about people and events.
- Spreading gossip throughout the organization.
- Competing for status and its symbols.
- Dwelling on past successes.
- Feeling more comfortable in small factions.
- Always seeking hierarchical superiority.

APPROPRIATE BEHAVIOR

- Establishing the facts using a pragmatic approach.
- Taking risks in an entrepreneurial fashion.
- Forming collegiate, collaborative, non-combative relationships.
- Insisting on detailed analysis before judgment.
- Practicing totally open communication.
- Recognizing achievement, not status.
- Learning from mistakes.
- Choosing to work in cooperative groups.
- Operating within flat, non-hierarchical structures.

UNDERSTANDING PEOPLE'S NEEDS

People's needs go far beyond basics, such as good working conditions and fair pay. But you cannot meet people's higher needs, such as pride in work and sharing in the corporate goals, without addressing basics.

> **3** Take care that people's lower-level needs are met.

▼ PRIORITIZING NEEDS

The psychologist Abraham Maslow has identified a five-stage "hierarchy of needs," starting with basic needs for food and shelter, and culminating in higher-level "self-actualization," or self-fulfillment, needs.

MEETING NEEDS

People have various kinds of needs. Examples of lower-level needs are salary, job security, and working conditions. You have to meet these basic needs, but doing so will not by itself give satisfaction. Failures with the basic needs nearly always explain dissatisfaction among staff. Satisfaction, on the other hand, springs from meeting higher-level needs, such as responsibility, progress, and personal growth.

3) Social needs are fulfilled by friendly interaction with other people

2) Secondary needs are for personal security

1) Basic needs are for food, shelter, and warmth

4) Higher-level esteem needs are met by recognition of achievements

5) Self-actualization needs are realized by achieving total individual potential

ENCOURAGING PRIDE

People need to feel that their contribution is valued and unique. Pride in work has two forms: individual and collective. If you work on an assembly line, for example, you are pleased with your own performance at, say, installing a car door. But you are also proud of the whole car to which you have contributed. As a manager, seek to exploit this pride in others, and be proud of your own ability to handle staff with positive results. Both management and staff should feel proud to belong to an admired company.

 4 Say thank you to people whenever it is merited.

 5 Add public praise to private words to raise pride.

IDENTIFYING SOURCES OF SATISFACTION

LOWER-LEVEL NEEDS

CONDITIONS
Reasonable hours, a pleasant environment, and adequate equipment: "I approve of the physical working conditions."

SUPERVISION
Empowerment and encouragement given by immediate managers: "I like the way I am treated by those who supervise me."

SECURITY
Confidence in the organization's outlook and a feeling of belonging: "I feel good about the future of the organization."

MANAGEMENT
An understanding of management methods: "I think the organization is making the changes necessary to be competitive."

COMMUNICATION
Full awareness of the organization's plans and involvement in the planning: "I understand and identify with the organization's strategy."

HIGHER-LEVEL NEEDS

JOB INTEREST
Satisfaction derived from the actual job content and its execution: "I like the kind of work that I do."

ACHIEVEMENT
Motivation to hit targets and to perform tasks at high levels of effectiveness: "My work gives me a sense of accomplishment."

COMMITMENT
Pleasure through belonging to the organization and identifying with it: "I am proud to say I work for the organization."

RESPONSIBILITY
Work requirements that stretch the individual, but are fair and rewarding: "I welcome the amount of work I am expected to do."

IDENTIFICATION
People understand how they fit into the overall plan: "I see how my work connects with the organization's strategies."

LEARNING THE BASICS

To understand people's attitudes, you need to be open to all the ways in which they communicate. Learn to listen to what they say – and do not say – and look out for other signals, such as body language.

LISTENING CAREFULLY

In many areas of a manager's job, from meetings and appraisals to telephone calls, listening plays a key role. Listening benefits both you and your staff: you gain a greater insight into people and potentially receive useful ideas about how your organization can be improved, while staff feel their views are being heard and will therefore respond more openly. Consider how you listen: do you interrupt frequently or cut people short to make your point? If so, practice remaining quiet and concentrating on the speaker; if necessary ask brief questions to ensure you have understood what they are saying. If you are easily distracted, practice focusing on the speaker's words, repeating key phrases silently to fix them in your mind. As well as actually hearing what a person says, you need to look and behave as if you are listening, for example, by appearing relaxed and open and nodding frequently.

7 Give people ample opportunity to express their true feelings.

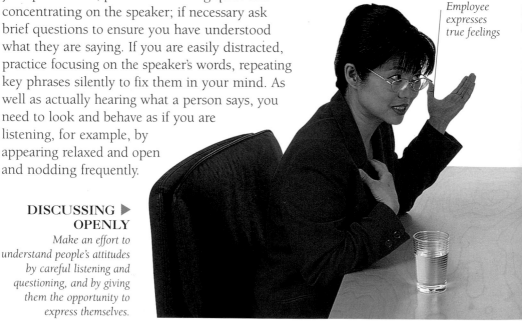

Employee expresses true feelings

**DISCUSSING ▶
OPENLY**
Make an effort to understand people's attitudes by careful listening and questioning, and by giving them the opportunity to express themselves.

INTERPRETING CORRECTLY

Listen to what a person says, and then mentally review their words to check you have understood their meaning. If you have not, ask them to clarify what they have said. You can also rephrase what they have said and repeat it back to them, giving them a chance to agree with or correct your statement. Look at the whole meaning of what a person is saying rather than selecting the parts you want to hear. Always take what you are told on trust, unless you have good reason not to. If the person is contradicting themselves or being evasive, they may not be telling the whole story, so continue questioning until you are satisfied.

8 Keep asking questions until you understand what someone means.

9 Practice reading people's body language.

READING BODY LANGUAGE

Body language is the term for the unconscious physical movements we all make that communicate thoughts and feelings. Interpreting body language correctly is a complex art, but you can easily learn to read broad messages. An open, relaxed posture and good eye contact are indications that a person is comfortable with themselves and what they are saying or hearing. A tense posture, perhaps with arms crossed and little eye contact, may indicate evasiveness, suppressed anger, or disagreement. Leaning forward when seated may indicate interest or agreement, while leaning back indicates lack of interest or resistance. Be aware of these signals in yourself as well as in others.

Manager encourages an open response by listening and asking affirming questions

BUILDING CONFIDENCE

Most people suffer from insecurity at some time. The many kinds of anxiety that affect people in organizations can feed such insecurity. Your antidote is to build confidence by giving recognition, high-level tasks, and full information.

10 Go to the rescue at once if people show that a task is beyond them.

REDUCING INSECURITY

Some people conceal their insecurity better than others, but do not be deceived. Everybody needs to be told that they are performing well and that they are respected, both for what they are and for what they have done and are doing. Praise is a very effective (and very economical) way of improving confidence, but be sure that it is deserved. Then suit the method of praise to the circumstances.

▼ WELCOMING INPUT
Bolster the confidence of all individuals, especially more reticent types, by allowing everyone at a meeting to speak in turn.

Committee leader invites input from all

Unconfident member is encouraged to speak

11 Avoid giving false reassurances – be frank if the news is not good.

ENCOURAGING ABILITY

Lack of confidence often holds people back from seeking out (or sometimes accepting) new challenges at work. Even very confident people operate at a small percentage of their maximum capacity or potential. Encourage staff to believe in their own abilities by giving them additional tasks – for instance, asking them to serve on committees tackling key issues. Do not accept the response "I'm no good at that." This is often merely an unconscious excuse for inaction.

ELIMINATING FEAR

People suffer from many kinds of fear: fear of personal failure; fear that the organization will fail or be taken over; fear that jobs will disappear through reorganization; or fear of the possible adverse consequences of change. None of these anxieties is irrational. They are only eased, though never completely eliminated, by full, frank, and open communication – with individuals and groups. The anxieties can be exacerbated by secretive management that uses fear as a way to control people. Drive out fear and you will find that trust, optimism, and kindness are much more effective.

Open, upright posture shows confidence

Withdrawn appearance shows lack of self-belief

▲ READING BODY LANGUAGE

The outward appearance of a person often gives insight into their feelings. An employee exhibiting defensive body language and a negative attitude may be feeling insecure.

12 Insist on people working together and communicating freely and openly.

ENABLING PARTICIPATION

Confidence in the workplace stems from true participation in the work. This can only happen when employees – singly or in groups – share information and therefore have a real influence over what actually happens. The advantages are democratic, motivational, and practical. Research shows that productivity is lower when jobs are closely prescribed, compared with situations in which people are allowed to contribute in their own ways to meeting goals.

POINTS TO REMEMBER

- Stepping back and letting others take the lead helps both you and your staff to be confident.
- Letting your own insecurity show will infect your team.
- Uncertainty always breeds low morale.
- It is important to inform people of company developments quickly and honestly.

COMMUNICATING CLEARLY

Sometimes highly organized, sometimes haphazard, communication happens all the time. Improve its quality by being open, honest, and accessible to everybody. You can never communicate too much, whether informally or formally.

13 Go out of your way to chat to staff on an informal basis.

THINGS TO DO

1. Keep appointments with all members of staff, regardless of their status.

2. Make sure you talk to or acknowledge people as often as you can.

3. On outside visits, talk to everybody, not just the boss.

4. If you want to speak with a staff member, make the effort to meet them in person rather than using the telephone.

OPEN PLANNING ▶
Open-plan offices encourage open communication and team spirit as well as making managers more accessible to staff.

14 Split large working units into several smaller ones with close links.

ENCOURAGING CONTACT

Many managers like to hide away behind closed office doors, keeping contact to a minimum. That makes it easy to be an administrator, but very hard to be a leader. It is far better to keep your office door open (as a general rule) and to encourage people to visit you when the door is open. Contact is made easier by open-plan work spaces, which is why some multimillionaire managers in Silicon Valley have abandoned their executive suites for desks in an open-plan office. If you have not talked to a particular member of staff for a while, make sure you do so. The more people who know you and can see you, the better working relationships are likely to be.

CUTTING BUREAUCRACY

If left unchecked, bureaucracy can severely impede communications, rendering attempts to improve productivity and morale ineffective. Although there is a need for some bureaucracy, it is important that you keep strict control over forms, reports, and other such documents. Avoid wasting time waiting for a proposal to be "rubber-stamped" when a decision can be taken in a quick, but effective, informal meeting.

 15 Clear out manuals and forms and replace only those that are missed.

CONSIDERING HOW ORGANIZATIONS COMMUNICATE

TYPE OF ORGANIZATION	EFFECTS ON COMMUNICATION
BUREAUCRATIC Dominated by hierarchies of power.	A domineering, "who reports to whom?" structure leads to rigid control, abundant manuals, systems, reports, and paperwork.
MATRIX Divided by product, geography, and function.	This type of organization is supposedly coordinated, but the leadership is divided and the bureaucracy is strong.
DECENTRALIZED Divided into separate operating units.	The individual units function separately or independently, so communication is difficult – the organization is primarily driven by budgets.
MARKET-ORIENTED Organized by product and/or geography.	A strong sales culture is dominated by commands from head office, so communication with outside staff is limited.
ENTREPRENEURIAL Flat structure with risk-taking philosophy.	The tendency to "hire-and-fire" people can lead to a culture of fear. Decisions are usually dependent on one or two key people.
PEOPLE-BASED Employees own shares and enjoy responsibility.	Staff are motivated by ownership in the company. People participate in and have responsibility for the company's management.

ONE-ON-ONE MEETINGS

Instead of relying on memos and other written communications, consider the immediacy of the one-on-one meeting as the most efficient way to deal with issues or problems that arise. Instant feedback and endorsements can be given at these personal meetings, and enthusiasm and commitment to new proposals or fresh ideas can be conveyed much more effectively and unambiguously than through written responses. Ensure that you have enough time available to give your full attention to matters under discussion, and that the meeting will not be unnecessarily interrupted or cut short.

QUESTIONS TO ASK YOURSELF

Q Has my message been well received and understood?

Q Do key customers think that I spend enough time visiting them and that my calls are productive?

Q Do I end meetings before people have had their say?

Q Do I hear rumors in enough time to dispel them?

Q Have I met everybody I should in the past week?

USING DIFFERENT MEDIA

One channel of communication is never enough – the more there are, the better. Your objective is to pass on information as quickly as possible, and to learn, just as speedily, about reactions to your messages. Noticeboards, newsletters, and magazines all have their place, as do suggestion boxes. But electronic media are more immediate and powerful. You can use digital noticeboards, Web sites, in-company television, video, and email. The same rules apply to all media: work to professional standards, match content to employees' needs, encourage feedback, and be prepared to change the format if the presentation is ill-received. Analyze the response to ensure that your message has been fully understood and has had the effect that you intended.

---

16 Ask customers for both suggestions and complaints.

Company Web site

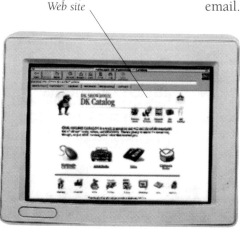

◀ USING NEW MEDIA
The wealth of new technology available to organizations means that company communications can be made more immediately and with greater impact than ever before.

USING THE "GRAPEVINE"

People at work form social networks and interact in the same way as all human groups. They value informal contacts, such as personal greetings and chats over tea and coffee. They also gossip. Some managers distrust the grapevine and worry that inaccurate, premature, and alarming information will spread. The grapevine, though, can be fed by management with accurate "rumors." Disarm its disruptive potential with swift information on matters that concern people. Often the best way to learn what is on people's minds is through informal meetings, so make sure that you participate fully in them.

▼ REMAINING INFORMAL

Informal chats are a useful way of finding out how your staff feel and of discouraging rumors and gossip.

Employee discusses team problems

Manager eases concern at source

---

17 Act swiftly to deny rumors if they are inaccurate.

18 Ensure that all those at meetings need to be there.

USING TEAM MEETINGS

In most organizations meetings occur more often than is necessary. Ensure that every meeting has a purpose, and that all attendees are directly concerned with that purpose. Regular team and management meetings are an important method of keeping people informed and answering their questions. Treat these meetings seriously. Unarranged meetings are also valuable, with any number of attendees from two upward. They require less formality but should be brief. Keep written notes of what has been decided or what needs to be done, and circulate the notes so that staff feel that they are fully involved.

GAINING TRUST AND COMMITMENT

A committed employee is extraordinarily valuable. You can gain staff commitment by meeting people's key needs, paying attention to people at all levels, trusting and being trusted, tolerating individuality, and creating a blame-free, "can-do" culture.

> **19** Give staff the opportunity to show that you can trust them.

QUESTIONS TO ASK YOURSELF

Q Do you trust others enough so you can delegate effectively?

Q Will you leave the delegate, after briefing, to complete the job without interference?

Q Do you show people that you trust them not to let you down?

Q Do you rely on rules and regulations to judge other people's work?

Q Do you instill trust in others by always being truthful and keeping your promises?

◀ WINNING TRUST
These are the key managerial qualities that inspire trust and commitment in employees. Work on developing such qualities in yourself to help create a fully committed workforce.

NURTURING TRUST

The quality and style of leadership are major factors in gaining employees' trust and commitment. Clear decision-making should be coupled with a collaborative, collegiate approach. This entails taking people into your confidence and explicitly and openly valuing their contributions. You should also make yourself as visible as possible, and show yourself to be approachable and willing to listen to others. People respond well to a collective ambition with which they can identify. Remember that to earn trust, you must first learn to trust those who work for you.

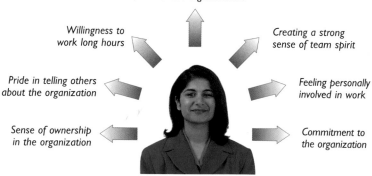

Holding personal values consistent with the organization's

Willingness to work long hours

Creating a strong sense of team spirit

Pride in telling others about the organization

Feeling personally involved in work

Sense of ownership in the organization

Commitment to the organization

20 Make sure you address people's intellectual and emotional needs.

21 Listen to unhappy employees – they may reveal serious problems.

WINNING MINDS, SPIRITS, AND HEARTS

The full commitment of staff cannot be realized unless you address people's psychological needs. Research has shown that most management activities are directed toward intellectual needs, some attention is paid to the expression of individuality, but even less attention is paid to emotional needs. By giving equal weight to all three areas, you are more likely to win the minds, spirits, and hearts of your employees. The means to achieve this include: allowing people some autonomy in creating their work environment; making them feel valued by openly recognizing their achievements; and empowering them by handing over as much control as possible in their areas of responsibility.

Remains loyal, despite unvoiced complaints

Loyal and enthusiastic

CHAMPION   **WALKING WOUNDED**

Highly critical of the company

Disenchanted and unproductive

DETRACTOR   **MISSING IN ACTION**

◀ **DEGREES OF COMMITMENT**
You must understand your staff in order to develop true commitment. One marketing classification of four customer types also applies to employees. Aim to build communication policies that reach those "missing in action," and identify the "walking wounded" and the "detractors." Then devise programs that will take them into the "champion" ranks.

22 Endeavor to transform all employees into "champions."

KEEPING STAFF COMMITTED

One of the most effective ways of keeping employees committed and raising retention, is to enrich their jobs and increase motivation. This can be achieved by a number of means, including raising interest levels, ensuring that each employee has a stimulating variety of tasks to perform, and providing the resources and training through which new skills can be developed. A multiskilled employee will be able to perform a range of interesting tasks, while a person with limited skills may be prone to boredom through repetition. Continually encouraging your staff to make suggestions for efficiency improvements will further motivate them, as well as give them a sense of involvement in a task or project and commitment to its success.

23 Investigate fully whenever figures for employee retention start to drop significantly.

▼ **DIFFERING PERCEPTIONS**
A survey conducted in several different organizations revealed that managers, in contrast to employees, have greater confidence in the personal development factors their organization provides.

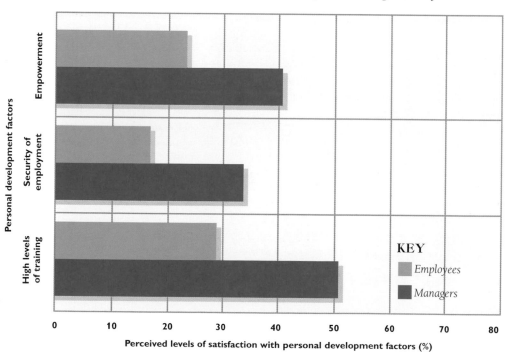

KEY
Employees
Managers

Perceived levels of satisfaction with personal development factors (%)

REWARDING EXCELLENCE

Acknowledging excellence is vital in maintaining an employee's commitment and job satisfaction. Consider rewarding exceptional performance and high productivity with financial incentives. These could include one-time salary raises, bonus payments, or, if appropriate, stock options. If an employee has substantially reduced the company's costs, this could also be financially rewarded. For more modest levels of achievement, other benefits – such as inclusion on senior staff training weekends – are highly motivating. Above all, never under-estimate the value of a simple "thank you."

QUESTIONS TO ASK YOURSELF

Q Have I devised financial reward programs for excellence?

Q Have I considered non-monetary rewards?

Q Do I always say "thank you" when a job is done well?

Q Am I creating "heroes" that other staff can admire?

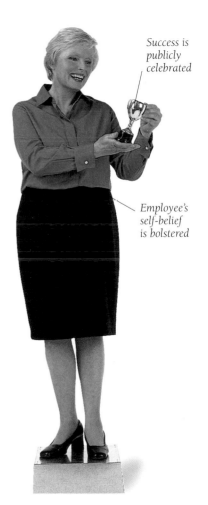

Success is publicly celebrated

Employee's self-belief is bolstered

---

24 Ensure you involve everybody in a personal project.

PROJECT ▶ "HERO"
Recognition of a popular leader encourages others to show commitment.

STAYING POSITIVE

To create a positive environment within your organization, it is important to create a "can-do" atmosphere. This should be built on mutual trust, in which people, whatever their self-doubts, are sure that the organization can achieve whatever it is asked to do. Actual achievement is essential to foster this confidence. Start group projects at every opportunity, choosing tasks that have a clear purpose and a positive, measurable outcome. Also, seek to create "heroes" – well-respected and productive employees (including project leaders) that other staff members admire. Be sure to celebrate each hero's successes: this not only bolsters the hero's self-belief, but also encourages others to trust in the can-do culture and to commit to the organization's goals.

ADJUSTING YOUR APPROACH

How you manage people has a deep impact on their behavior. It is useful to alter and direct your management methods to suit different people and different situations. Your aim is always to encourage people to motivate and manage themselves.

25 Apply discipline, but combine it with empowerment and trust.

COMBINING MANAGEMENT STYLES

Use Theory X to provide foundation of discipline → *Staff carry out instructions*

Use Theory Y to exploit employees' natural desire to succeed → *Employees act on own initiative*

Mix Theories X and Y to motivate, inspire, and continually challenge the team → *Peak performance is achieved*

26 People who enjoy their work will produce the best results.

THEORY X MANAGEMENT

The traditional "order and obey" approach to managing people can be an effective way of motivating them. Tell staff what to do and how to do it, and they either perform as ordered or pay the penalty, with dismissal as the last resort (sometimes the first). Researcher Douglas McGregor named this style Theory X management. You need a bedrock of Theory X discipline in any organization.

THEORY Y MANAGEMENT

In contrast to the Theory X approach, Theory Y states that self-discipline springs from enjoying responsibility. The better educated and skilled your workforce, the more you can rely on these natural drives. Theory Y works well only when people have strong objectives. Combine Theories X and Y to achieve the most effective management.

TRADITIONAL APPROACH

Job completed

RETHINKING METHODS

A traditional approach to allocating work is to split tasks into components that are given to a number of different workers. Although this gives you a high degree of control, it can be monotonous for staff. Also, because the task "waits" in a new line at every desk, this method tends to be inefficient. A better idea is to entrust all or most of a task to one person. This is quicker and more motivating, as the individual feels "ownership" of the task, even though that means more responsibility.

MULTI-TASKING

▲ OWNING THE PROJECT
Allocating a task to a single employee not only reduces the time needed to complete it, but also promotes job satisfaction.

27	Most people prefer responsibility over too little work.

28	Cut down layers after reforming processes.

CONSULTING PEOPLE

Aim to be flexible in your approach to people, but avoid following one system one day and another the next. Regularly ask your staff what they would like from you. They may like more responsibility or, conversely, more guidance – try to comply with their wishes as far as you can, while serving the best interests of the team.

DEVELOPING PEOPLE

Helping individuals to achieve their potential is in the best interests of the person and the organization. Aim to train, encourage, and provide opportunities for willing people.

PROVIDING TRAINING

Developing the abilities of staff at all levels is so important that some organizations have their own education facilities, and many engage outside trainers and advisers. Top-quality training and development are vital to all organizations.

29 Make training the last thing you cut back, never the first.

30 Ask people about their long-term goals and aspirations, and assist in their realization.

ARRANGING TRAINING

Try to allocate a percentage of revenues to training (1.5 percent at least), or to lay down minimum training hours – five days per year is a reasonable target. If such policies are sacrificed under short-term financial pressure, your organization loses the benefit of better-trained employees, and it is implied that training is not essential. Provide training that is *specific*, to improve current performance; *general*, to provide wider skills; and *in advance*, to prepare for promotion and change.

EVALUATING FORMS OF STAFF DEVELOPMENT

TYPE OF TRAINING	BENEFITS AND REINFORCEMENTS
TECHNICAL Training in the specifics of a particular job – usually provided in-house and during working hours by specialist instructors or supervisors.	● Enables high-quality performance of tasks. ● Must be repeated at regular intervals to maintain newly enhanced skills. ● Best coupled with an exam that gives a qualification.
QUALITY Training in the principles of total quality, together with the technical tools required for improvement – needs specialist instruction.	● Provides both "quick fixes" for immediate problems and longer-term, organization-wide benefits. ● Instils a philosophy of continuous practical improvement. ● Must be sustained indefinitely to become a way of life.
SKILLS Financial accounting, creative thinking, speaking, IT, writing, presentation, chairing, languages, interviewing, selling, etc. – in-house or external.	● All employees benefit from a general, multi-skill grounding. ● Nervousness about using skills in public is cured. ● Opportunities for practice are needed to build and maintain effectiveness.
PROFESSIONAL Education to obtain qualifications, for example, in accounting, law, banking, engineering – external and either full-time or part-time.	● Provides portable skills, which are valuable to the individual as well as to the employer. ● Specialization leads to a more select choice of future appointments in the organization. ● Requires effort over a considerable period.
FUNCTIONAL Education in marketing, planning, sales management, purchasing, human resources management, etc. – external, but not usually full-time.	● Functional training almost always leads to better performance and improved career paths. ● Must be linked with appointment to functional role. ● Area is often wrongly ignored by companies who simply "hope for the best."
ACTIVITY "Outward Bound"-type courses, in which people learn leadership and teamwork by engaging in physical tasks, such as rock climbing.	● Provides an effective means of team bonding and re-energizing the workforce. ● Must be supplemented by and coordinated with more direct management training.
MANAGERIAL Providing expertise and knowledge in fields such as strategy and change management – business school focus, either internal or external.	● Managers identify, work on, and solve real corporate problems. ● Invaluable grounding if learning is applied to the job. ● Both sides benefit if student remains committed.

IMPROVING SKILLS

Aim to train your staff in as many specific skills as possible. Mental abilities matter greatly in modern organizations, as do the skills needed to master computers. Training in thought processes will improve the execution of practical tasks.

31 Teach people to think analytically – this will benefit the whole organization.

THINKING CLEARLY

Like any other skill, thinking can be taught and improved on. The ability to analyze is basic to this, revolving around the question "Why?" – "Why do we need to cut our price?" or "Why have profits fallen?". Encourage your staff to analyze their work and to ask questions constantly. Analysis requires a high degree of mental organization, which can improve with practice if analysis is part of the corporate way of life.

USING MULTI-SKILLING

The more skills in which a person is trained, the more valuable they are as an employee and the greater their personal potential. In "manufacturing cells" within some factories, employees are given responsibility for an entire product – from initial research to sourcing materials, manufacture, and marketing. The people are interchangeable, which makes them flexible and provides them with a useful knowledge of each other's work. Office work can follow the same ideas on a project basis. Widening people's skills cuts down on cost and time, provides greater flexibility, and greatly encourages team spirit and collaboration.

WORKING IN "CELLS" ▼
Provide people with opportunities to operate in working cells or groups. They will learn the skills of other members of the group, which will increase their effectiveness and improve morale.

32 Get staff into the habit of constantly improving their range of skills.

▼ **USING NEW TECHNOLOGY**

Make sure that everybody who possibly can be is computer-literate. Both the individual and the organization will suffer in the long term if new technology is not mastered.

33 Invest heavily in training for key computer skills: this will improve the performance of your company.

On-line course gives practical experience

A trained employee benefits the company

Study aids help develop new skills

MASTERING COMPUTERS

The use of electronics in business is growing so fast that you should regard technology such as computers as something that everybody must know how to use. If your organization does not have an Intranet (internal computer system) or some way of connecting people and files, you must press hard for the installation of such a set-up. If portable computers can improve operations (for instance, those of service engineers), try to provide them. There will be problems to resolve, ranging from security and privacy to the overuse of email. But all these obstacles can be overcome. More difficulties will be created unless everybody who can usefully become computer-literate is given the necessary training and equipment.

QUESTIONS TO ASK YOURSELF

Q Have my staff been sufficiently trained in computer skills?

Q Is their training both up-to-date and updated regularly?

Q Do people have opportunities to practice their new skills in order to master them?

Q Have I listened to other people's suggestions regarding new technology?

Q Does the organization have sufficient technical support?

Q Is the company using all the computer programs available to improve performance?

GUIDING OTHERS

All managers coach. They tell people what they are doing right or wrong on the job, train them, assess them, and counsel them. The mentor's role overlaps with those of the coach and the counselor, but the three roles have separate purposes.

34 If mistakes are made, ask yourself if you played any part in them.

BEING A COACH

Giving clear instructions about what you expect is the first step of coaching. This stage often produces a drop in motivation as reality challenges the employee's ability. At this point you become a helper, coaching the employee to recognize his or her strengths and to form ambitions. Finally, the person is in control of him- or herself and the job. You then step aside and assume the role of adviser, to be consulted when needed.

At what point during the task did your approach fail, and are you personally responsible?

Can you pinpoint why your approach failed?

Would it help to do the same thing again, with improvements?

IIIII▷ NO IIIII▷

COACHING QUESTIONS

If someone you are coaching has experienced failure in his or her work, ask the person these questions in sequence. It may be that his or her work efforts can be improved with simple adjustments to current working methods. Alternatively, the person's basic approach to tasks may need reassessing.

Did you plan the task and, if so, how?

What wrong decisions were made?

YES

By analyzing what went wrong, and when and how the problems occurred, you can and should devise a series of improvement measures to ensure that failure does not occur on a similar task or project.

What must you do differently next time?

Design a program to correct defects.

▼ GUIDING OBJECTIVELY

Use your years of work experience and your knowledge of the organization to steer junior employees along the most appropriate career paths.

BEING A MENTOR

A mentor is a senior manager who establishes a special relationship with a particular junior. As a mentor, you should never be in a line relationship with the mentored (a "line" being the route along which orders pass from the top of the organization to the bottom), otherwise you cannot guarantee a disinterested, objective viewpoint. Do not consider mentoring only in times of trouble. Instead, take a continuous interest in the progress of the junior. He or she will expect to discuss work difficulties with you, and you can intervene with line managers if the situation demands it.

Experienced manager coaches an employee, helping his development

Employee receives valuable guidance and encouragement

BEING A COUNSELOR

As a counselor you are called upon to deal with personal problems. These may be problems at work or home. Either way, the junior employee needs to tell a sympathetic listener about his or her troubles. You should ideally help the person to find his or her own solution, though it may be necessary to make strong suggestions. Usually, the employee will turn to an immediate superior, especially since the problem may demand time off. Never turn away from a counseling need, and call in others (possibly outside experts) if the problem is beyond your powers.

35 Find every junior a wise mentor who gives good advice.

36 Encourage employees to suggest ways to solve problems.

TEACHING BY EXAMPLE

As the boss of a group you are likely to be a prime role model – the person who sets the tone of the unit. You must also create the right atmosphere for successful teamwork and use example purposefully to teach and encourage good practice.

37 Use opportunities to lead from the front and set a good example.

38 Teach by showing how, not by giving people your orders.

ACTING AS A ROLE MODEL

Employees expect their manager to set a positive example. It is therefore very important that you neither fall below the high standards that you set yourself nor behave disparagingly to members of staff who do fall short of them. Above all, you should behave consistently at all times.

COMPETENCE

SUPPORTIVENESS

CHARISMA

FAIR-MINDEDNESS

HONESTY

INSPIRING PEOPLE
According to research, there are ten personal qualities that are the most admired characteristics of respected organizational leaders. These qualities are less to do with making the right or wrong decisions and more to do with integrity and straightforward behavior.

VISION

INTELLIGENCE

COURAGE

BROAD-MINDEDNESS

DIRECTNESS

SHARING SKILLS

Team members often make very effective teachers, either by tutoring less experienced members or by sharing different sets of skills. You should consider an organized, on-the-job program of development with one team member sitting by another to learn about their job. This will help both parties reach a deeper understanding of the work of the team, as well as transferring new skills. You can achieve a similar effect by forming a mini-team or taskforce to tackle a particular issue, not necessarily related to the team's main objective. Adopting a strategy like this ensures that team members learn how to develop solutions and turn them into action.

39 Bring in outside trainers as often as possible.

CULTURAL DIFFERENCES

The emphasis placed on teaching varies from country to country, but the Japanese in particular place great importance on action learning. Germans tend to be more formal, expecting people to follow instructions. Americans are more likely to have been taught about managing and will often adopt new "empowering" methods, which may later be neglected. English managers are likely to improvise and regard skills as natural, untaught assets.

◀ **LEARNING ON THE JOB**
Action learning is more effective than sedentary learning involving books and lectures. Encourage more experienced staff members to take the lead.

Colleague is able to learn by practicing skills

Senior employee explains job to colleague

NURTURING TALENT

Identifying and using individual talent is one of the most satisfying and productive aspects of a manager's work. Finding good people is only part of the task – talented people can be difficult to manage, but the effort is well worthwhile.

40 Regard staff losses as opportunities to introduce new strengths.

QUESTIONS TO ASK ABOUT OTHERS

Q Do they have, or could they develop, a special expertise?

Q Can they combine talents such as research and management?

Q Do they show signs of organizational ability?

Q Are they successful at bringing in new business?

Q Have they shown the ability to lead others?

FINDING TALENT

Individual talents within organizations, especially large ones, are often underemployed or even unnoticed. Look out for signs of abilities that are not being fully used (or used at all) and find ways in which the individuals concerned can contribute more. People who engage in non-work activities, like running a company social club or event, may be sources of untapped talent. Bringing talent to the foreground not only relaunches the individual's career, but also strengthens the organization's success potential.

PLANNING SUCCESSION

The more successful subordinates are, the more likely they are to leave your company for "better" things. You should welcome this, as you are the friend and supporter who has helped them to develop and display their talents. However, their promotion will leave gaps. You should always have an answer to the question "What will I do if Jean or John leaves?". This may create an opportunity to reorganize work so that a replacement is not needed. More likely, you will be able to reward someone with promotion, thereby creating another vacancy. Maintain a succession folder, regularly update it, and pencil in potential successors for every key job.

41 Promote talented individuals, even if they excel in their current job.

42 Speak out if you believe someone is being moved to the wrong job.

| Personal qualities of drive and perseverance | Ability to form relationships and to communicate | Ability to identify and to recognize individual talent | Target-setting, appraising, coaching, and giving feedback |

 THE INDIVIDUAL'S CONTRIBUTION

 THE ORGANIZATION'S CONTRIBUTION

| Energy and strong needs, drives, and motives | Continual willingness to learn and develop | Giving rewards, incentives, and recognition | Investment in personnel training and development |

MAXIMUM DEVELOPMENT OF INDIVIDUAL TALENT

DEVELOPING ▲ TALENT

The development of talent depends equally on input from both the organization and the individual.

FOCUSING ON CONTRIBUTION

What is your attitude toward people who are "difficult, demanding, disagreeable, disobedient, dislikable, disorganized, disputing, disrespectful, and discordant"? An obvious answer is that you do not want them around. But the "9D" characteristics, according to American consultant Michael J. Kami, are those of the "talented gorillas," who may be the most productive employees you have. Above all, concentrate on people's contributions, not their personalities.

UNCONVENTIONAL EMPLOYEE ▶
Nonconformist staff members may be difficult to manage, but are sometimes the most productive.

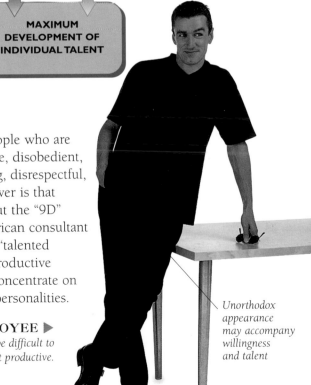

Unorthodox appearance may accompany willingness and talent

ENCOURAGING MANAGEMENT POTENTIAL

Avoid typecasting people and being typecast. Your staff may have abilities that go well beyond their present roles, and that will take them upward in the organization – perhaps into management.

43 Seek to promote from within in the first instance.

44 Encourage staff to apply for any internal openings.

POINTS TO REMEMBER

- People's abilities are more likely to be underestimated than rated too highly.
- Classroom learning is an essential element of management development.
- Lack of ability can usually be improved with training.

SPOTTING ABILITIES

The fact that somebody has mastered a particular job gives grounds for supposing that he or she could advance to higher levels. When vacancies or opportunities occur, always look first to see whether someone already employed in the organization could fill the post. Remember that technical deficiencies can generally be overcome by training. Look for personal characteristics (such as energy and perseverance), good interpersonal behavior, strong motivation, the ability and willingness to learn, excellent organizational skills, and flexibility. Task forces and other ad hoc groups provide a relatively risk-free way of testing whether a person has the ability to rise.

RECOGNIZING ▶
MANAGEMENT
QUALITIES
More people have management ability than is commonly supposed. Look out for employees with these key qualities, and earmark them for future promotion to management posts.

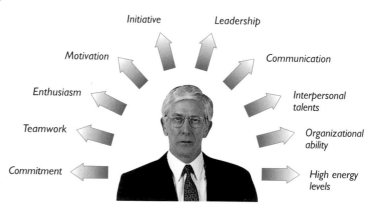

Initiative
Leadership
Motivation
Communication
Enthusiasm
Interpersonal talents
Teamwork
Organizational ability
Commitment
High energy levels

MAKING MANAGERS

In your search for management potential, remember that management is not a rarefied activity requiring a high degree of education. Although managers are supposed to spend their time on intellectual activities – such as planning, organizing, and coordinating – in reality their days are very fragmented and dominated by practical matters. They may have only half an hour of uninterrupted work every two days. You need to ask yourself if the person you are considering for promotion is capable of working effectively in these conditions. If your potential manager prefers to work on only one task at a time, then elevation to management may not be appropriate.

45 Allow people to show that they can manage.

▼ COPING WITH PRESSURE
Aspiring managers should be practical and able to handle several tasks at once. Give people the chance to demonstrate their ability and they may well prove to be candidates for promotion.

Employee is able to cope with interruptions

Several duties are managed simultaneously

46 Train staff for higher duties as early as you can.

47 Make a list of good coworkers and keep it for future reference.

FACILITATING PROMOTION

You may be tempted to keep people where they are – doing a good job – rather than move them onward and upward. Not promoting people is bad for their career development and for the organization, which is not using talent to the full. Some organizations even refuse to train adequately because they are frightened of losing the trained employee to someone else: this condemns them to having an undertrained labor force. Reconcile yourself to the fact that people are likely to move on from time to time. If you think the move is good for them, encourage and congratulate them.

MOTIVATING PEOPLE

Receiving orders is far less motivating than taking part in planning and decision-making. Enable your staff to achieve their ambitions and to manage themselves in order to achieve the desired results.

> **48** Use the strategic thinking of all employees.

MOTIVATING FACTORS

FACTOR	ACTION
SELF-FULFILLMENT	Enable employees to take on challenges.
RECOGNITION	Tell employees how well they are doing.
PEER RESPECT	Celebrate the individual's success publicly.
EXPERTISE	Encourage development of special knowledge.
COMPETENCE	Provide training to develop key skills.
ACHIEVEMENT	Agree on targets that are achievable.
AUTONOMY	Allow employees to plan and design own work.
SELF-CONFIDENCE	Make sure that allocated tasks can be done well.
SELF-RESPECT	Increase the individual's regard for self.
MEMBERSHIP	Ensure employees enter "club" of coworkers.

SHARING THE STRATEGY

It is very important to inform people about strategic plans and their own part in achieving the strategies. Take trouble to improve their understanding and to win their approval, as this will have a highly positive influence on performance. Never forget that employees invest their lives and financial security in the company.

Manager explains how task relates to overall strategy

▲ **ENRICHING A JOB**
Give people jobs that enable them to feel good about the organization and its management.

49 Allow others to make decisions that they can make just as well as you.

DELEGATING DECISIONS

Pushing the power of decision-making downward reduces pressure on senior management. It also motivates people on the lower levels because it gives them a vote of confidence. And, because the decision is taken nearer to the point of action, it is more likely to be correct. The main reasons for hoarding decisions that could be taken lower down are bad ones: you want to keep the decision power all to yourself, or you do not trust those in positions below to get things right (which calls into question the appropriateness of your appointments). You should certainly take all the decisions that only you as a manager can make; but even then you can draw on all the valuable input available from colleagues and subordinates.

HANDING DOWN POWER

MANAGEMENT DECISIONS
The manager sets out the agenda for a particular task, decides on the powers she must keep for herself, and selects the people who she thinks will best carry out the delegated duties.

DELEGATED DECISIONS
The delegates each have a clearly defined role that they have helped establish. They choose their own working methods, make decisions as necessary, and are responsible for meeting the agreed aim.

INTRODUCING SELF-MANAGEMENT

The standard approach to establishing self-management among staff is to define individual job requirements so that employees can carry out the processes effectively. This is contradictory because somebody other than the self-manager is managing the tasks, and probably explaining how to do the tasks as well. Motivational empowerment only develops if you can answer "yes" to four key questions (right). If any answers are "no," reassess your approach to self-management.

QUESTIONS TO ASK YOURSELF

Q Do individuals define their own tasks?

Q Do they define the behavior that is required to perform their tasks?

Q Do managers and the managed jointly define performance goals that are challenging for the individual?

Q Do individuals define the importance of the goal?

IMPROVING PERFORMANCE

All improvement programs run out of steam unless you make conscious efforts to renew people's support. Improvement stems from repetition, but greater gains come from focused planning and training.

---

50 Aim to improve the quality of all company processes.

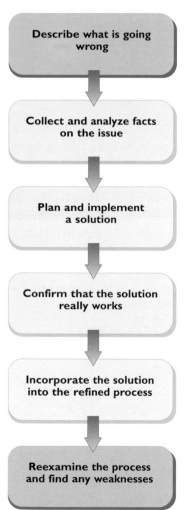

Describe what is going wrong

↓

Collect and analyze facts on the issue

↓

Plan and implement a solution

↓

Confirm that the solution really works

↓

Incorporate the solution into the refined process

↓

Reexamine the process and find any weaknesses

MANAGING QUALITY

Total Quality Management (TQM) is built around the idea that individuals can always improve their work by learning new techniques and applying them. In TQM workshops people master techniques, such as how to use the "six management and planning tools" required to resolve issues. This may sound complicated, but using such tools speeds up processes, eliminates task stages, and reduces costs quickly. The objective is to cut out waste and to increase customer satisfaction by improving product or service quality, employee performance, and economic value. This approach satisfies people's natural urge to do a better job and to see improvements.

◀ **SIX STEPS TO BETTER QUALITY**
These six steps can be applied by individuals or teams. Encourage staff at all levels to use them to examine and improve processes and systems.

---

51 Focus quality work on producing real customer benefits.

---

52 Use training in quality skills to increase people's general ability.

LEARNING BY EXPERIENCE

As people gain experience in a job, they see ways of doing it better, cutting costs, and saving time. Encourage staff to come forward with such ideas – this will improve performance and raise morale. Consider holding regular ideas meetings where people can make constructive suggestions. Such meetings often provide the inspiration for others to develop the ideas further. Always act on these proposals where possible – it is especially motivating if the person who brought forward the original idea is the one to implement it.

53 Listen to staff and ask for their improvement ideas.

54 Expect people to continue achieving better results.

◀ **LEARNING CURVE**
As people gain experience of their work, their performance will naturally improve. The pattern of a learning curve shows how a period of intensive development is followed by a "levelling-off" stage.

Skills learned

Time period

55 Concentrate on one initiative at a time to avoid confusion.

MAINTAINING MOMENTUM

A common mistake is to abandon an improvement initiative before it has a real chance to pay off, and to replace it with another, which then suffers the same fate. This "flavor of the month" policy breeds cynicism and lethargy. A far better policy is to stick to one basic program (such as TQM), but to revise and improve it all the time. At the same time, select new themes for the initiative (say, every year) to refocus and renew the forward drive. In a large team or department you could involve different groups in developing the new themes, and in this way everyone will feel more committed to the programme. The focus one year could be on responding to customers, the next target could be streamlining in-house systems, and the next could be boosting quality – but all of them would be aiming to deliver what the customer wants more quickly and cost-effectively.

MAKING PROGRESS

The more responsibility you give to people, the greater their interest and productivity are likely to be. The same principle applies to their knowledge of the organization and how they contribute to its success – the more knowledge, the better.

> **56** Make "right the first time" a key aim for everybody in your team.

QUESTIONS TO ASK YOURSELF

Q Do I enable people to take pride in the quality of their own work?

Q Do I constantly look for ways to increase group morale?

Q Have I considered setting up specialist groups within my organization?

Q Am I making best use of a deployment policy and annual review?

Q Am I setting objectives that will motivate people?

GETTING IT RIGHT THE FIRST TIME

Make people responsible for the quality of their own work and it will usually inspire them to do better. Quality used to be maintained by trained inspectors who would check the work and send back anything imperfect – an expensive and wasteful method. Instead, increase training and assistance to help people produce only perfect work in the first place. Use supervisors as "enablers" who help groups and individuals whenever needed. This will keep work that needs redoing to a minimum, and should allow you to greatly reduce the numbers of supervisors.

RAISING GROUP MORALE

High group morale can enrich individual motivation and performance remarkably. In difficult situations, when companies are in crisis and can only be saved by major effort, group morale often rises to far higher levels than before. Individual objections and objectives are bypassed in the collective drive to do what must be done. But you need not wait until crisis strikes to instil this attitude in your staff. This does not mean you have to create an artificial emergency: build urgency by setting important objectives to which everyone subscribes and has a clear, agreed plan for reaching.

> **57** Expect people to supervise their own performance.

> **58** Encourage acceptance of and desire for change at all times.

USING POLICY DEPLOYMENT

Policy deployment may sound daunting, but it is based on simple principles. First, a vision of the company's future is developed with the help of all its staff. "Improvement themes" are selected, again with people's help, that will produce better results. The themes, such as "Getting it Right the First Time" or "Increasing Competitive Advantage," generate objectives for every unit and everyone in every unit. Detailed plans are made for the theme's implementation, and progress is reviewed every month. An annual review is also necessary to modify the vision and associated themes when necessary. The goal is to align individual and team ambitions with those of the organization. Everyone, from the chief executive downward, shares in the vision and the strategy for realizing it, and knows their own part in achieving it.

ENRICHING JOBS ▶ USING DEPLOYMENT

By involving everyone in the organization with a new corporate vision and plans to realize that vision, you can enrich jobs and greatly increase people's motivation levels.

59 Ask questions to see if every person is aware of the team's strategy.

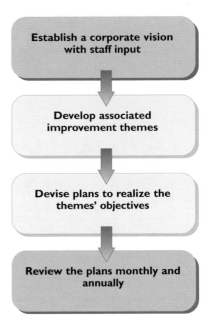

Establish a corporate vision with staff input

Develop associated improvement themes

Devise plans to realize the themes' objectives

Review the plans monthly and annually

OUTSOURCING TO INCREASE PROFITABILITY

Many companies have "outsourced" jobs by establishing their employees as independent suppliers of products or services. Sometimes these moves are driven by negative cost-cutting motives, which often backfire. Used positively, the approach enables the company to retain the services of highly skilled experts, whose full-time employment is not justified (for example). In return, the employees gain the freedom to work profitably on their own terms. The flexibility that outsourcing offers can enrich people's working lives greatly. You can, however, enrich jobs in this way without cutting the employee loose from the organization by creating a "firm within the firm" – an expert, in-house group with specific responsibilities.

Finding Solutions

Sensitive interpersonal skills are essential for creating a comfortable and productive working environment. Use your skills to resolve individual difficulties and to deal with conflicts.

Building Environments

Creating an atmosphere in which people feel appreciated and an essential part of a team is a challenge for every manager. A successful effort in this direction, however, will reduce the likelihood of problems.

60 If a group grows too large, divide it into smaller parts.

▲ **TEAM SPIRIT**
Encourage the workforce to consider themselves as an elite, closely knit team. A good analogy is a united football team.

Ensuring Cohesion

An employee who feels neglected and who is excluded from a cohesive working group is more likely to be unmotivated and prone to dissatisfaction than the person who has support and recognition from colleagues and managers. Encourage people to react positively and make effective contributions. This can be done by creating structures in which each staff member identifies with a group in which the responsibilities are clearly understood by all. An unselfish interest in the success of other group members is generated in a team that is closely bound together by common goals.

CONTROLLING OFFICE POLITICS

Strong feelings are aroused by the subject of office politics – anyone who has worked in an office will have experienced its effects. The negative side of office politics surfaces when it is used by individuals to increase personal power at the expense of colleagues and/or the organization. Strive to create a working environment in which status and hierarchy have as little importance as possible and the politics will stop.

61 Celebrate the achievements of your organization.

62 Whenever you can, involve people in specific tasks with clear aims.

CASE STUDY

Jan, a shopfloor worker, noticed that every so often her department had to write off stocks of components that had become obsolete. This was obviously expensive, and she wondered why the stock control was so ineffective. She found that the excess was held as "buffer stock" in case supplies became short. She reasoned that the cost of holding the stock must be so high that putting in a better system for ordering and locating needed parts would pay for itself many times over. Jan received full support from management and her colleagues to begin an improvement project, which she led from start to finish. She enlisted the help of other colleagues in completing her project. The stocks held in the department were halved, and the obsolete and obsolescent items reduced by 90 percent.

◀ **ENCOURAGING INITIATIVE**
Jan was encouraged by her superiors to embark on what could be termed a one-person "Quality Improvement Project" (QIP). Such projects involve detailed studies of significant areas where money is being wasted. They are only possible in working environments that support and nurture the initiative of the individual.

USING POSITIVE EMOTIONS

An openness and responsiveness to people's spontaneity and originality will generate a positive atmosphere in which creative ideas can flourish and demotivating boredom is reduced. Informality, and a reasonably tolerant acceptance of your staff's inevitable mistakes, will also generate an environment in which recognition for success, rather than blame for failure, is the dominant culture. Take every opportunity to generate excitement over what the company and individuals have achieved and what challenges must be met for the future of the organization.

OPENING CLOSED MINDS

People are often reluctant to accept ideas from outside sources. The "Not Invented Here" (NIH) syndrome occurs when individuals ignore ideas from other parts of the organization or other companies. Discourage this syndrome among your staff.

> **63** Clearly emphasize that new ideas will not be rejected as a matter of course.

ACCEPTING IDEAS

The consequences of NIH are often expensive and sometimes disastrous. Antidotes must come from the organization's management. Welcome all ideas, accept those that are good, and explain the reasons for any rejections. This will ensure a flow of ideas, and people will be encouraged to see plans as opportunities, rather than threats, and to welcome them. Also, encourage people to act as "spies," reporting on any good ideas they have spotted in other organizations, businesses, or countries.

Manager listens to idea and suggests changes

Employee's confidence is boosted

WELCOMING INPUT ▲
Always give new ideas careful thought and consideration. If you dismiss them, the flow of ideas will soon start to dry up.

> **64** Make creative contributions a part of all meetings.

ENCOURAGING CREATIVITY

Creativity involves exploring and adopting new ideas that may produce better results. Many people believe that they are uncreative: in fact, everybody has potential and can be taught resourceful techniques. Stage workshops in which people can apply their skills to real-life issues. People are often reluctant because they fear that the new approach may fail. Explain that not taking risks can lead to rivals seizing the best opportunities.

CHANGING MIND-SETS

Remember that people have a logical basis for rejecting a creative plan. Saying "no" means that no further action need be taken; saying "yes" may well mean extra work, as well as extra risk. People who start new projects and fail often suffer as a result, whereas managers are seldom sacked for the opportunities they missed. This helps to develop negative mind-sets, which mean that people spot the reasons for doing nothing and miss the benefits from taking new action. You can change negative mind-sets into positive ones by starting special projects that require creativity and by providing incentives for those involved. Regularly monitor such new initiatives, and ensure that senior management are aware of any progress or success and of who has contributed effectively.

CREATING POSITIVE MIND-SETS ▶

Provide incentives for creativity. Encourage managers to include in their monthly reports any creative initiatives that were taken in the period, who was involved, and what is planned for the future.

Establish a
special creative project to
encourage initiative

Include non-managerial
staff who will work effectively
in a team

Insist that such
new initiatives are recognized
throughout the company

Openly celebrate the
positive results of the creative
projects

65 Always insist that opportunities are seized after the risks are assessed.

66 Stress that not taking risks is usually due to lack of self-confidence.

TAKING RISKS

Since you want people to be active and to show initiative, you must make it clear that risk-taking is encouraged. Otherwise, the normal human tendency to prefer the known to the unknown will inhibit progress both inside the company and in the marketplace. Risk can be defined as "incurring the chance of unfortunate consequences by doing something." You should not let the threat of unfortunate consequences prevent action. Reward successful risk-taking, and do not penalize failure except in two circumstances:

● The person has not carefully analyzed and understood the risks before acting;
● The person has repeated past mistakes.

DEALING WITH CONFLICT

*C*onflict is unavoidable when people interact at work. If faced with conflict or an angry person, adopt a positive and rational approach to defuse any heightened emotions, then look for a resolution based on pragmatism and compromise.

67 Remember that you are concerned with behaviour, not with character.

QUESTIONS TO ASK YOURSELF

Q Where is the problem and what is it exactly?

Q What are the potential solutions?

Q Which solution out of all the alternatives is the best?

Q How is the solution best implemented?

FACING PROBLEMS

Dealing with conflicts between employees is an inevitable part of managerial life. Once you are aware of conflict, take immediate action and invite the disagreeing parties to voice their points of view in a meeting. The key is to minimize the emotive element and to substitute it with a rational pragmatism. Even if you believe one position to be correct, be prepared to consider the other point of view; if it is valid, then try to reach a compromise.

Manager acts as arbiter

Plans for a solution to the conflict are noted

Employee freely airs his point of view

▼ FINDING A SOLUTION
Provide an environment where disagreeing employees can openly voice their problems and then work towards effecting a resolution.

Employee voices her opinion

DEFUSING NEGATIVE EMOTIONS

Guilt, anxiety, and anger are common negative emotions that must be managed carefully. Try to impress upon your employees that guilt will not repair whatever action has caused the upset, that anxiety will not prevent a future event that causes fear, and that anger is not an appropriate or helpful response to any situation. A person usually reacts angrily because others have not acted as he or she wants. You can defuse this anger by presenting a more reasonable point of view.

68 Carefully analyze problems as they arise.

69 Ask a close colleague to help defuse your anger.

DEALING WITH ANGER

Discussing the negative effects of anger with a disgruntled employee may help to resolve a situation of conflict. Beset by emotions that will probably have been growing in intensity over a period of time, the person will benefit from your rational observations of their inappropriate and misdirected behaviour and your suggestions for dealing with these feelings.

SIGNS OF ANGER

- Projecting bad feelings on to others, and resorting to sarcasm and ridicule.
- Avoiding the need for rational, unemotional responses.
- Concealing the loss of an argument, and making excuses for failure.
- Making excuses for intimidating and manipulating others.

ANTIDOTES TO OFFER

- Analyze the reasons behind angry feelings.
- Remember that it is possible to disapprove without being angry.
- Turn to a trusted, uninvolved friend before venting your anger.
- Ask whether expectations of others are reasonable.
- Expect to be disagreed with and displeased sometimes.
- Apologize to the objects of anger.

◀ REGAINING COMPOSURE

By addressing some of the reasons and emotions behind a person's anger, you may be able to help them regain their composure.

WORKING COLLECTIVELY

*If general conflicts arise, resolutions may
be found through a frank and open airing
of grievances, or by rethinking current
working methods. Unions can play a vital
part in the proceedings as intermediaries
between an organization and its employees.*

70 Encourage your
workers to
recognize your
management skills.

71 Avoid demonizing
a union or any one
person, but treat
issues on merit.

▼ **BEING POSITIVE**
*When negotiating, restructuring, or
resolving disputes, always seek a firm
conclusion, and use a working method
that strengthens people's natural instincts
to be full members of a winning team.*

RESOLVING CONFLICT

If conflict occurs within teams, you must work
quickly to identify its causes and to implement
workable, mutually agreed solutions. Consider
whether a disruptive conflict is growing between
two or more members that is affecting the rest
of the team, or if the group as a whole is
expressing general dissatisfaction with an issue.
Conflicts between individuals should be resolved
through firm but even-handed intervention.
You may need to change the membership of
the team to resolve the issue finally.

HANDLING UNIONS

Employers tend to regard unions as the enemy, vice versa, but an orderly, sympathetic union can be helpful to a well-run organization. Employees like to have representatives who can look after their interests more effectively than they can as individuals. Do not, however, make the mistake of identifying the union as the workforce: your contract is with each employee. Reserve for the union only those matters that belong to the union (representing individuals in dismissals, for example), and treat union officials with the same respect you would show any associate.

---

72 Never give in to demands that are unreasonable, but seek compromise.

STANDING FIRM ▶

Alan's new working methods gave the workers much more say in their work, which improved quality and reduced costs. This enabled Alan to raise pay while still making large savings.

CASE STUDY

Alan was appointed to run the maintenance operation for a large vehicle fleet. It depended on skilled, unionized workers who had a long history of trouble-making. A strike broke out shortly after Alan took charge. The workers, testing the new boss, demanded pay raises that the operation could not afford. They would not make any concessions. Alan also stood firm, and the staff walked out. Calling his managers together, Alan offered a package that addressed some of the employees' grievances. His proposal was eventually accepted, the strike ended, and the staff resumed work. Alan had successfully asserted management's right to manage, but he felt that more needed to be done. He went on to devise new methods of working that would help prevent future conflict.

QUESTIONS TO ASK YOURSELF

Q Is the dispute caused by a deep-seated grievance?

Q How widespread is the dispute?

Q Will a financial reward resolve the problem?

Q Have I taken all factors into consideration?

Q Will the proposed solution be effective in the long term?

CONFRONTING TROUBLE

When major disputes arise, do not stop at analyzing the apparent difficulties. It is essential to look for the underlying causes of the problem. Once the root causes have been identified, you can produce plans for finding effective and long-term tactical solutions – whether they be strategic, financial, or otherwise. If you leave the causes untouched, however, the difficulties will only recur. Your object is not only to cure the present troubles, but to ensure that they are permanently eliminated – with beneficial results for everybody.

DEALING WITH PERSONAL DIFFICULTIES

All managers are ultimately personnel officers. From time to time, you may have to deal with difficult personal matters that your staff bring to you. Take fast action, because such issues rarely improve with time.

> **73** Encourage people to bring their complaints and problems to you.

Manager asks that grievances be discussed separately.

MEETING NEEDS

Performance at work can be affected by anything from illness and bereavement to marital break-up and financial woes. Whether or not performance suffers, the person concerned requires attention and sympathy. This can take the form of allowing time off, or insisting that it be taken. Often practical assistance is required, perhaps involving money or helping to find legal advice, for example.

◀ **UNEARTHING PROBLEMS**
Aggressive behaviour in the workplace may disguise personal difficulties – avoid leaping to conclusions and be prepared to listen.

ENCOURAGING OPENNESS

Develop a personal rapport with your staff – this will help you to recognize any changes in their behaviour. If an employee displays unusual irritability, tension, or other negative behaviour, do not hesitate to approach them. Do not reprimand them for their work performance, but encourage them to talk openly about their problem. Listen sympathetically. Your availability will contribute to a caring environment in which people feel they can share their concerns.

> **74** Never take sides in a quarrel – be clearly impartial.

> **75** Handle personal problems as a friend, not a boss.

CULTURAL DIFFERENCES

British managers tend to be sympathetic to people with difficulties, while Americans and Germans are generally less understanding. The Japanese expect people to work, even in times of personal crisis.

PROVIDING SUPPORT

A manager dealing with a troubled employee must be supportive without getting too involved. Some specific problems – such as alcoholism and other types of compulsive behaviour – can require professional help. Display a positive attitude towards therapy and encourage the employee to choose this option. In the workplace, make the employee feel that their services are still needed and valued. This will boost their confidence as well as maintain a level of normality.

Employee explains why her work is suffering

Manager listens and offers advice

◀ **OFFERING SYMPATHY**
It may be that an attentive ear will be enough to meet a need. Sometimes, however, you may have to refer a member of staff to a counsellor.

76 Make time to talk to any employee who comes to you with problems.

DEALING WITH GENDER ISSUES

The issue of gender in the workplace goes far beyond harassment, sexual or otherwise. Harassing women is both offensive and an offence and must not be tolerated. There is no acceptable alternative to both practising and preaching true equality: make sure that all employees are judged by what they contribute to the organization, not by their gender. If one of your employees is being subjected to patronizing behaviour, act swiftly. But do not expect to change intolerance overnight. Make the change a key objective, however, and be prepared to take any action necessary to create an atmosphere in which both men and women feel comfortable, and in which any family needs, such as child care, are understood and accommodated.

MANAGING CHANGE

Managers often focus on the mechanics of change, concentrating on ensuring that their plan is followed. If their staff are not satisfied, however, the plan is likely to fail. If you listen to people's needs, they will respond positively to change.

77 Treat resistance to change as a problem that can always be solved.

78 Motivate your staff by acting positively on their creative ideas for change.

79 Use measured, continuous change to stimulate staff and avoid staleness.

BALANCING NEEDS

Some managers fall into the trap of putting production needs ahead of other organizational needs; others put concern for people above that for production. Both styles are erroneous, though the latter is popular with employees. Change, both large and small, is managed effectively only by showing equal concern for both needs. Attention to employees as people, coupled with strong interest in their welfare, well-being, and wishes, pays off in terms of better acceptance of changes and better performance. Change management that pays inadequate attention to people threatens productivity and is likely to misfire.

INVOLVING PEOPLE

When employees feel excluded from the decisions that will determine the way they do their work, demotivation and resentment can be the negative results. Ensure, therefore, that staff are given the opportunity to contribute and involve themselves at many levels of the decision-making process before any changes have to be made. This could range from having a say in how the office is furnished, for example, to the all-important task of setting long-term objectives. Consulting people before major changes take place will also reinforce their commitment and trust.

THINGS TO DO

1. Consider all staff input, no matter how small.
2. Identify "change agents" and encourage them to meet.
3. Form clear plans for change and share your intentions.
4. Tackle resistance to change as early as possible.

IDENTIFYING A "CHANGE AGENT"

Is capable of thinking laterally

+

Is driven to improve and transform

+

Is strong and emotionally in control

+

Thinks forcefully and independently

+

Creates new frames of reference

80 Show people how they will gain personally from the changes that you consider are necessary.

MANAGING RESISTANCE

You are likely to encounter varying degrees of resistance from staff when initiating change or revising existing procedures. Do not dismiss or ignore these objections. Some may arise from fear of what lies ahead, so listen to people's objections and, when possible, focus carefully on unwarranted fears in order to reassure staff. Others may arise from reasonable concerns of which you may have been unaware; offer staff the opportunity to explain their worries to you, then clarify how the proposed changes will affect them. Once they feel fully informed, their fears should recede.

QUALITIES FOR CHANGE AGENTS

Organizational change can be blocked by having the wrong people in key roles. Identify members of staff who are open to change – "change agents" – and put them where their enthusiasm for change becomes infectious and allays the fears of other employees. Use them in meetings, allowing them to take a leading role in facilitating the acceptance of change. Place these agents at any level of the organization: they will help you gather feedback on staff morale and reactions to change.

81 Involve many people in producing plans for change.

ASSESSING AND REWARDING

People are employed to get good results for the company. Their rates of success are intrinsically linked to how they are directed, reviewed, rewarded, and trusted by management.

EVALUATING PERFORMANCE

When choosing methods of assessing your staff's performance, always make sure that the end result has a positive effect on motivation and increases people's sense of self-worth. Realistic targets, positive feedback, and listening are key factors.

82 Begin an appraisal by concentrating on what a person has done well.

CULTURAL DIFFERENCES

The British have formal appraisal systems, but are often lax in administering them. The French and Germans set high standards and expect compliance. In Asia, group performance is rated above individual action, whereas Americans are motivated to achieve personal targets.

APPRAISING TO MOTIVATE

Regular, one-to-one assessments with your staff provide an efficient two-way forum in which to set and review realistic achievement targets, provide feedback on performance, and listen to and consider any problems employees may have. For example, a sales executive may feel that he or she is underperforming, when in fact sales targets have been set too high. During the appraisal, these targets could be reviewed and set at more realistic levels. Remember that your chosen methods of assessment must have a positive effect on people's performance levels and motivation.

JUDGING FAIRLY

An appraisal should leave staff feeling motivated and happy about their work, so make a point of recognizing employees' achievements and unique skills, and offer guidance on ways in which they could improve their performance. Try to avoid using these meetings negatively to criticize and dwell on faults, although do not avoid giving constructive criticism as necessary.

83 If people fail, ask what you can do to help them.

▼ QUALITIES TO APPRAISE

Understand what personal attributes go with successful work behaviour, and your judgments and suggestions at appraisals will contribute more effectively to success.

APPRAISING PERSONAL ATTRIBUTES

POSITIVE	NEGATIVE
● Enjoys uncertainty	● Expects certainty
● Asks questions	● Accepts what he or she is told
● Tolerates ambiguity	● Dislikes ambiguity
● Looks for alternatives	● Ignores conflicting evidence
● Is self-critical	● Is impulsive
● Seeks and weighs evidence	● Values "gut feelings"
● Reflects on matters	● Uses "either/or" thinking
● Communicates effectively	● Is unresponsive
● Is willing	● Is reluctant to take on new tasks
● Gets on well with other staff	● Is unpopular
● Uses initiative	● Is not proactive
● Can work unsupervised	● Requires constant supervision
● Is flexible	● Is not adaptable

DEALING WITH UNDERACHIEVEMENT

If objectives are not achieved, ask three key questions (right), and avoid accepting excuses for the answers. You want to find out exactly why the person failed to meet the objectives to prevent it happening again. People regret underachieving, so agree objectives with them that are fair but reasonably stretching. Remember that what seems daunting often proves to be surprisingly easy.

QUESTIONS TO ASK YOURSELF

Q Was the situation understood but the objective too difficult?

Q Was the situation misunderstood or was the objective inappropriate?

Q Was the failure to meet the objective entirely due to causes within the person's control?

PROMOTING STAFF

*G*iving *people new or better jobs shows that you recognize their achievements and encourages them to achieve further success. Rewarding exceptional performance also inspires colleagues to improve their contribution in the workplace.*

> **84** Encourage people to set their own high targets for performance.

▲ **WILL DO – CAN DO**
The employee who shows the standard of behavior that you should always expect is a perfect candidate for promotion.

▲ **WILL DO – CAN'T DO**
The willing employee who experiences difficulties should respond positively to training and encouragement.

▲ **WON'T DO – CAN DO**
The unmotivated person is in danger of losing her job unless motivation can be raised.

▲ **WON'T DO – CAN'T DO**
The incompetent employee who is unwilling to improve should obviously not be retained.

CHOOSING STAFF FOR PROMOTION

A simple, effective way to promote people focuses on two main aspects. Are they able to do the work required? Are they willing to do the work? There are four possible combinations of staff attitude and ability. The willing and able person is the only one you should consider for promotion. At the other extreme, somebody who is neither able nor willing has no place in the organization, let alone on the promotion ladder. The people in-between, who are lacking in either motivation or ability, pose the real challenge to their managers. Motivating an unmotivated person is far more difficult than training a willing individual to perform better. The prospect of promotion, however, may push the unwilling person into trying harder.

THINGS TO DO

1. Prepare a clear and accurate job description.
2. Promote the person who best fits the job description, regardless of age.
3. Seek to promote an employee with a "will do – can do" attitude.
4. If there were other candidates, let them know why they were unsuccessful.
5. Ensure other staff members know the reasons why an employee was promoted.

PROMOTING THE RIGHT PEOPLE

In a traditional, hierarchical system, age comes before ability when people are selected for promotion. However, the diversity of skills in the modern workplace, and people's different aptitudes for them, means that this system is no longer appropriate. Avoid making promotions just because a person was successful in one job: they may not be suited to another. Others whose skills are more suited to the job may feel aggrieved, and the person being promoted will feel insecure. To get the best-qualified person for the job, start with an accurate job specification, and then match the skills and characteristics of the person to the job requirements. Let others know why you have chosen that particular person.

HANDLING DISMISSALS

Job losses are always traumatic and need to be handled sensitively. Whether dismissals are due to redundancies or individual performance problems, once you have made the decision to dismiss someone, implement it quickly. Delaying bad news is always counterproductive: rumors circulate and create anxiety. Set out the facts clearly in all cases of demotion or job loss, so that those affected can understand why the decisions need to be taken. Prepare yourself by considering objections, so that you can deal with them calmly. Be tactful and sympathetic, and as generous as possible with severance payment. In some cases you might consider counseling for those affected. You want those leaving to feel that they have been treated as fairly as possible, and you want to sustain the highest possible morale among your remaining staff.

85 Dismiss only as a last resort, and never fire just to set an example.

86 Be as generous as possible with all severance payments.

205

TURNING FAILURE INTO SUCCESS

*W*hen somebody fails on a project, always consider whether the failure can be turned into a success. Satisfy yourself that you will not be wasting time and money. Then, if there is a reasonable chance of saving the project and the person, take it.

| 87 | Think before you give up on people or plans – giving up is irreversible. |

ASSESSING FAILURE

Sometimes an employee does not complete a project successfully. Analyze these failures carefully. Perhaps you or the employee did not have all the necessary information or made false assumptions. Alternatively, if the assumptions were correct, they may have been invalidated by bad execution in which case, identify the mistakes and find out why they were made. The key question is whether, given the results of your research, you would assign another, similar project to the same person. Your answer will determine how best to deal with the employee so as to prevent future failures.

▼ DISCUSSING
PROBLEMS AT SOURCE
If an employee has failed on a particular project, you need to discuss the failure with them in detail. If the failure was due to a misunderstanding, for example, the project may be resurrected.

| 88 | Consider cutting your losses rather than carrying on in vague hope. |

IMPROVING PERFORMANCE

To improve the productivity of an employee who is not performing to the required standard, first consider the factors responsible for this failure. If the person is lacking skills, arrange appropriate training immediately. For minor reasons, such as time-wasting, a verbal warning should be enough. If the reasons are more complex, such as chronic demotivation, consider a plan of action to measure improvement in their performance over a given period. Reassess the situation at the end of this time, and discuss the progress made.

89 There is usually a good reason why an employee is not performing well.

DEALING WITH POOR PERFORMANCE

FAILURE FACTORS	REMEDIAL ACTION
DEMOTIVATION Lacks motivation and energy to improve.	● Tackle the problem immediately. ● Find out possible reasons for drop in motivation. ● Base the improvement plan on a schedule of achievement.
LACK OF SKILLS Cannot cope with the technical demands of the job.	● Find out exactly which skills the employee is lacking. ● Arrange training sessions as soon as possible. ● Assign a person with more appropriate skills to the task.
PROCRASTINATION Finds excuses for not getting on with work.	● Break down the job into more manageable stages. ● Do not let the procrastinator overestimate the time required. ● If necessary, provide hands-on help to get the job started.
ABSENTEEISM Avoids work and dodges responsibility.	● Sternly emphasize the negative effects of absenteeism. ● Ensure that the employee feels an important part of a team. ● Consider if more flexible hours would reduce the problem.
HABITUAL LATENESS Is invariably late and always has an excuse.	● Let it be known that you are not interested in excuses. ● Try a counselling approach before disciplining the employee. ● See if peer pressure from other team members helps.
PERSONAL PROBLEMS Lets personal worries affect work.	● Concentrate on a person's performance, not their problems. ● Consider giving sick leave or reassigning duties. ● If necessary, advise the employee to seek professional help.

REMUNERATING EFFECTIVELY

The way you pay people forms an essential foundation for effective people management. Money is by no means the only motivator of people, but too little money demotivates powerfully, and financial reward remains a strong incentive.

90 Keep basic pay below top rates – use bonuses to give top incomes.

PAYING THE BASICS

The key question for pricing goods – "How much is the market prepared to pay?" – applies just as strongly to remuneration. Ask yourself what level of basic wages and salaries will attract, retain, and motivate people of the caliber that you require. Large companies take pains to discover competitive levels for basic pay, so that they can aim toward the upper limits for their industry. But you should not be concerned only with comparability. You want exceptional results, not comparable performance. Exceptional productivity will more than cover the extra pay. People want to feel fairly rewarded – but they naturally prefer to be rewarded very well.

INCREASING PAY WITH ▶ BETTER PRODUCTIVITY

Higher levels of efficiency allow you to pay your staff more. Even with fewer labor hours, company A managed to achieve the same level of productivity as company B, making higher rates of pay possible. Company A reached its productivity target thanks to the commitment and motivation of its staff.

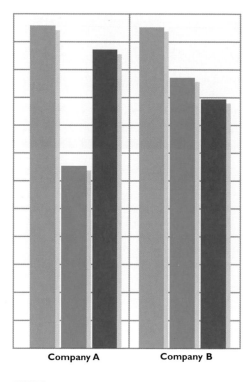

Company A   **Company B**

KEY
- *Productivity*
- *Labor hours*
- *Rates of pay*

PAYING BY RESULTS

The simplest form of payment by results (PBR) is piecework – the employee gets a fixed sum for each unit produced. In theory, this gives the employee the best incentive to maximize output. In fact, employees tend to put a ceiling on their earnings and thus on their effort, so this system has largely disappeared (especially now that more workers are in the information or service industries where piecework cannot be applied). The same principle – more pay for more production – still exists, however, in many forms. In sales, for example, commission can make up a very large proportion of total pay. In many cases, though, the PBR share of remuneration may be less than is necessary to add any real incentive – perhaps as low as five percent. Constantly revise any kind of PBR system that you are involved with to ensure that you are not overpaying for output or getting less output than you require.

TEST YOUR PAYMENT KNOWLEDGE

Answer True or False to the following propositions:
1. Wages and associated expenses determine the cost of labor.
2. The cost of labor determines how competitive your business is.
3. The main way to motivate people is to give financial incentives.
4. The primary incentive for most people at work is money.
(None of these propositions is true.)

91 Always involve employees in pay scale revisions.

92 Make it clear that extra pay is for special achievement.

93 Let team members decide how the team's bonus payment is divided.

GIVING BONUSES

Regard bonus payments as ways for the employee to share in the company's success – not as incentives. Avoid giving all employees an automatic 13 months' pay: they will come to take the annual bonus for granted as part of their basic income. Bonus programs can operate at any or all of three levels: company, team, and individual. Ideally, if the company does well, the individual gets a percentage addition to pay, and the same principle applies if his or her team (maybe a whole division) exceeds its targets. A bonus element tied to individual achievement alone must be reasonably large to be valued. Note the phrase "exceeds its targets": do not pay extra for what has been accepted as a sensible objective.

USING INCENTIVES

Non-cash incentives and fringe benefits can have a powerful influence on attitudes, which should in turn improve results. You can give employees the greatest incentive, however, by imparting a sense of ownership in the organization.

94 Use share schemes to reward people for contributing to team success.

95 Surprise people with gifts they do not expect.

96 Remember: giving people incentives of any kind sends a very positive signal.

SHARING THE SHARES

An employee who sees his or her efforts rewarded in company shares will, in theory, identify with the company, be committed to its success, and perform more effectively. In reality, it may be hard to tell whether the company's success is due to employees owning shares, or whether the success itself has led the company to issue shares. It is also difficult to know whether employees would have performed less effectively if no shares had changed hands. However, by giving people a stake in the company, you are making a highly positive statement about them, which encourages them to feel positive in return.

GIVING GIFTS

Expected remuneration has less impact than the unexpected. Even generous pay rises are taken for granted after a while, as salary aspirations increase accordingly. A far smaller "payment" – in the form of a gift – has a disproportionate worth in the eyes of the recipient. An employee could use a cash award to buy a gift (perhaps a weekend trip), but that provides less satisfaction than a payment in kind from you as reward for work well done. Presents are also a cost-effective method of motivating staff when cash is short or when competition does not allow an increase in pay.

QUESTIONS TO ASK YOURSELF

Q Have I ensured that rewards I have given are what people really want?

Q Am I acting to align the staff's interests with the goals and needs of the organization?

Q Do I always reward achievement and ability in preference to seniority?

Q Have I examined all possible ways of rewarding my staff?

OPTIMIZING BENEFITS

Fringe benefits have become much less effective financially in many countries because of tax changes. Good pension schemes, however, have become more attractive wherever state-funded provision has fallen. The same applies to medical insurance – the knowledge that the company cares for its people in sickness, health, and old age is a basic yet very powerful factor. Other benefits, such as company cars, paternity leave, education, and sabbaticals, improve the quality of people's lives. Electronic devices, from mobile telephones to computers, directly benefit the company, but the individual also gains personally from their availability. Ultimately, loyal and happy employees tend to work harder, leading to increased overall productivity.

▼ **BENEFIT PACKAGES**
Non-cash incentives, such as holidays, personal gifts, company cars, private medical insurance, help with children's education and care, and other benefits can greatly improve the way employees view and relate to the organization.

97 Make all welfare provisions as generous as possible.

98 Abolish status symbols that act in a divisive, "them and us" way.

ENDOWING STATUS

The modern company, with its flat structure, horizontal management, and open style, avoids status symbols that are divisive and counter-productive. Reserved parking places and separate dining rooms are rightly shunned. However, important-sounding job titles are an easy and economical way of providing recognition and psychological satisfaction. Moreover, outsiders like to deal with important people (although there is an obvious limit to the number of directors and vice-presidents you can appoint). Management can also confer status on those chosen to represent the company at prestigious events, such as conferences and key negotiations.

CREATING PARTNERSHIPS

W*hen people feel that their own success and that of the company are linked, they will be motivated to give their personal best for the good of all. Value the opinions of staff as partners in the company, and treat them with the care you give clients.*

99 Encourage people to work together as partners who help each other.

WORKERS AS PARTNERS

If a partnership is to work, you must treat employees like partners. Wherever possible, involve your staff in processes like decision-making and problem-solving to foster feelings of involvement and equality. Build a sense of community by providing opportunities to see how other departments within the organization operate. This will help everyone to relate to the company as a whole, and to understand the impact of their own contribution to its success. A shared vision is the strongest factor in the employee and organization partnership.

101 Make sure you let people know all the key facts about the business.

DO'S AND DON'TS

✔ Do enable your staff to understand the business.

✔ Do involve staff in decision-making.

✔ Do encourage staff to find partners to work with closely.

✘ Don't keep secrets that can safely be shared among staff.

✘ Don't leave staff in any doubt about future organization plans.

✘ Don't treat people as "cogs in a machine."

100 Value all your employees – they deserve the same treatment and respect as your customers.

WORKERS AS CUSTOMERS

Employees are valuable customers, and should be treated as such. They are customers in two senses. First, they rely on management for their livelihoods, and second, they might be potential or actual buyers of the company's goods or services. Look after your own people as carefully as you would your best customers. Happy people who feel valued will outperform those who do not.

CASE STUDY

One of the major problems at Pro-Act Inc., as with many firms, was that customer requests and inquiries were not passed on from department to department. The management felt that valuable feedback from the sales engineers' customer visits was being wasted, but was unsure how to resolve the matter. As part of a quality improvement exercise the issue was passed over to the engineers themselves for study and resolution. The engineers came up with the idea of a toll-free telephone line. If a customer asked them about a product other than the one they were selling, they could dial the free number, and a central desk would see that the inquiry reached the right place and monitor response. Sales increased, management was delighted, and the engineers were proud of their role.

◀ PROCESSING FEEDBACK

The case of Pro-Act highlights the significance of employee suggestions and the importance of acting on them. The toll-free telephone line program was adopted permanently and proved to be a major success. By adopting an employee-driven improvement plan, Pro-Act both increased sales (and therefore profits for the company) and raised the morale and sense of partnership and belonging felt by the engineers.

ACTING ON SUGGESTIONS

Formal suggestion programs are an easy way for you to make your staff feel involved in the company. Employees are usually deeply knowledgeable about the business, and will have valuable ideas about ways in which it could improve operations. Process suggestions and ideas rapidly, and let people know the fate of their suggestion – preferably by a note signed by their most senior manager. The acceptance of ideas is often accompanied by a small bonus. However, it is healthier if people regard improving the business as part of their normal activity, and expect and get warm recognition for their ideas and contribution to the company's success, rather than financial rewards.

THANKING PEOPLE ▼

Suggestion programs provide just one way of making your employees feel that they are in partnership with you and the company. Failure to acknowledge or act on suggestions, however, will have a detrimental effect.

Senior manager gives warm thanks for a helpful suggestion

Employee feels part of a winning team

ASSESSING YOUR ABILITY

Your ability to manage people should improve with experience, but many of the basic requirements can be mastered from the beginning of your career. The following questionnaire covers the key elements in getting people to work with you and for you to your mutual satisfaction – and to the benefit of the organization. If your answer is "never", mark Option 1; if it is "always", mark Option 4, and so on. Use your answers to identify the areas that need most improvement.

OPTIONS

1 Never

2 Occasionally

3 Frequently

4 Always

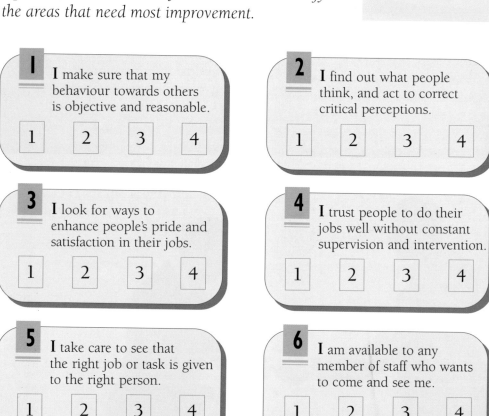

1 I make sure that my behaviour towards others is objective and reasonable.

1 2 3 4

2 I find out what people think, and act to correct critical perceptions.

1 2 3 4

3 I look for ways to enhance people's pride and satisfaction in their jobs.

1 2 3 4

4 I trust people to do their jobs well without constant supervision and intervention.

1 2 3 4

5 I take care to see that the right job or task is given to the right person.

1 2 3 4

6 I am available to any member of staff who wants to come and see me.

1 2 3 4

7 I prepare carefully for any meeting with individuals or with groups.

1 2 3 4

8 I involve people fully in plans for change and its implementation.

1 2 3 4

9 I rely on people's natural wish to do their work well, without orders.

1 2 3 4

10 I check to see that everybody is getting enough good-quality training.

1 2 3 4

11 I make a conscious effort to "talent-spot" among present and potential staff.

1 2 3 4

12 I discuss important issues with my people and ask for their opinions.

1 2 3 4

13 I motivate people with encouragement and example, rather than commands.

1 2 3 4

14 I welcome people's ideas for improvement, and implement good ones.

1 2 3 4

15 I ask for feedback on my performance from subordinates and peers.

1 2 3 4

16 I take opportunities to coach my people in ways to improve performance.

1 2 3 4

17 I give people the chance to demonstrate their management abilities.

1 2 3 4

18 I set high standards and insist that those standards are met.

1 2 3 4

19 I give people clear responsibility for a task that they can "own."

1 2 3 4

20 I form small groups or teams to tackle specific projects or needs.

1 2 3 4

21 I ask everybody in the team to come to a discussion with one or two new ideas.

1 2 3 4

22 I deal with people's personal problems swiftly and sympathetically.

1 2 3 4

23 I am prepared to listen to others and change my mind on issues.

1 2 3 4

24 I keep anger and other negative emotions out of my decisions and actions.

1 2 3 4

25 I try to understand the opposing point of view in cases of conflict.

1 2 3 4

26 I resolve interpersonal disputes quickly and without prejudice.

1 2 3 4

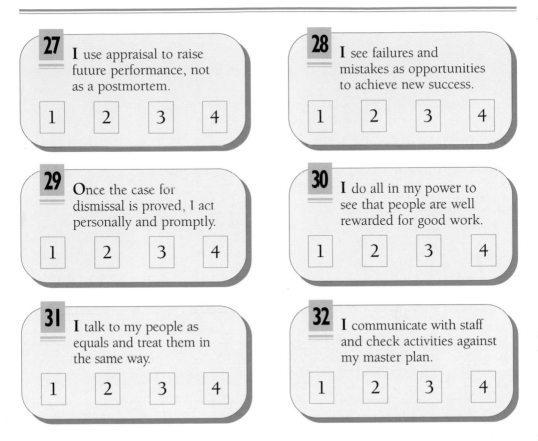

27 I use appraisal to raise future performance, not as a postmortem.

1 2 3 4

28 I see failures and mistakes as opportunities to achieve new success.

1 2 3 4

29 Once the case for dismissal is proved, I act personally and promptly.

1 2 3 4

30 I do all in my power to see that people are well rewarded for good work.

1 2 3 4

31 I talk to my people as equals and treat them in the same way.

1 2 3 4

32 I communicate with staff and check activities against my master plan.

1 2 3 4

ANALYSIS

Now that you have completed the self-assessment, add up the scores and check your performance by referring to the corresponding evaluations:

32–63: You are clearly having difficulties in dealing with people. The problems must be having a noticeable and unwelcome effect on your performance as well as your working environment. It is important to take action at once, probably with help from others, to begin badly needed improvement.

64–95: You are reasonably good with people but, in human relations at work, good is not enough. Use the questionnaire to identify your weaker areas, and work on them to get better results from yourself and others.

96–128: You should be pleased with your success with people, but remember that dealing with them is an ongoing process that can always be improved on.

COACHING SUCCESSFULLY

INTRODUCTION

The ability to raise the performance of your staff and seek long-term goals for them to work toward is an important element of being a good manager. Through coaching, you can develop staff to take on more responsibility and give yourself more time to get on with the job of managing. Coaching Successfully will help you get the best from your team and let you focus on achieving better results for your organization. Practical advice, including 101 concise tips, shows you how to develop the coaching approach in yourself and others, and a self-assessment test at the end of the book allows you to evaluate your skills as a coach. As you seek to instil coaching values in those around you, this book will be an invaluable source of reference and advice.

UNDERSTANDING COACHING

Coaching helps you bring out the potential of your staff. Use it to deal with immediate problems, as a constructive way to interact with your staff, and as an aid to their long-term development.

WHAT IS COACHING?

Coaching is the art of improving the performance of others. Managers who coach encourage their teams to learn from and be challenged by their work. Create the conditions for continuous development by helping your staff to define and achieve goals.

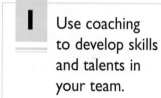

I Use coaching to develop skills and talents in your team.

▲ COACHING QUALITIES
A good coach listens first, asks searching questions, provides constructive feedback, and is ready to generate creative ideas.

HOW COACHING WORKS

The coaching process closes the gap between an individual's or team's present level of performance and the desired one. This can happen within a single coaching session, or over a long cycle of sessions. As a coach, you will help develop your employees by mutually assessing performance, discussing the present situation, defining achievable goals, exploring new initiatives, and supporting a coachee in their plan of action. Coaching refers both to specific interacting skills – used both in everyday situations and in more structured meetings – and the encouragement of long-term learning.

STRUCTURING COACHING

DEFINITION
Determine performance goals

ANALYSIS
Understand the present reality

EXPLORATION
Explore options to achieve goals

ACTION
Say when tasks will be done

LEARNING
Implement agreed actions

FEEDBACK
Review progress at next session

THE COACHING PROCESS

Coaching is an unending process – each new achievement forms a platform for the next challenge. However, for any single coaching goal there is a cycle of six basic stages from goal to completion. First, the coach and employee agree what the goals of coaching are; second, they discuss the present position; third, they explore the available options; and fourth, they identify and commit to a course of action. These steps can often be completed in a single coaching session. The coachee then implements the agreed action with the support of the coach, and with a view to permanently raising performance levels. In the final stage, the coach and coachee hold the next coaching session and consider what has been learnt and how to build on this knowledge.

2 Use the final stage of a coaching cycle to initiate the next cycle by defining the next achievable goal.

COACHING FUNDAMENTALS

It is not necessary to know everything about your employee's work to coach them well. In fact, much good coaching occurs when the manager is able to take an objective view of an employee's goals without being distracted by details. Good coaches help employees learn from their mistakes, identify their performance targets, and take responsibility for implementing the first step. As a coach, avoid trying to tell people what to do, but, instead, help them choose the best route to succeed in their objectives. Use coaching to teach your employees to adopt a positive approach to learning by encouraging them to say what they think.

POINTS TO REMEMBER

● A team with a positive attitude is more able to face new challenges.

● A good coach encourages team members to discuss their ideas.

● Staff should have the necessary resources to achieve their goals.

3 Encourage staff to come to their own conclusions.

WHY COACH?

B*y coaching, managers release their own time, improve their staff's performance, and enhance the productivity of their organizations. Coach and delegate more, and supervise less, to boost productivity and help team members fulfill their potential.*

4 Invest in people in the short term, and reap the benefits in the long term.

YOU CAN DELEGATE

You hand over more responsibility

Trust is established

Staff skills are increased

You do take time to coach

DELEGATING MORE

Managers with their eye on future success use coaching to develop skill and positive attitudes in their staff. It takes effort to maintain performance, let alone improve it, so be prepared to invest time in people's development. Once you have confidence in your staff's skills, and have developed a good relationship built on trust, you can begin to delegate some of your responsibilities to them.

◀ UPWARD SPIRAL OF RESPONSIBILITY
Investing time in improving the skill and confidence of your staff leads to an upward spiral of events, when you can delegate projects and get on with focusing on long-term managerial issues.

SUPERVISING LESS

Unless you develop your staff, they will be unable to cope with the responsibilities you want to give them. Coaching provides a solution. Coach your staff to accept their own responsibilities. This eases some of the pressure on you, so that you can focus on your own, longer-term responsibilities. In the meantime, your staff are achieving greater job satisfaction because they are allowed to make their own decisions and achieve independence.

DOWNWARD SPIRAL OF DEVELOPMENT ▶
If you do not invest time in developing the skills of your staff, you may need to supervise them to ensure work is done properly. This leads to long hours and stress for you and your staff.

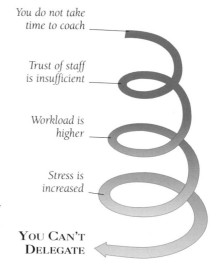

You do not take time to coach

Trust of staff is insufficient

Workload is higher

Stress is increased

YOU CAN'T DELEGATE

BRINGING OUT POTENTIAL

Asking searching questions and giving constructive feedback will encourage your staff to become more aware of their strengths and weaknesses. Help them to build on their strengths and to develop new skills, so that they can take on new challenges. Coach them to learn from both their successes and mistakes. As their competence and confidence improve, their self-esteem grows, and they will take more initiative in meeting agreed goals. Increasingly, by using all of their abilities and expressing their potential to the full, your whole team will benefit.

5 Use coaching to achieve increased productivity.

6 Identify, encourage, and build on your team's existing strengths and skills.

Coachee takes a confident role in the team; team benefits from shared strengths

THE NEEDS OF THE TEAM
Mutual support and increased skills

Coach benefits from an efficient team; team benefits from the manager focusing on long-term development

THE NEEDS OF THE COACHEE
Job satisfaction and fulfillment

THE NEEDS OF THE COACH
More time to be results focused

◀ **BENEFITS FOR ALL**
The role of the coach is pivotal to the needs of the team. Through coaching, the coachee has the benefit of personal and career development; the team is strengthened by having motivated and skilled staff; and the coach has more time to devote to management and results.

Coach and coachee aim for the same goals

7 Increase fulfillment by delegating responsibility for whole projects.

DO'S AND DON'TS

✔ Do make coaching one of your most important priorities.

✔ Do develop staff by delegating tasks that stretch their abilities.

✔ Do tell staff how coaching works.

✘ Don't delay coaching until there is nothing better to do.

✘ Don't just delegate the activities you would prefer not to do.

✘ Don't be afraid to take time coaching.

INVOLVING PEOPLE

Teams in business need high morale to perform well. Research shows that when people take part in decision making they have greater commitment to the final decision. Engage people in a search for ways of achieving their goals, rather than giving them ready-made answers. Remember that coaching is a two-way process that involves people in the choices that most affect them – in their jobs and their development. Your staff will benefit from the coaching approach because a sense of ownership for decisions is highly motivational.

8 Find out what your team values most in its work.

9 Involve your staff in decisions that affect them.

POINTS TO REMEMBER

- Team members who have been included in decisions feel empowered to achieve more.

- Teams and individuals should learn to recognize and use each other's strengths.

- Each team member should feel they play an essential role in the structure of the team.

- Team members should feel free to contribute their ideas about the team's goals and methods.

DEVELOPING POSITIVE ATTITUDES IN STAFF

When people's self-confidence and motivation grow, they take on more challenging assignments. They prove to themselves that they can handle these challenges, and they are able to solve many of the problems that inevitably arise. They know that if they do run into trouble you, their coach, will support them. This builds a positive attitude to change, and when your staff are presented with further challenges, they are more likely to accept them, rather than to give reasons why they cannot.

CASE STUDY

The subsidiary of one of Europe's biggest food producers had an ambitious goal to double shareholder value every four years. It implemented a decision-making process to evaluate and select products, activities, and markets adding greater value to the business. Their organization development manager recognized, however, that achieving strategic goals ultimately depended on staff –

their understanding, skill, and commitment were required in order to meet the inevitable new challenges. This reflected the chairman's publicized view that achieving strategic goals was 80 percent about people. In order to equip staff with the skills, the management development manager trained and encouraged all line managers to coach their people. The result was the hoped for increase in the productivity of the organization.

◀ **INVESTING IN EMPLOYEES**
In this case study, the director of the organization saw that it was necessary to equip staff with skills to enable them to respond positively to the challenge of new markets and increased competition. Coaching was used to develop the skills and attitudes of staff, which led to an increase in productivity.

INCREASING PRODUCTIVITY

Your team's ability to work efficiently increases as member skills improve through your coaching. The coaching goals you agree on make clear to everyone involved what good performance looks like. With this knowledge, teams can spot and correct mistakes more quickly, and can use their skill to deliver the required quality of work. The result is greater productivity. Just the increased attention coaching brings can improve performance. So, by coaching, you influence staff performance in two ways: first, through their professional development; second, through the positive attention of your coaching.

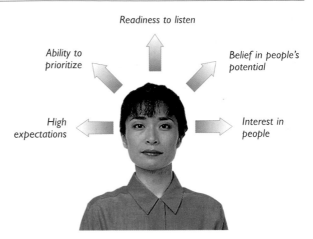

Readiness to listen

Ability to prioritize

Belief in people's potential

High expectations

Interest in people

▲ QUALITIES OF A GOOD COACH

There are a number of important qualities that a coach needs to possess in order to bring out the potential of staff, and in doing so, increase a team's competence and productivity.

10 Agree on clear performance standards so that the team has a level against which to assess itself.

THE HAWTHORNE EXPERIMENT

In the 1920s, physiologist Elton Mayo conducted experiments at the Hawthorne Electrical Works in Chicago. He was attempting to prove his theory that better lighting led to greater productivity. First, Mayo had the lights turned up on the factory floor. As he expected, production levels went up too. Mayo had proven his theory – or had he? As an afterthought, he decided to turn the lights down to see what would happen. To his surprise, production went up again. He found that whatever he did with the lighting, production went up. Mayo discussed his findings with the workers involved. They said that the interest shown in them by Mayo and his researchers had made them feel more valued. They were used to being ignored. The increase in morale led to an improvement in productivity. This effect is known as the "Hawthorne Effect."

DECIDING TO COACH

There are many applications to coaching. You can initiate coaching yourself or respond to requests for help. Look out for opportunities to coach on such issues as problem solving, career development, lack of motivation, and teamwork.

11 Look for every appropriate opportunity to coach your staff.

BUILDING SKILLS

Job satisfaction requires a continual supply of new goals and challenges to stretch the employee's potential to the utmost. As you prioritize personal development within your team they will naturally seek opportunities to extend their skills. Coaching is a natural follow-up to training. To bring out your team's potential, a combination of training, on-the-job learning, and coaching can be unbeatable.

Staff take steps to new challenges by building on skills learned

NEW GOAL

REVIEW

PRACTICE

COACH

TRAIN

INDUCT

CONSOLIDATING STEPS ▶

Help define step-by-step goals so staff can learn, understand, practice, and review skills before moving on to new challenges.

QUESTIONS TO ASK YOURSELF

Q Have I helped staff put their training to good use, by enabling them to practice their new skills on a project?

Q Have I offered support to staff to whom I have delegated challenging tasks?

Q Do I know each employee's goals and aspirations?

PROGRESSING PROJECTS

It is part of your role as a manager to delegate responsibility for projects, support staff in their work, and ensure that projects are completed satisfactorily. Coaching is an ideal way to keep individuals on track without undermining their responsibility. Hold coaching meetings over the life of a project so you are able to receive progress reports, troubleshoot problems, and monitor standards. When your staff come to you with difficulties, coach them to find a solution.

SOLVING PROBLEMS

You may be approached by a member of your staff for help, or you may decide that you need to address a performance issue with an individual. Either way, coaching can be used to help find solutions to a problem. This does not mean that you want to become the source of all solutions. If you did that, there would soon be little time to manage. Reduce precious management time spent on firefighting by coaching staff to think through problems for themselves and to come up with their own plan for resolution.

12 Avoid taking over problems from your staff.

13 Use coaching to explore ways of solving problems.

14 Groom your deputy to be ready to take over your projects.

DEFINING MILESTONES ▼
Use coaching to define the employee's next career milestone, give feedback, establish new training needs, and set achievable targets in the pursuit of these goals.

DEVELOPING CAREERS

A sense of career direction is essential if employees are to feel that they are valued by the organization. It is for this reason that regular performance reviews are standard practice in most organizations. The coaching approach can dovetail neatly with reviews, through which you can agree developmental goals with employees and give support while they achieve them. With particularly able staff, coaching can be an ideal way to keep them moving onward and upward.

Coach → Feedback → Set Targets

OVERCOMING CONFLICTS

Conflicts between individuals, between managers and staff, or between employees and customers are a fact of life. Reduce conflicts within your own team by encouraging openness, responsibility for high standards, and a creative approach to problems. Where your attention is drawn to disagreements, coach to explore the root of the issue and to resolve misunderstanding.

15 Defuse disputes and disagreements by encouraging staff to respect opposing viewpoints.

REMOTIVATING STAFF

Demoralized staff can quickly spread discontent. Often this occurs as a result of poor communication between managers and team members. Improve morale by helping people explore their differences honestly and to look at the causes of current problems. Another reason for a loss of motivation may be that individuals are bored or dissatisfied. When staff come to you expressing dissatisfaction, encourage them to talk openly about the causes of the problem as well as the problem itself. Managers who coach have a means of aligning staff personal goals with the mission of the organization itself.

FOCUSING ON ACHIEVING GOALS ▶
The best performers are focused on what they really want. Look for ways to remotivate dissatisfied staff by exploring their needs, recognizing their aspirations, and establishing new goals.

16 Make it clear that all ideas are worth hearing.

POINTS TO REMEMBER

- Coaching can be used whenever you want to improve performance or increase motivation levels.
- Coaching is not training, although it can help employees implement and practice new skills.
- To find a solution, problems should be looked at from as many points of view as possible.
- Coaching feedback should be specific, factual, and objective.
- New ways for staff advancement should be explored.

BRAINSTORMING

Despite the best efforts of your staff, projects will stall as problems arise from unforeseen difficulties. This can easily lead to a loss of responsibility for the project and a weakening of team spirit – often noticeable when staff start to blame others for delays. Unresolved difficulties can cause frustration or, worse, quick-fixes that solve nothing. When you notice that projects are stalling, or when your team comes to you with setbacks, coach them to move things on by defining the present state of affairs. Consolidate the team by inviting an open contribution of ideas from all team members to come up with possible solutions.

17 Use team coaching to foster mutual learning and support, and to create new initiatives.

DECIDING WHEN AND HOW TO COACH

REASON FOR COACHING	ACTIONS TO TAKE
BUILDING SKILLS Set up opportunities for new skills to be learned and practiced.	● Use coaching to break up large-scale tasks into smaller ones, gradually introducing new skills. ● Before selecting a training program, coach your staff to identify performance targets they want to achieve.
PROGRESSING PROJECTS Oversee progress and monitor any problems on projects.	● Link coaching sessions with progress reports over the life of the project. ● Work through problems that could hinder the successful completion of the project.
SOLVING PROBLEMS Help staff to identify problems and possible routes to a solution.	● Encourage staff to define the problem and to come up with their own route to a solution. ● Remain sympathetic to your staff's difficulties, while encouraging them to deal with problems robustly.
DEVELOPING CAREERS Prepare staff for promotion or show them a clear career path.	● Work on coaching goals that could result in recognition for staff achievements. ● Focus on long-term projects that are challenging and bring out potential, rather than small-scale jobs.
OVERCOMING CONFLICTS Defuse disagreements among team members.	● Coach staff to develop greater insight into others' perspectives and therefore avoid misunderstandings. ● Overcome friction by directing attention to results rather than personalities.
REMOTIVATING STAFF Restore enthusiasm and commitment within the team.	● Establish people's needs and aspirations and link these to performance targets. ● Be prepared to dig for the issues that really concern the employee and be ready to talk through them.
BRAINSTORMING Direct the creative input of the team to keep projects on track.	● Accentuate the generation of creative options rather than getting bogged down in problems. ● In team coaching, take a lead by offering creative ideas of your own, and then invite the team to assess them.

SELECTING A COACHING STYLE

Sometimes people like clear direction and definite answers to their questions. At other times, they want to be involved in a dialogue about their own development and goals. Select the style most appropriate for the coachee and to the objective of coaching.

18 Be ready to adapt your coaching style during a coaching session.

19 Ask questions and listen to the coachee, but also offer ideas and teach skills if necessary.

USING "PUSH" AND "PULL"

There is a spectrum of coaching styles ranging from "push" at one extreme to "pull" at the other. "Push" is akin to instruction. You give the coachee clear answers or show them how to perform a skill. At the opposite end of the spectrum is "pull," where you draw out a coachee's existing strengths. In the first style, you do most of the talking, while in the second, you do most of the listening. Both styles are used in coaching, and a skilled coach can move effortlessly between the two.

ADAPTING YOUR STYLE

"Push" style coaching can be useful in the early stages of a person's development, when they lack confidence and competence. The advantages of "push" are that it is quick and provides answers, teaching procedures step-by-step. The problem is that it leads to dependence on you for the answers to problems. Using the "pull" style, act as a catalyst to help staff find their own answers. Listen to answers and then probe further to help coachees create their own solutions. Such an approach results in coachees feeling accountable for results and being able to take the initiative.

POINTS TO REMEMBER

- "Pull" style coaching can irritate people who are used to being spoon-fed answers.
- "Pull" style coaching takes more time and more skill as a coach, but the benefits in terms of staff commitment are well worth it.
- If coachees develop their own solutions, they feel more motivated to achieve goals.
- If you use the "push" style, be sure that the coachee is able to reproduce the skill or procedure.

Coach does most talking

Coachee is quiet and dependent

Coach sees that coachee is ready to take initiative

Coachee is self-reliant and confident

Coach encourages and listens

PUSH   **TRANSITION**   **PULL**

CHANGING STYLES ▲

Match your coaching style to the motivation and skill level of your staff. Use a "pull" style as much as possible. Reserve a "push" style for those with low skill and low self-reliance, but change over to a "pull" style as they gain in confidence.

20 Introduce the "pull" style of coaching by asking more questions than you answer.

ADAPTING AN EMPLOYEE'S MOTIVATION LEVEL

LOW WILL/LOW SKILL

- "Pull" for coachee's reasons for being in the job. Find a motivational need and link learning to its fulfillment.

- "Push" to give plenty of direction and be ready to provide time and support.

LOW WILL/HIGH SKILL

- "Pull" to find motivational needs and aspirations, and find ways to focus on new challenges and goals.

- "Pull" to find if the employee is being stretched. Begin to establish trust.

HIGH WILL/LOW SKILL

- "Push" and give directions at first, then ease off and encourage the employee to find their own way.

- "Push" to teach new skills and set achievable goals to build confidence.

HIGH WILL/HIGH SKILL

- "Pull" by identifying challenges that provide opportunities for personal and career development.

- "Pull" by listening to the coachee's assessment, ideas, and options.

EMOTIONAL INTELLIGENCE AND COACHING

Top performers are distinguished by their self-motivation, self-awareness, self-regulation, and ability to influence others. These qualities are known as "emotional intelligence." Work on developing these qualities in yourself and in your staff.

21 Encourage your staff to analyze their own strengths and weaknesses.

22 Help people gain good relationship skills such as empathy and sensitivity.

WHAT IS EMOTIONAL INTELLIGENCE?

According to Daniel Goleman's theory, success in business depends on emotional intelligence rather than academic learning. People with emotional intelligence are self-aware, self-regulated, and motivated. They are sensitive to others' feelings and have the ability to influence people. Be a successful coach by developing these qualities in yourself and in others.

BEING AWARE

People who are self-aware know how they feel and how they are likely to react. They know that anger caused by an incident in one meeting can pollute the next if they do not discharge the bad feeling. Recognize and develop your own strengths: look for assignments that you will excel at. Seek coaching for areas you need improvement in. Self-awareness will enable you to make the best use of your skills.

QUESTIONS TO ASK YOURSELF

Q Am I aware of my limitations?

Q When do I take the time to analyze my own strengths and weaknesses?

Q Do I play to my strengths and develop skills in areas I am gifted in?

Q Do I know which times of the day I am able to work to my full potential?

Q Do I take a break when I feel jaded and unmotivated?

Q Do I delegate tasks to staff when I know they will get a better result than I will?

Q What important tasks can I reserve for the time of day I am most alert?

Q Am I able to see how my behavior can affect others?

REMAINING IN CONTROL

Self-regulation is the ability to accept and manage one's feelings. It goes hand in hand with self-awareness. Emotionally intelligent people work well within teams and develop good working relationships. Be aware of your nerves before a meeting. Call on memories of past success to trigger the necessary confidence for a task at hand. When conflicts arise, remain in control by analyzing your own reactions and responding appropriately, and encourage staff to do the same.

23 Persuade staff to overcome setbacks by focusing on past achievements.

24 Encourage staff to predict, and be prepared for, possible problems.

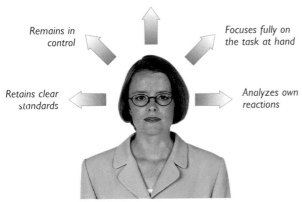

Recalls past successes to boost confidence

Remains in control

Focuses fully on the task at hand

Retains clear standards

Analyzes own reactions

◀ EMOTIONAL AWARENESS
A self-regulated person is able to focus fully on a goal. He or she has clear standards, but recognizes limitations and knows that he or she may need to take time out from a busy schedule in order to rejuvenate.

REMAIN FOCUSED ▶
Strong commitment to his goals, and an ability to remain focused were a deciding factor in the success of a top car-salesperson. His concentration on the task at hand was sharper and more consistent than that of his colleagues. His emotional intelligence meant he was also able to foster and retain good working relationships.

CASE STUDY

A salesperson in a car dealership exhibited a stronger ability to focus on a goal than his colleagues in the office. He remained able to manage his workload and was not distracted by things happening around him. This was most obvious when his colleagues chattered idly around his desk. He continued to make phone calls to follow up sales leads despite the distraction. In that year, he sold more than twice as many cars as the next best performing salesperson. At the same time, he was sociable and had a good working relationship with his colleagues and clients. However, his self-regulation meant that he spent more time than others working on the highest sales priorities, such as prospecting for sales, following up client meetings, and customer service. Consistently performing to his own high standards, he went on to become one of the car manufacturer's star performers.

UNDERSTANDING MOTIVATIONAL NEEDS

Feeling motivated is having the desire to excel for oneself and for the organization. Although high performers have a burning desire to be at the top of the ladder, they work within the interests of the organization. This gives them their long-term success, and is why their organizations value them highly. Link your own and your staff's desire to succeed with the motivation to continually seek new ways to improve your organization's service.

THINGS TO DO

1. Match personal priorities to those of the organization.

2. Learn from setbacks, rather than be defeated by them.

3. Focus on remaining positive and ahead of the game.

25 Motivate staff by linking their personal goals to the company's aims.

USING EMPATHY

Empathy is sensitivity to the feelings of others. As a good manager, you must understand what makes staff tick in order to maintain their firm commitment. Devote time to finding links between staff capabilities and goals. Your efforts will be rewarded by results. Learn to foster political know-how. Be aware of who wields power in your organization, which sensitive toes to avoid, and who is likely to support or oppose a proposal.

Looks attentive and interested

Uses calm voice tones

Matches body language to convey receptiveness

Coachee responds to coach positively and relaxes

Coachee explains problems

EMPATHIZING ▶
This coach can tell from nonverbal signals how others feel. By putting herself in the coachee's shoes, she knows how to sympathize, how to encourage, and how to push.

Open palm gesture emphasizes communication

INFLUENCING PEOPLE

People with influence have presence. This comes from their confidence in their strengths, their ability to manage crises, and their belief in their ideas. Show confidence and credibility in your demeanor. When confronted with conflict, seek out the other person's values and find ways of satisfying them with proposals. Fine-tune communication to suit the people you are influencing. If a colleague responds best to visual information, then influence them by using pictures or charts.

EXUDING CONFIDENCE ▶

Good managers listen to views different from their own. They hear employees' concerns and needs and take them into account before making any decisions of their own.

---

26 Be aware of nonverbal communication.

POINTS TO REMEMBER

- Good coaching requires high emotional intelligence.

- By demonstrating the qualities of motivation, empathy, sensitivity, and influence, you act as a role model to your staff.

- The more you encourage emotional intelligence in your staff, the easier it will be to coach them.

- When staff display emotional intelligence, praise them for it.

DEVELOPING EMOTIONAL INTELLIGENCE IN OTHERS

Coach your staff to improve their emotional intelligence by asking searching questions that prompt them to reflect on experience and learn from it. Give feedback that enables people to see themselves through others' eyes and discourage defensive thinking, while acknowledging the feelings of threat that underpin it. Ensure people take on responsibility for their own results and encourage them to consider the possible political sensitivities involved in their projects. Persuade staff to pursue challenging goals and provide the necessary support during difficult times.

▼ **COACHING TACTICS**

Question the coachee about past experiences and ask what can be learned from them. Challenge narrow thinking, and praise good work and performance to bolster the coachee's self-esteem.

Question ➡ **Challenge** ➡ **Praise**

DEVELOPING COACHING RELATIONSHIPS

Autonomy, initiative, decisiveness, and a sense of ownership for one's work are essential for both parties in a professional relationship. Encourage and develop these qualities in your staff to make them more receptive to a coaching approach.

27 Go out of your way to praise the achievements of your staff.

CULTURAL DIFFERENCES

Collaborative, participative attitudes to employee-manager working relations are fast gaining ground in both the US and the UK. In Japan, where the team is more important than the individual, participation is taken for granted within an overall structure of formal control.

ENCOURAGING AUTONOMY

Managers surrounded by independent staff will have more time to manage. Once managers have defined job responsibilities and reporting limits, then staff should be trusted to get on with the job in the best way they know how. Coaching is there to provide staff with a means of discussing pitfalls and brainstorming new ideas – not as a summons for orders and instructions. Let your staff learn to make their own decisions. Encourage autonomy by allowing your staff to learn from their mistakes and be ready to work with them to think through and build on what they learn.

ACHIEVING A GOOD COACHING RELATIONSHIP

A PRODUCTIVE RELATIONSHIP
A good coaching relationship is achieved by a combination of autonomy, shared responsibility, and the fostering of new skills.

● **AUTONOMY**
Coachee decides on the best options and relies on the coach for support when necessary.

● **RESPONSIBILITY**
Coach encourages the coachee to make decisions with a two-way coaching style.

● **FOSTERING LEARNING**
Coachee develops new skills with the support of the coach and sets new standards.

TREATING EMPLOYEES AS PARTNERS

Treating employees as partners fosters commitment and enterprise rather than compliance. Coaching is integral to this belief and places high emphasis on trust in the potential of individuals. Motivate employees by showing them that they have a valuable contribution to make.

Coach shows interest and respect for employee's views

Employee is confident about sharing ideas

SHARING IDEAS ▶

Encourage your team members to share their ideas on the best way to achieve your organization's goals.

QUESTIONS TO ASK YOURSELF

Q Am I letting fear stop me from delegating responsibility?

Q Do my staff each have a current project they can learn from?

Q Am I supportive of the ambitions of my staff?

Q Which members of my team are ready to step up a level?

Q Can I hand over a project to an able team member?

FOSTERING CONTINUOUS DEVELOPMENT

By asking "What can we learn from that?" or "What do we have to do next time to get a better result?," teams can come up with creative solutions that make the organization more efficient in the long run. Create a culture of opportunity in your team by continually setting new standards of excellence and using mistakes as springboards for new achievements. Keep looking for opportunities for your team to learn new skills, acquire new challenges, and expand their capabilities.

28 Set up progress reports for high risk projects and encourage the views of staff.

DO'S AND DON'TS	
✔ Do let staff find their own best way to do the job.	✘ Don't stifle effort and initiative with rules and regulations.
✔ Do give people as much responsibility as they can handle.	✘ Don't encourage staff to see you as the fount of all wisdom.
✔ Do use the phrase "How can we..?," not "Why did you...?"	✘ Don't coach people beyond their limits of competence.

INITIATING COACHING

The first steps in a coaching cycle lay the foundations for its likely success. Be clear about when to start coaching, and how to structure and follow up a session.

PREPARING FOR A SESSION

Coaching can be spontaneous or formal. It can be given on a one-time basis or can work long-term over many sessions. It may be requested by the coachee, or called for by the coach. Whatever the situation, always clarify the purpose of a session.

29 Be clear about what you will work on during the session.

30 Mentally rehearse planned coaching sessions, but always be ready to adapt your approach.

NOTICING OPPORTUNITIES

Having ensured that the right conditions for coaching are in place – good coaching relationships, developmental opportunities, and motivated team members – look out for opportunities to offer coaching. An employee may approach you to discuss the possibility of promotion, and, in a coaching session, you can work together to identify paths to career development. Or, you may decide to call a coaching session when you notice an employee is having problems on a project. Always be ready to implement coaching when you see an appropriate moment, or when staff request it.

CLARIFYING NEEDS

Once a coaching opportunity has been noticed, it is important for both parties to be clear about what they are doing and how, where, and when coaching is going to work. If a member of your staff raises an issue that you feel may be resolved by coaching, ask if they would like some time with you to explore the issue. If you have noticed a performance problem that needs attention, then make it clear that you want to collaborate on finding a way to resolve it. In either case, be sure to state the benefits of a session and be clear about what you will work on.

POINTS TO REMEMBER

● Coaching off site can encourage a more open discussion.

● A coaching session should be uninterrupted.

● It is not necessary to say that you are going to "do coaching."

31 Agree on where and when you are going to meet.

ARRANGING A COACHING SESSION

LOCATION	PLANNED SESSION	SPONTANEOUS SESSION
 **MEETING ROOM** A private office enables the discussion to be confidential and uninterrupted.	● **AGREE ON TIMING** Negotiate a time to meet and a length of session that suits both parties.	● **BE FLEXIBLE** Turn a question or complaint into an opportunity for spontaneous coaching.
	● **ALLOW SUFFICIENT TIME** Overestimate the time required for the meeting and make allowances for the unexpected.	● **BE CLEAR** Make clear how much time you have at the outset of a session.
OFF SITE An informal, neutral location lends a more relaxed, less guarded air to the discussion.	● **BOOK AHEAD** Book two meetings in advance to ensure continuity, because people's calendars fill quickly.	● **BE CONSIDERATE** Ask the coachee how much time they have, in case they are worried about other commitments.
	● **MEET REGULARLY** To make the best of time limitations, hold short coaching meetings on a regular basis.	● **REVIEW** Book a time and place for the next meeting, for feedback and further action.

STARTING A SESSION

Having prepared for coaching, you may want to hold a single session or you may decide to use the first session to initiate the coaching cycle. Whether coaching is initiated by you or by the coachee, outline what you aim to achieve in the session.

32 Start sessions positively and treat the coachee as an equal.

33 Divert calls to avoid unwanted interruptions.

MAKING A POSITIVE START

Your first remarks will set the tone for the rest of the session. Converse briefly about a positive, unrelated matter, such as a shared interest, to put the coachee at ease. Praise any achievements since you last met and allude specifically to work that has been well done. This will convey your positive interest and focus attention on performance. Agree on the length of the session so that you can set your sights on a realistic amount of ground to cover.

STARTING OUT ON THE RIGHT NOTE ▼

This coach warmly greets the coachee. His positive body language immediately puts the coachee at his ease.

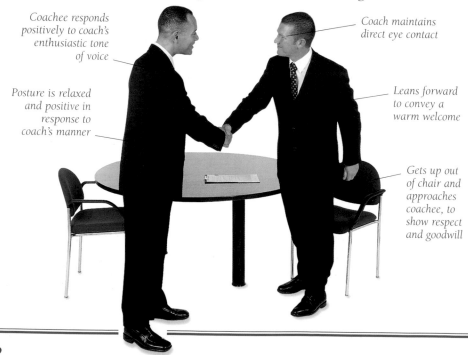

Coachee responds positively to coach's enthusiastic tone of voice

Coach maintains direct eye contact

Posture is relaxed and positive in response to coach's manner

Leans forward to convey a warm welcome

Gets up out of chair and approaches coachee, to show respect and goodwill

OUTLINING THE ISSUES

You may have called the session to focus on career development or to introduce a new procedure. In this case, outline the rationale for your interest. If you have called the coaching session to discuss a performance issue, then explain the problem. If the coachee agrees that the problem exists, then move on. If necessary, explain the consequences (to the coachee and the business) if the problem continues.

34 Emphasize your intent to support the coachee in solving issues.

THINGS TO DO

1. Acknowledge concerns and build a positive rapport.

2. Listen to comments and offer help in resolving outstanding issues.

3. Probe to find out what the coachee is aiming for.

WORKING WITH THE COACHEE'S AGENDA

If the session has been initiated by the coachee, restate your understanding of the reasons why the coachee has approached you and invite elaboration. Clarify points on which you are unclear, using simple questions such as "What do you mean by…?" If a developmental issue is on the agenda, find out what the coachee hopes to achieve and establish a clear basis for the session. Then begin coaching in a collaborative way.

ACHIEVING MUTUAL UNDERSTANDING

GIVING FEEDBACK

- **RELAX**
  You are offering an opinion, not imposing your interpretation as fact.

- **BE SPECIFIC**
  Call attention to the person's past behavior and its consequences.

- **INTERACT**
  Be prepared to listen, clarify, and expand. Be tactful and avoid casting blame.

- **SEEK AGREEMENT AND ACTION**
  Ask for the coachee's view and how he or she will act on your feedback.

RECEIVING FEEDBACK

- **BE OPEN**
  Feedback is crucial to development and learning, so listen attentively.

- **EVALUATE**
  Assess the validity of the feedback and the consequences of acting on it.

- **CLARIFY**
  Ask questions to clarify your understanding of the points made.

- **STATE YOUR VIEW**
  If you have a different view, offer it as another interpretation rather than as the "right" one.

SHAPING THE COACHING SESSION

Coaching is an organized way of generating ideas that raise individual performance. Use the GROW model to structure your work: define the Goals, explore present Reality, discuss Options, and agree on When an action will take place.

> **35** Well-defined, clear goals are at the heart of successful coaching.

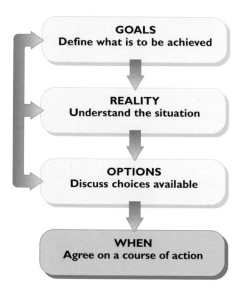

GOALS
Define what is to be achieved

REALITY
Understand the situation

OPTIONS
Discuss choices available

WHEN
Agree on a course of action

SETTING GOALS

Good coaches ensure that both they and the individual know precisely what specific results are being sought. Many coaching sessions are based on little more than an exploration of what is to be achieved – and how, when, where, with whom, and why. Aim to form a coaching goal that is workable, operates within a realistic time frame, and is also achievable on the employee's present level of experience.

◀ **USING THE GROW MODEL**
You can start with any of the first three coaching steps, so long as they are all covered in one session and an agreement to a course of action is achieved.

CHECKING REALITY

Sometimes the coachee may begin a session by focusing on the reality of the situation. Be an excellent listener. In an atmosphere of attentiveness and support, employees are more likely to speak frankly about their problems and their personal limitations. Do not dwell on doubts, however. Encourage the coachee to move on as soon as possible to the consideration of options or goals.

> **36** Encourage staff to actively imagine doing better at something – they often go on to do so.

DISCOVERING OPTIONS

Coaching creates worthwhile opportunities by giving attention to the employee's strengths, to past accomplishments that can be adapted to the present, or by taking an imaginative look at new solutions. Some individuals may begin the session by wishing to discuss their good ideas and options with you. If so, praise their imaginative ideas, but be sure that you clarify what it is they will achieve (the goal) and how this will fit in with present conditions (reality).

DISCUSSING POSSIBLE OPTIONS ▶
Draw out ideas and solutions from the coachee. Opportunities can be discovered by going outside the individual's present frame of reference to other, more fruitful, perspectives.

37	Help the coachee look at a situation from a fresh angle.

38	Build on the coachee's past achievements.

DECIDING WHEN

Once goals have been defined, reality explored, and options established, it is up to the coachee to select the most inspiring or useful option and consider how it might be put into practice. Ensure that the session ends with a commitment to a specific action within a given time. This might be to gather information, confer with a colleague, or complete a task. Schedule the next coaching session so that the employee can report back on results. The coaching process can then begin again, using feedback as the basis for the next session's "reality."

DO'S AND DON'TS

✔ Do make rapport an important priority.

✔ Do be open, honest, patient, and persistent.

✔ Do consistently end coaching sessions by receiving commitment to an action.

✘ Don't close any options until the employee is ready to choose.

✘ Don't stop looking for opportunities to pin down achievable goals.

✘ Don't stop noticing nonverbal responses.

39	Arrange the next session before the meeting comes to an end.

DEFINING GOALS

Goal setting, the crux of coaching, is used to provide a structure for the coaching session itself and as a clear focus for resulting action. If time is limited, agree on a realistic goal for the session. Use the mnemonic SMART to focus on achievable results.

40 Use imagination to create, define, and explore an ideal outcome.

ANALYZING SITUATIONS

In order to establish definable goals, ask the coachee to imagine that he or she is working in an ideal way. Find out how this ideal differs from his or her current working patterns and procedures. Then ask what aspects of this "ideal" the coachee could realistically start to put into practice immediately.

AGREEING ON A COACHING GOAL

A goal for the meeting helps to focus coaching on the highest priorities. Agree on a coaching goal that can be achieved in the available time. Use it by asking yourself and the coachee if the meeting is progressing toward the goal. If not, work out how the session needs to change. If the goal is only partially addressed in the time, then schedule another session.

CREATING IDEAL GOALS

People often describe a means to an end rather than the end itself when they are asked to state their goals. The coachee may have an attractive goal in mind but rejects it because he or she sees too many problems in the way. Probe for what coachees really want. Uncover goals they will be motivated to achieve. Find out how things would look if there were no limits to what they could do. Once you have an ideal goal, find practical ways of achieving it.

▼ **IDENTIFYING IDEALS**

In this case, the coach acted as a catalyst and helped the manager recognize the real root of the problem, which she had previously overlooked.

CASE STUDY

In a coaching session between a sales director and a sales manager, the initial goal identified by the sales manager was to improve her forward planning. However, in reality, her ability to do this was hampered by many demands on her time. The coach asked her to imagine an ideal working environment. By looking at the problem from a different perspective, the big picture began to emerge.

In fact, the sales manager wanted a greater sense of control, rather than feeling she was reacting to others' demands. She wanted a better balance between her life at work and at home. After the coaching session, the manager made agreements with her sales director about her priorities and work schedules. She worked at home for one day each week on projects, and the result was an improvement in her planning.

SETTING SPECIFIC GOALS

The ideal aim becomes the specific goal to work toward. Use the mnemonic SMART as a tool for turning an ideal coaching goal into a specific goal. The "S" of SMART stands for Specific: you must precisely define the aim. "M" stands for Measurement: identify standards with which to assess achievement. "A" stands for Achievable: ensure the coachee has the resources needed to accomplish the goal. "R" stands for Relevant: check that the goal is worthwhile for the coachee. "T" is for Timed, representing the completion date.

 41 Ask the coachee to imagine what they will see, hear, and feel when they have achieved a goal.

REACH THE MOON

President John. F. Kennedy's speech to Congress on May 25, 1961, is a superb example of a goal that combines the ideal with SMART. In it, he stated his belief that the US should work toward the goal of landing a man on the Moon within 10 years. He emphasized the magnitude of the project for mankind, and he outlined specifically what would need to be done to achieve the goal. In a sense, the entire nation would be working together to put one man on the Moon.

QUESTIONS TO ELICIT SMART GOALS

ELEMENTS OF SMART	USEFUL QUESTIONS
SPECIFIC Ensure everyone knows the aim.	● What will you be doing when you have achieved the goal? ● What do you want to do next?
MEASURED Define standards to work toward.	● How will you measure the achievement of the goal? ● What will you feel when the goal is reached?
ACHIEVABLE Ensure that the goal is realistic.	● What might hinder you as you progress toward the goal? ● What resources can you call upon?
RELEVANT Make sure the goal is worthwhile.	● What do you, and others, get out of this? ● Have other parties involved agreed to it?
TIMED Agree on a time frame.	● When will you achieve the goal? ● What will be your first step?

CHECKING REALITY

Before looking at potential ways forward, it is vital to compare the coachee's present skill level with the desired one. This comparison may be obscured by worries and concerns. Listen attentively to these and be ready to assess present performance levels.

42 Keep things clear and simple by asking direct questions.

43 Always keep the purpose of the session in mind.

44 Let staff vent their true feelings and clear the air.

DEALING WITH CONCERNS

Some employees may view coaching as a chance to offload complaints rather than work on their performance. Let the coachee feel heard without allowing the session to be deflected from the coaching aim. Distinguish between complaints about matters that are beyond the coachee's control and concerns that they can do something about. Ask if they have already explored a solution.

▼ LISTENING WITH CARE

In this coaching session, the coach draws out the coachee's worries to get to the root of the problem. He watches the coachee's body language to gain valuable insights into the issue.

Coach adopts sympathetic tone of voice

Direct gaze shows attention and interest

Coachee's averted gaze denotes uncertainty

Relaxed posture invites trust

Open body language conveys willingness to help

Defensive posture shows lack of confidence

Hand gesture shows eagerness to communicate

- The flow of ideas should be maintained during the session.

- It is important to understand what the speaker is saying from his or her perspective.

- Show interest with nonverbal communication and use phrases such as "I see" and "Mm-hm" to signal understanding.

- You can subtly control the conversation by an exhalation of breath or a change of expression.

CONTROLLING THE FLOW

Listen to the coachee's responses to your questions. Avoid becoming overwhelmed with information. If the session starts to lose direction, politely stop the coachee and summarize what has been said. Ask a question that clarifies a point or leads on to considering a possible option. Alternatively, challenge what has been said and ask how it is relevant to the coachee's or team's goals. Use hand gestures to signal a pause for reflection or a slow-down in the flow of information, and ask the coachee where he or she thinks the session is going.

USING THE EARS MODEL

Attentive listening and effective questions based on what is heard are prerequisites to good coaching. Good listeners require the attitudes and skills summed up in the mnemonic EARS.

LISTENING WITH EARS

Empathize — Understand the perspective of the speaker

Acknowledge — Use responsive communication such as "Mm-hm"

Reflect — Repeat key words and pause to think

Summarize — Frequently summarize what has been said

Coach acknowledges point made

Leans back to denote a pause

Gestures to slow speaker down

Pauses to reflect

Retains open, positive body language

COACH

45 If you find yourself getting confused then say so, and ask for clarification.

RECOGNIZING NONVERBAL SIGNALS

People rely as much on the way things are said as on what is said. During a coaching session, take note of tones of voice, facial expressions, and hand gestures. Is the speaker coming across as active, positive, and focused? Or passive, confused, and self-divided? If the former, then press on with questions concerning options and goals. If the latter, then make time to explore the basis of the problem and be ready to lend more support. Listen to concerns that are barriers to achieving goals.

46 Understanding body language gives you insight.

47 Be aware that your expressions mirror your thoughts.

Restless gaze indicates thoughts are elsewhere

Hunched shoulders are defensive

Folded arms form a barrier to communication

Frown denotes disagreement

▲ SHOWING PREOCCUPATION
Avoidance of eye contact and fidgeting may indicate preoccupation with other matters. Ask the coachee if there is something on his or her mind.

▲ SHOWING DISAGREEMENT
A frown and hunched shoulders may reveal skepticism or even anger. Ask for the coachee's thoughts on what has just been said.

Averted eyes indicate evasiveness

Watching the time denotes restlessness

Ear pulling indicates doubt

Faraway look shows uncertainty

▲ REVEALING DISINTEREST
Restless movements, checking the time, and averted eyes could denote lack of interest. Ask the coachee how the session can be brought back on track.

▲ INDICATING UNCERTAINTY
When hands touch the face, particularly the ears, this can demonstrate uncertainty or doubt. Ask if there is a matter that the coachee needs to discuss.

ASSESSING WITH SCALES

Scales are a simple way of establishing present skill level and comparing it to the desired one. By asking the coachee for their thoughts on their own performance, it is possible to get to the roots of potential problems and establish what has to happen for performance to be improved. Ask the speaker to rate their assessments on a scale of 0–10 (with 10 representing the highest point on the scale). Then ask: "What has to happen for you to move up another point on this scale?" Self-ratings can be applied to confidence or motivation levels, and past performance.

Ask the coachee "What will you be doing when you reach 9 on the scale?"

Ask "What needs to happen before you can rate at 8 or 9 for motivation?"

Ask "What would have to happen for your confidence level to go up to 7?"

Ask "What can be done on a future project, for your rating to go up to 9?"

Assessing Performance

What rating would you give yourself for the way you handled that meeting?

1 2 3 4 5 6 7 ⑧ 9 1 0

How motivated are you to complete this?

1 2 3 4 5 6 ⑦ 8 9 1 0

Are you confident that you have the necessary skills to complete this project satisfactorily?

1 2 3 4 ⑤ 6 7 8 9 1 0

How confident are you that you can finish this project on time?

1 2 3 4 5 ⑥ 7 8 9 1 0

How did you rate your performance on the project you have just completed?

1 2 3 4 5 6 7 ⑧ 9 1 0

▲ MOVING UP THE SCALE

By establishing a present level of skill, confidence, or motivation, the coach can help identify a route to improvement.

---

48 Use a scale to help staff assess their present skill levels, and to assess their commitment to a goal.

CODE OF CONFIDENTIALITY

The golden rule of coaching is that everything that is said between a coach and coachee is confidential. You may hear of things that call for action outside the coaching session. If so, make it clear that you intend to preserve the anonymity of the coachee. If this is impossible, then ask for permission to share the information with those who need to know. However, aim to achieve openness in your team.

QUESTIONS TO ASK THE COACHEE

Q What do you notice is unusual about...?

Q What is another way of looking at this problem?

Q Can I check that I have got this right...?

Q How is this relevant to what we have been saying so far?

Q What has to happen for us to solve this?

Q Is there anything important that we've missed?

Q What will you have to do to move up the scale?

LOOKING FOR OPTIONS

Present strengths, past successes, and the difference between effective and less effective performance, all represent a gold mine of resources to be used in the service of achieving desired goals. Ask questions that encourage creative answers.

49 Make it known that you have high expectations of success.

THINGS TO DO

1. Find out what the coachee is good at and how these strengths can be utilized.

2. Match these strengths to the goal aimed for.

3. Find out about the coachee's past successes.

4. Use successful past actions to solve present problems.

5. Identify specific tasks that employ the coachee's skills.

EXPLOITING STRENGTHS

Mobilize people's talents and capabilities in the search for new ways to achieve goals. If you ask people what they like or enjoy, very often they will tell you what they are good at. When they reply, notice what excites or enthuses them. This is a good clue to what their strengths and preferences are. Chatting about work or nonwork matters during the session can also reveal people's abilities, as they tend to talk naturally about what they are enjoying at the moment or what interests them. Once you have identified a strength, determine how this particular skill can be used to good effect in the future. Use your creativity to link strengths to future tasks or projects.

CASE STUDY

A manager was made chief executive of a subsidiary in Europe. Socializing with customers was key to success in the designated country. Unfortunately, the manager considered himself to be socially inept, scoring himself 0 out of 10 for social confidence and skill with senior customers. Working with an external coach, he identified personal strengths he could employ in such social situations. These were a love of sports, strategic thinking, and project management. His coach encouraged him to make detailed plans to entertain customers at major sporting events. He decided who he would take with him from his own organization to help with conversation and how he would prepare himself prior to meeting senior customers. Through coaching, he was able to tackle his new role with confidence.

◀ **BUILDING ON STRENGTHS**
Through the help of a coach, this manager was able to identify what he was naturally good at and what he found difficult. He was able to adapt his working situation to build on his strengths and plan around his weaknesses.

NOTICING DIFFERENCES

Raise awareness in a coachee of the difference between effective and ineffective performance. In this way, the coachee can learn to recognize, and put into action, behavior appropriate for a particular situation. If, for example, the coachee is having a problem handling a "difficult" colleague, then ask the coachee to remember a time when the colleague was handled well. Eventually, the coachee will learn to be reflective about personal performance without your help.

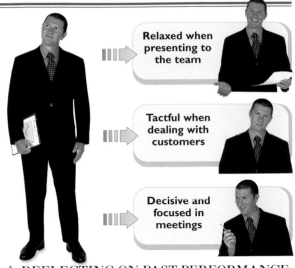

Relaxed when presenting to the team

Tactful when dealing with customers

Decisive and focused in meetings

▲ REFLECTING ON PAST PERFORMANCE

Encourage your coachees to actively recall a past situation where they performed well. Ask them to imagine doing the same thing in the future in a situation where that particular quality is called for.

50 Draw out the difference between present experience of a problem and a past success.

FINDING EXCEPTIONS

An exception is an instance in a person's past when a similarly challenging goal was achieved. To find such exceptions, ask when, in the past, the coachee has risen to a similar challenge. Set up a scale of 0–10, with 10 as the ideal solution. Ask the coachee to rate the present situation on the scale. Then ask if, in the past, the person would have rated higher up the scale than now, and why this should be.

ASSUMING SUCCESS

Encouraging high expectations leads to better performance. Do this by choosing words that assume success. For instance: "As you walk into the meeting feeling confident, what will you be thinking?", or "When you have broached this difficulty with the customer, what difference will it make to how you feel?". These questions assume a successful and constructive outcome. People accept positive expectation and are likely to live up to it.

QUESTIONS TO ASK THE COACHEE

Q What has worked in this situation before?

Q What was different about a past success?

Q When you achieve the goal, how will you feel?

Q What would a person you admire do?

CREATING NEW PERSPECTIVES

In the search to perceive new possibilities, focus on, or "frame," a situation to look at an issue from a different viewpoint. Use as much creativity as you can to help individuals to develop frames that foster creativity and solve problems.

51 Look at problems from every angle in order to find possible solutions.

52 Always listen to opposing points of view.

FRAMING PERSPECTIVES

One way to think about perspectives is as a series of frames. Each time we adopt a particular point of view we frame the things around us so that we can categorize them, understand them, and respond to them. When listening to the coachee's opinions, always bear in mind that the description is created from one particular viewpoint. This is especially true when an individual is stuck with what seems like an irredeemable problem.

▼ CONSIDERING DIFFERENT VIEWS
A salesperson has a customer who has problems with a product. Her coach encourages her to consider the points of view of her colleagues before taking discussions with the customer further.

The manager focuses on how to improve the service

The salesperson focuses on the problem with the product. The coach encourages her to talk to her colleagues for their points of view

As a result of the salesperson's consultations with her colleagues, the team re-presents the issue in a constructive way to the customer

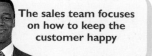

The sales team focuses on how to keep the customer happy

CREATING FRAMES

Creative people use frames to look at things from fresh angles. Leonardo da Vinci framed paint blots on the wall as landscapes, to get ideas for his drawings. Similarly, an advertising agent might frame a new toy from a child's point of view to note product features that can be emphasized in an advertisement. Develop frames by asking how things look from the point of view of an existing customer, in a year's time or five years' time, or from the point of view of two very different customers.

53 Use imaginative frames to get new ideas on a project.

DEFINING FRAMES

TYPE OF FRAME	DEFINITION
PROBLEM FRAME	When everything is seen as a problem.
LEARNING FRAME	When everything is seen as a learning opportunity.
DETAIL FRAME	When the focus is on one element of an issue.
BIG PICTURE FRAME	When the focus is on the whole issue.
PERSONAL FRAME	When you focus only on what is happening to you.
TEAM FRAME	When you notice how events affect the team.
CONFLICT FRAME	When the focus is on disagreement.
NEGOTIATION FRAME	When the focus is on resolving conflict.

FRAME SWITCHING

An issue can appear to be an insurmountable problem. Encourage your team to view issues through another "frame," so they can be seen instead as a challenging goal, or as part of a bigger picture. Here are some useful questions to encourage "frame switching":

Problem Frame to Learning Frame

66 *What can we do about that?* 99

Detail Frame to Big Picture

66 *Can we step back from this for a moment?* 99

Personal Frame to Team Frame

66 *What is best for the team?* 99

Conflict Frame to Negotiation Frame

66 *What do you think would motivate them?* 99

TAKING ACTION

The focus of a coaching session is to pinpoint issues and to plan a course of positive action made up of specific tasks. At the end of a session, gain agreement and commitment to an action plan, which can be reviewed and assessed at a later date.

54 Prepare for a challenging event with constructive mental rehearsal.

SETTING TASKS

The options uncovered during the session provide the basis for action. The tasks agreed upon must move the coachee nearer to the agreed upon goal. Choose tasks that match the coachee's competence and level of confidence. Agree on a task that extends the coachee, but not so far that there is an unacceptable chance of failure. Ensure that the tasks are within the coachee's scope and will help build on or develop new skills. In either case, you should be ready to support coachees as they learn from any mistakes they make while following through the action plan.

55 Agree on and set achievable tasks that stretch a coachee's talents.

EXAMPLES OF TYPICAL TASKS

TASK SET	AIM OF ACTION
REVIEW COMMITMENTS	The coachee needs to prioritize the most important issues.
MEET WITH DECISION-MAKER	The coachee aims to get approval on a new business approach.
DISCUSSION WITH THE TEAM	A new way of working can be found by assessing feedback with the team.
TAKE TIME OUT TO CONSIDER	The coachee needs to ensure that the project is on track.
MEET WITH COLLEAGUE	The coachee needs to implement a changed approach to a meeting.
MEET WITH CUSTOMER	The customer needs reassurance about the progress of a project.

GETTING AGREEMENT

When staff are involved in decisions, and agree to a task, they are more likely to feel a sense of ownership for it. Ensure agreement at this stage by summarizing the options discussed and asking which ones are most likely to be successful. Once a selection has been made, test your understanding in order to solidify agreement. For example, you could consolidate the agreement by saying: "Let me check that I understand so far. You have decided that when an unexpected assignment is handed to you, you will ask for time to think it over. Once you have considered the implications, you will take it on or not, consulting your manager as necessary."

56 Make your staff accountable for their results.

57 Be prepared to offer your own opinion, without imposing it.

Asks questions

Leans forward

SHOWING COMMITMENT

Unresponsive to questions

Turns away

SHOWING NONCOMMITMENT

ASSESSING COMMITMENT

When an ambitious action plan is discussed, commitment needs to be high, as it may require a significant change in behavior. If commitment is low, then other priorities are likely to override change. Assess commitment by asking questions that probe for enthusiasm. Watch carefully for nonverbal signs that indicate motivation. Increase commitment by asking how the coachee will feel when the job is done. Ask the coachee what can be done to resolve any doubts.

◀ **NOTING COMMITMENT**
When the coachee is replying to your questions, notice signs of commitment, such as an interested posture and definite answers. A wavering look and a slouching posture can both denote noncommitment.

OFFERING SUPPORT

As the coachee prepares to take action, offer support without undermining the coachee's sense of responsibility. Make it clear that you are available to be used as a sounding board to work out ideas or explore solutions to problems. In this way, you act as a catalyst, enabling change rather than directing it. Provide your support if your seniority is needed to influence other senior managers, or to gain the cooperation of other team members.

COACHING TO SUCCEED ▼

As a coach, you should be supportive, act as a mediator of ideas, ensure there are no barriers to success, and, if necessary, mobilize the resources needed to achieve the goal.

THINGS TO DO

1. Ask the coachee to identify issues or tasks for which he or she needs support.

2. Let the coachee know when you are going to be available to give support.

3. Make sure other team members are working toward the same goal, so that there are no conflicts.

Be supportive	Act as a catalyst	Use your influence

PLANNING ACTION

The tasks agreed on must be turned into a solid action plan that can be reviewed. Either work out the plan with the coachee during the coaching session, or agree that the coachee can develop a plan before the next coaching session. Set a review date and agree on the location for the next session. This gives a point in time to work toward so that the coachee knows that certain tasks have to be completed by this date. Once agreed on, the coachee needs to make notes on results achieved and further actions to be taken.

Course of action decided, and tasks set

Sales manager gives necessary support

Goal is outlined

SAMPLE ACTION PLAN ▶

This coaching plan was formed between a sales manager and his assistant to agree on how a customer complaint will be dealt with.

Plan is formed to deal with a customer complaint

Coaching Plan
Resolving a Complaint

Action:
Sales assistant to telephone the customer and ask for details of the wrong delivery.
Organize meeting with Operations Manager.

Deadline for Action:
7th May.

Resources Required:
Sales Manager to look at discount policy and speak to Operations Manager before meeting.

Results Required:
Customer to send in receipt and Operations Manager to investigate problem and offer customer a discount.

Review:
On May 20th, in main meeting room.

Review date and location is set

Coach offers support and acts as a catalyst to overcome problems

Completion and review dates are agreed

Coachee has doubts

Solid action plan is determined

Ambitious action plan is discussed

Coach and coachee consider options

▲ AGREEING ACTION

In this example, the coach and coachee meet to form an action plan. The coachee has doubts about the plan, and the coach must work to keep the meeting on track.

Coach and coachee fail to reach agreement

MANAGING RISKS

Although you want to stretch the capabilities of your staff, you need to insure against failure. Any task with a high risk attached to it is one in which failure could damage the reputation of yourself, the coachee, or your organization. Manage risks by discussing the actions the coachee plans to implement. Then monitor the results and agree on reviews without undue interference. When the risk is low because staff are competent or the task is simple, ask them to act first and then report.

QUESTIONS TO ASK THE COACHEE

Q What option do you think will work best?

Q How soon are you able to start working on this?

Q What will be your first step toward achieving your goal?

Q When will you take the action we have agreed on?

Q When can we meet to review your progress?

58 Show loyalty to your staff even if things go wrong, and help them identify lessons for the future.

FOLLOWING UP

Coaching – like any learning process – is continual. Each coaching session leads to action, followed by either success or feedback on what must be done next time. Put in place follow-up procedures that initiate an upward spiral of achievement.

59 Ask your staff to tell you what they have learnt from recent projects.

60 Keep spaces in your calendar so you are able to give extra coaching if necessary.

FOLLOWING UP SESSIONS

Keep up the momentum of learning. Make links between the work completed in the current session and the agreed action plan, and then to follow-up sessions. Arrange the next meeting at the end of each session, and aim for this to coincide with the completion of the agreed action plan. Explain that this next meeting will begin with a briefing from the coachee about how the action plan has been carried out and what the results were.

MONITORING CHANGE

When arranging projects that consolidate new skills, ensure your staff feel confident about what they are to do. Smaller projects are favorable if the employee is inexperienced. Small successes lead to bigger wins, gathering momentum with each new achievement. The other thing you can offer as a coach in between sessions is support. Let your staff know that you are always on hand for consultations if they need them. Once you hear that goals have been achieved, acknowledge success and deliver praise.

▼ ASSESSING DEVELOPMENT

A key role of a manager is to develop staff's potential. By offering support, you are also in a position to assess progress.

Coach gives constructive feedback

RESETTING STRETCH GOALS

Momentum for existing changes will slow down as the employee becomes more experienced. Coaching requires that the coachee is continually being stretched, or challenged, in order to improve on past levels of performance. As you continue to coach, periodically reset employees' performance goals by asking them to come up with new challenges. If they do not have any ideas themselves concerning their next performance targets, then look out for new responsibilities to assign to them, and get ready to delegate.

REACHING FOR SUCCESS ▶
Encourage your staff to reach slightly beyond their perceived limits when reviewing their next goal. Ensure that each new goal represents a definite advance on the previous level of competence.

---

61 Encourage team members to coach each other.

---

62 Set an example by seeking coaching yourself.

COACHING VALUES ▼
Encourage staff to coach themselves and team members to coach each other, either formally or informally.

INSTILLING COACHING ATTITUDES

As a manager, your eventual aim as a coach is to build a coaching team. To do this requires that all members of the team are able to coach themselves, and each other. Advance this teaching process by explaining the four steps of coaching (GROW) and encouraging employees to use it whenever working problems and opportunities arise. Ask participants to prepare for team coaching sessions by defining goals, writing a brief description of the issues at stake, mentioning some options, and recommending a proposed course and date of action. In this way you will be encouraging your staff to be their own coaches.

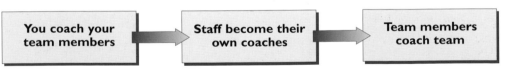

You coach your team members	→	Staff become their own coaches	→	Team members coach team

MAKING COACHING WORK

When coaching attitudes are introduced into traditional business environments, misunderstandings can arise. Overcome doubts with tact, persistence, and insight.

COACHING ATTITUDES

For the coaching approach to become an accepted working practice on your team, you should be seen as a good role model for coaching. Act on the beliefs, values, and attitudes that underpin the approach, and encourage your team to participate in them.

63 Discourage perfectionism – always seek to develop realism.

64 Treat achievements as stepping stones to future success.

65 Treat setbacks as lessons to be learned from, and then move on.

APPRECIATING SUCCESS

Coaching is based on appreciative inquiry. It actively assumes that successes are inevitable and looks for opportunities to acknowledge these when they occur. Coaches recognize success in teams that cope with adversity, in individuals who learn to master skills, and in organizations that adapt to change. This does not mean that all successes are to be rewarded, but that there is a focus on gains as opposed to losses. Gains represent actual and potential success and are there to be used in the future. Celebrate your team's achievements and find ways to use these in the future.

FOCUSING ON THE POSSIBLE

Problems are easy to find and magnify. The complex nature of many organizations, and the markets in which they operate, means that control over outcomes is often beyond the scope of managers. In practice, you have to make do with the possible rather than with the ideal. Be pragmatic rather than demanding. Be practical rather than perfectionist.

Solution focused: looks for options

Self-starting: shows strong motivation

Practical: focuses on the achievable

Responsible: sees job through to the end

Proactive: plans ahead

Takes initiative: makes decisions

▲ COACHING ATTITUDES

Coaching is an approach that develops good attitudes and a set of values in your staff. As you display these qualities yourself, your good example spreads to the rest of your team.

POINTS TO REMEMBER

- A good coach remains composed under pressure, focusing on what is in their power to change.
- When crises occur, you should lead by example and show staff you are helping to solve the issue.
- Everyone benefits when you influence the situation rather than blame others.
- Staff should be responsible for any mistakes they make.

TAKING OWNERSHIP

Ownership means taking responsibility for oneself and one's work. Managers who take ownership will accept that they are accountable for the work of everybody in the team, not just their own work. When the work of an individual team member is criticized, support the individual and be seen to be taking responsibility for corrections. To encourage responsibility in your team, delegate ownership for a task to an employee, within the limits of their present skills. Exercise a hands-off policy unless the employee asks you for help.

ACKNOWLEDGING VIEWS

The efforts of each individual team member are reliant on the efforts of all the other members. To this end, make room for a variety of specializations, ideas, and approaches within a team. A team can benefit from having, for example, a creative planner, a dynamic go-getter, and a reflective critic. Accepting personal differences between team members means ensuring that their voices are heard and their contributions appreciated. Encourage team members to share their ideas.

66 At meetings, stick to the agenda, while encouraging suggestions from all parties present.

DEALING WITH BARRIERS TO COACHING

Coaching is a modern approach to management, and it can raise fear or distrust in those unfamiliar with it. Deal with misconceptions about coaching by explaining its benefits and be ready to defuse misunderstandings.

67 Treat suspicion as a comment on the past, rather than on the present.

POINTS TO REMEMBER

- Openness can be built by encouraging employees to voice concerns.
- Coaching should develop at a pace the coachee is comfortable with.
- Differences of opinion should be worked through.
- If you practice what you preach, resentment can be avoided.

HANDLING MISTRUST

Coaching works only if there is a bond of trust between the parties involved. The coach must ensure that the employee is speaking openly and honestly. In turn, the coachee needs to feel sure of the coach's loyalty and willingness to understand. Suspicion can be based on a sense that the organization or its management are not practicing what is being preached. If so, be ready to give evidence that you and your organization are actively practicing coaching attitudes.

OVERCOMING RELUCTANCE

The most common reason for avoidance of coaching lies in misunderstanding. Check that your staff realize that coaching is designed to help them achieve success. Stress the benefits of coaching and its potential for gaining the coachee greater recognition within the organization. It is also important to check whether there is a need for coaching. Often, highly motivated and able employees may not require coaching for the work they are currently doing. In this case, ask the employee to list their longer-term career aims and make this the basis for agreed upon coaching goals.

68 Be ready to resolve past conflicts openly.

69 Ask how staff would like to be coached and adapt your approach.

DEALING WITH MISCONCEPTIONS

MISCONCEPTION

"COACHING IS FOR STAFF WHO ARE FAILING IN THEIR WORK"
Coaching is stigmatic and disciplinary. It is a form of retraining for people who are unable to do their job properly.

"COACHING IS A FORM OF COUNSELING"
Coaching is an excuse for people to offload problems or complaints, and discuss personal emotions.

"COACHING IS A NEW MANAGEMENT FAD"
Coaching has been introduced because other initiatives have failed.

"COACHING MEANS MORE WORK FOR LESS MONEY"
Coaching will lead to an increased workload, without any rewards for staff.

RESPONSE

Coaching is for people who want to do better and meet new challenges. It helps people explore their potential beyond the work they are currently involved in.

Counseling is reactive. Coaching is the opposite. It is proactive, goal focused, and seeks to improve personal and organizational performance.

Coaching has potential benefits for the employee, the team, and the manager. It is worth making it work, irrespective of people's past experiences.

When performing at their best, staff find work easier and more rewarding. Coaching can focus on those areas of work in which you would like to solve problems, simplify the issues, and streamline your efforts.

DO'S AND DON'TS

✔ Do practice what you preach.

✔ Do look at problems from the individual's point of view.

✔ Do keep stressing the benefits of coaching.

✔ Do remain calm in the face of opposition.

✘ Don't lose patience – old habits die hard.

✘ Don't wait for confusion to spread – deal with it at once.

✘ Don't coach if the time isn't right.

✘ Don't worry if progress is slow.

70 Show others that coaching works by outlining successful examples.

TROUBLESHOOTING

Despite your best efforts, coaching may not always work. Most of the pitfalls are common, however, and can be thoughtfully dealt with. If necessary, go back to basics, ask searching questions to find the root of the problem, and refocus priorities.

71 Be open to a dialogue with staff and take heed of their suggestions.

72 Introduce coaching gradually to staff with misgivings.

73 Always address causes rather than symptoms.

ADDRESSING MISGIVINGS

Some people are skeptical. They distrust the coach or doubt the benefits of coaching. Be open to a dialogue with staff and take heed of their suggestions. If the culture does not immediately support coaching, introduce it slowly. Ask questions rather than give answers, but do not overdo it. Be aware that there are occasions when people need straight answers, for example, a quick decision during the heat of a negotiation. As a manager, make decisions when needed, and coach people before and after the event.

FINDING THE CAUSE

In the long term, a coaching cycle that addresses causes rather than symptoms is more likely to succeed. For example, you could deal with a workload problem by relieving an employee of certain tasks. This could solve the immediate problem but not the long-term one. Reflect on the stages in the project where the problem could have arisen. The cause could be that the employee takes on too much work to please you, without considering the consequences.

Coach thinks through possible roots of problem

ASSESSING ROOTS OF PROBLEMS ▶
There may be a number of barriers to coaching. Search for the underlying roots to a problem, such as fear of change, dependency, or skepticism.

DEALING WITH BACKSLIDING

Problems can occur when the coachee does not have the know-how, commitment, or resources, including time, to do a job. Ensure that the necessary conditions exist for the goal to be achieved by equipping the coachee with the necessary skills. Focus their commitment by showing how the challenge will benefit the coachee personally. Check that there are no organizational barriers to the goals and that the coachee has the necessary resources and time to do the job.

75 Break down challenges into smaller, less daunting steps.

ASSESSING CONDITIONS

SETTING GOALS
In order to achieve a goal, the coachee needs to know what to do, will want to do it, and will have the opportunity to do it.

KNOW-HOW
The coachee has been trained in the skills necessary for the job.

COMMITMENT
The coachee is motivated and understands how success will be personally rewarding.

OPPORTUNITY
The coachee has the necessary support and resources to do the job.

74 Support your staff by freeing up their time so that they are able to concentrate on achieving new goals.

OVERCOMING THE FEAR OF CHANGE

Being daunted by challenges, such as a change of role, or communication with the senior management team, can interfere with people's development. The new challenge may be daunting, and the employee may feel ready to give up when setbacks occur. Often, at the heart of the matter is a fear of failure and its consequences. You can lessen this by using a coaching approach: learning from mistakes rather than punishing errors. Another way of helping people take on new challenges is to find ways in which they can apply their present strengths by, for example, asking a good organizer to draw up a difficult work schedule for the team.

OVERCOMING DEPENDENCY

If your style in the past has been to give answers to your staff rather than to coach them, or if you have inherited a team from such a manager, then team members may habitually look to you to solve their problems. Deal with this by clarifying expectations. Agree on the kinds of issues you are prepared to discuss and how you expect these issues to be presented. Gradually, ask staff to outline their ideas for solutions so that you can discuss them. Ask them what they have already thought of and what other solutions exist.

76 Encourage staff to use their own initiative.

77 Learn to notice signs of over-dependency.

RECOGNIZING SIGNS OF DEPENDENCY

SIGN	SYMPTOM
NO THOUGHT	Staff nearly always ask you for the answers rather than working through a problem and coming up with a solution themselves.
NO CONFIDENCE	People have a tendency to ask you to do things for them, rather than making decisions and taking concerted action.
NO FORESIGHT	Problems and opportunities are missed through lack of foresight or an inability to see the whole picture.
NO INITIATIVE	Staff rely on you to get things going rather than risk making mistakes and failing in the task themselves.

78 Show your staff that you trust and believe in their capabilities.

DO'S AND DON'TS

✔ Do watch out for signs that staff are getting too dependent on you.

✔ Do build confidence by showing that you expect staff to do well.

✘ Don't allow your staff to feel inadequate if they are unable to solve an issue alone.

✘ Don't change your style of management too abruptly.

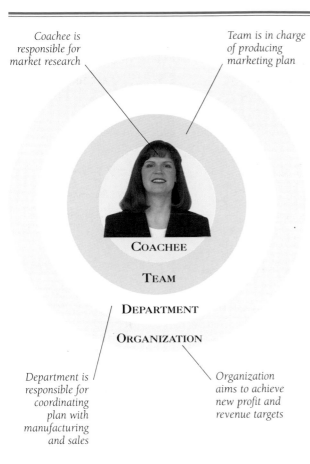

Coachee is responsible for market research

Team is in charge of producing marketing plan

COACHEE

TEAM

DEPARTMENT

ORGANIZATION

Department is responsible for coordinating plan with manufacturing and sales

Organization aims to achieve new profit and revenue targets

◀ **TAKING AN OVERVIEW**
As a coach, help show your coachees how their roles and goals fit with those of their team, department, and organization. In this way, the coachees can learn to see the value of their contribution to the whole.

FOCUSING ON PRIORITIES

When coaching is not achieving its aim, it is important to listen to employees' problems and focus on priorities. When you talk about the actions people have taken to achieve a goal, talk around the subject and find out what enthuses them. Realign coaching goals with what you observe to be the most important priorities for your staff. Motivate your staff by showing them how their priorities align with the organization's interests, and by explaining how their work directly affects results. This leads to self-motivated staff.

RECOGNIZING ▶ STRENGTHS
In this case study, the coach was able to build a coachee's confidence. By drawing on the coachee's existing strengths, he showed how these could be used in situations that seemed new or challenging.

CASE STUDY
A manager asked a coach for help in putting complex information given in meetings into logical order. The coach gave advice about note taking, mind mapping, and questioning techniques. However, the coach found that the manager already knew these techniques. The breakthrough in the coaching session came when the coach asked if there were times in the past when the manager had converted complex information from a meeting into logical notes. The manager acknowledged she had been able to do this in past meetings when her knowledge of the subject had given her mental pegs on which to hang the information. The coach subsequently focused on how the manager could do research before meetings so that she had mental pegs in mind and could approach note taking with new confidence.

DEALING WITH ORGANIZATIONAL BARRIERS

Barriers typically occur as organizations move from a traditional, directive management style to a coaching approach. Deal with these barriers by recognizing old attitudes and working to overcome them through education, example, and persistence.

79 Get the support of colleagues who also favor a coaching approach.

80 Encourage your staff to be more autonomous.

LEARNING TO LET GO ▼
Coaching can become impossible if you are doing the work of others as well as your own. Coach yourself to be disciplined about delegating tasks.

DEALING WITH OVERLOAD
Managers may be overloaded with responsibilities for a variety of reasons. You may be overloaded with work because you are carrying your employees' responsibilities. This may reflect the old attitude that managers are the only people who know how the job should be done. If so, deal with this gradually by encouraging your employees to make decisions without relying on you. Coach your employees to think through their own options.

Manager tries to concentrate on a coaching plan

Manager does tasks left undone by team

Administrative tasks interrupt manager's day

MANAGING YOUR TIME

Coaching can take time in the short term, but it is a worthwhile investment of your hours. Coach your team to assume the responsibility for solving problems, while you get on with the job of managing. Prioritize important items and cut down on inefficient demands on your time. Coach yourself to do this by setting a goal of increasing the time available to you, analyzing your present workload, and generating options for reducing it.

81 Focus on long-term development rather than fire-fighting problems for short-term benefit.

QUESTIONS TO ASK YOURSELF

Q Does senior management adopt a coaching approach?

Q Does my senior manager support team development?

Q Does my team feel the organization supports its initiatives?

Q Do I set projects off on the right note by consistently using a coaching approach?

DEALING WITH INERTIA

For the coaching approach to become widely adopted it must be supported by all levels of management, as well as by the teams and employees involved. If it is not, then employees may become discouraged if they feel that their initiatives and improved performance are not achieving recognition from the organization. Old attitudes die hard, and it may take time before the coaching philosophy takes root. Deal with inertia by becoming an active agent for change.

OVERCOMING IGNORANCE

Talk to other managers about what you are trying to achieve with coaching. Give seminars on the coaching approach, explaining how it can influence the organization. Ask senior managers to hold briefings emphasizing the organization's support for coaching. Be ready to enter into a dialogue with critics by anticipating their objections and linking the benefits of coaching to their personal values. Show how coaching can free up management time once team members learn to become more independent.

▼ INITIATING CHANGE
Educate people in your organization and enlist their support by explaining how the coaching approach works and how it differs from other approaches to management.

REFINING COACHING

Be prepared to use coaching in a variety of situations. Coach your team, your external staff, and your colleagues to adopt coaching values, and delegate so you have time to manage and lead.

TEAM COACHING

The coaching process can be of equal value in coaching teams. Use the GROW model and adapt your coaching style by ensuring that teams share in the work of defining goals, generating options, and assuming responsibility for tasks.

82 Check that each team member is committed to the team's goal.

▲ **WORKING AS A TEAM**
Ask your team to work together to create inspirational goals. By asking them to imagine a desired future, the team can then work on turning an ideal into a goal.

AGREEING ON GOALS

It is essential that a team agree on shared goals in order to achieve optimum performance. Clarify goals at the start of a project, or when an operational problem needs to be solved. At a coaching session, ask team members to summarize their understanding of present goals or to suggest new goals. Encourage your team to come up with creative ideas, then use ideal goal questions. Take the shared ideas and make them work by turning them into SMART goals.

ASSESSING REALITY

Each person's view of reality depends on his or her perspective. Ensure these different views are aired. During the session, set up a scale to represent the extremes of performance at, for example, project start and finish. Ask the team members to give their present assessment ratings privately. Then, ask them to declare their ratings. Explore the reasons for differences of opinion.

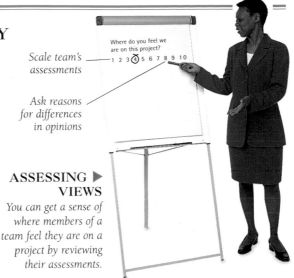

Where do you feel we are on this project?
1 2 3 4 5 6 7 8 9 10

Scale team's assessments

Ask reasons for differences in opinions

ASSESSING ▶ VIEWS
You can get a sense of where members of a team feel they are on a project by reviewing their assessments.

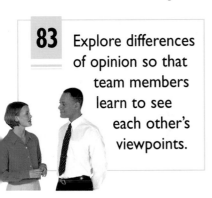

83 Explore differences of opinion so that team members learn to see each other's viewpoints.

EXPLORING OPTIONS

The gap between goals and reality now needs to be closed. Searching for exceptions and brainstorming are two ways that can help. To find exceptions, the team can discuss successful projects of the past. The lessons can then be applied to the present project. Encourage the team to brainstorm ideas and suspend criticism. Then evaluate the ideas against an agreed upon set of criteria to select the most promising for action.

DECIDING WHEN

In the coaching session, make a point of taking a break between the options and action phase of GROW. A coffee break can be an ideal way to punctuate a session and make an action plan memorably stand out against the background of a meeting. On resumption of the session, identify the specific tasks to be done. Be sure that accountability for each task is assigned clearly and agree on the completion dates. Check that everyone agrees to the plan. If you see signs of uncertainty, ask questions to find out the reasons behind it.

84 Clearly assign specific tasks to individuals.

85 Resolve issues at the early stage of an action plan.

273

COACHING LONG DISTANCE

Managers with team members who work in the field, or at some distance from the office, may communicate mainly by phone or email. Make sure face-to-face meetings are utilized to maximum effect and that responsibilities are clear-cut.

| 86 | Maintain contact with field staff at the same time each week. |

ORGANIZING LONG-DISTANCE COACHING

The coaching process can be completed with any combination of telephone coaching, email correspondence, video conferencing, and face-to-face meetings. Conduct the first session in person, so that a mutually agreeable format for coaching can be discussed. Further communications may be used to provide progress reports, feedback on results, and discussions on how actions could be amended. However, performance issues are best dealt with face-to-face.

Salesman agrees to method of coaching

▼ **OUTLINING METHODS**
Meet your field staff to discuss the coaching cycle. Explain that you will use face-to-face sessions for big issues, telephone calls for reviews, and emails for progress checking.

Coach outlines coaching cycle

| 87 | Always keep communications interruption-free. |

| 88 | Provide regular briefings on issues to field staff. |

DO'S AND DON'TS

✔ Do make sure you coach face-to-face at regular intervals.

✔ Do consider video conferencing facilities if available.

✔ Do be punctual for telephone meetings.

✗ Don't let telephone calls lose the point.

✗ Don't forget to follow up telephone calls with written summaries.

✗ Don't address complex coaching issues by email.

REVIEWING BY TELEPHONE

If the first progress report is to take place by telephone, plan the call to last around 15–20 minutes. Start by restating the goals and agreed upon actions, and ask for a brief summary of results. If things are going well and further coaching is not required at this point, then the telephone call can be rescheduled for a later time. If further coaching is required then begin by asking the coachee how they would like to use the available time in relation to the goal.

Uses questions to guide coachee

Updates coaching notes

▲ COACHING BY PHONE
Keep telephone coaching direct and to the point. Use simple questions, reminders, and suggestions to keep staff on track.

88 Use emails for suggestions or reminders.

89 Hold regular social events for all of your team.

E-COACHING

An effective means of virtual communication, emails are widely used by professional coaches. However, they should never be used as substitutes for personal coaching. Instead, they should be employed strictly as a follow-up to a personal coaching session. Email etiquette dictates that messages should be brief, condensed, and informal. Avoid long-winded messages and defer complex matters for personal communication.

CHECKING PROGRESS THROUGH EMAILS

When following up via emails, avoid messages that focus on problems. Use well-defined, simple, and constructive questions about goals. Keep communication short, simple, and direct. You are then more likely to receive quick and direct responses.

❝ *Where are you with that project?* ❞

❝ *Have you discovered a better way to reduce costs?* ❞

❝ *The managing director is really excited by our ideas. Do you have any new ones for her?* ❞

❝ *I've heard that the project office has some experience with that client. Have you spoken to them recently?* ❞

COACHING AND APPRAISING

Appraising can mean an informal evaluation by you of an individual's work or a more formal review process. Use coaching to enhance the appraisal process by identifying achievements and making sure new performance targets are realistic.

91 Give constructive and supportive feedback on past performances.

92 Praise staff achievements and link them to the prospect of future success.

HOLDING REVIEWS

Your organization may have a performance review process by which employees' past performance is evaluated and new goals set for the future. Apply a coaching approach to the review process. Look for opportunities to praise an employee's achievements and link them to the prospect of achievements to come. If it is necessary to discuss failures, invite the employee to discuss what happened, and what options are available for corrective action.

DEVELOPING EMPLOYEES

Within the appraisal interview, use open-ended questions to explore your employee's needs and aspirations. Ask about the next step needed to take the employee up to his or her desired standard of work. Coaching is a complementary process to the development of skills. When carrying out the appraisal, identify the skills required to achieve the agreed upon goals and set up training opportunities if necessary. This may be on-the-job or out-of-house training. Develop a plan through which employees can gradually introduce their newly acquired skills to specific projects.

REVIEWING AS A FORM OF COACHING ▶

Integrate coaching values and techniques into the review session by defining goals, assessing reality, discussing options, and agreeing on a schedule for when actions will be carried out.

Compare recent performance against past objectives

Ask about learning experiences and give feedback and praise

Identify and prioritize development options

Agree on new objectives and when they are to be achieved

Specify actions to be taken and devise schedule

LINKING TO REWARDS

Coaching is built on the premise that individuals are capable of using their abilities to become more successful than they are now. Bear in mind that a good result needs to be encouraged by linking it to rewards. These need not be material. Some of the most worthwhile rewards include praise, recognition, awards, and visible respect. Material rewards can range from company benefits to promotions, and salary increases. Reward each completion of a coaching performance target by a public recognition of the individual's achievement.

CULTURAL DIFFERENCES

Americans celebrate and praise success with great enthusiasm. In contrast, the British tend to mark success with a quiet, appreciative word. Formal recognition in German organizations may be followed up by more enthusiastic comment outside the work environment.

SETTING TARGETS AFTER A REVIEW ▼

Here is an example of a review carried out between a credit control supervisor and his manager, which resulted in a single developmental goal plan supported by training and coaching.

93 Achievements that are rewarded tend to be repeated.

Clear notes are used as a basis for the next review

A Coaching-Based Review

Last Period's Objectives:
Create new credit control system

Examples of achievements:
Developed new procedures. Learned to supervise new employees.

Employee's self-rating:
7. Would like to expand customer liaison.

Manager's Comments:
8. Kevin's results exceed expectation.

Next Period's Objectives:
Reduce average credit period to 40 days.

Employee's comments: Need to focus on problem spotting.

General Comments:
Coaching will establish ways in which Kevin's existing expertise can be applied.

Coach recognizes coachee's natural flair with customers

Achievements are recorded

Goal is established

Employee assesses own performance

New targets are identified

A timeline is agreed on

Agreed upon plan is put in writing after review

Development Plan

Long-Term Objectives:
To increase customer-liaison role.

Immediate objectives:
To increase response rate with customers delaying settlement.

Competencies required:
Effective liaison skills

Training needs (if any):
2-day customer relations course.

Actions Agreed:
Take course within next three months and use follow-up coaching to implement new skills.

Review Date Agreed:
Date set for review of results.

COACHING THROUGH DELEGATION

Coaching and delegation are complementary. As the continual learning cycle moves upward, team members become ready to assume responsibility for more complex tasks. You are then in a position to delegate, set new targets, and lead.

94 Raise your expectations and ask people to live up to them.

DELEGATING PROJECTS

Identify priorities and capabilities of coachee

↓

Ensure that the delegated work represents more responsibility

↓

Brief employee on what is to be achieved

↓

Ask for ideas and show confidence and trust

↓

Be available to offer support if necessary

↓

Arrange for periodic reports on progress

PREPARING TO DELEGATE

Coaching requires the identification of ever-new performance targets for the next cycle of achievement. Remember that the latent talents to achieve new targets probably already exist within your team. Coach people in order to draw out these talents. As you notice that an employee starts to attain the necessary level of competence, get ready to delegate some of your own work. When coaching, bear in mind that the delegated work should represent an opportunity for genuine advancement in terms of increased skill and responsibility. Above all, empower your staff by letting them see your increasing confidence in them and by giving them opportunities to do things their way rather than yours. Use coaching to brief team members thoroughly, asking for ideas and then leaving them to get on with it under their own initiative.

95 Resolve any doubts by offering support and explaining how difficulties can be overcome.

DELEGATING PROJECTS

Let the team member know that they are progressing well and that you are ready to delegate an important project. Be sure to praise the employee's past performance. Set the agenda for the coaching session by introducing the project. Seek agreement from the coachee that they are ready for new responsibility and ensure that they are committed to the new venture.

Coachee expresses enthusiasm and interest

Coachee takes notes

Coach tells coachee she is ready for more responsibility

Project is presented and explained

96 Delegate work before it overwhelms you.

97 Allow people to learn from their own mistakes.

POINTS TO REMEMBER

● People remember more from their mistakes than from their successes.

● People have hidden talents that emerge when they are challenged.

● Staff blossom when they are trusted with jobs they do well.

▲ HANDING OVER RESPONSIBILITY

When you hand over a project, explain the background and specify the deadlines, available resources, and levels of authority in place. Make it clear what the employee is to achieve before considering the possible options for achieving it.

OFFERING SUPPORT

Coaches position themselves as supporters rather than authority figures. Offer support to the team members to whom you delegate. Make it clear that you are available for further brief or extended coaching sessions in relation to the delegated task. Avoid interference and do not give advice unless it is asked for. Exercise a "hands-off" policy once action plans have been agreed upon and leave employees to get on with things in their own way. Refrain from interfering in order to "save time" on the project and let delegates learn from their own mistakes. If you are called upon to help, ask the delegate to think through the problem prior to the coaching session and be ready to talk through their options with you.

EMPOWERING EMPLOYEES

Let employees know that they are entrusted with carrying out the work in the way they think best, within the parameters set for the job. Be aware that their approach may differ radically from yours. Work through any questions or doubts, and make suggestions that are designed to enhance options rather than replace ideas with your own. If you have concerns about any risks attached to the delegated task, then you should set up further coaching sessions at specified stages in the project before important decisions are made. During those sessions your comments should be informative rather than directive.

98 Coach your successor to assume a managerial role.

99 Assume everyone can be a manager, unless it is proven otherwise.

EMPOWERING THROUGH DELEGATION

STAFF BENEFITS   MANAGER BENEFITS

Staff are empowered and challenged

DELEGATE WORK
Assign responsibility for part of your own work

More time for concentrating on leadership

Staff are motivated by their own decisions

STEP BACK
Resist the urge to control, so staff can form their own approach

More time to manage and less stress incurred

Staff retain initiative but benefit from support

MONITOR RISKS
Answer questions, make suggestions, assess progress

Risk of failure can be recognized and acted on

Staff enjoy success and an enhanced reputation

REVIEW SUCCESS
Give constructive feedback, and praise good results

Successful results are a reflection of good management

REINFORCING LEARNING

When you integrate delegation opportunities into your coaching work, follow up by asking about what has been learned during work on a project. On completion of the work, arrange for a meeting with the employee in order to discuss how the individual has developed as a result of their involvement on the project. Make links between these achievements and those needed on other assignments. Establish what new knowledge and skills were acquired as a result and how these can be used in future work.

100 Call a meeting to review what has been learned.

101 Identify proven strengths in your staff.

QUESTIONS TO ASK YOURSELF

Q Which responsibilities am I hanging on to for fear of appearing not to be "in charge?"

Q How would I like my manager to coach me to take on more responsibility?

Q Have I delegated interesting and rewarding jobs?

EXAMINING ATTITUDES

The hallmark of a first-class coach is often summed up in their attitude to delegation. Poor coaches see delegation as a way to make life easier for themselves, while retaining control. Good coaches use coaching as a means of developing people even though this may mean taking risks and spending more time supporting personnel. Look honestly at your own attitudes and question any limiting beliefs you may have about human potential.

COACHING TO LEAD

Good coaches want to help people develop because, in the long run, they know that this will enable them to develop their leadership skills, rather than just managing. The manager focuses on running things well; a leader focuses on innovation. Leaders have an obvious interest in coaching and delegating because these are the means through which they can move from being a manager to being a leader.

SHOWING GOOD LEADERSHIP ▶

If you have a positive attitude to your staff and to delegating, you can concentrate on getting the best results for your organization. Give staff your support and encouragement.

ASSESSING YOUR COACHING SKILLS

*E*valuate your performance as a coach by responding to the following statements, and mark the option that is closest to your experience. Be as honest as you can: if your answer is "never," mark Option 1; if it is "always," mark Option 4, and so on. Add your scores together, and refer to the Analysis to see how you scored. Use your answers to identify areas that need most improvement.

OPTIONS

1 Never

2 Occasionally

3 Frequently

4 Always

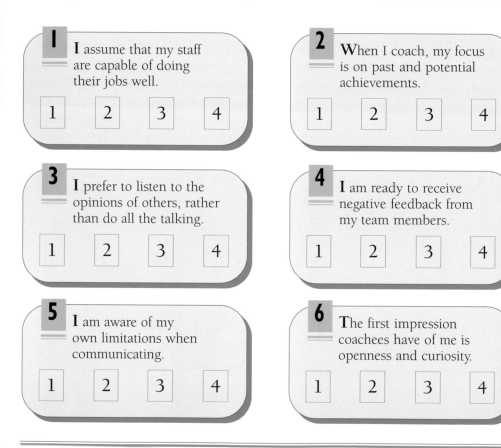

1 I assume that my staff are capable of doing their jobs well.

1   2   3   4

2 When I coach, my focus is on past and potential achievements.

1   2   3   4

3 I prefer to listen to the opinions of others, rather than do all the talking.

1   2   3   4

4 I am ready to receive negative feedback from my team members.

1   2   3   4

5 I am aware of my own limitations when communicating.

1   2   3   4

6 The first impression coachees have of me is openness and curiosity.

1   2   3   4

7 I seek to involve staff in making important decisions on a project.

1 2 3 4

8 I treat my staff as partners rather than subordinates.

1 2 3 4

9 My coaching sessions are free of interruptions and distractions.

1 2 3 4

10 I am flexible in switching between discussing goals and exploring problems.

1 2 3 4

11 I believe that people will exercise responsibility when empowered to do so.

1 2 3 4

12 I make links between my staff's motivational needs and their goals.

1 2 3 4

13 I seek to establish what is at the heart of my employees' concerns.

1 2 3 4

14 I am alert to small nonverbal clues when interpreting communication.

1 2 3 4

15 I presuppose that everybody has underutilized strengths and talents.

1 2 3 4

16 I summarize and reflect on what is said in order to check mutual understanding.

1 2 3 4

17 I assume that positive changes can be simple to achieve.

1   2   3   4

18 I prefer to ask open-ended questions rather than closed ones.

1   2   3   4

19 I am not afraid to coach my superiors and colleagues as well as my staff.

1   2   3   4

20 I believe good communication is based on seeing different views.

1   2   3   4

21 When coaching, I assume that my staff can find their own solutions.

1   2   3   4

22 I believe that some of the best coaching results come from creative insight.

1   2   3   4

23 When I give feedback on weak performance, I am constructive and specific.

1   2   3   4

24 I close coaching sessions by getting a specific commitment to a task.

1   2   3   4

25 I control coaching sessions by linking what has been said to the goal.

1   2   3   4

26 I follow up coaching by asking for briefings on progress.

1   2   3   4

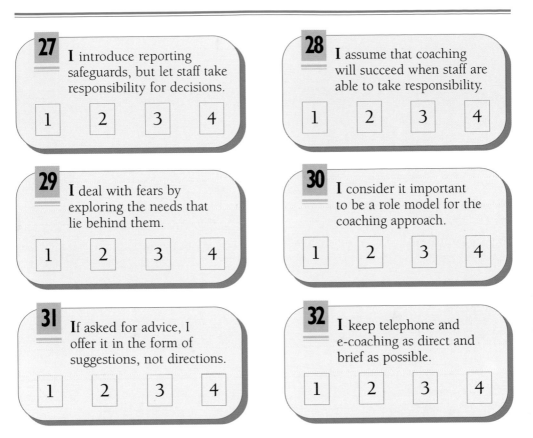

27 I introduce reporting safeguards, but let staff take responsibility for decisions.

1   2   3   4

28 I assume that coaching will succeed when staff are able to take responsibility.

1   2   3   4

29 I deal with fears by exploring the needs that lie behind them.

1   2   3   4

30 I consider it important to be a role model for the coaching approach.

1   2   3   4

31 If asked for advice, I offer it in the form of suggestions, not directions.

1   2   3   4

32 I keep telephone and e-coaching as direct and brief as possible.

1   2   3   4

ANALYSIS

Now you have completed the self assessment, add up your total score and check your performance by referring to the corresponding evaluation below. Identify your weakest areas, and refer to the relevant sections in this book to develop and hone your coaching skills.

32–64: There are many skills that you need to practice in order to be a successful coach. Work on your personal attitudes to coaching values, as well as specific skills.

65–95: You have reasonable coaching skills, but certain areas require improvement. Focus on improvement in the areas of your test where you scored low marks.

96–128: You are a successful coach, but do not become complacent. Keep striving to get the best from your team, and to develop coaching values in others.

MANAGING PROJECTS

INTRODUCTION

To be successful in today's competitive business world, managers must deliver results on time and within budget. By applying the processes, tools, and techniques shown in Managing Projects you will maximize performance and ensure optimum results every time. Suitable for managers at all levels, this book equips you with the know-how you need to lead any project, large or small, to a successful conclusion. From starting a project effectively to motivating a team and overcoming problems; every aspect of professional project management is clearly explained. Included is a step-by step guide to project planning, while 101 tips offer further practical advice. Finally, a self-assessment exercise allows you to evaluate your ability as a project manager, helping you to improve your skills, and your prospects for the future.

UNDERSTANDING THE BASICS

Project management provides structure, focus, flexibility, and control in the pursuit of results. Understand what running a project entails and how to improve the likelihood of success.

DEFINING PROJECTS

A project is a series of activities designed to achieve a specific outcome within a set budget and time frame. Learn how to distinguish projects from everyday work and adopt the discipline of project management more widely to improve performance.

1 Greet a new project as an opportunity to develop your skills.

2 Review your work to determine which tasks would be better tackled as projects.

WHAT IS A PROJECT?

A project has clear start and end points, a defined set of objectives, and a sequence of activities in between. The activities need not be complex: painting the staff restaurant is as valid a project as building a bridge. You may be involved in a project without realizing it – for example, if you work in a special team, perhaps outside the normal business schedule, to a deadline. Routine work, on the other hand, is usually ongoing, repetitive, and process-oriented. Some everyday work may lend itself to being managed as a project – tackling it as such will greatly increase your efficiency.

QUESTIONS TO ASK YOURSELF

Q What projects am I involved in at the moment?

Q Has my organization been trying to make changes that might be more likely to happen if tackled as a project?

Q Would I work more effectively if I regarded certain tasks as part of a project?

Q Could project management techniques help to make me more efficient?

WHY USE PROJECT MANAGEMENT?

In today's competitive business environment, a flexible and responsive approach to changing customer requirements is essential. Project management enables you to focus on priorities, track performance, overcome difficulties, and adapt to change. It gives you more control and provides proven tools and techniques to help you lead teams to reach objectives on time and within budget. Organizing activities into a project may be time-consuming initially, but in the long term it will save time, effort, and reduce the risk of failure.

IDENTIFYING THE KEY FEATURES OF PROJECTS

FEATURES	POINTS TO NOTE
DEFINED START AND END All projects have start-up and closure stages.	● Some projects are repeated often, but they are not processes because they have clear start and end points. ● Routine work can be distinguished from projects because it is recurring, and there is no clear end to the process.
ORGANIZED PLAN A planned, methodical approach is used to meet project objectives.	● Good planning ensures a project is completed on time and within budget; having delivered the expected results. ● An effective plan provides a template that guides the project and details the work that needs to be done.
SEPARATE RESOURCES Projects are allocated time, people, and money on their own merits.	● Some projects operate outside the normal routine of business life, others within it – but they all require separate resources. ● Working within agreed resources is vital to success.
TEAMWORK Projects usually require a team of people to get the job done.	● Project teams take responsibility for and gain satisfaction from their own objectives, while contributing to the success of the organization as a whole. ● Projects offer new challenges and experiences for staff.
ESTABLISHED GOALS Projects bring results in terms of quality and/or performance.	● A project often results in a new way of working, or creates something that did not previously exist. ● Objectives must be identified for all those involved in the project.

EXAMINING KEY ROLES

Projects can involve a wide range of people with very different skills and backgrounds. However, there are several pivotal roles common to all projects, and it is important to understand the parts that each of these key people play.

3 Draw up a list of all the people who might be able to help you.

CULTURAL DIFFERENCES

North American projects need a senior sponsor to get off the ground and be accepted by stakeholders. Australia's flatter management structure means that projects also depend on senior support. In the UK, the sponsor can be at a lower level, provided that there is a strong business case for the project.

UNDERSTANDING ROLES

As project manager, you are in charge of the entire project. But you cannot succeed alone, and establishing good relations with other key players is vital. Important project people include the sponsor, who may also be your superior, and who provides backing (either financial or moral); key team members, who are responsible for the overall success of the project; part-time or less senior members, who nevertheless contribute to the plan, and experts or advisers with important roles. There will also be stakeholders, or people with an interest in the project, such as customers, suppliers, or executives in other parts of your organization.

INVOLVING STAKEHOLDERS

Aim to involve your stakeholders at an early stage. Not all stakeholders will be equally important, so identify those who could have a significant effect on the project; and when you draw up the project plan later, consider how regularly they should be consulted. When stakeholders are enthusiastic and strongly supportive of the project, seek their assistance in motivating others. Make sure that you forge strong alliances with those stakeholders who control the resources. Finally, check that everyone understands the reason for their involvement in the project and what its impact on them will be.

4 Build up a good rapport with your main stakeholders.

5 Make sure that your core team consists of people you really trust.

IDENTIFYING KEY PLAYERS AND THEIR ROLES

KEY PLAYER	ROLES

SPONSOR
Initiates a project, adds to the team's authority, and is the most senior team member.

- Ensures that the project is of real relevance to the organization.
- Helps in setting objectives and constraints.
- Acts as an inspirational figurehead.
- May provide resources.

PROJECT MANAGER
Responsible for achieving the project's overall objectives and leading the project team.

- Produces a detailed plan of action.
- Motivates and develops project team.
- Communicates project information to stakeholders and other interested parties.
- Monitors progress to keep project on track.

STAKEHOLDER
Any other party who is interested in, or affected by, the outcome of the project.

- Contributes to various stages of the planning process by providing feedback.
- Might only be involved from time to time.
- May not be a stakeholder for the entire project if his or her contribution is complete.

KEY TEAM MEMBER
Assists the project manager and provides the breadth of knowledge needed.

- Makes a major contribution in examining feasibility and planning a project.
- Lends technical expertise when needed.
- Is directly responsible for project being completed on time and within budget.

TEAM MEMBER
Full or part-time person who has actions to carry out in the project plan.

- Takes responsibility for completing activities as set out in the project plan.
- Fulfills a specialized role if involved as a consultant, or as an individual who is only needed for part of the project.

CUSTOMER
Internal or external person who benefits from changes brought about by the project.

- Strongly influences the objectives of the project and how its success is measured.
- Dictates how and when some activities are carried out.
- Provides direction for the project manager.

SUPPLIER
Provider of materials, products, or services needed to carry out the project.

- Can become very involved with, and supportive of, the project.
- Delivers supplies on time and provides services or goods at a fixed cost, agreed with the project manager at the outset.

IDENTIFYING THE ESSENTIALS FOR SUCCESS

To achieve the desired outcome, a project must have defined and approved goals, a committed team, and a viable plan of action that can be altered to accommodate change. Abide by these essentials to keep you on course for success.

> **6** Make sure that people understand what you are aiming to achieve.

> **7** Ask colleagues to read your goals. If any comments are negative, revise the goals.

HAVING CLEAR GOALS

To be successful, a project must have clearly defined goals. These goals must be agreed by all involved, so that everyone proceeds with the same expectations. The scope of the project must remain consistent so that it achieves what it set out to accomplish. Whoever agreed to the initiation of the project, usually the project sponsor or customer, should not need to make significant changes to its scope or extent. People who are key to the success of the project must commit their time to it, even if their involvement is only on a part-time basis.

GAINING COMMITMENT

An eager, skilled, and committed team is vital to the success of any project. To this end, the motivational and people management skills of the project manager are paramount. As project manager, it is your responsibility to develop the best team that you can, guide it in the right direction, and ensure that members benefit from the experience. Choose your team carefully and provide training, if necessary. The ongoing support of your superior, sponsor, and other interested parties must also be gained from the outset.

QUESTIONS TO ASK YOURSELF

Q Could I respond to a customer's demand by initiating a project?

Q Whom should I approach to get the project under way?

Q Am I confident that key people will lend their support to make this project successful?

Q Do the overall aims of the project seem achievable?

8 Expect to revise and enhance your project plan at least several times.

PLANNING AND COMMUNICATING

For a project to run smoothly, the resources required must be available at the time you need them. This demands effective front-end planning, taking into account not only people, but also facilities, equipment, and materials. A detailed, complete plan guides the project and is the document that communicates your overall objectives, activities, resource requirements, and schedules. It is also vital that you keep everyone involved fully informed of the plan and update them whenever it changes.

◀ **ACTING EARLY**
Check with your superior that a sufficient budget and realistic time frame have been agreed for the project from the outset. This avoids the success of your project being threatened later because time or money has run out.

BEING FLEXIBLE

In a rapidly changing business environment, the ability to think ahead and anticipate can make the difference between achieving project objectives or not. You must be prepared to change your plans in a flexible and responsive way. It is unlikely that your original plan will be the one you follow all the way, since circumstances and requirements generally change as the project unfolds. This means that you will have to reevaluate the plan regularly and adapt it accordingly. If your project is to succeed, you must be able to anticipate and recognize the need for change, implement it, and measure its impact effectively.

9 Learn to accept the inevitability of change.

10 You can hope for the best, but always plan for the worst.

DEFINING THE STAGES

There are five stages to a project: initiation, planning, motivating, monitoring, and closing. Start with a burst, end positively, and recognize the different techniques and skills required to negotiate the three key stages in between.

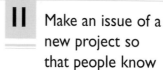

11 Make an issue of a new project so that people know it is happening.

PLANNING A PROJECT

Whether you initiate a project yourself, or your manager or a customer suggests it, the first step in the planning process is to agree a vision for the project, stating exactly what it will achieve. To do this, you will bring together your core team members and people with a close interest in the project's result, known as stakeholders. Having defined a vision, you can identify objectives, agree on actions and resources, order and schedule tasks, and finally validate the plan with all concerned and gain their commitment to it.

IMPLEMENTING THE PLAN

The success of the implementation phase rests with the project team and, ultimately, your ability to lead them. You will have to think about team selection, understand how the team will develop as the project progresses, encourage teamwork, agree on key decisions, and adopt different leadership styles to inspire and motivate different personalities. To gain the commitment of all concerned, make sure that you start with a well-prepared burst, using the authority of your sponsor, manager, and customer to focus everyone on the plan. You must ensure that everyone has access to key project information, and keep communication flowing at all times.

12 Monitor the project consistently from start to finish – problems can occur anywhere along the way.

MONITORING PERFORMANCE

Once the project is under way, you will need to assess how it is faring against objectives and time targets. An efficient monitoring system is vital if you are to deal with problems and changes before they throw a project off-course. During this stage, you will be asking for regular progress reports, organizing team meetings, and identifying milestones that will measure your progress. Once you have identified potential problems and threats, you can then use logical processes to overcome them, and to manage and incorporate changes to the plan when required. Finally, you will gain maximum benefit for your organization by recording your experiences for future reference.

UNDERSTANDING PROJECT DEVELOPMENT

Initiators of project agree a vision

Key people outline project purpose and objectives

Activities and resources are agreed and prioritized

Project plan is approved by all involved

Project manager executes plan, guiding team to achieve goals

Progress is monitored and plan revised as necessary

Project is successfully completed on time and within budget

Project manager greets new colleague with enthusiasm

◀ MAKING AN IMPRESSION

Bring the project team together as early as possible to introduce them, and yourself, informally. It is important to start off on a good footing, so be positive and stress how much you are looking forward to working together as a team.

Checking Feasibility

Before starting on a project, you need to be certain that there is a good chance it will be successful. Take the relevant steps to find out whether a project is appropriately timed, feasible, and worthwhile before going ahead with it.

13 Make sure you are not undertaking a task that cannot be achieved.

14 Find out where a project is in danger of failure.

15 Examine whether a given schedule is realistic.

Timing It Right

However promising and desirable a project may seem, always carefully examine whether it is the right time to initiate it. Take into account other projects that have already started. Some organizations have so many projects in place that it is not possible for them all to succeed, so you may have to consider postponing the new project or curtailing those that are unlikely to produce valuable results. Since all projects require access to limited or even scarce resources, it is vital that each has a clear reason for existing and that now is definitely the right time for it to happen.

Identifying Driving Resources

Every project is driven by the needs of the organization. The stronger these driving forces, the more likely the project is to succeed. If, for example, a project involves winning back lost customers, the driving force is very strong. To create a list of driving forces, or reasons why your project should go ahead, decide which business concerns the project will have an impact on, and then compare your project with other projects. For example, if there is a driving force behind two projects to increase sales, then the one that, say, doubles sales is more likely to succeed.

Questions to Ask Yourself

Q Are there any ongoing projects with a higher priority than my own that are taking up key resources?

Q Are my project goals in line with the long-term objectives of my organization?

Q How will the outcome of the project affect the performance of the organization?

Q Could this project damage the chances of another project being successful?

IDENTIFYING RESISTING FORCES

There are always reasons why projects may not be completed. Such forces include people's resistance to change, the weight of the current workload, lack of information or resources, or a dearth of people with the necessary skills. Identify these resisting forces early on so that you can overcome them, or change the timing of the project. A strong resisting force emerges in organizations that frequently initiate projects to change the way people carry out their jobs but fail to see the projects through. If people view a project as simply another management initiative, it will take great skill to motivate them to make it happen.

▼ SEEKING EXPERT ADVICE

Ask a key team member with technical expertise to help you identify reasons why your project may not be successful. They may be able to pinpoint flaws that you had not previously considered.

▼ USING FORCEFIELD ANALYSIS

Create a simple diagram, such as the example below, to compare driving and resisting forces. List the driving forces against a vertical grid, and give each column a number between one and five. Do the same with the resisting forces but give them a negative measurement.

PREDICTING SUCCESS

A useful technique, known as forcefield analysis, will help you to decide whether the driving forces outweigh the resisting forces, and, consequently, whether the project has a good chance of success. By creating such an analysis, you will be able to see at a glance whether the balance is weighted toward success or failure. To assess the relative impact of each force, remember that drivers range from "one," a weak driver, to "five," an essential need. "Minus one" describes a resisting force that is not much of a threat to the success of the project, while "minus five" shows a force that is very strong, and that, unless you can minimize its impact, is likely to hinder you in achieving the desired project results.

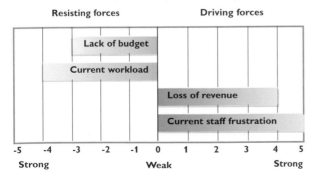

Resisting forces — Driving forces

Lack of budget
Current workload
Loss of revenue
Current staff frustration

-5 -4 -3 -2 -1 0 1 2 3 4 5
Strong   Weak   Strong

PRIORITIZING PROJECTS

W*hen managing several projects, you must evaluate which is the most important to your organization in order to allocate time and resources. Seek advice from key people and use the discipline of a master schedule to prioritize effectively.*

16 Put your projects in order now and avoid damaging conflicts later.

17 Check that project and organizational priorities align.

SETTING PRIORITIES ▼

In this example, the project manager is assigned several projects by her superior. By prioritizing effectively, she is able to complete all the projects successfully. A failure to prioritize, however, leads to disorganization, resulting in none of the projects achieving their intended value.

CONSIDERING VALUE

Before starting a new project, consider how many people and what resources it needs to meet its objectives. Your aim is to deploy the organization's resources to projects that offer the greatest value in their results. Discuss with your superior, and/or the project initiator, the relative importance of your project. You may wish to hold meetings with your customer or other project team members. The more complex the project, the more important it is to seek the opinion of others before you prioritize.

Project manager reviews projects but cannot decide which is most important

Project manager takes responsibility for three new projects

SCHEDULING PROJECTS

To help you decide early on how best to tackle a string of projects, create a form known as a master schedule. You need not identify all the resources in detail at this stage but write down an estimate. This will enable you to see where there are potential resource clashes between projects and confirm or deny the feasibility of a new project. If, for example, two projects require a crane at the same time, and you only have one available, you must reschedule one project to ensure that the crane is available for both.

Master Schedule

	JAN	FEB	MAR	APR	MAY	JUNE	JULY
Project 1							
Project 2							
Project 3							
RESOURCES							
Project manager	1	2	2	3	2	2	1
Engineers	2	4	4	5	4	1	0
Installation staff	0	3	3	4	2	2	1
Computers	3	5	5	7	4	3	2
Low loader	0	1	2	2	0	0	0
Heavy crane	0	0	1	2	0	0	0

▲ **CREATING A MASTER SCHEDULE**

Create a series of monthly (or, for complex projects, weekly) columns running to the right of the form. List all your ongoing projects and, underneath, detail the resources (people, equipment, materials) you think you are likely to need.

Project manager seeks superior's opinion on which projects should take priority

Project manager completes all three projects successfully

Project manager falls behind with projects because she has failed to prioritize

THINGS TO DO

1. Decide which projects offer the greatest potential value to your organization.

2. If in doubt, seek advice from a superior or the project initiator.

3. Create a master schedule to outline the resources each project requires.

4. If available resources are in conflict, rethink priorities.

PLANNING A PROJECT

An effective plan maps out your project from start to finish, detailing what needs to be done, when, and how much it will cost. Prepare your plan well, and it will guide you to success.

DEFINING THE VISION

Having a clear idea of what a project will achieve is essential if you are to ensure that it will accomplish something of perceived value. With your key team members and sponsor, produce an overall statement that describes the project vision.

18 Be as ambitious as you can, but avoid committing to the impossible.

19 Create a precise vision to avoid ambiguous results.

20 See if others agree with your vision of the future.

DEFINING DESIRABLE CHANGE

Ensure that everyone knows exactly what a project is expected to attain by summarizing its aims. With your key team members and sponsor, create a statement that describes the project vision. For the statement to explain your proposal properly, it must answer the question, "What are we going to change and how?". Check the vision statement with your customers, who may help to refine it by describing what they would expect from such a project. If the project creates something of value for the customer, that is a good indicator of its desirability.

EXAMINING THE IDEAL

To help you outline your vision, try to define what would be ideal. Start from a blank sheet of paper and ask the team to describe what, in an ideal world, the project would change. Avoid being held back by the situation as it is now. While you must remain realistic, you must also be creative in your thinking. Do not allow the way in which you have always done things to deter you from coming up with alternatives. If you involve the customer in this process, avoid giving them the impression that this is how the world will be, but how you would like it to be. Check how feasible the ideal is to arrive at your vision.

CREATING A PROJECT VISION

Identify a need for change

Meet with key team members and sponsor

Define what the project would ideally change

Assess the likelihood of attaining ideal vision

Produce a feasible vision statement

DO'S AND DON'TS

✔ Do compromise on the ideal if that is what it takes to arrive at the vision.

✔ Do make the vision statement explain why the project is needed.

✘ Don't ignore obstacles at this stage – they may prove to be major stumbling blocks.

✘ Don't involve too many people this early in the process.

AGREEING A VISION ▶

Encourage team members to question every aspect of the vision to check that it is truly workable and achievable. Make sure that everyone agrees on the way ahead, so that they are committed to attaining the vision.

21 Check at this stage that the vision is clearly worth attaining.

SETTING OBJECTIVES

Once you have agreed on the project vision, you must set objectives that will measure the progress and ultimate success of the project. Expand the vision to clarify the purpose of the project, list the objectives, and then set priorities and interim targets.

22 Gain agreement on objectives from everyone involved in the project.

23 Make sure that your objectives are measurable.

24 Think how relevant an objective will be when it is achieved.

DEFINING PURPOSE

Expand the vision statement to explain what you are going to do, how long it will take, and how much it will cost. Your statement of purpose should reflect the relative importance of time, cost, and performance. For example, if you aim to create a product that competes with the newest solutions available, the key purpose is performance. Time frame is the key driver if you must install a new system before starting international operations. Cost is the key purpose if you cannot, under any circumstances, spend more than last year's budget.

DEFINING OBJECTIVES AND INDICATORS

List the specific objectives you wish to achieve, covering the areas of change that the project involves. Avoid listing an activity, such as "complete a pilot," instead of an objective, which would be to "demonstrate that the project will achieve the planned business impact." Ensure that progress against objectives is measurable by setting an "indicator" against each one. For example, if your objective is to increase sales of a new drink, use the indicator of sales volume to measure success. If you are having difficulty in arriving at the indicator, ask the question, "How will we know if we have achieved this objective?"

▼ RESEARCHING STANDARDS

Nominate a team member to read up on industry standards. These will provide a benchmark for your own indicators and a check on your competitiveness.

Team member studies competitors' brochures

SETTING PRIORITIES AND TARGETS

It is unlikely that all the objectives will be equally important to your organization. Give each a priority of one to ten, where one is least important. It will probably be obvious which objectives are significant and which are not, but priorities of those falling in between will be less clear. Discuss and agree these with the team. Then set targets. These may be simple, such as increasing sales by 50 percent, or they may be more complex. If, for example, your objective is to improve customer satisfaction, and the indicator is based on complaints, you must count the number of complaints you now receive, and set a target for reducing them.

▼ DECIDING ON PROJECT EMPHASIS

Write down your objectives, indicators, priorities, current performance, and targets. This will help you to decide which aspects of the project require most effort and resources.

25 Be prepared to drop any objective that has a low priority.

Key objectives that determine project's success

Priority of objective

Objective	Indicator	P	Current	Target
Improve sales of non-standard products	Increase volume of orders	10	5 million	7.5 million
Improve the speed of decision-making	Reduce time taken to respond to a customer request for a quotation	8	8 weeks	4 weeks
Improve efficiency of preparing customer quotations	(a) Reduce time spent on preparing quotations (b) Cut number of days spent on product training courses	6	(a) 4 days per month (b) 5 days per year	(a) 2 days per month (b) 0 days per year
Improve management accountability for proposals	Make a single manager accountable for producing each customer proposal	6	Not done	In place

Measure of the objective's success

Current level of performance

Desired level of performance

ASSESSING CONSTRAINTS

Every project faces constraints, such as limits on time or money. Occasionally, such constraints may even render the project unfeasible. Make sure that team members understand the constraints in advance, and that they are able to work within them.

> **26** You can overcome most constraints by planning how to get around them.

▼ LIMITING CHANGE

Talk through any changes you wish to make with your superior, but be prepared to accept that some will not be approved. There may be valid reasons for keeping certain processes or practises intact.

PROTECTING WHAT WORKS

There is little point in change for the sake of it if you can work within the constraints of what currently exists. Even if you identify an area for improvement, it may be better to include the change in a later project, rather than deal with it immediately. This is because too many changes can put a project at risk as people try to cope with too fluid an environment. Also, by taking on too many changes, there is the danger that you will not be able to identify those that have resulted in the success of the project, or indeed, its failure.

ASSESSING TIME CONSTRAINTS

A fast-moving business environment often gives projects a specific window of opportunity. If you are facing a competitor who is to deliver a new product into the stores for the fall season, you must work within that time constraint. You will not benefit from working hard to deliver a competitive product if you cannot launch the new line in time for your customers to place orders. Whether you like it or not, the time constraint has been set and you must work within that boundary.

> **27** Face up to constraints in a logical fashion.

> **28** Do your best to find short cuts to success.

EXAMINING RESOURCE LIMITATIONS

Most organizations work within limited resources and budgets, and projects are subject to similar constraints. A new project may entail an extravagant use of resources, so you will need to make sure that they really would be available. But if the success of your project depends on a level of resources that is unlikely to be forthcoming, think again, and alter the objectives of the project. For example, if you can complete the project with fewer resources, then you should make that your plan. Alternatively, if you are in a position to negotiate for more time and money to enable the project to go ahead, do so.

THINGS TO DO

1. Assess whether time is of the essence.
2. Analyze what resources you will need and whether you can afford them.
3. Look into using existing processes or resources.
4. Identify any external constraints, such as legal or environmental regulations.
5. Decide whether to proceed within the given constraints.

29 Explain the constraints to all who agree to take part in the project.

USING EXISTING PROCESSES

In order to reduce project time frames, look at what currently exists. For example, other departments may have plans for change in an associated area that you could capitalize on, product parts that would shortcut design, or current technologies that would avoid the need to invent something new. It is important to consider these issues and reuse as much as possible. It is rarely a good idea to start from scratch, no matter how appealing that may seem.

◀ **CAPITALIZING ON INVESTMENTS**
By studying systems in other departments within your organization, you can capitalize on internal expertise and experience, at the same time saving your organization money.

CASE STUDY
Robert was asked to create a website for his department. Since he did not have the expertise to do this alone, he asked two outside companies that specialized in setting up and maintaining websites to quote for the work.
Robert's sponsor thought that both quotations were too high, and advised Robert to look at the websites already created by other departments within their organization.
Robert particularly liked the site designed and maintained by Anne-Marie, who showed him how to use the software she had bought especially to create her site.
As a result, Robert was able to create the website for his department. In doing so, he not only saved the money that had been allocated specifically for that purpose but also made further use of the software investment originally made by Anne-Marie.

Listing Activities

Having identified your objectives and constraints, you can now plan in greater detail. List all the activities needed to achieve the objectives and divide them into groups to make it easier to assess what must be done, when, and by whom.

30 Make sure that you consult widely when creating your activity list.

Why List Activities?

Breaking the project work down into smaller units, or activities, makes it much easier to see how work overlaps, and how some activities may affect the timing or outcome of others. Since the list can be long, it helps to divide activities into groups so that each set of tasks becomes more manageable and easier to track when monitoring performance and progress. Grouping activities also helps you determine how they fit into a logical sequence for completion, which aids scheduling and enables you to assess the number of people and the skills that will be needed. Listing activities in this way also reduces the risk of misunderstandings, since everyone knows what their tasks are.

Team member records each activity on a flip chart

Team member with experience of similar project lends experience to the brainstorm

31 Try to describe each activity within a short sentence or two.

DRAWING UP A LIST

Start the process by brainstorming a list of activities. You may need to include more people at this stage. It is often useful, for example, to ask various stakeholders for their views on what it will take to complete the project, especially if it is a complex one. You may also wish to consult other potential team members. Such consultation makes sensible use of other people's expertise and experience. Ideally, if someone in the organization has previously completed a similar project, consult the original project manager and use the previous plan as a checklist. At this stage it is not necessary to concern yourself with the order in which the activities will occur; this comes later.

32 Keep checking your list to see if anything is missing.

PLANNING PROJECT ACTIVITIES

Brainstorm a comprehensive list

Group activities into a logical order

Check that nothing has been missed

Give each group and activity a unique identifying number

Document the activity list

Project manager guides team but does not judge contributions

Team member feels free to suggest an activity

Colleague is aware that this is not the time to pass comment

◀ **BRAINSTORMING ACTIVITIES**

Use a brainstorming session to generate ideas on all the activities needed to complete the project. Note every activity suggested, no matter how inconsequential. Your aim is to draw up a comprehensive list that can be refined later.

GROUPING ACTIVITIES

Break down your long list of activities into smaller, more manageable units by putting the activities into logical groups. You can ask the team to help you or, as project manager, you can do it yourself. Most groups will be obvious. Perhaps certain activities are all concerned with one event occurring later in the project, or some may all involve the same department or people with similar skills. If an activity does not fit into a group, question whether it is really necessary, or leave it as a separate entity.

GROUPING ACTIVITIES ▶

To group activities effectively, consider the logical order in which they will have to happen. One group, for example, may not be able to start before another is complete. The extract shown lists groups of activities involved in bringing a new product to the manufacturing stage.

33 Present your activity list so that it is clear and easy to understand.

ACTIVITIES AND GROUPS

1 **Conduct analysis**
  1.1 Interview customer representatives
  1.2 Consolidate findings into a report
  1.3 Present report to board
2 **Agree product outline**
  2.1 Hold discussions with departments
  2.2 Gain budget approval
3 **Complete design**
  3.1 Take first draft to representative customers
  3.2 Amend to answer customer comments
  3.3 Gain top level agreement to design
4 **Arrange logistics**
  4.1 Order materials
  4.2 Train personnel
  4.3 Engage subcontractors

34 Ask specialists for advice when grouping activities.

35 Put the list away and review it a week later with a fresh perspective.

IDENTIFYING TYPICAL GROUPS

Every project has a start-up phase, or a group of activities that signifies the launch of the project, introduces team members, and records what each person has committed to achieving. Similarly, there should be a group of activities marking the project's closure, involving final checks on performance indicators and finalizing project records for the benefit of subsequent project managers. Finally, most projects need a group of communications activities, for example issuing weekly progress reports or holding a presentation shortly before a planned pilot program goes live.

CHECKING FOR GAPS

Review your list of activities and groups to ensure that it is complete. If you miss this step now and realize later that you have overlooked something, it could have serious implications on the project's budget, schedule, or other resources. Have you identified every activity needed in each group? Go through the planned activities step-by-step: is there anything missing; are you assuming that something will have happened in between activities that you have not actually listed? Once you are confident that each group is complete, give each group and each activity within the group a unique identifying number.

QUESTIONS TO ASK YOURSELF

Q If we complete all the activities listed, will we have done everything required to meet the project's objectives?

Q Will the activities ensure that we hit our indicator targets?

Q Does our activity list reflect the priorities we originally set for each objective?

Q Have we written down all our activities in sufficient detail?

Q Are all of the activities listed really necessary?

PLANNING A PILOT

Another group of activities that features in many projects, especially when the purpose is to create something entirely new, is a pilot implementation. Typical activities include choosing a limited number of people as a pilot team, implementing the whole project on a limited basis, and keeping records of the experience. By building a pilot phase into the plan, you will have a far less stressful and error-prone time when it comes to rolling out the entire project.

Choose your people for the pilot program carefully and make them aware that they are, for this particular project, guinea pigs. Make sure you communicate your thanks to them after the project, since their agreement to be involved at an early stage probably caused them some problems.

RUNNING A TRIAL ▶
Testing a new idea, even one as complex as an automated production line, allows problems to be solved before a new system is introduced more widely.

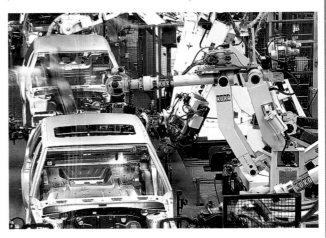

COMMITTING RESOURCES

Before starting to implement a project, you must study resource requirements and budgets. The feasibility of the project depends on you and your team being able to justify the expenditure by comparing it favorably with the proposed benefits.

> **36** Estimate costs carefully – once approved, you are bound by them.

ESTIMATING MANPOWER

Think about who needs to be involved in each activity and for how long in actual worker days. A team member may need to work on a project for a period of 10 days, but if he or she has to work on it for only 30 minutes per day, the total commitment is just five hours. If the member can usefully work on other projects for the rest of the time, the cost to your project will be a fraction of the member's 10-day earnings or charge. But if he or she can make no contribution elsewhere, then your project's budget must bear the full cost.

> **37** Provide the best supplies, facilities, and equipment you can afford.

CONSIDERING KEY RESOURCES

PEOPLE

How many people do you need? → Assess who will take on each activity

What type of skills do they require? → Identify levels of expertise required

OTHER RESOURCES

Are facilities, materials, or supplies essential? → Look at what each activity requires

Is information or technology needed? → Examine using existing systems

MONEY

What is the total cost of project? → Consider the cost of all the resources

Are sufficient funds available? → Check the budget that was agreed

IDENTIFYING OTHER RESOURCES

While the major cost of a project is generally the people, there are other resources that will have an impact on the budget. For example, you may have to commission market research. Facilities, equipment, and materials may also involve expenditure. Failure to identify all the costs will mean that you lose credibility when others examine the project to balance its costs against its benefits. A comprehensive estimate of costs at this stage also reduces the risk that you will have to request extra funds once the project is up and running.

QUESTIONS TO ASK YOURSELF

Q Can I estimate costs or resources more accurately by asking someone with relevant expertise for advice?

Q Is there another way to achieve the goals that would not require expenditure on particular resources?

Q Is the cost estimate that I have drawn up realistic rather than optimistic?

38 Ensure that the budget will allow you to complete all your activities.

EXAMINING THE DETAILS

It is not enough to know that the team will need a training room for a month during the project, you will also need to know how large that room needs to be and what kind of equipment you should install in it. The better the detail at this stage, the more likely you are to avoid problems during the implementation. This will enable your team to focus on achieving objectives rather than on fixing matters that were poorly planned.

CHOOSING A COSTING METHOD

Whatever resources you consider, you can calculate their cost in one of two ways: absolute costing or marginal costing. Absolute costing means calculating the exact cost of the resource. If, for example, a new computer is essential for the project, the amount you pay for it becomes a project cost. If you can use an existing computer, allocate a proportion of its cost to the project. Marginal costing means that you only allocate costs to the project if they would not be incurred if the project did not take place. For example, if an existing computer, which is not being used, is required, the marginal, or extra cost, of the computer is nil. The cost of the computer should not be in the project budget. With practice, marginal costing is easy to calculate and is generally a more accurate measure of the cost of a project to an organization.

MAKING COMPROMISES

In an ideal world, you would gain approval for all the resources you need. In reality, you will probably have to cope with less. The person you most want for a certain task may be unavailable, or the best premises for the project occupied, and you will have to make compromises. Look for compromises that will not threaten the overall aims and objectives of the project. For example, you may be able to recruit a highly skilled worker part-time and allocate the remainder of the work to a less experienced, yet able, team member.

39 Avoid cutting back on tools that the team really needs.

40 If resources are scarce, consider your alternatives.

41 Refine a resource plan until anyone could work from it.

CREATING A ▼ COMMITMENT MATRIX

When you have identified all the resources and estimated costs, document these on a commitment matrix and seek your stakeholders' agreement to it.

DOCUMENTING RESOURCES

The key to ensuring that the resources you require will be available when you need them is to produce a document that all the stakeholders can agree to. This is known as a commitment matrix, because it can be used to remind people of their commitments. Check that the matrix is complete and that every group of activities is comprehensive so that you can be sure that you have identified all the necessary resources.

Activity as identified by number on activity list

Team members assigned to carry out activity

Resources required to carry out activity

Total cost involved

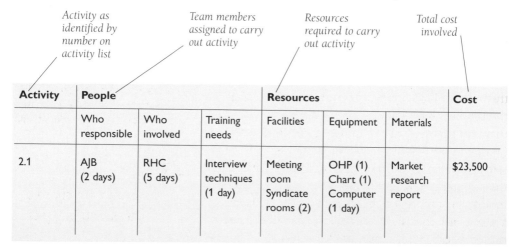

Activity	People			Resources			Cost
	Who responsible	Who involved	Training needs	Facilities	Equipment	Materials	
2.1	AJB (2 days)	RHC (5 days)	Interview techniques (1 day)	Meeting room Syndicate rooms (2)	OHP (1) Chart (1) Computer (1 day)	Market research report	$23,500

USING OUTSIDE RESOURCES

While many resources will come from within your team or organization, you will need to go outside for others. Make sure that you get competitive quotes from potential suppliers and reach an agreement on costs and performance that makes it easy for both parties to monitor progress tightly. You may need to brush up on your negotiating skills beforehand to ensure that you can win the best deal. While it may seem unnecessary to go into such detail at the outset, the tighter the agreement, the more likely you are to avoid conflict.

MAKING CONTACTS ▶

Ensure that you meet with several potential suppliers and keep their details on record. Even if you decide not to use them this time, an extensive network of contacts could well prove useful for future projects.

GETTING SIGN-OFF

Before you can obtain the official go-ahead for a new project, it must be proven that it is still a business priority and that its benefits to the organization considerably outweigh its costs. This is known as investment appraisal, or cost-benefit analysis, and it is a discipline used widely in many organizations which often have formal systems for the process. If the costs are the same or more than the benefits, the sponsors have three alternatives: they can proceed with the project regardless (although this is seldom desirable unless the strategic value of the project is very important to the long-term aims of the organization); they can modify the objectives and change the activities in a way that reduces costs; or they can cancel the project because it is considered unfeasible.

POINTS TO REMEMBER

● If your organization has an official system for obtaining sign-off for a project, this should be followed.

● Finance departments can provide useful feedback on your estimates by comparing your project's costs with others.

● The benefits of a project should never be exaggerated – promises will be expected to be delivered.

42 Be prepared to justify your choices, dates, and budgets.

ORDERING ACTIVITIES

*N*ot all activities can, or need to, start at the same time to meet the project's planned completion date. Put activities into a logical sequence, estimate the duration of each, and then use clear documentation to help you devise a project schedule.

43 Remember that activities can be carried out in parallel.

44 Ask whoever is responsible for an activity to give you their estimated start and end dates.

CONSIDERING ORDER

Having completed a list of the activities required to complete the project, look at how they interrelate. Decide which activities should start immediately or first, which need to be completed before moving on to the next, and work through all the activities until the end of the project. Some activities will be the culmination of a number of others. For example, the team will probably need to complete several activities before it can make a presentation to the people involved in a pilot program. Important activities will be review meetings.

ESTIMATING ACTIVITY TIMES

To draw up an effective schedule, you need to know how much time each activity is likely to take. It is important to estimate these durations accurately, since poor guesswork may throw the entire project off course. Team members should also have input to ensure that they agree with the estimated activity times and will be able to work to the schedule that you produce. If there is major doubt as to how long an activity could take, estimate best and worst case scenarios and work out a compromise between the two. If a project is under time pressure this will help to identify where you could reduce the overall time frame.

QUESTIONS TO ASK YOURSELF

Q Do I have time to do a trial run of an activity to test how long it might take?

Q Could I estimate the duration of an activity more reliably if I sought expert advice?

Q Have I looked at previous project plans to see how long similar activities took?

Q Could I ask other project managers for their advice?

Q Am I confident that my estimates are realistic?

45 Get expert help to draw the first network diagram.

Key

Critical path (minimum duration 19 days)

Noncritical path (minimum duration 6 days)

Activities that can be undertaken simultaneously

Activity that can only start once previous activities are complete

WORKING WITH A NETWORK DIAGRAM

A network diagram shows the relationship between activities, and which ones depend on the completion of others. The diagram may be simple or highly complex, according to how many activities there are and how they interrelate. Where there are several routes through a network, there is a chance to complete tasks simultaneously. Indicate the duration of each task and add up the total time required to complete each route to find the longest route through the network. This longest route is known as the critical path, which shows the shortest possible duration for the project.

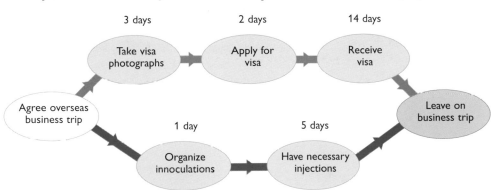

LOOKING FOR SLACK

You can also use the the network diagram to find opportunities for shortening the project schedule. This involves looking at where you can cut the amount of time it takes to complete activities on the critical path, for example, by increasing the resources available to that activity. Take another look at the diagram to identify where any other routes might have some slack. You may then be able to reallocate resources to reduce the pressure on the team members who are responsible for activities on the critical path.

▲ CREATING A NETWORK DIAGRAM
The network above sets out activities to be completed before a business trip. Progress on the critical path must be monitored closely, since a delay in carrying out these activities will affect the project end date.

46 Keep to the critical path to stay on schedule.

AGREEING DATES

Having identified how the activities follow on from one another, and worked out the minimum duration of the project, you can now set real dates. Plot these carefully, taking any potential conflicts into account, and then agree them with the team.

47 Start noncritical tasks as early as possible to free up resources later.

48 Remember to keep your Gantt chart up to date at all times.

USING A GANTT CHART ▼
This Gantt chart lists tasks on the left and the project timeline in weeks across the top. The bars show when tasks start and finish, providing a clear visual overview of project tasks and timings.

CALCULATING DATES
Use the network diagram to help you calculate start and end dates for each activity. Begin with the first activity and work through all the others, starting each as early as possible to allow as much time as you can. If an activity is not on the critical path, start and end dates can be more flexible, since these will not necessarily affect the overall project duration. Finally, plot the dates against a timeline to produce a Gantt chart. These charts are useful for early schedule planning, for showing individual timelines on complex projects, and for comparing progress to the original schedule.

Timeline shows length of project

Each activity is listed separately

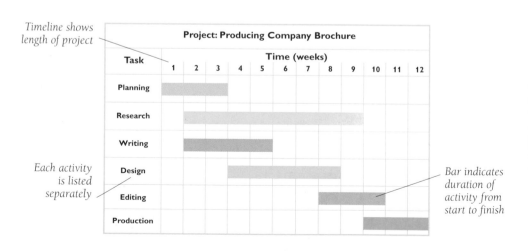

Bar indicates duration of activity from start to finish

Project: Producing Company Brochure

Task	Time (weeks)											
	1	2	3	4	5	6	7	8	9	10	11	12
Planning												
Research												
Writing												
Design												
Editing												
Production												

LOOKING FOR OVERLAP

To check that the dates you have calculated are realistic, refer to your Gantt chart, commitment matrix, and master schedule. The Gantt chart shows you immediately where project activities overlap. Where an overlap exists, the commitment matrix will reveal whether an activity requires the same resource at the same time. In these circumstances, you will have to amend that activity's start and finish dates. The final piece of information comes from looking at the master schedule, which will tell you whether there is any overlap in resources between two projects or more.

POINTS TO REMEMBER

- The earlier an area of overlap is identified, the more likely it is that a way round it can be found.
- Noncritical activities may also be scheduled as late as possible in order to show how much work can be delayed without causing the critical activities to slip.
- When team members have too many commitments on several projects, it may be possible to reduce the overlap by assigning some of their activities to others.

---

49 Encourage your team members to be realistic about dates.

GAINING AGREEMENT

Discuss the dates you have set with the key people to make sure that they are truly available at the time they are needed. You may have to hold discussions with their managers if they are being held to other commitments elsewhere in the organization. On long projects, remember to allow for the fact that team members will not necessarily be available every day, even if they are theoretically working full-time on the project. The percentage of time they will be available is often around two-thirds of the calendar year, or 240 days. Use that number to check that you have allowed time off for vacations, sickness and training.

◀ **PLANNING VACATIONS**
Ask team members to book in their vacation time as early as possible in order to avoid last-minute alterations to the schedule. Use a wallchart to show the team's vacation commitments.

VALIDATING THE PLAN

N*o matter how well you have written your plan, the unexpected is bound to occur and circumstances are certain to change. It is vital to work closely with the team and stakeholders to anticipate and preempt potential problems.*

50 Make a point of discussing the final plan with your customers.

51 Use other project managers' experience to identify threats.

ANTICIPATING ▼ PROBLEMS

Bring together a representative group of stakeholders, particularly customers, and those with relevant experience, and ask what could, in their opinion, go wrong.

IDENTIFYING THREATS

Now that you have a schedule for all the activities needed to complete the project, brainstorm a list of potential threats and analyze each for its impact on your plan. People outside the team can be very helpful in this process, which also encourages the team to defend the plan against constructive criticism, making them more determined to overcome any obstacles. Deal with every threat in turn, paying most attention to those that have an impact on activities on the critical path so that you can work out your best counterattack in advance.

Customer identifies potential problem

Sponsor weighs up impact on project

Project manager suggests a way of overcoming threat

Team member notes threats and suggested counterattacks

PREEMPTING PROBLEMS

Now get the team to focus on preventing the problems from occurring. The question is, "What can we do to reduce the probability that each potential problem might occur?". If the plan is dependent on the weather, for example, you may change the timing of the work schedule. If key materials are in short supply or there is the possibility of a labor strike in your own organization or that of your supplier, you must consider ways to address these problems early on.

52 If you suspect that someone may be promoted off the team, take steps to train a replacement.

53 Check contingency plans with whoever supplies resources.

54 Table the plan, with contingencies, at a review meeting.

CONTINGENCY PLANNING

It is not possible to preempt every eventuality that could harm the project. Get the team to consider what it will do if certain threats occur, and how to minimize the impact of the threats. If the project needs a new piece of software, for example, look at what you could do if it were to be delivered late. If the software is late, and you need a contingency system, it will probably add to the cost of the project. Bring this to the attention of those in control of budgets. You may then have to revisit your cost-benefit analysis.

COMPLETING THE PLAN

From the list of threats and the discussion on preempting problems and contingency planning, you will be able to decide what changes to make to the plan. Make these alterations and the plan is complete. The team has its "baseline" or starting point. It knows what the situation is now, and what will be the result of implementing the plan. Remember, though, that you must ensure that the team is prepared for the fact that the planning and implementation process is rarely sequential. It is likely they will have to recast some of the plan as activities are carried out and changes occur.

POINTS TO REMEMBER

- The more stakeholders who validate a plan, the more likely it is to be implemented.
- If there is a strong likelihood that a contingency plan will be needed, that course of action should become the actual plan.
- Time spent validating the plan and preparing for problems in advance is rarely wasted.
- The entire plan should be double-checked by the project manager before implementation.

IMPLEMENTING A PLAN

The success of a project plan relies on the people who execute it. Equip yourself with the leadership skills necessary to build a strong, committed team and guide it to the desired outcome.

EXAMINING YOUR ROLE

To successfully implement a project plan, it is important to understand what is involved at the outset. Familiarize yourself with the key tasks, responsibilities, and skills involved, and you will be better prepared to lead a project team successfully.

55 Know the project plan inside out and answer questions authoritatively.

56 Keep the business priorities in mind, especially when the project goal is to make a profit.

DEFINING YOUR RESPONSIBILITIES

As project manager, you have overall responsibility for the project's success. Having negotiated the planning process, you must now translate the plan into action. This involves selecting the right team members, focusing and motivating them to achieve project goals, and helping them to develop both as individuals and as team workers. The project manager must also build good relationships with stakeholders, run team meetings effectively, administrate and coordinate, and communicate clearly on all levels every step of the way.

TAKING THE LEAD

A successful project manager is both a manager and leader. Leaders command authority and respect, follow up plans with actions, and are able to inspire and motivate others. They also adopt different leadership styles as circumstances dictate. You can develop these skills through training and experience: try practicing outside work by taking office at your local civic club. Mainly, you develop leadership skills by taking responsibility for objectives. You may have to start by becoming accountable for a group of activities before you can take on an entire project.

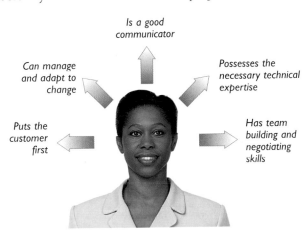

DEFINING YOUR ROLE

Select final team members and allocate responsibilities

Launch the project successfully

Motivate and focus team on objectives

Organize information systems

Communicate key information

◀ **EVALUATING SKILLS**
To be an effective leader, you must develop several important attributes. This example shows some of the essential qualities of a successful project manager.

QUESTIONS TO ASK YOURSELF

Q Are you willing to stay with the project for its entire term?

Q Are you interested in developing people and helping them to become leaders?

Q Do you have a real interest in working on the project?

Q Can you delegate objectives to the team as well as tasks?

ASSESSING YOURSELF

If you are not sure whether you have what it takes to be a leader, ask someone whose opinion you respect for objective comments. For example, you could talk to people with whom you have worked in the past to ascertain how they regard you. If they plainly feel that they could work for you, then that is a good indicator. Once you have gathered the facts, you can create a picture of where you want to be in the future, and put together a plan for developing the necessary skills.

Building a Team

*H*aving *planned the project with a core team, now ensure that you have the full complement of people with the right mix of skills and personalities to see it through. Choose your team carefully, bearing in mind the vital team roles that should be covered.*

57 Try not to have preconceived ideas about people – judge as you find.

Assessing Availability

Refer back to your commitment matrix to identify the skills and people needed to complete the project. The chart will tell you who is required, for how long, and when. Draw up a list of candidates who might be suitable for each part and find out whether they are available. You may need to negotiate with other managers if you wish to appoint staff working in different areas of the organization. Your own project is almost certainly not the only one in progress, so you may also need to talk to whoever is coordinating the resources deployed on all of the projects.

Choosing the Right People

Apart from having the necessary skills, the people you want to attract are those who will come willingly. It is much easier to work with people who are enthusiastic about the project, so it pays to hold discussions with potential team members to find out whether they are eager to work on the project. Think also of the team as a whole. Will each team member fit in with the others? Is there any conflict between potential members? You will, of course, help them to form a team under your leadership, but it is better to start off with people who are sympathetic to each other.

58 Be frank with potential team members – ask if they identify with the project's aims.

59 Build a team that takes advantage of each individual's skills without overburdening their weaknesses.

CONSIDERING ROLES

In any team you will look for people to carry out a team role as well as their functional role. To operate efficiently you, as the team leader, will want someone to perform the roles of critic, implementer, external contact, coordinator, ideas person, team builder, and inspector. Most team members will fit strongly into one or more of these roles. You need them all, and if one is not present, you will have to take the role on yourself. If, for example, you see that no one is challenging the team's standards, quality, and way of working, you are lacking a critic. Keep challenging the team yourself until you see someone else leaning toward this role. Discuss these roles in an open manner, encourage friendly conversations, and you will build one of the most important qualities of a group – team spirit. Remember that only as a team will you be able to achieve the project's objectives.

DO'S AND DON'TS

✔ Do allow people to settle into roles without being pushed.

✔ Do double or treble up on roles when a project team only has a few members.

✔ Do ask a stakeholder to take on a role if it is not being played.

✘ Don't attempt to shoehorn a personality into a particular role.

✘ Don't expect people to continue playing a role if they become uncomfortable in it.

✘ Don't take on a role yourself if it means appearing insincere.

KEY TEAM ROLES

COORDINATOR
Pulls together the work of the team as a whole.

CRITIC
Guardian and analyst of the team's effectiveness.

IDEAS PERSON
Encourages the team's innovative vitality.

IMPLEMENTER
Ensures smooth-running of the team's actions.

EXTERNAL CONTACT
Looks after the team's external contacts.

INSPECTOR
Ensures high standards are maintained.

TEAM BUILDER
Develops the teamworking spirit.

60 Encourage criticism, but ask the critic to supply alternatives, too.

STARTING POSITIVELY

Once you have the right team in place, it is important to launch a new project in a positive manner. Encourage teamwork by inviting everyone to an informal gathering at the outset, and record the project's existence formally to clarify its purpose.

61 Ask the most senior person possible to attend a project launch.

62 Listen to reactions from newcomers and be prepared to review activities.

USING YOUR SPONSOR ▼
The first team meeting offers your sponsor an important platform. Invite him or her to address the team and express belief and commitment in the project. This is invaluable for encouraging team spirit.

STARTING ACTIVELY

At an early stage, gather the team together for a full initiation session to let them know exactly what the project is all about. Explain what the targets and constraints are, let everyone know how the project will benefit them, and establish ground rules relating to the sharing of information and decision-making. Keep the session two-way so that people can ask questions. By the end of the meeting, everyone should understand what needs to be done and feel motivated to achieve it.

Colleague feels valued in his new role

Sponsor greets team with positive enthusiasm

Team member learns of the project's importance

Team member is impressed by sponsor's confidence in the project manager and team

326

WRITING A START-UP REPORT

A start-up report should make everyone aware of the vision that has inspired the project and the measures of success the team will be aiming for. You may also document the resources allocated to the project, and give some indication of the risks that are involved. Finally, it is a good idea to name all the stakeholders so that everyone knows who they are, and ask key people who are underpinning the project to endorse it by adding their signatures to the document. These will include the project manager and project sponsor.

63 Keep reports free of jargon and complex language.

64 Ask for signatures to the plan as a formal agreement.

STRUCTURING A START-UP REPORT

PARTS OF A REPORT	FACTORS TO INCLUDE
VISION An explanation of the overall aim of the project.	● Clarify exactly why the project has been initiated and what it is setting out to achieve. ● Spell out the benefits of the project to the entire project team and to the organization as a whole.
TARGETS A summary of indicators, current performance, and target figures.	● Provide clear information on how the success of the project will be measured. ● Explain what business results are expected to have been achieved by the end of the project.
MILESTONES Special events or achievements that mark progress along the way.	● Summarize milestones to remind everyone of what they will have to deliver at each stage of the project. ● Set out your milestones so that they divide the project into logical, measurable segments.
RISKS AND OPPORTUNITIES A list of the potential risks and additional opportunities.	● Explain what needs to be avoided when team members carry out their roles. ● Highlight any areas where improvements could be made in order to gain even greater benefit from the project.
LIST OF STAKEHOLDERS A directory of all the stakeholders involved in the project.	● Name all interested parties and list their credentials to add to the credibility of the project. ● List all your customers, and state what each customer expects to gain from the project.

LEADING EFFECTIVELY

There are many different styles of leadership, but because projects rely on good teamwork, it is important to favor a consensus-building, rather than a dictatorial, approach. To lead a project well, you must be able to motivate your team.

65 Be a manager whom people want to seek out, rather than avoid.

66 Show your enthusiasm for the project, even when under pressure.

UNDERSTANDING STYLES

There is a spectrum of possibilities in leadership styles, and you will need to adopt them all at certain points in the project. While your approach may need to vary from a dictatorial style to a consensus-seeking one, the predominant style you adopt should depend on your organization, the nature of the project, the characteristics of the team, and your own personality.

CHOOSING A LEADERSHIP STYLE

LEADERSHIP STYLE	WHEN TO USE IT
DICTATORIAL Making decisions alone, taking risks, being autocratic and controlling.	This style may be appropriate if the project faces a crisis, and there is no time to consult. However, since it discourages teamwork, it should be used sparingly.
ANALYTICAL Gathering all the facts, observing and analyzing before reaching decisions.	This style, which requires sound analytical skills, may be used when a project is under time pressure or threat, and the right decision must be made quickly.
OPINION-SEEKING Asking for opinions from the team on which to base decisions.	Use this style to build team confidence and show that you value people's views, as well as to impress stakeholders, who like to be consulted.
DEMOCRATIC Encouraging team participation and involvement in decision-making.	This is an essential style to be used on a regular basis to empower team members, and help strengthen their commitment to a project.

CULTURAL DIFFERENCES

Project managers in the UK often create an inner circle of key team members to speed up decision-making, while in the US, the entire team is brought together frequently. In Japan, decisions are reached by consensus, in which unanimous agreement is reached through a laborious process.

CHANGING STYLES

Be prepared to change your leadership style to suit the circumstances and the team, even if you feel uncomfortable for a while because the style you are adopting does not come naturally. For example, some managers find consultation annoying and time-wasting, while other managers are so intent on gaining consensus that decisions take too long, and the project suffers as a result. The key to making good consensus decisions is to listen carefully to everyone before indicating which way they are leaning. A decision is then reached accordingly, unless someone can argue most convincingly that it is the wrong move.

LEADING APPROPRIATELY

Each member of a team has a unique personality and style. Take time to study each individual and understand what motivates them so that you can provide the level of guidance they need. Some team members will prefer to be set objectives, with the project manager delegating responsibility to them for how they should be tackled. Others will react better to being given specific tasks. Use the appropriate style for each individual.

▼ ADOPTING A HANDS-OFF APPROACH

Motivate an experienced, capable team member by allowing them to use their own initiative. Provide support and guidance but avoid interfering too heavily.

◀ BEING HANDS-ON

Explain clearly what you expect from a new or less confident worker, who will need close supervision and encouragement.

OBTAINING RESULTS

There are two major factors to consider when deciding which style of leadership to use. If the project is under time pressure, there may be no alternative to the dictatorial style because you do not have the luxury of time to consult. If you want to gain commitment, you must involve others in the key decisions to increase their willingness to make the decision work. Whichever style you choose, the quality of the decision is vital. Before you impose a decision, ensure that you have all the facts to prove that it is the right thing to do.

> **67** Look for ways to use conflict constructively.

RESOLVING CONFLICT

Personality clashes are inevitable when many people work together. There may be differences of opinion or disputes that arise from people having different standards on quality of work, or there may be one or two team members who simply do not get along. If team members disagree, find a way of resolving the conflict either by taking on the role of decision- maker yourself or by using diplomacy in talking to the people concerned.

Conflicts can sometimes arise as a result of schedules. For example, one team member might want more time for a group of activities, which a colleague feels is unnecessary. Work through the schedule with both parties to arrive at a solution that suits everyone.

◀ BEING A DIPLOMAT
When a conflict between team members threatens the project's success, you will have to mediate. Look for a solution that brings some source of satisfaction to each party. Such a compromise will allow the project to move on.

CASE STUDY

Sally, a key member of the project team, was responsible for leading a small team of her own. As the project got under way, Tom, the project manager, was surprised to see that Gerald, one of Sally's most competent and confident team members, was contributing very little to team meetings. He took Gerald aside informally and asked how he was getting on. Although Tom was reluctant to criticize Sally,

by listening carefully, Tom realized that Gerald had been used to far more involvement in making decisions on other project teams he had worked for. It was evident that Gerald found Sally too abrupt. Tom approached Sally and asked her to think about her leadership style with Gerald. As a result, she spent more time discussing issues with him, and Gerald went on to play a far more active part in team meetings once again.

◀ **LEADING WISELY**

Sally's abrupt approach and her tendency to make all the decisions was very demotivating for Gerald, who liked to be able to use his initiative. Rather than take matters into his own hands, Tom asked Sally to consider the matter and take any action she deemed appropriate. Sally decided to make a point of involving Gerald more to make him feel valued. As a result, his performance soon began to improve.

STANDING BACK

It can be a hard lesson to learn that a good leader will allow people to make a mistake. You may, from your experience, know that the team is taking a decision that is not in the best interests of the project. But if you take control, you are not necessarily helping them to improve. If they never see the effects of their decisions, they will never learn which ones led to difficulties. Obviously, you must use your discretion as to when to step back. The team's development is important, but not as vital as achieving the objectives of the project.

68 Show your team respect, and they will show it to you.

69 Introduce new ideas to maintain the team's interest.

EXERCISING LEADERSHIP SKILLS

To lead your team effectively, you must:
- Ensure that everyone is working toward agreed, shared objectives;
- Criticize constructively, and praise good work as well as find fault;
- Monitor team members' activities continuously by obtaining effective feedback, such as regular reports;
- Constantly encourage and organize the generation of new ideas within the team, using techniques such as brainstorming;
- Always insist on the highest standards of execution from team members;
- Develop the individual and collective skills of the team, and seek to strengthen them by training and recruitment.

DEVELOPING TEAMWORK

For a team to be successful, people must learn to pull together. Encourage teamwork by promoting a positive atmosphere in which people compete with ideas rather than egos, and recognize the team's changing needs as it progresses through the project.

70 When individuals perform well, praise them in front of the team.

CULTURAL DIFFERENCES

Project managers in the US often use rousing speeches and rhetoric to motivate staff and build team spirit. In the UK, an eloquent speech will also strengthen commitment, but the approach has to be far more subtle. In Japan, managers seek to build strong ties of loyalty by emphasizing the importance of the project to the company.

ENCOURAGING TEAMWORK

Make sure that each member of the team recognizes the value that everyone else is bringing to the project. Encourage them to appreciate one another's skills and capabilities, and to work together to achieve the highest standards. Praise the team as well as individuals so that everyone feels that they are doing a good job. If everyone understands who is playing which role and who has responsibility for what, there should be no reason for conflict and uncertainty. As project manager, you must be seen to be fair to everyone, since showing any favoritism can also lead to dissent. Use project review meetings to strengthen teamwork and help build team confidence.

UNDERSTANDING TEAM DEVELOPMENT

All teams go through a series of stages as they develop, described as forming, storming, norming, and performing. Your aim is to move the team on to the performing stage, where they are working well together, as quickly as possible. With strong leadership, the difficult initial stages of bringing the team together and settling them into the project can be negotiated smoothly. Use your authority to swiftly defuse any conflict and put a stop to any early political maneuvering.

POINTS TO REMEMBER

- Not every team member will be equally committed to the project at the outset.
- It should be expected that everyone will have to go through the storming stage, but this can be creative if managed positively.
- It is important to develop creative team members rather than conformists.
- People need to be comfortable to work well together.

DEALING WITH STAGES IN THE LIFE OF A PROJECT TEAM

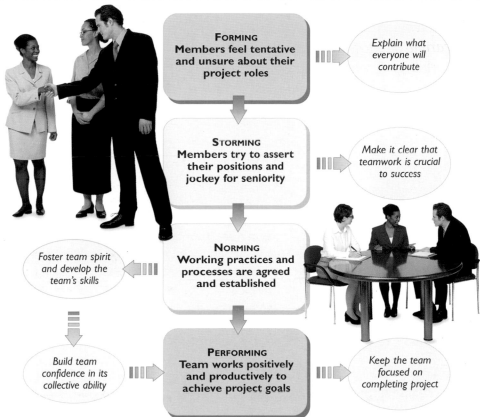

FORMING
Members feel tentative and unsure about their project roles

Explain what everyone will contribute

STORMING
Members try to assert their positions and jockey for seniority

Make it clear that teamwork is crucial to success

NORMING
Working practices and processes are agreed and established

Foster team spirit and develop the team's skills

Build team confidence in its collective ability

PERFORMING
Team works positively and productively to achieve project goals

Keep the team focused on completing project

MAINTAINING MOMENTUM

There are two more stages that occur in a team's long-term life, known as "boring" and "mourning." The first applies to a project lasting a long time, where team members may stop looking for new challenges or new and improved ways of doing things. Put in effort at this stage to encourage innovation. Mourning occurs when a team has bonded well and reacts to a member's departure by grieving their loss. Decide how to replace that person and reassure remaining team members that you have every confidence in their ability.

71 Help people to define problems for themselves.

72 Remember that relationships will change over time.

MAKING TEAM DECISIONS

When mapping out the future course of the project, quality decision-making is paramount. To ensure that you make the right decisions as a team, establish a logical process that you follow every time. Then use feedback to double-check quality.

73 Ensure that you know all the facts before making a decision.

POINTS TO REMEMBER

- Using a decision-making process may take time initially, but speed will improve with experience.
- The decision-making process can be clearly explained to sponsors and stakeholders.
- People implement decisions more willingly when they have participated in them.

USING A LOGICAL PROCESS

Following the same process in making every decision has several benefits. The team becomes faster at decision-making, since if everyone knows the process, they quickly eliminate invalid options and come to the most sensible alternative. The quality of decisions improves because using a process removes some of the guesswork and, finally, any team members who might initially have been against a decision are more likely to accept it if it has been reached via a process of consensus.

DEFINING THE IDEAL

The team must agree on the criteria against which they wish to measure a decision and the ideal performance against each criterion. Suppose, for example, you are looking at two options for a supplier of services to the project. Ask team members to brainstorm what an ideal solution would look like. Ask the questions, "What do we want this solution to do for us?", and "What benefits should we look for?". This list then gives the team a way of filtering options and comparing the alternatives.

▼ AGREEING CRITERIA
Brainstorm a list of criteria against which you will measure decisions, and ask a team member to record each suggestion on a flipchart so that everyone is using the same wording to describe the ideal.

EVALUATING OPTIONS

With the team's help, identify which criteria are the most important. You may find that three or four stand out as being vital. Now measure all your options against the ideal agreed for each criterion. The process is logical, but good creative thinking is still needed to evaluate the options effectively. Having carried out this evaluation, you may find that the decision is obvious. If not, take the next most important criterion and repeat the exercise. Continue until one option stands out, or until the team is certain that, say, two options have nothing between them. Where that is the case, choose the option you believe will be the most acceptable to your sponsor and other stakeholders.

74 Encourage debate on all the options to gain a wider perspective.

75 Ask an objective critic to look at your decision and give you feedback.

MAKING SAFE DECISIONS

What would be the impact if you made a wrong decision? If it would be catastrophic, you may want to think again and find a less risky route. Finally use the acronym SAFE to validate the choice. SAFE stands for:

- Suitable: is the decision really the most suitable one, given the current state of the project?
- Acceptable: is the decision acceptable to all the stakeholders who have an interest in it?
- Feasible: will it be practical and feasible to implement the solution, given the project's time and resource constraints?

- Enduring: will the solution endure to the end of the project and further into the long term?

Remember that the SAFE test can be applied as a quick and useful check for any decision made by teams or individuals.

VALIDATING DECISIONS ▶

Check that you have made the right decisions by asking your sponsor or other stakeholders, such as customers or suppliers, for their views.

MANAGING INFORMATION

*E*veryone must have easy access to key project information whenever they need it. You can ensure that all the project data is kept up to date and recorded efficiently by setting up a knowledge center and appointing a coordinator to manage it.

76 Keep notes of errors made and lessons learned for future reference.

77 Index information clearly to make it more accessible.

78 Check that data is being updated on a regular basis.

ASSESSING INFORMATION

During the life of a project you will produce a wealth of data. Each item of information should be regarded as potentially valuable, either to your own project or to a subsequent one. It will be obvious what must be stored, but try to think more widely. If, for example, a project involves researching a benchmark for productivity, remember that this may be of interest to other parts of the organization. Any work undertaken on risk management, new techniques used, or even the way in which the team has been structured could prove valuable in the future.

ORGANIZING DATA

Project data can be grouped into two types: general planning information, such as the vision statement, objectives, master schedule, and network diagram; and general data, such as any background information that might be needed to carry out activities. It may be a good idea to divide activity information into three further groups: completed activities; activities currently in progress; and activities still to be started. In this way, everyone will know exactly where to look for the information they need. Beware of amassing lots of unnecessary data, however, because this will simply clog up what should be an efficient, easy-to-use system.

THINGS TO DO

1. Explain to the team what type of information is to go into the knowledge center.
2. Ensure that the knowledge coordinator has the necessary software tools to run the center efficiently.
3. Ask the coordinator to remind people of deadlines for completing activities and progress reports.

APPOINTING A COORDINATOR

In projects where the information flow is limited, you will probably be able to manage the data yourself. However, in a large project with a mass of information, it will pay dividends to put a team member in charge of the knowledge center, either full-time or part-time. Such a person is known as the knowledge coordinator, and the most likely candidate for the job is the team member who most takes on the role of coordinator. He or she will keep the planning documentation up to date and collect, index, and make available all the important project information gathered by the team.

CULTURAL DIFFERENCES

Business organizations in North America tend to lead the way when it comes to saving information and making it available to the organization as a whole. Most organizations in the US employ knowledge coordinators at several levels, meaning that project managers are able to access information quickly and easily. Knowledge coordinators are gradually making their presence felt in Europe as their importance becomes recognized.

Team member updates coordinator on progress of an activity

Coordinator records information for knowledge centre

◄ UPDATING PROJECT INFORMATION

The knowledge coordinator plays an important role as the administrator of the project plan, collecting progress reports, updating network diagrams, Gantt charts, and activity reports.

COMMUNICATING CLEARLY

The better the communication, the more smoothly a project will flow. Make sure that everyone who needs it has easy access to project information, and that you encourage two-way communication by listening and asking for feedback.

79 Avoid sending any message that could hinder, rather than help, your project.

80 Tell the team what they want and need to know.

81 Meet often with team members on a one-on-one basis.

SHARING KNOWLEDGE

Consider who needs what information, in what format, and when. Refer to the list of stakeholders in the start-up report to ensure that noone is forgotten. Concentrate on people whose access to information will be crucial to the project, but do not ignore others with less significant roles. Plan how you are going to make the information available, bearing in mind that these activities should take up as little time as possible. Your knowledge coordinator must know what the priorities are. For example, if a customer changes requirements, the team needs to know urgently.

USING INFORMATION TECHNOLOGY

Make the most of new technology to improve communications. Email is an extremely useful time-saving device, provided it is handled correctly. The main point to remember is that you receive as many emails as you send, which means that you should think carefully before writing each message. Is it absolutely vital to send a message now? Is it the most effective means of communication for the current situation? As a guideline, send as few emails as possible to do the job well, and you will get the best out of electronic communication. Take care too, with compatibility. Emailing an electronic file to someone who does not have the same software results in an immediate communication breakdown. This wastes time.

ENCOURAGING TWO-WAY COMMUNICATION

The team is the primary conduit for information between the customer, other stakeholders, and you, the project manager. It is important to encourage honest feedback. Use open questions, such as the ones below, to ascertain their real feelings and opinions.

How do you think we could improve the way we are working on this project?

How are our customers reacting to the work we are doing – do they appear to be satisfied?

Having completed that activity, is there anything you would change if you had to do it again?

Are you aware of any negative reactions concerning the progress of the project?

LISTENING TO OTHERS

Encourage the project team to be open and honest with you by showing that you value their opinions and are willing to listen to them. Make it clear that even negative feedback is viewed as a positive opportunity for improvement, and ensure that team members are not intimidated by fear of any repercussions when they do express criticisms. Keep your door open for stakeholders, too – it is important that they feel they can approach you with queries or problems. Always listen to people carefully – because only through listening can you determine whether your messages have really been understood.

82 Be interested both in what people say and how they are saying it.

Colleague provides both negative and positive feedback

Team member feels free to voice an honest opinion

INVITING ▶ FEEDBACK
Take team members aside, either individually or in small groups, and solicit feedback by asking for their comments on how they think the project is progressing.

MONITORING PERFORMANCE

Effective monitoring keeps a project on track in terms of performance, time, and cost. Focus on your plan while acting fast to tackle problems and changes in order to stay on course.

TRACKING PROGRESS

Even the best-laid plans can go awry, which is why it is crucial to have an early-warning monitoring system. Make sure that you understand what effective monitoring involves and how to set up a process that will highlight potential problems.

83 Keep comparing current schedules and budgets against the original plan.

84 Never relax control, even when all is going to plan.

85 Ask the team for ideas on speeding up progress.

MONITORING EFFECTIVELY

Keeping control of a project involves carefully managing your plan to keep it moving forward smoothly. Effective monitoring allows you to gather information so that you can measure and adjust progress toward the project's goals. It enables you to communicate project progress and changes to team members, stakeholders, superiors, and customers, and gives you the justification for making any necessary adjustments to the plan. It also enables you to measure current progress against that set out in the original plan.

MONITORING SUPPLIERS

External suppliers can be a threat, since you do not have direct control over their resources. Remember to ensure that you monitor their progress, too. Make them feel part of the team by inviting them to meetings and informal gatherings. This will help you to track their progress throughout their involvement in the project, rather than only when they are due to deliver.

USING REPORTS

Anyone responsible for an activity or a milestone must report on progress. Encourage the team to take reports seriously, and to submit them on time. Reports should record the current state of the project, achievements since the last report, and potential problems, opportunities, or threats to milestones. As project manager, you review the reports and summarize the current position for your sponsor and stakeholders. Having gauged the importance of issues reported, use a red, amber, and green status system to help you draw up your review meeting agenda, so that the most urgent items, or those with red status, take priority.

UNDERSTANDING THE MONITORING PROCESS

Team members prepare progress reports

Project manager summarizes for sponsor and stakeholders

Items for discussion are listed on regular review meeting agenda

Regular review meeting is held to resolve issues and assess progress

Periodic meetings are held to monitor milestones

Plans are updated if necessary to keep project on track

POINTS TO REMEMBER

- If the project is a large or complex one, reports will be required more frequently.

- When a project involves tackling issues for the first time, tight and frequent controls should be established.

- If team members are used to working on their own, too frequent monitoring may be counterproductive.

CONSIDERING TIMING

Think about how often you will need progress reports and review meetings. You may require weekly or even daily reports, depending on the potential harm a problem could do to the project were it not detected and reported. Regular review meetings provide an opportunity to resolve issues, discuss progress, and review performance. You should hold reviews at least once a month, and probably more often on a complex project, or a project going through a very demanding phase.

HOLDING REVIEW MEETINGS

Review meetings are held throughout the life of a project to discuss progress and achievements and mark milestones. Run these meetings effectively to encourage teamwork and provide all involved with an accurate picture of how the project is faring.

86 Encourage team members to speak out on any aspect of the project.

87 Ensure that review meetings are not tediously long.

88 If progress has been made, praise people's efforts.

PLANNING A REVIEW

There are two types of review meeting. A regular formal review occurs at least monthly to monitor detailed achievements and issues in implementing the plan. An event-driven review, to which stakeholders, such as your sponsor, will be invited is held as certain milestones are arrived at. These meetings are concerned with the business objectives of the project. They may be called to check that the project is meeting certain criteria. It is sometimes true that if the criteria are not met, the future of the project will be in doubt.

SELECTING ATTENDEES

You will need your sponsor at some meetings, but probably not all. Key team members will almost certainly attend all reviews, while other members should attend only if there is a valid reason for their attendance, or their time will be wasted. If someone need only be present for one or two items, estimate when you will reach those items and ask them to arrive a few minutes earlier. If you need to make a decision, ensure that the person with the authority to make the decision is present and that all the necessary information is available.

QUESTIONS TO ASK YOURSELF

Q Will every attendee have a valid contribution to make?

Q Are there some team members who only need to attend part of the meeting?

Q Is this team member attending the meeting because they have always done so, rather than for a specific purpose?

Q Does the absence of anyone pose a threat to the project?

| Use progress report to compile agenda | Decide who needs to attend review | Circulate agenda to participants |

CHAIRING A REVIEW

The key to chairing a review meeting successfully is good discipline. Summarize the objectives at the outset and allocate time to each item on the agenda. Focus the team on appraisal rather than analysis, using questions such as, "How is the project going?" and "What new issues have arisen since the last meeting?". Your aim is to keep everyone up to date with progress and give them a shared understanding of what is happening.

ESTABLISHING ▶ DISCIPLINE
Be prepared to be tough on latecomers. Make it clear from the outset that such behavior is unacceptable, stressing the fact that one person's lateness wastes everyone's time.

▲ PREPARING FOR MEETINGS
Key decisions are made at review meetings, so it is essential to prepare for them well. Send out agendas in advance to give the team time to do preparation work, too.

Team member arrives late for meeting

Project manager sets standards for punctuality in future

89 Remind people of the agenda when they stray from it.

90 Always seek to end a meeting on a positive note.

REINFORCING OBJECTIVES

Ensure that you return to the objectives throughout the meeting, recording which have been achieved, which remain, and how the meeting is going against the time plan. If people are straying from the point or talking irrelevantly, bring the discussion back to the main issue by saying, for example, "We are not here to discuss that today – let's get back to the point." At appropriate moments, summarize the views and decisions made. As objectives are achieved, consider releasing those people who are no longer needed.

OVERCOMING PROBLEMS

However sound the project plan, once you start to operate in the real world, problems will occur. Encourage team members to raise concerns, and use the discipline of problem-solving techniques to tackle difficulties as they arise.

91 Look at every aspect of a problem before trying to resolve it.

92 Remember that forewarned is forearmed.

93 Ask team members to bring you solutions as well as problems.

RAISING CONCERNS

Your primary aim is to identify problems early enough to prevent their becoming crises. It is far more difficult to take action when a problem has become urgent. Although you may create extra work by examining problems that do not ultimately occur, it is better to err on the side of caution than to find that a problem has escalated without your knowledge. With experience, the team will get better at judging whether and when to raise a concern. You should be particularly concerned to see that problems with a high impact on the project are spotted and action taken before they become high urgency as well.

CASE STUDY

John was put in charge of a new project to improve the inventory control system in his organization's main warehouse. However, once the project was under way, he was approached by Tom, the warehouse manager, who told John that he and his warehouse staff were having to spend an inordinate amount of time chasing up deliveries deemed to be late by a member of the project team. Tom explained that most of the queries raised by the team member were unnecessary, because the goods were generally delivered only a few hours late, and so asking warehouse staff to chase them seemed pointless. John called Tom and the project team together to agree when a query really needed to be raised. This reduced the strain on warehouse staff, and gave everyone more time to chase up deliveries that really were late.

◀ **HANDLING TENSIONS**
Since projects tend to be carried out alongside regular business operations, problems often result when the two are ongoing. In this case, the project members were trying to make improvements by identifying late deliveries. But by raising concerns too early, they were disrupting the usual warehouse work. By agreeing when to raise concerns, both teams were able to do their jobs more effectively.

DEALING WITH PROBLEMS

> **Listen to concerns raised by team members**

> **Discuss their impact and, if significant, look at the options with the team**

> **Take an overview and make a final decision**

> **Update the plan if the decision involves altering course**

> **Send updated plan to knowledge coordinator**

RESOLVING DIFFICULTIES

A useful problem-solving technique is to home in on four areas to find out which is causing difficulty. For example, if production is falling short of target, consider which of the following four P's could be the culprit:

- **People** Is the problem occurring because people do not have the right skills or support?
- **Product** Is there something wrong in the design of the product or the production method?
- **Process** Would an improvement in one of your business processes cure the problem?
- **Procurement** Is it something to do with the products and services we buy?

DO'S AND DON'TS

✔ Do keep in constant touch with suppliers who may be causing you problems.

✔ Do correct a recurring problem by changing a process.

✘ Don't start to resolve an issue until you have understood the whole problem.

✘ Don't assume that team members have problem-solving skills

UPDATING THE PLAN

Ask your project coordinator to document ongoing problem-solving activities in the knowledge center as open items, and assess them at your regular review meetings. Major issues may result in the need to make significant changes to the plan. It is even possible that new information or a change in the external environment will invalidate the project as it stands. Suppose, for example, that a competitor brings out a new product using components that makes your project irrelevant. This would be unfortunate, but since your priority is to deliver value to your organization, the best value may lie in scrapping the project.

94 Keep stakeholders informed if you change the plan.

95 Identify the cause of a problem to prevent it from happening again.

DEALING WITH CHANGE

Change is inevitable on projects, so flexibility is vital. Whether customers revise a brief or senior managers alter the scope of a project, you must be able to negotiate changes, adapt the plan, and keep everyone informed about what is happening.

96 Look at alternatives before changing a major component of the plan.

97 Explain the benefits of change to those affected by it.

98 Seek approval for any changes as quickly as possible.

UNDERSTANDING CHANGE

Some changes will be within your control, such as shortening the schedule because you and your team are learning how to complete activities more quickly as you work through the plan. Other changes will be imposed upon you, such as when a customer asks for something different, or a superior decides to poach two of your key team members to do another job. Alternatively, your monitoring system may have highlighted the need for a change to avoid a potential problem or threat. Whenever the need for change arises, it is vital to be able to adjust the project plan as necessary. You must also be able to measure whether the desired effect on the project has been achieved, so that you will know if the change has been successful.

◀ **DISCUSSING CHANGE**
Bring the team together to evaluate how changes might affect the project plan, looking at the proposed alterations against your original goals, order of activities, budget, people, resources, and time.

ASSESSING IMPACT

Before you commit to making any changes, assess their impact on the project. Ask the team to review how they will affect the schedule, budget, and resources. Examine the alternatives: is there another way to accomplish the project's objectives? If changes have to be made for the project to move forward, document them on the original plan, and gain approval from superiors, sponsors, and stakeholders before implementing them.

RESISTING UNNECESSARY OR DETRIMENTAL CHANGES

When change is dictated, perhaps by a superior or sponsor, it may not always make sense. Determine whether carrying out the change will affect the eventual outcome of the project. If the change seems to be frivolous, or will have a negative impact on the project, make those imposing it aware of the benefits that will be lost. Be prepared to fight your corner, or to offer alternative solutions that will ensure your project still meets its objectives.

TACKLING CHANGE EFFECTIVELY

Discuss impact of change with the team

If change has a major impact, look at the alternatives

Document necessary changes on original plan

Seek approval from stakeholders and superiors

Inform everyone on the project of changes as soon as possible

THINGS TO DO

1. Talk to the team about how changes will affect them.
2. Explain the rationale behind the changes and why they had to happen.
3. Redefine new objectives, time frames, or roles.
4. Discuss issues individually if anyone is still unhappy about the changes.

COMMUNICATING CHANGE

If your team has been working hard to achieve one set of objectives and is suddenly told that the goal posts have changed, people will inevitably feel demotivated. Talk to the team about change as soon as possible, particularly if roles are affected. Focus on the positive aspects of change, and be frank about why it is happening. Take people's concerns seriously, listen to their ideas, but stress the need to adapt as quickly as possible. Finally, spell out clearly any new expectations, schedules, or objectives in writing, so that everyone understands what should happen next.

MAXIMIZING IMPACT

As a project draws to a close, it is important to evaluate exactly what has been achieved and what can be learned for the next time. Take your project through a formal closure process that ties up all loose ends and marks its success.

99 Evaluate this project well to better manage the next one.

QUESTIONS TO ASK YOURSELF

Q Is the sponsor satisfied that the original aims and business objectives of the project have been met?

Q Is the customer satisfied that he or she is receiving an improved service?

Q Have we spoken to all our stakeholders about final results?

Q Have I thanked all the contributors to the project?

Q Have all new insights and ideas been recorded?

SEEING PROJECTS THROUGH

Inevitably toward the end of a project, some team members will start to move to new assignments. It is important to keep remaining team members focused on final objectives until the very end of the project, when you write a formal closure report and hold a final meeting. You may have to protect your resources from being moved off the project too early, particularly if you want to avoid an untidy ending where the benefits are dissipated because final activities are completed haphazardly. Finally, you want your organization to learn as much as possible from the exercise and to ensure that the results you predicted are delivered in full.

LEARNING FROM PROJECTS

Talk to your knowledge coordinator about publishing a report explaining what the project achieved, and detailing relevant information such as facts gathered and processes used. If the project is likely to be repeated, meet with team members to go through the project from start to finish. Ask people to point out where, with hindsight, they could have made improvements. Your organization may benefit significantly if you produce a template for such a project plan, including an outline network and Gantt chart.

100 Ensure that you have not left any jobs unfinished.

101 Publicize the achievements of the project team.

COMPILING A CLOSURE REPORT

PARTS OF REPORT	FACTORS TO CONSIDER
PERFORMANCE INDICATORS A comparison of what the project has achieved against the original targets set.	● Explain in full the reasons for any variances between targets and actual achievements. ● Word the comparison in a way that validates the original investment appraisal.
RESOURCE UTILIZATION An assessment of the resources planned and those that were actually used.	● If the project used more or fewer resources than expected, state the reasons why. ● Include any information that will validate the budget allocated to the project.
STRENGTHS AND WEAKNESSES An appraisal of what went well on the project and what went wrong, or caused problems.	● Ask team members for input in order to conduct as thorough an analysis as possible. ● Make sure that the information recorded enables others to learn from this experience.
SUCCESS FACTORS A record of the top 10 factors judged as critical to the success of your project	● List your success factors with the help of the team, sponsor, and stakeholders. ● Create a list that will provide focus for future project managers.

THANKING THE TEAM

It is important that all the members of the team go their separate ways feeling as positive as possible, especially since you may want to work with the same people on subsequent projects. Indeed, good relationships should be kept up with all the stakeholders. Talk to everyone individually to thank them for their contributions. Hold a final meeting at which your sponsor can confirm that the project has indeed brought benefits and thank the team for its efforts. Your customers, in particular, may welcome an opportunity to express how they have found the results of the project.

▼ **CELEBRATING SUCCESS**

Mark the end of a project with a celebration in recognition of the team's hard work and effort. This allows people to say their farewells and realize their achievements in a convivial atmosphere.

ASSESSING YOUR PROJECT MANAGEMENT SKILLS

*E*valuate your ability to think strategically by responding to the following statements, marking the option closest to your experience. Be as honest as you can: if your answer is "never," circle Option 1; if it is "always," circle Option 4, and so on. Add your scores together, and refer to the Analysis to see how well you scored. Use your answers to identify the areas that most need improvement.

OPTIONS
1 Never
2 Occasionally
3 Frequently
4 Always

1 I check whether I should treat a series of actions as a project.

| 1 | 2 | 3 | 4 |

2 I set specific, measurable objectives for projects.

| 1 | 2 | 3 | 4 |

3 I take time to plan a project thoroughly before starting work.

| 1 | 2 | 3 | 4 |

4 I fully understand the difficulties I face in achieving a project's objectives.

| 1 | 2 | 3 | 4 |

5 I have identified which of my project's resources are occupied on other projects.

| 1 | 2 | 3 | 4 |

6 I keep in regular contact with all stakeholders involved in my projects.

| 1 | 2 | 3 | 4 |

7 I always consider what the ideal outcome of a project would be.

1   2   3   4

8 I ensure that everyone clearly understands the project's objectives.

1   2   3   4

9 I set business targets for each part of a project.

1   2   3   4

10 I check that a project will not unnecessarily change what already works.

1   2   3   4

11 I compile a full list of project activities before I place them in correct order.

1   2   3   4

12 I calculate manpower time and elapsed time of all project activities.

1   2   3   4

13 I make sure all the key people have approved the plan before I start a project.

1   2   3   4

14 I liaise with the finance department to check the costs of a project.

1   2   3   4

15 I generally start project implementation with a pilot.

1   2   3   4

16 I keep a network diagram up to date throughout a project.

1   2   3   4

17 I inform all interested parties of changes to project resource requirements.

1 2 3 4

18 I prepare contingency plans for all major risks to the project.

1 2 3 4

19 I adapt my leadership style to suit circumstances and individuals.

1 2 3 4

20 I consider how best to develop my teams' skills.

1 2 3 4

21 I consider how well new team members will fit in with the rest of the team.

1 2 3 4

22 I make sure each team member knows exactly what is expected of them.

1 2 3 4

23 I use my sponsor to help motivate my team.

1 2 3 4

24 I have documented and circulated the primary milestones of the project.

1 2 3 4

25 I ensure that every team member has access to the information they need.

1 2 3 4

26 I avoid keeping secrets from the project team and stakeholders.

1 2 3 4

27 I ask people to attend review meetings only if they really need to be present.

| 1 | 2 | 3 | 4 |

28 I use the same standard method of reporting progress to all stakeholders.

| 1 | 2 | 3 | 4 |

29 I prepare the objectives and agenda of meetings.

| 1 | 2 | 3 | 4 |

30 I use a logical process to make decisions with my project team.

| 1 | 2 | 3 | 4 |

31 I keep my sponsor fully up to date with progress on the project plan.

| 1 | 2 | 3 | 4 |

32 I use problem-solving techniques to arrive at decisions.

| 1 | 2 | 3 | 4 |

ANALYSIS

Now you have completed the self-assessment, add up your total score and check your performance by referring to the corresponding evaluation below. Whatever level of success you have achieved, there is always room for improvement. Identify your weakest areas and refer to the relevant sections to refine your skills.

32–64: You are not yet sufficiently well-organized to ensure that a complex project will achieve its objectives. Review the planning process thoroughly and make sure that you follow it through step-by-step.

65–95: You are a reasonably effective project manager, but need to address some weak points.

96–128: You are an excellent project manager. Be careful not to become complacent or to let your high standards slip.

THINKING STRATEGICALLY

INTRODUCTION

The ability to plan long-term while maximizing performance in the short term is a must for managers. Thinking Strategically will help you to map out the route to success and build your analytical and team-planning skills. From researching and gathering the background information and arriving at a new strategy to reviewing and adapting it – all the key aspects of developing and implementing a strategy are clearly explained. There are 101 tips scattered throughout to give you further practical advice, while a self-assessment exercise allows you to evaluate your effectiveness as a strategic thinker. As you raise your ambitions to plan for the future, this will be an invaluable reference book to keep your thinking on course.

UNDERSTANDING STRATEGY

A strategy is a declaration of intent, defining where you want to be in the long-term. Understand the processes involved and how to avoid potential pitfalls to help you plan successful strategies.

DEFINING STRATEGY

S trategy was once defined as "the art of planning and directing large military movements and the operations of war." In business, a strategy maps out the future, setting out which products and services you will take to which markets – and how.

1 Understand why a strategy is important for you and your business.

2 If you are unsure of the strategy of your organization, ask your superior to clarify it for you.

WHY HAVE A STRATEGY?

Having a strategy enables you to ensure that day-to-day decisions fit in with the long-term interests of an organization. Without a strategy, decisions made today could have a negative impact on future results. A strategy also encourages everyone to work together to achieve common aims. Most organizations have a strategic plan at the highest level, but some do not communicate it all the way down. A strategy is equally important whether you serve external customers (those outside your organization) or internal customers (those in departments or sections within your company).

LOOKING TO THE FUTURE

Today's business environment puts pressure on people to complete urgent tasks, meet day-to-day objectives, and overcome short-term problems. This is operational, or short-term, planning – and it often tends to take precedence over planning for the future. Strategy concerns itself with what is ahead, looking at where you are going, and how to get there. Even if you already know which products and services you are taking to which markets, you will still need a strategy to make it happen.

FOLLOWING THE STRATEGIC FRAMEWORK

Analyze information to understand your position

Pinpoint your competitive advantage

Define the scope of your products and markets

Decide where you want to focus your resources

Identify, prioritize, and implement change

Continuously monitor performance and review strategy

Balances short- and long-term needs

Sees problems as opportunities to improve

Keeps calm when the unexpected occurs

Is a team player

Is a skilled communicator

▲ BEING A GOOD STRATEGIST

Effective strategists look at what is happening now in the context of where they want to go. They react positively to problems, can inspire and motivate people, and communicate well.

INVOLVING THE TEAM

To get the best from your people, it is important to work within a clear framework that details how they will be expected to help you to develop and then implement a strategic plan. Think of the methods and processes involved as a "map" that the team can follow to achieve success. By creating such a framework, you encourage the team to pull together and work to a common goal. You also promote their personal development by teaching them to think strategically.

EXAMINING THE PROCESS

There are three distinct phases to developing a new strategy: analysis, planning, and implementation. It is vital to devote time and effort to the first two stages, but also to maintain momentum throughout implementation to ensure ultimate success.

3 Involve everyone on the team in gathering information.

4 Encourage people to look objectively at the facts.

DELEGATING RESEARCH ▼

Assign fact-finding exercises to members of your team. Information can be gleaned from publications, the Internet, and from talking to customers and contacts.

ANALYZING THOROUGHLY

During the analysis phase, you will collect as much background information as you can to help you make informed decisions. This stage is crucial because the facts you have at hand will influence the direction you decide to take. You will analyze what is happening inside your organization, looking carefully at aspects of your own and other parts of the company that may influence the plan. You will also find out what your customers want, how your competitors operate, and what the research trends or developments in your industry are. Your aim is to draw up a clear statement of the strengths and weaknesses of your position as well as a list of opportunities for the future.

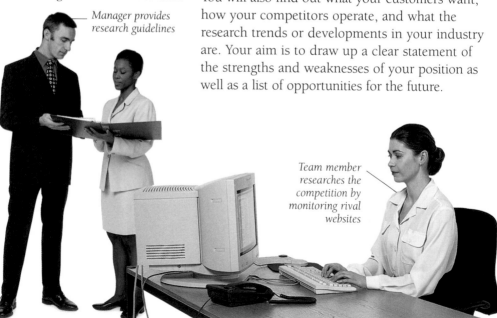

— Manager provides research guidelines

Team member researches the competition by monitoring rival websites

PLANNING STRATEGY

Having gathered all the necessary facts, the next phase is to make strategic decisions that will bring you closer to your overall aim. You will need to take into account where you have advantages over the competition and establish the boundaries within which you will operate. The first step will be to list the products and services likely to be in demand in the future, and the markets that are available to you. You will then choose which of these markets you wish to develop, whether with existing products and services or new ones. Similarly, you will choose which markets it would be beneficial to leave. The decisions you reach will help you to establish your future financial position and work out a realistic budget.

5 Set aside ample time now to avoid rushing the planning stage.

6 Be prepared to listen to your team – every step of the way.

QUESTIONS TO ASK YOURSELF

Q Can I outline the strategic process to others?

Q Do I know where to look for the information I require?

Q Am I prepared to put enough time into the first two phases of developing a new strategy?

Q Can I get the support of my superior in establishing a new strategy?

BUILDING A STRATEGY ▼
There are three stages in the strategic process: analysis provides the basis for making choices, planning provides direction, and implementation brings the results.

IMPLEMENTING STRATEGY

During the final phase of developing a strategy you will determine, on the basis of your analysis, what you are going to do and how you are going to do it. It may be possible to achieve your aims with little change to the way the team works. On the other hand, you may find that success depends upon making far-reaching changes and learning new skills. Do not make the mistake of working so hard on the analysis phase that planning and implementation receive less overall effort – this will result in less effective strategies and incomplete implementation. You will also need to communicate the strategy to everyone who needs to know about it, and adapt it to take onboard any changes in circumstances and in the activities of the rest of the organization.

Analyze ▶ Plan ▶ Implement

THINKING SHORT-
AND LONG-TERM

*The ability to differentiate between short-
and long-term thinking and strike a
balance between the two is an integral part
of strategy. Understand the importance of
both in strategic planning and you will find
it easier to achieve the right combination.*

7 Be confident about
the future but
realistic about what
you can achieve.

8 Work hard for
long-term goals
while striving for
immediate results.

KNOWING THE PITFALLS

Short-term planning deals with the here and now,
or a few weeks hence, while long-term thinking
takes you far into the future. If you focus entirely
on short-term success, you risk long-term failure.
For example, you may find yourself selling out-of-
date products or targeting markets whose
requirements have changed. If you place undue
emphasis on long-term planning, today's business
will inevitably suffer. The key is to focus on the
present to achieve the growth you need now, and
to keep one eye on the
future to ensure that good
decisions today are just
as beneficial tomorrow.

**◀ LOOKING AT THE
LONG TERM**
*Sometimes the delivery of a
quick sale is not in the best
long-term interests of the
business. Although this may
mean that you face a difficult
time with your customer in the
short term, you are more likely
to give them maximum
satisfaction in the long term.*

CASE STUDY
Elizabeth worked for a
company that sold automated
warehouse equipment. One
of her customers was
experiencing problems caused
by a lack of capacity on a
moving belt. Elizabeth wished
to sell her customer two new
belts to rectify the situation.
However, when she placed an
order for the belts with her
production department, she
was told that there was a new
strategy to replace the old

belts with new, superior, higher-
tech products in about nine
months' time. She informed
her customer of this fact and
also worked out a temporary
solution to alleviate his
problem. Although Elizabeth
did not receive an order for
short-term delivery, she did
offer a much better solution to
her customer, which resulted in
a larger order at a later date,
as well as the customer's
continued goodwill and
assured long-term business.

9 Make the effort to build strategic thinking into your everyday life.

ACHIEVING BALANCE

Striking the right balance between short- and long-term thinking takes effort and discipline. If you cancel a strategy meeting, it will have no short-term impact, but if you fail to return a customer's call, you could lose an order. It is hardly surprising, then, that unless a team is determined to give time to strategic issues, short-term operational tasks will always take priority. Allocate the appropriate time and resources to operations and strategy and stick to that plan. For example, you might decide to set aside three months to develop a new strategy, allocating two days of meetings to get started, and one day a week thereafter. That still leaves plenty of time for dealing with operational issues.

◀ **WORKING OUT A TIMETABLE**
By working out a timetable for producing and maintaining your strategic plan, you are committed to focusing on the long term. Keep to that timetable and avoid being distracted by operational issues.

WORKING STRATEGICALLY

Strategy is a continuous process; even when your plan becomes operational, you cannot neglect future planning. Set aside one day each month to discuss maintaining and developing the plan with the team. The most successful business people allow at least half a day per week to implement the strategic part of their jobs. They talk to customers regularly and review the roles of their team. Do a little work often on the plan to keep it fresh and ensure that team members stay committed and focused.

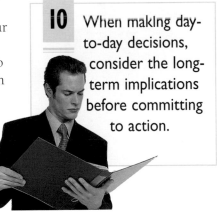

10 When making day-to-day decisions, consider the long-term implications before committing to action.

PREPARING FOR STRATEGIC SUCCESS

*A*n effective strategic plan has accurate information, strong ideas, and committed people at its core. Involve the right people from the outset, then encourage them to research facts, and brainstorm for ideas to achieve the best possible plan.

 11 Make every step in the planning process practical and achievable.

QUESTIONS TO ASK YOURSELF

Q Will this person add to the quality of the plan?

Q Do I need his/her commitment to implement the plan fully and successfully?

Q Does the plan require people with specific knowledge and/or expertise?

Q Will this person work well with the rest of the team?

INVOLVING KEY PEOPLE

An effective team is essential for a successful strategy. Involve the whole team early on in the planning so that they feel part of the process. Managers sometimes avoid team planning at this stage because they are not sure that all the people involved will play a significant role in implementing the strategy at a later date. Yet team planning is always useful: it allows you to assess team members as well as giving them the chance to decide if they are happy to work within the new strategy as it develops, or whether they feel they could make a greater contribution in another environment. Your core team should comprise all those people responsible for implementing the plan and achieving its aims.

◀ ASSESSING TEAMS
Involving key team members in strategy planning from the outset enables you to assess whether they have the qualities necessary to help you implement the plan in the future.

INVOLVING OTHERS

People with an interest in or an influence on the new strategy are known as "stakeholders." Foster good relations with them, since they often provide experience or information, or can help with the analysis and decision-making. Strategic planning often requires people from different areas of the organization, such as sales and production staff, to formulate a plan together. This spirit of cooperation invariably produces the best results. The more involved key people feel in the process, the more likely they are to support the output and help during the implementation phase. Beware of involving too many people, however, as this may slow down the whole process. Too large a team is also likely to operate like a committee where finding an agreed decision becomes more important than finding the right one.

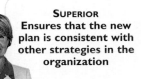

SUPERIOR
Ensures that the new plan is consistent with other strategies in the organization

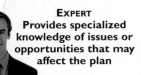

EXPERT
Provides specialized knowledge of issues or opportunities that may affect the plan

BACKER
Lends support to the strategic plan by providing resources or budgets

TEAM
Relies on support from stakeholders inside and outside the organization

KEY CUSTOMER/SUPPLIER
Provides valuable information on future requirements and new possibilities

12 Change the make-up of the team if you feel you need to strengthen it.

Gaining Commitment

Once you have developed your strategy, it is vital that the team does not start to lose interest during implementation. It is your role as manager to ensure that everyone understands the importance of the long-term strategy and is dedicated to making it happen. First, everyone should agree that a new strategy is needed. Second, everyone involved in the strategic process must feel confident that, guided by their manager, they have developed the right plan. Third, everyone must feel personally committed to making the strategy happen. Make the team aware that operational pressures are not an excuse for missing target dates involved in implementing the strategy.

13 Make sure team members remain committed to achieving the plan.

14 Beware of jumping to conclusions before you have all the facts at hand.

Points to Remember

- A positive, motivational atmosphere can be created by involving everyone and being open to suggestions.
- Your own commitment to the strategy can be used as an example for others.
- The team should be encouraged to check the facts.
- Brainstorming begins at the beginning and never stops throughout the strategic process.

Getting the Right Facts

The importance of basing your strategy on the right information cannot be stressed enough. Poor data may lead to a crisis when the correct facts come to light, meaning the whole plan may need to be changed. The same goes for using out-of-date facts or for failing to collect all the information. Bear in mind that a poor strategic plan can lead to long-term failure and disappointing short-term results. At some stage, you will have to stop gathering facts in order to move on, even if you do not have everything you need. Resolve that at a later date.

Avoiding Guesswork

Successful strategies must have strong factual foundations. Relying on guesswork or estimates could lead to a strategy collapsing, so avoid these at all costs, no matter how convincing they appear. Get all the relevant information before reaching a conclusion. Where there is a lack of data, look at the range of options on which you will base decisions once the information becomes known.

15 Know when to move on – over-analysis can lead to paralysis.

BRAINSTORMING IDEAS

Coming up with ideas is paramount in strategic planning, whether it is thinking of key trends to be monitored, pinpointing possible product choices that could be made, or suggesting new and innovative ways to gain a competitive advantage. Throughout the strategic process, you and your team should meet regularly to brainstorm ideas. Write down a number of ideas in no particular order on, say, a flipchart, refine them, and then sort them into groups. The finished list will become part of the plan, although it will take several sessions to create the final strategic plan.

 16 Give everybody at a meeting the chance to air their views in turn.

▼ ENCOURAGING CREATIVITY

To get the most from a brainstorming session, create a comfortable, relaxed environment where everyone feels free to express ideas. Seating should be kept informal, with no desks.

Each team member takes a turn to record ideas on a flipchart

Team member feels encouraged to be spontaneous

Team member listens and contributes without taking notes

Team leader expresses opinions but does not dominate the debate

LOOKING TO THE FUTURE

Continuous strategic thinking in a changing world is vital if you and your business are to maintain a winning position. Anticipate change rather than simply react to it, and adapt your strategy as necessary to keep moving ahead.

17 Remember that the planning process never comes to an end.

18 Adjust plans as circumstances change – radically, if necessary.

AVOIDING STRATEGIC DRIFT ▼
This diagram illustrates how, by anticipating change in the external environment, the proactive team manages to give customers what they want before they even ask for it. The reactive team, on the other hand, is always one step behind.

REVIEWING DECISIONS

Your strategy must be reviewed on a regular basis; the market does not stand still and neither do your competitors. A product or service that a customer has found interesting and satisfying over a long period of time may not be viewed so favorably in the future. Whole organizations have fallen flat because a product feature introduced by a competitor has been taken up by the consumer and become desirable, even fashionable. It is extremely important to be ready to embrace such changes in the market and react quickly and positively if you failed to anticipate them in the first place. But, above all, aim to be the proactive person who first brings out a new feature, not the person who simply reacts to it.

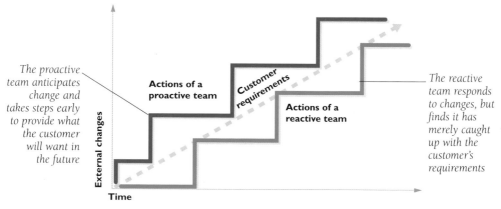

The proactive team anticipates change and takes steps early to provide what the customer will want in the future

Actions of a proactive team

Customer requirements

Actions of a reactive team

The reactive team responds to changes, but finds it has merely caught up with the customer's requirements

External changes

Time

AVOIDING PITFALLS

The best teams strive to be leading players rather than followers. Teams operating without a strategic plan find themselves constantly trying to gain lost ground. For example, customers may complain that a product lacks a desirable feature, so you put through a special order to get as near as you can to their request. Then your premium service is offered as standard by a competitor. Consequently, you lower prices or spend money to improve the service, but you still remain one step behind your customers' expectations. Their criteria for buying have changed from what they were when you devised your strategic plan initially.

▲ DETERMINING CUSTOMERS' NEEDS

Meet with customers periodically to find out what they expect from you, and carry out extensive market research on a regular basis to help you to anticipate their future needs.

19 Think the unthinkable; you can make it happen.

20 Never assume that you know what people think; always ask them.

STAYING AHEAD

To succeed in the future, it is necessary to put time and effort now into predicting what your customers will want and then guide the market toward adopting your customers' view of the future. Use the information your team gathers from sales and support staff, who have direct customer contact, to get a step ahead, and then work to maintain that lead. The most effective teams use innovation to stay in front of the market and the competition; take the example of the forward-looking garage that negotiated with a bank to install a cash machine on its forecourt long before any of its competitors.

ANALYZING YOUR POSITION

A strong strategy is derived from an analysis of your business. Assess environmental influences, customers, competition, and internal capabilities before forming your strategic plan.

EXAMINING INFLUENCES

There are many factors that may affect your performance. Study the economy, technology, and any legal and political changes related to your organization to identify new product and market trends that could influence your strategic planning.

> **21** Use analysis to lead you to strong conclusions and good decisions.

QUESTIONS TO ASK YOURSELF

Q How strong is our local currency, and will that affect our export business?

Q Does our organization take a strong line on environmental issues? If so, what does that mean for this team?

Q Are fuel prices expected to rise in the future, possibly because of tax increases, thereby reducing profits?

LOOKING AT THE ECONOMY

Most strategies depend to some extent on what is happening in the local and global economy. Look for issues that may have a radical impact first. For example, if you anticipate that interest rates will go up in the next six months and then stabilize, this may determine how and when you spend money on developing new products. Alternatively, if you sell products to or provide a service for tourists, you will want to know the best predictions for the growth of tourism in your area. Make a note of that trend and use the information when working out budgets.

EXAMINING TRENDS IN TECHNOLOGY

The dramatic pace of technological change has had an enormous impact on most organizations. The merging of communications techniques with computer information is steadily changing the way we all have to work. Guard against any dangers or problems that new technology may introduce by discussing the latest relevant technological developments at your planning meetings. If necessary, consult an expert or familiarize yourself with analysts' reports. Ask someone on the team to read the appropriate journals and give brief but concise updates to colleagues on a regular basis.

ASKING "SO WHAT?"

In analyzing your position, you will create a huge pool of data, some of it irrelevant to your strategic plan. Make the information more manageable and appropriate by subjecting it to the "So what?" question. If the answer is "So nothing," then that information has no impact on the strategy. Disregard it and move on.

22 Read widely to keep up to date with new trends and ideas.

UNDERSTANDING LEGAL AND POLITICAL CHANGES

As an increasing number of organizations, particularly in the public sector, find themselves operating within regulatory frameworks, it is vital to understand exactly what the rules are. If you are part of a government organization, you may have to take into account a change in the political party of the executive. In any case, you are subject to current employment laws which may have an impact on your strategic plan. Internal policy documents may need to be made available to the team, or you may need to ask a legal adviser to help you with your fact-gathering. Again, if you are not sure what data you need, brainstorm the possibilities with the team.

Employment lawyer advises on downsizing legislation

◀ **TALKING TO EXPERTS**
If you need information about the effect that certain legal or political changes may have upon your strategic plan, ask an expert in that field for advice.

UNDERSTANDING YOUR CUSTOMERS

The driving force behind any plan is what the customer wants from you as a supplier. Analyze why your customers buy from you and what their ideal is, then prioritize their needs to ensure that you design your strategy to serve them better.

23 Look at the service you provide from your customers' point of view.

24 Appoint a team member to discuss your organization's performance with customers.

IDENTIFYING BUYING CRITERIA

Customers trade product or service features against the price they are willing to pay for them. They also judge the quality of their relationship with a company's representatives and whether business processes give them customer satisfaction. To build customer loyalty, understand their buying criteria. What questions will they use to compare you with your competitors? Ask people in your organization who deal directly with customers for their input, and take into account potential customers as well as existing ones.

DEFINING THE IDEAL

Find out what your customers see as the ideal offering in four main areas: product, process, people, and price. Ask for their opinion either in a meeting, on the telephone, or by inviting them to be present at part of the planning session. An internal customer, for example, will tell you why he or she might turn to an external supplier to replace your service. These points make up the buying criteria and will fit into one of the four factors mentioned above.

POINTS TO REMEMBER

● Not all customers have the same desires and expectations.

● If customers are asked the right questions, they are more likely to tell you exactly what they want.

● Achieving a customer's ideal may be impossible, but knowing what it is will help you to come close.

● New or potential customers should not be overlooked.

PRIORITIZING CRITERIA

Having identified your customers' buying criteria, the next step is to decide which are the most important to them. The priorities you set now will have an impact on the decisions you make later in the planning process regarding your products, processes, people, and prices. Think about the relative importance of the criteria to each other when it comes to deciding on which changes to make to improve your service; you do not want to work hard on issues that the customer thinks less significant, particularly if that means putting less effort into issues they believe to be vital. If the team finds it difficult to agree on priorities in any of these areas, go back to your key customers again for their views and, if necessary, make good use of the brainstorming technique to discuss the possibilities.

25 Make sure that your customers' real requirements drive the plan.

▼ **SETTING PRIORITIES**
Work out customers' priorities by listing their criteria in four key areas: product (what you supply); process (how you deal with customers); people (the quality of those who deal with customers); and price (cost to the customer). Note what customers would ideally want against each one. Finally, prioritize the criteria by rating how important the ideal is to the customer on a scale of 1–10. The higher the figure the greater the priority.

A first-class product is listed as an important criterion

	Criteria	Customer Ideal	Priority
PRODUCT	Quality	Zero faults	7
	Ease of use	No special training required	10
PROCESS	Ease of ordering	Fast and efficient order systems and delivery	8
	Administration	Accurate invoices and statements	6
PEOPLE	Knowledge of their product and services	One person able to answer all questions	3
	Customer knowledge	Able to relate products to customer's needs	4
PRICE	Competitive	Lowest price available	7
	Payment terms	Favorable credit terms to allow spread payments	6

Supplying a product that is simple to use is given highest priority

Ensuring that one person can respond to all queries is rated as a lower priority

ANALYZING COMPETITORS

Understanding your customers and meeting their expectations will only result in success if your performance exceeds that of the competition. Analyze your competitors' capabilities to identify potential opportunities and threats.

26 Learn from your competitors' failures as well as their successes.

27 Use competitive analysis to build team spirit.

FOCUSING ON ANALYSIS ▼

Remember that at this stage you are not making decisions. Do not take action, even if you spot an opportunity, until you move into the planning process. Then use your findings to make the right strategic choices.

EXAMINING COMPETITORS

If you have many competitors, choose a few key ones to analyze. Obtain competitors' brochures and promotional material to ascertain what they see as their strengths and how they present them to customers, and look at trade journals for product comparisons and reviews. Customers can be a source of competitive knowledge, as can new recruits who have come from a competitor. Make a chart of your competitors' ability to meet your customers' criteria, so you can see where they are nearer to the customers' ideal than you are.

Team member looks over competitors' brochures

Leader controls meeting to prevent rash decisions

Colleague highlights weakness in a rival organization

Team member notes opportunity and resolves to exploit it in the plan later

CULTURAL DIFFERENCES

North Americans tend to have a quicker and more widespread acceptance of new technology opportunities than Europeans; this can give them a competitive advantage over their rivals in Europe. It also means that if you are marketing a new technology in Europe, the North American market cannot be used as a benchmark for its success.

ENVISAGING THE FUTURE

Most organizations see their current competitors as providers of similar products or services. But in the future this may not be the case. There is often more than one way of doing things. If, for example, you run a helicopter service ferrying people out to an exclusive conference center, a current competitor may be another contractor offering to run the same route. But future competitors might be videoconferencing companies who would render the journey completely unnecessary. Think about what your customers' requirements are likely to be in the future and research additional ways of meeting their needs. Bear in mind that your competitors are certain to be doing this, too.

ASSESSING OPPORTUNITIES

Once you have completed your competitive analysis, you will be able to see clearly where there are major differences between your capability to meet your customers' priority criteria and your competitors' ability to do the same. Where you are significantly nearer to meeting your customers' ideal than your competitors, you will probably find that later on in the planning process you will have an opportunity to exploit this fact and, by so doing, to sell more products and services.

28 Keep information on the behavior of competitors – it may come in useful later.

29 Never ignore a threat but build a way of dealing with it into the plan.

IDENTIFYING THREATS

Where your approach and abilities are similar, the customer will see no particular advantage in buying from you or your competitor. Where the competitor has a significant advantage, you may choose to reduce this threat to your success when it comes to making decisions later. Think widely about the possibilities, because other organizations will be doing the same when considering their prospects in terms of your customers.

ASSESSING YOUR SKILLS AND CAPABILITIES

*A*nalysis of processes, information systems, resources, and team skills enables you to plan within your capabilities. However, rather than allow weaknesses to limit strategy, note areas for improvement and aim to build them into the plan later.

30 Remember that no business process lasts for ever.

31 In a changing environment, everyone must find ways to improve their skills.

EXAMINING INTERNAL BUSINESS PROCESSES

Your business processes must be efficient if you are to impress customers. Examine them all closely and note those that need working on. You may need to review the way you take and confirm orders, revise terms and conditions, change how you inform staff of an order and distribute your products, and reassess the after-sales service you provide. Look particularly for duplication, gaps, and frequent areas of complaint.

ACCESSING INFORMATION

Examine how well your information systems, whether computerized or manual, provide people with the right information in the right format at the right time. Ask members of the team to note instances when their work has been delayed because they have had to spend precious time chasing information that could have been included in an easily accessible standard report or document. You may need to brainstorm to draw up a comprehensive list of information gaps. Finally, decide which of these gaps prevents the team giving a first-class service to its customers.

QUESTIONS TO ASK YOURSELF

Q Can I easily find the answers to customers' questions if I do not already know them?

Q Do I have to regularly correct information I receive?

Q Do I ever have to ask someone to wait because a certain piece of information has not yet reached me?

Q Am I always aware of how close my results actually are to my targets?

REVIEWING TEAM SKILLS

Ask people to talk about their strengths and weaknesses in relation to meeting customer needs. Try to make them feel positive about the process; after all, you are discussing formulating a new strategy that will bring the team greater success and more opportunities in the future. Review resources so you can be sure that nothing is preventing you from giving first-class service to the customer. Look at office accommodation, factory space, and warehousing, and assess how well they meet your needs now, and how suitable they will be in the future. Similarly, think about machinery, vehicles, and computer equipment.

▼ PUTTING THE TEAM AT EASE

When assessing the team's strengths and weaknesses in an open meeting, make sure everyone feels at ease. Use positive body language such as direct eye-contact.

Review internal business processes

Examine information systems

Evaluate facilities and equipment

Assess the skills and experience of the team

Agree internal capabilities

Note areas for improvement

DISCUSSING STRENGTHS AND WEAKNESSES

While some people feel secure enough to speak about their strengths and weaknesses openly, many do not. Start by discussing everyone's strengths, and it will then be easier to talk about areas for improvement, particularly if you use positive questions such as the following:

❝ *How has your job changed since you started work here?* ❞

❝ *How, broadly, could we all improve our performance?* ❞

❝ *Do we offer enough training?* ❞

❝ *Are there times when you find yourself in a difficult situation and are uncertain of how to tackle it?* ❞

SUMMARIZING THE ANALYSIS

Analysis produces a wealth of information. It is important to extract the most valuable elements, or those that will have the greatest effect on your strategy, and document them in a summary. Use this as the starting point for the planning process.

32 Make sure the team understands the purpose of the summary.

33 Use a quick SWOT analysis to solve any problems as they arise.

CREATING A SWOT SUMMARY

Bring the mass of information you have collected during the analysis phase into a manageable summary using a SWOT matrix. SWOT is an acronym for Strengths, Weaknesses, Opportunities, and Threats. You have already listed external trends, studied your customers and competitors, and reviewed your internal capabilities. Now pick the key elements and group them under the SWOT headings. The SWOT summary is a structured exercise that helps to clarify the team's views, acts as a powerful "driver" of the plan, and provides a way of measuring progress.

ASSESSING YOUR SWOT ▼
A SWOT summary details your strengths, weaknesses, opportunities, and threats, often in the form of a matrix. The chart below highlights questions you can ask to help you decide which key elements from your analysis belong under which headings.

UNDERSTANDING YOUR TEAM'S SWOT

STRENGTHS
What is the team competent at? What is the team really good at?

WEAKNESSES
Where is the team short of resources or capabilities? Where does it have competitive disadvantages?

OPPORTUNITIES
How could the team boost its sales to customers and improve its service? Where are there new markets?

THREATS
How might your products and services be overtaken? Which markets are deteriorating?

CULTURAL DIFFERENCES

Business people in Asia tend to fear "losing face" if they admit to deficiencies, so they tend not to list so many weaknesses. The British concentrate too much on their weaknesses, overlooking their strengths. The French have a reputation for original thinking during SWOT brainstormings.

DOCUMENTING FINDINGS

When compiling your summary, make sure that the strengths you have identified are truly of benefit to the customer. For example, if the customer wants a fast response to problems and you have set up a software-based help desk, then that is a strength. If you have highly skilled staff but no help desk, that is a weakness. By listing your weaknesses, you will be able to identify key areas where you could improve performance and service (which you document as opportunities). List as threats those issues in your analysis that, if ignored, may damage your ability to succeed.

SHARING THE SUMMARY

Before you use the summary as a basis for your strategic plan, show it to your stakeholders. This allows them to point out any areas of misunderstanding or issues that are already being addressed elsewhere in the organization. It may also be useful to share your summary with key customers. You may choose to remove any sensitive information from the summary before showing it to them, but remember that most relationships benefit from openness. When you eventually produce the strategic plan, the summary will give you a number of drivers. Look for ways in which you can use your strengths, remove your weaknesses, exploit your opportunities, and avoid or overcome threats. Since you have spent time analyzing what is important to the customer, you can be confident that your final plan will be "customer driven."

QUESTIONS TO ASK YOURSELF

Q Is it easy to see the main drivers of my business by looking at the SWOT summary?

Q Is the language used in the SWOT summary clear, concise, and simple?

Q Have I validated the summary with enough stakeholders by discussing it with them?

Q Does the entire team agree to all the points in the summary?

▼ REVIEWING THE SWOT SUMMARY

Use the SWOT summary as a tool to determine the underlying assumptions of your strategic plan. Remember that it needs to be reviewed regularly and kept up to date for it to be effective.

Use the SWOT summary as basis for strategy ➤ **Review every three months** ➤ **Amend SWOT to reflect the current situation**

PLANNING A STRATEGY

An effective strategic plan is developed methodically, drawing on the in-depth analysis that has been carried out. Now is the time to make a series of choices that will form the basis for change.

STAGING THE PROCESS

A strategic plan is formulated in stages, involving the team and any stakeholders you may wish to include. The decisions you make at each step will give your strategy direction, while a final test will check that the focus is right prior to implementation.

34 Always consider the implications of a decision before finalizing it.

35 Enlist the help of others to make the plan as successful as possible.

SETTING OUT THE STAGES

The first stage in building a strategy is to define your aims. Once you have a clear direction, you will be able to determine where your competitive advantage lies, or what your team or organization has that is unique and that customers want. You will then need to set boundaries and choose areas on which you wish to focus, decide which stakeholders you wish to consult as you go through the process, and work out a timeline. As a guideline, a simple plan can probably be worked out within a couple of days, while a complex one could take up to three months.

PLANNING STRATEGY IN STAGES

STAGES	FACTORS TO CONSIDER
DEFINE PURPOSE Create a definitive statement of future goals, agreed with superiors, team members, and stakeholders.	● Your purpose must fit in with the strategic aims of other departments and teams in the organization. ● The statement should be kept brief and clear, concentrating on simple definitions of intent.
DETERMINE ADVANTAGE Compose a brief statement identifying why customers will buy from you rather than anyone else.	● Other stakeholders, such as the marketing team, may help in deciding on your competitive advantage. ● The advantages must be enduring, since strategy focuses on the long term.
SET BOUNDARIES List the products and markets you will deal in and those you definitely will not, approved by the entire team.	● Too many boundaries will make the team inflexible; too few will prevent the team from focusing clearly. ● If team members have plans for products or services, they should air them when setting boundaries.
CHOOSE AREAS OF EMPHASIS Identify products and markets that are considered worthwhile areas for more time and resources.	● Dividing products, services, markets, and customers into groups will help with choosing priorities. ● Emphasis will need to be reviewed on a regular basis as circumstances change.
ESTIMATE A BUDGET Examine the costs of allocating resources to product markets and forecast expected profits.	● In organizations with a standard budgeting process, an expert in this field should be involved. ● Other stakeholders may be needed to supply information for cost estimates.

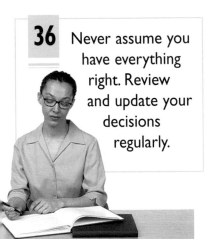

36 Never assume you have everything right. Review and update your decisions regularly.

CHECKING THE STRATEGY

At the end of the strategic planning process, you will list the key criteria of the new strategy in a template, known as a "business case template." This is used to test both current activities and future ideas, or business scenarios, to ascertain whether or not they will fit in with your strategy. If, for example, a criteria is to keep service staff to a minimum, an idea for new, high-maintenance product would fail to measure up against the template. You could either discard the idea, or make it fit the template by altering the product or service, or putting more resources into that market.

DEFINING YOUR PURPOSE

E*very business must have a primary purpose. Why do you and your team exist in your own organization and in the context of the outside world? Define your aims and agree on a statement of purpose to keep you focused as you develop the plan.*

> **37** Make sure that your team is able to state its purpose.

CONSIDERING AIMS

> **38** See that your purpose fits in with that of your organization.

If your superior has asked you to start the strategic planning process, you may be given a definite set of aims at the outset. If you are creating the strategy for yourself, then define your aims by discussing them with others. Think about the wording you use, since your purpose forms the first boundary for the strategic plan and should help all stakeholders understand where the strategy will lead.

INVOLVING OTHERS IN DEFINING PURPOSE

MANAGER
As manager, you have overall responsibility for deciding on your team's purpose, but it is important to discuss your aims with colleagues throughout the organization, and outside it if necessary, in order to agree on the direction to take.

SUPERIORS
Talk to superiors about your aims, since they will have to check that your strategic purpose fits in with that of the organization overall.

STAKEHOLDERS
Involve stakeholders to help draft your aims and refine the wording. They may have valuable suggestions to make on getting the focus right.

TEAM MEMBERS
Ask key members of the team to agree the final definition of aims, taking into account any suggestions made by superiors and stakeholders.

39 Talk through your aims with other teams to foster good relations.

DISCUSSING AIMS WITH COLLEAGUES

Teams fit within organizations and, to operate effectively, need good links with other teams. Make sure that your team understands how its strategy fits in with those of other teams within the organization, and appreciates the aims of cross-functional teams with whom it has dealings. Some organizations have a formal structure in place for communicating strategic aims among staff; but if one does not exist, it is up to you to ensure that your team's aims are made known.

CREATING A PURPOSE STATEMENT

Ask your team to come up with a simple definition of what it is going to sell to what markets. Do not be tempted to write a "mission statement" because these tend to be long and rather vague. Instead, make sure that the team concentrates on creating a statement that is succinct and clear, based on the good research it has carried out on customers and competitors.

40 Keep your statements of purpose short, to the point, and action-oriented.

> We will provide quality training courses for call center managers statewide

STRENGTHENING PURPOSE STATEMENTS

WEAK STATEMENTS	QUESTIONS RAISED	STRONG STATEMENTS
"We will concentrate on exploiting our considerable experience in food products."	Will you only be selling products? Where do you intend selling them?	"We will supply food products and services to North American markets (mainly Canada) in the first two years of our overseas operation."
"We will become the center of excellence for the company in information technology."	Who and where are your customers? What do you think you will be doing for them?	"We will provide computer hardware, software, and application systems to all the departments in head office."

DETERMINING COMPETITIVE ADVANTAGES

Your distinctive capabilities, or whatever your team or organization does that sets it apart, form the backbone of your strategy. Carefully review your analysis in order to create a statement that clearly sums up your enduring competitive advantages.

41 Remember that whoever won yesterday may not win tomorrow.

42 Check that your customer agrees with what you see as an advantage.

STARTING A REVIEW

To pinpoint your enduring advantage, first review your findings from the initial three analysis stages. Look at the trends identified in your analysis of the environment to see where you are ahead in terms of products or markets, then list any strengths that have been brought to your attention while analyzing your customers. Finally, list the capabilities revealed by your internal review. To qualify as a true advantage, a strength must be recognized as such by the customer. For example, your staff may be highly qualified and motivated, but they can only be considered a strength if they provide your customers with a fast and efficient service.

◀ **SEEKING OPINIONS**
Meet with customers or suppliers and ask them for their views on where you have the advantage over the competition. They will have an objective opinion and may well offer interesting suggestions or insights.

SUMMARIZING COMPETITIVE ANALYSIS

Examine your analysis of the competition. If your performance is no better than that of your rival, ask yourself why your customers have not switched to another supplier. The answer will reveal your true source of advantage. Alternatively, if your team supplies internal customers, imagine that a new manager has challenged you to justify your existence. The statement of competitive advantage should help you to understand how to win against the competition.

QUESTIONS TO ASK YOURSELF

Q Is our statement of competitive advantage useful in determining which products and services we should sell?

Q Does each advantage put us ahead of all our competitors?

Q Would our main customers agree with the statement?

Q Do our brochures reflect the same advantage?

---

43 Once you have identified an advantage, use it.

▼ USING YOUR ANALYSIS

A systematic review of your analysis will enable you to agree on lots of advantages. It is up to you to then decide which ones you are really going to depend upon.

DETERMINING ENDURING ADVANTAGES

There is little point in the team agreeing on a source of advantage that will be lost in the near future. Any advantage should have the potential for surviving at least into year two of the plan. One reason why it is extremely dangerous for organizations to rely on slogans such as "our people are our main source of advantage" is that it makes the organization vulnerable; employees will not stay in the same job forever. Finally, make sure that you express your competitive advantages in terms familiar to your customers to show that they offer real value to them.

Enduring competitive advantages			
Product and market trends	Product and service strengths	Opportunities in the marketplace	Skills and capabilities
Environmental analysis	Customer analysis	Competitive analysis	Internal audit

SETTING BOUNDARIES

Your customers and prospects will make many demands. You cannot fulfill them all. Draw up definite parameters so that the team is clear about what it will and will not focus on, and ensure that everyone agrees to abide by the boundaries set.

 44 Planning what *not* to do is as vital as planning what to do.

 45 Choose customers who will be there for the long term.

▼ **AGREEING BOUNDARIES**
If team members have plans or products that they are convinced particular customers would love, now is the time to sell those ideas to the rest of the team. However, they must be prepared to accept boundaries, even if their ideas are rejected – or face leaving the team.

IMPROVING EFFECTIVENESS

Setting boundaries is essential to prevent people from wasting time and energy chasing opportunities that are not exactly what the customer needs or what the team wants to deliver. Trying to be all things to all people leads to a lack of team focus, thinly spread resources and, ultimately, failure. Clarifying boundaries early on will help to restrict the choices to be considered later in the planning process. It will also improve operational effectiveness by concentrating on those points that the team believes to be important.

Plan is rejected, since it oversteps boundaries

Manager notes team member is unhappy

Team member's plan comes up for consideration at team meeting

TARGETING MARKETS AND CUSTOMERS

Rejecting markets and customers is difficult, but understanding the boundaries is vital here, too. It is far better to identify and target customer groups than adopt a "shotgun" approach where any expression of interest is investigated. Draw up a list of what you are going to sell to whom, and what you will not sell. A commercial organization will often target people who pay the best price and give the highest profit margin. An internal organization may focus on customers in the fastest developing part of the business. Make sure the decision on markets is good for the long term.

After discussion, team member agrees to accept decision and keep to boundaries

Manager fails to gain full support of team member

Team member elects to leave the team because he cannot accept boundaries

DRAWING UP BOUNDARIES

Refer to your analysis for guidance

Decide what you are going to sell

Identify who you are going to sell to

Decide what you are not going to sell

Agree who you will not sell to

Write down boundaries and abide by them

46 Make it clear that exceptions to the boundaries set are not allowed.

CHOOSING
STRATEGIC EMPHASIS

Your strategic emphasis dictates where you should allocate time and resources. To get the priorities right, look at your products, services, markets, and customers in terms of groups. Bear in mind that circumstances change, so review your emphasis regularly.

47 The more you focus, the faster your effectiveness will improve.

48 Talk to your suppliers to check that you have grouped products correctly.

GROUPING PRODUCTS AND SERVICES

If you have many different products and services, you will find them far more manageable if you consider them in terms of groups when deciding which are most important. Group products by whatever criteria is appropriate, such as by their complexity. A simple group might require little after-sales support, a complex one might need a lot of support, for example. Or you could group products according to value, size, maturity, or manufacturing process. Exploring creative options for groups can often spark new ideas.

SEGMENTING MARKETS AND CUSTOMERS

Markets and customers can be grouped, too, allowing you to focus clearly on a shorter, more specific list. Bear in mind that a more creative approach may reap benefits. The first bank to set up a telephone banking service realized that there was a new group of people to cater to during a strategic planning session. These people wanted to bank using technology rather than visit branches, and to bank outside normal business hours.

POINTS TO REMEMBER

- The more your team focuses its energy and resources, the more effectively it will perform.
- Concentrating on a specific market will make you more knowledgeable about your customers' business.
- Markets and customers could be segmented by region, size, growth potential, value, or selling process or channel.

ESTABLISHING PRIORITIES

In order to identify which groups are important for today's cash flow and which are going to be important for the long term, examine potential volumes and sales values over the next two to three years. In terms of market forecasts, look at each group in the same way and estimate their current and future sales revenues and/or profits. Consider what each group needs in order to be successful. For example, you may find that one group of products may need automatic packing, while another requires extremely quick distribution. Decide what you have to do to be successful with each product and market group and remember to use this information when you look for gaps in your capabilities later.

49 Encourage debate on priorities to help focus the team.

Manager seeks advice on future sales figures

Marketing manager reveals forecasts

FORECASTING SALES ▶
Accurate forecasts of sales volume and value will help you to decide which are the most important areas for emphasis. Ask a colleague from the marketing department for an expert view.

CASE STUDY
Having agreed with her team to choose a new area of emphasis, Jane, the manager, was aware that one of her team members, Derek, was not entirely happy. The change meant that he would be selling to retailers rather than to the distribution customers with whom he had been working for a while. When his performance began to suffer, Jane called Derek into her office at a time when she knew they would not be interrupted and asked for his concerns. He admitted that he felt he knew very little about the retail business and was not confident about his ability to improve sales. Jane was then able to send him on a familiarization course. She also organized a good customer to spend time with Derek explaining the details of retailing. Derek soon got his confidence back, and his sales figures improved dramatically.

◀ ADAPTING TO NEW EMPHASIS
A shift of emphasis can often lead to changes in the way that team members work. In this case, Jane acted promptly when she realized that Derek was having problems in his new area. By arranging extra training and help, she was able to give him confidence and he adapted well to his new area of responsibility.

50 Be realistic; remember that resources for new areas must come from somewhere.

AGREEING EMPHASIS

If the team is to work together to improve overall performance, each member must agree where the strategic emphasis should lie. A split in focus can cause conflict and adversely affect performance, particularly when team members come from different areas of the organization. For example, people who deal with customers may believe that the focus should be on easy-to-sell products, while those responsible for manufacturing more complex products completely disagree. Check that your stakeholders agree with the areas you have chosen to emphasize, too. Use a simple matrix to encourage the team to think about the importance of each product and market. This will help you to agree on the amount of time and resources you are going to put into them in the future.

CULTURAL DIFFERENCES

Nobody doubts the wisdom of trying out markets on a pilot basis. The North Americans tend to be more adventurous in tackling high-volume sales, since their domestic market is so huge. They are less likely than their European colleagues to "wait and see" and risk rival organizations taking the opportunity from them. Asians like to be sure that the market is there before they hit it hard with quality, quantity, and competitive pricing.

▼ DOCUMENTING CHANGES IN EMPHASIS

Devise a product-market matrix showing where you plan to upgrade and reduce emphasis on products or services. The team can then use this for easy reference.

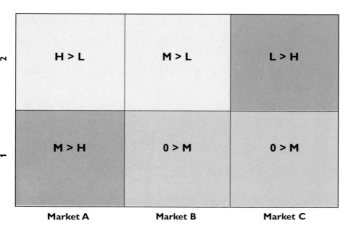

Current > Future

Products/services	Market A	Market B	Market C
2	H > L	M > L	L > H
1	M > H	0 > M	0 > M

Key

H *High level of activity, that is, occupying many staff and other resources*

M *Medium level of activity*

L *Low level of activity*

0 *No activity at all*

> *Change of emphasis from now to the future*

CHANGING EMPHASIS

As you change products or there are changes to your markets, you will have to change emphasis in each product-market segment as a result. If your customer group is putting such an emphasis on low cost that your profit margin is being badly squeezed, you may choose to downgrade your effort and, over time, withdraw from that segment. How often you do this depends on the volatility of your product markets. Change is particularly rapid in the technology industry, for example, so a software developer may have to review its emphasis on product markets at least twice a year. In the steel industry, on the other hand, emphasis would probably need reviewing only occasionally.

QUESTIONS TO ASK YOURSELF

Q Why are we getting such poor sales results from this product market?

Q Are we sure that this product market is going to continue at this growth for another two years?

Q If sales in this area take so much effort, is it worth it?

REVIEWING EMPHASIS ▶
It is very easy to become complacent when all is going according to plan. Encourage team members to keep asking questions to make sure that the strategic emphasis is absolutely correct.

51 Use logic rather than emotion to find focus.

52 Discuss and agree emphasis with everyone involved.

RESOLVING PROBLEMS

As circumstances change and you review your emphasis, you are likely to notice anomalies and discover areas that no longer deserve so many resources and as much time. Plan to reduce the amount of effort in declining areas and take resources away before the sales value becomes insufficient to pay for the people involved. If you find an area of good potential, now is the time to put in more resources and achieve competitive advantage. Communicating the product-market matrix throughout the company could greatly contribute to getting a cross-functional "one team" view of the whole or part of the organization.

ESTIMATING A BUDGET

Understanding the financial implications of a strategy is fundamental to its success. Look at potential sales volumes, take into account your areas of strategic emphasis, and estimate future costs to arrive at an overall budget.

53 Understand your plan's financial implications to improve its quality.

54 Check that your customer would agree with your sales forecast.

55 Base your budget on realistic sales estimates.

FORECASTING REVENUES

It is important to forecast sales in detail for the next year and at least in outline for two years after that. This is a difficult exercise, but if you miss it out or do it without thought, you risk producing an unrealistic plan; either you will not achieve the sales to make the budget work or you will not be able to supply the number of orders received. Think through your likely sales in terms of optimistic, most likely, and pessimistic, for each product market. In the end, the forecast of what you are committed to sell drives all the other budgets, such as production and distribution.

BECOMING NUMERATE

Accounting is not a natural talent for most people, but in order to plan and follow through strategy successfully, it is important to understand the basics of budgeting and forecasting. If there is any financial issue you do not fully understand, take steps to improve your knowledge, either by reading up on the subject or by taking an accounting course. Once you understand the principles of accounting, you will learn from the experience of actually drawing up budgets, writing business plans, doing management accounts, and studying financial reports. This may be a rather laborious process at first, but as you grow increasingly comfortable with managing figures, you will become faster and more skilled at all aspects of accounting.

ESTIMATING COSTS

From your sales forecasts and understanding of your customers' needs, you can make an estimate of any costs involved. Generally, it is useful to break down costs into five categories: people, supplies, facilities, equipment, and information. You may need the help of other stakeholders to complete this stage. For example, it may be useful to know what the IT department intends charging you for information services over the next two to three years. Concentrate on getting numbers that are realistic rather than wholly accurate.

56 Look at every cost now to avoid major revisions later.

▼ **SETTING OUT BUDGETS**
The items of expenditure on this concise budget form have been broken down into five separate categories. The total expenditure and income are then given, followed by the estimated profit.

Budget

The cost of supply for products or anything purchased

The charge that the organization makes for space and other facilities

The total of forecast revenue

Expenditure	Year 1	Year 2	Year 3
People	33,500	36,850	40,535
Supplies	22,000	24,200	26,620
Facilities	12,000	13,200	14,520
Equipment	6,500	7,150	7,865
Information	2,500	2,750	3,025
Total expenditure	76,500	84,150	92,565
Total income	102,000	121,000	139,000
Forecast profit	25,500	36,850	46,435

The total cost of the people in the team

The costs of equipment that the team rents or buys

The charges made for administration

57 Always ask yourself what would happen if sales were to fall.

CALCULATING MARGIN

To work out the operating margin, deduct expenditure from income. In most organizations, there is a standard way of doing budgets. In small organizations, the availability of cash is most important, and it is likely that the team will produce a "cash flow," which is a document showing the timing of payments and receipts. In large organizations, a cash flow is necessary for any team operating in an area where the volume of sales is likely to grow or fall away dramatically.

INTEGRATING STRATEGY

Whan formulating your plan, make sure that it will integrate well into the organization as a whole. Its aims must be consistent with the plans of other departments to avoid internal conflict and confusion in the marketplace.

58 Always present one consistent strategy to your customers.

59 Think about your interfaces with other departments.

60 Be prepared to give ground in order to reach agreement.

IDENTIFYING POTENTIAL CONFLICT

At every stage in the creation of your plan, look for areas of potential conflict that could jeopardize its success. For example, if strategic thinking is not common practice in your organization, you may, unintentionally, highlight the outmoded and ineffective methods of working of other teams, so act sensitively. Consider whether other teams will understand the need for the changes that you propose. Be sure of your reasons for change before discussing the plan with other teams. Try to work out a mutually acceptable way ahead, and always be prepared to compromise as you move along.

MAKING PROCESSES COMPATIBLE

Always develop your plan with the rest of the organization in mind. If you cannot initiate a new process while an old process remains in place for other teams, determine how this situation can be rectified. Open negotiations with other teams and stimulate thoughts of change and improvement. As team manager, discuss matters with your peers to make the planning process a cycle, so that if one team formulates a plan, the changes required to another team's plan will be anticipated and easy to initiate. As a result, both plans will be improved.

61 Focus people on the positive aspects of change.

62 Organize informal discussions on strategy with other teams.

ALIGNING STRATEGIES

The whole process of aligning strategies is made easier where teams follow an agreed procedure, as well as standard techniques and documents, when creating their plans. If your organization does not currently standardize the formulation of its strategic plans, you could always suggest a simple, step-by-step approach. Computer software, for example, has a vital role to play in standardizing procedures, allowing organizations to communicate and update their planning process online. Stress the benefits to your organization of all teams being able to learn from each other's experiences, as well as from their own.

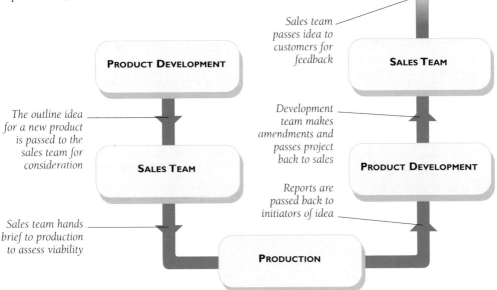

Sales team passes idea to customers for feedback

The outline idea for a new product is passed to the sales team for consideration

Development team makes amendments and passes project back to sales

Sales team hands brief to production to assess viability

Reports are passed back to initiators of idea

▲ USING PROCESS MAPS

When projects involve different teams, use a process map to identify where each stage of a process moves between them. The danger points lie at the handover stage, where delays or misunderstandings may occur. To avoid problems, ensure that each team sees its own part in the process in the context of everyone else's.

63 Many people in your organization have knowledge and experience – make use of these resources.

TESTING THE STRATEGY

You now have a strategic plan to which everyone should be committed, until events require you to review and amend it. To maintain the plan's effectiveness, it is important to be able to test current activities and new ideas for strategic fit.

64 Ensure that everyone knows the key tests for a new idea.

65 Keep referring people back to the strategy to maintain focus.

BUILDING A BUSINESS CASE TEMPLATE

A business case template enables you to assess whether new ideas fit with your strategy. To create the template, list the most important criteria of your strategy. One criteria, for example, might be to maximize short-term sales. Give each criteria a rating out of 10 that reflects its importance, with 10 being the highest priority. To test a new idea, define how you would ideally meet each criteria. For example, if a criteria is to keep staff to a minimum, you might define the ideal as a reduction in staff. Rate the new idea out of 10 according to how close it comes to the ideal, then multiply the two scores to give a weighting. Ideally, the new idea should score 10 against each criteria, so calculate this. Add up each set of scores to give you total ideal and actual weightings, then work out a percentage.

▼ **TESTING A NEW IDEA**

In the template below, a new idea is measured against three criteria. It scores well against the first and third criteria but not so well against the second. Added together, the weighting scores give a total figure that is translated into a percentage. With 61 percent, this idea has a reasonable strategic fit.

Criteria (main criteria of strategy)	Priority rating (score 1–10)	New idea (score 1–10)	Weighting (multiply scores)	Ideal weighting (priority x 10)
Increase short-term sales	7	7	49	70
Protect long-term sales	5	2	10	50
Keep staff to minimum	7	8	56	70
Total scores			**115**	**190**
% of ideal				**61%**

To calculate percentage, multiply total weighting score by 100 and divide by total ideal weighting score. The figure reveals how well the idea fits with strategy

USING BUSINESS CASES

It is no good having a well-defined strategy on what you are going to sell and to whom if, in reality, everyone ignores it. Encourage the team to use the business case as a matter of course, both to check what they are doing currently (are they concentrating on the agreed strategic emphasis?) and to test every new opportunity for viability. Adopting such a logical process for assessing current and new plans encourages team members to view issues objectively. The more the business case template is used, the more experienced the team will become at evaluating suggestions. Additionally, once team members realize exactly what the criteria and ideal are, they will be more likely to make suggestions that come close to these important requirements.

66 Make it clear that all new ideas must be tested against the template.

67 Look at the risk of ideas not going as well as hoped.

CLARIFYING THE ▶ PROCESS
Make sure that the team understands how new opportunities will be evaluated. Having a formal process for reviewing ideas emphasizes that all suggestions are important and will be taken seriously.

CASE STUDY

Peter, a sales executive for a frozen foods company, had the idea of offering a new home delivery service to domestic clients. A survey of customers revealed that many would welcome the service. He decided to test his idea against the business case template to see whether it fitted the company strategy. The template had three criteria: short-term sales had a high priority; quality of service medium priority;

and long-term sales high priority. He had a high score against the first criteria but needed to score highly against the third, too. In a trade newspaper, Peter found results of a national survey showing that home delivery, with orders coming from the Internet as well as the telephone, were set to grow hugely. This meant that his proposal scored well against the template, and a project to start home delivery was put into place.

◀ USING A BUSINESS CASE
Peter's boss had made him fully aware that any new ideas for the company should be tested against the business case template. This meant that Peter could take it upon himself to come up with a well-argued and easy-to-implement idea. He knew that the idea would work with the overall strategy because he had been able to test its viability himself.

COMMUNICATING CLEARLY

For your strategy to succeed, it is vital that everyone who needs to know about it is informed. Communicate your plan to every stakeholder so that they understand what the strategy will do for them, and you will gain their commitment to it.

> **68** If people do not know what you are trying to do, they cannot help.

> **69** Be as frank and open as possible with colleagues.

> **70** Keep everyone up to date on any proposed changes.

KEEPING STAKEHOLDERS INFORMED

Since stakeholders – whether superiors, colleagues in other departments, team members who have not been involved in the entire planning process, or customers and suppliers – have a vested interest in the strategic plan, each of them needs to be kept informed of developments relevant to them. Keep the language you use simple and define all important terms; even a word such as "sale" can have different meanings to different people within the same organization.

GETTING FEEDBACK

Whichever method of communication you use, make sure that there is a feedback mechanism in place whereby stakeholders can let you know what they think of the plan and its impact on them. Everyone in the organization should be viewed as the eyes and ears of the team. The salespeople, for example, know what the customers are saying, just as site engineers will have an insider's view of how work is progressing. Each has a role to play in checking and molding the final version of the strategy. So make sure communication is two-way and listen. Then listen some more. Use feedback in a review meeting to spark changes and improvements to the plan.

CULTURAL DIFFERENCES

In the UK and, to a certain extent, Scandinavia, metaphors, similes, and irony are used extensively in business dealings, not to be impolite but to strongly emphasize a point. In the US, Canada, and Germany, such figures of speech are more likely to be taken literally, causing possible, unintended offense.

COMMUNICATING THE STRATEGY

METHOD OF COMMUNICATION	FACTORS TO CONSIDER

DETAILED REPORT
The whole plan, including the planning process and change projects.

● Documentation should be clearly laid out and backed up with the analysis information.
● Only superiors and key team members should receive the plan in its entirety.

OUTLINE REPORT
A one-page outline of the strategy; extracts of the plan relevant to the stakeholder.

● This report should be personalized for stakeholders, stressing factors that will have a direct effect on them.
● Any other parties who might benefit from the information can receive an outline report.

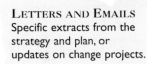

PRESENTATION
A summary of the strategy and implementation plan using visual aids.

● Presentation material must look professional and convincing.
● Team members, internal stakeholders, and manager's peer group should be invited.

NEWSLETTERS
Updates on the progress of the strategy and plan.

● Reports should be kept brief and circulated to team members and stakeholders regularly.
● Preparing newsletters can be delegated to a key team member.

LETTERS AND EMAILS
Specific extracts from the strategy and plan, or updates on change projects.

● These are quick to produce and useful for keeping a large number of people updated.
● Stakeholders with a limited interest in the strategy need only minimal information.

GAINING COMMITMENT

When communicating the strategy, encourage your audience to ask themselves the question, "So what does this mean to me and the way I do my job?" This helps them to understand the strategy. Ask people to commit to their role in the plan, and, where it is important, confirm those commitments in writing. Communicating the plan is also a continuous process. Ensure you keep those who need to know regularly updated on progress.

71 Aim to finish off communications with a summary of agreed actions.

IMPLEMENTING A STRATEGY

Implementing a strategic plan involves setting change projects in motion that will achieve strategic aims. Learn how to change for the future while maximizing performance today.

PRIORITIZING CHANGE

The first step in implementing a strategy is to identify areas for improvement. Compare the current situation with the ideal to see where there are gaps, then group changes that are critical to your strategy into areas for immediate action.

72 Learn to live with business processes that you are unable to change.

73 Always aim for the best possible result.

74 Deal with the most important areas for improvement first.

LISTING IMPROVEMENTS

Draw up a comprehensive list of between 50 to 100 issues that need improvement in order for the new strategy to succeed. This will provide you with the starting point for planning the changes. You can compile this list yourself if it comes easily to you, or you can ask key members of the team to brainstorm it with you. Pose the question, "Given what we are trying to achieve, how, in an ideal world, would our organization operate in the areas of business processes, technology, and people?". This will lead to several answers. You now know what would be ideal.

IDENTIFYING GAPS

By reviewing your current situation and comparing it to the ideal, you will reveal gaps. These will probably never be fully closed, since there is always room for improvements. Nevertheless the major gaps – the ones you must do something about – will be clear. At the opposite end of the scale, there will be much less important gaps where improvements would be desirable but not necessarily essential.

SETTING PRIORITIES

List each area for improvement and mark it as high, medium, or low under the categories of impact and urgency. You have no option but to deal with those changes that have a high impact and high urgency. Use the measure to prioritize the changes, then group them so that you arrive at, say, eight to 10 areas for change. These groupings are called "change projects." As you implement your strategy, the team should find itself tackling high-impact changes before they become high-urgency.

THINGS TO DO

1. Look at your processes, such as how you handle customer orders.
2. Assess whether you need to upgrade your technology.
3. Look at staffing structure: might smaller teams serve the customer better?
4. Check that you have the right people with the necessary skills on the team.
5. Look at support resources: does the team have backup?

▼ COMPARING PRIORITIES

The good prioritizing team looks ahead and tackles critical jobs first, giving them control over the strategy. Bad prioritizers react to the past and put off demanding activities, leading to loss of control.

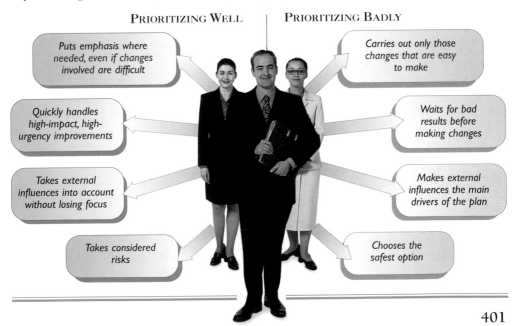

PRIORITIZING WELL | PRIORITIZING BADLY

Puts emphasis where needed, even if changes involved are difficult

Carries out only those changes that are easy to make

Quickly handles high-impact, high-urgency improvements

Waits for bad results before making changes

Takes external influences into account without losing focus

Makes external influences the main drivers of the plan

Takes considered risks

Chooses the safest option

PLANNING CHANGE

B ringing *about effective change is vital to strategic success. Take a disciplined approach and work out action plans for all your change projects with objectives, milestones, and timelines. These then form part of your overall implementation plan.*

75 If change will not bring definite benefits, it is not worthwhile.

MOVING FORWARD

Change projects are aimed at improving long-term operational effectiveness and could take from a few weeks to two years or more to complete, depending on the complexity and degree of change involved. Break down each project into an action plan, with estimated start and end dates. As you change for the future, continue with operational plans and targets that rule how you run today's business. Once change projects are under way, you may then need to review operations to accommodate them.

76 Look for big improvements from change projects.

LEARNING FROM THE PAST

Keep good notes as you tackle each change project, so that you or your colleagues can refer to them in the future when similar challenges present themselves. Find out whether anyone in the organization has had experience of making the same type of changes that you are planning and ask to borrow their notes. Referring to what has been done before may give you valuable insights into the task at hand.

KEEPING A RECORD ▶
Update progress notes regularly so that you can make them immediately available to colleagues who may need to carry out similar activities urgently.

77   When wording objectives, make them unambiguous.

POINTS TO REMEMBER

- The wording of the objective should be clear enough to enable people who are new to the team to understand it.

- Each change project may have several objectives.

- Most people prefer a set objective to a list of tasks because it provides more of a challenge.

DEFINING OBJECTIVES

Before deciding on an action plan, make sure you have defined exactly what each change project is trying to achieve and by when. It is important to produce objectives that are as tight and specific as possible. Follow the SMART rule, a useful management acronym that defines objectives as:

- Stretching – they should challenge the manager and the team;
- Measurable – they must be quantifiable;
- Achievable – they must be realistic;
- Related to the customer – they should improve service to them;
- Time-targeted – they must have an end date.

By setting such objectives you ensure that everyone has a clear definition of what you hope to gain and a better understanding of the value of the change.

ALLOCATING RESPONSIBILITY

Change projects can be tricky to implement since many people are resistant to change. A major change in attitude, such as changing your customers' perception of your company, can also be a long and difficult process. Yet for the change to happen, someone must take overall responsibility for it. Usually, the team member with the most relevant experience takes charge. If it is not obvious who this should be, then it falls to the manager.

Team member takes ownership of the project

Colleague agrees to assist but does not take responsibility

TAKING ▶ RESPONSIBLITY

Each change project should be overseen by a single team member who is held accountable. The person responsible then has the task of making sure that everyone else in the team does what is required.

SETTING MILESTONES

Change projects, by their nature, are often far-reaching. If, for example, you are trying to redefine all your business processes, you will not be able to succeed overnight. Having established the objective of the change project, it is important to set some milestones as steps on the way to success so that the team can check if the change project is on track. Ask yourself, "What do I need to do to reach each milestone?", and break down the work into a series of tasks. Milestones may be events, such as producing a report, or they may be achievements – for example, getting the agreement of a director to allocate resources to review the sales order processing system.

THINGS TO DO

1. Set out milestones that allow you to measure progress periodically.

2. Draw up clear and unambiguous directives that everyone will understand.

3. Keep stakeholders up to date with progress and any changes to the plan.

4. Check that team members feel confident of achieving their milestones.

78 Make sure the team's priorities are the same as yours.

SETTING TIME TARGETS

Achieving change takes time. However, if the change is urgent but the problem has little short-term impact, there is a danger that the team will put a low priority on their part in the change project. By setting time targets you make sure that people are not sidetracked by operational issues. Emphasize to the team that failure to change now will seriously hurt performance in the future. If you have effectively specified accountability and set a timeline, you will be able to answer the question, "If this change does not occur by this date, whom do we hold responsible?"

◀ AGREEING TIMELINES
Make sure that time targets are demanding but achievable. It is a good idea to discuss targets with team members to ensure they are realistic and stress that you expect them to be met.

RECORDING PROGRESS

Each change project action plan should be updated regularly and made available to any team member who needs it. Put all the plans, together with all the necessary backup documents available, into one large folder, as a record of all aspects of the implementation of your strategic plan. You should also include the research carried out during the analysis. You may also wish to store all the information in an electronic file, to which all members have access. Keep the data practical. Refer back to the folder or electronic file yourself and encourage the team to do so to keep the document dynamic and in use from day to day.

- Documentation should be consistent and easily accessible.
- When the plan describes actions clearly and simply, it makes it easier for the person responsible to carry them out.
- Teams should be encouraged to consult and update the action plan regularly.

79 Remember that an action plan is not complete until it is written down.

▼ DOCUMENTING CHANGE PROJECTS

Teams must take change projects as seriously as they take a project involved in delivering products to a customer. Use the discipline of clear documentation.

A clear, SMART statement of the project objective

The deadlines by which the changes need to be made

An event or achievement marking the progress of a change project

Key events that allow you to monitor if the project is on track to finish in time

CHANGE PROJECT ACTION PLAN

Objective To implement a new sales ordering processing system within a budget of £50,000

Measure A reduction in our debt collection days from 80 days on average to 50 days on average

Deadline Pilot by end January next year, and full implementation by September	**Owner** RHC
Actions Agree the attributes of the new system with internal departments and customers	**Time** March 28
	Responsibility ASD
Milestones Recommendation agreed by Board	**Time** June 11
	Responsibility RHC

The qualification by which the objectives may be measured

The person with overall responsibility for achieving objective

Date by which action should be completed

Person responsible for the action

405

ASSESSING THE RISKS

Having tested the strategy for problems during the planning stage, now review the change project plans to ascertain what might prevent them from succeeding. List potential threats and, if necessary, alter the plans to minimize them.

80 Always rehearse a contingency plan to make it more useful.

81 Ask stakeholders what they think could go wrong.

82 Greet the unexpected as an opportunity rather than a threat.

PREDICTING PROBLEMS

Bring the team together with the sole purpose of brainstorming a list of possible future problems. Look at each action plan in turn and ask the question, "What could prevent this from happening?". This process encourages the team to defend the plan against constructive criticism, with the result that they will be even more confident in working within the strategy and more committed to overcoming any future obstacles. Avoid listing every potential problem but concentrate instead on those that have at least a 50 percent chance of actually occurring.

ASSESSING IMPACT

Since potential problems will vary in importance, look at the likely impact of each problem, and ask the team to assess whether such problems could prevent the change project from being completed on time. Consider whether the impact of each problem on the project will be high, medium, or low. Assess the probability that each threat will occur. Mark these high, medium, or low. As your team members implement the strategy and begin to think long term, they will inevitably spend more time on high-probability but low-impact threats. When this occurs, they will be in better control of their business environment and strategy.

POINTS TO REMEMBER

- People should be encouraged to treat problems as another challenge of change.
- By changing the plan, it might be possible to completely avoid a potential problem without affecting the strategy.
- It is important not only to look at the current situation when assessing problems but also at two to three years further on.
- A change of customer or supplier could pose a significant threat to success.

AVOIDING TROUBLE

The most significant threats are those with the potential for the greatest impact and with the highest probability of occurrence. Change or add to an action plan to prevent them. For example, another stakeholder may be able to mitigate a certain threat. Approach them to find out whether the problem can be avoided, or whether the milestone or objective under threat is not feasible. If the latter is the case, you will have to think again.

Stakeholder envisages what could go wrong

Team member explains a change in procedure

SEEKING NEW INSIGHTS ▶

It is important to talk to stakeholders, either in the normal course of events or in a special meeting, about how change projects will affect them. The stakeholders may provide valuable new insights into potential problems.

PREEMPTING TROUBLE ▼

By taking early action, Laura ensured that software delivery was delayed for less than a month, customer service was maintained, and problems caused by the delayed completion date were minimized.

CONTINGENCY PLANNING

You will not be able to preempt all significant problems, but you can certainly think through alternative ways of achieving the milestones or objectives under threat. This is called contingency planning, and it ensures that the team reacts smoothly and quickly should a predicted potential problem occur. Sometimes you may just have to wait to see if a problem arises, and then respond; but if you have assessed the risks well, you will be far better prepared to react swiftly and effectively. It makes sense to install the sprinkler system before there is a fire.

CASE STUDY

Laura ran a computer help desk for her head office. She and her team planned a major change project to improve the computer system and provide a better service to customers. A vital piece of software they needed for this was in the final stages of testing, and Laura knew that if the software was supplied late, they would be unable to switch over to the new system on time, or even maintain their current level of service. It was, in Laura's opinion, a high-impact, high-probability risk. She talked to her supplier, who agreed that if the software was not delivered on time, he would lend her two staff until it was. They also agreed that Laura would pay their salaries for the first month but that the supplier would pay them thereafter. The team then warned its customers about the potential delay to the new system and explained the contingency plan.

REVIEWING OPERATIONAL TARGETS

A new strategy will almost certainly mean changes to operational targets. Agree new targets collectively for the team, and individually for each team member; then, as targets are achieved, look for ways of making further improvements.

83 Treat people as if they want to succeed, and they will do their best.

84 Set targets that will help to develop the team.

85 Allow people to decide how to meet their targets.

SETTING NEW TARGETS

Translate the top-level objectives of the plan into specific measurable targets at the next level, and so on down the team. For example, when a sales team agrees to a strategy it may well agree on what market share the team is trying to achieve. This is then broken down into individual sales targets which, if all are hit, will achieve the overall target for market share. Performance targets, even when there are only two levels, are part of a hierarchy where top-level performance is delivered through achieving targets spread around the organization.

ENSURING REALISTIC TARGETS

Make targets stretching but achievable. If you set a target that carries little challenge, you will not get the best from people. If you set a target that is virtually impossible, either they will not try or they will come under too much pressure. As manager, it is a good time to make people enthusiastic about the new opportunities and challenges ahead. Make sure team members are committed to their new targets and feel good about their ability to achieve them.

POINTS TO REMEMBER

● If everyone hits their targets and most people over-achieve significantly, the targets were probably too low.

● It is better for people to succeed on a realistic target than, for the same performance, to fail on an over-ambitious one.

● The sum of the team's targets should be greater than the overall target set, in order to allow for any shortfalls.

86 Explain to the team how strategic thinking will benefit performance today as well as tomorrow.

MAKING IMPROVEMENTS

As the team achieves new targets, the strategy will develop and you will be able to look for further progress and improvement. Most organizations compete in markets where customer expectations are increasing regularly and competitors are getting better at satisfying them. Ensure that your internal targets keep in step with this. You may have brought costs down below last year, but can you keep them at that level and improve on quality? Do not wait for the start of a new company year to discuss targets. Review them continuously and encourage people to want to be more productive.

Implement a new strategy

Carry out change projects

Review operational targets

Produce a team operating plan

Create individual operating plans

Achieve improved results

Superior agrees to put in more resources in the expectation of better results

Manager explains how a new opportunity will enable her to achieve higher targets

◀ USING TARGETS TO WIN BACKING

Targets can be used as bargaining tools. If you need more resources to exploit an opportunity, you are likely to gain approval if you can meet higher targets and show when, and in what quantity, the improved results will come.

MOTIVATING PEOPLE

A new strategy brings fresh challenges and opportunities. Motivate everyone involved by ensuring that they appreciate the part they have to play in making it a success. Then encourage the team through training and rewarding their achievements.

87 Always assume that people really want to achieve more.

REVIEWING ROLES AND RESPONSIBILITIES

If a team adopts a new strategy, almost all of its members and other stakeholders will have to change their behavior and adjust to the new requirements of the job. Take the opportunity to review all roles and responsibilities. Create an attitude that says, "It is no longer enough to turn up to do the job we did yesterday; instead we all have a responsibility to find ways in which we can improve." Hold discussions individually with team members, perhaps at the same time as you discuss new operating targets, to ensure that they are happy with any changes. Then ask appropriate team members to talk to stakeholders. It is important that everyone involved understands their new responsibilities, including managers in your organization, customers, and suppliers.

▲ **INVOLVING CUSTOMERS**

Customers will be far more enthusiastic and cooperative if you make them feel involved. Appoint a key team member to explain the strategy and the reasons for any changes, and ask customers to confirm their agreement. Get written confirmation if the changes proposed are significant.

DO'S AND DON'TS

✔ Do encourage suggestions from the team on ways to change and improve.

✔ Do ensure that team members completely understand their new roles.

✘ Don't allow incentive programs to reward people for working outside the strategy.

✘ Don't imagine that roles set at start of the year will still be appropriate at the end.

88 If raising targets, listen to feedback to improve the chance of success.

89 Set the highest standards, both for yourself and for others.

INVESTING IN TRAINING

By changing roles and responsibilities, you may find that previously well-qualified team members now lack the skills to achieve new targets. What skills will your staff need for future roles? For example, given that technology is changing so rapidly, do they possess the know-how to work with the latest computer software? You will encourage people to implement strategy more effectively if it integrates into their normal business lives, such as by building the use of computers and software into the implementation. Bear in mind that people will not need to master new skills or learn facts that can be provided through technology when required.

REWARDING PEOPLE

Check that the old reward system still fits the new environment. If you have changed targets, roles, and responsibilities, you may have to offer new rewards and incentives. Remember that mentoring and coaching are an essential part of an environment where you are continuously trying to improve service to customers and team performance. Give your team the support it needs to do the new job well, and help stakeholders to play their roles as fully as possible. Recognition and feedback are as important as financial rewards. Give people feedback when they get it right as well as when they get it wrong. Is anyone on your team likely to say, "I do not know whether or not I am doing a good job"? If the answer is yes, you still have some work to do to agree targets, roles, responsibilities, and rewards.

▼ **SAYING THANK YOU**
One of the easiest and most effective forms of reward is to say thank you for a job well done. Praising an individual in front of fellow team members reinforces the message and inspires confidence.

MONITORING PERFORMANCE

To keep the plan on track, closely monitor progress in both operational plans and change projects. Organize team reports that signal shortfalls or problems to be corrected, and look at progress across the organization where it impacts your plans.

| 90 | Give people only the level of detail they really need. |

▲ INDICATING PROBLEMS
Use a green, amber, and red "traffic light" system to monitor progress. Amber or red indicators denote issues that must be tackled at the next review meeting.

ORGANIZING REPORTS

Performance reports must show what progress has been made to date toward the targets set. A useful technique is to use red, amber, and green indicators to chart progress. For example, if you are halfway through a year in which the target is to produce 1,000 units, and you have made about 500, the status of this target is "green." If production problems have led to only 380 units being made, the status of this target should be recorded as "amber," and the item should be discussed at the next review meeting. If you have only produced 150 units, the status indicator will be set at "red." This signals that urgent action is required or that the target has become impossible to achieve.

MONITORING CHANGE PROJECTS

You can also use green, amber, and red status indicators to monitor change projects. If most milestones are being achieved, the status should be green. If there are problems, it is the responsibility of the manager or the team member in charge of the project to alert the team that the status has changed to amber. If there are serious problems, the team must be informed of the red status immediately, and a course of action must be proposed to remedy the situation.

ASSESSING THE PROGRESS OF OTHERS

In addition to producing your own reports, it is important to keep a close check on the performance of people outside your team if their progress is likely to affect your targets or change projects. If, for example, production is falling behind on a new range of goods and you are a sales manager with a target of selling a specific number of units, you will need to know about any shortfall. Try to persuade people in other departments to use the same standard methods of producing reports, since this will make understanding them far easier. To make certain that the information contained in a report is timely and accurate, someone must also be responsible for it. Allocate this task to a team member who is responsible for some of the items in the report itself. Stress the importance of keeping reports clear and up-to-date – and hope that others will follow your good example.

91 Monitor informally by listening, observing, and communicating.

92 Keep up to date with changes in other areas of your organization.

▼ MONITORING EFFECTIVELY
The diagram below shows how important it is to have a monitoring system that warns of the gap between target and progress before it becomes critical. After that point, it may be impossible to get a change project back on track. Operational targets may need monitoring weekly rather than monthly.

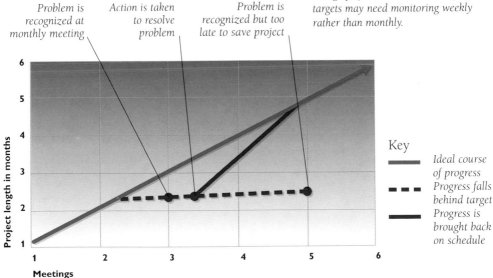

Problem is recognized at monthly meeting

Action is taken to resolve problem

Problem is recognized but too late to save project

Project length in months

Meetings

Key

— *Ideal course of progress*

- - - *Progress falls behind target*

— *Progress is brought back on schedule*

HOLDING REVIEWS

Monthly review meetings allow you to examine the operational issues of the day and resolve any problems highlighted by progress reports. It is also important to set aside time to look at the overall strategy and ensure that it is still relevant.

93 Be firm when running meetings; keep them strictly to the point.

94 Make it a hard and fast rule to start and finish meetings on time.

CONDUCTING REVIEWS ▼

Address urgent issues first, giving each team member the opportunity to come up with solutions. If a solution is not obvious, delegate the problem to the appropriate people to be resolved after the meeting.

REVIEWING PROGRESS

Like a board of directors, teams typically meet once a month. Use the status indicators – red, amber, or green – to establish the order of your agenda. Monitor the operational past by asking how you have done, and consider the likely outcome if you leave things as they are. Look at change projects and assess whether you are actually making changes in the way you intended. Finally, check your assumptions. Is your plan still valid in all aspects? The answers will prompt a number of suggestions for changing how you work.

Team leader begins review by discussing urgent, or "red," item

Team member responsible for change project explains problems

Colleague suggests possible remedial action

Team member agrees to assist in getting objective back on track

RESOLVING ISSUES

Discuss indicators that show that immediate action is required. For example, if there is a delay in delivering products to an important customer, the team must decide what it is going to do about it, agree who is responsible for resolving the issue, and put a time limit on finding a solution. Discussion of progress against change projects is almost always useful, and often the whole team will have a contribution to make. If a point comes up regularly and shows no improvement, check what action is feasible and change the plan rather than leaving the subject to fester.

95 If plans are not working, change them now rather than later.

96 Use review meetings to test new ideas against the business case.

REVIEWING STRATEGY

Use monthly meetings to concentrate on operational targets and change projects that are already under way. You should also hold longer meetings on a regular basis to review the strategy itself if your plan is to retain its relevance, and to make sure it is still the best plan the team can devise. Check the assumptions you identified at the fact-gathering stage to confirm they are still the best estimates. It is unlikely that you will need to go back to stating purpose or to examine your competitive advantage or boundary setting at every quarterly meeting, but you may have to regroup product markets, change emphasis on product markets, and have another look at budgets.

DO'S AND DON'TS

✔ Do remind people that completed change projects will ultimately benefit them.

✔ Do expect everyone to carry out their actions in change projects.

✘ Don't accept excuses that everyday pressure is preventing work on change projects.

✘ Don't leave more than one month between reviews.

97 Consider changes to the business case template itself, if necessary.

BEING FLEXIBLE

An army general once said: "No plan survives contact with the enemy." Similarly, it is said that no strategic plan survives contact with the marketplace. Be prepared to change the plan in the light of new circumstances and the unforeseen.

98 Aim to improve continuously to be flexible strategically.

EXPECTING THE UNEXPECTED

Not all eventualities can be predicted. External events may force you to review a basic part of the plan only a short time into implementation. A radical change, such as a competitor launching a new product or an important customer merging with another company, will have a major impact on the strategy. Whenever this happens, and certainly every year, you must reexamine the plan for its overall statement of direction.

In a review meeting, team spots the need to change the plan

Team postpones review and fails to recognize that change is needed

Team finalizes the strategic plan

Team fails to deliver and customer expresses lack of confidence

▲ ADAPTING TO CHANGE

In this example, a team is faced with external changes in the market. The effective team discusses the changes, decides to change its plan, and informs the customer, boosting his confidence in the team. The team that fails to spot the changes, or ignores them, risks losing its customers.

99 Listen to what suppliers say about changes in their industry.

ALTERING COURSE

Be prepared to change the strategic plan as and when necessary. In fact, one of the paybacks of developing a good strategic plan is that even in fast-moving business environments, the strategy provides the basis on which to evaluate opportunities. To be effective, you and your team must constantly challenge your current methods of conducting business and seek to change and improve the ways in which you meet customer needs. Review meetings offer an excellent platform for the discussion of these ideas. A difficult situation arises if, for example, a pet project for a new product has been made irrelevant by a competitor offering something radically better. Just as your reviewing system must allow for new opportunities, it must also provide a mechanism for discarding ideas that were originally sound. New opportunities require resources, and it is not unusual for these resources to come from existing activities or projects.

Customer is impressed by forward-thinking and increases business

RETESTING STRATEGY

The strategy at the end of a planning year may differ significantly from the initial plan, but, provided that the team has applied the agreed criteria for assessing business cases, it will still reflect the best speed and direction of development. The benefit of using the business case template will be seen again when the team makes a change to the strategy. By subjecting a change, such as a new emphasis on a product market, to the business case template test, you will see which opportunities you should exploit. Finally, there will be times when even the business case template may need reviewing. But that is what strategic thinking is all about: keeping up to date and improving all the time.

100 Make sure you react to change with courage and resolution.

101 Remember that strategic thinking should be fun as well as challenging.

ASSESSING YOUR STRATEGIC THINKING

E*valuate your ability to think strategically by responding to the following statements, marking the option closest to your experience. Be as honest as you can: if your answer is "never," circle Option 1; if it is "always," circle Option 4, and so on. Add your scores together, and refer to the Analysis to see how well you scored. Use your answers to identify the areas that most need improvement.*

OPTIONS

1 Never

2 Occasionally

3 Frequently

4 Always

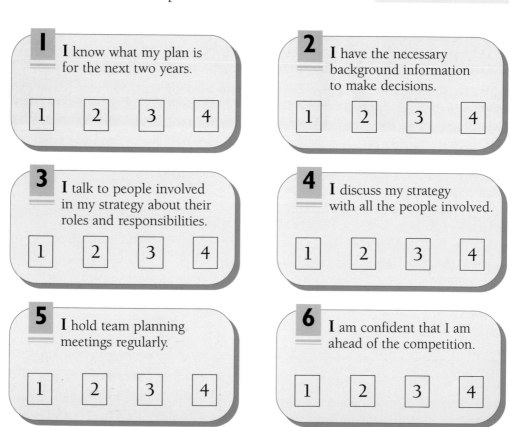

1 I know what my plan is for the next two years.

1 2 3 4

2 I have the necessary background information to make decisions.

1 2 3 4

3 I talk to people involved in my strategy about their roles and responsibilities.

1 2 3 4

4 I discuss my strategy with all the people involved.

1 2 3 4

5 I hold team planning meetings regularly.

1 2 3 4

6 I am confident that I am ahead of the competition.

1 2 3 4

7 I am able to accurately predict my customers' requirements.

| 1 | 2 | 3 | 4 |

8 I know how to get the best from new technology.

| 1 | 2 | 3 | 4 |

9 I can state my customers' up-to-date buying criteria.

| 1 | 2 | 3 | 4 |

10 I know the contents of my competitors' websites.

| 1 | 2 | 3 | 4 |

11 I regularly discuss internal business processes with my team.

| 1 | 2 | 3 | 4 |

12 I use SWOT analysis on an everyday basis.

| 1 | 2 | 3 | 4 |

13 I understand my up-to-date competitive advantage.

| 1 | 2 | 3 | 4 |

14 I consult with other team leaders on strategy.

| 1 | 2 | 3 | 4 |

15 I discuss changes to my strategy with my customers and suppliers.

| 1 | 2 | 3 | 4 |

16 I use a business case template to check that new ideas fit with my strategy.

| 1 | 2 | 3 | 4 |

17 I ensure that my team members know the criteria for adopting new ideas.

1　2　3　4

18 I ensure that my team always operates within the strategy.

1　2　3　4

19 I have drawn up appropriate priorities for product markets.

1　2　3　4

20 I put resources into new markets with potential but little short-term profit.

1　2　3　4

21 I know what my costs are against budget.

1　2　3　4

22 I know what my actual sales are against target.

1　2　3　4

23 I know exactly where my team needs to improve on its skills.

1　2　3　4

24 I ensure that team members take change projects seriously.

1　2　3　4

25 I have a documented and up-to-date strategic plan.

1　2　3　4

26 I know what the threats are to achieving my objectives.

1　2　3　4

27 I see that everyone who needs to know about my strategy is kept informed.

| 1 | 2 | 3 | 4 |

28 I know that my team members see their targets as reasonable but challenging.

| 1 | 2 | 3 | 4 |

29 I review and update my plan on a regular basis.

| 1 | 2 | 3 | 4 |

30 I adopt company-wide standards when producing my reports.

| 1 | 2 | 3 | 4 |

31 I require only those who need to be present to remain in review meetings.

| 1 | 2 | 3 | 4 |

32 I ensure that my own strategy fits in with the strategies of my colleagues.

| 1 | 2 | 3 | 4 |

ANALYSIS

Now that you have completed the self-assessment, add up your total score and check your performance by reading the corresponding evaluation. Whichever level of success you have achieved in thinking strategically, it is important to remember that there is always room for improvement. Identify your weakest areas, and refer to the relevant section and chapters where you will find practical advice and tips to help you to develop and refine your skills.

32–64: You operate reactively and do not spend enough time thinking strategically. Take one or two individual steps from the planning process and see them through to a result.

65–95: You are a reasonable strategic thinker, but should address some weak points.

96–128: You are a good strategic thinker, but do not become complacent.

MANAGING BUDGETS

INTRODUCTION

The managers most likely to succeed in today's business environment are those who understand how to use budgets as business tools for departmental and personal success. Managing Budgets is an informative and practical guide to the essential skills needed to produce accurate and useful budgets. The three key stages to budgeting – preparing, writing, and monitoring – are clearly explained to help you significantly improve the quality of your budgets. Practical advice is given on how to challenge figures logically and how to monitor procedures sensibly. One hundred and one concise tips scattered throughout the text give further vital information. Finally, a thorough self-assessment exercise allows you to evaluate and improve on your budgeting skills.

UNDERSTANDING BUDGETING

Budgeting is the process of preparing, compiling, and monitoring financial budgets. It is a key management tool for planning and controlling a department within an organization.

WHAT IS A BUDGET?

A budget is a plan for future activities. It can be expressed in a number of ways, but usually it describes all of a business in financial terms. It is the yardstick by which an organization's performance is measured.

 Always remember that if you fail to plan, you are planning to fail.

MANAGEMENT SKILLS ▲
As a manager, you must be able to communicate your budgetary requirements effectively.

DEFINING A BUDGET

A budget is a statement of monetary plans that is prepared in advance of a forthcoming period, usually one year. Budgets are often thought to include only planned revenues and expenditures (the profit and loss account), which show the income that each part of an organization is expected to generate and the total cost that it is authorized to incur. However, a budget should also include an organization's plans for assets and liabilities (budgeted balance sheet) and the estimates for cash receipts and payments (budgeted cash flow).

Overall expenditure type is divided into component parts, including a clear description of each cost

A total figure for departmental expenditure types is calculated (this figure is then put into expenditure totals for the whole organization)

MARKETING DEPARTMENT BUDGET YEAR 2		
ADVERTISING EXPENDITURE	YEAR 2 BUDGET	YEAR 1 ACTUAL
Gizmo pre-launch leaflet research	110	100
Gizmo launch Geneva	60	52
TV spring year 2 offensive	700	680
Radio advertisements March year 2	600	554
Newspaper quarter-page monthly	70	63
Stall at Berlin Trade Fair	450	512
Dealer incentive program	60	54
National Trade Body funding	80	90
Stall at Birmingham Trade Fair	40	44
Radio advertisements May year 2	100	67
TV fall year 2 offensive	80	68
TOTALS	2350	2284

Heading gives business department and budget period currently being prepared

Financial amounts anticipated to be spent are presented alongside actual amounts spent in previous period

2 Manage your business, do not let it manage you.

QUESTIONS TO ASK YOURSELF

Q Has my organization been budgeting successfully for many years?

Q Did anything go particularly wrong in last year's budgeting?

Q Does the business have any unusual features that will cause budgeting problems?

Q Are there any managers that are particularly good at budgeting?

▲ **LISTING A TYPICAL BUDGET**
In this example, a marketing department has prepared next year's expenditure budget by listing the activities on which they anticipate spending money, compared with what they spent in the current year.

BUDGETING IN BUSINESS

Using budgets is vital for the planning and control of a business. Budgets help coordinate actions of different managers and departments while securing commitment to achieving results. Budgets also give authority for departmental managers to incur expenditure by their department and provide targets for earning revenue.

By providing benchmarks against which actual activities are monitored, budgets are a reliable way of analyzing actual business performance. Budgets are therefore a way for an organization to generate information so that it can measure how it is progressing, and how it might adapt to an agreed business plan in view of actual performance.

WHY BUDGET?

Budgets help an individual, department, and organization achieve planned objectives. Budgets also help to illustrate the financial responsibilities of the organization to several groups of people: lenders, suppliers, employees, customers, and the owners.

3 Use budgets effectively and they will be key tools for success.

RECOGNIZING YOUR RESPONSIBILITIES

While budgetary systems are more common in larger organizations, where sophisticated and formalized management techniques exist, the usefulness of budgeting in smaller organizations is just as great. You must recognize what your personal and departmental responsibilities are to your organization and budget appropriately. The validity and usefulness of a budget depend on the people who put it together. Budgets are only as good as the individuals who prepare them.

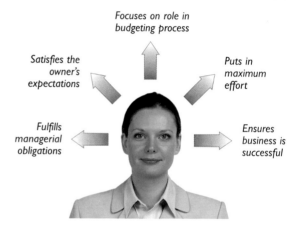

Focuses on role in budgeting process

Satisfies the owner's expectations

Puts in maximum effort

Fulfills managerial obligations

Ensures business is successful

▲ **RESPONSIBILITIES FOR BUDGETING**
Just as budgets must achieve a number of aims within an organization, so, as a manager, you must be prepared to fulfill a number of responsibilities as part of the budgeting process.

4 Decide on the role and responsibility of your budget to suit the whole organization.

THE ROLE OF BUDGETING

Budgeting creates a framework within which individuals, departments, and whole organizations can work. Budgets encourage individuals and departments to look and plan ahead using a standardized agenda that can enhance effective communication of their objectives. Drafting assorted budgets and collating them can help coordinate and motivate employees. Budgets also provide a focus for evaluation of the various aspects of a business in a controlled fashion.

THE SIX MAIN AIMS OF BUDGETING

AIMS	DESCRIPTION
PLANNING	To aid the planning of an organization in a systematic and logical manner that adheres to the long-term business strategy.
COORDINATION	To help coordinate the activities of the various parts of the organization and ensure that they are consistent.
COMMUNICATION	To communicate more easily the objectives, opportunities, and plans of the business to the various business team managers.
MOTIVATION	To provide motivation for managers to try to achieve the organizational and individual goals.
CONTROL	To help control activities by measuring progress against the original plan, adjusting where necessary.
EVALUATION	To provide a framework for evaluating the performance of managers in meeting individual and departmental targets.

5 Remember, budget planning and control go hand in hand.

6 Plan what you are going to do, do not just react to changes.

EVALUATING THE DISADVANTAGES

A conscientious and effective budget brings numerous benefits to an organization, yet a budget can be inconvenient. Assess the disadvantages of preparing a budget in the light of its many advantages.

- Budgets increase paperwork and can be a drain on management time, especially early on.
- Budgets are slow to work, since the benefits will not be seen until the next year.
- Budgets require standardization, which can lead to inflexibility.
- Budgets can meet with resistance from managers reluctant to embrace new procedures.

BUDGETING AND BUSINESS STRATEGY

The budgeting process is a relatively short-term measure that is just one part of the overall business strategy. It is a tactic that is used in the implementation of activities and programs for which senior management will have planned.

7 Tell your money where to go; do not worry about where it went.

8 Make sure your organization has clearly thought out long-term plans and strategies.

UNDERSTANDING BUSINESS STRATEGY

Business strategy is the vision of where the organization wants to be in three to five years' time. This will include setting overall objectives so that the organization can determine what it hopes to achieve. The business strategy also identifies courses of action. This involves analyzing the environment in which an organization operates and the resources that it possesses using the SWOT analysis – an assessment of the business strengths, weaknesses, opportunities, and threats.

DEVELOPING THE BUSINESS PLAN

Whereas organizations plan for the long term using a strategic plan, they plan for the short term using a business plan – what the organization must do now in order to achieve the strategic plan. In order to put into practice the business plan, the organization must consider appropriate planning procedures to work out what to do when, and the necessary controls (including budgeting) to ensure that anticipated results are actually achieved.

THINGS TO DO

1. Inspect the strategic plan.
2. Review the SWOT analysis.
3. Examine other business assessments.
4. Inspect the business plan.
5. Understand the context of your budget within the overall business.

USING A BUDGET AS A BUSINESS TACTIC

Budgeting is the tactical implementation of the business plan. It is incorporated in both the business planning and control processes. Senior management choose the strategic options that will have the greatest potential for achieving the organization's objectives and will create long-term plans to implement those strategies. You can transform those long-range plans into your department's budgeted annual operating plans. Use budgets as a benchmark against which you can measure actual future performance by using regular internally-generated financial reports called the management accounting package. This package is made up from the profit and loss accounts, balance sheets, and cash flow financial reports, and shows what was expected compared to what actually happened.

9 Consider the market trends of your organization's products.

10 Use budgets to judge performance and as an authority to spend.

THE BUSINESS PLANNING AND CONTROL PROCESS

STAGE	ACTIONS TO TAKE
SHORT-TERM PLANNING	● Prepare operating plans and programs. ● Compile annual financial budgets. ● React to changes in the marketplace. ● Continually reassess validity of plans.
LONG-TERM PLANNING	● Determine the organization's business objectives. ● Evaluate strategic market and product options. ● Analyze the organization's strengths and weaknesses. ● Identify financial, physical, and human resource needs.
CONTROL	● Prepare management reports. ● Evaluate discrepancies between actual and plan. ● Decide on how to remedy discrepancies. ● Take effective corrective action.

MAINTAINING A BUSINESS BUDGETING CYCLE

There is a popular misconception that the annual budgeting event is a ballistic process: you do a lot of work, then you press a button and you're off. Everything is then put away until next year. In fact, quite the opposite is true. Far from being a discrete once-a-year activity, budgeting requires continuous and simultaneous tending of budgeted and actual figures from several accounting years. In every month in the year, there will be a budgeting-related activity taking place in an organization. This activity could be for one of several years – the year just gone, the current year, the year to come, or several years to come. This activity could also be of several types – budget preparation, budget monitoring, updating estimates, finalizing whole year results, or looking ahead longer-term.

 Ensure that your budgeting is a year-round continuous process.

12 **Schedule your budgeting-related tasks in financially less busy periods.**

13 Allow sufficient time in your budgeting schedule to do justice to your budgeting process.

POINTS TO REMEMBER

- Budgeting activity may be for this year, next year, or several years into the future.
- Budgeting activities repeat themselves, usually over the course of a year, and should therefore be anticipated.
- Realistic planning will help you to carry out budgeting-related tasks in a logical order.

CULTURAL DIFFERENCES

Most European countries regard budgeting as a necessary management tool without which an organization cannot survive. However, the US and certain Scandinavian countries are increasingly seeing budgeting as a tool of repression that does little to improve business health. These countries see little value in continuing to work to figures from a budget that bear little resemblance to the actual figures that are produced from the changing real world. Many of the techniques used in these countries as an alternative to traditional budgeting follow a more holistic approach. An example is the balanced business scorecard technique, which considers all aspects of a business rather than just its financial concerns.

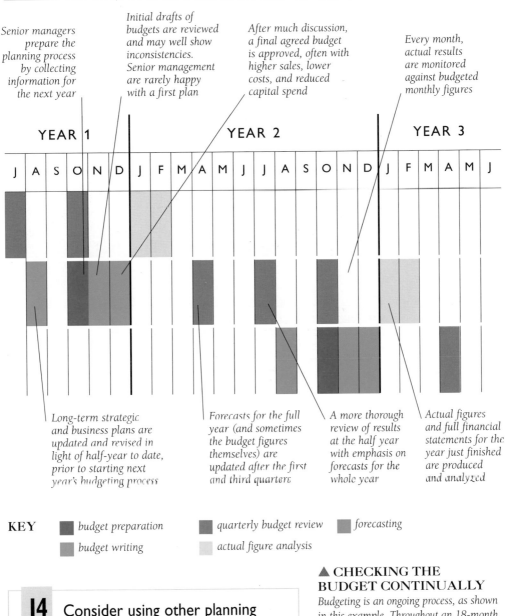

Senior managers prepare the planning process by collecting information for the next year

Initial drafts of budgets are reviewed and may well show inconsistencies. Senior management are rarely happy with a first plan

After much discussion, a final agreed budget is approved, often with higher sales, lower costs, and reduced capital spend

Every month, actual results are monitored against budgeted monthly figures

YEAR 1   **YEAR 2**   **YEAR 3**

| J | A | S | O | N | D | J | F | M | A | M | J | J | A | S | O | N | D | J | F | M | A | M | J |

Long-term strategic and business plans are updated and revised in light of half-year to date, prior to starting next year's budgeting process

Forecasts for the full year (and sometimes the budget figures themselves) are updated after the first and third quarters

A more thorough review of results at the half year with emphasis on forecasts for the whole year

Actual figures and full financial statements for the year just finished are produced and analyzed

KEY
- ■ *budget preparation*
- ■ *budget writing*
- ■ *quarterly budget review*
- ■ *actual figure analysis*
- ■ *forecasting*

14 Consider using other planning techniques for your organization, in addition to budgeting.

▲ CHECKING THE BUDGET CONTINUALLY

Budgeting is an ongoing process, as shown in this example. Throughout an 18-month budget period the same activities are repeated every financial year (each row). In every month of the year, there is an aspect of budgeting that requires attention.

MANAGING THE BUDGETING PROCESS

Just as budgeting is part of the structured business model of planning and control, so is there a structured model for managing the budgeting process itself. It is important to use a model as a blueprint for the process to ensure consistency and quality.

15 Ensure that you know what you intend to do at every stage.

16 Always plan, even if the future is unpredictable.

17 Co-ordinate your budget with other departments.

TAILORING THE MODEL

Budgeting is too important to get wrong, and a manager will often not get a second chance. Within reason, make your budgets as accurate as possible on the first attempt. Following a model will help you to get it right the first time. It will not guarantee success, but the quality of what is produced will be greatly improved. As with all models, tailor your budgeting process to suit your departmental needs in tune with your business environment. If something in the model is not relevant to your organization, do not do it.

COPING WITH AN UNCERTAIN FUTURE

The future is uncertain, so what is the point of trying to predict it accurately? Many will claim that the uncertainties specific to their business make budgets impractical for them, yet one can always find companies in the same industry that use budgets successfully. Even in fast-moving sectors, such as information technology and telecommunications, you will find that many of the companies that regard budgets as indispensable are among the industry leaders. As a manager, it is important that you grapple with any uncertainties early on, and that you are prepared to be flexible in your approach to budgeting. Always bear in mind that the benefits of good budgeting will always exceed the cost.

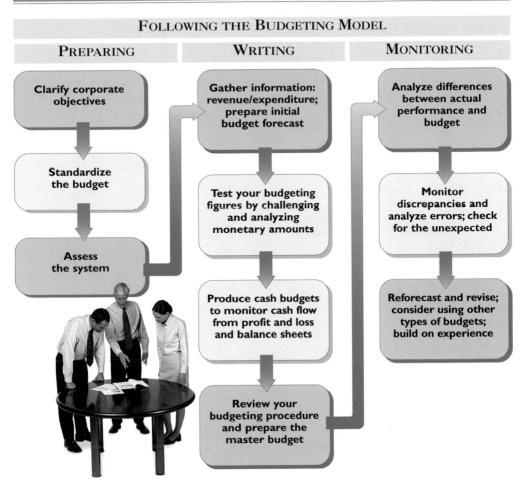

Following the Budgeting Model

PREPARING	WRITING	MONITORING
Clarify corporate objectives	Gather information: revenue/expenditure; prepare initial budget forecast	Analyze differences between actual performance and budget
Standardize the budget	Test your budgeting figures by challenging and analyzing monetary amounts	Monitor discrepancies and analyze errors; check for the unexpected
Assess the system	Produce cash budgets to monitor cash flow from profit and loss and balance sheets	Reforecast and revise; consider using other types of budgets; build on experience
	Review your budgeting procedure and prepare the master budget	

Following a Structure

Build three distinct, but equally important, tasks into your budgeting model. First, you should prepare the budget; second, you should write the budget; finally, you must monitor the budget. Research has shown that most budgets that fail to achieve their purpose have been neither properly planned nor properly monitored. Organizations often jump straight into writing a budget, without any thought or preparation, and have nothing to refer to later on in the budgeting cycle.

THINGS TO DO

1. Plan your budgeting model.
2. Decide on the personnel that you want involved.
3. Communicate the plan to key people.
4. Allocate sufficient budget resources.

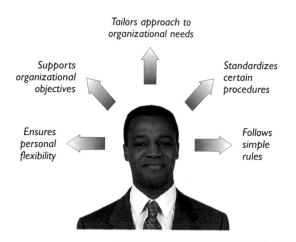

Tailors approach to organizational needs

Supports organizational objectives

Standardizes certain procedures

Ensures personal flexibility

Follows simple rules

BEGINNING TO BUDGET ▲

There are a number of qualities that a manager must possess in order to manage budgeting effectively. If any one of these qualities is absent, your budgeting efficiency will soon be reduced.

18 Write out the important tasks on a calendar to help with the timing of key steps within your budget.

PREPARING TO BUDGET

The importance of "planning the plan" can not be over-emphasized, and you must understand how a budget can be made to work for your organization. Rather than expecting someone else's budgeting model to work for you, you must tailor your budget to your organization. A superb document is worthless if it does not comply with your organization's strategic plan. Preparing to budget also involves standardizing procedures. It can be useful to create a budgeting manual that provides budgeting guidelines which, depending on the size of your organization, can be monitored by a committee.

DO'S AND DON'TS

✔ Do encourage your team to plan ahead to reduce the number of ad hoc decisions.

✔ Do communicate management plans and listen to the problems that others foresee.

✔ Do provide a yardstick against which other managers and their departments' performances can be evaluated.

✗ Don't expect to reconcile and merge separate functional budgets without any co-ordination.

✗ Don't accept anything other than reasonable, well-defined targets to encourage motivation.

✗ Don't forget to allocate resources appropriately and openly for managers and departments.

19 Consider using project-planning software for more complex budgets.

20 Ask friends in other departments to show you how they budget.

WRITING A BUDGET ▼

If all managers follow the same standard procedures for writing budgets, senior management will be able to evaluate all budgets in relation to each other, for the good of the whole organization.

WRITING A BUDGET

There are a number of logical steps to writing a meaningful budget. Initially, you must gather information about what your organization wants to achieve, what its limits are, and what the relevant internal and external business influences are that will affect the organization. It is crucial that you focus on the types, amounts, and timings of both revenue and costs to give you better estimates for income and expenditure. To be more efficient, provide more valid figures, and know how to challenge budgeted amounts you must understand cost types and behavior. Linking the capital expenditure budgets to revenue and expenditure will give senior management a clearer picture of the feasibility of a budget, and you must carry out an all-important consolidation process to finalize the budget.

Chairperson evaluates the requirements of all departments

Manager reports on own department

MONITORING A BUDGET

It is vital that you monitor a budget by checking what actually happened against what you budgeted to happen, investigating the reasons why there are discrepancies, taking corrective action, then assessing how you could improve your budgeting in the future. It is important to know what to do when the budget seems to be plainly wrong: whether it should be left alone or changed, and how changes should be made. Some of the inaccuracies in a budget may be due to human errors rather than business issues, so it is important to consider all the various factors before you begin to build for the future.

21 Tailor writing your budget to those aspects that you want to monitor.

22 See if there is a trend in the accuracy of previous budgets.

RECOGNIZING POTENTIAL PROBLEMS

In some organizations, budgets are regarded as something to be feared rather than as positive business tools that enhance performance. This is because budget systems serve several interests, some of which may conflict with each other.

23 Demanding but achievable targets are the most successful.

Managers meet to discuss and attempt to resolve conflicts

UNDERSTANDING CONFLICTS

By predicting potential conflicts of interest you will be able to set a realistic budget.

- Planning a demanding budget may lead to higher than realistically achievable figures, which can lead to demotivation among staff and poor performance.
- Business decisions that look good from an individual's perspective might prove to be less good for the department or whole organization.
- The business environment may be so fast-moving that the budget, as a tool or prediction, cannot keep up with events fast enough.

Conflicts remain unresolved and budget is likely to fail

DEALING WITH CONFLICTS

Budgeting is an imperfect science, and it is important to recognize that without corrective action conflicts can be become very disruptive.

- To motivate staff without compromising departmental plans, produce two budgets: one for planning purposes and one for setting management targets.
- Give clear instructions to managers that they must act in accordance not only with their own interests but also those of the department.
- To ensure the budget is up to date, allow for a short budget timeframe, such as three months.

> **24** Communicate with others to avoid potential budgeting problems.

Managers understand each others' needs and agree how to keep to budget.

DISCUSSING ▲ WITH OTHERS

This illustration shows how by resolving potential conflicts early on, a budget can be successfully adhered to.

> **25** Organize training sessions that deal with budgeting best practice.

DO'S AND DON'TS

✔ Do recognize that budgets are used for more purposes than simply predicting next year's results.

✔ Do accept that depending on the purpose and use of the figures, budgets can conflict.

✔ Do collaborate with other departmental managers to reach agreement.

✘ Don't confuse the organization's needs with what you want to achieve.

✘ Don't get so drawn into interdepartmental politics that you begin to lose sight of the organization's aims.

✘ Don't keep to a budget that is clearly out of step with a fast-moving business; revise the budget.

PREPARING TO BUDGET

The better prepared your budget, the fewer problems you will have in the future. Link your budget to the objectives of your organization and provide a procedure that all can follow.

TAILORING A BUDGET

Your ultimate goal should be to create a budgeting system that actively supports the success of your organization. To achieve this you must prepare a budget that is tailored to your department and that fits in with the ambitions of your organization.

26 Learn from those who have done their budgets well in the past.

27 Take care not to be overambitious; it is a common error in a first budget submission.

WHY TAILOR THE BUDGET?

It is very important early on that you determine how you are going set out your own budgeting style. Budgeting can fulfill a number of functions. It can be a means by which to help achieve business targets, measure business performance, appraise managers and departments, and motivate staff. Consider which functions are most important to your department and organization and build your budgeting style and reporting around them. Remember that the budgeting process is a means to an end, not the end in itself.

DEVISING A RELEVANT BUDGET

Make sure that you do not devise a rigid and unyielding budget in which everything is categorized as a success or failure. You will not set a useful budget if you set unrealistic targets and try to measure performance against them. Approach budgeting in a pragmatic manner so that it is effective as a business tool and not an impediment to your success. Do not be tempted to slavishly follow someone else's budget model. Set the headings yourself based on your own assessment of your needs. Keep in mind that budgeting priorities can change and that you may need to adapt your budget to serve a constantly changing business environment. It can be helpful early on to review those budgeting activities that have taken place within your organization in the past. How successful were they, what should be improved upon, and what should be added to make this year's budgeting even better? Finally, as a rule of thumb, bear in mind that it will take one or two years to set up a reliable system that can run effectively.

28 Avoid unnecessary jargon to help convey your budgeting aims.

THINGS TO DO

1. Publicize the fact that budgeting will take place.
2. Educate staff about what the budgeting process will do for the department.
3. Consider how accurate you want your first budgeting attempt to be.
4. Establish your department's goals for success and prepare a budget that reflects those aims.

BUDGETING ▶ FOR YOUR NEEDS

No two organizations are the same. Every organization will budget differently and should not blindly borrow practices from others. You need to decide why you are budgeting, what you want to achieve from it, what your particular business problems are, and how your approach to budgeting will meet these aims.

CASE STUDY

Felicity's Foods maintained food vending machines in corporate offices. The company had never really budgeted for any future activities before, but was anxious to do so as its sales were growing fast.

The accountant suggested a budgeting model that he used in his last job at Megahuge plc, a manufacturing company, which he said worked well.

However, senior managers were worried that the budget model would not be relevant for a business of their size.

The accountant resolved the problem by revising the budget model to include only those elements of the borrowed budget that were relevant to the size of Felicity's Foods' business, and he omitted any details that were inappropriate.

As a result, senior management were much happier, and agreed to use the tailored budgeting model as a pilot run for the following year.

CLARIFYING OBJECTIVES

Base your budget on a clear, objective organizational strategy. Determine this strategy early on by reviewing your departmental business to compare actual results with ideal results, then prepare a budgeting plan to close that gap.

29 Clarify objectives in a brainstorming session with other managers.

30 Be innovative with the financial ratios you choose.

THE FOUR STEPS ▼

Base budgets on a four step approach that will help you to clarify your department's business objectives in financial terms.

STEP 4
Set financial targets

STEP 3
Decide objectives

STEP 2
Plan for the future

STEP 1
Review the business

REVIEWING THE BUSINESS

You must carry out a thoroughly realistic and honest departmental review that looks at all parts of the business that affect its capacity to deliver what the customer wants. The review procedure gives you an opportunity to look at your department with an objective budgeting eye, which can be both an exhilarating and leveling process. The important thing is that it must be well-informed and honest. This is not the time for fault-finding or fantasy. The lessons of the past should only be viewed as a tool for acting effectively in the future. The popular SWOT analysis (strengths, weaknesses, opportunities, and threats) is a good starting point for the review, though other structured and objective techniques can be just as effective.

DO'S AND DON'TS

☑ Do make sure that you fully appreciate the true strengths and opportunities that your department and organization possess.

☑ Do be fully aware of the enormous amount of time and effort that budgeting requires.

☒ Don't be afraid to recognize honestly the weaknesses and threats that your business faces.

☒ Don't copy business objectives from other departments, make sure you generate your own.

PLANNING FOR THE FUTURE

The strategic plan sets out the major long-term business and financial plans for your organization and is the basis on which you will set your department's objectives. The strategic plan could simply state the definition of your business and how your organization plans to grow in terms of size, quality, security, and competitiveness.

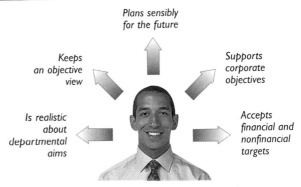

Plans sensibly for the future

Keeps an objective view

Supports corporate objectives

Is realistic about departmental aims

Accepts financial and nonfinancial targets

▲ **FOLLOW BUSINESS OBJECTIVES**
It is from the definition of the strategic plan that you will be able to set your all-important business objectives and link your organization's strategy to your department's operational control.

31	Avoid too many backward-looking measures.

32	In business, there is always something to be standardized.

DECIDING CORPORATE OBJECTIVES

Business objectives consider the business as a whole and may be only partly quantifiable. Some objectives are general; others relate specifically to marketing, organizational, or financial concerns. Setting objectives for your department allows you to define your aspirations in ways that can be used to measure the business. You will achieve much more by remembering to balance what is achievable with what is aspirational.

SETTING FINANCIAL TARGETS

Convert your department's objectives into a formal financial budget. This should take into account marketing, production (or provisions of services), purchasing, personnel, and administration. Express these financial targets in profit and loss accounts, balance sheets, and cash flow statements, year by year, for the whole budget period.To cover all aspects of your business, you should also include in your budget nonfinancial perfomance measures, such as recorded complaints and compliments.

CHOOSING THE BUDGET PERIOD

The budget period is the length of time the budget covers, usually one year. It is often sub-divided into control periods of varying lengths, usually monthly. Choose your budget period by defining the level of budgetary control you wish to exercise.

STANDARDIZING A BUDGET

To coordinate budgets within your organization, managers should use a standard budgeting format. This will help with collaboration over budget content and enable budgets to be compared and linked throughout your organization.

33 Issue blank budgets as spreadsheets for electronic completion.

34 Publicize the purpose of the budget committee and its activities.

DEVISING A MANUAL ▼

A budget manual need not be much more than a few sheets of paper listing key facts to make sure that everyone is working with the same basic figures in mind.

COMPILING A MANUAL

An effective budget manual needs to include the following:

- An introduction to the importance of budgeting.
- A timetable showing when the master budget will be prepared from all other budgets.
- Guidelines to common key assumptions to be made by managers in their budgets.
- Copies of forms to be completed, including explanations concerning their completion.
- An organizational chart with names of those that are responsible for each budget.
- Departmental account codes and names of contacts to help with budgeting problems.

Shows standard assumptions about external matters affecting the budget preparation

Gives the organization's estimate for likely prices and market conditions

Shows nontrading items, such as tax, exchange, interest, and inflation rates

EXTERNAL MATTERS
1. The market is not expected to grow by much more than 20% per a each of the next 5 years. O is that 10% is likely to be th growth rate in sales that w achieve.
2. Markets are currently pric and our economic forecast no early end to this trend. zero price increase next y
3. Interest rates of 6.5% are for all calculations.
4. For those with foreign cu exposure in Europe assu For other currency rate contact Treasury depart
5. Assume 2.5% inflation board.
6. Tax rates will remain u throughout the year.

INTERNAL MATTERS
1. Headcount is to be maintained at current levels and wage increases will be limited to 3% at all levels.
2. The timetable below highlights key milestone dates in the budget - please be aware of them.
3. This year certain departments are being asked to prepare budgets on a different basis - see zero based budgeting.
4. Below is an organization chart showing how your budget fits in, and who to go to for help.

5. We aim to pay all suppliers within 60 days and collect monies from customers in the same time.

Gives details of estimates about internal matters affecting the budget

Presents structural matters, such as changes to employee numbers and likely wage settlements

Provides consistent benchmarks for dealing with customers and suppliers

QUESTIONS TO ASK YOURSELF

Q How could we possibly improve on the effectiveness of last year's budget?

Q Are all managers in the budgeting process familiar with the standardized procedures?

Q How far in advance of the budgeting process should the manual be issued?

Q What is the minimum number of people I need on the budgeting committee?

Q Does the budgeting committee have the right mix of skills, seniority, and relevant people?

FORMING A COMMITTEE

A budget cannot be prepared without reference to other departmental budgets, and so some degree of budgetary coordination is required. By forming a budget committee that includes representatives from the various business departments, you will be able to monitor the departmental budgeting progress and resolve any problems that might arise. The budgeting committee should set the guidelines for the budgeting manual, review departmental budgets by studying budget forecasts at meetings, create a master budget, be a general budgeting trouble-shooter, and ensure that the whole process is completed effectively and on time.

COMMITTEE MEMBERS ▼

A budgeting committee should comprise senior managers from the major business segments, the management accountant, and heads of all departments involved in the budget preparations.

35 Arrange for the budget committee to meet regularly.

Accountant is committee's technical advisor

Chairperson controls and mediates

Manager represents his department

CREATING A FORM

A budget form is the standardized actual layout that is used to collect and display all the information that goes into a budget. While most organizations should insist on standard forms (especially for the key areas of income, costs, and capital), some do allow a degree of flexibility appropriate to specific individual circumstances. Keep five principles in mind to ensure that the form looks good, is easy to use, and is efficient:

- Keep the form simple and straightforward, with only necessary details.
- Avoid amateur and overenthusiastic artwork.
- All forms should be consistent, with similar layout, typeface, and design.
- The form should be logically presented, well-organized, and be understandable without instructions.
- Wherever possible, use spreadsheets or the equivalent to ensure easy capture of data and ease of subsequent processing.

▼ **USING FORMS**
Everyone involved in filling in a budget form will do things differently. To end up with figures that are homogenous and can be easily added together, you must design a form that can be used by everyone.

A well-presented, standard form is easy for everyone to use

Notes on specific details can be taken and referred to at a later date

QUESTIONS TO ASK YOURSELF

Q Is the form good enough to stand on its own?

Q Are its contents clear and easy to understand?

Q Does it answer all likely questions?

Q Will the budget committee need more details?

Q Has it been fully completed in all significant respects?

Q Will other managers be able to fill in similar forms?

COMPLETING A FORM

When filling in a form, always keep one question in mind: "Am I completing the form correctly?" Ensure that you have inserted figures accurately and they have been added or subtracted correctly. Check that information is correctly arranged in columns and rows and that decimal points and commas are in the right places. Try to make the form as intelligible as possible. Correct all grammar, spelling, and punctuation; avoid using jargon, slang, technical, or vague expressions; and keep words and phrases short. Give the form to someone else, perhaps another manager, to check that they can understand its content.

| TRADING RESULTS | YEAR DATE | | | | | | | | | | | | | FORM TR1/99 |

CENTURY COPIERS

TRADING RESULTS	YEAR DATE												TOTAL
	Jan	Feb	Mar	Apr	May	Jun	Jul	Aug	Sep	Oct	Nov	Dec	
TURNOVER	940	1,100	1,200	960	980	1,150	1,060	850	1,200	1,250	1,500	1,310	13,500
COST OF SALES	705	840	910	740	730	880	820	650	910	950	1,100	980	10,215
GROSS PROFIT	235	260	290	220	250	270	240	200	290	300	400	330	3,285
GROSS PROFIT MARGIN	25%	24%	24%	23%	26%	23%	23%	24%	24%	24%	27%	25%	24%
OVERHEADS:													
Salaries	56	57	57	54	60	62	55	58	56	55	52	53	675
Pensions	6	6	6	6	6	6	6	6	5	5	5	5	68
Motor and travel	6	7	7	7	7	7	6	6	7	7	7	7	81
Equipment rental	1	1	1	1	1	1	1	1	1	1	1	1	12
Telecom	10	9	11	11	10	10	11	10	9	10	10	11	122
Print, post, & stationery	4	4	5	5	5	6	4	4	4	5	4	4	54
Marketing	10	11	11	12	12	11	13	12	11	11	11	10	135
Storage	3	3	3	4	3	3	3	4	3	4	4	4	41
Maintenance	12	12	11	12	13	12	12	14	12	13	13	13	149
Heat, light, & power	20	20	20	22	20	19	19	18	19	22	21	23	243
Insurance	8	8	8	7	9	9	9	10	8	8	8	9	101
Rent and rates	34	34	34	34	34	34	34	34	34	34	33	32	405
Legal & professional	1	1	1	1	3	1	1	1	1	2	1	2	16
Sundries	3	3	3	3	4	4	4	4	4	4	4	5	45
Depreciation	22	22	22	20	21	21	21	23	25	24	24	25	270
Bad debts	2	2	3	4	2	2	3	2	3	3	4	4	34
Profit on sale of assets	1	1	1		1	1	1	3	1	1	1	2	14
TOTAL OVERHEADS	199	201	204	203	211	209	203	210	203	209	203	210	2,465
OPERATING PROFIT (LOSS)	36	59	86	17	39	61	37	-10	87	91	197	120	820
Interest payable	5	5	5	5	5	5	5	5	5	5	5	5	60
NET PROFIT	31	54	81	12	34	56	32	-15	82	86	192	115	760

Reference code/number that can be quoted in later discussions

Clearly-defined columns and rows help to structure information

Black figures on a white background are easy to refer to for subsequent processing

Key calculations are segregated for easy reference

List of essential revenue and expenditure headings, ordered in a logical and progressive way

36 Use only listed options in spreadsheet cells to ensure there is consistency.

▲ DEVISING THE LAYOUT

Time spent on a well-created form is never wasted. Not only will it portray a well-presented and professional image, it can be understood easily by colleagues, and, importantly, can be easily referred to during later budget discussions.

Reviewing Your System

Once all the preparations for the budget have been made, you are ready to begin writing the budget and drafting the figures. Before you do that, review your system to ensure that your budget will provide you with correct and relevant information.

37 Deliberately putting padding into budgets achieves nothing.

38 Responsibility and accountability must go together.

39 Ensure you check the budget with the right people.

Keeping to Your Plan

Try not to dive straight into the budget. Remember the pareto rule: you can get 80 percent of the result with only 20 percent of the effort, but without proper planning the remaining 20 percent of the result can take up to 80 percent of the effort. Achieve successful preparation by ensuring that you have personalized and tailored your approach, linked the budget to organizational objectives, and used a few standardized procedures. Much of this is simply common sense and good practice, but it is often ignored in the rush to produce figures.

Following the Golden Rules

While budgets should be flexible and tailored to suit individual and departmental circumstances, you must also double-check that your budget is compatible with others and that there is a degree of standardization throughout the organization. You can achieve this not only through the use of budget manuals and forms but also by ensuring that everyone involved in the budgeting process keeps to the same principles of budget preparation. Keep following a list of rules for the whole budgeting process to ensure greater consistency and to realize the budget's full potential.

Points to Remember

● Use your colleagues' expertise and knowledge in the business review and planning process.

● Challenge present limits to your business and be inventive about how these could be overcome.

● Widen the organization's measurement perspective to beyond purely financial matters and include other significant objectives.

● Be pragmatic: a budget is a practical tool so it must be realistic and easy to use.

EIGHT GOLDEN RULES FOR EFFECTIVE BUDGETS

GOLDEN RULES	PUTTING THEORY INTO PRACTICE
BUDGET CONTINUOUSLY Budgeting and planning are not just one-time events.	Consider budgeting as more than an annual activity. Remember that the future is uncertain, so revise budgets regularly to reflect changes in the business environment.
TAKE YOUR TIME Budgets are the key part of planning and require careful thinking.	Do not underestimate the time needed to gather relevant information, formulate plans, and make a budget a realistic planning proposal.
INVOLVE EVERYONE Include all those that should be involved in the budgeting process.	Make your budgeting more than just a high-level activity. Involve relevant people with appropriate knowledge and skills and encourage them to commit to the process.
BE REALISTIC Focus on what your department actually needs in a particular budget.	Be aware that if resources are scarce there will be competing demands for items within the organization, which can often lead to deliberate overestimation.
LOOK AHEAD Look to the future, not to the past when deciding budgeting amounts.	Keep focused on future targets. Do not rely on historic figures to guide next year's budget, which, although approximately right, might be completely wrong.
BE AWARE OF POLITICS The size of budget does not equal its importance in the organization.	Understand that the size of a budget should not be confused with importance, and avoid all traditional budgetary game-playing around this.
MONITOR EVENTS Priorities and amounts may need to be changed in line with events.	Be prepared to amend your budget while still challenging all expenditures and trying to resolve unforeseen problems in other ways.
ALLOW FLEXIBILITY Budgets do not have to be slavishly followed.	Avoid the temptation to spend all that you were authorized to, and do not guard an underspend in your budget when others could well use the resource.

WRITING A BUDGET

To write a budget you must gather information, estimate figures for income and expenditure, and bring everything together in one agreed overall document.

GATHERING INFORMATION

By gathering information on all the possible internal and external influences on your budget, you will be able to determine what can and what cannot be achieved and what limiting factors might constrain your organization's activities.

40 Be aware of changing business laws and requirements.

CULTURAL DIFFERENCES

Government legislation in different countries can make the business environment liberal or authoritarian, and employment costs can affect labor mobility and the availability of skills. There are also different cross-cultural attitudes to payments from customers and to suppliers.

ASSESSING EXTERNAL INFLUENCES

External influences can have a greater effect on the success of a business than internal influences, so pay them close attention. Many organizations fail because they simply do not take the time to understand what is happening and what is about to happen around them. The main external influences that can affect your budget can be grouped into three areas: economic, population, and labor matters; governments and statutory bodies; and the business relationship between customers and suppliers.

POSSIBLE EXTERNAL INFLUENCES ON A BUDGET

AREA OF INFLUENCE	FACTORS TO CONSIDER
ECONOMIC, POPULATION, AND LABOR	**ECONOMY** Structure, cycle, inflation rates, interest rates, taxation levels, world influence, stock markets. **POPULATION** Types, number, location, mobility, births, deaths, future trends. **COMMUNITY** Neighbors, pressure groups, environmental issues, local differences, social trends, cultural trends. **LABOR** Types, number, availability, response to training, demands, expectations, skill sets.
GOVERNMENTS AND STATUTORY BODIES	**LEGISLATION** Employment law, consumer protection, health and safety, competition laws, statutory bodies. **GOVERNMENT** Types, fiscal and monetary policy, industrial and competition policy, incentives and initiatives. **INTERNATIONAL TRADE AGREEMENTS** Exports and imports, trade tariffs, tax harmonization, trade quotas, exchange rates. **ORGANIZATIONS** IRS, state tax bodies, creditors, lenders, stakeholders, management, regulatory bodies.
BUSINESS RELATIONSHIP BETWEEN CUSTOMERS AND SUPPLIERS	**CUSTOMERS** Types and numbers, demand levels, financial viability, likely growth, wants and needs. **COMPETITORS** Location, products, activities, strengths and weaknesses, attrition rate, aggression, growth rates. **SUPPLIERS** Types and numbers, cost and levels of supply, partnership, reliance, financial viability, location.

ASSESSING INTERNAL INFLUENCES

Assessing the influence that internal factors will have on a budget may seem simple enough but, because the focus is now inward-looking, sometimes obvious matters can be overlooked. There are three main areas of influence: business influences such as products and services; higher-level factors such as directors or shareholders; and resource availability. Since checklists cannot be exhaustive, always consider what other factors might apply; from the volatility of the business, through restructuring or change initiatives, to quality of management.

41 Recognize the importance of good management.

POINTS TO REMEMBER

- Internal factors may change and should be assessed continuously.
- Internal discussions can be the best source of information.
- Significant events should be anticipated.

POSSIBLE INTERNAL INFLUENCES ON A BUDGET

AREA OF INFLUENCE	FACTORS TO CONSIDER
BUSINESS INFLUENCES	**PRODUCTS AND SERVICES** Types, number, production methods, prices, pricing methods, stock levels
	BUSINESS UNITS Sales, production, purchasing, marketing, finance, administration, personnel
HIGH-LEVEL FACTORS	**PEOPLE** Directors, shareholders, unions, employees
	BUSINESS OBJECTIVES Short term, medium term, long term
RESOURCE AVAILABILITY	**AVAILABLE RESOURCES** Capital, profits, land, buildings, plant and equipment, machinery
	DEPARTMENTAL BUDGETS Sales, production, purchasing, marketing, finance, administration, personnel

ASSESSING THE LIMITING FACTOR

A limiting factor is a dominating influence that has a constraining effect on your department and organization. Although it may seem theoretical, the concept is only too real for most businesses. Identify limiting factors early in the budgeting process because they will determine the order in which you prepare individual budgets. If you fail to recognize a limiting factor you may set yourself targets that are just not achievable. There will probably be only one limiting factor; usually it is sales or the capacity to produce, though sometimes the marketplace may be the limit, especially if it is monopolistic and anticompetitive, stagnant, or subject to quotas. Other limiting factors include shortages or irregularities in raw materials, labor investment and machinery, or there might be physical constraints on property and premises.

QUESTIONS TO ASK YOURSELF

Q Does the organization's constitution allow us to perform planned activities?

Q Is planning permission for expansion likely to be granted?

Q Do we have access to enough capital to achieve our plan?

Q Are we in a small marketplace with a limited customer base?

Q Can we attract people with sufficient skills to our location?

42 Be aware that it is not always sales that limit an organization.

---

43 Be honest and objective with your assessment of internal influences.

44 Keep informed by reading your internal business communications.

LIMITING FACTOR REMEDIES

What can be done to stop something being a limiting factor? Constraints can be temporary, so recognize that a limiting factor can change from year to year.

- If the limiting factor is sales, consider cutting the price of goods and services, and increase the media advertising budget.
- To remove capacity constraints, spend more on plant and machinery or contemplate outsourcing production.
- If labor is scarce, either pay more or recruit from other, non-traditional, labor pools.

ANTICIPATING REVENUES

Most budgets are driven by the overall level of sales, so to produce an accurate budget you must correctly estimate the type, amount, and timing of revenues. Focus on the sources of income, their likely volume and price, and the timing of receipts.

45 Customers usually take twice as long to pay than you would expect.

ASSESSING REVENUE TYPES

Estimating overall sales revenues is likely to be the hardest task in the budgeting process, since you can only guess what the future holds. However, if you divide revenues – which will be almost entirely sales of goods and services – into subheadings, such as types of product, market segment, and geographical location you can at least make your estimates easier to access. The purpose is to make subsequent analysis, discussion, and monitoring of revenues easier to undertake; so organize your revenue types into sufficient detail without being excessive.

Manager explains why his sales figures underachieved last year

New products to achieve increased sales next year

DO'S AND DON'TS

✔ Do liaise with other departments to anticipate next year's new revenue streams.

✔ Do be realistic about how far to subdivide income types for analysis purposes.

✘ Don't be constrained by looking only at the revenue types that arose last year.

✘ Don't restrict analysis to ongoing revenues; consider capital and one-time events.

▲ **ESTIMATING REVENUES**
Analyze recent history, anticipate the future, and liaise closely with other departments to ensure an accurate budget.

46 Estimate the likely price elasticity of demand for sales.

ESTIMATING REVENUE AMOUNTS

Arriving at a realistic figure for sales revenue owes much to inspired guesswork and luck. Typically, figures will be based on what happened in the previous year, since this approach is based on some reality. It is important to get an estimate of what really could be achieved with commitment and effort, rather than through minor marginal improvements. Ask the sales department to build up figures based on customer histories, current developments, and local intelligence. Management's instinct, albeit subjective, is also a valid tool.

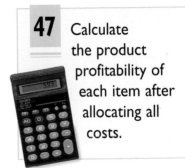

47 Calculate the product profitability of each item after allocating all costs.

▼ **PREDICTING INCOME**
To obtain an accurate prediction of income, focus on the three steps of income assessment.

| **Types** | **Amounts** | **Timing** |

48 Always keep an open mind when you look into the future.

PROJECTING REVENUE TIMING

The single most important control that you should exert within your department is monitoring cash flow. Most organizations can trade profitably, but run out of cash – the lifeblood of a business. Typically, expenditure is paid before revenues are received, especially during times of growth, so it is essential that you control your cash timings. Be realistic, and even a little pessimistic, since most customers do not pay within their agreed terms. Talk to the accounting department about historical payment trends, and talk to the sales department about individual customers' current financial health and their likely future payment positions.

◀ **ANALYZING TIMING TRENDS**
Generally, sales revenue arrives later than expected. Look at payment trends and anticipate how these might change in the future, both overall and on an individual customer basis.

455

ESTIMATING EXPENDITURE

Actual expenditure is usually greater than that budgeted for. Organizations are often surprised by this, even though it happens every year. To ensure an accurate expenditure forecast, focus on the types, amounts, and timing of expenditure.

49 Remind yourself that not everything in a budget has to be spent.

ESTIMATING COSTS ▲
By understanding which of the four types of expenditure your costs are, you can assess how easy they will be to control.

ASSESSING EXPENDITURE TYPES

There are four main types of expenditure. Ongoing specific costs (costs driven by particular products and services) and ongoing shared costs (shared costs incurred for the whole organization) will be incurred by most organizations all the time on a routine basis. These are true annual recurring expenditure items, which should be relatively easy to estimate and control. Startup costs (incurred when starting or growing a new operation) and capital (or nonrevenue) costs are one-time items. They are usually harder to estimate because they do not happen often, and when they do the costs are likely to be different each time.

ESTIMATING THE AMOUNT OF EXPENDITURE

Expenditure must be estimated in terms of both quantities used and prices paid. There is no doubt that a list of possible activities and costs may appear limitless. Ask every relevant department and colleague about the probable quantities needed, prices payable, and total amounts for all the different possible costs. Although all the estimates will largely be based on previous experiences in similar circumstances, your intuition will play a significant part.

50 Check the previous year's expenditure to prevent omitting costs from this year's budget.

PROJECTING EXPENDITURE TIMING

Timing of expenditure is crucial to producing an accurate cash flow forecast, especially the timing of the largest expenditure. It is important to liaise with the purchasing department since they might have recently negotiated some expenditure timings; for example, they may have traded supplier prices with the timing of supplier invoices. Often, payments are made quarterly rather than monthly, and while some expenses are payable in advance, others are paid in arrears. Do not forget that there are significant infrequent (rather than one-time) costs, the most important one being taxation on profits.

51 Allow for the impact of inflation on anticipated expenditure.

52 Be aware that technological changes will affect your costs.

TYPES OF EXPENDITURE

TYPE	EXAMPLES
ONGOING SPECIFIC COSTS	Raw material and component parts, purchased services, goods for resale, labor and wages, after-sales support and service.
ONGOING SHARED COSTS	Rent, rates, utilities, insurance, repairs, infrastructure, finance charges, postage, stationery, advertising, telephone, transportation, and professional fees.
ONE-TIME STARTUP COSTS	Drawings, pre-trading items, setup costs, specifications, production lines, sales and marketing literature, and employment and retraining costs.
ONE-TIME CAPITAL NON-REVENUE COSTS	Tangible assets such as buildings, plant and equipment, office machinery, fixtures, fittings, motor cars, and intangible assets such as goodwill, brands, and intellectual property.

Understanding Costs

It is important to fully understand costs so that you can produce a more accurate budget that contains better predictions and provides a better basis for analysis and decisions. View costs from two perspectives: fixed or variable, and direct or indirect.

53 Remember, a fixed cost is a cost that remains even if an activity is not done.

Points to Remember

- Your budgeted fixed and variable costs must be checked to ensure they make financial sense – before your accountant sees them.
- Costs are often neither clearly fixed nor variable, but a combination of the two.
- Indirect (or shared) costs should be used in assessing the true profitability of products.
- Cost terminology can be disconcerting, but should be overcome.

Studying Cost Behavior

You should understand what drives costs, so as to be clear on cause-and-effect (have you spent more because you are busier, or just less efficient?), to gain more accurate expenditure estimates, and to get more useful analysis. If an organization doubles its sales, will all, some, or none of its costs also double? Will raw material purchases double? They probably will. But will head office costs double? Almost certainly they will not. Why are certain costs incurred; is it for one, or for many purposes? How should the cost then be allocated between the goods, services, and departments that use the cost?

Understanding Fixed and Variable Costs

Judge cost behavior in terms of the way that the cost is linked to your organization's volume of activity, usually sales. Costs that stay the same when volume increases (or decreases) are fixed costs, for example, finance, personnel, head office building, administration. Costs that increase in proportion to volume are variable costs, for example, goods for resale, productive labor, raw materials, distribution. Stepped fixed costs are those costs that are fixed until capacity is reached, when another fixed cost is added.

54 Understanding cost behavior is fundamental.

55 Challenge any increases in shared costs.

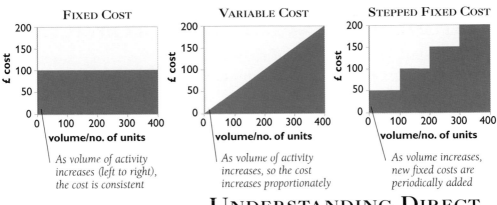

FIXED COST

As volume of activity increases (left to right), the cost is consistent

VARIABLE COST

As volume of activity increases, so the cost increases proportionately

STEPPED FIXED COST

As volume increases, new fixed costs are periodically added

DEFINING COSTS ▲

Other than for fixed costs, where cost is consistent, the price of costs changes as volume of activity increases.

56 Always try to get to the bottom of what drives indirect costs.

UNDERSTANDING DIRECT AND INDIRECT COSTS

A direct cost is incurred for the benefit of just one product or service, whereas an indirect cost is incurred for the benefit of many. Indirect costs are therefore sometimes known as shared costs. You must understand how to allocate indirect costs back to products and services. For example, you will need to decide how much of the head-office cost each item will bear. This will affect each product's profitability and can be used by senior management to assess its financial viability.

DIRECT AND INDIRECT COSTS

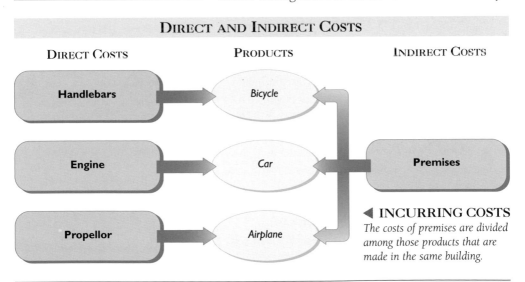

DIRECT COSTS

Handlebars

Engine

Propellor

PRODUCTS

Bicycle

Car

Airplane

INDIRECT COSTS

Premises

◀ INCURRING COSTS

The costs of premises are divided among those products that are made in the same building.

PRODUCING THE FIGURES

C *hallenge the monetary amounts in your budget by testing the validity of your figures. Do this early on since initial budget submissions are rarely right; often sales figures will be optimistic and expenditure figures pessimistic.*

57 Understand costs more clearly by showing them as a percentage of sales.

58 Remember, costs are driven by what must be achieved.

59 Check whether last year's figures are obviously wrong.

CHALLENGING MONETARY AMOUNTS

You should check and double-check your figures carefully. When the budget committee examines your first budgeting attempt you must be confident that you have submitted accurate figures. Budget committees are usually aware that experienced managers often build budgetary slack into their first submissions in anticipation of them being trimmed. In recognition of this common occurrence, you must allow for the budgeting committee simply to reduce your first budget submission by 10 percent.

USING THE OUTPUT/ INPUT METHOD

The Output/Input method is how you should approach producing the figures for your budget. Assess what your department produces (output), and ask yourself how this can be done, and then decide what resources are required to achieve this (input). It is all too easy to get this sequence the wrong way around. Avoid starting by assessing what resources you have and then trying to assess what can be achieved for the department. Categorize resources, people, and budgeted expenditure as inputs. Things that are made, work done, and services provided are outputs.

POINTS TO REMEMBER

- Inputs are determined by outputs, not the other way around.
- The required outputs, targets, and timings of the organization must be clarified.
- Alternative and challenging ideas can be generated in brainstorming sessions.
- The cost of required resources should be quantified financially.
- The quality and quantity of resources should be identified.

BUDGETING CORRECTLY

THE RIGHT WAY TO BUDGET

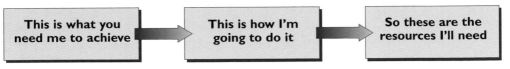

| This is what you need me to achieve | → | This is how I'm going to do it | → | So these are the resources I'll need |

THE WRONG WAY TO BUDGET

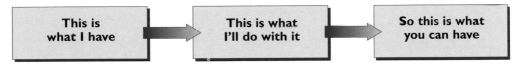

| This is what I have | → | This is what I'll do with it | → | So this is what you can have |

USING TOP-DOWN BUDGETING

Although budgets should be prepared using the output/input method, many managers use the top-down approach (often called "last year's plus"). This very simple method works out what was spent in the previous year and then adds or subtracts a percentage. The flaw in this approach is that the previous year's figures could be wrong, and it is very unlikely to give optimum resource allocations. It may also miss hidden gradual cost changes and can perpetuate inefficient practices. However, top-down budgeting is still the most common way to produce budgeted figures. Often a manager will have had the budget forms in the in-tray for several weeks, and yet, by using this approach, can still produce a budget in one day without reference to any other part of the business.

USING THE ▶ TOP-DOWN APPROACH

A listing of all revenue items for last year's actual results or last year's budget should be used as the incremental basis for estimating the figures for this year's budget.

QUESTIONS TO ASK YOURSELF

Q Have I challenged figures and eliminated excess?

Q Where figures have been derived from the top-down approach, is there another way to challenge their validity?

Q Have I met with other managers to discuss their figures in relation to mine?

EXPENDITURE BUDGET			
	LAST YEAR	CHANGE	THIS YEAR
Salaries	10,000	6%	10,600
Pensions	1,200	6%	1,272
Motor & travel	500	10%	550
Equipment hire	100	5%	105
Telecom	600	-10%	540
Print, post, & stationery	240	-2%	235
Marketing	300	8%	324
Storage	60	3%	62
Maintenance	120	10%	132
Heat, light, & power	480	-5%	456
	13,600		14,276

Only items from last year will appear in current year budget

Add or subtract increments to or from last year

USING BOTTOM-UP BUDGETING

60 Introduce bottom-up testing gradually for selected departments.

61 Be sensitive to the concerns that bottom-up cost-cutting can cause.

Consider using bottom-up, or zero-based budgeting (ZBB), which questions the relationship between costs and benefits. State the purpose and outcome of varying expenditure for each activity, starting from a base of nothing (or zero). This means you will have to justify all expenditure, from the ground up. Bottom-up budgeting is best suited for discretionary and support costs, such as marketing costs, rather than tangible costs (easily measurable costs), such as production costs. Bottom-up budgeting is very time-consuming. Some managers prefer not to use it because it is considered to be an aggressive approach.

TOP-DOWN COMPARED WITH BOTTOM-UP BUDGETING

	TOP-DOWN	BOTTOM-UP
STARTING POINT	Last year's budget or actual	Zero: assume no spending at all
BASIS FOR BUDGET	Last year plus or minus a sum	Activity-based building blocks
AMOUNT BUDGETED	Normally a single sum	Range of amounts
NEEDS AWARENESS OF	Individual function/department	Whole of the business
PEOPLE INVOLVED	Manager and owner only	Cross-functional groups
TIME AND EFFORT	Can be significant	Often very substantial
FREQUENCY	Usually annual	Periodically over years
ALTERNATIVES	Only mentioned briefly	Subjected to detailed review
PRIORITIES	Often not stated	Wants and must-haves discussed

ACTIVITY-BASED COSTING (ABC)

To generate accurate figures and gain a better feel for which products and services make money, you must understand what drives the costs in your department. Often, costs are allocated back to each product and service in proportion to sales revenue only. However, this does not take account of other business features, such as office space, head count, and units of product sold. Activity-based costing is a more complete way to understand what drives costs as it allocates each cost in proportion to several business features. By keeping detailed timesheets and cost records for everyone and every activity, you can make a more accurate costing allocation based on the whole organization.

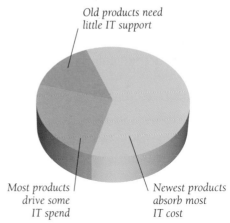

Old products need little IT support

Most products drive some IT spend

Newest products absorb most IT cost

▲ ALLOCATING COSTS

Information Technology (IT) costs are driven by newer products that are difficult to support, rather than high volume, easily administered older ones.

QUESTIONS TO ASK YOURSELF

Q Should I introduce zero-based budgeting for certain support departments?

Q Would the "What if?" analysis provide a useful insight to my budgeted amounts?

Q Have I considered obtaining a range of forecasts, instead of working to just a single figure?

62 Use ranges of outcomes to get away from "single figure syndrome."

USING OTHER METHODS

Other ways of testing the figures assess how artificial changes to the budget can affect the outcome. The "What if?" analysis (usually adding 10 percent to key costs and deducting 10 percent from certain revenues) shows up clearly financial sensitivities within the budget. Since budgets typically produce one final figure, such as "Sales will be $15m," you should also consider what might be achievable with favorable conditions, and what might be the worst outcome. By ascribing each single figure outcome a probability, and multiplying the outcome by the probability, a more accurate figure, called the expected value, can by calculated. Calculating a range of best/most likely/worst-case scenarios can help the budget committee decide whether to add one manager's best to another's worst, and so on.

UNDERSTANDING CAPITAL BUDGETS

*E*xpenditures on large capital items such as premises, equipment, and machinery are not included in departmental budgets. Yet assessing capital spending is crucial for your organization's success, so it is vital that you understand capital budgeting.

63 One wrong capital spend can undo all the perfect profit planning.

64 Remember, capital spending is often poorly controlled.

65 Ensure profit and loss sheets reflect capital spending.

CONTROLLING CAPITAL

The constraints exerted by organizations over their capital spending can come as a surprise to the inexperienced, yet the price of making mistakes over it can be bankruptcy. Capital spending often takes place early on, and if it is not controlled it can have a domino effect on the rest of the business. Life-sustaining cash can disappear in significant amounts, often on frivolous purchases. Typically, spending overruns the budget, the project starts late, receipts from sales take longer to arrive, and suddenly there is a cash flow problem.

AUTHORIZING CAPITAL

Organizations have developed sophisticated and often long-winded procedures for authorizing capital. Many organizations have a capital-investment committee (which includes senior management) that sets the limits for how much capital can be spent on a project and how the timing of that capital spending is regulated within the organization. There are also capital-approval forms and various other policies and procedures that organizations devise to apply rigorous checks on the authorization of capital spending.

POINTS TO REMEMBER

- An environment should be created that will generate ideas for future capital investment.
- Procedures for authorizing capital must be understood.
- The financial hurdles a project must overcome to be viable should be clearly understood.
- Acquisition of new assets must be examined using a capital-appraisal method.

ASSESSING PROJECTS

Consider whether capital investment is needed

Assess the risks, and plan how they will be managed

List the tangible and intangible benefits

Write the business case and obtain approval

Carry out the plan, and review project's success

JUSTIFYING CAPITAL SPENDING

To assess the viability of a project, you must justify, in financial terms, how much capital you will have to spend on it. A project can be measured in terms of how many dollars of profit it returns per dollar invested (known as the "return on capital"). A more useful indicator is the "payback period," which is the time taken to recoup the initial investment. However, both these methods fail to take into account the time value of money. We all instinctively know that $1 today is worth more than $1 tomorrow. When looking at future amounts, we should therefore express them in terms of today's value – known as present value or discounted cash flow (DCF). For example, assuming 10 percent interest, $1 in a year's time is worth 91 cents today, and $1 in two years' time is worth 83 cents today. Only discounted cash flow recognizes the time factor, and reduces the real value of future amounts before adding up costs and revenues.

LINKING CAPITAL BUDGETS

Once a capital budget has been authorized, remember that it will have a domino effect to other budgets and will have a profound effect on cash flow. As a result of capital spending on new machinery, for example, the sales budget should reflect the benefits to the organization of the increased capacity or efficiency afforded by the purchase. For costs budgets, apart from depreciation (which is a fixed cost), different assets will influence the type of additional cost incurred. Motor vehicles will increase gas, insurance, and tax costs, whereas buildings will affect utility and maintenance costs.

66 When assessing projects, always consider the "do nothing" option.

67 Be aware that revenue and capital spending are related.

PRODUCING CASH BUDGETS

*C*ash flow is the movement of money into and out of a business. If you do not have enough cash flow, then your business will be threatened. Create a cash budget to help you predict cash flow over time and to keep an informed eye on your business.

68 Be aware that cash flow usually turns out to be worse than you plan for.

UNDERSTANDING CASH BUDGETS

A cash budget takes figures from a profit and loss budget and estimates the timing of income and costs, thus budgeting for actual incoming cash receipts and outgoing cost payments. Just as business health will ebb and flow, so will the demands on cash; yet often the cash needs of a business can seem at odds with the profits generated. A growing business will often have short-term financing problems, whereas a mature declining business can often generate surprising amounts of cash.

▲ CHECKING CASH FLOWS
Producing cash flow forecasts involves the whole business producing realistic and consistent assumptions about timings.

69 Always remember the saying, "Profits are vanity, cash is sanity."

QUESTIONS TO ASK YOURSELF

Q Have the effects of sales tax on cash flow been assessed?

Q How definite are the capital plans, both amounts and timings?

Q Are the timings of receipts realistic, especially for new initiatives?

Q Has there been an increase in trading overseas, on different terms?

Q Is the interest that builds up on borrowings realistic?

Q Will new laws on late payments affect cash flows

DO'S AND DONT'S

✔ Do be sensible about the timings of cash flows; they are often made more difficult by optimistic budgets.

✔ Do ask plenty of "What if?" questions about cash flows, should timings of significant amounts change.

✗ Don't assume that cash flow will not be a problem for you just because it has not been in the past.

✗ Don't assume that everyone will always keep to their terms about payments into or out of the organization.

FILLING IN A CASH BUDGET ▼

Extend the profit and loss account items and estimate the likely timings for each item. Add the projected cash flows for each month to indicate cash surpluses or funding requirements.

PREPARING A CASH BUDGET

Prepare a cash budget from the profit and loss and balance sheet. Often, an organization has standardized cash flow forecasting forms to make it easier. Working monthly, combine the budget amounts with cash flow timing predictions for each item of revenue and expenditure. Remember to include the one-time events. Repeat the process every time amounts or predictions change.

Annual budgeted profit and loss account figures are divided into annual and monthly amounts

Timing of cash flow is estimated for the individual profit and loss account items

Actual cash receipts and payments are filled for each month

PROFIT AND LOSS ACCOUNT			TIMING PREDICTIONS	CASH FLOWS					
ITEM	ANNUAL	MONTH		JUL	AUG	SEP	OCT	NOV	DEC
Sales	+1920	+160	One month credit	0	+160	+160	+160	+160	+160
Purchases	-720	-60	One month credit	0	-60	-60	-60	-60	-60
Direct labor	-576	-48	Immediate	-48	-48	-48	-48	-48	-48
Rent	-60	-5	One month in advance	-10	-5	-5	-5	-5	-5
Heat, light, & power	-48	-4	One month credit	0	-4	-4	-4	-4	-4
Insurance	-12	-1	Six months in advance	-6	0	0	0	0	0
Marketing	-72	-6	One month credit	0	-6	-6	-6	-6	-6
Salaries	-192	-16	Immediate	-16	-16	-16	-16	-16	-16
			Monthly cash flow	-80	+21	+21	+21	+21	+21
PROFIT	+240	+20	Cumulative cash flow	-80	-59	-38	-17	+4	+25

Annual profit is calculated by deducting expenditure from revenue

Monthly figure for total cash receipts and payments is calculated

Cumulative cash flow figure for the period is calculated, representing actual money in the bank

CONSOLIDATING BUDGETS

Once you have prepared your budget you will have to submit it to the budgeting committee so that the master budget can be prepared. In light of what the overall figures look like when consolidated, you may have to amend your budget.

70 Keep to a time-table, especially during the final budgeting stages.

71 Make sure figures are consistently prepared once guidelines are set.

REVIEWING DEPARTMENTAL BUDGETS

Before departmental budgets are brought together you must review your own budget and ensure the following steps were undertaken:

- Limiting factors were correctly identified.
- Relevant background information was gathered.
- Both external and internal influences were recognized and considered.
- Other material sources of information and advice were taken into account.
- Types, amounts, and timing of revenues, expenditures, and significant one-time items were conservatively predicted.

Committee chairperson collates all departmental budgets

Departmental manager submits individual budget

SUBMITTING BUDGETS ▲

Only when you are satisfied that you have extensively reviewed your budget, tested the figures, and made any necessary amendments should you submit it to the budgeting committee.

THINGS TO DO

1. Review your budget
2. Test for consistent preparation
3. Prepare initial draft
4. Send out for amendments
5. Collate amendments
6. Resubmit for approval
7. Submit to committee

GAINING APPROVAL

Submit/resubmit your budget to committee

Committee checks budget for feasibility

Committee specifies amendments

Budget is revised

Committee approves final budget

PREPARING A MASTER BUDGET

A master budget is the summary budget of all the budgets that have been individually prepared by departmental managers. It is a single document that the budget committee prepares to describe the whole organization's aims and expectations for future income, cash flows, and financial status. As with the departmental budgets, the focus will be on key areas, such as sales, production, and finance. The master budget provides information in a summarized form, so that senior management can determine whether the budget is acceptable and can be approved. The master budget should include budgets for profit and loss, balance sheet, and cash flows. The criteria senior management use to approve it will vary with each organization, though they will usually relate to higher level measures, such as adherence to long-term objectives, as well as to traditional shorter-term measures such as profitability, return on capital, solvency, and liquidity.

FOLLOWING THE ITERATIVE PROCESS

If the first draft of the master budget does not meet the expectations of senior management, then it will need to be redrafted. Senior management might insist that fundamental changes are made right away, or they might want to assess the impact of certain progressive changes on the overall plan. Each time this happens, you will have to change figures and again resubmit them for approval. A new master budget will be drafted, which will again be presented to senior management. This process will be repeated until a final plan is accepted. This ongoing redrafting and reapproval is known as the iterative process.

72 Consult with everyone involved over changes to the budget.

73 Record any changes, in case you have to refer to them again.

FINALIZING A BUDGET

Once your budget has been consolidated, the budget committee will be ready to finalize the master budget. Be well prepared for dealing with the committee so that you are in a position to put forward the best possible case for your department.

74 Be efficient by budgeting for only appropriate resources.

75 Be effective by achieving all your stated objectives.

76 Probe the budget by using "What if" scenarios.

REVIEWING THE FIGURES

The budget committee's role is to review the figures and assess their viability. You must be prepared to answer questions such as "What if sales rise or fall more than anticipated?", "How will costs for personnel, purchasing, production, marketing, finance, and administration affect the budget?", and "How will interest, inflation, taxation, duties, and quotas affect the budget?". You will need to decide which factors could affect your budget, in what ways, and whether there are any other circumstances that might be relevant to your department and to the whole organization.

PREPARING FOR THE COMMITTEE MEETING

You should be fully prepared for the budget committee meeting. Make sure you are ready and able to answer the following questions before you attend the meeting:

- Why do you have to attend the committee meeting and how important is it?
- Do you know the role of a budget committee, both generally and in your specific business, and are you aware of who sits on this committee?
- How do you intend to put across the case for your department?
- What follow-up might be required?

POINTS TO REMEMBER

- Develop the skills of interpreting a profit and loss account and balance sheet by using relevant financial ratios.
- Make sure that any questions about forecasting budgets have been answered satisfactorily.
- Understand the relevance of the master budget to the budgeting process.
- Make effective personal contributions to the key budget committee meetings.

PARTICIPATING IN BUDGET MEETINGS

As your individual departmental budgets are brought into the negotiation process, they are examined in relation to each other. You may simply not be aware of other plans, conditions, and constraints that could affect what your department has budgeted for. Remember that high level executives will be present at budget meetings, representing the major parts of the organization, as well as the chairperson and accountants. The chairperson advises and liaises with departmental heads and coordinates the final agreements. Accountants are there to assist you in your budget preparation rather than to determine the actual content of all the various budgets.

Factory manager has budgeted for new equipment

Chairperson mediates and finds agreed solution

Accountant identifies there is insufficient cash

FINISHING THE BUDGET

Once the budget committee has agreed on the master budget, all departmental and subsidiary budgets will have been consolidated, comprising budgeted profit and loss accounts, balance sheets, and cash flow statements. These documents and the supporting subsidiary budgets are used to plan and control activities for the following year. Your budget will remain the centerpiece of control in your department, linking long- and short-term planning in the overall strategy of the organization.

▲ NEGOTIATING BUDGETS

Participating effectively at budget meetings requires an understanding of the agendas of each member of the budget committee, understanding why they are there, and what they are trying to achieve.

 77 Remember, budgets can lose credibility when cuts are announced.

MONITORING A BUDGET

Once you have written the budget, revenues must be achieved and expenditure must not be exceeded. To check this, you should constantly review your budget and adjust as necessary.

ANALYZING DISCREPANCIES

There will always be discrepancies between your budget and actual performance results. To make constructive adjustments for the future, provide for a framework with which to understand and analyze all such discrepancies.

78 Ignore differences that will correct themselves the following month.

79 Allow sufficient time in your schedule to identify any discrepancies.

UNDERSTANDING DISCREPANCIES

It is important to understand why there are discrepancies, no matter how small, between your budget and actual performance. What might seem an insignificant discrepancy to you and your department could be crucial to the whole organization, especially if other departments are also not meeting their budgets. By assessing why discrepancies have occurred, you will be able to ensure that the chances of them recurring are reduced and that future discrepancies are more efficiently anticipated.

COMPARING ACTUAL WITH BUDGET

Comparing actual performance with budget is the traditional device used by senior management to measure managerial and business performance. A good business-management system asks questions such as, "Do I have the correct plans in place?" and "How is each part of the business contributing?". A budget managed properly and taken seriously becomes a more forward-looking document that can assist senior management to identify trends, predict year-end results, and avoid any unpleasant financial surprises.

THINGS TO DO

1. Give equal weight to monitoring and planning.
2. Decide what is important to monitor in your budget.
3. Allow sufficient time to monitor budgets properly.
4. Arrange to be sent regular financial information.

THE CONTROL CYCLE ▶

In order to properly monitor the budget, work through the four actions of this feedback loop. This will ensure you have a reliable control activity built into your budgeting process.

80 Allow time for all four steps of the control cycle.

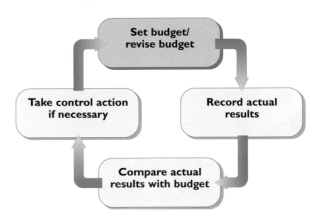

Set budget/ revise budget

Take control action if necessary

Record actual results

Compare actual results with budget

CASE STUDY

For several years, Video Visual had been producing budgets. However, Video Visual's managers found the process of budgeting time-consuming and a significant drain on management resources. Their industry was fast moving and at the leading edge of innovation and technology, and time was very precious to them. As a result they did not make the time to do much with the budget once it had been finalized. They did not monitor what actually happened in the business, and any comparison of actual performance against budget was done only at a very superficial level. Video Visual failed to follow logically the four steps in the control cycle. It learned very little from each year's budget, and so each consecutive year's budget was never likely to be better or more useful to the organization.

◀ FEEDBACK IN ACTION

Making budgeting a learning process need not be time-consuming, but it does require management to assess why figures are not achieved and what might be done in future to correct this. Writing a budget without using it for monitoring purposes is performing only one half of the required task – the two activities go hand in hand.

MONITORING VARIANCES

The discrepancies revealed by comparing actual and budgeted results are called variances, which you must analyze in order to prioritize subsequent action. Overspending is an adverse variance and underspending a positive variance.

81 Define your reporting system when starting the budget process.

82 Prioritize those variances that will be more useful.

83 Use "Flash" reports to define problem areas.

ESTABLISHING PROCEDURES

Continually monitor discrepancies and understand how they have arisen. Variances are generally categorized as either budget errors or unexpected variances. Constant monitoring helps promote a greater overall understanding of cost behavior, which will help you produce a more accurate budget next time around. However, to do this well, you must establish suitable monitoring procedures. Experience shows that to be truly effective, your procedure must be regular, easy to administer, and sufficiently detailed.

CHOOSING AND MEASURING VARIANCES

Identify significant variances so you can ensure that your budget is adhered to as closely as possible. To select which variances to look at further, consider the likelihood of the variance being controllable, the probable cost of investigating the variance, and the chance that it might arise again in the future. The key question to ask when deciding what to examine is why do you want to look at this variance and, importantly, what will you do with it once it is measured. If it is not going to be of practical use, do not measure it.

QUESTIONS TO ASK YOURSELF

Q What is the procedure for monitoring variances?

Q Are the procedures regular, easily followed, and do they contain sufficient detail?

Q Do the variances measured actually provide useful forward-looking information?

Q Is it realistic to investigate why the variance might have arisen?

Q Are variance reports intelligible and do they contain appropriate comparisons?

UTILIZING VARIANCE REPORTS

There are no rules about how to produce variance reports, and there is no definitive layout. Because variance reports are prepared internally, you can devise any style, though bear in mind that it should be designed specifically to suit your department. Useful reports in one department may well be useless in another. Try to base all reports on the original budget documents to ensure consistency of style. On a practical level managers benefit little from overly elaborate budgeting- and variance-analysis reports. These will be little used because of their complexity, and the result is no improvement in operations. Additional columns are added to show both the price and percentage difference between budget this year and actual last year.

84 Assess the value of your organization's reports to you.

85 To maintain flexibility, include or delete figures as appropriate.

▼ TYPICAL VARIANCE REPORT

Whatever the department, a variance report should show items categorized into actual, budget, and prior year sections.

Actual results are compared to budget and expressed as a variance

Heading is month of year of variance report

Actual results are compared to last year's results and expressed as a variance

ITEM	ACTUAL $	BUDGET $	VARIANCE $	%	LAST YEAR $	VARIANCE $	%
DEPARTMENTAL VARIANCE REPORT APRIL YEAR 2							
Heat	1,200	1,300	100	8%	1,100	-100	-9%
Light	500	550	50	9%	525	25	5%
Telephone	660	700	40	6%	650	-10	-2%
Postage	100	90	-10	-11%	110	10	9%
Stationery	200	180	-20	-11%	160	-40	-25%
Books	50	80	30	38%	50	0	0%
Insurance	240	240	0	0%	220	-20	-9%

Costs item is described in sufficient detail to help subsequent analysis

Difference between actual results and budget is expressed in dollars

Difference between actual results and last year's results is expressed as a percentage

ANALYZING BUDGET ERRORS

Budget errors occur as a result of poor preparation of the original budget. Sales will be lower than expected while costs will be out of control. It is vital that you understand where you went wrong so that you do not make the same mistakes again.

86 Do not fall for the trap of expecting optimistic income, pessimistic costs.

87 Check all variances; smaller ones might hide larger amounts.

DISSECTING ERRORS ▲

When analyzing budget errors, concentrate on dissecting the validity and accuracy of the original budgeted amounts.

STUDYING THE FIGURES

Actual budget errors may be due to insufficient research into budgeted amounts, a lack of understanding of what drives the business financially, or inadequate challenging of the figures. The obvious solution to low revenues and high costs would be for you to reverse the situation and increase sales while reducing expenditure. But you must analyze why things went wrong and ask yourself the following questions:

● What are the most common variances encountered when monitoring costs, their cause and effects, and possible remedies?

● In particular, what are the main variances in sales revenue, likely causes and effects, and possible remedies?

It can help to understand where errors have crept in by categorizing revenue and expenditure variances into price, volume, and timing.

88 Focus on the root of the problem and do not be overawed by technical variance analysis.

	SALES $s	SALES TIMING	SOURCES OF INFORMATION
SALES PER PRODUCT GROUP	✔		"Annual Product Sales Report"
SALES PER REGION	✔	✔	regional sales projections
SALES PER MARKET PLACE		✔	"Account Manager's Report"
OTHER SALES			

Confirmation that sales amount per product group has been checked

Confirmation that timing of sales per region has been checked

Name of relevant report

Sales are described in logical categories

	SALES $s	SALES TIMING	SOURCES OF INFORMATION
SALES PER PRODUCT GROUP	✔		"Annual Product Sales Report"
SALES PER REGION	✔	✔	regional sales projections
SALES PER MARKET PLACE		✔	"Account Manager's Report"
OTHER SALES			

CHECKING OFF SALES REVENUE ▲

Use a checklist to help investigate the source of errors when predicting sales revenues. It will help to uncover possible explanations in a logical and systematic way.

ANALYZING EXPENDITURE

Use a step-by-step approach to identify expenditure variances. To tackle expenditure queries in a way that is most likely to ensure a successful analysis, ask yourself the following questions:

- Is the price paid for items more or less than budgeted? Is there a cure for this price expenditure variance, and what are the likely financial consequences of the cure?
- Are the amounts purchased more or less than budgeted? Is there a remedy for this volume variance, and what are the possible domino effects of the remedy?
- Is there an expenditure timing difference, can it be fixed, and at what price?

STUDYING INCOME

Though identifying important sales revenue variances is relatively easy, how to remedy them and achieve the original plan is harder and you must keep asking yourself some key questions. First, is there a price variance (selling for more or fewer dollars than expected), what is its impact on the budget, and is there a way to solve it? Second, is there a volume variance (selling more or fewer items than expected), what does it do to the budget, and is there a way around it? Finally, is there a timing variance (not receiving money when expected), and what is its impact on cash flow?

POINTS TO REMEMBER

- All expense types in the cost section of the budget should be checked.
- All sources of income must be tracked – by region, product, market, and salesperson.
- Variances should be categorized into price, volume, and timing to help work out a cure for them.
- Variances should be analyzed in terms of cause, remedy, and the domino effect of the remedy.
- Not all variances have a logical cause or an actionable remedy; some things can just happen.

INVESTIGATING UNEXPECTED VARIANCES

There are often cases where a variance could not possibly have been foreseen or avoided. Even though these variances are unexpected there may be something you can do about them and ways that you can learn from their consequences.

89 Do not blame staff for genuinely unforseeable variances.

90 Only spend time on those variances that you can do something about.

91 Distinguish between poor planning and poor performance.

AVOIDING CRITICIZING OTHERS

One of the main problems with variance analysis is that often a scapegoat is sought when results fall short of plans. Blaming someone for a variance that is effectively unavoidable is very demoralizing. At the time of budgeting there was nothing that the department could, or should, have done differently. Although a variance could not possibly have been foreseen, it may be easily explained with hindsight. So to be more constructive when analyzing unexpected variances you should look beyond apportioning blame and dig a little deeper.

QUESTIONS TO ASK YOURSELF

Q Did you define your measurement and variance reporting system when first setting budgets?

Q Have you checked positive variances for opportunities that could be exploited further?

Q Do you combine variance reporting with investigation into causes and possible cures?

Q Have you considered selecting the key variances that are critical to your business?

92 Keep your perspective and do not be drawn into examining variances in too great a detail.

THINGS TO DO

1. Once you have analyzed variances, take action.
2. Investigate favorable as well as adverse variances.
3. Ignore all variance and budgeting alibis.
4. Determine whether a variance is controllable.

93 Remember, foresight is better than hindsight.

STUDYING CONTROLLABLE COSTS

Once unexpected variances have been identified, there may be a lot that you can do about them. A controllable cost is one that can be influenced by the budget holder. If a cost is controllable, then senior management will expect you to exercise your influence and adjust your expenditure where appropriate. Consider the situation where the cost price of a raw material has increased significantly during the budget period. Although you cannot change the price of the raw material, perhaps you could use a cheaper alternative. If skilled labor shortages drive up rates, consider using other grades or even de-skilling the job to avoid this constraint. Using alternatives is not the only type of control you can exercise. You could, for example, consider reducing your discretionary costs by choosing not to spend money on advertising, training, staff parties, and bonuses.

PLANNING AND OPERATING VARIANCES

A meaningful way of looking at unexpected variances is by considering the variance as a planning variance or as an operational one. A typical budget (an ex-ante budget) contains information that was thought to be correct at the time of preparation (ex-ante means "before the event"). An ex-post budget is written after the period to which it relates (ex-post means "after the event"). It is used to produce, with hindsight, the best possible achievable budget. A planning variance is a variance generated by an ex-ante budget that is changed to an ex-post budget. An

example of this may be the variance that occurs when an original budget does not take into account a significant increase in raw material price due to a world shortage. This ex-ante budget would be changed to an ex-post budget that builds in this factor for the original time period. An operational variance is where an ex-post budget is compared with actual performance in the current time period. It shows how the department might be currently performing in line with hindsight, which is all that might be reasonably expected.

MAKING ADJUSTMENTS

Having assessed budget variances, you are now in a position to make informed alterations to your budget. The process of comparing actual figures with budget is a continuous one. You should constantly adjust the budget.

94 Change your budget to reflect changes in the world.

REFORECASTING BUDGETS

As changes in internal or external factors occur, so actual results begin to diverge from the budget. It can become frustrating for departmental managers when performance reported against budget becomes increasingly less relevant to the actual daily management of the business. It is therefore important that you reforecast the budget periodically (typically quarterly, or at least every six months) to reflect any changing real circumstances.

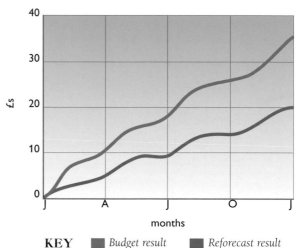

KEY ■ Budget result ■ Reforecast result

▲ JUDGING REALITY

The increasing disparity between the original budget and the latest forecast means that, for monitoring purposes, the original budget has become meaningless and might as well be ignored.

95 Remember that flexing a budget can benefit staff motivation.

USING FLEXIBLE BUDGETS

A flexible budget takes into account changing real activity. For example, if budgeted sales were 100 units, yet only 80 were sold, in a normal budget all the cost variances would be unfavorable; but this is not particularly informative. A flexible budget, however, shows the expected revenue and expenditure for the actual volume produced and sold (80 units), and so gives a much more valid comparison of real activity against budget.

REVISING A BUDGET

Take great care to ensure that when you amend a budget using flexible budgeting it is as well controlled and structured as the original budget. Often, it is the timing of certain key factors in your budget that give cause for a budget revision. Examples include: change in the timing of sales income, deferral of a new product launch, significant movement in currency rates, new capital investment, unexpected national wage increases. Try and anticipate timing changes and always keep a record of what these changes are so that you can assess their influence on your budget and you can allow for them in future budgets.

THINGS TO DO

1. Revise budgets as soon as necessary.
2. Abandon original budgets if superseded.
3. Have the confidence to change figures.
4. Revise equally rigorously.
5. Measure against flexible budgets.
6. Consider rolling budgets.

96 Ask yourself, "Am I too busy to plan because I do not plan enough?"

ROLLING BUDGET ▼
Budgeting activity for a month is added onto the budget period twelve months into the future, so that, at any time, the budget will stretch twelve months ahead.

USING ROLLING BUDGETS

During a normal annual budget there will come a time when the budget covers only a month or two ahead. Some organizations therefore use a rolling budget, which continuously updates the budget each time actual results are reported, by adding on a further period of budgeting activity. In practice, this involves adding a month or quarter at the end of the existing budget, while dropping off the month or quarter just finished. Be aware, however, that the quality of this type of budgeting is often not the same as a traditional annual budget, because of insufficient time or resources.

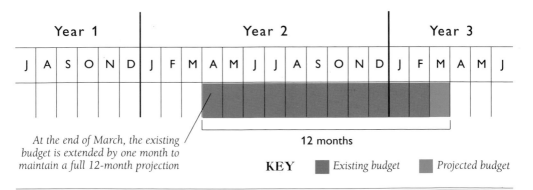

| Year 1 | | | | | | Year 2 | | | | | | | | | | | | Year 3 | | | | | |
| J | A | S | O | N | D | J | F | M | A | M | J | J | A | S | O | N | D | J | F | M | A | M | J |

At the end of March, the existing budget is extended by one month to maintain a full 12-month projection

12 months

KEY ■ *Existing budget* ■ *Projected budget*

RECOGNIZING BEHAVIORAL PROBLEMS

As part of the budgeting process, you will have to manage not only financial affairs but also the staff in your department. The success of a budget will depend on the cooperation of all those who are involved in all stages of the budget process.

97 Recognize the human aspects of budgeting, not just financial concerns.

98 Always value the importance of staff motivation to your budget.

ORGANIZING YOURSELF ▼
To use a budget as a key management tool for your department, you must be able to project yourself as a motivator and as an efficient and organized manager.

UNDERSTANDING PEOPLE AND BUDGETS

Be aware that your staff are key to the budgeting process and that inaccuracies in a budget can cause staff demotivation. You should not revise a nonperforming budget by making short-term adjustments that neglect the concerns of your staff. For instance, an easy solution to meeting financial targets would be to reduce discretionary costs, such as staff training, but this results in staff missing out on crucial skill development and could lead to further staff demotivation.

POOR MANAGEMENT ATTRIBUTES

Being too busy to worry about budgets

Slavishly following what the boss plans

Being unenthusiastic about future plans

POSITIVE MANAGEMENT ATTRIBUTES

Producing a challenging budget that is realistic

Producing motivational incentives and targets

Being in control of budget operations

RESOLVING PEOPLE PROBLEMS

Adapt management control systems to meet the differing personalities and attitudes of your staff. Recognize and respond to behavioral issues that arise from using budgets as planning and control tools and you will achieve much better results. Follow these practical solutions:

- Get the best from people by using budgets that are participative and consultative. They are more likely to be successful than ones imposed by senior management.
- Explain to the relevant people what the budget is all about and exactly what they are expected to achieve and how they are to perform.
- Acknowledge achievement promptly.
- Do not set your targets too high or too low. People can become demoralised when actual results are compared with unattainable budgets. You must judge the correct balance of what is achievable and what is motivational.

CULTURAL DIFFERENCES

The general rule in western countries is that management has to include a motivation factor in its budgets. In countries such as Japan, the focus is more on a cooperative approach to management since motivation is taken for granted. In such countries, being told what to do by management rarely gets the best out of staff.

99 Cultivate accountability with responsiblility.

RECOGNIZING ALIBIS

We have all heard them before – the excuses people use to avoid personal responsibility. It is important to recognize when an excuse is genuine and when it is not, since covering up the truth can result in a poor budget that is not carried out effectively.

ALIBI

66 *I've got demanding clients and problems with suppliers.* 99

66 *I just had to spend everything in my budget this year.* 99

REAL REASON

66 *I'm too busy to produce a meaningful budget and do not value the budgeting process.* 99

66 *I believe that I must spend everything or I will not get as much for my department next year.* 99

BUILDING ON BUDGETING

*S*ome time after your budget has been
set and monitored, you should look
back over your budgeting activities to learn
from your experiences. You should do this
after the first three months of your budget
and at regular intervals thereafter.

100 Learn from each year's budget so that next year's effort is better.

101 Commit yourself to budgeting and you will significantly improve your management performance.

PREPARING THE BUDGET

Sometimes a budget goes exactly to plan, or
at least there are only minor discrepancies that
are financially insignificant. Often, however,
the differences are more than 10 percent and
you should ask yourself why that has happened,
starting with the planning phase. Were the
advantages and disadvantages of budgeting
considered? Did you fully find out about all
the types of budget your organization uses
and what its budgeting procedures are?

WRITING THE BUDGET

Using hindsight, how well did you do at
actually writing the budget? Can you spot any
patterns within your budgets? Most companies
find that the original budget is hopelessly
overoptimistic, the first reforecast is then unduly
pessimistic, while the final figures turn out to
be close to the target. Assess how you can put
your experience into practice in next year's
departmental budget. Were certain members
of staff persistently inaccurate? Was it more
difficult to predict figures for particular products
or regions? Was forecasting capital expenditure a
major difficulty? Essentially, were you particularly
skillful at budgeting, or were you just lucky?

POINTS TO REMEMBER

- Your level of success should be analyzed so that you can plan for greater success next year.
- Budget improvements come only by following a logical and structured model.
- Everyone in the business should be carried along throughout the budgeting process.
- Your appraisal of your own and departmental competence should be honest and frank.
- Budgeting success or failure depends heavily on the people in your department.

LOOKING AT RESULTS ▲

Focus on year-end results, reforecast continuously, and try not to be too proud to learn from your mistakes.

MONITORING THE BUDGET

How well did you monitor the budget? Were your procedural checks and investigations all properly designed and executed so that you knew what had happened when? Could you effectively take the required controlling actions? Perhaps you had deliberately either over- or under-estimated revenues and costs to make results more achievable and expenditure easier to control? Consider the impact of doing this on both your department and the rest of the organization. In doing this, you have probably undermined some of the point of doing a budget in the first place; what should you do differently next time to make sure it does not happen again?

LOOKING TO THE FUTURE

You can manage budgets much more effectively by following a planned procedure and keeping to practical checklists and tips. However, even taking everything into account, things can still go wrong – people, competitors, organizations, and markets are all in a state of constant change. But you must be aware that whatever changes occur, budgeting must go on, and as a manager you must ensure that each year it becomes more effective than ever.

▼ TURNING THE SITUATION AROUND

Just producing a budget is not enough. You must prepare the budget using proper procedures and ensure that everyone understands how it works. Only when everyone is working together can you use the budget as a successful management tool.

CASE STUDY

In their first year Growth.com produced budgets that management did not fully understand. Their first budgeting effort was plagued with problems: everything was late, figures were wrong, and the quality of budgeting in general left a lot to be desired. Senior management were anxious that they should learn from their experiences and that the fiasco should not be repeated in the following year.

They decided to deliver a training program based on the benefits of budgeting. Managers were taught the importance of keeping closely to the timetable, keeping everyone informed and consulted, insisting on high quality figures, and ensuring that the budget was closely and accurately monitored. As a result, the situation was comprehensively turned in the second year and the budget was a great success.

ASSESSING YOUR SKILLS

This very simple questionnaire will help you to evaluate how well you have carried out the budgeting process. The most important part of this exercise is to discover the relationship between what you see as your strengths and your weaknesses. You must be honest with yourself. Check 1 or 4 and only score 2 or 3 where you are in doubt. Add your scores and consult the analysis on page 69. The profile may suggest new avenues for you to explore.

OPTIONS

1 Never

2 Occasionally

3 Frequently

4 Always

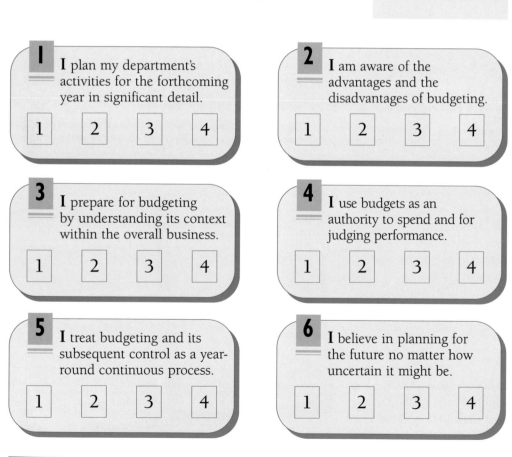

1 I plan my department's activities for the forthcoming year in significant detail.

1　2　3　4

2 I am aware of the advantages and the disadvantages of budgeting.

1　2　3　4

3 I prepare for budgeting by understanding its context within the overall business.

1　2　3　4

4 I use budgets as an authority to spend and for judging performance.

1　2　3　4

5 I treat budgeting and its subsequent control as a year-round continuous process.

1　2　3　4

6 I believe in planning for the future no matter how uncertain it might be.

1　2　3　4

7 I communicate plans to my department and listen to their comments and ideas.

1   2   3   4

8 I separate the needs of the organization from my personal ambitions.

1   2   3   4

9 I select a budget model that is relevant to my department.

1   2   3   4

10 I fully appreciate the strengths and opportunities my business possesses.

1   2   3   4

11 I refer to the budget manual and study its contents when I do the figures.

1   2   3   4

12 I understand the role of the budget committee and how it impacts on me.

1   2   3   4

13 I prefer to use standardized budget forms to help get the figures right.

1   2   3   4

14 I use my colleagues' expertise and knowledge throughout budgeting.

1   2   3   4

15 I exhaustively consider how external factors will affect my budget figures.

1   2   3   4

16 I know my department's limiting constraint and how to overcome it.

1   2   3   4

17 **I** estimate revenues by looking at their likely type, amount, and timing.

1 2 3 4

18 **I** check through all last year's expenditure so as not to miss costs.

1 2 3 4

19 **I** use my knowledge of fixed and variable costs when predicting future expenditure.

1 2 3 4

20 **I** follow the Output/Input method when I work out the budget.

1 2 3 4

21 **I** prefer to budget from a base of zero rather than just adjusting last year's figures.

1 2 3 4

22 **I** assess the financial impact of capital expenditure on my department.

1 2 3 4

23 **I** understand and use the budgeted cash flow forecast for my department.

1 2 3 4

24 **I** insist on being included in the iterative consolidating process.

1 2 3 4

25 **I** prepare for and participate effectively in budget-committee meetings.

1 2 3 4

26 **I** use the four-stage loop: set budget, record actual, compare, and control.

1 2 3 4

27 I choose which variances to focus on because some are more useful than others.

| 1 | 2 | 3 | 4 |

28 I am rigorous in rooting out discrepancies in my budget.

| 1 | 2 | 3 | 4 |

29 I distinguish between poor predictions and poor work.

| 1 | 2 | 3 | 4 |

30 I change my budget if there are major differences between it and actual results.

| 1 | 2 | 3 | 4 |

31 I recognize the importance of people's behavior in budgeting.

| 1 | 2 | 3 | 4 |

32 I make sure that I learn from and improve upon each year's budgeting.

| 1 | 2 | 3 | 4 |

ANALYSIS

Now that you have completed the self-assessment, add up your total score and check your performance by referring to the corresponding evaluations.

32–63: Your lack of budgeting skills means that you must rethink your approach to budgeting; refer to the relevant sections in this book on the fundamentals regarding your role and best practice in budgeting.

64–95: You have made considerable progress and are reasonably proficient at budgeting. Make renewed efforts to rectify areas of weakness and work on them to get better results from your budgeting.

96–128: You are skilled and competent at budgeting, but do not become too complacent. Remember that your development, like budgeting itself, is a continuous and ever-changing process.

UNDERSTANDING ACCOUNTS

492

INTRODUCTION

F*inance is probably the most important function in any organization, and an* understanding of the fundamental figures and financial statements is key to successful management. Understanding Accounts shows you how to master the language of finance, enabling you to contribute more effectively to overall business performance and improve your leadership skills. This book clearly explains how financial statements are compiled and shows you how to uncover a wealth of information about financial activity within your own, or a competitor's, organization. Packed with helpful hints, 101 tips, real-life case studies, and practical advice and information, it provides an indispensable guide to using and interpreting a set of financial statements.

UNDERSTANDING THE BASICS

Financial statements are produced periodically to measure how well an organization is performing. Learn how they are prepared and what they reveal about your own, or a competitor's, business.

EXPLAINING ACCOUNTS

A set of accounts, also known as financial statements, provides an invaluable insight into business performance. Learn what the three key financial statements are and how they link to give an overall picture of just how well an organization is faring.

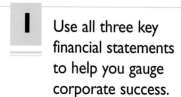

1 Use all three key financial statements to help you gauge corporate success.

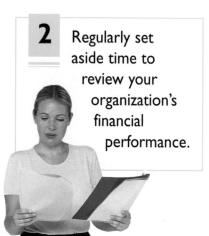

2 Regularly set aside time to review your organization's financial performance.

PRODUCING RELIABLE FINANCIAL STATEMENTS

When Italian monk Fra Pacioli first invented double-entry bookkeeping some 500 years ago, he introduced the civilized world to reliable accounting. Transactions were recorded twice (once to show where an item came from, and then to show where it went), so that nothing could be missed. Accountants today use the same principles – as well as following standards laid down by their own profession – to produce meaningful financial statements that summarize both the past and current financial position of an organization.

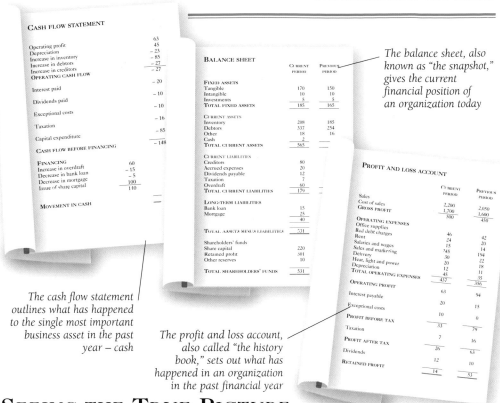

CASH FLOW STATEMENT

Operating profit	63
Depreciation	45
Increase in inventory	– 23
Increase in debtors	– 85
Increase in creditors	– 27
OPERATING CASH FLOW	– 27
	– 20
Interest paid	– 10
Dividends paid	– 10
Exceptional costs	– 16
Taxation	– 85
Capital expenditure	
CASH FLOW BEFORE FINANCING	– 148

FINANCING	
Increase in overdraft	60
Decrease in bank loan	– 15
Decrease in mortgage	– 5
Issue of share capital	100
	110
MOVEMENT IN CASH	

BALANCE SHEET

	CURRENT PERIOD	PREVIOUS PERIOD
FIXED ASSETS		
Tangible	170	150
Intangible	10	10
Investments	5	5
TOTAL FIXED ASSETS	185	165
CURRENT ASSETS		
Inventory	208	185
Debtors	337	254
Other	18	16
Cash	2	
TOTAL CURRENT ASSETS	565	
CURRENT LIABILITIES		
Creditors	80	
Accrued expenses	20	
Dividends payable	12	
Taxation	7	
Overdraft	60	
TOTAL CURRENT LIABILITIES	179	
LONG-TERM LIABILITIES		
Bank loan	15	
Mortgage	25	
	40	
TOTAL ASSETS MINUS LIABILITIES	531	
Shareholders' funds		
Share capital	220	
Retained profit	301	
Other reserves	10	
TOTAL SHAREHOLDERS' FUNDS	531	

The balance sheet, also known as "the snapshot," gives the current financial position of an organization today

PROFIT AND LOSS ACCOUNT

	CURRENT PERIOD	PREVIOUS PERIOD
Sales	2,200	2,050
Cost of sales	1,700	1,600
GROSS PROFIT	500	450
OPERATING EXPENSES		
Office supplies	46	42
Bad debt charges	24	20
Rent	15	14
Salaries and wages	245	194
Sales and marketing	30	22
Delivery	20	18
Heat, light and power	12	11
Depreciation	45	35
TOTAL OPERATING EXPENSES	437	356
OPERATING PROFIT	63	94
Interest payable	20	15
Exceptional costs	10	0
PROFIT BEFORE TAX	33	79
Taxation	7	16
PROFIT AFTER TAX	26	63
Dividends	12	10
RETAINED PROFIT	14	53

The cash flow statement outlines what has happened to the single most important business asset in the past year – cash

The profit and loss account, also called "the history book," sets out what has happened in an organization in the past financial year

SEEING THE TRUE PICTURE

Each time you examine the financial statements that make up a set of business accounts, keep some key points in mind. First, since all businesses have different accounting policies and calculation methods, no two sets of financial statements will be the same. Second, different business formats (partnerships or publicly traded companies, for example) and types (such as manufacturing or service organizations) will operate in different ways, with the result that some financial statements are straightforward and others complex. Financial statements may also be produced for a variety of reasons, such as calculating tax liability, assessing investment potential, or establishing a value for sale. Remember this when you interpret the figures.

▲ IDENTIFYING THE KEY FINANCIAL STATEMENTS

There are three financial statements that will help you assess the success of a company. Broadly, the profit and loss account reveals the income minus expenses, the balance sheet shows the assets minus the liabilities, and the cash flow statement records the increase or decrease of cash.

3 Understand that accounts do no more than reflect financial reality.

WHO USES ACCOUNTS?

Financial statements are of interest to the organization that produces them and to outsiders such as competitors and tax officials. Add to your understanding of financial statements by learning how to look at them from different points of view.

4 Recognize that accounts are produced for different purposes.

5 Be clear on why it is vital to examine your company's accounts.

WHO NEEDS ACCOUNTS?

There are two main groups of people who use accounts: those who are interested in the financial performance of an organization (such as investors, shareholders, or suppliers), and those who take a broader view (often for taxation, regulatory, or legal reasons). The latter are more interested in general issues such as compliance with appropriate legislation than in detailed financial analysis.

DEFINING PERSPECTIVES

In addition to annual reports and financial statements for external consumption, most organizations produce internal, or management, accounts. These are used only within the organization and are helpfully flexible in measuring different (sometimes nonfinancial) aspects of performance because they are not subject to the rules and regulations that govern the preparation of external figures. However, because internal accounts do not have to adhere to any rules, they often bear little or no resemblance to annual external accounts. The internals can simply be wrong, causing problems for managers who are using them to drive the business forward.

Manager wants to know where performance can be improved

INTERNAL ACCOUNTS

Tax official checks that correct tax has been paid on profits

EXTERNAL ACCOUNTS

LOOKING AT DIFFERENT ACCOUNTS ▶
External accounts show consistency and comparability. Internal accounts need not follow any rules and can be more flexible and useful to a business, but also more open to error.

IDENTIFYING USERS OF FINANCIAL STATEMENTS

USERS OF ACCOUNTS	WHAT THEY LOOK FOR
OWNER Has a vested interest in the organization's future and success; tends to be financially cautious.	• How well the business is doing compared with previous years and with competitors. • Reassurance that the family source of income is safe and secure.
INVESTOR/SHAREHOLDER Invests money or has shares in an organization; their analysis is often detailed and ruthless.	• Information on an organization to allow comparisons with other businesses, with a view to choosing between them. • Indications that returns will be maximized.
CREDITOR Advances loans; needs to know that the interest is affordable and that the debt can be repaid.	• Evidence that an organization will be able to pay the interest on any debts. • The worth of an organization should the debt be unpaid and the business wound up.
COMPETITOR Has an interest in the relative financial performance and business statistics of rivals.	• Growth in sales, market share, net profits, and overall business efficiency. • Information about the cost structure and operations of competitors.
MANAGER/EMPLOYEE Works for and is paid by the organization on a full-time or regular basis.	• Reassurance that the organization will continue to operate competitively. • End-of-year figures that reflect his/her competence favorably.
CUSTOMER/SUPPLIER Needs to know whether he/she is dealing with financially sound and reputable organizations.	• Continuity of supply and business without disruption to the flow of goods or services. • Ability of an organization to pay for goods and deliver on time.
TAXATION OFFICIAL Reviews financial statements for accuracy and reasonableness, then checks the amount of tax payable.	• Properly prepared and computed financial statements and profit and loss statements. • Validity of financial statements when compared with similar businesses.

EXAMINING REGULATIONS AND PRACTICE

The preparation of financial statements is governed both by strict legal requirements and by guidelines created by the accounting profession. Understand the principles and the influences that have shaped the way in which accounts are prepared.

6 Understand the impact of the law and the accounting profession.

7 Accept that minimal information is usually disclosed.

8 Keep up to date with accounting methods.

FOLLOWING THE LAW

In most countries the primary rules for producing financial statements are laid down by law. This states exactly what must be done in creating, managing, and closing down a company – in short, the law establishes the overall framework, or "skeleton," for producing accounts. While the law is usually clear on the "what" and "when" of accounts, it is often vague on such issues as "How should inventory be valued?" or "How should profit be recognized on a particular transaction?". This detailed, practical level of accounting is usually left to accountants.

ASSESSING GUIDELINES

For those accounting issues where the law gives insufficient guidance, accountants have established their own set of guidelines and standards known as Generally Accepted Accounting Principles (GAAP). Country specific, GAAP advises on how certain key transactions are best treated. Because GAAP is not compulsory, compliance with it may be less than perfect, which is why abuse of the system is possible. Additional rules may also apply to certain businesses, depending on company size, ownership, and listing rules of stock exchanges.

QUESTIONS TO ASK YOURSELF

Q What size of business am I looking at, and what level and detail of accounting disclosure should I expect to see?

Q What does the law require the accounts to contain, and how informative will I find this?

Q Are the accounting policies of the organization typical and reasonable for a business of its size and type?

COMPARING PRACTICE IN DIFFERENT COUNTRIES

The rules governing the preparation and structure of accounts are unusual. Strict legal requirements laid down by a country's law, together with generally accepted but more informal practice typically created by the accounting profession of that country, may be either strong or weak, depending on the country. Countries with strong "codified" legal and tax systems (Continental Europe, in general) tend to have weaker GAAP, and vice versa. Strong and open stock exchanges typically have strong GAAP, since, unlike laws, GAAP guidelines can be drawn up relatively quickly in response to real-life issues.

CHOOSING POLICIES

Operating within both the law and GAAP, organizations choose how they will treat certain financial transactions. Known as accounting policies, these are generally selected by the directors of an organization and their business advisors as being the most appropriate to the company's current circumstances and also the best way of fairly presenting their results and financial position. Since no two organizations are the same, they will obviously all calculate their accounts in a slightly different way.

9 Realize that calculation methods vary worldwide.

▼ **DEFINING INFLUENCES ON ACCOUNTS**
Of the five key influences on accounting statements, company law and accounting practice have the most impact on the form that accounts take, followed by regulatory and taxation rules, and international laws.

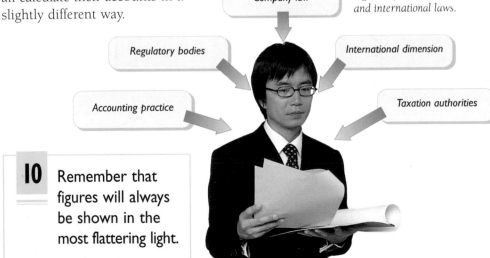

Company law

Regulatory bodies

International dimension

Accounting practice

Taxation authorities

10 Remember that figures will always be shown in the most flattering light.

DEFINING KEY CONCEPTS

There are certain fundamental themes or concepts, such as accruals, prudence, consistency, and viability, that are seen as the cornerstones of good accounting. In order to understand accounts it is vital to appreciate the importance of these.

11 Commit the four basic accounting principles to memory.

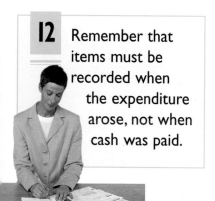

12 Remember that items must be recorded when the expenditure arose, not when cash was paid.

USING ACCRUALS

The principle of accruals, or matching, sets out when a transaction should appear in the accounts. An item is always recorded when the income (or expenditure) arises – not when cash is received (or paid). For example, even when a sale is made on credit terms and cash may not be received until the next accounting period, the sale must still be recognized now. While applying this fundamental accounting principle is commonsense, it nevertheless causes the most accounting problems.

SHOWING PRUDENCE AND CONSISTENCY

Financial statements must be prudently or conservatively presented, which means that profits must not be overstated, and costs must be realistically and fairly estimated. In other words, figures should be on the pessimistic side. Prudence addresses the question: "How much should an amount be?" and is the most important of the key concepts. Accounts should also be produced using consistent assumptions and treatments. This means that an organization should use similar principles year after year, so that accounts can be compared sensibly. Changes to assumptions and treatments can, of course, be made, but the financial implications must be highlighted and quantified.

POINTS TO REMEMBER

- The accruals principle asks the question: "in which accounting period" or "when" should the impact of a transaction be shown?

- Prudence, or financial conservatism, effectively overrides all other accounting principles in importance.

13 Know that prudence governs fair accounting.

ASSUMING VIABILITY

When producing a set of financial statements it is necessary to assume that the organization will be in business, or a going concern, the following year. This is a silent assumption, since it would be almost impossible to produce accounts if the business were likely to fail. The value of inventory in a warehouse, a plant, a piece of equipment, or any other item in the accounts would be affected if the business were to cease to exist.

 14 Be aware that any change in calculations often indicates a cover-up.

EXPLAINING KEY TERMS

KEY TERM	DEFINITION
ASSET	Anything owned by an organization that has a monetary value, from plant and machinery to patents and goodwill.
AUDIT	Independent inspection of accounts, according to set principles, by accountants who are qualified auditors.
DEPRECIATION	Annual cost shown in the profit and loss account of writing off a fixed asset over its expected useful life.
EQUITY	Share capital and reserves of a company, which represent what shareholders have invested in the organization.
FIXED ASSET	Asset used in a business and not held for resale, typically with a life of more than one year.
LIABILITY	Amount owed at a set time, often split into short-term (less than one year) and long-term (more than one year).
RETAINED EARNINGS	Profits made by a business, which have been reinvested in the business rather than paid out in dividends.
WORKING CAPITAL	Capital available for daily operations of an organization, usually expressed as current assets minus current liabilities.

MASTERING THE ACCOUNTS

Mastering accounts means understanding the three key financial statements: the profit and loss account, the balance sheet, and the cash flow statement. Learn how they all fit together.

UNDERSTANDING A PROFIT AND LOSS ACCOUNT

The profit and loss account is an organization's statement of earnings; it shows all the income minus expenses over the year. Make sure that you know how the profit and loss account is structured and what type of items are included.

15 Check how the accounting policies show that profit is measured.

16 Remember only "revenue" items appear in a profit and loss account.

RECORDING THE PAST

The profit and loss account is a "history book" of the past year. It tells how well a business has performed, listing all the "ins minus outs," or sales minus costs. Working on the accruals principle, only items arising during the year are shown. They must also be of a "revenue" nature (goods, services, and general annual expenditure), never items of a "capital" nature (purchase or sale of fixed assets such as equipment and machinery).

READING THE LINES

A profit and loss account measures various levels, or "lines," of profit. First is gross profit: sales (sometimes called gross income or fees billed) minus the cost of sales (the costs of providing goods or services). Next is operating profit: gross profit minus all the expenses supporting the infrastructure and administration of an organization. Profit before tax is the operating profit minus interest incurred on borrowings for the year, plus interest received. Profit after tax is calculated by deducting the tax due as a result of being in business for the year. Retained profit is the after-tax profit minus any dividends paid to the shareholders.

PROFIT AND LOSS ACCOUNT

	CURRENT PERIOD	PREVIOUS PERIOD
Sales	2,200	2,050
Cost of sales	1,700	1,600
GROSS PROFIT	500	450
OPERATING EXPENSES		
Office supplies	46	42
Bad debt charges	24	20
Rent	15	14
Salaries and wages	245	194
Sales and marketing	30	22
Delivery	20	18
Heat, light, and power	12	11
Depreciation	45	35
TOTAL OPERATING EXPENSES	437	356
OPERATING PROFIT	63	94
Interest payable	20	15
Exceptional costs	10	0
PROFIT BEFORE TAX	33	79
Taxation	7	16
PROFIT AFTER TAX	26	63
Dividends	12	10
RETAINED PROFIT	14	53

DECIDING WHAT COUNTS

Items included in the profit and loss account must all have passed the accruals test, but there are times when deciding what should be counted as sales or expenses is tricky. For example, should a sales invoice be included in the accounts if the work has not been completed? Accountants use various signposts to help them recognize what and how much to include, and when to do so. These signposts include the following:

- Completion: Is the work substantially completed?
- Ownership: Has ownership passed from the vendor to the customer?
- Measurement: Can the profit be accurately and prudently estimated?
- Irrevocability: Could the customer cancel the sale, causing the loss of profit?

▲ **RECOGNIZING THE FORMAT**
A typical profit and loss account is consistently structured into set rows and columns to show the profit or loss for the year; that is, the difference between income and expenditure.

17 Understand what the main headings in a profit and loss account mean.

LOOKING AT GROSS PROFIT

The gross profit, or first line of profit, provides an important early measure of a business's well-being. Ensure that you understand which types of expenses are deducted to calculate gross profit and what the gross margin can tell you.

18 Remember that the gross profit percentage should not be falling.

19 Compare your company's accounts year to year and with competitors'.

20 Be aware that gross profit measures a company's basic viability.

RECORDING SALES

The first item on a profit and loss account records a business's overall volume of activity and is called either sales, turnover, income, or fees billed. This is the full amount of all the sales invoices raised during the accounting period that have met the correct accruals criteria for being included on the statement. These are stated minus any sales-related taxes (since tax belongs to the taxation authority, not to the organization itself).

▼ DETECTING GROSS PROFIT
The first three lines of a profit and loss account show an organization's fundamental financial performance in black and white. From it, the well-being of the business can be determined.

The previous period's figures are shown so that they can be easily compared with this period's results

PROFIT AND LOSS ACCOUNT

	CURRENT PERIOD	PREVIOUS PERIOD
Sales	2,200	2,050
Cost of sales	1,700	1,600
GROSS PROFIT	500	450
OPERATING EXPENSES		
Office supplies	46	42
Bad debt charges	24	20
Rent	15	14
	245	194

Gross profit is the key result of a business and the first figure that investors or owners are likely to be interested in

DEDUCTING COST OF SALES

There are two types of costs in the profit and loss account, and these are deducted separately. The first group is known as cost of sales (COS), sometimes referred to as cost of goods sold (COGS). These are all the costs expended to make or produce the product or service that is being sold, and usually includes materials, production staff, production premises, and machinery costs – typically "factory" costs.

21 Look beyond the figures to the type and structure of the organization.

PROVIDING A MEASURE

While gross income, or the full amount of sales, is an important sign of life for a business, gross profit, or the full amount of sales minus COS, is more informative about its health. This "factory result" is often more usefully expressed as a percentage of sales. Since different businesses have different COS, they will have different gross profit percentages. These must be looked at in relation to what would be expected from the type of business.

PERFECT PRINTERS
PROFIT AND LOSS ACCOUNT

	CURRENT PERIOD	%	PREVIOUS PERIOD	%
Sales	2,200	100.0	2,050	100.0
Cost of sales	600	27.3	560	27.3
GROSS PROFIT	1,600	72.7	1,190	72.7
OPERATING EXPENSES	46	2.1		
Office supplies				

▲ COMPARING GROSS PROFIT MARGINS

Gross profit margins vary significantly between different types of businesses, and a low margin is to be expected from a business with a high cost of sales, such as a supermarket or travel agency. On the other hand, a service business with a lower than normal cost of sales will have a higher than average gross profit margin.

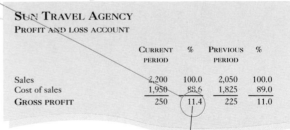

SUN TRAVEL AGENCY
PROFIT AND LOSS ACCOUNT

	CURRENT PERIOD	%	PREVIOUS PERIOD	%
Sales	2,200	100.0	2,050	100.0
Cost of sales	1,950	88.6	1,825	89.0
GROSS PROFIT	250	11.4	225	11.0

Profit margins for low cost of sales businesses are typically between 50 and 90 percent; for high cost of sales businesses they rarely exceed 10 percent

DETERMINING OPERATING PROFIT

The second line of profit is operating or trading profit, which is a clear measure of a business's performance after all its operating costs have been deducted. Identify which costs apply to ascertain how successfully a business has been managed.

22 Examine operating costs to gauge management efficiency.

23 Look at trends in certain costs to anticipate any future problems.

CALCULATING ▼ OPERATING PROFIT

Operating profit is struck after the remainder of costs in a business have been deducted. It is usually expressed as a percentage of sales.

DEDUCTING OTHER COSTS

The second type of costs in the profit and loss account, which are now deducted to determine operating profit, are called selling, general, and administration (SG&A) costs, or operating expenses. These cover any expenses not listed in the cost of sales category. SG&A includes marketing and advertising under "selling," while "general and administration" covers head office, accounting, information technology, marketing, personnel, directors, and central costs. All costs must be either COS or SG&A.

Sales		
Cost of sales	1,700	1,600
GROSS PROFIT	500	450
OPERATING EXPENSES		
Office supplies	46	42
Bad debt charges	24	20
Rent	15	14
Salaries and wages	245	194
Sales and marketing	30	22
Delivery	20	18
Heat, light, and power	12	11
Depreciation	45	35
TOTAL OPERATING EXPENSES	437	356
OPERATING PROFIT	63	94
Interest payable	20	15

Total operating expenses are deducted from the gross profit

Operating profit made from business, before the deduction of tax, interest, and dividends.

UNDERSTANDING DIFFERENT CYCLES

All businesses have two cycles – an operating cycle and a capital investment cycle. The operating cycle is straightforward: A business buys goods or services in order that they can be sold at a profit. The capital investment cycle, on the other hand, is a measure of how much is invested in the fabric of a business (such as plant, tools, or machinery) in order that a business may carry out its operating cycle. More than one operating cycle is generally needed to fund one capital cycle. A set of financial statements simply reflects how much money is tied up in an organization at any time in both of these cycles.

▼ REVIEWING THE CAPITAL INVESTMENT CYCLE

Capital investment, or the purchase of onetime items needed for an organization to operate, involves a substantial cash outflow. Several operating cycles are therefore needed to fund one investment cycle.

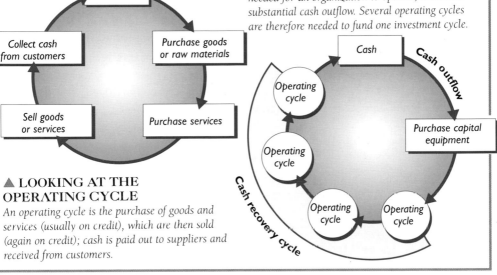

▲ LOOKING AT THE OPERATING CYCLE

An operating cycle is the purchase of goods and services (usually on credit), which are then sold (again on credit); cash is paid out to suppliers and received from customers.

REACHING A SUBTOTAL

Deducting SG&A costs from gross profit gives the subtotal of operating profit. This is effectively the end of the "first half" of the profit and loss account, which measures how well a business has performed in its core operations. Operating profit is often more usefully expressed as a percentage of sales – a typical range being between zero and 10 percent.

24 Compare operating profit percentages among organizations.

EVALUATING THE BOTTOM LINE

The second half of the profit and loss statement, down to the "bottom line," relates to other expenses, including taxation and interest. It is vital to learn how to interpret these items, since their financial impact can often be significant.

25 Determine whether an interest bill is really affordable.

26 Check if onetime costs are warning signs of problems.

LOOKING AT INTEREST

Below the operating profit the next deduction to be made is the amount of interest incurred on all loans and borrowings over the period covered by the profit and loss account. This is often an issue because the amount payable can call into question the viability of an entire business. Affordability can be calculated by comparing the interest charges for the year to the operating profit. For example, if operating profit is $63 and interest $20, the interest could be paid about three times over and interest cover is said to be "three." There is no absolute target; what is important is the trend in interest cover, which can change from year to year.

REACHING THE ▼ BOTTOM LINE
The difference between operating profit and retained profit will be due to varying amounts of interest, exceptional items, taxation, and dividends.

TOTAL OPERATING EXPENSES		356
OPERATING PROFIT	63	94
Interest payable	20	15
Exceptional costs	10	0
PROFIT BEFORE TAX	33	79
Taxation	7	16
PROFIT AFTER TAX	26	63
Dividends	12	10
RETAINED PROFIT	14	53

Profit after tax is what is left for shareholders after interest, exceptional costs, and tax have been deducted

After paying shareholder dividends, the business reinvests the retained profit

EXAMINING EXCEPTIONAL COSTS

Occasionally you will come across other items of a onetime, nonrecurring nature, and traditionally these are shown separately from the core gross and operating profit figures so as not to distort them. Such items are referred to as exceptional items and typically include provisions for large future events (recognizing costs now even though the event will happen in the future), currency movements, gains and losses on sales of assets or businesses. Assess whether these seem reasonable or if they indicate problems.

EXAMINING TAXATION

The operating profit minus interest gives profit before tax (PBT), which is subject to taxation; the profit and loss account details the tax charge on the year's profits. The amount shown is unlikely yet to have been paid in full to the tax authorities and is also probably a best estimate. Whatever the annual tax charge is computed to be, it is deducted from PBT to give profit after tax, or PAT, which, in principle, belongs to the shareholders. PAT also provides a basis for calculating shareholder measures such as earnings per share.

27 Investigate a tax charge if it is not the expected rate.

28 Spot the trend in, and sufficiency of, retained profits.

▲ SPLITTING PROFIT

For a publicly traded company, profit before tax is split three ways. One-third represents tax (where corporate tax rate is approximately 30 percent), one-third is typically paid to shareholders by way of dividends, and the final one-third is retained in the business.

PINPOINTING RETAINED PROFIT

At the bottom line of the profit and loss account, once declared dividends have been deducted, are retained earnings. These represent the profit kept behind by an organization in order to help it grow. Bear in mind that profits make a balance sheet grow, so the amount of retained profit should correspond to the increase in the balance sheet. However, in large companies this simple accounting truth may be obscured by technical shuffling. It may also be unclear exactly where the retained profit will be; it is hoped that it would be in cash form in a successful organization, rather than in a less liquid item, such as inventory.

UNDERSTANDING BALANCE SHEETS

*T*he balance sheet is effectively a listing of everything a business owns minus all that it owes. Learn how this key financial statement is structured and how the figures work to provide you with a picture of the total net assets of an organization.

29 Think of the balance sheet as an aerial photograph.

BALANCE SHEET	CURRENT PERIOD	PREVIOUS PERIOD
FIXED ASSETS		
Tangible	170	150
Intangible	10	10
Investments	5	5
TOTAL FIXED ASSETS	185	165
CURRENT ASSETS		
Inventory	208	185
Debtors	337	254
Other	18	16
Cash	2	10
TOTAL CURRENT ASSETS	565	465
CURRENT LIABILITIES		
Creditors	80	109
Accrued expenses	20	18
Dividends payable	12	10
Taxation	7	16
Overdraft	60	0
TOTAL CURRENT LIABILITIES	179	153
LONG-TERM LIABILITIES		
Bank loan	15	30
Mortgage	25	30
	40	60
TOTAL ASSETS LESS LIABILITIES	531	417
Shareholders' funds	220	120
Share capital	301	287
Retained profit	10	10
Other reserves		
TOTAL SHAREHOLDERS' FUNDS	531	417

EXAMINING HOW BALANCE SHEETS WORK

The balance sheet shows the present financial performance of a business. It can be compared to a snapshot of an entire organization taken at the close of business on a specific day, and it is therefore correct only at that one precise moment. The snapshot shows everything that the business owns – its assets – and all that it owes – its liabilities. Balance sheets are generally drawn up each year at the same time as the profit and loss account. But bear in mind that pictures can be flattering. If, for example, a fashion retailer's balance sheet is done after the summer sales (when there is plenty of cash in the bank and inventories are low), it will look particularly good.

▲ READING THE BALANCE SHEET

The balance sheet lists assets and liabilities comparing both previous and current accounting periods, grouping them into meaningful subtotals and totals that explain what is happening financially within an organization.

QUESTIONS TO ASK YOURSELF

Q Does the year-end fit the annual nature of the business?

Q Would a different accounting date alter the balance sheet?

Q Have there been major changes in any totals year to year?

Q Have assets shown at current value been estimated fairly?

GROUPING FIGURES

The balance sheet is split into sections, according to strict accounting rules. The first section lists an organization's assets split between fixed (or long-term) and current (or short-term) assets. The second section itemizes liabilities (again split between fixed and current). The third shows shareholders' funds, or money invested in the business by its owners.

30 Understand the importance of how liabilities and assets are grouped.

Fleet manager informs team that new vans are needed

Colleague reminds fleet manager that their major client has unsettled bills

Accountant also notes that the company has excess inventory

Senior manager decides that it is too risky to purchase new vans at present

USING THE ▲ BALANCE SHEET

As a manager, it is important to look at, understand, and act upon what the balance sheet tells you. In this way you will be able to make better quality financial decisions.

31 Appreciate that balance sheets show cost and not value.

INTERPRETING THE TOTAL

All assets and liabilities are generally shown on the balance sheet according to an accounting convention called historic cost, which means that they are shown at their original cost to the business. The balance sheet total, also referred to as total net assets, is arrived at by adding up the cost of all assets and then deducting the total of short- and long-term liabilities. Remember that the balance sheet normally shows only costs, and it should not be seen as an indication of an organization's market value. Nothing could be further from the truth, yet this remains a popular misconception.

EXAMINING FIXED ASSETS

Fixed assets are used by a business on a permanent basis to create wealth in the normal course of operations. Learn to recognize the three types of fixed assets (tangibles, intangibles, and investments) and understand the concept of depreciation.

32 Investigate any significant additions in unusual fixed assets.

33 Scrutinize closely any asset that is shown at current value.

UNDERSTANDING ▼ FIXED ASSETS

Fixed assets are generally grouped into tangible, intangible, and investments held for the longer term. They are listed in order of the frequency in which they are encountered. Amounts are stated after depreciation.

RECOGNIZING TANGIBLE FIXED ASSETS

Assets needed for a business to be in a position to operate are known as fixed assets. These are typically tangible items with a life of more than 12 months (otherwise they would be shown as a cost on the profit and loss). Spending on fixed assets is called capital expenditure, and this reflects how much is invested in the fabric of a business in order that it may carry out its operating cycle. Typical fixed assets are land, buildings, equipment, machinery, computers, fixtures, and vehicles. Manufacturers generally have high fixed assets and are capital intensive. Service businesses have low fixed assets and are not capital intensive.

BALANCE SHEET	CURRENT PERIOD	PREVIOUS PERIOD
FIXED ASSETS	170	150
Tangible	10	10
Intangible	5	5
Investments		
TOTAL FIXED ASSETS	185	165
CURRENT ASSETS	208	185
Inventory	337	254
Debtors	18	16
Other	2	10
Cash	565	465
TOTAL CURRENT ASSETS		

Total fixed assets shows how much is invested in a business to enable it to operate

ANALYZING DEPRECIATION

Fixed assets are shown at cost minus depreciation, known as net book value. Depreciation writes off the cost of the asset (minus any anticipated residual value, often assumed to be zero) over its effective useful life. For example, assuming a computer costs $900 and has a useful life of three years, it will be depreciated by $300 a year. This means that it will be written down to $600 after one year, $300 after two years, and $0 after three years. Depreciation simply spreads the cost of a fixed asset over its lifetime; it does not write the asset down to secondhand value, nor does it provide a fund of money for replacement.

34 See that an asset's life and depreciation rate seem fair.

▼ CALCULATING DEPRECIATION

With the "straight line" method, a computer would be written off by an equal annual amount throughout its depreciable life. Using the "reducing balance" method, the depreciation of a car would be recalculated every year based on the net book value (or written down value) reached to date.

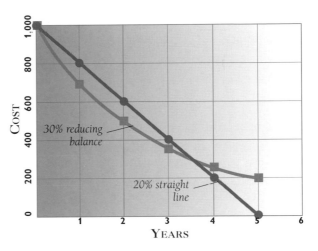

30% reducing balance

20% straight line

COST / YEARS

FLYING ON TIME ▼

The useful economic life of an asset is usually written off over a number of years. With an aircraft, however, the number of hours flown is considered to be a far better determinant of age.

SETTING A RATE

The depreciation life/rate of each asset is set by the business, so although different companies are making the same business profit, because their fixed assets have different depreciation lives, each will show a different accounting profit. In addition to the straight line on cost and reducing balance methods of depreciating an asset, there are any number of other ways to depreciate assets, most of which are simply based on commonsense and generally accepted practice.

DEFINING INTANGIBLES

Most fixed assets are real and tangible; in other words, they physically exist and can be touched. Yet balance sheets recognize that certain long-term assets may not be tangible. There are two main types of intangibles: traditional and modern. Traditional intangibles include items such as patents, intellectual property rights, and know-how, while modern intangibles (or those that have recently become popular) are goodwill and brands. Intangibles, by their very nature, are often difficult to value, but – like all fixed assets – once their worth has been calculated, they must be depreciated over their useful economic life.

POINTS TO REMEMBER

- Certain intangibles have been shown in financial statements for many years without creating problems.
- Goodwill is no more than an amount needed to get the figures to balance; it might also represent something intangible of value.
- Including the value of brands in a balance sheet involves much subjectivity and can often be very controversial.

35 See if intangibles make up a realistic proportion of the balance sheet.

EXPLAINING GOODWILL

Goodwill is generally taken to mean the value of a business's good name, reputation, and client base. Goodwill is shown as a fixed asset by an organization when it buys another business at a higher price than the value of its assets. Any decent business will be worth more than simply its assets, but the problem is how to get the accounts of the buyer to balance. When buying a business for $10 that has assets of only $6, the difference of $4 is called goodwill. Goodwill is shown as an intangible asset and is amortized (depreciated) over its useful economic life.

Purchase price is established by mutual agreement

NOTES TO ACCOUNTS

COMPANY	A	B	C
Amount paid for company	155	15	23
Fair value of acquired assets	95	2	-2
Goodwill	60	13	25

Amount of goodwill depends on the purchaser's perception of worth

Purchaser is so eager that it pays money to acquire liabilities

◀ **BALANCING THE BOOKS**
This extract from the notes to accounts shows an organization that has bought three companies during the year. The purchase price reflects the value of the acquired company as a whole, not just its assets. The amount of goodwill is simply the difference between the purchase price and the fair value of the assets acquired.

UNDERSTANDING BRANDS

A new development has seen the concept of goodwill taken even further, which is known as brand accounting. The idea is that because some organizations do not want to show a cost to the profit and loss account every year when depreciating goodwill (either because their profits will not stand it or because they do not believe that the asset in question should be written down), they categorize the asset as a "brand" rather than as goodwill. They argue that any spending on marketing and advertising means that the brand does not fall in value – and so is not being depreciated.

36 Check whether any brands should have been reduced in value.

CASE STUDY

Peter, the sales manager of a confectionery company, was disappointed that profits were down in spite of increased sales. In the latest set of accounts, Peter discovered that large amortization (depreciation) charges had been made because his company had acquired two businesses. Since the assets of the new businesses had been bought for more than their book value, the shortfall had been categorized as goodwill, which had to be written off over its useful life. As a result, profits were being reduced by the amount of the annual write-off. Peter approached David, the finance manager, to suggest that since so much money was being spent on marketing and advertising (expenditure in support of the brands), the goodwill should be classified as a brand. David agreed, and profits increased again.

EXPLORING INVESTMENTS

The final category of fixed assets is called investments, which covers any monies or shares held outside the company. These may be shares in another organization held for the long term, investments, or any other asset that will be sold, but not within the next 12 months. Again, the issue is that of cost. For example, should shares be valued at the price originally paid for them or according to the stock market price as at that day? It is generally agreed that they should be shown at market value.

▲ AVOIDING DEPRECIATION CHARGES

Peter's understanding of the issues of goodwill and brands prompted him to approach the finance manager with a sound proposition. By classifying goodwill as a brand, David was able to amend the company's financial statements so that there was no annual write-off. As a result, Peter was happy to see his team's improved sales performance reflected in the increased profit shown on the next period's profit and loss account.

QUESTIONS TO ASK YOURSELF

Q Are all fixed assets fairly stated in cost and depreciation?

Q Do the figures demonstrate adequate investment for the future?

Q Should any intangibles be ignored when analyzing figures?

Q Have investments been valued and accounted for correctly?

WORKING WITH CURRENT ASSETS

Current assets are short-term assets that a business holds that will convert into cash within the next 12 months. Learn to recognize the four main types of current assets and why it is important to convert the first three into cash quickly.

37 Look at current assets with care – they represent a business's lifeblood.

38 Check that debtors change only in proportion to turnover.

UNDERSTANDING ▼ CURRENT ASSETS

Current assets, or items that will turn into cash in the next year, include inventory held for resale, debtors owing for credit sales made, miscellaneous items paid for in advance, and cash itself.

LISTING CURRENT ASSETS

Included under current assets is cash, plus anything that will turn into cash in the next 12 months. The importance of current assets is that they show how much an organization has in the way of cash, or near cash, and therefore how viable the business is. There are three main categories of current assets: inventory, debtors (people who have bought goods and owe payment), and other current assets, which include other monies owed and items known as prepayments. There is also cash (received when debtors pay their bills, and including petty cash or monies held in the business bank account or on short-term deposit).

TOTAL FIXED ASSETS	185	165
CURRENT ASSETS		
Inventory	208	185
Debtors	337	254
Other	18	16
Cash	2	10
TOTAL CURRENT ASSETS	565	465
CURRENT LIABILITIES		
Creditors	80	109
Accrued expenses	20	18

Current assets in a business should be as "liquid" (close to cash) as possible

DEFINING INVENTORY

There are three components of inventory: raw materials, work in progress, and finished goods. What is of interest is how much cash is tied up in each component, because the more raw materials there are, the further they must go to be converted into cash, incurring costs along the way. Finished goods are safer assets because they are more liquid. However, inventory overall is the least liquid of all current assets.

LOOKING AT ASSETS WITHIN THE OPERATING CYCLE

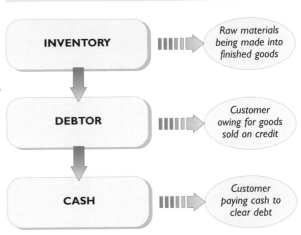

INVENTORY → Raw materials being made into finished goods

DEBTOR → Customer owing for goods sold on credit

CASH → Customer paying cash to clear debt

VALUING INVENTORY

Inventory is usually valued either at cost or at net realizable value (whichever is lower), since it should never be overstated. Cost is the price paid for items when bought; realizable is what they could be sold for, net of expenses. An item bought for $5 with a selling price of $20 should be shown in inventory at $5. If it could be sold for only $1, then that is how it should be shown, with an inventory write-down of $4 ($5 minus $1) appearing as a cost of sales in that year's profit and loss account. The higher the inventory at the end of the year (closing inventory), the lower the cost of sales on the profit and loss account, hence the higher the reported profit.

39 Appreciate how inventory on the balance sheet impacts profit on the profit and loss account.

DO'S AND DON'TS

✔ Do look for surprise increases in inventories and debtors.

✔ Do be cynical about the valuation applied to inventories.

✘ Don't believe that more current assets are always good news.

✘ Don't overlook other current assets and what they tell you.

40 Realize that obsolete inventory is a common problem.

IDENTIFYING INVENTORY

Assuming that prices of inventory are rising, then raw materials purchased earlier will cost less than those bought later. Accountants generally choose one of two methods for charging a material out of the stores and on to the job: FIFO (first in, first out) or LIFO (last in, first out). The method chosen will affect reported profits and assets, since under FIFO the profit and loss account profit and balance sheet closing inventory figures will be higher. Under LIFO, both figures will be lower.

41 Check that your inventory has not been overvalued – reject amounts that do not seem right.

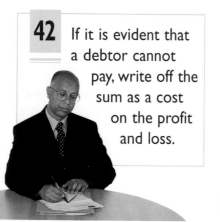

42 If it is evident that a debtor cannot pay, write off the sum as a cost on the profit and loss.

EXAMINING DEBTORS

Debtors, or amounts owed by customers for sales made on credit terms, is a more liquid asset than inventory. The amount shown is the total of the invoices outstanding (issued but not yet paid) at the accounting period end and it represents cash that is being held, albeit temporarily, by customers. Debtors will invariably be an organization's largest current asset – in which case it is vital that a business has them under control. This means making sure that customers pay, preferably on time and the full amount.

DEFINING DEDUCTIONS FROM DEBTORS

The problem with debtors is that not all of an organization's customers will end up paying – some may default on the debt. Since accountants must follow the prudence principle and state all assets at a realistic figure, they must anticipate that a certain amount of debt will not be paid and make a provision for it. This bad debt provision, which is estimated at the end of the year, is deducted from the debtors figure shown on the balance sheet. The difference between this year's and the previous year's provision then becomes a sales, general, and administration cost on the profit and loss account. Bad debts also impact on accounts during the year if, at any time, customers are unable to pay what they owe. Once this is apparent, their debt should be immediately canceled. This is called a bad debt charge or write-off, and is also an SG&A cost on the profit and loss account.

IDENTIFYING OTHER CURRENT ASSETS

CURRENT ASSET	POINTS TO NOTE
ASSETS HELD FOR RESALE Items about to be sold.	When a fixed asset such as land is about to be sold, it is shown on the balance sheet as a current asset, rather than as a fixed asset, because it will convert into cash within one year.
LOANS Advances to employees.	When an organization has lent or advanced money to its employees or directors, this is shown as a current asset of the business, since generally the monies will be fully repaid within the next year.
PREPAYMENTS Payments made in advance.	If bills are paid in advance, cash has been paid out – but the expense relates to a future accounting period. This means that a prepayment is, in effect, a current asset.
OTHERS Miscellaneous items.	Insurance claims, tax refunds, deposits paid to secure goods, payments received by installments, and stage payments represent sums owed that should be received within one year, hence they are current assets.

LISTING OTHER ITEMS

There are other items listed under current assets that can also be significant. Again the principle is that these will convert into cash within the next 12 months. Other assets typically include monies owed by people other than customers (such as a tax refund that is due), and items that have been paid for in advance (such as rent), which could theoretically be reimbursed.

43 Think of your current assets as cash temporarily looked after by someone else.

44 Examine in detail the movement in cash for the period in question.

CLASSIFYING CASH

The most liquid of all current assets is cash – either at the bank or in hand. Cash includes everything that is a liquid asset, ranging from money in a bank account to cash in store cash registers and petty cash boxes. Money in a certificate of deposit or with limited access rights is not strictly cash, so is listed under other current assets.

UNDERSTANDING LIABILITIES

*L*iabilities are debts payable in a future
period because of events that have
already happened. They are either current
(due in the next 12 months) or long term.
Learn to identify both types of liability and
why the split between the two is important.

45 Check that an organization's liabilities do not exceed its assets.

46 Make sure that all possible liabilities have been included.

SPLITTING LIABILITIES ▼
*Liabilities are split into immediate and
future obligations. On some balance sheets,
current liabilities are deducted from current
assets to give a net current assets subtotal.
Then long-term liabilities are shown.*

EXAMINING CURRENT LIABILITIES

Typical current liabilities are large items such as
creditors (people who are owed money for goods
purchased) and bank overdrafts (always repayable
on demand). A business does not want what it
owes (current liabilities) to exceed what it has
coming in (current assets), since this is a recipe for
insolvency. However, an enterprise that uses its
creditors as a source of funding from a position of
strength is not a cause for concern; if it cannot
afford to pay its creditors, that is a sign of trouble.

Cash	565	465
TOTAL CURRENT ASSETS		
CURRENT LIABILITIES	80	109
Creditors	20	18
Accrued expenses	12	10
Dividends payable	7	16
Taxation	60	0
Overdraft	179	153
TOTAL CURRENT LIABILITIES		
LONG-TERM LIABILITIES	15	30
Bank loan	25	30
Mortgage	40	60
TOTAL ASSETS MINUS LIABILITIES	531	417

Current liabilities are typically listed in order of liquidity

Deducting current and long-term liabilities from total current assets gives the balance sheet total

IDENTIFYING OTHER CURRENT LIABILITIES

LIABILITY	POINTS TO NOTE
CREDITORS Sums owed to suppliers for purchases.	Some purchases of goods or services used during the year may not have been paid for; amounts owed to suppliers are shown as creditors, which are usually due within the next 12 months.
TAXATION Amounts owed in taxes.	Tax on profits, tax on capital gains, and other taxes may not have been paid in full – especially if not legally required to be paid until later. Outstanding amounts are shown as current liabilities.
DIVIDENDS Monies payable to shareholders.	Dividends are typically paid twice a year, with the second (or final) dividend declared but not yet paid. This is a current liability since it will inevitably be payable within the next 12 months.
LEASING Sums owed to leasing and rental companies.	Amounts shown in current liabilities are only those that must be paid to the leasing or rental company within 12 months. Installments due after that year are long-term liabilities.
ACCRUALS Payments owed to providers of goods and services.	General bills (such as for telephones and electricity), accounting fees, auditing costs, and so on will have been incurred but not yet paid for. These are all shown under the general title of accruals.
SHORT-TERM DEBT Sums payable to a bank or providers of finance.	A bank overdraft is a current liability, since it is strictly repayable on demand. A repayment toward long-term debt that must be made in the next 12 months is also a current liability.

RECOGNIZING LONG-TERM LIABILITIES

Amounts payable by a business more than one year from the balance sheet date are long-term liabilities. These are items such as long-term debts and loans, mortgages, and formalized borrowing instruments such as debentures. They may be more technical, as in the case of provisions, which are taken out of this year's profits to pay for something in a future period. The point of splitting liabilities into current and long-term groups is to see how comfortably the business can repay its immediate debt.

POINTS TO REMEMBER

- Liabilities are amounts owed by an organization because of transactions that have already taken place.

- In time, all long-term liabilities will become short-term liabilities, which will, in turn, have to be paid off.

- Any increase in debt should be for a good reason, whether to increase transaction volumes or to acquire fixed assets.

ANALYZING SHAREHOLDERS' FUNDS

This part of the balance sheet shows the funds put into or left in an organization by its shareholders. It must therefore equal the total net assets, or balance sheet total. It is here that you can learn where the money invested in the balance sheet has come from.

47 Remember that the funds of shareholders are always at risk.

48 Look at retained reserves to discover past profitability.

LOOKING AT SHARE CAPITAL

Share capital is essentially the money that shareholders have put into the business, for no guaranteed return or guaranteed payment. If a company raises, for instance, $1 million of share capital, the share capital account and the bank account both increase by $1 million.

UNDERSTANDING RETAINED PROFIT

The second major source of shareholders' funds is retained profit. Calculated from the profit and loss account, this is essentially the cumulative retained profit made each year since the company started. Retained profit is usually the most important source (in terms of size) of continued funding of a business.

▼ CALCULATING SHAREHOLDERS' FUNDS
This part of the balance sheet looks at where the money has come from in a business and will typically consist of share capital, retained profit, and technical reserves.

The total equity and reserves must equal the balance sheet total of assets minus liabilities

Shareholders' funds		
Share capital	220	120
Retained profit	301	287
Technical reserves	10	10
TOTAL SHAREHOLDERS' FUNDS	531	417

DEFINING TECHNICAL RESERVES

There are other items shown in this part of the balance sheet that are known as technical reserves. Two types that appear most frequently are share premium and revaluation reserve. A share premium is the result of a company selling shares for a higher price than their nominal value. For example, if a $1 share is sold for $5, then it has been sold at a premium of $4. This share premium is not strictly retained profit, because it has not been made in the course of business, so it has to be shown separately under technical reserves. A revaluation reserve occurs when an organization revalues an asset (such as a property) to show its current value rather than its original cost. Again, this is not strictly retained profit since it is merely a revaluation, and no profit has yet been realized.

▲ REVALUING ASSETS

Sometimes an organization chooses to show an asset, such as a building, at a higher current value rather than at its original cost, and the difference is shown in a revaluation reserve. This informs the reader of accounts that the profit exists but cannot be distributed because it is, as yet, unrealized.

LOOKING AT LINKING STATEMENTS

Although the principle is that the retained profit must equal the increase in the balance sheet, often there is so much information that a linking statement is needed to clarify the situation. This statement sets out recognized gains and losses, and movement in shareholders' funds, and it reconciles the profit and loss account with the balance sheet. In addition to listing the retained profit for the year, this statement may detail gains and losses in currency fluctuations on foreign assets, issuance of additional share capital, and other technical items. In essence, shareholders' funds show how much money shareholders have chosen to leave behind in the business, which is all at risk should the business fail.

CHECKING FOR CLARITY ▶

Ask an accountant to guide you through a linking statement, showing why shareholders' funds have increased in the year.

USING CASH FLOW STATEMENTS

The cash flow statement is key to understanding how well cash, which is the lifeblood of a business, is being managed. Give this statement the attention it deserves, since the profit and loss account and balance sheet can provide only a part of the picture.

49 Remember the adage that profits are vanity and cash is sanity.

50 Bear in mind that profits do not repay loans – only cash can do that.

CASH FLOW STATEMENT

Operating profit	63
Depreciation	45
Increase in inventory	– 23
Increase in debtors	– 85
Increase in creditors	– 27
OPERATING CASH FLOW	– 27
Interest paid	– 20
Dividends paid	– 10
Exceptional costs	– 10
Taxation	– 16
Capital expenditure	– 85
CASH FLOW BEFORE FINANCING	– 148
FINANCING	
Increase in overdraft	60
Decrease in bank loan	– 15
Decrease in mortgage	– 5
Issue of share capital	100
	140
MOVEMENT IN CASH	– 8

FOCUSING ON CASH

The third of the key financial statements, the cash flow statement, is practically the most important yet is often underused. When cash stops circulating, a business will die. The profit and loss account shows the profits made in the accounting period, but profits are not cash – and it is crucial to know how much actual cash has been received or paid out. The balance sheet shows the often large flows of investing activities, such as the purchase of fixed assets or the acquisition of a business, but it does not reveal whether the business has an excess (or lack of) cash. The cash flow statement links the other two key statements using cash as an objective, no-nonsense measure that is verifiable against the bank balance.

◀ REVIEWING A CASH FLOW STATEMENT

Starting with operating profit, the statement shows how cash has been generated or consumed. It reveals aspects of a business that are difficult to gauge from the profit and loss account alone.

UNDERSTANDING THE PRINCIPLES

Cash flow statements generally follow a standard format, and, while variations on the theme exist, similar principles are used worldwide in order to make the statement more useful and easily understood. The document is sectioned into meaningful blocks and subtotals, providing clear information on the cash movements within an organization's key activities. These include normal business activities, interest and dividends, taxes, investing activities, and financing. To understand the statement, you must know what is counted as cash. The generally accepted definition is that cash items are those to which an organization has immediate or one-day access, which means actual cash, bank accounts, and short-term deposits.

51 Manage your own working capital and control your cash aggressively.

52 Think of working capital as a sponge: it absorbs cash if left alone and releases it if squeezed.

CULTURAL DIFFERENCES

Two attempts have been made by different countries to quantify just what a statement based on the flows of cash should contain. The first is the Source and Application of Funds Statement, but this does not clarify what a flow of cash is, and has generally fallen out of favor. The second is a Cash Flow Statement, which more closely defines cash and produces an overall more meaningful document.

CALCULATING OPERATING CASH FLOW

The first and most important subtotal on the cash flow statement is operating cash flow, which shows how much is generated from running a business. To calculate this, the operating profit (from the profit and loss account) must be adjusted. First, noncash items, such as depreciation, which had already been deducted, must be added back in. (Remember that depreciation is not – and never will be – a pile of cash.) Next, the working capital, or net current assets, from this and last year's balance sheet are adjusted, with the increase in inventory, debtors, and creditors being the difference between the two. If there is more inventory now than a year ago, then cash must have been paid out. If debtors owe more, then they temporarily hold cash, so there is less in the business. If suppliers are owed more (because they haven't been paid), then the business temporarily has more cash.

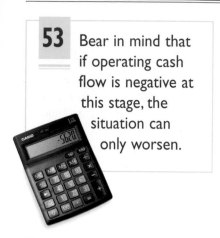

53 Bear in mind that if operating cash flow is negative at this stage, the situation can only worsen.

DETERMINING CASH FLOW BEFORE FINANCING

The subtotal of cash flow before financing shows how much the organization has either generated or will need to find to stay afloat. To calculate this, nonbusiness items such as interest, dividends, and taxes must first be deducted or credited. Any interest paid or received in the year is shown, as are any dividends paid or received. The point is to reflect how much the organization is paying out simply to "service" its debt and share capital. Finally, taxation on business profits is deducted.

DETAILING CASH FOR CAPITAL EXPENDITURE

Once interest, dividends, and taxes have been accounted for, then capital expenditure comes into the equation. Cash spent on purchasing, or received from the sale of, normal fixed assets is detailed here. If fixed assets are bought on rent-to-own contracts or leased agreements, then only the cash paid is shown. Onetime items such as the purchase of a business are also shown. If an item is large compared to normal year-to-year cash flow and requires significant financing effort, this part of the statement reveals whether that item can be afforded or not.

54 Note that spending on fixed assets will often exceed profit.

Planning to open a new branch office, manager reviews cash flow statement and finds that cash is critically low

**KEEPING UP ▶
WITH CASH FLOW**
This illustration shows two possible outcomes to managing cash flow. A manager who looks only at profits may not even realize that there is virtually no cash in the business. A successful manager reviews the cash flow statement thoroughly before making any commitments and is able to prevent financial disaster.

Manager sees from profit and loss account that profits are up

MANAGING CASH FLOW

Controlling cash flow is management's prime financial task. It is critical that managers understand where cash flow comes from and how it is spent by an organization, since this can make the difference between financial success and disaster. When operating cash flow is negative, there are four levers that can be pulled to improve it: make more profit, decrease inventory, decrease debtors, and increase creditors. These may not help, however, if an organization is expanding because growth inevitably means increasing sales, which results in larger debtors and inventory, hence worse cash flow. This may be inescapable but must be recognized and planned for. Another key consideration is whether the annual dividend and interest bill is affordable. If not, does the funding of the organization need overhauling? Finally, buying certain assets may be entirely discretionary and should be carefully thought through before making commitments. Remember, cash is critical.

Prompt action to boost cash flow ensures that cash flow crisis is avoided

Manager postpones expansion and acts to collect cash from debtors

Manager fails to review cash flow statement

Manager goes ahead with expansion, runs out of cash, and the business fails

CALCULATING MOVEMENT

Two main sources of financing are debt (loans) and equity (share capital). Loans taken out or share capital issued are sources of cash; loans repaid or share capital repurchased are uses of cash. The difference between cash flow before financing and the subtotal of financing indicates the overall movement in cash for the year, which must agree with the difference between this and last year's cash in the balance sheet.

55 See that movement in cash and the bank account tally.

PRODUCING CASH FLOW FORECASTS

The forward-looking cash flow forecast is often forgotten because it is not required by law or regulations, yet it is an invaluable document. Use the forecast to help you predict cash flow in the future and keep an informed eye on your business.

56 Be aware that cash flow usually turns out to be worse than you plan for.

57 Remember to control capital spending properly.

58 Note that revenue and capital spending are often related.

ANTICIPATING PROBLEMS

Cash flow forecasting differs from cash flow statements in the perspective it adopts – it is forward rather than backward looking. Its purpose is to predict at what point the demands on an organization's cash resources become so great that cash is exhausted – whether from normal business demands or planned growth.

▼ **PRODUCING FORECASTS**
Involve colleagues regularly in forecasting cash flow. By planning in advance you can ensure that you have the cash available for future commitments and solve problems before they arise.

Colleagues check that timings of receipts are realistic, especially for new initiatives

Accountant ensures consistent assumptions about cash flow timings

Manager asks whether forecast capital spending plans are definite

USING A CASH FLOW FORECAST

Prepare a cash flow forecast from the profit and loss account and balance sheet. Working monthly, combine the anticipated amounts with cash flow timing predictions for each item of revenue and expenditure, remembering to include any likely onetime items. Then calculate the closing balance sheet, representing what is owed or owing from what you have not paid or received.

DO'S AND DON'TS

✔ Do be sensible about the timings of cash flows; they are often made more difficult by optimistic budgets.

✔ Do ask plenty of "what if?" questions about cash flows, should timings of significant amounts change.

✘ Don't assume that cash flow will not be a problem for you just because it has not been in the past.

✘ Don't presume that everyone will always keep to their terms about payments into or out of the organization.

▼ CREATING A CASH FLOW FORECAST

Extend the profit and loss account items and estimate the likely timings for each item. Add the predicted cash flow timings for each month to indicate cash surpluses or funding requirements.

Profit and loss account figures are divided into annual and monthly amounts

Timing of cash flow is estimated for the individual profit and loss account items

Actual cash receipts and payments are recorded for each month

PROFIT AND LOSS ACCOUNT			PREDICTION	CASH FLOW					
Item	Annual	Month	Payment	Jan	Feb	Mar	Apr	May	Jun
Sales	2,400	200	One month credit	0	200	200	200	200	200
Cost of goods sold	-1,800	-150	One month credit	0	-150	-150	-150	-150	-150
Office supplies	-48	-4	One month credit	0	-4	-4	-4	-4	-4
Rent	-24	-2	One month advance	-4	-2	-2	-2	-2	-2
Salaries and wages	-264	-22	Immediate	-22	-22	-22	-22	-22	-22
Sales and marketing	-36	-3	One month credit	0	-3	-3	-3	-3	-3
Delivery	-24	-2	One month credit	0	-2	-2	-2	-2	-2
Heat, light, and power	-12	-1	One month credit	0	-1	-1	-1	-1	-1
Interest payable	-24	-2	Immediate	-2	-2	-2	-2	-2	-2
			Monthly cash flow	-28	14	14	14	14	14
Profit	168	14	Cumulative cash flow	-28	-14	0	14	28	42

Annual profit is calculated by deducting expenditure from revenue

Monthly total for cash receipts and payments is calculated

Cumulative cash flow is calculated, showing actual money in the bank

MEASURING PERFORMANCE

Ratios are essential tools for interpreting the messages behind lines of figures. Learn how to use ratios and how to translate supplementary reports for a clear view of business performance.

UNDERSTANDING RATIOS

A ratio is calculated by dividing one figure by another. Used logically and consistently, performance ratios can provide important indicators and highlight trends. Understand where ratios are useful and what they can reveal about performance.

> **59** Analyze profitability first, closely followed by asset efficiency.

> **60** Always look at performance ratios in the context of the business as a whole.

USING RATIOS

Ratios are most useful when produced and analyzed regularly to help identify important trends in areas such as cash and profit management. They can also be used to help make comparisons year-to-year and between organizations. However, since no two businesses are alike, this is fraught with practical difficulties. There are many ways of calculating ratios and there is no one correct method. Avoid relying on ratios alone to provide a full answer as to why one organization is performing better than another – you must examine the business as a whole.

61 Obtain sets of comparative ratios for your business.

62 Show ratio results graphically to help you spot trends.

ANALYZING EFFECTIVELY

When interpreting accounts, most people are interested in four key areas: profitability, efficiency, financing, and liquidity. Profitability measures how much income is made from sales, and is assessed by analyzing the profit and loss account; efficiency measures the use to which assets are put; financing shows the degree and affordability of funding; and liquidity measures whether there is sufficient cash to continue operating. Efficiency, financing, and liquidity can be evaluated by analyzing the balance sheet.

MEASURING ROCE

The most important overall ratio for measuring performance is called Return on Capital Employed (ROCE). This reveals how much profit is being made on the money invested in the business and is a key measure of how well management is doing its job. ROCE is calculated by dividing the operating profit by the capital employed (shareholders' funds plus long-term liabilities on the balance sheet). The rate of return should be higher than a shareholder could make by depositing their funds elsewhere, such as in a bank or savings and loan. The ROCE also needs to be higher than the cost of borrowings, or a business will be paying more in interest than it makes on the money borrowed.

USING ROCE TO ASSESS YOUR PERFORMANCE

Calculate your organization's ROCE

Assess whether your ROCE ratio is adequate for shareholders

Check whether this period's ROCE has improved on the last

Check your ROCE against that of your competitors'

To boost ROCE, increase profit and reduce capital employed

DO'S AND DON'TS

✔ Do use ratios that are appropriate to the nature, type, and size of the organization under scrutiny.

✔ Do take a balanced and holistic view or ratio analysis.

✘ Don't be hidebound and inflexible in your choice of ratios for assessing performance.

✘ Don't be too accurate about the results you calculate from accounting figures.

ANALYZING A PROFIT AND LOSS ACCOUNT

*L*ine-by-line analysis of the profit and loss account provides a valuable insight into business performance. Find out what the figures really mean using a series of measures that show how profits are being utilized and determine whether they can be improved.

63 Always perform a quick top to bottom line review of profits.

64 Assess revenues and expenditures as a percentage of sales.

USING COMMON SIZING ▼
Express each line of the proft and loss account as a percentage of the top line – sales. Do this particularly for gross profit, total operating expenses, operating profit, and retained profit.

EXAMINING KEY LINES
Start by taking an overview. First, look at the top line of sales: Are figures up or down on last year, and is any increase or decrease reflected in the retained profit on the bottom line? If not, examine the statement to ascertain where the profits have gone. Use commonsense, look for obvious trends, and watch for factors that may affect your analysis; has the accounting period been a long one, for example? Then, to make year-to-year or industry comparisons easier, calculate each of the key lines as a percentage of sales. Known as common sizing, this strips out the effects of both volume and size.

Salaries and wages as a percentage of sales has increased; find out why and take corrective action

65 Concentrate on operating profit, but also note what follows.

PROFIT AND LOSS ACCOUNT
(INCLUDING RATIOS)

	CURRENT PERIOD	%	PREVIOUS PERIOD	%
Sales	2,200	100.0	2,050	100.0
Cost of sales	1,700	77.3	1,600	78.0
GROSS PROFIT	500	22.7	450	22.0
OPERATING EXPENSES				
Office supplies	46	2.1	42	2.0
Bad debt charges	24	1.1	20	1.0
Rent	15	0.7	14	0.7
Salaries and wages	245	11.1	194	9.5
Sales and marketing	30	1.4	22	1.1
	20	0.9	18	0.9

ANALYZING FIGURES ▼

Calculate ratios for interest payable, taxation, and dividends. Compare the current accounting period figures with the previous period to ascertain whether a business's health has improved or deteriorated, and pinpoint reasons why.

ASSESSING AFFORDABILITY

Interest payable, taxes, and dividends are not directly related to business performance, but how easily an organization can afford to pay them is a key measure of its health. Assess the affordability of these items using specific ratios. First, divide operating profit by interest payable to work out how many times an organization could afford to pay that amount of interest (interest cover). Use the same method (PAT divided by dividends) to assess the affordability of dividends. Finally, divide taxes by profit before tax to give the apparent taxes as a percentage, which should approximate to the official tax rate on business profits. Investigate any glaring discrepancies.

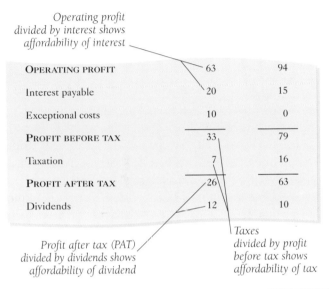

Operating profit divided by interest shows affordability of interest

OPERATING PROFIT	63	94
Interest payable	20	15
Exceptional costs	10	0
PROFIT BEFORE TAX	33	79
Taxation	7	16
PROFIT AFTER TAX	26	63
Dividends	12	10

Profit after tax (PAT) divided by dividends shows affordability of dividend

Taxes divided by profit before tax shows affordability of tax

---

EVALUATING PROFIT IMPROVEMENT METHODS

To boost profits, a well-run organization may use a profit improvement checklist This is an accepted list of things to do in order of preference. Look at the following areas of the profit and loss account to gauge whether an organization has been putting this checklist into practice:

● Has it increased the selling price of products or services? (This could mean stopping any discounts, which would have the same effect.)

● Has it reduced the cost of sales (COS)?

(This could involve either buying more effectively or introducing more efficient business processes.)

● Has gross profit improved? (This would be the effect of taking both steps above.)

● Has volume increased? (An efficient organization would take this step only after assessing the profitability of its products and services to decide which items make a real profit.)

● Have sales, general, and administration (SG&A) costs been reduced?

READING A BALANCE SHEET

A nother way of improving business performance is to reduce the amount of capital tied up in the balance sheet and increase the uses to which it is being put. Examine the balance sheet thoroughly to gain some clear measures of efficiency.

66 Note that figures in a balance sheet may be seasonal or unrepresentative.

67 Look at the notes to accounts to find the right figures to use.

GAUGING EFFICIENCY

Assess the overall efficiency of a business by measuring the number of times its assets (you can use fixed, current, or total assets) divide into the top line of sales. This is called asset turn and it shows whether more sales are being made with the same number of assets. On its own the ratio is meaningless, but when compared to the asset turn of previous years, it can indicate whether a business is becoming more, or less, efficient.

EVALUATING CASH MANAGEMENT

The amount of time that inventory is held before being sold (inventory days), how long customers take to pay (debtor days), and how long a business takes to pay its suppliers (creditor days) are classic efficiency measures. Using the inventory, debtor, and creditor figures for the end of the current accounting period, calculate the number of working capital days. Compare your figures against the industry average. Too many working capital days can cause a cash crisis; too few mean that a business cannot operate properly.

Inventory divided by COS x 365 gives inventory days

Debtors divided by sales x 365 gives debtor days

Creditors divided by COS x 365 gives creditor days

▼CALCULATING WORKING CAPITAL RATIOS

To calculate working capital days, use the balance sheet figures and the two lines of sales and cost of sales on the profit and loss.

BALANCE SHEET	CURRENT PERIOD	PREVIOUS PERIOD
FIXED ASSETS		
Tangible	170	150
Intangible	10	10
Investments	5	5
TOTAL FIXED ASSETS	185	165
CURRENT ASSETS		
Inventory	208	185
Debtors	337	254
Other	18	16
Cash	2	10
TOTAL CURRENT ASSETS	565	465
CURRENT LIABILITIES		
Creditors	80	109
Accrue... ...nces	20	18
Divide	12	10
Taxati		
Overd		

PROFIT AND LOSS ACCOUNT

	CURRENT PERIOD	PREVIOUS PERIOD
Sales		
Cost of sales	2,200	2,050
GROSS PROFIT	1,700	1,600
	500	450

68 Calculate the cost effect of one extra day of debtors.

▼ USING BALANCE SHEET RATIOS
The key ratios of fixed asset turn, working capital days (inventory, debtors, and creditors), and current and quick ratios are calculated to measure efficiency.

BALANCE SHEET RATIOS

	CURRENT PERIOD	PREVIOUS PERIOD
FIXED ASSET TURN	11.9	12.4
Inventory days	44.7	42.2
Debtor days	55.9	45.2
Creditor days	(17.2)	(24.9)
TOTAL	83.4	62.5
CURRENT RATIO	3.16	3.04
QUICK RATIO	2.00	1.83

Deleting inventory from current assets in the numerator will reduce the ratio, but it will still be comfortably more than 1

Dividing current assets by current liabilities gives a ratio comfortably more than the target of 1

ASSESSING FINANCING

Lenders and investors in particular like to assess how long-term financing is structured, since an organization that borrows heavily is riskier than one that has borrowed little. The key ratio used is known as debt to equity, or gearing. To calculate this, divide long-term liabilities by total shareholders' funds plus long-term liabilities, expressed as a percentage. For example, if long-term debt is $70 and shareholders' funds $30, gearing is 70 percent. There is no target figure here; instead, closely monitor trends.

EXAMINING SOLVENCY

To assess whether an organization has enough money to cover its debts, or is liquid, there are two commonly used measures: the current ratio and the quick ratio (or acid test). To calculate the current ratio, divide current assets by current liabilities. Most textbooks suggest that the target for this ratio should be at least one or, in other words, that current assets should be greater than current liabilities. To calculate the acid test, divide current assets less inventory by current liabilities, on the grounds that inventory will not convert to cash quickly. Remember that businesses showing a ratio of less than 1 are not always a cause for concern. For a cash retailer, for example, zero debtors, low inventory, and high creditors equal efficiency, not inefficiency, as such ratios might suggest.

69 Remember that the popular current ratio has its limitations.

70 Assess whether a business is properly financed and structured.

UNDERSTANDING INVESTORS' RATIOS

The world of the stock exchange and external investors uses its own ratios to determine the viability of a business. These hard-nosed measures can be very revealing, so learn how to assess financial statements from an outsider's point of view.

71 Note that investors focus on performance within industry sectors.

72 As with all financial analysis, always look at more than one ratio or measure.

DETERMINING WORTH

A stock exchange index lists the largest publicly traded companies on the stock market as measured by their overall worth, or market capitalization. If your employer, a customer, a supplier, or a competitor is a publicly traded company, market capitalization will give a crude estimate of its worth in the marketplace.

CALCULATING MARKET CAPITALIZATION

Market capitalization is calculated by multiplying the number of shares that the company has issued (a finite, known figure)

by the share price (a fluctuating figure). Share prices are irrelevant on one level because the price at which they are traded will not affect a firm's daily production or selling routines. However, the market's perceived worth of a company may well affect its ability to borrow or raise more funds from the investment community.

◀ **LEADING THE MARKET**
Companies in stock markets are ranked according to their total worth, with the highest valued businesses forming that country's stock market index (such as the Dow, FTSE, DAX, and CAC).

LOOKING AT PROSPECTS

The price earnings (PE) ratio provides a good indication as to how the market views a business's prospects. To arrive at this ratio, first calculate earnings per share (the profit that each share has generated) by dividing profit after tax (from the profit and loss account) by the number of shares that have been issued. Then divide the market price per share by earnings per share to give the PE ratio, which reveals how a share is currently valued compared to the profits that it made last year. A high PE ratio is a sign of confidence in a company, a low PE ratio indicates the reverse.

73 Pay particular attention to what the price earnings ratio tells you.

▼ WATCHING THE FIGURES

Investors and interested parties use the financial press's figures of corporate performance to see how key organizations are performing and to make comparisons between similar business types.

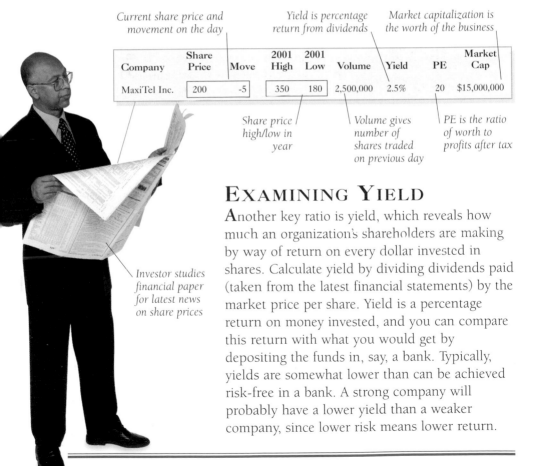

Current share price and movement on the day

Yield is percentage return from dividends

Market capitalization is the worth of the business

Company	Share Price	Move	2001 High	2001 Low	Volume	Yield	PE	Market Cap
MaxiTel Inc.	200	-5	350	180	2,500,000	2.5%	20	$15,000,000

Share price high/low in year

Volume gives number of shares traded on previous day

PE is the ratio of worth to profits after tax

Investor studies financial paper for latest news on share prices

EXAMINING YIELD

Another key ratio is yield, which reveals how much an organization's shareholders are making by way of return on every dollar invested in shares. Calculate yield by dividing dividends paid (taken from the latest financial statements) by the market price per share. Yield is a percentage return on money invested, and you can compare this return with what you would get by depositing the funds in, say, a bank. Typically, yields are somewhat lower than can be achieved risk-free in a bank. A strong company will probably have a lower yield than a weaker company, since lower risk means lower return.

Gathering More Information

In addition to the key statements, large organizations disclose a wealth of extra information, either voluntarily or because they are legally obliged to do so. Know where to look for these details and what you can glean from them.

74 Get to know what is contained in a published report and accounts.

75 Examine reports and notes carefully – you may uncover some very important details.

Interpreting Auditors' Code

The role of the auditors is to report on whether financial statements have been properly prepared in accordance with company law and GAAP. Rather than stating that accounts are correct, however, they choose such phrases as "give a true and fair view" or "fairly represent," which mean that these accounts are said to be "unqualified," or clean. Watch out for "qualified" opinions, as these point to areas where there is either uncertainty or, more worryingly, disagreement.

Understanding Qualified Phrases

Phrase	Example	Meaning
"Subject to"	"Subject to continuing support from its bankers…"	Without the bank's support, the business will fail.
"Except for"	"Except for the valuation of certain inventory items…"	There has been a fundamental disagreement between auditor and management about a matter.
"Do not"	"The financial statements do not…"	The accounts have not been properly prepared.

READING THE DIRECTORS' REPORT

When annual reports are published, a company's directors often comment on the results. Since there are strict laws on disclosure, whatever is said must be objective rather than propaganda led. Pay attention to the section on salaries (companies today are sensitive about what they pay their directors, since salaries must be seen to be commensurate with overall corporate performance) and look at details on share options. Both sections provide clues as to how well the directors think that they and the company have done in the year.

76 The larger the organization, the greater the scope for information.

COMPARING REPORTS ▶

In their report, directors generally outline how they expect the organization to perform in the coming year. Most will be optimistic to reassure shareholders, but watch for cautious qualifications or predictions of a "tough year ahead."

77 Read the reviews by key directors for optimism about prospects.

78 Dig into the notes for interesting further detail and information.

FOCUSING ON NOTES TO ACCOUNTS

Copious notes are attached to the main financial statements of balance sheet, profit and loss account, cash flow, recognized gains and losses, and movement in shareholders' funds. It is important to read these in conjunction with the actual statements. While the notes to accounts may appear daunting at first, persevere with them since they are an integral part of the message and must be understood. Domestic and housekeeping items, such as important dates for the calendar and a timetable of the annual general meeting and immediate future events, are also to be found in the notes.

BROADENING YOUR KNOWLEDGE

The complexity of accounting means that "gray" areas abound. Learn where anomalies arise, how accountants deal with them, and how to improve the quality of your own internal accounts.

EXPLORING INTERNATIONAL ISSUES

Many organizations today operate on an international level, yet, despite increasing globalization, accounting practices and formats still differ significantly around the world. Understand the differences to help you pinpoint where problems can arise.

79 Always be clear about on which rules the accounts are based.

80 Accept that profits and assets can vary significantly between countries.

HIGHLIGHTING PROBLEMS

Accounting measurements are dependent on the rules of individual countries, and this is often a hindrance to international business transactions. Investors must negotiate cross-border obstacles, multinationals face differences in profits concepts and taxation, and governments creating trading blocks face unequal opportunities and economic distortions. As a result, efforts are being made to reduce differences through harmonization.

DEFINING DIFFERENCES

Because countries have different legal systems, taxation systems, historical influences, and business practices, their accounting systems are also different. Continental Europe's strong legal framework of accounting plans and commercial codes contrasts with the UK and US combination of legal principles and a separate set of accounting rules. Some countries require the figures in financial statements to be the same as for tax purposes, while in other countries no connection is needed. Political and historical factors also play their part, with much of the world influenced by the UK system. The need for open information for shareholders has ensured that appropriate financial statements have evolved.

81 Get to know the key international differences that affect you.

▼ EVALUATING SYSTEMS

Countries influenced by the UK and the US tend to have a more pragmatic approach to accounting, the onus being to inform shareholders. In other parts of Europe and in Japan, strict taxation and legislation rule out any subjectivity or deviation, so that financial statements are less useful and informative to interested outsiders.

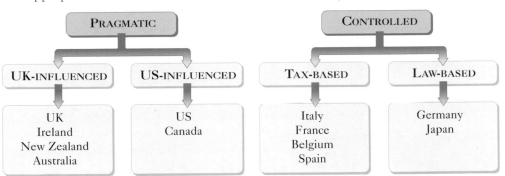

PRAGMATIC		CONTROLLED	
UK-INFLUENCED	**US-INFLUENCED**	**TAX-BASED**	**LAW-BASED**
UK Ireland New Zealand Australia	US Canada	Italy France Belgium Spain	Germany Japan

HARMONIZING ACCOUNTS

Since accounting systems around the world measure items such as assets and profits differently, international comparison and analysis are difficult. As a result, there has been mounting pressure to harmonize accounting. For 10 years, an international accounting body has been working to produce International Accounting Standards (IAS). These now provide the benchmark worldwide and are used by many multinationals, some of which even prepare two versions of accounts. One version will comply with Generally Accepted Accounting Principles of the country in which the organization is based, and another will be in accordance with IAS. The EU is a useful example where law-based harmonization has taken place but no GAAP convergence has occurred.

LOOKING AT COMMON PROBLEMS

Accounting is technical by nature and there are many complex issues facing accountants. As a manager, there is little to gain from poring over technical details, but it is useful to know where problems can occur and how they can be dealt with.

82 Grasp the essentials, not the details, of technical accounting.

83 When dealing with unfamiliar technical issues, seek advice from an expert.

LISTING LEASED ASSETS

One type of fixed asset that causes controversy is a leased asset. This is an asset that a business uses for three years or more but that it does not legally own (unlike all other fixed assets). At some point in the future, annual lease costs may be substantial, but organizations prefer to omit this liability from their accounts to avoid giving the impression that they are borrowing more now. Accountants prefer to treat a leased asset as if it were owned in order to give a fairer picture. The debt can then be shown on the balance sheet for all to see.

CONTROVERSIAL INTANGIBLE ASSETS

Goodwill and brands can cause controversy (see pp.514–515), and other intangibles can do the same:

● Patent (an object or process patented by someone else and bought by a company). The amount paid for the patent is written off over the period of time for which it has been acquired.

● Know-how (similar to a patent but the

object or process purchased may not have been formally registered).

● Copyright and intellectual property, typically on music and books.

● Research and development. Costs are taken out of the profit and loss account and shown as an asset in the balance sheet. If this is the case, current profits and assets may be overstated.

MAKING PROVISIONS

When the cost of a future event, such as a reorganization, will seriously hit profits, an appropriate figure must be deducted from the current year's profits. This is known as making a provision and is a way of alerting users of financial statements to what lies ahead for the organization. If an impending event may potentially hit profits (perhaps there is the threat of legal action, for example), it is often not included in the financial statements but should be noted in the accounts as a contingent liability. Finally, if an event with significant financial impact should occur between the balance sheet date and the date of signing off accounts, this must also be noted.

ACCOUNTING FOR GROUPS

Gleaning useful information from the accounts of a group of companies, where some businesses are controlled by others, can be a difficult exercise. Financial statements should give a picture of the whole business entity, but that picture may be blurred if, for example, the holding company has been juggling with the figures of one of its subsidiaries. As a manager, you will probably be interested in the performance of other companies in your group, as well as in the group's performance as a whole. Financial statements of groups of companies are sometimes called "consolidated" accounts.

POINTS TO REMEMBER

- You should try to form an opinion on the financial health of an organization.
- Provisions have traditionally been devices for "smoothing out" the fluctuations in profits.
- It helps to appreciate the principal accounting logic behind each technical treatment.

▼ UNDERSTANDING GROUP ACCOUNTS

Subsidiary companies produce their own accounts, which are incorporated into those of the parent company to give more meaningful results for the group as a whole.

Parent company prepares the financial statements for the entire group

GROUP HEAD OFFICE

Company directors pass individual sets of accounts to the parent company

Individual company prepares its own accounts separately

COMPANY A   **COMPANY B**   **COMPANY C**

RECOGNIZING CREATIVE ACCOUNTING

An accountant is expected to present a company's figures in the best possible light, while being accurate and truthful at all times. Learn to recognize when the figures are being manipulated, since this is a sure sign of creative accounting at work.

84 Recognize that one person's smoothing is another's creative accounting.

85 Check if creative accounting is increasing or suppressing profits.

WHY HIDE THE TRUTH?

Every organization has its own agenda for creative accounting: the larger company wants to report bigger profits, the smaller to pay less taxes. Being creative need not involve adjusting figures: merely choosing an accounting date to paint a rosy picture, extending an accounting period to bolster profits or confuse the picture, or failing to file accounts at all are popular ways of hiding the truth.

REVIEWING PROFITS

On the profit and loss account, watch for a high number of invoices at the year-end, which is a method of boosting profits. Similarly, postponing invoicing until the start of the new accounting period ensures that tax is payable later. Depending upon whether a business has had a good or bad year, it may lower income by recognizing too many costs, or raise it by not recognizing enough. To determine disproportionate activity, look at the first month of the next accounting period: discrepancies will often be compensated for here.

▼ SMOOTHING THE RIDE

Making profits is unlikely to be a smooth process, so a creative accountant will smooth out peaks and valleys to show a steady, well-managed line of profitability.

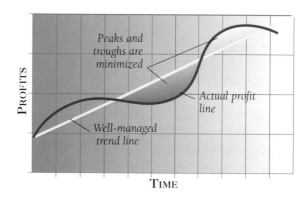

Peaks and troughs are minimized

Actual profit line

Well-managed trend line

PROFITS

TIME

COOKING BOOKS ▶

Accounts can be based on books and records that might range from being lightly cooked to completely burned. But the task of the reader to distinguish between what is acceptable and what is simply going a little too far will always be difficult, since creatively produced accounts will always look normal on the surface to the untrained eye. Always seek technical advice if you suspect that anything is not right with the figures.

CASE STUDY

Happy Nappies wanted to increase its profits and decided to use some typical creative accounting techniques. First, it recognized revenue on sales earlier: on confirmation of order rather than on delivery of goods, thereby increasing sales revenue. Second, it reduced costs by taking out of the profit and loss account expenses relating to a new factory and adding them to the factory's costs – again

increasing profits and the balance sheet. Third, it extended the depreciation lives on certain high-value assets, again increasing profits and the balance sheet. Finally, it changed the method for translating the value of foreign-located assets into domestic currency, again manipulating the value of its balance sheet. Not all of these treatments are within the spirit of accounting law and practice, but they are commonplace nevertheless.

TAKING INVENTORY

On the balance sheet, the first item to watch is inventory. If its value is too high, inventory on the balance sheet (and profits) will be too high. Look at creditors as well: Managing working capital efficiently involves stretching creditors (suppliers), but within reason. Payment of bills may be postponed before the year-end, increasing creditors and giving the impression of a good relationship with suppliers who are willing to extend credit. Check the first day of the next accounting period to see whether large checks are subsequently despatched to suppliers.

86 Remember that the balance sheet and profit and loss move together.

▼ CHECKING THE BALANCE

Remember the principle that when profits increase, so does the balance sheet. Think of two ends of a dumbbell moving in tandem, so that what affects one statement will also affect the other.

PROFIT AND LOSS

BALANCE SHEET

Undervaluing closing inventory results in higher cost of sales and lower profits

Undervaluing closing inventory gives a lower balance sheet inventory amount

BENEFITING FROM MANAGEMENT ACCOUNTS

The fact that management accounts need not follow any rules makes them usefully flexible but more open to error. Recognize the uses and drawbacks of internal accounts and how you, as a manager, can improve the information they contain.

87 Remember that management accounts lack standardized rules.

88 Understand the purpose and use of management accounts.

UNDERSTANDING MANAGEMENT ACCOUNTS

Prepared and distributed internally within an organization, management accounts are governed by the needs of managers. They are used to help keep control of, and make decisions regarding, the everyday running of a business. As a result, they often contain more than mere financial information. They generally focus on four main areas: past scorekeeping, present problem solving, present controlling, and future planning.

COMPARING EXTERNAL AND INTERNAL ACCOUNTS

EXTERNAL ACCOUNTS	INTERNAL ACCOUNTS
Are published externally and are available to the public.	Are distributed internally within an organization and kept confidential.
Must conform to legal requirements and GAAP principles.	Are not bound by any rules or regulations, and may follow any format.
Are generally published once or twice a year and look backward at the past year's results.	Are produced on a regular basis and focus both on previous and future periods' results.
Reflect the financial reality of what has happened in an organization.	Provide a means of controlling the financial side of an organization now and into the future.

DRAWING CONCLUSIONS

A striking feature of management accounting is that, having been liberated from the usual accounting format straitjacket, endless different layouts and formats can be used. Unfortunately, because there is no one correct way of producing these financial statements, there is considerable room for error. But how can you gauge the accuracy of your management accounts? A useful exercise is to attempt to reconcile the internal figures to the external financial statements, since the external ones will inevitably be more accurate. If internal accounts differ seriously from the external statements, there is cause for concern.

89 Try to reconcile internal to external statements.

90 Examine your company's internal accounts package.

▼ **INFORMING MANAGERS**
The content of management accounts should reflect what managers want them to show, namely how well the business has performed according to plan, and what corrective action, if any, should be taken.

The current month's actual figures are compared to the budget

The year to date is perhaps a better indicator of long-term trends

MANAGEMENT ACCOUNTS FOR AUGUST

| ITEM | MONTH | | | | YEAR TO DATE | | | | FULL YEAR |
	ACTUAL $	BUDGET $	VARIANCE $	%	ACTUAL $	BUDGET $	VARIANCE $	%	FORECAST
Sales	195	200	-5	-3	1,520	1,600	-80	-5	2,300
Cost of sales	-150	-150	0	0	-1,190	-1,200	10	1	-1,770
Office supplies	-5	-4	-1	-15	-35	-32	-3	-9	-53
Rent	-2	-2	0	0	-16	-16	0	0	-24
Salaries and wages	-21	-22	1	5	-166	-176	10	6	-250
Sales and marketing	-4	-3	-1	-33	-30	-24	-6	-25	-40
Delivery	-2	-2	0	0	-18	-16	-2	-13	-27
Heat, light, and power	-1	-1	0	0	-8	-8	0	0	-12
Interest payable	-2	-2	0	0	-16	-16	0	0	-24
PROFIT	8	14	-6	-43	41	112	-71	-63	100

Actual results are compared to budget and expressed as a variance

Variance is also expressed as a percentage

A forecast is made for the full year's results

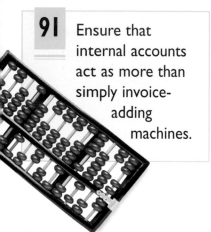

91 Ensure that internal accounts act as more than simply invoice-adding machines.

ASSESSING QUALITY

The quality of management accounting varies considerably. Even large, successful organizations can produce poor management accounts. Yet it is vital for managers to have financial documents in excellent user-friendly shape. Your accountant is bound to feel happier giving you a traditional profit and loss account – it is, after all, what he is used to. But this will not always contain the information you need to help you to manage your business into the future. If your management accounts are sub-standard, take steps to improve them.

IMPROVING EFFECTIVENESS

As a manager, it is important to take a more enlightened view as to how well your company is performing. This involves moving away from accountant-dominated management accounts toward those that are tailored specifically for you. Think of the quality of management accounts as a spectrum. At one end of the spectrum are traditional accounting statements, midway along are financial statements containing targeted management information, and at the opposite end are manager-led accounts containing indicators tailored specifically to your particular needs. Make sure that your organization is evolving in the right direction.

92 Take responsibility for improving management information.

Manager looks for practical measures that will help him in the future

Accountant suggests showing information graphically for greater clarity

ASKING FOR ▶ INFORMATION
Ask your accountant what information is available internally that will help you in your role as manager and discuss ways of presenting that information to make it easy for you to use.

USING PERFORMANCE INDICATORS

To ensure that the information you receive from accountants is valuable, consider using a set of measures known as key performance indicators (KPIs). These can be whatever you want them to be, provided that they are important to you and your organization. Generally, KPIs will include a financial component in their calculation, but this may not always be the case. Typical KPIs could be made up of the following: sales per employee, cost of sales per customer, marketing costs per new customer, labor cost per dollar of sales revenue, percentage of leads converted into sales. Often KPIs can indicate standings of performance internally.

▼ BRAINSTORMING MEASURES

Sit down with your fellow managers and decide which indicators would be most valuable in helping you to monitor and improve your performance.

Manager invites group to make suggestions for appropriate performance indicators

POINTS TO REMEMBER

- Your traditional financial accounting information should be up to date and bulletproof.

- The measures you take should be meaningful to you in your role.

- Developing a package of easy-to-obtain management information with your accountant will help you manage your department.

93 Consider using scorecard-type performance measures.

TAKING A HOLISTIC APPROACH

Just as some say that a business should be measured on more than its financial results, it is also necessary to use more than one performance indicator. A popular management information tool, the balanced business scorecard sets out the following four cornerstones for measuring performance holistically:

- Customers: Are we pleasing them? Are they coming back? What is our market share?
- Internal business processes: How can we improve processes to serve customers better?
- Learning and growth: Are we equipped to deal with customer and business process demands?
- Financials: How is the organization faring financially? The scorecard suggests that if the first three aspects are right, this will be, too.

MAKING FUTURE FINANCIAL DECISIONS

For a business to succeed, it must focus on using accounting concepts and techniques that look to the future. Set an example by basing your calculations on the right costs and using simple but effective tools for sound financial decision making.

94 Remember that future-looking decisions require new financial skills.

95 Accept that future-looking decisions of most companies are flawed.

ADOPTING A NEW MINDSET

To make the right accounting decisions for the future, you need to rethink the way that you look at figures. Rather than rely on the backward-looking perspective of the past, accountants, organizations, and managers must learn to adopt a new, forward-looking mindset. Traditional accounting uses historic costs and bases all analysis on those figures. However, when looking at decisions into the future, simply adding up the figures will not give the right answer.

COMPARING PAST AND FUTURE ACCOUNTING NEEDS

PAST	FUTURE
Traditional accounting uses historic costs and what has happened in the past.	Future decisions ignore sunk costs and what has already happened.
Traditional decision-making uses the concepts of profit and return on assets.	Future decisions use the concepts of incremental cost and opportunity cost.
Traditional measurement treats all money as being of the same value – whenever it arises.	Future decision making looks at discounted cash flows rather than simple profits.
Historic accounting arrives at a simple result of dollar profit.	Future-looking decision making compares projects and the option of doing nothing.

IGNORING SUNK COSTS

Getting the costs right is paramount to correct decision making. A golden rule is to always ignore "sunk" costs, or those that have already been paid and cannot be recovered – hence sunk. Although someone will try to allocate blame for what has been spent, you should reject it as a cost when assessing whether to go ahead with spending in the future. How often do you hear, "We have to go ahead because of all the money spent so far?" This is a common yet potentially calamitous approach.

> **96** Compare the cost of doing a project with the cost of doing nothing.

FOCUSING ON INCREMENTAL COSTS

Costs that are incremental are those that increase or decrease – the point is that they do in fact change – as a direct result of something taking place, hence the term incremental. If a project uses two people for a month and there are none available internally, then you will have to bring in people from outside; this is a true incremental cost. If, however, people are available internally and you use them, there is no incremental cost to the business as a whole, so these are not relevant costs. The rule is to ignore irrelevant costs and count only incremental costs.

> **97** Only costs that are incremental to a company as a whole are relevant.

▼ **COUNTING COSTS**
There are three golden rules to follow when considering which costs should be taken into account to help you make a decision on future spending: ignore sunk costs, disregard irrelevant costs, and count only incremental costs.

Money spent on hiring Tom to conduct market research could not be recovered

Alice was asked to take over the project in addition to continuing with her own projects

Peter was recruited from outside the organization to finish the project

PROJECT

SUNK COST **IRRELEVANT COST** **INCREMENTAL COST**

98 Ask your accountant what the cost of money is to your company.

99 Be aware that future cash flow predictions need not be accurate.

USING SIMPLE MEASURES

Once the costs are right, consider whether the outlay will be worthwhile using measures known as accounting rate of return and the payback period. To calculate the rate of return, simply add up all the figures and express them as a percentage. For example, an outlay of $1,000 with returns of $400 for the next three years gives a profit of $200, or a return of 20 percent (about 6 percent per annum) on the initial investment. Then assess the amount of time taken to recover the initial outlay – the payback period – which in this case is two-and-a-half years. Acceptable payback periods vary from six months to several years, depending on your organization and its view of the future.

APPLYING DISCOUNTING

When making decisions about the future, it is essential to recognize the time value of money. The example of a $1,000 outlay providing returns of $400 per year over the next three years is misleading, since the $400 will be worth a different amount in the first, second, and third year. To add together future sums of money fairly, you must first discount a future sum back to its value today, or "present value." Assuming a 10 percent interest rate, $1 in one year's time is worth only 91c today (91c plus 10 percent equals $1). The value today of 91c in one year's time is about 83c. Multiplying cash flow by the discount factor gives the discounted cash flow, or DCF, and the sum of them is called the net present value, or NPV.

▼ CALCULATING DISCOUNTED CASH FLOW

Multiply the amount of the cash flow by the discount factor to give discounted cash flow. Add down to give the sum of all the discounted cash flows, or net present value (NPV). Normally, a project will be undertaken if its NPV is positive.

Cash outflows typically happen at time zero; inflows occur annually thereafter

Total anticipated future cash flows are estimated

Discount factor will typically be around 10%

TIME	CASH FLOW	9% DISCOUNT FACTOR	DISCOUNTED CASH FLOW
0	$–1,000	1.00	$–1,000
1	400	0.92	368
2	400	0.84	336
3	400	0.77	308
TOTAL	$200		$12

Sum of all the discounted cash flows gives the NPV

AVOIDING PITFALLS

There are some drawbacks to be aware of when using discounted cash flow:

- Timescale: For how many years should a project run? (The longer it runs, the better it will look.)
- Accuracy: Predicting future events will always be difficult and subjective,

especially when projected several years.

- Significant figures: Keep it simple and do not try to get too much unrealistic accuracy into predictions.
- Cost of money: Use actual cost, average cost to the organization, or even a "hurdle" rate in order to sleep at night.

USING A HIGHER FACTOR

Applying a higher discount factor will make future cash flows more attractive and a project appear more viable. There will be a point (or discount factor) for a project where the NPV is $0. The discount factor that gives a NPV of $0 is called the "internal rate of return," or IRR, and is approximately the project's inherent profitability. NPV and IRR both point to the same conclusion, but many people prefer the easily compared IRR because it is expresssed as a percentage.

▼ **USING INTERNAL RATE OF RETURN**
A 9% discount factor gives an overall project a NPV that is just positive. A higher discount factor will give lesser weighting to future cash flows, so the figures are reworked using a discount factor of 9.7%. This factor gives a NPV of $0, which is the IRR of the project, or its inherent profitability.

100 Use spreadsheets to check your calculations when discounting.

101 Remember your decision is only as good as your estimated figures.

Timescale same as for previous example

Individual undiscounted cash flow amounts are unchanged

Since the NPV was positive at 9%, a higher factor is used

TIME	CASH FLOW	9.7% DISCOUNT FACTOR	DISCOUNTED CASH FLOW
0	$–1,000	1.00	$–1,000
1	400	0.91	364
2	400	0.83	332
3	400	0.76	304
TOTAL	$200		$0

Revised NPV is $0, so 9.7% is the project's IRR

ASSESSING YOUR ACCOUNTING SKILLS

A knowledge of accounting practices and the three key financial statements will ensure that you can interpret and use the information supplied in any set of accounts. Use this questionnaire to test your understanding. Answer the questions as honestly as you can. If your answer is "Never," mark Option 1, and so on. Add your scores together and refer to the Analysis at the end of the questionnaire.

OPTIONS

1 Never

2 Occasionally

3 Frequently

4 Always

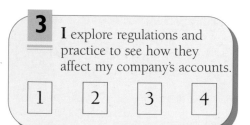

1 I am aware of the financial statements that my organization produces.

1   2   3   4

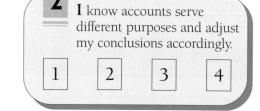

2 I know accounts serve different purposes and adjust my conclusions accordingly.

1   2   3   4

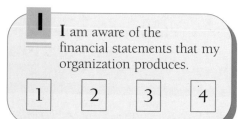

3 I explore regulations and practice to see how they affect my company's accounts.

1   2   3   4

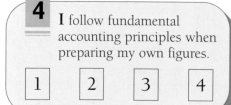

4 I follow fundamental accounting principles when preparing my own figures.

1   2   3   4

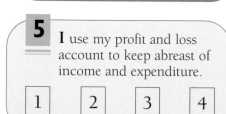

5 I use my profit and loss account to keep abreast of income and expenditure.

1   2   3   4

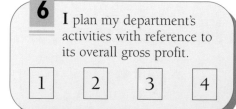

6 I plan my department's activities with reference to its overall gross profit.

1   2   3   4

7 I understand what operating profit contains and how to interpret it.

| 1 | 2 | 3 | 4 |

8 I refer to retained profits as the key measure of growth potential for a business.

| 1 | 2 | 3 | 4 |

9 I explore my balance sheet to investigate how to become more efficient.

| 1 | 2 | 3 | 4 |

10 I closely assess my capital expenditure amounts by analyzing fixed assets.

| 1 | 2 | 3 | 4 |

11 I am aware of the meaning and impact of intangible assets.

| 1 | 2 | 3 | 4 |

12 I refer to the type and amount of current assets to manage working capital.

| 1 | 2 | 3 | 4 |

13 I pay attention to whether inventories and debtors are long-standing.

| 1 | 2 | 3 | 4 |

14 I consider the impact of the amount of debt and its repayment date.

| 1 | 2 | 3 | 4 |

15 I examine shareholders' funds to see how a business has grown.

| 1 | 2 | 3 | 4 |

16 I understand the difference between profits and cash.

| 1 | 2 | 3 | 4 |

17 I analyze the cash flows that my organization generates.

1 2 3 4

18 I plan my department's future with reference to a cash flow forecast.

1 2 3 4

19 I use only accounting ratios that are specific to what I want to understand.

1 2 3 4

20 I express all lines in a profit and loss account as a percentage of sales.

1 2 3 4

21 I have certain preferred balance sheet ratios that I use and fully understand.

1 2 3 4

22 I understand the external investor ratios commonly used in stock exchanges.

1 2 3 4

23 I read the supplementary disclosure statements in my company's annual reports.

1 2 3 4

24 I am aware of how key international differences in accounting affect me.

1 2 3 4

25 I accept that I will need to seek help with some technical accounting issues.

1 2 3 4

26 I consider how creative accounting may have influenced the figures.

1 2 3 4

27 I refer to management accounts to help me control my department's finances.

| 1 | 2 | 3 | 4 |

28 I seek to improve the content and quality of internal financial information.

| 1 | 2 | 3 | 4 |

29 I realize that I must use different financial criteria in making future decisions.

| 1 | 2 | 3 | 4 |

30 I use discounted cash flow to appraise the financial viability of a project.

| 1 | 2 | 3 | 4 |

31 I recognize that accounts contain certain subjective and flexible elements.

| 1 | 2 | 3 | 4 |

32 I learn from and continually improve upon my accounting analyses.

| 1 | 2 | 3 | 4 |

ANALYSIS

Now that you have completed the self-assessment, add up your total score and check your performance. Whatever level of success you have achieved, there is always room for improvement. Identify your weakest areas, then refer to the relevant sections of this book, where you will find practical advice and tips to help you establish and hone your accounting skills. **32–64:** Your understanding is not as thorough as it should be at manager level.

65–95: You are reasonably proficient in your understanding of accounting. Make renewed efforts to improve areas of weakness to ensure better results from your accounting skills. **96–128:** You are a highly competent user of accounts. However, do not become complacent: Keep using your accounting skills by practising them regularly.

SELLING SUCCESSFULLY

INTRODUCTION

*E*ffective, high-performance selling is *important to the success of almost every kind of business. Whether you are a salesperson working at the customer interface or a sales team manager, achieving the best possible results will be determined not only by your knowledge of your own product, but also by your understanding of your customers and the communication skills you can bring to bear to close a sale. Selling Successfully covers every aspect of the sales process, providing advice on taking the right mental approach, organizing yourself, understanding and working with your customers' needs, and building essential skills such as presenting and negotiating. It includes invaluable advice on running a sales team, and is supplemented by 101 useful tips scattered throughout the section. A self-assessment exercise helps you to evaluate and improve your skills.*

PREPARING TO SELL

Selling is the basis of all business success. Lay the foundations for successful selling by following long-term principles and practices and by developing key personal skills.

AIMING FOR SUCCESS

In truly successful selling, everybody wins. Good salespeople make good deals for their customers. Bad salespeople give their customers bad deals. Customers who feel that they have made the right purchase will be happy and will be likely to come back for more.

MAKING A "WIN-WIN"

The win for salespeople is not just making the sale – the truly successful "win-win" consists of:
● Creating a satisfied customer;
● Earning satisfactory profits for the company. The degree of satisfaction depends on the real strength of the proposition offered and delivered. Salespeople's performance tends to be judged on sales volume alone, which is simple to calculate, but can give a seriously misleading picture. This happens when, for example, the seller offers discounts or terms of trade that ultimately make that particular sale unprofitable.

Supportive sales manager recognizes the long-term benefits of the sale

PROMOTING CUSTOMER PARTNERSHIPS

The sales relationship most likely to result in a "win-win" is the supplier partnership. Many companies are giving all or much of their business to one or two suppliers and working closely with them. Any savings from the collaboration are often shared between the two parties. To form such a relationship with another party, you must invest time and effort in finding solutions to their needs. Be prepared to share business plans and to collaborate on research and development. Partnerships work best where power is balanced equally between the two parties. Where the purchaser dominates the relationship, take steps to strengthen your own position, and vice versa.

1 Find out what the customer really wants as early as possible.

Salesperson secures a deal that benefits his or her company's interests

⬇

Customer realizes that the deal represents poor value for money

⬇

Relationship between the salesperson and the customer ends

▲ **MAKING A NO-WIN SALE**
A salesperson who pursues a policy of making deals that are good for the seller but bad for the customer will ultimately fail to benefit from the value that a customer's long-term business represents.

◀ **MAKING A WIN-WIN SALE**
The ideal sale consists of a salesperson creating a satisfied customer, with the support of sales management, so that the business relationship continues.

Salesperson agrees to mutually beneficial terms

Customer receives the product or service that he wants

GAINING SELF-CONFIDENCE

*S*elling can sometimes seem like a form of confrontation. That explains why many salespeople find the process difficult or nerve-racking. Substitute positive expectations of success for negative fears of failure, and selling becomes an enjoyable experience.

> **2** Always approach prospective customers expecting to sell.

◄ **PACING YOUR SPEECH**
Speak clearly and succinctly, avoiding the temptation to rush.

PRESENTING CLEARLY

If you are nervous, you may be tempted to rush your sales pitch. Approach the sale with positive expectations, and deliver your lines at a steady pace. Speak with clarity and force, and avoid babbling. Look out for signs that your speech has delivered the message by watching the other party's body language, and by asking questions related to what you have just said. Always be prepared to slow down, and do not be afraid of silences.

ASSESSING YOUR SELF-CONFIDENCE

Answer "true" or "false" to these statements:
- My mind is my own.
- I can control my feelings.
- I can motivate myself.
- I do not need the approval of others.
- I follow my own principles of conduct.
- I do not complain if things go wrong.
- I have high self-esteem.
- I am not dependent on others.
- I do not blame and find fault.

- I do not worry about the future.
- I do not procrastinate.
- I do not get angry.
- I learn lessons from my failures.
- I treat others as I would expect to be treated myself.

Your answers should all be "true." If not, work on the areas concerned until all your answers are positive. This will provide a firm foundation for your self-confidence.

GIVING THE RIGHT IMPRESSION

How you look and behave has a direct bearing on confidence on both sides of the table. Dress with care, knowing that a well-pressed suit or outfit, like a neat haircut, conveys a message to the client. A good stance, direct eye contact, a firm handshake, and excellent manners all send positive messages. However, do not rely on your personal attributes and appearance to cover up inadequate preparation and knowledge. The effort to conceal ignorance and unreadiness creates insecurity, which will undermine your efforts to feel confident.

UNTIDY

Hair is messy

Shirt is unpressed

Tie is loose

SMART

Stance is positive

Clothes are neat

Shoes are casual

3 Take the advice of others about your appearance and your presence.

LOOKING ▶ THE PART
Always make an effort to look well groomed and to appear positive.

COPING WITH REJECTION

The potential customer may not like you, what you are selling, or how you are selling it. The risk of being rejected by a customer is always daunting. The first lesson in building self-confidence is to understand that negative feelings are counterproductive and ill-founded. Be aware that what you think of yourself matters more than what you believe others think of you. Never say or think "no" for somebody else, but recognize that they, like you, have the right to refuse an offer. Remember that their refusal is not your failure, but their lost opportunity.

4 Have confidence in yourself if you want others to believe in you.

5 Record your presentation and correct any faults.

PRACTICING SELF-DEVELOPMENT

The best salespeople are ardent self-improvers. They read books, play tapes, videos, and CD-ROMs, and attend courses. These people know that paying attention to personal and professional development underpins successful careers.

6 Plan your reading and courses to meet specific, measurable aims.

Video material

General business and management books

Self-development audio tapes

Multimedia study courses

WIDENING HORIZONS

Being a professional demands a comprehensive and up-to-date knowledge of the principles and practices of the profession. Widely available literature, CD-ROM and Internet courses, and videos on sales skills and techniques cover every sales activity. These "knowledge kits" are as important as specific product and company knowledge. General business and management books are important in giving background information, including accounts of how effective selling companies and salespeople have succeeded. They provide both factual information and inspirational impact.

▲ KEEPING AHEAD

Success is founded on knowledge gained from reading and study. Aim to know as much, if not more, than your customer to create an equal business relationship.

7 Revise your new knowledge at regular intervals, and keep practicing your acquired skills.

LEARNING FROM A MASTER

These ten maxims are derived from the *Golden Rules of Customer Care* written by top American car seller Carl Sewell:

- Ask customers what they want and give it to them again and again;
- Have systems that ensure you do the job right first time, every time;
- Under-promise, over-deliver;
- The answer to a customer is always "yes";
- Give every employee who deals with clients the authority to handle customer complaints;
- No complaints? Something is wrong;
- Measure everything;
- Pay people like partners;
- Show people respect;
- Learn best practice, imitate it, then improve it.

IMPROVING ABILITIES

All human activities can be improved by training, and most training can be self-taught. Every salesperson can markedly improve key critical personal abilities (see below). Gain as much knowledge of each ability as possible, and then aim to develop each one in turn. Make a personal development plan that includes a time-scale, a reading list, a schedule of courses, and, where relevant, targets for getting to the desired level of performance. When your objectives have been realized, set some new targets.

8 Try out selling maxims to see if they work for you.

9 Talk to others about what you learn. It will increase recall.

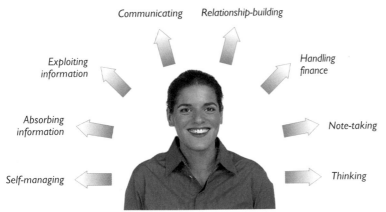

Communicating Relationship-building

Exploiting information

Handling finance

Absorbing information

Note-taking

Self-managing

Thinking

◀ **TEACHING YOURSELF**
Improve your chances of selling successfully by learning how to use time more effectively (including how to speed-read and use short-hand). Develop skills for management accounting, handling conflict, and for increasing memory capacity and creativity.

GETTING ORGANIZED

Selling must be matched to very clear business purposes and planned to enable the realization of those aims. By organizing office documentation and systems, and by managing your time, your business aims will be met with greater ease and efficiency.

> **10** Track paperwork processes from start to finish to cut out waste.

CUTTING OUT PAPERWORK

Sales departments breed paper in large quantities. Aim to counteract this tendency as much as possible for two reasons: paperwork is demotivating to most salespeople; and much of it is unnecessary. Call reporting, in particular, can take up ten percent of a salesperson's time, without making any contribution to higher or better sales. Suggest reducing the number of forms used by your company to a minimum and making the forms as simple as possible. One approach is to abolish them all and then reintroduce only those that are missed. Remember that proper planning before selling is much more valuable than subjective accounts after a sales visit.

▲ **USING SUPPORT STAFF**
Delegate tasks such as filing to support staff when possible, leaving yourself free to concentrate on more productive activities.

> **11** Free an early morning period to catch up on undone tasks.

IMPROVING SYSTEMS

Use electronic documents whenever possible, rather than hard copies, to speed up reporting, to eliminate paper filing, and to make data easily transferable. Whether computerized or not, tailor forms to be built around the questions you want answered. You are only interested in accurate data and information that helps you to improve your performance and optimize business results.

USING TIME-LOGS

A time-log is a means of improving your use of time. Record your daily activities and note how much time you spend on them every day for two or three weeks. You may be surprised by how many tasks appear unnecessary or superfluous on reflection. List those activities that only you could have done, those that could have been delegated to subordinates, and those that did not need doing at all. If the latter have been ordered by superiors, take the matter up with those concerned. Your time is your most precious asset and it must not be squandered. Once the analysis is complete, replan your time around effective activities that you alone can do.

Period	Action
9.00–9.30	*Went through mail, faxes, and emails*
9.30–10.00	*Replied to all emails, including three personal ones*
10.00–10.30	*Introduced a new recruit to the rest of the sales team*
10.30–11.00	*Spoke to Norman about new computer equipment on order*
11.00–11.30	*Spoke to human resources about June's maternity leave entitlement*
11.30–12.00	*Made follow-up calls to five of our major customers*
12.00–12.30	*Chaired weekly sales meeting – continued through lunch hour*
12.30–1.00	*Sales meeting continued*
1.00–1.30	

12 Plan days daily, months monthly, and years annually.

▲ RECORDING ACTIVITIES
Divide your time-log into hourly or half-hourly slots, and record exactly how you spend your time each day. Use the log to pinpoint any wasted time.

CULTURAL DIFFERENCES

Attitudes to time vary from country to country. Germans dislike interruptions or changed schedules. The French work long hours because of long lunches. The British work longer hours than other Europeans, and Americans are the most likely to plan their working time strictly.

SETTING TARGETS

One super-salesman had a daily activity target of making four visits, writing four letters, and making four telephone calls. Similar discipline will pay off for anybody. Ask yourself what you want to accomplish each day, week, month, and year. Recording and revising these targets focuses your mind and enables you to ensure that enough time is available for each objective. If you find that each day is ending with targets unmet, reconsider how your time is spent. Almost certainly, nonessential activities are reducing the number of effective hours available to you.

Using Electronic Aids

Selling and marketing have been moved into a new dimension with the advent of cyberspace. Portable computers and mobile telephones, to name just two modern devices, have become indispensable sales tools.

13 Contact people by telephone, fax, or email to avoid unnecessary visits.

Exploiting Mobility

Advances in telecommunications have created the salesperson of no fixed abode. One immediate advantage, apart from lower sales overheads, is the elimination of the need for coming into the office daily. Sales reporting can be handled over the computer network, automatically increasing the amount of selling time available. Face-to-face meetings, supplemented by conferencing – with or without video – remain essential, but can be planned only when necessary.

Mobile phone can be used to call clients from any location

MODERN SELLING ▶
The benefits of portable computers and telephones are considerable and enable salespeople to manage time effectively.

Carrying Computers

Portable computers and electronic organizers have revolutionized key aspects of selling. The best equipped salespeople "carry" their desks and filing systems in their briefcases and have them linked to central office files. They can answer questions in customers' offices or homes at the click of a mouse. While talking to the customer, they can configure a potential order and check on availability, delivery, and prices. If a sale is made, they can enter the details immediately for clearing into the company system.

Portable allows salesperson to work at any temporary space

OPERATING ONLINE

The Internet is potentially the greatest aid to selling ever invented. Every company can advertise using websites, and individual salespeople can set up their own sites. Some sites allow the customer to order, pay, and make queries without going near a salesperson. Companies of all sizes offer packages to help you get started on the Internet. You can have your website written, designed, programmed, and maintained, or you can choose to receive advice that enables your company to create and operate the site itself.

14 Make websites useful as well as useable.

◀ **SELLING BY EMAIL**
Unsolicited email can result in negative responses if it is seen as blanket mailing. Be selective when targeting potential customers for this form of marketing.

USING EMAIL AND FAX

Email, or electronic mail, has advantages in terms of cost and convenience compared with faxes. However, faxes are still heavily used – through both dedicated machines and computers. Email has the advantage of supplying an electronic version of the text, which the recipient can then manipulate, but faxes are more suitable for sending contracts and other legal documents requiring a signature. The prime advantage of email is also a main drawback – its ease of use results in a large number of messages. Encourage colleagues to send only important messages.

15 Act right away on any criticisms of your website.

16 Limit your email usage to business rather than personal matters.

DEALING WITH CUSTOMERS

Understanding customer attitudes is the key to increasing sales. Make an effort to research prospective customers, maximize customer contacts, and maintain strong relationships.

UNDERSTANDING TYPES OF CUSTOMER

The buying decisions of customers are influenced by many issues – not just competitive pricing, as is commonly supposed. Familiarize yourself with the range of customer needs, but keep an open mind when dealing with individuals.

17 Regard your customers as allies rather than as opponents.

18 Do research into customers' actual needs, and respond to findings.

DEVELOPING AWARENESS

Different customers have different needs over time, according to how their business is developing. While you should avoid pigeonholing customers, it is possible to recognize types and use this knowledge to target your products and techniques. Build up a profile of customers so you can emphasize features that are most attractive to them. Remember that by making people feel that your offering meets a basic need, they will feel justified in buying from you.

IDENTIFYING MOTIVES

Aim to match your sales strategy to your customer's motives and situation. Your customers will be receptive if you can offer a solution to their immediate problems or improve their business's performance. Some types of customer may be primarily motivated by security needs and will be looking for a guarantee of reliability. People who are driven by a desire to belong will buy what others buy, while those whose ego is the main motivator will want to be seen to have the best product available. Other customers, however, may be predisposed to reject your sales pitch without examining the potential benefits. In these cases, it is important not to waste time or lose heart.

19 Note that your customer's priorities probably differ from what you expect.

20 If you promise anything to your customer, always keep the promise.

RELATING TO THE CUSTOMER'S POSITION

POSITION	SIGNS	PROGNOSIS
GROWTH The customer perceives a gap between current and desired business performance.	Typically uses words like "more," "better," and "improve." This person is prepared to accept a proposal.	A good likelihood of sales success if you concentrate on showing that you can fill the perceived gap.
TROUBLE The customer is aware of a gap between required results and those that are achieved.	Will not admit to the difficulty directly, but may be prepared to discuss circumstantial problems.	The easiest type to sell to, if you can really fill the gap. Buyer is eager to say "yes" to somebody's proposal.
EVEN KEEL The buyer believes that the current position is satisfactory, and is unreceptive to change.	May use phrases such as "Don't rock the boat." Your proposal is seen as a threat, not an opportunity.	May switch to the Growth or Trouble position due to circumstances or persuasion – a hard sell otherwise.
OVERCONFIDENT This buyer thinks performance is satisfactory, rejects change, but may well be mistaken.	Will make it clear that "business has never been better," and that any change can only be for the worse.	Difficulties are almost certain to arise, but until they do, the chances of selling to this buyer are negligible.

FINDING CUSTOMERS

Making the right proposition to the right customer at the right time cannot be left to chance. Carry out research about customers and their companies before approaching them to increase the probability of finding the winning combination.

21 Pay equal attention to new and existing customers.

22 Save time and effort by targeting your sales drives.

FOLLOWING LEADS ▼
The pointers below indicate key sources of potential customers. Investigate each lead to establish a list of people who are most likely to buy your product or service. You can then focus your selling efforts on them.

IDENTIFYING PROSPECTS
New salespeople often think that the best sales prospects come from new customers. In fact, existing customers provide the best opportunities for sales, followed by former customers who have moved their business on. A common fault is to regard everyone as a potential customer, which can result in wasted effort. You want "qualified" prospects, or people who have been identified by market research as likely customers. These customers will have been identified by other companies, so competition may be strong.

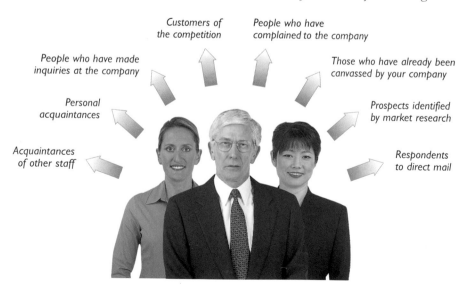

Customers of the competition

People who have complained to the company

People who have made inquiries at the company

Those who have already been canvassed by your company

Personal acquaintances

Prospects identified by market research

Acquaintances of other staff

Respondents to direct mail

TARGETING THE BUYER

Salespeople can waste time by negotiating with someone who has no budget for a purchase, or who lacks the authority to say "yes" to the sales proposition. There is a tendency to make the sales approach at too low a level – because the salesperson feels uneasy dealing with senior people, or because he or she has not identified the key decisionmaker. Even if you know who the decision-maker is, you may be unable to make direct contact. The key is to persevere. If you have identified a real need in a target company, the need will eventually outweigh the obstacles.

23 Spend time finding out who makes the final decision to buy in the target company.

▼ **MAKING CONTACT**
Find out who has the ultimate buying power, and persist in making contact. Existing and former customers are especially worth pursuing at senior levels as they yield the best results.

CONTACTING CUSTOMERS

Establish a well-researched list of prospective customers

⬇

Double-check the name and title of the person you need to deal with

⬇

Initiate contact with prospective customers by telephone, letter, or both

⬇

Confirm proposals and meeting times by letter

RESEARCHING CUSTOMERS

You can discover much about potential customers without leaving your desk. Once you have identified a prospective client, spend time learning about his or her needs and aspirations while constantly looking for opportunities to increase sales.

> **24** Work closely with customers to find the best selling opportunities.

QUESTIONS TO ASK YOURSELF

Q What reason does the client have to buy from me?

Q What "special value proposition" would be of interest to the customer?

Q Why is our company and our product or service either the best or better choice for the customer?

CARRYING OUT RESEARCH

Your desk is where to begin asking some vital questions about potential customers. Use these as starting points. Against the questions, write where the information can be found – in your own files, on relevant websites, or through personal contacts – to make your research more time efficient. Next, brief yourself thoroughly on your own company and its offer, and on the competition – your own and the customer's.

◄ **FINDING KILLER OPPORTUNITIES**
Research your client's needs and desires to discover "killer opportunities" that customers will clamor for. Aim to sell a product or service that delivers so much competitive advantage the opposition cannot compete. Such products or services are known as "killer applications." The term comes from the field of Information Technology and was originally applied to software applications that were so popular, people bought new computers just to run them on. To interest the customer in finding such a winning product or service, research and present examples from other businesses.

IDENTIFYING NEEDS

Thorough knowledge of the customer's business and requirements is fundamental. It will help you to pinpoint the factors most likely to close a deal. Emphasize the following outcomes if they are likely to meet the needs of the prospective customer:

- Improved performance and better results;
- A product or service that is new to the buyer and will offer valuable benefits;
- Greater value for money;
- An opportunity to strengthen the buyer's position in the company;
- Removing a serious problem or bottleneck;
- Rivaling or outreaching the competition.

25 Find out about customers from the best source – your customers.

26 Think about the customer as your most valuable business asset.

27 Concentrate on the benefits that your company will be able to supply.

EXPANDING SALES

While researching your customers, endeavor to discover the wider business needs that promise further and larger sales. The sale of a product system complete with components, for example, is much more valuable than selling a component alone. By looking beyond the immediate product and its characteristics, you can expand the size of your selling proposition.

DO YOU KNOW YOUR CUSTOMER?

It is easy to concentrate on product knowledge, but much harder to gain a thorough understanding of the customer. Use the following statements as a checklist. Make sure you adapt your strategy and tactics according to any insight gained.

I have learned everything I need to know about my customer and the product I am selling.

I know what the customer really wants and what I really want to sell.

I have checked who makes or influences the buying decision and which influences are sympathetic.

I understand the customer's current and potential business worth in profit terms.

COMMUNICATING EFFECTIVELY

Your key objective when communicating with a customer is to secure a sale. Ideally, a meeting should result in a satisfactory outcome for both parties. Honest and open communication is the key.

BEING OPEN

You must be confident in order for your customer to have confidence in you. Eye contact and body language play a very important part in building rapport. Smile and use open, nonthreatening gestures. Watch the customer's body language for clues as to how they are responding to you, and modify your behavior accordingly. Question and listen instead of making statements, and take careful note of objections and complaints – they may give you further clues as to the needs of the customer.

28	Adapt your style to that of your customer.

29	Do not be afraid of silences – use them to collect your thoughts.

Open arms indicate customer is receptive to suggestions

Body language remains positive throughout meeting

KEEPING ▶ POSITIVE
Be positive and honest when communicating. Lean forward, make eye contact, and emphasize key points with hand gestures.

USING COMMUNICATION TECHNIQUES

TECHNIQUES	KEYS TO ACHIEVEMENT
EMPATHY Put yourself in the customer's shoes to help you understand the issues from his or her point of view.	● Ask for as much information as possible about the other person in a genuine, straightforward manner. ● Use questions that encourage openness. ● Be supportive in your pose, nodding or making approving noises to show that you are listening.
RESEARCH Find out about the facts surrounding a customer's situation to understand why they think as they do.	● Ask the customer open questions to draw out as much information as possible. ● Keep the emphasis on fact-finding. ● Listen to the answers carefully for clues that will help you understand more about the other person.
SYNTHESIS Aim to resolve any conflicts and guide the discussion toward a desired objective.	● Make statements that will encourage the other party to respond constructively. ● Show by your responses that you value what they have said and that their responses have influenced your actions.
NEUROLINGUISTIC PROGRAMMING (NLP) Use this technique to attain conversational harmony with the customer.	● While listening intently, match your spoken language and body language to that of the customer. ● Mirror the customer's imagery, phraseology, posture, and gestures, modifying any that are counterproductive.
BODY LANGUAGE Use positive body language to encourage the customer to move toward a commitment or to adopt your ideas.	● Keep an open posture – relax your arms, lean forward, slightly tilt the head, and avoid slouching. Maintain eye contact and keep smiling. ● Respond with reassuring gestures if the customer betrays signs of nervousness or negativity.
CLEAR REACTIONS Show that you have listened to and understood the other person by responding directly to their concerns and requests.	● Listen for any concerns that may be underlying a discussion and seek to resolve them. ● Follow up requests promptly; if you cannot deliver the full promise at once, explain why and say when the promise will be kept.

MOTIVATING CUSTOMERS

Getting a prospective customer on your side means striving to recognize what motivates him or her. That will seem easier when the customer is friendly and informative. If the customer initially shows hostility, work hard to overcome the barrier between you. There are two key behaviors that motivate customers. The first is empathy: put yourself in the other person's position, talk straightforwardly, and use gentle persuasion when the customer seems uncertain. Get to the point quickly if someone is busy or impatient. The second is projection: use your strength of character to gain compliance. The best way to motivate a customer is to use a combination of the two techniques.

> **30** Complete all the research you can before meeting the customer.

▼ **ASKING FOR FEEDBACK**
If a customer appears hostile or confused, encourage him or her to provide you with feedback, however negative, in the hope that you can allay any fears.

Salesperson solicits feedback in an open and friendly manner

CULTURAL DIFFERENCES

When communicating internationally, cultural factors must be considered. Japanese customers, for example, can be hard for others to read. They may say little during a meeting, yet suddenly make an offer. You may have to wait before the French get to the point of a long business lunch. The British like a give-and-take conversation, which may even end inconclusively. Americans may show great enthusiasm for your offer, but may not accept it.

ANSWERING QUESTIONS

How do you handle questions when you do not know the answers? If possible, do not admit your ignorance, since it undermines your credibility. One technique is to answer a question with another question. When asked "Who is your biggest competitor?", for instance, reply "Do you think that size is the crucial factor in your market?". At some point, however, you must be able to show knowledge of the market. Always listen carefully to questions before answering them, and use positive body language to reinforce your answers.

Customer's body language shows hostility to proposition

31 Avoid speculating about how a meeting went.

32 Encourage customers to reveal their aims.

33 Always strive to obtain feedback from the customer toward the end of a meeting.

STEERING DISCUSSIONS

Customers will influence the course of the discussion, and may be working to their own agenda. They may seem unwilling to listen to you or to discuss issues that you want to cover. Keep returning to your strategy after handling queries with sympathy and honesty:

● Do not be led easily into repetitive debate;
● Counter arguments toward the end of a meeting in which you have successfully put across your main points;
● Respond to all of the customer's arguments with total honesty.

PROVIDING CUSTOMER SERVICE

T*reat sales and customer service as one and the same. Regard sales as a front-line activity – looking after customers' needs by providing what they want, when, and how they want it, and by following up the sale to ensure they are satisfied.*

34 Check up on the effectiveness of your service by personal trial.

35 Monitor customer response, and act immediately if you find it inadequate.

36 If customers complain, assume they are right.

RESPONDING TO CUSTOMER INQUIRIES

An essential aspect of sales is responding to customer inquiries, but it is often badly handled. Figures for responses on the World Wide Web highlight the problem. Only two out of ten contactors get replies within a day, and 13 percent of people receive no response at all. Ideally all inquirers should get a response the same day. Always answer your telephone – it is counterproductive to avoid contact with customers.

RESPONSES TO ▶ WEB INQUIRIES
World Wide Web sites have been set up on the Internet to generate sales inquiries and, presumably, to answer them. Yet most companies are failing to take advantage of this fast-growing sales medium, as the figures on this chart show.

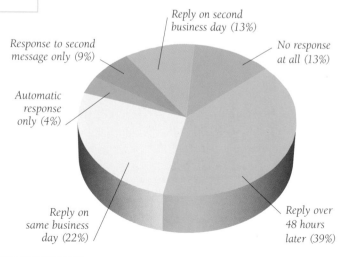

Reply on second business day (13%)

Response to second message only (9%)

No response at all (13%)

Automatic response only (4%)

Reply on same business day (22%)

Reply over 48 hours later (39%)

DEALING WITH COMPLAINTS

All customers who complain are valuable assets. The complaints tell you necessary truths about the quality of your company's product or service. By handling complaints swiftly and effectively, you create a high degree of customer satisfaction:

● Apologize and own the problem;
● Act quickly – within five days;
● Assure the customer the problem is being fixed;
● Deal with it in person or on the telephone.

You must make it clear at the outset that you are 100 percent on the customer's side. Even if the complaint is factually unjustified, the client's perception is otherwise and that perception is what matters. Never rest until the matter has reached a conclusion acceptable to the customer.

CUSTOMER CONFIDENCE

When handling complaints, follow these rules to retain customer confidence and avoid antagonizing them further:

● Paraphrase the customer's complaint to show that you have heard and understood.
● Tell the customer that you understand how they feel.
● Assure the customer that their feedback is invaluable.
● Apologize for any inconvenience, and do all you can to make up for it.

37 Establish a habit of calling your customers after a sale to check that they are satisfied.

▼ MONITORING PROGRESS

Endeavor to maintain client contact and continue to reinforce customer relationships whatever the size of the sale.

MAINTAINING CONTACT

Customer service must not end with the sale. How well you identify with and handle the needs of the customers has a marked effect on their loyalty. The principle is the same with a machinery buyer or a vacation customer: always ask "Is the customer satisfied?" and "Will he or she buy again?". If the answers are "No," find out why and what can be done about it. Make a note to call customers regularly to check levels of satisfaction.

Call your customers regularly to check they are satisfied

Make a note of any complaints and act on them immediately

SATISFYING CUSTOMERS

Y*ou can never satisfy all of the customers all of the time. But you can never stop trying to do so. Find out what the customer's requirements are, and then discover whether those needs have been met by constantly monitoring the customer's reactions.*

38 Keep first-class service standards to please and retain customers.

ESTABLISHING PRIORITIES

The primary target of selling – to exceed customer expectations and earn an "excellent" rating from clients – depends on knowing in advance what matters most to the buyer. Do not assume that price is the top priority. Salespeople often damage profits by taking this for granted. Customers may have a number of different factors on their list of priorities, such as delivery times or technical support. If you have researched what customers want most, and how your company's product or service ranks against the competition, then successful selling will be considerably easier.

Read company reports to assess the needs of your customers

▲ **RESEARCHING NEEDS**
Use all sources available to research your customers, from company literature to press reports.

◀ ASSESSING PRIORITIES
Keep an open mind about what your customer values the most about your propositions.

Use customer feedback to establish their priorities

KEEPING CUSTOMERS

The only sure way to find out if you are fulfilling your customers' needs is to ask them. Invite customer groups to tell you what would make your products or services more attractive. Send out questionnaires, and call customers personally to ask them for their comments. Make use of the routine contact that other staff may have with customers, since they may be able to provide useful insights. Above all, make it clear to customers that you want their comments and will act on them.

MEETING CUSTOMER NEEDS

QUESTIONS TO ASK	ACTIONS TO TAKE
BRAND AND IMAGE Does your company and its products have a strong rating in the marketplace?	● Find out if the customer has a high opinion of the brand and the company. ● Check if the customer feels that they are buying the right product from the right company.
SALES TECHNIQUE Is the sales process being conducted so that the customer likes doing business with your company?	● Provide your salespeople with training in customer care and communication skills. ● Establish that the buyer is being helped to make the right decision and is not being put under pressure.
KEEPING COMMITMENTS Is your company doing what it says it will, when it says it will?	● Deliver the right product to the right place at the right time in the right quantity. ● Live up to your word, and avoid making promises that you may not be able to fulfill.
ADMINISTRATION Is the sale being handled with efficiency and without unnecessary bureaucratic procedures?	● Ensure that invoices and other documents are clear and accurate and easy to use correctly. ● Encourage your company to be flexible in drawing up and interpreting terms and conditions.
RESPONSIVENESS Is the customer being answered and responded to swiftly and effectively at all times?	● Clarify any ambiguous communications with the customer as soon as possible. ● Deal with customer's complaints by acknowledging mistakes and rectifying errors immediately.
INFORMATION Does the customer know everything that they need to know about the product or service they are buying?	● Make sure that your salespeople are knowledgeable about the product or service they are supplying. ● Provide the customer with all the information and assistance needed to use the product or service.
PRODUCT OR SERVICE Does the purchase live up to or exceed the customers expectations?	● Ensure that agreed specifications are met, including any special concessions made when negotiating the sale. ● Check that the customer is happy with the performance of the service or product.
AFTER-SALES SERVICE Is the customer relationship being looked after successfully post-sale?	● Make sure that customer inquiries or complaints are always dealt with promptly and courteously. ● Be proactive in contacting the customer to monitor how satisfied they feel with their purchase.

39 Employ proven research firms to measure customer satisfaction.

40 Back up survey results by posing questions to a customer sample.

MEASURING SATISFACTION

Customer satisfaction must be researched, and preferably measured. There are two main types of research method: quantitative and qualitative. Quantitative research, usually based on questionnaires, can be measured for statistical analysis. "Closed" questions are used, which means responses are limited – for example, to a scale of one to five. This type of research is very well-established and widespread, but fairly expensive. You should supplement quantitative results with qualitative research, which is based on interviews. Both methods should be carried out as part of your follow-up routine to ensure that the customer remains content.

QUANTITATIVE SURVEYS

This type of survey uses questions that prompt specific answers from customers, since the results are calculated for use in charts and tables. But do not assume that all such results are accurate. Errors can be introduced, and a high score may conceal customer dissatisfaction that will have a serious impact on future sales. Research by Xerox has shown that customers who give a "Very Satisfied" rating, for instance, are six times more likely to buy from you again than those registering as "Satisfied." So, if the questions used in quantitative surveys are not clearly defined (if "Very Satisfied" and "Satisfied" are combined, for example), results can be misleading.

POSING KEY QUESTIONS ▶

Quantitative research, like an opinion poll, poses identical questions to a representative sample of people. Any research should address three basic questions that really matter when assessing customer satisfaction. If your research provides you with customer responses to each of these questions, you will have your essential research information.

Ask if customers would buy from you again

Ask if customers would be prepared to recommend you to other people

Ask if customers would rate your product or service as excellent

Assess the customers' response, and make any changes that are necessary

QUALITATIVE SURVEYS

The qualitative survey method involves asking customers personally how they feel about a product or service. The survey uses questions that encourage customers to volunteer their feelings. It can be conducted in-house or out-of-house. In-house methods often involve either group interviews with a customer panel or individual interviews as follow-ups to questionnaires. Face-to-face, in-depth interviews are the most telling methods, but you should take care not to influence the answers. Ask "What do you think of the service?", rather than "Do you think the service is good?".

▼ **USING TEST PANELS AND FOCUS GROUPS**
An external researcher may ask questions of panels, or focus groups, if the company has many customers (such as a retail chain). This research is most effective when carried out in an informal setting.

COMMUNICATING SENSIBLY

Just as you can over-sell to the customer, so you can overdo the effort to delight. Companies are now encouraged to embark on "relationship marketing," which provides (and often bombards) the customer with follow-up letters, telephone calls, and special offers. Keep follow-up activities within careful control. Have a clear reason for each act of communication, and do not make too frequent calls on the customer's time and patience. On the other hand, never fail to accept or return a customer's call or to reply promptly to any correspondence. Failure to do so can undo much hard-won customer loyalty.

41 Good is not good enough – only excellence takes you forward.

42 Pose as a customer to test how your company handles customer calls.

MAKING A SUCCESSFUL SALE

Effective selling involves planning and strategy. Your strategy may initially involve a team presentation or a simple mail shot, but all sales ultimately depend on negotiating skills.

PLANNING THE APPROACH

Selling operations need military-style planning to improve success rates. The customers must be clearly identified, the market properly covered – with salespeople covering carefully allocated areas – and the sale must match customer needs.

43 Make sure your sales strategy makes sense to everybody.

44 Assess your brand image and current market position to strengthen your sales strategy.

ADOPTING A STRATEGY

Whether you are selling an existing product, or launching a new one, a successful sales strategy is based on a thorough analysis of product, market, and competition. Your strategy may be aimed at finding new customers, or at building strong relationships with existing customers. But before you commit resources to a sales drive, consider the size of the market, its potential, and the strength of competition from other organizations. Once you have established your market, ensure that your sales force covers the areas in which customers or potential customers are located.

45 Look for the most exciting customer propositions.

FOLLOWING A SALES STRATEGY

Investigate the customer's objectives by desk research and by asking colleagues

Plan an arresting presentation, keeping the customer's objectives in mind

Make your presentation, supplying as much information as possible

Negotiate terms that meet both your goals and the needs of the customer

Close the deal, summarizing the key points and emphasizing benefits

SELLING IN STAGES

Your selling process should go through key stages before you attempt to close a deal. Each of these stages requires its own mini-plan. Set down your desired outcome, the tactics you will employ to win that outcome, and your response to foreseeable deviations. Revise your plan at every stage to incorporate any new knowledge or information you have gleaned. Your assessment of the customer's needs and expectations will provide the starting point for planning your sales and negotiation strategies and your presentation. Ensure that you have all the relevant facts and figures available to enable you to answer any questions the customer may have, and always conclude a meeting by reiterating the unique benefits of your product or service.

KNOWING YOUR PRODUCT AND MARKET

A successful sales strategy depends on the key skills of persuasion and negotiation – skills that can only be effectively deployed if they are reinforced by familiarity with, and confidence in, the product or service being offered. Customers rely on salespeople to tell them what they need to know, so it is essential that you have the answers for any line of enquiry that might arise. It is not sufficient to limit your knowledge to your own product – you must be able to put it into context with similar products so that favorable comparisons can be made. Use every method available to become an expert in your field. Study market literature, discuss relevant issues with technical, operations, and production staff, and take advantage of training. Above all, use every sales call as an opportunity to increase your knowledge, and therefore your competence.

USING AIDCA

The acronym AIDCA stands for the key words Attention, Interest, Desire, Conviction, and Action. These are the five stages that you should lead your prospective customer through in sequence to maximize the chances of a successful sale.

FOLLOWING AIDCA PRINCIPLES

Direct-mail sellers have long used the AIDCA formula as a guide to writing sales letters. But the principles apply strongly to all aspects of selling. Following them gives you an organizing tool that provides your sales pitch with shape and direction, and makes the proposition coherent as well as attractive to the prospective customer. First catch the customer's Attention, then arouse Interest. Convert Interest into Desire for your product or service before creating the Conviction that will result in Action – the sale.

ATTRACTING ATTENTION

You need to gain the attention of the customer in order to make a sale. Attention can be grabbed by an all-singing, all-dancing act, by an arresting proposition, or by an introduction from an influential or admired person. Whatever technique you use, your aim is to be noticed. Assume that the customer is besieged with propositions and proposers. Carefully design your opening gambit, whether delivered in person, over the telephone, or in writing, to distinguish yourself from the competition. You have to win the customers' eyes and ears before you can win their minds, hearts, and wallets.

46 Work hard on developing a "story" that will interest buyers.

47 Consider how to grab attention in a mail shot.

ATTENTION

Salesperson writes an arresting mail shot

▲ **AIDCA IN ACTION**
The first stages in the sequence determine whether your approach will be successful. Make your mail shot as striking as possible, and include interesting information that will tempt the reader to find out more.

48 Keep "features" in reserve as aids to tip the balance to your advantage.

49 Make the best possible use of the first minutes with the customer.

DEVELOPING INTEREST

Capitalize on Attention by turning it into Interest. This depends on understanding and pressing a customer's "hot-spot." That is the promise (explicit or implicit) that the potential purchase will meet a genuine customer need. "What I have to offer will halve your telephone bills" is the kind of proposition that is likely to interest anybody. On its own, the statement that excites Interest will not make a sale. It sets up the customer to be receptive to further information.

Key points in the mail shot arouse customer interest

INTEREST

DESIRE

Salesperson meets customer to provide extra information and stimulate desire

INSPIRING DESIRE

Attention and Interest are not enough to clinch a sale. The customer has to be brought to a condition of Desire. The process of booking a vacation illustrates the progression. An advertisement in the press attracts Attention, the details about the resort arouse Interest, and the pictures in the brochure sent by a travel agent inspire Desire. The extras, like discounts or preferential payment schemes, provide additional attraction. The basic need is all-important, but the embellishments can tip the scale and, in some cases, can be seen as the main objects of Desire.

50 Ask yourself "Why is my product unique?" and use the answer.

Customer realizes offer is unbeatable

CREATING CONVICTION

The customer must be drawn to the conclusion that they must buy from you, and you alone. In advertising terms, you must present the Unique Selling Proposition, or USP. This is the attribute that persuades the buyer that your product or service is different and better. Comparing a vacation with more expensive alternatives, for example, encourages the Conviction that the buying decision is correct. So does an attractive insurance package, or a concession on payment methods. The more you let customers convince themselves, as opposed to being convinced, the better for the sale.

◀ **CONCLUDING THE SALE**
The final stages in the AIDCA sequence aim to persuade the customer that they will not get a better deal elsewhere, and to make the decision to buy.

CONVICTION

INCITING ACTION

The test of effectiveness is Action. The famous sales pitch "Act now while supplies last" sums up two key principles: immediacy and urgency. You want the customer to place their order now, so you make it appear that the opportunity will not last for ever. This situation may be artificial, but unless elements of urgency can be created, the sales process may drag on, and impetus may be lost. Then the whole AIDCA sequence will have to be repeated, with lower chances of success. Properly timed, the sequence is logical and highly effective.

ACTION

Salesperson urges customer to act promptly to avoid missing out

Customer decides to purchase

51 Give customers a final incentive to "sign on the dotted line."

52 Employ jokes and vivid words to engage clients.

CHANGING PREFERENCES

The object of AIDCA is to persuade the buyer to prefer your offering to all alternatives and, you hope, to shift from their current product or service to yours. The most effective method is to offer the best solution to the buyer's identified problems, and to demonstrate the solution when possible. Putting yourself across as a humorous and helpful person who is strongly associated with the company or brand assists the sale. Provide vivid descriptions of the beneficial results of buying from you, and give the customer plenty of news about new features and applications. Novelty needs backing with security, so come armed with testimonials from satisfied clients.

Customer tries out the product first-hand

Salesperson demonstrates product benefits

◄ **DEMONSTRATING A PRODUCT**
Do not forget the power of demonstrations, if applicable, to create the Conviction that will eventually result in Action.

DO'S AND DON'TS

✔ Do stress the unique benefits that can be obtained by buying from you.

✔ Do focus on the last "A" in AIDCA: get the customer to act now.

✘ Don't "knock" rivals when convincing clients that they should buy from you.

✘ Don't let the sales process drag on if AIDCA has failed.

53 Use "free" or extra features to help persuade the customer to buy.

COMMUNICATING BY MAIL

Writing is required for most types of selling, so the better its quality, the higher the likely volume of sales. Direct mail, which relies upon excellent writing, is a highly effective and fast-growing sales method – a whole selling campaign can be based on it.

54 Have your letters read by someone else to help spot any errors.

55 Test different letters on groups of customers and select the best.

56 Make sure that all mailed material reinforces your brand values.

WRITING FOR SUCCESS

Letters are effective sales methods to use as introductions and as precursors to direct mail shots. If you receive a letter in response, never allow it to go unanswered, and always follow it up by telephone. If your correspondence is successful and you meet the customer, write to confirm what has been discussed (a letter then acts like the minutes of the meeting), and to advance the negotiation. Always ensure that matters of substance are recorded on paper. Finally, if the sale should fall through, do not forget to send a letter that is designed to keep you in mind for future opportunities.

IMPROVING YOUR WRITING

Use the following guidelines, which follow the principles of AIDCA, to write an excellent introductory letter that will grab and hold the customer's attention.

- Plan ahead, giving your writing an introduction, middle, and short end.
- Improve your physical writing speed.
- Write as you talk – naturally.
- Visualize the reader and address them.
- Use as few words as you need.

- Make sure that your meaning is clear.
- Keep your sentences simple and short.
- Preserve a smooth and logical flow.
- Never strive for effect.
- Avoid circumlocutions and archaisms.
- Use short words rather than long ones.
- Use active voice instead of passive voice.
- Avoid jargon and double negatives.
- Speak your written words to yourself.
- Revise only when you have finished.

SELLING BY MAIL

Direct-mail selling eliminates telephone calls. It also allows for controlled experiments – varying sales methods until you find a combination that attracts the most custom. Writing an effective letter is obviously vital, but the most important factor is the mailing list. It is essential to have an up-to-date list of potential customers, either compiled from your own database, or bought in from a mailing-list company. Sending out large mailings is expensive, and the letter should always be tested first on a small, random sample to ensure that profit on the investment will more than cover the costs of preparation, printing, and postage.

Logo adds corporate identity

Consistent style reinforces brand recognition

◀ **ELEGANT DESIGN**
Spend time choosing the style of your direct mail shots. The design should be clear, consistent, and eye-catching.

RECOGNIZING BRANDS

Organizations spend heavily on brochures and other material, which is distributed by mail, at trade fairs, or on sales visits. The materials vary from glossy leaflets to price lists. Whatever its nature and cost, any production must answer one key question: "Will it give the customer clear reasons to buy from us, and nobody else?". That means adopting a consistent, high-quality design to sustain brand recognition, delivering messages with clarity and impact, and avoiding an excessive and dense quantity of material.

WRITING AN EFFECTIVE DIRECT-MAIL LETTER

Promise the most important product benefit at the very beginning

Enlarge upon the benefit (or benefits) immediately after the opening

Tell the reader what they are going to get in as much detail as possible

Back up the product or service details with proof of sales and endorsements

Tell the reader what they may lose if they fail to take up the offer

Rephrase the prominent benefits in the closing section of your mail shot

Incite action – let the reader know that they must act immediately

USING THE TELEPHONE

Persuading a customer by telephone to meet you, especially someone who has never heard of you, is a sales skill in itself. Use well-practiced telephone techniques for establishing contact, booking meetings, and selling direct by telephone.

57 Arrange to meet your customer face to face, however hard it may seem.

BREAKING THE ICE

It is important to give a valid reason for your call. Try developing an initial icebreaker for securing appointments over the telephone. Suitable questions are: "Has anybody visited you from Selling Inc., lately?"; or "Has my name been mentioned?". Your answer, whatever the reply, needs to be positive. "Did you get my letter?" can be used if you have made initial contact by letter. Make a point of following up any correspondence with a telephone call. If the other party cannot remember your letter or its contents, you have the perfect opportunity to explain your reason for calling.

POINTS TO REMEMBER

- Matching your vocal pace to that of the person you are talking to will establish a rapport.
- Interrupting the other party should be avoided.
- The use of "I" should be kept to a minimum; instead use your own name five times during the call.
- On the first call, "This is" rather than "My name is" makes a good opening.
- Pauses should be avoided during your telephone conversation.

Hold the telephone firmly

Have a script in front of you

Look at a mirror to encourage you to smile

◀ **IMPROVING TECHNIQUES**

Securing an appointment by telephone will be assisted by concentrated effort. Preparing a script and monitoring your facial expressions in a mirror will help you achieve a positive outcome.

MAINTAINING INTEREST

When dealing with a customer, show genuine interest in them. Ask, "How are you?" as if the automatic answer ("Fine, thanks") is meaningful. If either party has limited the call, say, to ten minutes, do not exceed this limit unless the other party plainly wants to carry on. Ensure that you maintain a sympathetic response, even if the conversation becomes objectionable and includes criticisms. Use stock responses like "That's understandable," or "We find that is the case with most people."

58 Like the people you deal with, and show your liking in word and deed.

59 Confirm the time before you leave for a meeting.

Smile to maintain a positive tone of voice

Note down any follow-up actions to take

REMAINING ▶ POSITIVE
Make the customer feel that you are on his or her side. React to any hostility with sympathy, and always keep calm. Avoid making promises you cannot fulfil.

SECURING AN APPOINTMENT

When cold-calling strangers to get an appointment, you should expect to succeed every time. Explain briefly the reason for the call, and use these questions or statements to help secure a meeting, which you must confirm before ringing off:

❝ *You've probably heard my name already. Has anybody mentioned me to you?* ❞

❝ *As you may know, Selling Inc. has recently introduced the first fully digital...* ❞

❝ *I'd be happy to drop by and give you the opportunity to learn about this new product.* ❞

❝ *I'll be in your area on Tuesday around 3 p.m. Will you be there for seven minutes if I drop by?* ❞

MAKING THE MOST OF MEETINGS

O nce you have made the effort to understand your customers' needs and objectives, you can start to plan how to use your time with them effectively, and how to present your sales proposition so that it is as attractive as possible.

60 Only give your customers product information that they really want.

PLANNING CUSTOMER MEETINGS

Every aspect of a customer contact needs to be carefully thought out. Choose a neutral location, and remember that formality helps concentration, but may be intimidating. Conversely, a relaxed environment can be unbusinesslike. Be clear about your objective – is it to make a sale or to build up data on customer needs? Ensure that you have all the facts and figures on your own and rival products. Estimate the time it will take to cover the essential points, and have copies of relevant data – a brochure, for example – that you can leave with the customer. Always be clear about how much you are prepared to compromise.

DO'S AND DON'TS

✔ Do plan questions that will get a positive response.

✔ Do allow time to listen to the customer.

✔ Do memorize all the unique aspects of your offer and the company.

✘ Don't overwhelm the customer by including too much information.

✘ Don't plan to bully the buyer into the deal.

✘ Don't worry about failure – expect to be successful.

PROMOTING YOUR PRODUCT

When you meet the customer, ensure that you provide all the information that they need to choose your product or service:

● Tell the customer what you know of his or her current activities and ambitions;

● Stress how your product can benefit the customer;

● Elaborate on product or service features, benefits, and company knowledge;

● Know your competitors' strengths and weaknesses, and be knowledgeable about their products and services;

● Anticipate negative points that the customer may raise, and be ready with positive remedial suggestions;

● Provide references from satisfied customers.

LISTENING TO CUSTOMERS

Allow customers to tell you what they need before you tell them what you have to offer, and ask questions to ensure that you have understood them. Always be courteous, addressing the customer by name, and avoid jargon. Aim to exceed expectations by asking the customer if there is anything that might make your product or service more attractive. Try to end a meeting by offering them an extra, unsolicited concession (however small) to make them feel that they are a favored customer. Thank them for their time, and tell them how much you value their custom.

61 Be aware of your objective when planning a customer meeting.

CULTURAL DIFFERENCES

American salespeople are known for giving slick presentations when meeting customers. The British are often shy about selling and will take time getting to the point of the meeting. Germans are more formal and may use meetings mainly to give the customer a mass of product information. A French salesperson may take an intellectual approach and do most of the talking.

62 Be absolutely sure that your company is able to deliver any service promises that you make.

MAKING ▼ FOLLOW-UP CALLS

It is usually appropriate to follow up meetings with a telephone call. This will establish a relationship with the customer and keep you uppermost in their minds.

Keep an up-to-date contact list

Refer to records of previous customer meetings if necessary

MAKING A PRESENTATION

Putting over the message in a face-to-face presentation or in front of a large audience is the leading edge of selling. The difference between an excellent and poor presentation is very often the difference between making and losing a sale.

63 Keep your talk as short as you can, keep to the point, and end positively.

PLANNING YOUR PRESENTATION

Although each sales presentation needs to be tailored to both customer and product, there is a basic sequence that will ensure that the audience's initial interest results in action:

● Explain the unique advantages of your particular product or service;
● Emphasize all the successes that the product has achieved, and back up your claims with up-to-date statistics and endorsements from other customers;
● Explain that it would be dangerous to lag behind in the marketplace;
● Aim to persuade the audience that the purchase of your product or service will improve their status in the market;
● Finally, encourage the audience to act immediately to guarantee fulfilment of their order.

TIMING THE TALK

The rules of a presentation are the same as those for a good speech. First of all, set down the key points you wish to make in the AIDCA sequence (see pp. 34–7). The shorter the time taken to present them the better: 20–40 minutes is the typical attention span of most people. Divide the number of points into the allotted time, and you then know how long to spend on each point. If using visual aids, as you should if possible, three minutes is probably needed to make each point. This means that you can make only ten to twelve points in all, but this is usually sufficient.

▼ USING EMPHASIS
Reinforce the main points of your presentation by first giving the audience an introduction to your speech, then discussing the issues you raise, and by finishing off with a clear summary.

| Tell them what you are going to say | Say it | Tell them what you have said |

USING AUDIO-VISUAL AIDS

The mind remembers speech less well than images, and images alone are registered less efficiently than an audiovisual (AV) combination. Using top-quality AV is far easier than ever before – thanks to personal computers and the software that creates colored texts, images to order, and animations, and projects them digitally onscreen. For face-to-face meetings, a standard computer screen is fine. But to create maximum impact, you should go for a full-color projection, with dynamic, moving elements, a soundtrack, and perhaps lighting effects. Always tailor the AV presentation to the perceived needs of the customer.

▲ AUDIOVISUALS
High-level technical AV aids may require specialized help to set up. Always have a technical rehearsal before the presentation.

64 Develop a new set of audiovisual images for each new talk you give.

65 Do not read your speech – memorize as much as possible.

ACHIEVING IMPACT

Effective messages are easy to recall, convincing and distinctive, and are stimuli to action:
- Be emphatic about the benefit you offer, and start with an arresting statement;
- Follow the golden sales rule of addressing solutions not problems, and introduce your product or service (visually and aurally) at the earliest possible moment;
- Repeat the company or brand name frequently;
- Never knock the competition: explain that your excellent offer improves on their good solution;
- Do not overemphasize technology, which can lose a nontechnical audience;
- Sincerely mean what you say, and say only what you mean;
- Finally, end with a repeat image of the product or service and the company.

NEGOTIATING TERMS

Even when the customer has agreed to give you business, you still have to negotiate terms and conditions. Any two negotiating sides will probably have different objectives. Be prepared for these differences, and work toward mutual satisfaction.

66 Analyze what you would do if you were in the other party's shoes.

PREPARING TO NEGOTIATE

Anticipating what the buyer may say or ask gives you a critical advantage at the negotiating encounter. If you are unprepared, a single question may ground your whole strategy. Poor preparation has lost many sales contracts. Prepare to your best ability by rehearsing with colleagues, asking them to assume the role of the customer. Concentrate on what questions are likely to be raised, how best to answer the questions, and how, through your use of body language, to gain the customer's confidence.

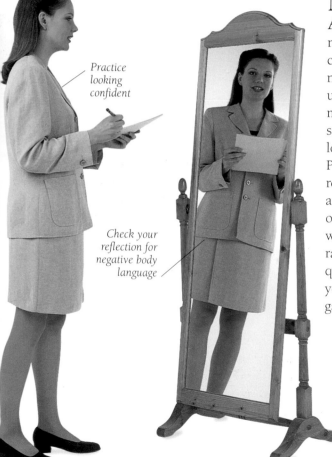

Practice looking confident

Check your reflection for negative body language

◄ **TRIAL RUN**
Practice what you will say to customers before a negotiation, preferably in front of a mirror so that you can check your expression and body language and keep both positive. You will then feel better prepared and less anxious about the possible outcome of the meeting.

MEETING THE NEEDS OF BOTH PARTIES

Your goal is to make a sale on terms that satisfy the needs of your business. That goal should always include meeting the needs of the buyer. Come into the negotiation, therefore, with a clear idea of your own and your company's best, medium, and lowest acceptable outcomes. You require an equally clear idea of the customer's expectations. The first task in the negotiation is to confirm that your analysis of your own and your company's needs is correct. If not, adjust it accordingly. Next, be seen to work toward the customer's needs as far as possible.

▼ COMBINING OBJECTIVES

Clearly explain your objectives to the customer, and listen carefully to theirs, then work toward combining both sets of objectives for a successful sale.

Customer confirms her requirements

Salesperson explains his objectives

67 Avoid thinking in an adversarial, pugnacious style – keep your tone sympathetic.

STRESSING BENEFITS

The purchaser will never mind beating you down to an unprofitable figure. You can try to escape this trap by emphasizing valuable features. However, it is far more effective to stress benefits in terms of time, efficiency, and competitive advantage to the customer. The absolute price is less important (provided it is within the customer's means) than the perceived value for money.

COPING WITH THE COMPETITION

In any negotiation there is usually an invisible third party: your competitor or competitors. Their existing offers have set a ceiling on what deal you may make. The customer will pay more than the lowest competitive offer (or accept less than the best terms) only if you provide a convincing argument for your superiority. Find out all you can about the competition and tackle it head-on.

68 Never criticize the competition, but always aim to outperform it.

SETTING THE PRICE

Effective selling means avoiding price reductions for two reasons. First, price is often not the customer's major preoccupation or need. Second, price holds the key to your profit. Offering price reductions as your chief negotiating ploy may threaten a company's financial returns without making the sale more certain. You will do better to negotiate the price upward. Car dealers, for example, achieve this by offering desirable extras. Given the chance, however, salespeople will generally discount prices as much as they are allowed. Equally, they will resist price rises for fear of damaging volume. The mathematics show that it is much harder to gain profits by cutting prices than by raising them. So, give way on price reluctantly and as little as possible.

POINTS TO REMEMBER

- The most effective negotiating tactic is to stress benefits.
- Emphasizing valuable features is always worthwhile.
- Improving the customer's knowledge of your product or service is a major key to a successful outcome.

69 Initially, ask for the highest price that the market will bear.

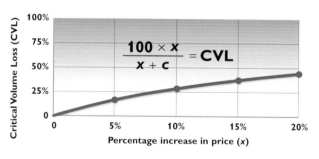

KEY x = Percentage increase in price
y = Percentage decrease in price
c = Price minus direct costs (%)

◀ RAISING PRICES

This equation helps you decide if you can set a higher price by showing how far sales can fall before profitability declines. In this example, where c equals 25, if the product price is raised by 20 percent, profits will not fall until sales drop by more than 44 percent (Critical Volume Loss), making this a risk worth taking.

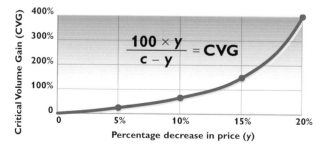

◀ LOWERING PRICES

This equation helps you decide if you can cut your product prices by showing how far sales must rise at the new price in order to sustain profits. If the product price is dropped by 20 percent when c equals 25, sales must rise by 400 percent (Critical Volume Gain) to maintain profit levels. This is clearly not a viable strategy.

USING HIGHER AUTHORITY

If you reach an impasse on price, try making a concession that will leave the buyer feeling victorious. Turn to higher authority to achieve this, or encourage your team to turn to you. This backup is needed to maximize the appearance of flexibility, and also for support when standing firm. One Dickensian character used to deal with clients by reference to a senior partner who, in truth, had taken no part in the firm's affairs for years. Avoid making exceptions, however, that seriously undermine the value of the sale.

70 Try to keep the negotiation on a friendly level at all times.

▼ **SEEKING CONSENT**
Leave the room to find or call your superior, and come back with a special concession for the buyer: "My boss says he can make an exception in this case."

71 Be ready to refer upward any sales problem that you cannot resolve.

Manager's involvement increases perceived value of concession

Salesperson seeks senior approval for special deal

CLINCHING THE DEAL

To close a sale you need to lead the customer to the point at which he or she feels confident in accepting your offer. Provide as much information as possible, resolve any objections, and ask for a decision – but avoid applying pressure.

72 Take note of any considered objections.

Salesperson deals with objections by stressing the benefits of the sale

CONSIDERING THE CLOSE

To close you need to behave in a way that directly or indirectly prompts the buyer to commit to the sale. Avoid acting according to a predetermined formula at this stage – you are dealing with an individual and should plan your closing with that in mind. Some customers like a direct approach; others find this hostile and prefer a choice of options, or some last-minute reassurance.

Customer likes benefits and accepts terms

REACHING A ▲ CONCLUSION
Avoid set rules to close a sale. Instead, stress benefits and, if necessary, use a final concession to secure your sale.

73 Thank your customer warmly, whatever the outcome has been.

OBTAINING FEEDBACK

Customer objections can be discouraging, but high objectors are nearly three times as likely to buy than prospective customers who offer no objections at all. Non-objectors give the salesperson low feedback of any kind and make the selling task harder. In contrast, the objector is reacting, entering into a dialogue, and giving the salesperson a cue for the next move. Never lightly dismiss objections from customers, but take them as serious matters for discussion toward the closing stages of a negotiation.

GUIDING THE CUSTOMER

Wait until you feel that you have given and received as much relevant information as possible to enable you to guide the negotiation to a successful conclusion and generate a decision to buy. Then summarize all the key points made, emphasizing the strong links between the customer's objectives and your product or service. Ask the customer if all concerns have been satisfied, as this helps to clarify the situation and gives you a final opportunity to defuse any lingering resistance.

FINALIZING THE SALE

It is important to act swiftly and not to allow the buying moment to pass. When the time has come to sign the contract, the customer will clearly see that the benefits you are offering correspond exactly with their needs, and the buying decision should be a mere formality. Have your pen and the order form on the table during the negotiation to avoid introducing them suddenly, which may give the impression that you are pushing the customer into the purchase.

74 Identify success criteria beforehand, and always work toward them.

75 Analyze your successes as closely as your failures, and repeat techniques that lead to success.

76 Look for lessons when you fail, and learn from them.

PHRASING YOUR CLOSING QUESTIONS

Asking the buyer for a decision can be awkward, so find some closing phrases that you feel comfortable with. Aim to introduce the close as a natural progression of the negotiation by asking questions that assume a positive decision has already been made:

What delivery date would be most convenient for you?

Do you have an order number or any other order references that I need?

Should we send the invoice to the delivery address, or would you prefer it to go to head office?

Of course it's cheaper to order in bulk, but would you prefer a smaller batch to begin with?

MANAGING SALES TEAMS

Short-term sales management involves daily administration, while long-term management requires decisions affecting the future of the team. Aim to acquire skills for both needs.

LEADING A TEAM

T*he key to effective sales management is to keep control while motivating salespeople to maximize their contribution as members of a strong team, including key people from different departments.*

 77 Give rewards for team success if you want better team performance.

THE NINE SKILLS

Better managers will result from training that covers these skills:
- Recruiting salespeople
- Training salespeople
- Coaching salespeople
- Allocating customers
- Monitoring call rates
- Monitoring performance
- Analyzing sales results
- Rewarding achievement
- Dealing with failure

ACQUIRING SKILLS

The sales manager has a challenging role. You are responsible for hitting sales targets, but you probably do no selling yourself. You may be a promoted salesperson with no experience of, and perhaps little aptitude for, management. This is a common problem. If it applies to you, try to secure yourself some training, and make sure that members of your sales team are provided with training before promotion to management. In your role as manager, always avoid reverting to the role of salesperson, and watch out for this tendency in other members of your team.

RETAINING PEOPLE

The keys to running a successful sales team are providing motivation and recognizing success. Be aware of levels of satisfaction among your team. The best salespeople differ from the worst in their reasons for leaving a company. The champion sellers are most demotivated by bureaucratic restraints on their activity. The low performers put reward first and restraints bother them least. Having unnecessary controls is a poor reason for losing your best sellers.

TOP REASONS WHY STAFF LEAVE

TOP PERFORMERS	POOR PERFORMERS
1 Excessive restrictions	1 Inadequate rewards
2 Dissatisfaction with job	2 Lack of prospects
3 Lack of prospects	3 Dissatisfaction with job
4 Inadequate rewards	4 Relations at work
5 Relations at work	5 Excessive restrictions

▼ PROMOTING A TEAM APPROACH

Encourage all departments to exchange information constantly. This will improve each department's understanding of the business as a whole and create a more competitive workforce.

HARMONIZING TEAMS

Your sales teams should work closely with marketing, customer services, and product manufacturing departments. Ensure a flow of information between departments at all times. This will instantly create a competitive advantage. High-level selling, for example, may be hogged by the marketing staff, but this kind of clannish departmental thinking is as counterproductive as having too many people calling on the same customer.

SALES

MARKETING

MANUFACTURING

CUSTOMER SERVICES

TRAINING YOUR TEAM

Make use of the fact that training works more effectively in sales than most other areas of business. Listen to and learn from the best experts, engage them to speak directly to your team if possible, and allocate sufficient time to training needs.

78 Take notes of what the experts teach, and refer to the notes regularly.

QUESTIONS TO ASK YOURSELF

Q Does the team need to know more about the company's products and services?

Q Do they have a high enough level of technical knowledge?

Q Does the team need to know more about the marketplace?

Q Would performance improve with general sales training?

Q Should training be in-house or out-of-house?

BROADENING KNOWLEDGE

Salespeople are, unfortunately, often treated as technicians who require only sales techniques and product knowledge. Send your salespeople on courses on general business principles and practices to help both them and the customer. The salesperson will better understand the customer's financial needs, for example, and the needs of his or her own company. Such training will also enable the development of more effective lists of high-probability potential customers. Basic knowledge of marketing, additionally, will align the salespeople's message to that of the company's promotional activities.

CASE STUDY

John was the team's new sales manager in a company whose practice it was to fire each month's bottom performer. When that happened to Alan, he complained to John that even Jane, the top performer, would do no better in his difficult territory. The sales manager realized that Alan would benefit from on-the-job training and coaching. John sent Jane to the area and she accompanied Alan on the calls, observed his mistakes, told him how to correct the errors, and continued to train him until Alan eventually topped the league. As sales manager, John responded by pairing all the underperformers with top performers to achieve similar results. The aces were trained in teaching, and the incentives were altered to reward team success as well as individual performance. John's team rapidly improved until it outperformed all other teams.

◀ TRAINING IN TEAMS

The sales manager in this case could have easily continued with the crude system the firm used to motivate sales teams. Instead, he listened to an objection, and found a superior system built on training and coaching within teams.

79 Try to engage the experts you respect most.

▼ **FORMAL TRAINING**
An expert trainer covers a wide range of topics according to the needs of the group. Ideally, the trainer will also be an experienced sales manager.

USING THE EXPERTS

The extent of expertise available in sales training is greater than in any other field of management, partly because so much training is carried out, and partly because it is eminently practical. Professional expertise can be acquired either in person or in recorded form for the reinforcement and expansion of internal training. It may seem costly, but it will pay for itself in improved company-wide performance. Learn how to train other people yourself, as sales managers should be excellent trainers as well.

Salespeople pick up training skills as they learn

Expert entertains with vivid rules of thumb and advice

80 Teach all salespeople business finance principles, no matter how unfamiliar they may be with money matters.

81 Keep your team's technical knowledge right up to date.

USING ROLE PLAYING

The chief value of role playing, with the participants alternating in the roles of buyer and seller, is to train people to recognize and handle a variety of reactions. Different kinds of buyer will react differently: some types will always be eager to buy; others will be almost impossible to sell to. A key issue is how realistic you or your team members are about what your performances can achieve. Buyers can be divided into easily recognizable types (aggressive or suspicious, for example). Acting out how to handle each of the types ensures that selling opportunities are not misread and that time is not wasted.

82 List those who require coaching, and provide suitable training.

83 Make role-playing as realistic as you can for maximum effectiveness.

Salesperson

Hostile customer

Interested customer

Salesperson

▲ **REVERSING ROLES**
Acting out different selling scenarios is an enjoyable method of training. Encourage people to explore a variety of customer responses by reversing the roles each person plays.

ACTING AS COACH

You cannot teach sales skills solely in the classroom. The coach, or mentor, has to accompany the salesperson into the field, taking care to leave the sale to the person being coached. It should go without saying that a manager's coaching skills are just as important as his or her other sales skills. Enhanced coaching abilities will actually improve these other skills. The well-versed coach knows how to concentrate on one skill at a time, and does not use team coaching as a substitute for individual mentoring.

84 Let the salesperson take the glory. It brushes off on you.

▼ **MONITORING PROGRESS**
Constantly monitor performance after training. Give regular feedback to staff to avoid the development of bad habits.

POINTS TO REMEMBER

- Constructive demonstrations of different selling scenarios can be made a part of training.
- The temptation to interfere in a training sale must be resisted.
- The defects of trainees should not be harshly criticized.
- Good progress should be observed and faults noted.
- Anything that has been done well should always be praised.

Salesperson learns from constructive advice

Manager gives feedback

USING ▶ COACHING
As this example shows, it is worth making coaching an integral part of working in a team, allocating regular time to it. Combined with an organized approach to planning the working day, coaching can improve the skills and productivity of the whole team.

CASE STUDY
George took over a sales operation that was seriously underperforming, even though the salespeople were well-trained and enthusiastic. He analyzed the sales records and discovered that the morning hours were the most productive for sales, but were used for daily meetings. He also found that one major distinction of the top sellers lay in their use of the telephone to find new customers ("cold calling"). All training and sales meetings were moved to the afternoons and mornings were used for work with coaches. George paired high-achievers and low-performers to coach the latter in the best methods, stopping them, for instance, from apologizing for taking somebody's time; the product was valuable "so he should be thanking you." The results improved dramatically.

MANAGING SALES CALLS

The times of the day when customers can be telephoned are times for selling. Sales calls must always be put above non-sales activities, such as reporting customer contacts and administration. The calls must be planned and their effectiveness measured.

85 Analyze the success of sales calls continuously.

TARGETING THE CALLS

An increase in sales calls should result in more orders, but you have to target your calls to make them effective. Trying to sell vacuum cleaners to people who already own them, for example, will not sell more of them. With large contracts, a team will make fewer calls because of the greater complexity of the orders. In such cases, pushing for an increase in calls may be asking for failure. Always ask the question "What is the ratio of orders to telephone calls?" to monitor the effectiveness of calls.

Add up the number of calls made

⬇

Work out the average length of each call

⬇

Work out the percentage of calls that turn into sales

⬇

Calculate the average value of each sale

⬇

Use these figures to monitor the efficiency of your calls

FOCUSING ▶ ON RESULTS
Call management is important for control of sales, but only if it is coupled with close focus on delivered results. Ensure that team members monitor their calls and report the results to you.

Team member records length and outcome of call

▲ CALCULATING SUCCESS RATES
Calculate call success rates to minimize wasted time on unsuccessful calls.

86 Focus on how many calls result in sales, not on how much time is spent on the calls.

MEASURING TEAM EFFECTIVENESS

The ratio of orders to calls will vary widely within most sales teams. The worst performer may need to make three times more calls than the best. You will also find discrepancies between teams and departments. Such findings enable you to improve the performance of tail-enders until their allocated time is used better. You should be able to raise the average ratio substantially by transferring the successful habits and methods of top performers to those of underperformers. Achieve this by allowing less successful callers to sit with top performers while calls are made.

SOLVING PROBLEMS

Both managers and salespeople must manage their call times effectively. Activities that seem highly commendable, such as trouble-shooting, may divert managers from their prime duty of maximizing overall customer calling performance. A problem sale may benefit from intervention, but if a manager dashes to every trouble spot, time will be swallowed up or wasted. Treat each difficulty on its merits. Only handle particularly problematic issues, and always consider whether the salesperson – perhaps with some advice – can handle it alone. If so, the experience gained will benefit both the company and the individual.

87 Use your most successful callers to coach weak performers.

88 Resist the urge to interfere or take over every time problems appear.

89 Assume that salespeople can handle problems with minimal help from you.

DO'S AND DON'TS

✔ Do watch closely the call-order ratio.

✔ Do analyze the results of top performers.

✔ Do allow enough time for essential non-sales activities.

✘ Don't push for more calls without a clear objective.

✘ Don't treat tail-end performers as no good.

✘ Don't feel you have to solve all problems.

PROVIDING REWARDS AND FIXING TARGETS

You may pay your sales team a basic salary, or offer commission or bonuses tied to sales targets. Linking the right payment or incentive to the right target is difficult, but your careful consideration of the link is crucial to your staff's motivation.

90 Keep payments and incentive systems simple and transparent.

91 Make targets ambitious, but keep them within reasonable reach.

BALANCING PAYMENTS

The usual form of payment based on results (PBR) is individual commission, although some companies reward salespeople with salary alone. It is impossible to say which method works best because each has disadvantages. Salary-only provides no reward for exceptional effort, but 100 percent commission provides no security and great fluctuations in earnings. The best schemes combine elements of basic salary, commission, and group rewards.

Salesperson is rewarded for exceptional effort

Manager pays a basic salary plus special bonus

▼ **GETTING THE RIGHT BALANCE**
Combine basic salaries with commissions and group rewards to provide security with added incentives for outstanding performance.

Provide basic pay to cover normal needs	→	Add commission for exceptional success	→	Complete pay with group incentives

▲ ELEMENTS OF PAY

Group incentives provide significant extra income for the salesperson. Individual commission provides sufficient extra funds to retain and encourage top performers. Basic pay covers normal personal needs.

SETTING TARGETS

In most companies, salespeople are subject to PBR and targets to a far greater extent than other employees. How you set targets is important, since it determines when commissions are triggered. Involve salespeople in setting all targets – whether standard targets or "super" targets for extra incentives – to establish a logical payment system. This ensures that all targets are set within the upper ranges of possibility and are related to market realities. If this produces a shortfall against goals, then take other actions to fill the gap. Never confuse targets with budgets. A budget is based on what is most likely to happen, while targets are designed to improve on the budget.

92 Involve your sales team in setting realistic targets.

93 Minimize changes to your target schemes. Targets need revising, but too many changes will confuse and demotivate the salesforce.

REVISING TARGETS

Give exceptional rewards only for exceptional performance. If a promotion campaign has already been paid for by the company, do not pay for it twice in undeserved commissions. Target payments have to be revised to recognize changes, to reflect competitive reward structures, and to refresh motivation. Too many and too frequent changes, however, destabilize the salesforce and divert managers' attention. Above all, keep targets and related incentive elements simple and sensible. Many schemes, for example, have a sliding scale for individual rewards that rises to "super" target levels. This can have damaging consequences. For example, salespeople may be encouraged to give away expensive discounts to clinch the "super" sale target.

RECOGNIZING ACHIEVEMENTS

Ensure that you have effective and accurate measures for monitoring the performance of your team. Watch for early indications of success and failure, and provide a solid basis for rewards and incentives.

94 Keep incentive schemes under constant review.

95 Put actual profits above volume for effective incentives.

USING INCENTIVE SCHEMES

Commissions and bonuses in many companies are supplemented by reward schemes using incentives ranging from Caribbean cruises and weekends in sports cars to membership of select "super-sales" clubs. These schemes work well as morale-boosters, but they do not serve as a substitute for proper organization, training, coaching, or daily management of the salesforce. Regard and treat the incentives as additions only.

MONITORING SUCCESS

Regular checks on sales performance are essential to success, and as sales manager you are responsible for ensuring that these are carried out effectively. You should be constantly aware of several success factors, including market position and realized profits – not just sales volume. The overall objective of sales activities is to achieve optimum revenue and profit while strengthening the competitive position. Thanks to computers, this objective can be monitored more readily and efficiently than before on a daily basis. Once you have identified any gaps between targets and performance, you can initiate corrective actions.

CHECKING PERFORMANCE

For maximum profits and competitive strength, constantly monitor these success factors:
- Realized prices;
- Gross profit margins;
- Company market share;
- Selling costs as a proportion of company income;
- The number of successful sales made by your team.

AVOIDING UNFAIRNESS

The immediate results of salespeople's efforts are visible and measurable. They can point instantly to their successes, but equally they can be blamed for failures. Some companies automatically fire those who miss their quotas. Others fire the unfortunate who comes bottom of their monthly sales league. Both approaches are counterproductive. The prospect of dismissal is intended to motivate, but in reality it achieves the opposite effect. The policy is seen as unfair, and morale is lowered. You should be interested solely in raising the results of the whole team, partly by helping its weaker members.

96 Treat your sales staff as people who can always perform better.

REWARDING SUCCESS

The stick with which "failures" are penalized is usually combined with the carrot – the offer of monetary rewards. Judge performance by measuring customer satisfaction as well as sales volume. Financial rewards and incentives are effective motivators, but are not the only necessary responses to success. People need to feel that their achievements have been recognized. Tell your team how much you appreciate their efforts, and single out the top performers for special praise.

97 Make a public fuss over those who produce excellent results – both one-offs and multiple sales.

DEALING WITH FAILURE

Successes will be accompanied by some failures, which require equally careful analysis. Remember that failure can stem from three main causes:

● The wrong customers were targeted – businesses who are not in the market for your products;
● The customer was right, but the product or service was wrong;
● The salesperson mismanaged the sale.
Penalizing failure only makes any kind of sense in the third set of circumstances. You still need to know, however, why the selling failed.

QUESTIONS TO ASK YOURSELF

Q Was the failure due to lack of selling skills?

Q Was it due to lack of product knowledge?

Q Could knowledge of the customer be lacking?

Q Were any personal problems to blame?

Q Is the salesperson totally unsuitable for selling?

HOLDING SALES MEETINGS

Meetings, conferences, and seminars are valuable for building team spirit, celebrating success, reporting on progress, developing customer relations, and unveiling new plans. Meetings will be most effective if they allow for feedback from the sales teams.

98 Review the annual conference in detail, and always apply the lessons.

99 Ensure that communications can be two-way.

100 Make the team a reality, not just a word that means little to anybody.

BOOSTING MORALE

The mood of a sales meeting will be affected by the latest sales performances, be they acceptable or poor. Whatever the case, do not make the meetings punitive. Constructive criticism, coupled with an objective analysis of the causes of failures, can motivate salespeople and stimulate the desire to do better. However, the goals of achievement, recognition, and reward are more important. Place emphasis on the future, in particular, to boost morale. Make people feel they are part of a team that, despite inevitable and avoidable disappointments, is a real, long-term winner.

CASE STUDY

Anna, who was in charge of a sales operation in the US, regularly received messages from her UK head office berating her for missing her quarterly sales forecasts. If she lowered her forecasts, the pressure became greater still. Anna called her salespeople to an emergency meeting to seek a solution. The teams decided to try pulling in more business for the following three months. After that time, though, they faced even more pressure. The sales force agreed with Anna that the quarterly emphasis made no sense in an industry with a three-year selling cycle, and it was stopping them from winning new accounts. They all agreed that they should shift the emphasis toward three-year plans, broken down into annual targets. Head office accepted the idea, new business flowed in, and the pressure on Anna subsided.

◀ **THE POWER OF MEETINGS**
Anna had a problem stemming from the company's head office. However, by meeting with her sales staff and encouraging them to work together to solve the problem as a team, Anna was able to develop a local solution that met the needs of head office.

HOLDING ANNUAL CONFERENCES

The internal sales conference is often an annual affair, primarily designed to build morale and motivation by celebration and exhortation, and not by specific development of the sales force.

There may be guest speakers – a management guru or a sports personality – but the focus is mostly on rewards. This approach often wastes the invaluable opportunities presented by having all the salespeople together at the same time. Always have clear business objectives, and plan the event around training needs, reaching targets, and giving people a sense of moving forward as part of a dynamic, successful team.

INVOLVING CUSTOMERS

Persuading customers to attend a sales seminar or conference is an excellent method of building the confidence of the salesforce. Your company has the opportunity to associate itself with an authoritative presentation on an important subject (a telecommunications company hosting a seminar on the use of the Internet is one example). Your salespeople can mingle with their customers. Careful choice of speakers will inevitably encourage customers to consider your products and services as first choices. Too hard a sales message, however, will defeat the purpose. That can be left until after the event when you make the necessary follow-up calls.

▼ RALLYING THE TEAM
Selling is a social activity, but the socializing must be wedded to very clear business purposes and planned to enable the realization of those aims.

| 101 | Use your seminar as an opportunity to boost customer confidence in your company. |

ASSESSING YOUR SKILLS

*S*elling is the foundation of success in many areas of management. Your sales skills need to be kept strong and up to date by practising and learning. This questionnaire will test the quality of your present performance as a salesperson and show you where you need to improve. To assess your sales skills, add the scores together and refer to the Analysis. If your answer is "never", mark Option 1; if it is "always", mark Option 4, and so on. Use your answers to identify the areas that need most improvement.

OPTIONS
1 Never
2 Occasionally
3 Frequently
4 Always

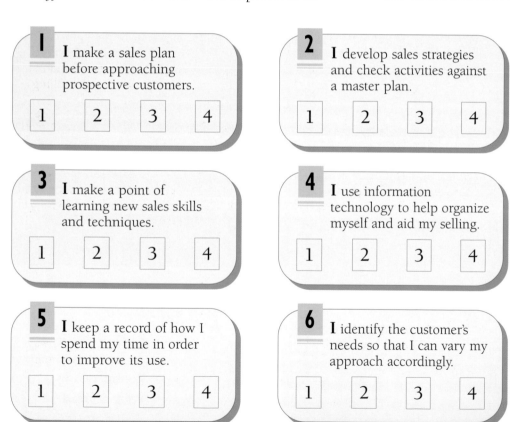

1 I make a sales plan before approaching prospective customers.

  1   2   3   4

2 I develop sales strategies and check activities against a master plan.

  1   2   3   4

3 I make a point of learning new sales skills and techniques.

  1   2   3   4

4 I use information technology to help organize myself and aid my selling.

  1   2   3   4

5 I keep a record of how I spend my time in order to improve its use.

  1   2   3   4

6 I identify the customer's needs so that I can vary my approach accordingly.

  1   2   3   4

7 I prepare myself carefully before going into a sales meeting or interview.

1 2 3 4

8 I approach companies knowing exactly who is the right person to contact.

1 2 3 4

9 I use research to build my knowledge of the industry and the customers.

1 2 3 4

10 I keep meetings with customers friendly, brisk, and focused.

1 2 3 4

11 I know and use the best techniques for getting sales results by telephone.

1 2 3 4

12 I take great care over my letter-writing and develop writing skills to aid selling.

1 2 3 4

13 I put myself in the customer's shoes when preparing for negotiations.

1 2 3 4

14 I end sales presentations on a positive note, inviting a definite action.

1 2 3 4

15 I ask for feedback on my presentations so that I can improve my effectiveness.

1 2 3 4

16 I adapt my selling approach to match the way the customer reacts to me.

1 2 3 4

17 I tell the truth, even if the truth is not what I want the customer to hear.

1   2   3   4

18 I search for the key sales point that will persuade customers to buy.

1   2   3   4

19 I endeavor to get the other party to name their price objectives first.

1   2   3   4

20 I stress value for money in negotiations, rather than price alone.

1   2   3   4

21 When I complete a sale, both sides are satisfied with the deal.

1   2   3   4

22 I try to anticipate any objections the customer may present to me.

1   2   3   4

23 I respond quickly to inquiries or complaints from any customer.

1   2   3   4

24 I get feedback to ensure that my customers are very satisfied with the purchase.

1   2   3   4

25 I keep other salespeople free from bureaucratic restrictions.

1   2   3   4

26 I use teaching methods to develop my own skills and improve those of others.

1   2   3   4

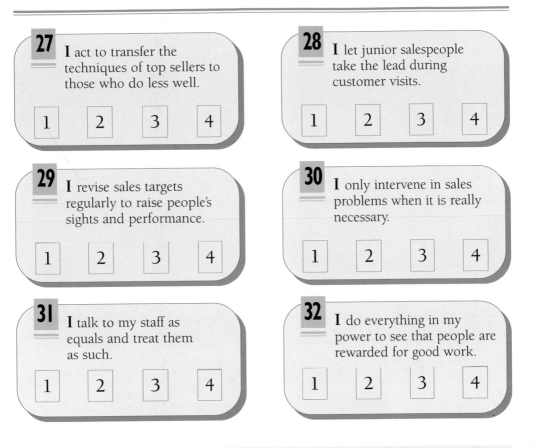

27 I act to transfer the techniques of top sellers to those who do less well.

1   2   3   4

28 I let junior salespeople take the lead during customer visits.

1   2   3   4

29 I revise sales targets regularly to raise people's sights and performance.

1   2   3   4

30 I only intervene in sales problems when it is really necessary.

1   2   3   4

31 I talk to my staff as equals and treat them as such.

1   2   3   4

32 I do everything in my power to see that people are rewarded for good work.

1   2   3   4

ANALYSIS

Now you have completed the self-assessment, add up your total score and check your performance by reading the corresponding evaluation.

32–63: Your lack of sales skills and good practice must be affecting your performance and, possibly, putting your job at risk. Begin at once to master the lessons in this book, and apply them in the office and the field.

64–95: You have made considerable progress and are probably performing well, but you have not raised your sights high enough. Make renewed efforts to improve in the weaker areas revealed by your assessment answers, and continue until your scores take you to the next level.

96–128: You are a skilled and effective salesperson. Continue working to improve your abilities, however, to stay at the top.

MARKETING EFFECTIVELY

INTRODUCTION

M arketing is an essential business
discipline, and its vital contribution to
the success of an organization is widely
recognized. Successful marketing results in
stronger products, happier customers, and
bigger profits. Whether the whole marketing
function within your business is your
responsibility, or whether it is a peripheral
activity, Marketing Effectively will show you
how to take a strategic approach to the task.
Stay on course with helpful hints, advice, and
information and evaluate your skills with a
self-assessment exercise. Covering basic
concepts such as the marketing mix, essential
skills including direct mail, and the
fundamentals of marketing strategy, this
book is an invaluable guide to improving
your marketing performance.

PUTTING
CUSTOMERS FIRST

Marketing is key to the success of any business and must be customer-driven in order to be effective. Make customers your prime focus and reap the rewards.

UNDERSTANDING MARKETING

Marketing is often confused with publicity and promotion, but these are just part of the discipline. Understand all the components of marketing, particularly the central role that customers play, and you will be a step closer to business success.

> **1** Design your whole business around your customers' needs.

> **2** Gather as much information as possible on the requirements of potential new customers.

DEFINING MARKETING

Effective marketing is often described as "making what you can sell, not selling what you can make". Organizations that sell what they can make are product-led: they make the product first, consider customers afterwards, and see marketing simply as a means of persuading customers to buy. The most successful organizations make what they can sell. They are customer-led, creating products and services in response to customer need.

630

TAKING MARKETING SERIOUSLY

Focus on every aspect of marketing, not just on promotion and sales techniques, to persuade customers to buy. By taking the discipline seriously and acknowledging its influence, you will reap all the benefits that effective marketing has to offer: satisfied, loyal customers, a growing customer base, popular and successful products, increased turnover, more recommendations and repeat business, as well as fewer complaints. The end result of all this is bigger profits, which is one of the most powerful reasons for improving marketing performance. You are also far more likely to enjoy overall business success, and be the envy of your competitors.

FOCUSING ON CUSTOMERS
Research is conducted into customers' wants
Product or service is designed to meet need
Product or service is made public
Customers buy product or service
Product or service meets customers' need
Customers buy product or service again

3 Try to develop an outward-looking approach to marketing, as opposed to an insular one.

IDENTIFYING MARKETING COMPANY TYPES

TYPE OF COMPANY	CHARACTERISTICS
FOREFRONTER Consistently anticipates customers' needs and gets its products to the market first.	Innovative and proactive. This type of organization truly understands marketing. It invests in research and product development and devises innovative solutions.
FOLLOWER Dislikes taking risks. Prefers to play it safe and see which way the market will go before deciding whether to take any action.	Lacks pioneering spirit. This type of company might attain success, but its attitude will always limit achievement. A more proactive approach would improve marketing success.
FOSSIL Has always conducted business in the same way and sees no reason to change.	Conservative, insular, and complacent. Such organizations need to develop a more outward focus. Activity must be driven by customer need, not company habit and tradition.

ANALYZING THE MARKETING MIX

The marketing mix is a very simple and successful recipe to follow. Blend its key ingredients – product, price, place, and promotion – in the correct proportions, and you will reap the many benefits of effective, strategic marketing.

4 Look at each element of the mix and determine its importance.

5 Create the right balance between price and quality.

6 Concentrate your efforts on the key elements of the mix.

UNDERSTANDING THE MIX

The marketing mix of product, price, place, and promotion is known as the "Four Ps." Marketing involves developing the right product (one that meets customer need); setting the right price (one that delivers a profit and keeps customers happy); getting the product to the right place (where customers can buy it); and promoting it (to encourage customers to buy it). The ingredients of the mix are the same for all organizations, only quantities vary. Where customers are price-conscious, for example, price dominates the mix and setting the right price is vital.

COMPARING ▶ DIFFERENT MIXES

Two hotels can have very different marketing mixes. For a five-star hotel, product (excellent restaurant, health club facilities, and superior rooms) is the principal ingredient of the mix. Guests expect luxury and accept that they must pay a price for it. For a budget hotel, cost is paramount. Its customers want to be able to stay at an affordable price.

FIVE-STAR HOTEL   BUDGET HOTEL

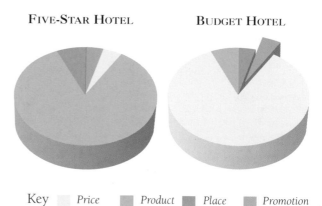

Key ▪ Price   ▪ Product   ▪ Place   ▪ Promotion

EXAMINING PROPORTIONS

Devise the right marketing mix, and you will maximize profits. Focus on each element of the mix to determine its importance to your business. Remember that the mix is not static; the perfect proportions today may not produce the desired results next year, or even next week. From time to time you will need to vary the recipe, by reducing prices during quiet periods, for example. There is an interrelationship between the four ingredients of the mix. If a product's price is high, customers will have high expectations. If advertising and promotional activity are significant, these costs will have to be recouped in the price.

7 Re-examine your marketing mix from time to time.

8 Compare your mix to that of your competitors.

CREATING THE RIGHT MARKETING MIX

KEY ELEMENTS	FACTORS TO CONSIDER
PRODUCT OR SERVICE Bought by customers to meet a need. The need may be practical (to get rid of stains), emotional (to feel good), or basic (to satisfy hunger).	● Products and services usually fulfill a number of needs, and it is important to identify which ones your products and services satisify. ● A product or service may satisfy a need that consumers did not even realize they had.
PRICE A crucial part of the mix, the price must be right if customers are to buy a product in sufficient quantities to ensure a profit.	● The right price for quality goods is a fair one. Price and quality must be balanced successfully. ● Fair does not necessarily mean cheap – set the price of a product too low, and customers may assume that its quality is inferior.
PLACE The "bridge" connecting customers and products, such as a wholesaler, retail outlet, or other distribution system.	● For some niche businesses, place is not an issue – enthusiasts and collectors, for example, are willing to travel long distances to shop. ● The internet provides a new mechanism for bringing customers and company together.
PROMOTION Promotional activity, such as advertising and direct mail, that informs customers what you have to offer and persuades them to buy.	● For most enterprises, promotional activity is essential for attracting customers. ● For businesses that rely on passing trade, promotion is less important, since the right location and products will ensure success.

SETTING THE RIGHT PRICE

Price is the most flexible element of the marketing mix, since you can change it quickly and easily. But your profits depend on getting it right. Selling at low prices means tight profit margins and an over-reliance on high sales volume. A downturn in your market can put you out of business. There is no fixed link between price and cost: you can raise prices even if your costs have not increased, and lower them without a cost decrease. Monitor competitors' prices so that you know exactly what is happening in the marketplace, and aim to understand what your competitors' strategies are. Then develop your own pricing strategy. Supply and demand will inevitably affect what you can charge, but aim at a Goldilocks pricing strategy: not too cheap, not too expensive, but just right.

POINTS TO REMEMBER

- Low price is often equated with low quality. Customers might prefer to pay more for an identical product because they are convinced that it is better than a cheaper one.

- Customers do not buy a product simply because it is cheap; they buy because of need. However inexpensive your lawnmowers, you will not sell one to someone without a garden.

- Customers can be less "price aware" than you might expect. Test to see. Find out more about your customers' buying habits and whether they shop around for the best price.

9 Make sure you know what price your competitors are charging.

10 Employ market research to find out how you are perceived by your clients.

SELLING ON VALUE

Consider selling on value rather than price. Price-based sales pitches attract price-sensitive customers who are already in the market for what you are selling. A value-based pitch can woo customers who did not realize they needed your product. For example, a £300 mattress will appeal to customers who are looking for a new mattress at a good price. A mattress guaranteed to ease back pain will open up a new market by appealing to bad back sufferers who were not even considering such a purchase.

QUESTIONS TO ASK YOURSELF

Q What is the value of our offering in terms of saving customers time and effort?

Q Are we demonstrating that a purchase is not a cost but a good investment?

Q Is our offering giving value by enhancing beauty or status?

Q Have we asked what customers most value about our products?

FITTING PR INTO THE MIX

Public relations (PR) is often regarded as the fifth "P" of the marketing mix, standing for perception. A good image is a prerequisite for successful marketing. An attractive product at the right price will not guarantee a sale. Customers do not like to buy from companies with poor reputations. Use PR techniques to enhance your image and shape positive customer perceptions. Consider ways of boosting your image: perhaps your organization could support or sponsor a charity, a worthwhile cause, or local venture, for example. Take the opportunity to build a strong profile by publicizing your achievements in the media.

11 Involve PR staff in marketing decision-making.

12 Use research rather than gut feeling to assess customers' needs.

CREATING THE RIGHT IMAGE

Look at the various aspects of your business that customers use to form their view of you. These might include your premises, the telephone manner of staff, and your publicity materials. Examine each of them in detail and work out what kind of image is being conveyed to your customers. Is that the image you want to put across? If not, draw up a plan of action for bringing your desired image into line with your actual image.

◀ CONVEYING A GOOD IMAGE

Attractive physical surroundings, committed staff, and well thought-out procedures are all important in conveying a caring and friendly image and giving an organization an edge over its competitors.

GETTING TO KNOW YOUR CUSTOMERS

Good customer information is key to boosting profit, so it is vital to build up a clear picture of who your customers are. Watch them, talk to them, ask them questions, and find out all that you can in order to give them what they want and keep them happy.

13 Avoid gathering facts for the sake of it – look only for what you can use.

14 Collect information on an ongoing basis by asking new customers a few marketing questions.

COLLECTING DATA

Many organizations have huge customer bases, but it is those who respond to customers' needs to be treated as individuals who are most likely to succeed. By collecting and processing customer data to produce a customer profile and identify customer segments, you can tailor-make products and services for particular groups of key customers. Meet identified customer need and you will sell more products and lose fewer customers. A better understanding of your customers will also enable you to target publicity more accurately.

PROFILING CUSTOMERS

A customer profile provides a picture of your typical customer. Some companies require an in-depth profile, detailing sex, age, income, lifestyle, address and type of housing, number of children, and so on. For others, a simpler profile will suffice. Decide which common characteristics it would be useful to look for in your customers. Business-to-business organizations, for example, may wish to analyze factors such as company size, vehicle fleet size, turnover, and location. Identify the kind of data you need, then plan how to uncover it.

QUESTIONS TO ASK YOURSELF

Q What age groups are our customers in, and what is the male/female split?

Q Where do our customers live, and do they travel far to buy?

Q Do they make onetime purchases, or is there an on-going relationship?

Q How much do they spend each month/year?

IDENTIFYING SOURCES OF INFORMATION

SOURCE	FACTORS TO CONSIDER
COMPANY RESOURCES Includes invoices, dispatch notes, mailing lists, and sales statistics.	Existing information can often provide valuable marketing data, such as size of purchase, date of last purchase, and geographic location of customers.
CUSTOMER INTERACTION Includes face-to-face surveys and focus groups.	A good way of eliciting qualitative information about your customers' motivations. Explain that their insights will help you to develop products and services to meet their needs.
CUSTOMER FEEDBACK Includes comment cards and feedback via your website.	Create as many channels as possible for customers to give you their views. Ask what they think about your products and services, but also seek relevant data about them.
STATUTORY BODIES Regulatory bodies holding data on company performance and finances.	Use statutory sources of information to build a company profile of your typical customer based on factors such as size or turnover. Use this data to target similar companies.

SEGMENTING CUSTOMERS

Break your customer base into segments. You may have low-value regular or occasional customers, or high-value regular or occasional customers. Identify your principal segments and target marketing activity accordingly. High-value customers, for example, may merit more attention, while loyalty programs or discounts may persuade low-value customers to buy more and more often.

15 Turn low-value occasional clients into high-value regular ones.

USING THE INFORMATION

Influence your marketing decisions with profiling and segmentation. A profiling exercise might reveal that products aimed at one group are actually bought by another. If a men's underwear company finds that 75 percent of its customers are female, this suggests that men leave their underwear buying to mothers, wives, and girlfriends. In such a case, use mailshots and other advertising to target women, not men.

16 Identify which factors will help you target new customers.

UNDERSTANDING CUSTOMER BUYING

F ind the key to why customers buy and you have unlocked the secret of how to sell to them. Discover what your customers buy, how often, when, and why. Then use this important information to influence your marketing decisions.

 17 Emphasize your buying points in publicity and sales pitches.

18 Ensure that both buying and selling points coincide.

IDENTIFYING SELLING POINTS

A selling point is a powerful factor that you identify internally as helping to clinch a sale. To determine your strongest selling points, you must understand what a customer looks for when making a sale. This is known as a buying point. To ensure success, the points you highlight when selling should be the same factors that customers most value when buying. You may, for example, decide that being "established for a century" is a good selling point because your company takes pride in this. But your customers' key buying point is likely to be quite different.

◀ **ANALYZING BUYING**
In a large shopping mall, where stores compete for the same customers, those that promote customers' key buying points – such as good prices – as their selling points are more likely to succeed.

UNDERSTANDING THE BUYING PROCESS

KEY STAGES	CUSTOMER ACTION
RECOGNITION Becoming aware of a need.	Prospective customer realizes that something is required: more space at home, for example.
APPRAISAL Investigating what is available to fufil need.	Customer reads brochures, magazine articles, looks for information on price, durability, etc.
NEGOTIATION Approaching supplier of produce or service.	Having made a choice, customer asks supplier for quotations, looks at warranties, etc.
PURCHASE Buying preferred option.	A decision is made and the customer goes ahead with purchase.
RECOMMENDATION Commending product or service to others.	Customer evaluates the product and, if happy, recommends it to friends, colleagues, etc.

BEING ADAPTABLE

If your customer is a company, as opposed to an individual, bear in mind that its buying process will probably be very specific. This means that to succeed in selling to a company, particularly a business customer, you must understand what its buying process is and adapt your approach to suit. Ask the following questions:

- "Do you consult a list of approved suppliers? If so, how can we get on that list?"
- "Do you ask for tenders? If so, how can we get on the tender list?"
- "Do you always shop around for the best deal?"
- "Do you go by recommendation or use contacts?"
- "Do you always use the same supplier? What would persuade you to try a different one?"

Time spent getting to know how other people's customers buy is time invested in learning how to turn them into your own customers.

QUESTIONS TO ASK YOURSELF

Q How often do our customers buy?

Q What is the average transaction size?

Q Which payment methods do they use?

Q Which customers are most profitable?

Q Which customers are least profitable?

 19 When dealing with a company, find out who influences key buying decisions.

USING SURVEYS

Work out some reasons why customers might choose to buy goods or services from you, then use survey techniques to discover the facts. Ask customers to rank the factors you have identified in order of importance, as well as adding their own. Your list might include:

- quick or free delivery;
- competitive price;
- excellent after-sales support;
- easy payment terms;
- friendly staff.

Self-completion questionnaires are an excellent way of reaching customers quickly and cheaply.

20 Collate buying information as an ongoing task.

21 Set a deadline to encourage the return of mailed questionnaires.

MAKING THE MOST OF SURVEY TECHNIQUES

TECHNIQUE	USING IT EFFECTIVELY
MAILED QUESTIONNAIRE An excellent way of reaching a large number of geographically dispersed customers quickly and cheaply.	● Boost return rates by enclosing a stamped self-addressed envelope and use a follow-up mailing to encourage nonresponding customers. ● Make sure that questionnaires have an attractive layout and, above all, are easy to complete.
ONE-ON-ONE INTERVIEW Although time consuming, this is seen as the best type of survey and tends to elicit the best response rate.	● Look at location options carefully: would interviews in the street serve your purpose better than interviews in a hotel, or in your customers' homes or workplaces? ● Rapport is important, so ensure that interviewers explain the purpose and value of the survey.
CUSTOMER PANEL Comprises a group of your customers with a strong interest in your organization or products.	● Use customer panels as a sounding board for new ideas, and a source of valuable feedback. ● Ensure that panels retain their objectivity: if they become too integral a part of the organization's structure, customers can feel more like employees.
FOCUS GROUP A small discussion group led by a facilitator. Its aim is to uncover attitudes, motivations, and qualitative insights.	● Ensure that focus group members are representative of your customers and that the facilitator encourages them to add their input. ● Remember that, although structured, these should be less rigid than questionnaire-based interviews.

UNDERSTANDING MOTIVATION

Usually there will be a combination of several motivating factors to buy, not just one. Easy payment terms might prove to be the clinching factor, but friendliness of staff, or the availability of the product from stock, may also influence the decision to buy from you. It is important to learn what motivates your customers and find ways to build on this knowledge.

MOTIVATING FACTORS ▶

These three customers frequent the same bar, although their reasons for doing so are very different. Being able to identify the principal selling points allows for more effective marketing.

Phil is a regular because the bar serves an extensive range of quality French wines

Tracy uses the bar because it is convenient, just two minutes' walk from her office

Aziz travels some distance to the bar because it has a no-smoking policy

---

CALCULATING LIFETIME VALUE

Use a simple formula to calculate roughly what the average regular customer is worth to you during your relationship. You can then decide whether to treat high-value customers in a special way, for example by inviting them to special events. The example here shows that although the average sale is only $40, the customer is, in fact, worth $3,200 to the company.

A Value of average sale (divide annual sales in $s by number of transactions)	$40
B Number of transactions each regular customer makes annually	4
C Average number of years a customer buys from you	5
D Average number of referrals/recommendations a customer makes annually	3
E Sales per customer per year (A x B)	$160
F Sales per customer over a lifetime (E x C)	$800
G Potential gross sales from referrals (F x D)	$2,400
TOTAL VALUE OF CUSTOMER (F + G)	**$3,200**

BUILDING RELATIONSHIPS

Selling to existing customers is far cheaper and easier than finding new ones. Use marketing to nurture customer loyalty through good service and quality products, backed up by a strong, lasting, mutually rewarding relationship.

22 Examine every area of customer service and seek to improve it.

MONITORING FOR QUALITY OF SERVICE

Review all aspects of your working practices

⬇

Set measurable standards so that quality is not left to chance

⬇

Make sure that staff are trained to be able to meet standards

⬇

If necessary, issue staff with a customer service manual

⬇

Measure performance to check that quality is being attained

⬇

Review standards to keep improving customer care

DELIVERING SERVICE

Customers today expect first-class service, and rightly so. Think about how you felt when you last received poor service. Disappointed? Angry? Cheated? This is exactly how your customers feel when they experience similar treatment. Compare this with how you feel when you receive exceptional service. Remember that customers are not an irritation standing in the way of you and your work, they are your work. Without them you have no business. List areas where you feel that you can improve customer service. Look at how staff interact with customers, how orders are processed, and how correspondence is dealt with. Tackle each area for improvement in turn.

QUESTIONS TO ASK YOURSELF

Q Do we answer the phones quickly and courteously?

Q Are our staff neat, helpful, friendly, and knowledgeable?

Q Are our premises clean and comfortable?

Q Do we reply to mail promptly?

Q Do we provide good after-sales service?

Q How swiftly are orders processed?

Q Could we do more to eliminate ordering errors?

Q How many compliments or complaints do we receive?

TACKLING COMPLAINTS

Complaints should always be taken seriously. Some companies have found that customers who have complained, and have had their complaints dealt with to their satisfaction, are more loyal than customers who have never complained. This underlines the importance of handling complaints well. Devise a fair and efficient procedure, set timescales for responding to complaints, and never let a complaint drift on. If you are in the wrong, admit it, apologize, and, if necessary, compensate the customer. Learn from errors and revise procedures so that mistakes are not repeated.

23 Remember that an existing client is more valuable than a potential one.

24 Ask dissatisfied customers how you can win them back.

▼ RESOLVING COMPLAINTS

This illustration shows two outcomes following a customer complaint. When the case is handled badly, the customer not only feels poorly treated enough to take her business elsewhere, but discusses her bad experience with others. When prompt remedial action is taken, the customer feels that her business is valued. Fair, courteous treatment also helps to ensure her continued loyalty.

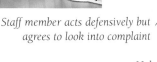

Staff member takes call from customer who complains that her order has been delivered late

Staff member apologizes and promises an immediate investigation

Offers to refund 50 percent of the invoiced amount

Customer feels satisfied with the way the complaint has been resolved and is happy to leave her business where it is

Puts complaint to one side and forgets all about it

Staff member acts defensively but agrees to look into complaint

Unhappy customer tells everyone about the poor service she has received and takes her business elsewhere

KEEPING IN TOUCH

When a customer places an order, it is not the end of selling, it is just the beginning. Turn that onetime purchase into repeat sales by developing a relationship with your customers. Relationships do not sustain themselves. They take effort, and all the responsibility lies with you. Your customer may not even want a relationship. You have to take the initiative, not them. Find ways to remind customers that you are there. Tell them when their maintenance contract is due for renewal, offer them upgrades, invite them to exclusive previews, give them special discounts, and make sure they are among the first to hear about new developments. Devise valid reasons for communicating and so keep your company's products or services fresh in their minds.

THINGS TO DO

1. Call customers with news and developments.
2. If you cannot get in touch with customers by phone, send an email.
3. Drop in on business clients, if necessary, having checked first that your visit will be convenient for them.
4. Devise new ways of keeping customers informed of special offers or events, sales, and improvements in service.

25 Maintain healthy relationships with customers by being helpful and pleasant at all times.

▼ USING CUSTOMER CONTACT CARDS
Sustain relationships by mapping out planned customer contact. Keep records of the contact made with each customer, any follow-up required, and the outcome.

Customer contact card

Customer name: Thelma Driver, Trepark Limited

Due	Action	Completed	Outcome
April 21st	Call to check that new system is working well	✔	System working well. Agreed to meet for lunch
May 3rd	Call to arrange date for lunch	✔	Met and discussed new projects. Have promised to send free tickets to the next trade exhibition
July 16th	Send complimentary tickets to the trade exhibition	✔	Thelma visited trade exhibition with Trevor James, a friend from Davis Company. Have added Trevor's details to mailing list
August 20th	Send copy of customer newsletter	✔	

TESTING THE STRENGTH OF RELATIONSHIPS

There are two tests of a relationship's strength: is a customer satisfied enough to remain loyal?, and is a customer happy to recommend you to others? Find out by asking them. A good way to elicit honest answers is to use a questionnaire, or try an after-sales phone call to customers. Some companies ask these questions on the product warranty registration card. If customers plan to use a different company next time, or are unwilling to recommend you, discover why.

26 Thank people for their business to make them feel valued – the human touch can make all the difference.

NURTURING LOYALTY

Customers need a reason to remain loyal. They may expect more than simply excellent products or services. How do your competitors nurture customer loyalty? Could you introduce ways to show customers actively how much you value their business? Loyalty or reward programs have been proven to work for many businesses. Give people a card that records their business with you. After a number of transactions, or after reaching a certain total, they can qualify for special treatment, free gifts, discounts, or other perks. In a competitive market, where customers tend to shop around for the best deal, a voucher offering a reduction off their next order can help attract repeat business. A discount that escalates with each order, while still making a profit for you, might make you irresistible to otherwise fickle customers.

ADVOCATE

If really happy, client becomes an advocate who recommends you to others

CLIENT

If happy, the customer makes repeat purchases and becomes a regular client

CUSTOMER

New customer makes a onetime purchase

PROSPECT

Prospective customer is considering buying, possibly from you, or possibly from a rival

TARGET

Target customer receives information (advertising, sales visit, or other)

UNKNOWN

Unknown customer is not familiar with your company or products

▲ MOVING PEOPLE UP THE LOYALTY LADDER

Successful marketing can turn a casual customer into a committed advocate of your company. Aim to advance everyone to the top of the loyalty ladder.

WINNING NEW CUSTOMERS

Customer loss is inevitable: people move, change jobs, and, of course, they die. Losses may be gradual and easy to overlook, but the effects are cumulative. Maintain a thriving business by finding new customers faster than you lose them.

27 Consider setting up a special introductory offer for new customers.

28 Provide incentives to your sales team to help them improve their overall selling performances.

UNDERSTANDING CUSTOMER LOSS

You are sure to be losing some customers, even if you have a full order book. But is this due to natural loss, or could you be driving customers away? Contact former customers and ask them. If losses are due to your own underperformance, take action to correct it. If your traditional customer base appears to be a dying breed, your business is heading for terminal decline. The only cure is to find a new market and possibly also to develop new products or services. Replacing customers is an endless task, but an essential one.

FINDING NEW BUSINESS

It is vital to go out and find customers, since they cannot be relied upon to come to you. Plan how you are going to win new business. Follow up all leads and get in touch with people who have made an inquiry or requested information. Contact former customers in a bid to win them back. Identify potential customers and let them know how you can help. Approach competitors' customers and make them a better offer. Review your publicity strategy to see if there is a better way of reaching potential customers. Would cold calling or a direct mail campaign be useful in attracting new business?

QUESTIONS TO ASK YOURSELF

- Do we know how many customers we lose?
- Do we know the reasons why customers desert us?
- Are there any compelling reasons why customers should remain loyal to us?
- How do we show our customers that we value them and their loyalty?
- Could we do more to retain our customers?

INCREASING YOUR CUSTOMER BASE

There is a well-established technique, known as member-get-member, or MGM, that many businesses use to good effect in the endless challenge to win new business. Try to get each of your existing customers to provide just one productive lead. You can literally double the size of your customer base using this method; but obviously your customers will be willing to participate only if they feel happy with your products and your organization generally. Use incremental incentives to encourage customers to provide leads.

▼ TURNING CUSTOMERS INTO YOUR SALES FORCE

Happy customers can do as good a job for you as the most highly trained sales force, and at a fraction of the cost. Harness the enthusiasm of satisfied customers and ask them to help you spread the word to their friends and family. An easy-to-complete card sent to regulars can result in valuable leads.

USING INCENTIVES

Ask customers for details of colleagues/friends who might like to be on your mailing list

Offer a small incentive, such as a prize drawing, to encourage customers to supply leads

Send your mailing to leads, explaining that a friend recommended them

If necessary, offer a bigger incentive, such as a free gift, if a lead places an order

---

Highlight the incentive in the headline

RECOMMEND US AND ENTER OUR PRIZE DRAWING

As a loyal customer you already know how great our products are. Don't keep it a secret! If you have friends or family who might like to find out what we have to offer, please include their details, and we will make sure they receive a copy of our latest catalog free of charge. In return for your help, we will enter you into our PRIZE DRAW for the opportunity to win a case of champagne. If your friend goes on to place an order with us, we will also send you a COMPLIMENTARY BOX OF CHOCOLATES as a thank you.

Make the incentive incremental, with a small incentive for supplying details and a larger one if the prospective customer places an order

You may want to ask customers for additional details, but remember that the more information you ask them for, the less likely they are to respond

Your name and address:

Your friend's name and address:

Make it easy for respondents to reply by, for example, using prepaid envelopes

Include your address on the card just in case the prepaid envelope is lost

Please return this card, in the prepaid envelope, by March 30th to qualify for the prize drawing. Send to Garden Tools Limited, Unit 17, Anytown Business Park, Anytown, US.

Include a reply-by date to encourage customers to act

BUILDING STRONG PRODUCTS

Quality products, backed by a strong brand, are vital for success. To keep your customers and stay ahead of competitors, you must develop first-class new products and improve existing ones.

IMPROVING PRODUCTS

Products generally have some kind of life cycle: some age and die, while others need restyling to remain fresh. Change, enhance, repackage, rebrand, remodel, or upgrade your products to ensure that they appeal to today's market.

29 Tell former customers about improvements to your products.

30 Use comment cards to elicit useful feedback.

31 Regard feedback from customers as valuable marketing intelligence.

ENHANCING PRODUCTS

Before investing considerable time and effort in developing new products, look at your current line. It is important to avoid creating new products at the expense of existing ones. For the best ideas on how to improve your products, consult the experts: your customers. Seek their opinions and suggestions using questionnaires, comment cards, focus groups, or customer panels, so that you can introduce real enhancements based on customer demand. Keep products fresh by introducing new variants, limited editions, add-ons, special recipes, and improved versions.

32 Always look for ways to improve your products.

33 Always thank your customers for their comments, even if they are negative.

PROMOTING PRODUCT IMPROVEMENTS

Whenever you introduce product improvements, tell your customers. You can use this as an excuse to write, telephone, or visit them. Ensure that your ads mention the enhancements, and use product packaging to draw attention to them. You can also highlight improvements in your publicity material. Brief your sales team on new features so that they are able to promote them. If there is a news angle, issue a press release to attract positive media coverage. Significant improvements to products will provide a launchpad for renewed promotional activity aimed at reviving sales.

LEARNING FROM YOUR COMPETITORS

Study your competitors; you may find that some of their ideas or working practices are worth copying or adapting. As a member of the public, sample any improvements they make to their products and services. Send for their publicity material. Phone their switchboard. Read their advertisements. Visit at one of their outlets. Examine organizations in other sectors. Is there anything they can teach you? Which of their good ideas are transferable or adaptable? Be on the lookout for ideas that you can adopt, adapt, borrow, or steal. Aim to improve existing products by taking the best of the rest and incorporating them to create a product that cannot be beaten.

▼ MONITORING COMPETING PRODUCTS

An easy way to compare your product with rival products is to search the internet and see what other companies are offering. Make sure you monitor the competition periodically, not just once.

Manager looks at competitor's brochure

Colleague checks competitor's website

DIFFERENTIATING YOUR PRODUCTS

F*ew products are unique. Often the challenge lies in finding a way to differentiate your products from a rival's near-identical offerings. Make use of a combination of techniques to give you an advantage over the competition.*

34 Review company processes to make them more customer focused.

35 Ask customers what your unique selling point is.

36 Identify something you offer that your rivals do not.

UNDERSTANDING COMPETITIVE EDGE

When your products are better than those of your competitors, and when customers recognize this superiority, you have a real advantage. Few organizations are in this position. Most find that there is little or nothing to distinguish their own products from a competitor's. To gain competitive advantage, uncover not just differences but also attributes that customers value. Make sure the differences are meaningful to customers, so that your product is preferable to the others available.

RECOGNIZING WHAT IS IMPORTANT

Often it is the little things that count. Customers may choose your product over a competitor's identical product simply because they prefer your packaging, or because you give them coffee while they wait. Pay attention to details that could make a difference. A genuine customer-centric approach will differentiate you from competitors. Show your commitment to customers and ensure that staff are empathic. Review company systems and processes to make them more customer focused.

QUESTIONS TO ASK YOURSELF

Q Why should customers buy from us rather than from our competitors?

Q What makes us different from our competitors?

Q How are we better than our rivals?

Q What strengths do we have that we can effectively capitalize on?

ADDING VALUE

When there is nothing intrinsically different about your product, look to your strengths as an organization to find your competitive edge. A combination of the following may differentiate you from your rivals:

- free/same-day delivery
- products held in stock
- free trial
- on-site demonstration of product
- choice of payment terms/ interest-free credit
- free parking
- personal service from trained staff
- better warranty
- good after-sales service/ on-site repairs
- 1–800 customer helpline

37 Gain advantage over your competitors by achieving total customer satisfaction.

IDENTIFYING USPs

Even an indistinguishable product can have a claim to uniqueness, and you may still have a unique selling point (USP). Perhaps you are the only local company to offer such a service, or were the first to make it available. You may be the newest, the nearest, or the largest. You might be the most experienced, the only family-owned firm, or the longest-established. Perhaps you are the only supplier to have achieved a coveted award, or maybe your staff have all reached a certain level of training or experience. Scrutinize your company for a claim to uniqueness. Check that none of your competitors is making a similar claim. Even a weakness can be turned into a strength. Being the smallest, for example, could be a USP. It means that you can offer a more personal, flexible service.

CASE STUDY

Vanessa and Susan ran two flower shops, which were situated only a short distance apart on the same street. Both florists had to compete for the same customers, and since their stock and prices were similar, there was no strong reason for customers to favor one florist over the other. Searching for a way to increase business, Vanessa came up with the idea of making special bouquets to coordinate with

interior color schemes. It was not more expensive for Vanessa to offer this new service, nor did customers have to pay any more to use it, yet the scheme gave Vanessa the competitive advantage she was looking for. Customers were delighted and made a point of returning to Vanessa's shop rather than to her rival's. Just over a year later, the shop managed by Susan closed, increasing Vanessa's business even further.

◀ **CREATING AN ADVANTAGE**

By differentiating her own business from her near-identical neighboring competitor, Vanessa succeeded in making her florist's shop far more profitable. Her idea was simple but clever: adding value for customers without increasing cost. Creative thinking is free, but can result in significant business gains.

PROVIDING INCENTIVES

Even without uniqueness you can still build a competitive edge. Ask yourself, "Why would a customer choose us rather than one of our competitors?" If you cannot come up with at least one compelling reason, consider using incentives. These can encourage customers to opt for you over a rival. Be sure to work out costs and benefits very carefully before taking this route. If you offer an expensive incentive, you or your customer will end up paying the price; it needs to be cheap to you but attractive to the customer. Choose a relevant incentive, such as a free tie with every suit, or free on-site servicing with every photocopier.

UNDERSTANDING THE BUYING PROCESS

Select incentive

Will incentive persuade customer to buy from you rather than from a competitor?
YES   NO

Will incentive result in a boost to sales sufficient to cover extra costs incurred?
YES   NO

Go ahead with incentive and carefully monitor results

Discard incentive

38 Choose an incentive that will enhance your reputation; tawdry gifts may tarnish your image.

SEEKING ENDORSEMENTS

Endorsements can be powerful persuaders, providing customers with a strong reason to buy from you. Who could resist saucepans promoted as the professional cook's favorite? Or the home computer that programmers choose? Or the vacation resort where travel agents take their vacation? Customers like the safety and security that an endorsement provides. A relevant endorsement can result in a dramatic sales boost.

CULTURAL DIFFERENCES

Before using endorsements and testimonials, check the relevant legislation. In the United States, the Federal Trade Commission regulates the use of endorsements and testimonials in advertising. Strict rules apply to any advertising message that consumers are likely to believe reflects the opinions, findings, or experience of a third party other than the sponsoring advertiser.

USING TESTIMONIALS

Testimonials serve exactly the same purpose as endorsements, but the difference between them is that a testimonial quotes a named person who has used the product and wishes to recommend it. Famous faces, relevant professionals and experts, and even ordinary people can provide testimonials. Customers are more likely to believe third-party testimony than to accept your company's claims of excellence. Testimonials reproduced in your publicity material in a handwritten form appear to be more persuasive and believable than typewritten ones. Always get written consent before using any testimonial, and make sure that the views expressed in it can be supported by independent evidence.

39 Ensure that views expressed in testimonials can be supported.

40 Choose an incentive that is relevant to the product.

41 Brief your sales team to highlight product benefits, not features, when talking to customers.

EVALUATING FEATURES AND BENEFITS

When promoting products, companies have a tendency to focus attention on a product's features. But customers do not look for features; they want to see benefits. Regard features merely as a way of creating benefits. Start by listing the features for each of your products and then add the benefits that customers derive from them. Make sure that all your publicity material and packaging highlights the latter.

COMPARING FEATURES AND BENEFITS

FEATURE	BENEFIT
"Uses the latest microchip technology"	"Never again burn a slice of toast"
"Built-in moisture reader"	"Transforms stale bread into fresh toast"
"Audible toast-completion alert"	"Bell lets you know when the toast is ready"

DEVELOPING A BRAND

Strong, well-known products provide companies with a real competitive advantage. Use the power of branding to imbue your products with personality and meaning, ensuring they achieve a prominent position in the marketplace.

42 Establish trust in your brand and customers will remain loyal.

NAMING PRODUCTS

The right name helps to sell products and services. It bestows individuality and personality, enabling customers to identify with your offerings and to get to know them. It makes products and services tangible and real. Choose names that enhance your company image and that are appropriate for the product and its positioning in the marketplace. Check that the name is available and register it so that it cannot be used by others. If your market is international, ensure that the name is pronounceable in other languages and does not translate into a vulgar word or one with negative connotations. Aim for a name that is short, apt, easy to spell, and memorable. Strict rules govern the naming of organizations, so check them out with the relevant official body.

▼ TESTING YOUR BRAND NAME

Show your shortlist of product names to target customers and ask them what images each name conjures up. Use their feedback to help select a name with the most positive associations.

International customer considers whether names will be appropriate in her country

Regional customer rejects two names because they have negative connotations in her area

Target customer gives his view on the appeal of suggested product names

COMPARING BRAND ATTRIBUTES

SERVICE ATTRIBUTES

Friendliness

Creativity

Courtesy

Helpfulness

Knowledgeability

PRODUCT ATTRIBUTES

Durability

Reliability

Usefulness

Value

Aesthetic value

43	Extend branding across your entire product line.

HARNESSING BRAND POWER

Manager asks selected customers for feedback on new product names

An effective way of differentiating your products from those of your competitors is to use branding. Branding means developing unique attributes so that your products are instantly recognizable, memorable, and evoke positive associations. Some brands have a solid and reliable personality, others are youthful and fun. Choose your company and product name, corporate colors, logo, packaging, and promotional activity to help convey a personality and build a brand. Branding conveys a complex message quickly. A customer should be able to look at one of your products and assimilate all that you stand for in a second by recalling the brand values.

44	A strong brand is not a substitute for quality, but an enhancement to it.

45 Look out for opportunities to reinforce your corporate identity.

46 Maintain corporate identity consistently by issuing written guidelines for staff.

PROMOTING A CORPORATE IDENTITY

The creation of a corporate identity is a vital element of branding. Present an integrated, strong, instantly recognizable, individual image that is regarded in a positive way by your customers, and seize every opportunity to strengthen your corporate identity. Devise a distinctive logo and corporate colors, and use them on stationery, packaging materials, and on your vehicle. Work the branding into the design and layout of your premises. Big hotel chains, for example, reinforce their corporate identity through color-coordinated staff uniforms, carpets, soft furnishings, and towels. They also have napkins, coasters, tableware, and cutlery bearing the company logo.

▲ CREATING A STRONG IDENTITY

Utilizing distinctive corporate colors and logos on company vehicles helps to build a strong identity. This ensures that an individual company is easily distinguishable from others that may offer very similar services.

POINTS TO REMEMBER

● A logo forms a central part of your corporate identity and should convey something about your business.

● It may incorporate a baseline – a summary of your mission or your business.

● A logo can be typographical or a design in its own right.

● The logo's colors will become your corporate colors.

47 Be aware that colors can have cultural or political connotations.

48 Keep corporate colors to a minimum to keep printing costs low.

49 Ensure all aspects of company behavior reflect brand values.

COMMISSIONING A VISUAL IDENTITY

If your organization lacks a strong visual identity, or has an outmoded image, consider a restyle. Give a full brief of your brand values and positioning to a graphic designer whose style you like, and ask them to produce some ideas. Explain how you intend to use your new corporate identity. Will it be placed on vehicles, for example, or on storefronts? Ask to see your proposed new visual identity on mock-ups of items on which it will ultimately appear: product packaging, stationery, and so on. Test your shortlisted design on a focus group comprising your key audiences, such as customers and suppliers. Find out what associations it produces. Take time to develop a new identity; you will have to live with it for a long while.

MAINTAINING BRAND VALUES

Having established a brand, work to maintain its positive values. Use patents, trademarks, design rights, and other devices to protect your brand and prevent others from cashing in on its success. Live up to your projected image. Ensure that standards of customer care, service, and product quality remain high, giving real substance to the brand. It can take years to create a successful brand yet seconds to destroy it. Check regularly that the brand values are still relevant, since brands can become outdated. Gently reposition the brand over time where necessary, or opt for a major repositioning and use media exposure to promote your new image.

▼ **GAINING RECOGNITION**
Successful brands have such a strong visual identity that they are instantly recognizable, even when seen in a foreign language. Companies can often charge more for winning brands, since customers feel, often subliminally, more confident in the value of the product.

ACHIEVING GROWTH THROUGH PRODUCTS

Selling more products is the most effective strategy for ensuring big increases in profitability. Achieve growth in this way by expanding your share of the existing market, finding new markets, developing new products, or diversifying.

50 Use the internet as a vehicle for reaching global markets.

51 Be prepared to restructure in order to grow.

52 Use related products to expand your product range safely.

PENETRATING THE MARKET

One way to ensure growth is to achieve a larger share of the market. This strategy is widely used because it is considered a "safe" way to grow. Security lies in the fact that you are dealing with two known entities: your offerings, i.e. your products, and the market. You have already spent time getting to know this market and refining your products to meet customer need, so you avoid the need to invest in new research, or in new product development. Your goal is simply to make contact with previously unreached potential customers.

DEVELOPING THE MARKET

Market development involves finding new markets for your existing products. Start by drawing up a list of possible new markets. Conduct research to check whether they would be interested in your offerings and that you could satisfy potential new customers with your existing products. Some product remodeling may be necessary if you are to appeal to your new market, but remember that you are not looking at totally new products. Finally, plan how you will reach your new markets.

POINTS TO REMEMBER

- It is possible to increase sales by simple but valued product improvements.
- You may combine, for example, product development with market penetration.
- It is a good idea to develop new products that will be bought in the same transaction as your existing products.

IMPLEMENTING GROWTH STRATEGIES

GROWTH STRATEGY	IMPLEMENTATION METHODS
MARKET PENETRATION Improving market share by reaching previously unreached potential customers.	● Use heavy advertising, promotional offers, direct mail campaigns, or cold calling to find new customers matching the profile of existing ones. ● Focus on winning customers from competitors.
MARKET DEVELOPMENT Identifying and breaking into new markets to increase sales of existing products.	● Use targeted advertising, direct mail, and the internet. ● Consider an internal restructuring, such as setting up a sales arm to deal with large companies, or remodel products to appeal to new markets.
PRODUCT DEVELOPMENT Introducing new product lines or add-ons to existing products to appeal to current market.	● Research new product ideas, ask customers for opinions, and examine successful rival product lines. ● Examine your market carefully to ensure that it is not already oversaturated.
DIVERSIFICATION Expanding through the development of new products to be sold to new markets.	● Remember that the rules applying to setting up a new enterprise also apply to organizations seeking to diversify. ● If you decide to diversify, you will need to develop a separate marketing strategy.

CREATING NEW PRODUCTS

Achieve growth and keep risk to a minimum by introducing new product lines to your existing market. Products introduced to an existing line can be very successful. A curtain manufacturer, for example, may add coordinating bedlinen to its line of curtains. Customers will often buy an existing product (a mobile phone) and a new one (a colorful, snap-on cover) in the same transaction.

53 Ask customers what new products they would like to see on the market.

54 Be sure to explore all the alternatives before risking diversification.

DIVERSIFYING

The riskiest growth strategy – diversification – involves developing totally new products to sell to new markets, and it is a journey into the complete unknown. Essentially you are embarking on an undertaking not dissimilar to a complete new business start-up. This is not often a first choice for boosting profits, but it can be – and has been – done. Explore all the alternatives first.

MAXIMIZING PUBLICITY

To buy from you, customers must know what you have to sell, which is why promotion is a vital part of the marketing mix. Learn to make the most of publicity to boost sales and profits.

PLANNING A CAMPAIGN

A successful publicity campaign can lead to an enhanced profile, increased sales, and improved profits. Before embarking on a campaign, map out exactly what you wish to achieve so that you can choose the right method to attain your goals.

55 Use calendars and desktop giveaways to keep your name in view of clients.

56 Use directories and annuals as publicity tools.

57 Use launches and previews to reach customers.

SETTING OBJECTIVES

The first step of a publicity campaign is to consider the outcome you desire and then set one or more clear, specific, measurable, time-framed objectives to achieve it. Avoid vague outcomes, such as "to attract more orders," and be explicit, for example, "to attract orders valued at $100,000 within four weeks" or "to attract 5,000 inquiries, leading to 1,000 sales in two months." Only by setting measurable objectives will you be able to identify what works and what does not. This will allow you to concentrate your publicity budget where it will produce the best results.

EVALUATING KEY METHODS

By far the most popular methods of gaining publicity are press and radio advertising, direct mail, and the internet, since these have high impact and are affordable for most businesses. When considering which method to use, bear in mind the following:

- Advertising in print allows excellent targeting, since most publications have detailed readership profiles.
- Radio ads are easier to digest than print ads, but they are more transient.
- Direct mail is highly effective, provided that it is efficiently targeted, although it does have a rather poor image.
- The internet is a booming growth area with a vast potential for publicity.

ORGANIZING A SUCCESSFUL CAMPAIGN

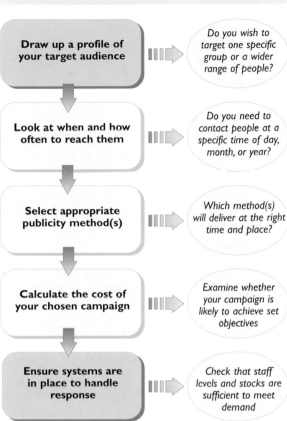

Draw up a profile of your target audience
Do you wish to target one specific group or a wider range of people?

Look at when and how often to reach them
Do you need to contact people at a specific time of day, month, or year?

Select appropriate publicity method(s)
Which method(s) will deliver at the right time and place?

Calculate the cost of your chosen campaign
Examine whether your campaign is likely to achieve set objectives

Ensure systems are in place to handle response
Check that staff levels and stocks are sufficient to meet demand

COMBINING METHODS

The best way to obtain maximum publicity is to organize an integrated campaign combining several methods. This allows optimum penetration of the market: one technique builds upon the work achieved by another. A software company targeting business start-ups, for example, could place a coupon response ad in the national press offering a free business software package to business start-ups. This would bring in names and addresses of target customers, to whom direct mail and publicity could be sent with the free packages.

POINTS TO REMEMBER

- Check that any claims made in your publicity materials can be substantiated.
- Avoid making false or exaggerated claims.
- Ensure publicity is both accurate and unambiguous.
- Be sure that publicity does not mislead or deliberately give the wrong impression.

GETTING THE MOST FROM ADVERTISING

Advertising is a paid-for, persuasive promotional activity that uses the media and other publicity channels, such as the internet. Use it to build and maintain awareness; to publicize special offers, sales, and events; to promote new products and services; to announce price changes, revised opening hours, or product modifications; to invite inquiries, and to find new customers. Above all, use it to sell. Direct response advertising (incorporating a response device, such as a coupon or fax number) brings you and your customers together.

58 Ensure relevant staff know which ads are appearing when.

CALCULATING COST ▶

Use a simple formula to check that an advertising campaign will produce results. When adding up the total cost of your campaign, include every item, not only the cost of buying space or airtime. If forecast sales exceed the break-even figure (C), success is likely. Allow a margin of error: response rates are a guideline and not a guarantee.

(A) **Total cost of campaign**	$1,000
(B) **Profit per sale**	$20
(C) **Number of sales needed to break even** (A) ÷ (B)	50
(D) **Mailing quantity, circulation figures, or listening/viewing statistics**	5,000
(E) **Expected response rate** (based on figures supplied by publication/station)	80
FORECAST SALES	62.5

DEFINING THE KEY STEPS TO SUCCESSFUL PUBLICITY

KEY STEPS	HOW TO TACKLE THEM
GRAB ATTENTION	Use a striking design, a hard-hitting headline, strong colors, large lettering, powerful photography, or other devices to get noticed.
HOLD INTEREST	Devise an appealing, persuasive proposition that will make potential customers sit up and pay attention.
STIMULATE DESIRE	Make your offer irresistible: show how good the deal is and highlight valuable extras, such as easy payment terms or quick delivery.
GAIN CONVICTION	Convince customers that they need what you are selling by giving powerful reasons that will appeal to them.
PUSH FOR ACTION	Urge customers to act using words such as "time-limited offer." Make action easier with coupons, 1–800 numbers, credit card payment, etc.

USING EXPERTS

If you are planning a major campaign, or intend to move into a specialized area, such as television or movie advertising, consider calling in the experts. Media professionals should be able to run a campaign more effectively on your behalf, and sometimes for less money than you would pay, and usually more quickly. If you plan to spend a lot on advertising, it could be to your advantage to use an advertising agency. Agencies earn a commission for buying media space or airtime, and this may cover their creative and account management costs. This effectively means that you are receiving their services for nothing. Approach a few advertising agencies and find out how they structure their fees.

MAKING IT LEGAL

Strict industry and legal codes govern advertising in the United Kingdom and the United States. In the US, for example, Federal Trade Commission regulations cover advertising, marketing and promotional activities, and sales practices in general. In Canada, the industry adheres to a Code of Advertising Standards. In the UK, over 150 statutes and regulations relate to a host of advertising issues.

---

59 Investigate using an outside company to handle the extra work for you.

PREPARING TO RESPOND

Be ready for the response to your campaign by ensuring that there are plenty of staff to answer telephone calls as well as process, pack, and dispatch orders. Organize extra telephone lines, if necessary. Check that you have sufficient stock, packaging materials, brochures, or information packs to fulfill responses. Delays will reflect badly on your company and may lead to customer loss. If you cannot cope with a big response, stagger your advertising. Target one geographic area or customer group, fulfill orders, then place your next batch of advertisements. Alternatively, employ a specialized fulfillment house to handle all the extra work on your behalf.

◀ BEING PREPARED
Be ready for the increase in customer response once your marketing takes effect. If necessary, employ more telephone staff and ensure that they are fully briefed.

ADVERTISING IN PRINT

Press advertising offers the cheapest way to reach a large audience and is highly effective for direct response advertising, where the public buys straight off the page. Choose the right publication, craft your ads carefully, and negotiate the best deal.

60 Bear in mind that spaces between paragraphs will increase readership.

61 Avoid too much small print; it is difficult to read.

62 Keep your idea or proposition as simple as possible.

REQUESTING MEDIA KITS

Draw up a list of possible publications in which to advertise and ask each one to send a media kit, with information on readership profiles and circulation details. Choose the best title for your product and target audience. Details and dates of special features contained in the kit will help you to decide the best time to place your ad. Try to book space for the time when your chosen publication is running a feature on your market sector. The kit will set out the deadlines for placing an ad, as well as technical data explaining the form in which to supply artwork.

NEGOTIATING THE BEST PRICE

Never agree to pay the quoted rate card price for advertising space without first trying to negotiate it down. It is almost always possible to arrange some kind of reduction. Various factors affect cost, including the time of year, demand, the size and position of your ad, circulation of the publication, and whether the ad is in black type or color. If demand for space is slack, a discount is usually available. Even if you cannot get the price reduced, try to negotiate a bigger ad for the same price, a second ad at half price, or a more prominent position for it.

QUESTIONS TO ASK YOURSELF

Q What do we hope to achieve as a result of advertising?

Q Whom do we want to reach, and what do we want to say to them?

Q Which publications do our target customers read?

Q How often do we need to advertise to get our message across successfully?

Q How large will our ad need to be?

USING THE RIGHT PUBLICATION

TYPE OF PUBLICATION	ADVANTAGES AND DISADVANTAGES
FREE LOCAL PAPERS Usually weekly, these contain editorials on the local area and are delivered free through the door.	• These rely solely on advertising for income, so there are many more ads competing for attention. • It is cheap to advertise in these papers and easier to get away with less sophisticated ads.
"PAID-FOR" PAPERS Daily and weekly, local and regional, these are generally paid-for titles serving local cities and communities.	• Good for local organizations, or national ones, wishing to target areas where they have outlets. • Short lead-in times. • Daily papers have a short shelf life.
NATIONAL NEWSPAPERS These are daily publications, usually with a Sunday edition.	• Good for reaching a mass audience since readership profiles allow wide socioeconomic targeting. • National advertising can be prestigious. • Expensive and with a short shelf life.
CONSUMER MAGAZINES This huge range of publications includes women's, lifestyle, music, health, and sports titles.	• Good for targeting special interest groups. • High reader interest so more likely to be read. • Longer lead-in times. • Competitors are likely to be advertising in them, too.
PROFESSIONAL PUBLICATIONS These include publications for particular professions and trades, from architects to pig farmers.	• Excellent for targeting a particular professional group. • Often retained for reference, extending their shelf life. • Often passed around the workplace and read by more than one person.

TARGETING ADS ▶

Andrew found that advertising in the wrong place produced no new leads, whereas a well-placed advertisement generated a steady stream of new work. He learned that an advertising campaign in itself will not necessarily produce an upturn in sales. For his ads to be effective, they needed to reach the right target. Readership profiles helped him to pinpoint the right publication – the one that was read by his potential customers.

CASE STUDY

Andrew ran an architectural practice in a large city, working on domestic projects. He first advertised in an architectural magazine but realized that it was the wrong vehicle for him, since only those in the trade were reading it. Andrew then drew up a profile of the clients he wanted to reach: reasonably well-off people who lived within a 50-mile radius of the city in which he practiced. He placed an ad in the regional glossy lifestyle magazine for his area. The readership profile stated that the magazine was bought by relatively affluent property owners interested in homes and interiors, and they all lived within reach of the city. The profile was perfect. Andrew's first ad produced 15 inquiries, which led to nine commissions. He decided to advertise there monthly and gained 80 percent of his work this way. As a result, turnover increased by 60 percent.

WRITING A PRESS AD

Make sure that the elements making up your ad – style of language, tone, colors, graphics, photographs, and illustrations – are chosen with your target reader in mind. Check competitors' ads, too, to see how they promote their products. Do you want to take a similar approach, or a radically different one? Create a clear, simple proposition, and avoid complex ideas that require hard work from readers. Ensure that all the elements of your ad work in harmony. Use text to reinforce any photos or illustrations, and eye-catching design to hold the various aspects together, thereby creating an unmissable and persuasive ad that makes readers act.

63 Give a small ad a heavy dashed border to increase its impact.

▼ **MAKING YOUR PRESS AD WORK**

When readers see an ad for the first time, their eye follows a set route. Take account of this route when designing your ad. Readers tend to look first at the picture, then at the headline, bottom right-hand corner, captions, subheads, and body copy, in that order.

Use the headline to attract attention; remember that 80 percent of people will stop reading at this stage

An illustration or photo is the first element readers look at, and it will encourage them to read further

Captions on photos attract twice the readership of the main text

Code coupons so that you know which publications produced the best response and on which days

MAIN HEADING
Subhead

The body copy expands on the headline and photograph to tell the story. About 80 percent of readers will not get this far. However, those who are still reading at this point are genuinely interested.

The caption for the picture

Please send me your brochure.
Name
Address

Telephone   Fax
Mail now to: Van Village, Freepost, Anytown 12345
NB122

(logo)

Readers quickly scan subheads and crossheads, illustrations, and graphs

Body copy must be readable, informative, persuasive, and directive, but also simple

A reply device such as a coupon response makes it easy for customers to take action

Readers expect to see a company logo here, which helps to reinforce corporate identity

PRETESTING ADS

Before spending your budget on buying media space, ask your staff, passers-by in the street, or, best of all, your target audience what they think of your ads. Discover whether they find the ads attractive, the copy readable, and the proposition persuasive. See which of two ads they like best. Both ads might be yours; or one could be your competitor's. After the ads have appeared, you can then assess their effectiveness using objective measures, such as the number of inquiries generated, the number of sales, or the percentage upturn in people through your doors. Measuring outcomes can occur only after an ad has been placed.

64 Appeal directly to readers by using the "first person" in advertising copy.

65 Use color ads to attract twice the readership of mono ones.

ANALYZING DIFFERENT TYPES OF HEADLINE

HEADLINE TYPE	EXAMPLE	WHEN TO USE IT
DIRECT Presents your proposition in a direct and concise form.	"Any van serviced for just $80 at Van Village"	To present a simple proposition requiring little or no explanatory body copy.
FILTER Shows the relevance of your ad by flagging up the target audience.	"Attention all van owners"	To attract the right prospective customers and ensure that they do not overlook your ad.
CRYPTIC Attracts the reader's curiosity but makes no sense as a stand-alone headline.	"It's what everyone's talking about"	To hook your readers and lure them into your body copy, providing you with an opportunity to persuade them.
COMMAND Issues the reader with an instruction that cannot be ignored.	"Contact us today to arrange your cheap van service"	To prompt readers to take action and respond to your ad.
QUESTION Poses a query to which the answer should be "yes."	"Want to save money servicing your van?"	To engage readers' interest and push them toward accepting your proposition.

ADVERTISING ON RADIO

Since customers listen to the radio at home, at work, and in their cars, it is an effective way of plugging your message. Weigh up the pros and cons of using local and national commercial radio, investigate what is involved, and carefully assess costs.

66 Find out if the radio station can help with production.

67 Ask to listen to ads that agencies have already produced.

QUIZZING A STATION REPRESENTATIVE ▼

Have a list of questions ready to ask the representative. Find out what the listener profile is, whether it changes at night, and what costs are involved. Remember that the representative wants to sell airtime to you, so may be economical with the truth.

MAKING GOOD ADS

The most successful radio ads induce listeners to prick up their ears. Sound, music, voices, accents, both a male and a female voice for extra rhythm, and a conversational style in which speakers talk directly to the listener are all elements of a good ad. Since a studio and specialized equipment are needed, appoint an advertising agency, or commission the radio station's in-house creative team to script and produce the ad for you. Look at the station's listener profile and think of a real person you know who fits that profile. Try the ad out on them. Would they like it? Would they be persuaded to buy?

Radio representative provides information about the station and its listeners

Manager asks questions from a prepared list

Colleague notes facts and sales points

ADVANTAGES	DISADVANTAGES

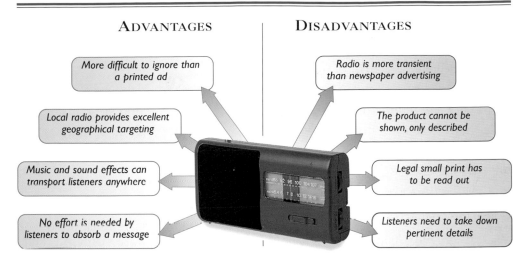

More difficult to ignore than a printed ad

Local radio provides excellent geographical targeting

Music and sound effects can transport listeners anywhere

No effort is needed by listeners to absorb a message

Radio is more transient than newspaper advertising

The product cannot be shown, only described

Legal small print has to be read out

Listeners need to take down pertinent details

PLANNING COSTS

There is more to radio advertising than buying airtime, so it is important to budget for extra costs. You may need to pay a copywriter to write the script for your ad, as well as actors or voice-over artists. If you commission your own music or jingle, you will need to pay a composer, musicians, and singers. Existing music will require permission to play and involves airplay royalties. Studio time, technicians, and sound effects all have a cost, too.

 WEIGHING UP THE BENEFITS
Consider both the pros and cons of radio advertising. You may find that spreading your advertising budget over a range of mediums will be more effective.

68 Remember that radio ads are heard, not seen.

ADVERTISING ON TELEVISION

It is possible to produce radio ads without using an advertising agency, but television advertising is far more specialized and technical. Commission an agency to advise on where, when, and how to advertise, as well as coming up with creative ideas and overseeing production. Contact at least three agencies with a written brief explaining what you wish to achieve. Ask each to do a presentation outlining their credentials, explaining how they would approach your assignment, and detailing costs. Look at examples of their work and ask for their client list. Select your agency on their experience and ability, creativity and approach to the campaign, their understanding of your needs, enthusiasm, and total cost.

MASTERING DIRECT MAIL

Direct mail is a form of advertising that delivers targeted, individually addressed communications through the mail. Select the contents of your mailshot carefully, ensure it hits its target, then test the effectiveness of the campaign.

> **69** Make sure you keep your mailing list up to date at all times.

> **70** Ensure that people's names are correctly spelled.

UNDERSTANDING DIRECT MAIL ▼
Direct mail is a carefully targeted mailshot sent only to people with a proclivity to buy the product or service being promoted. Junk mail is irrelevant mail sent to the wrong people.

IDENTIFYING USES
Direct mail has many marketing applications. Use it to find and convert new prospects, to distribute product samples or newsletters, and as a selling tool targeting current customers. Launch new products, win back lapsed customers, and announce changes to your service or forthcoming sales, events, and special offers – all via the post. Use the technique to build and maintain customer relationships. Keep in touch with clients, send them Christmas cards, tell them all the latest news and developments. Send out questionnaires and gather valuable marketing information.

DIRECT MAIL RECIPIENT

A regular skier, recipient reads about promotion offering cut-price skiing equipment with great interest

JUNK MAIL RECIPIENT

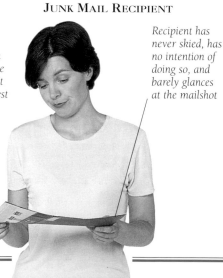

Recipient has never skied, has no intention of doing so, and barely glances at the mailshot

TARGETING YOUR MAILSHOT

Your mailshot is only as good as the address printed on it, which is why a good mailing list is essential if you are to target customers effectively and maximize your returns. Mailing to people who have moved or changed jobs, who hate direct mail, or who are just not interested is a waste of your marketing budget. Existing customers are three times as likely to respond to a mailing as cold prospects, so make them the basis of your list and then start looking for names to add. People who have inquired in the past and former customers could be worth testing, as could people whose business cards you have collected.

71 Write "you" in your mailshots – it is a powerful lure.

CULTURAL DIFFERENCES

Some countries operate mailing, telephone, and fax preference programs that allow consumers to opt-out of receiving direct mail, so-called "junk" faxes, and cold calling on the telephone. Before embarking on a direct mail campaign, check the legislation and codes that affect direct mail in your country, including any laws relating to the use of information on databases.

RENTING A LIST

When seeking new customers, you may wish to approach a list broker who can provide names and addresses of people who match the profile of your existing customers. Note that mailing lists are usually rented, not bought; you buy permission to use the list a certain number of times. If you attempt to use it more often, be warned: brokers plant "seed" names to check that their lists are not reused without permission. The names you rent are called "cold prospects." However, if they respond to your mailing, they become "warm prospects" and you can legitimately add them to your own mailing list and contact them again. Make sure you ask the broker the following questions:

- How was the list compiled?
- When was the list last updated?
- How has the list performed?
- What are typical response rates for others who have used it?
- Can we have the list in a form that suits us, such as on disk or adhesive labels?

IDENTIFYING ITEMS TO INCLUDE IN A MAILSHOT

A mailshot can comprise nothing more than a simple postcard with a printed message. More usually, it is made up of an envelope containing one or more of the items shown:

- cover letter
- leaflet, brochure, or catalog
- promotional video
- customer newsletter
- product sample
- free gift
- money-off voucher
- order form
- coupon response device
- prepaid envelope

USING ENVELOPES

The envelope is a vital ingredient of your mailshot and has an important job to do. If you cannot encourage people to open the envelope, it is not worth spending money on what is inside. Some companies have found that envelopes resembling regular mail are most successful because customers tend to open a mailshot that looks like an ordinary letter. Other organizations have found that undisguised mailshots bring better results. Printed envelopes that urge the recipient to open the mailing, or that highlight the offer inside, are also effective. Innovative envelopes have novelty value and can attract attention, as can unusual sizes, shapes, textures, or color combinations, or unexpected materials such as foil, rubber, or plastic. Use gimmicky envelopes such as inflatables, or unusual fastenings such as Velcro. All can boost response rates, although they may be more expensive.

72 Make it easy for clients to update their details for your mailing list.

Unusual envelope and amusing free gift prompt recipient to read mailshot

ATTRACTING ATTENTION ▶
Regard your envelope as more than just a container for your mailshot. Consider using an unusual envelope which, although more expensive, can boost response rates.

CREATING THE PERFECT MAILSHOT

Maximize your marketing budget by developing the perfect mailing. You can achieve this by testing what works best, working with one variable at a time. Try out different mailing lists to find the best one, experiment with different offers to ascertain which is most attractive to customers, send mailings at different times to identify the best timing for a mailshot, and try out a variety of response devices to see which produces most replies. You can also use a technique known as split test mailing. If, for example, you want to test whether a price reduction produces a greater response, send half of your mailing list the standard offer and the other half the discounted offer. Then compare the take-up from each half.

73 Think about expanding your mailing list into a database.

▼ GAUGING COST

A standard method of accurately measuring the impact of a direct mail campaign is known as "cost per response," which tells you how much you are paying to elicit each response.

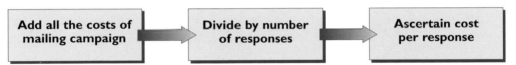

| Add all the costs of mailing campaign | Divide by number of responses | Ascertain cost per response |

74 Use bullet points to make benefits stand out from the main text.

75 Read your cover letter aloud. If it sounds stilted, rewrite it.

MEASURING CONVERSION

In addition to the "cost per response," there is another measurement that provides an insight into the effectiveness of a campaign. The "cost per conversion" tells you how much it costs to attract each sale. Divide the total cost of the mailing by the number of sales. At the outset, establish an allowable cost per conversion. Only you can decide what is acceptable. If an average customer spends $10,000 a year with you, $100 appears an acceptable investment to win such a customer. However, $100 is too much to pay if the annual transaction value per customer is only $35. If your allowable cost per conversion is $100, and you mail 10,000 packs (which cost $1 each), you will need to make 100 sales to break even.

USING THE INTERNET

*E*veryone seems to want a presence in cyberspace, and more organizations are getting online daily. Make sure that you stay ahead of the competition by developing your own website, and learn how to use the internet as a powerful sales channel.

76 Avoid hyphens in domain names; they complicate a web address.

77 Visit competitors' sites and collect useful ideas for your own.

78 Onscreen reading is harder on the eye, so keep text legible.

DEVELOPING A WEBSITE

Since your website may be the first point of contact for customers, it is very important that it reflects the right image. Templates enabling you to build your own website are available to download from the internet, but it takes an expert to design a well-executed site. Professional web designers know all the tricks. They can help ensure that your site pops up when potential customers use a search engine to hunt for you and link you to other sites. They can also advise on domain names, as well as securing and registering one for you, and they will, for a fee, maintain your site and keep it up to date on your behalf.

THE PROS AND CONS OF INTERNET SELLING

ATTRIBUTES	LIMITATIONS
Conveys a massive amount of information.	Fraud presents problems for buyers and sellers.
Provides a gateway to new markets.	Buying online concerns some customers.
Enables instant feedback from customers.	Hacking and viruses are an ever-present threat.
The number of "hits," or visitors, attracted can be measured.	It is impossible to go to consumers; they must come to you.
Available 24 hours – the internet never sleeps.	Not everyone is online.

MAKING THE MOST OF YOUR WEBSITE

Consider carefully how you will use your site and have it constructed around your needs. Think about how the internet will fit into your overall marketing plan. It should be tackled not in isolation but as a component part of a much wider-ranging strategy. Your site can be used for:

- interactive publicity;
- customer support via email;
- maintaining relationships with existing customers and attracting new clients;
- generating interest in and building awareness of your product, service, or organization;
- conducting market research;
- selling products and services online;
- providing product information and current availability.

◀ **VESTING CONTROL**
Traditional publicity is relatively passive: organizations push it at consumers. The internet is a proactive medium: customers pull the information that they want.

ADVERTISING IN CYBERSPACE

Advertising on the internet continues to develop. It is inexpensive and measurable, interactive, sometimes fun, and can be viewed anytime. Use it to reach new markets locally, nationally, and globally. Make your website a promotional tool in its own right, so that it acts as an interactive brochure. Advertise on others' sites, perhaps with banner advertisements, which are the main advertising vehicle on the net, or animated or static ads, often found on search engine sites, which, if clicked on, lead viewers directly to your site. Sponsor other related sites that can provide a route to your own site. Web brokers will offer demographic information to help you decide where and how to advertise on the net, and they will also negotiate the space for you.

POINTS TO REMEMBER

- Your website should be designed to reflect your corporate image.
- A website should be easy and quick to navigate.
- Prospective clients may leave your site and visit those of competitors if your pages are elaborately designed and take a long time to download.
- It should be possible to return to the home page with one click.
- Including an email link will allow visitors to get in touch easily.
- Registering with directories may help publicize your site.
- A site needs maintaining to keep it fresh, current, and relevant.

CREATING A VIRTUAL STORE

E-commerce is a major growth area because it provides a fast, cost-efficient, "open all hours" way of selling. Setting up shop on the web is a very different undertaking from simply having a website. Once you begin to sell online, you are entering a new world, and internal restructuring will be needed. Set about establishing an order management system, comprising interactive order forms, order handling and tracking, a safe and secure payment environment, automated invoicing, and order fulfillment and delivery systems – orders may arrive from anywhere in the world. Some products do not lend themselves well to online selling (those that need to be touched or felt), while others are made for it (music or software, which can be downloaded directly from the net). Consider how an online storefront will affect your existing selling channels.

79 Register with net directories to ensure that your site is publicized.

▼ ANALYZING WEBSITE USES

A website can have numerous marketing applications. Use it to build and maintain customer relationships via email, for selling, promoting awareness of products or services to a wider market, giving up-to-date information, and so on.

80 Update the information on your site regularly.

81 Decide whether your products are suitable for selling online.

QUESTIONS TO ASK YOURSELF

Q Are our customers online?

Q Is our product or service suitable for online sales?

Q Do we want to limit our online presence to the publicizing of our venture?

Q Are our competitors online?

Q Do we have the skills to create and maintain our site?

Q Do we want to sell via the internet and could we handle the extra orders?

Emailing Customers

While poorly targeted direct mail is called junk mail, the email equivalent is known as "spam." Mass emailing (or spamming) to cold prospects is bad netiquette and will only result in damage to your reputation. However, email contact with customers and prospects can work to your advantage. Email provides an extremely cheap way to maintain a lasting relationship. Ask visitors to your website if they want to receive emailed updates, information, special offers, or details of new products; many will say yes. Ask current customers for their email details. Always keep an up-to-date emailing list and find legitimate excuses to get in contact. Remember to include a simple opt-out so that customers can ask to be removed from your emailing list if they wish.

Reassuring Virtual Customers

The internet is no longer new, yet there is still wariness about internet shopping. Scare stories about fraud and unfulfilled orders abound. Give customers confidence in your website. Explain how credit card payments can be made securely and safely. Create a customer charter or statement of rights to reassure people that it is safe to buy online from you. Explain clearly what your refund policy is. Publish your complaints procedure. Include an address, telephone and fax number, and a contact name, so that customers have other means of getting in touch if necessary.

82 Create a short domain name that is easy to spell and remember.

Customer is impressed that he is able to exchange goods bought on the internet at one of the supplier's retail outlets

INSTILLING ▶ CONFIDENCE
Where possible, allow customers to use both your virtual store and traditional outlets, if you have them. If customers buy on the net, let them exchange goods through your retail stores.

DEVELOPING A STRATEGY

A strategy gives businesses a defined route to follow and a clear destination. Build a marketing strategy, and you will ensure that marketing is a long-term way of working, not a onetime activity.

THINKING STRATEGICALLY

When devising a marketing strategy, getting started can be the hardest part. Bring together a strong team to help plan your approach, and make sure that everyone understands the strategic elements that contribute to marketing success.

83 Allow plenty of time so that key decisions are not rushed.

84 Work on your marketing strategy when it is quiet to aid concentration.

GAINING FROM A STRATEGIC APPROACH

A marketing strategy provides organizations with a shared vision of the future. All too often, an organization will perform a marketing task, such as a direct mailshot, then sit back and see what happens. Or, as a knee-jerk reaction to falling sales or competitor activity, it might follow it up with a promotional offer, almost as if the organization is making up marketing as it goes along. A strategic approach will ensure that you maximize returns on your marketing spending and boost the profits of your organization.

STRATEGIC MANAGER	NON-STRATEGIC MANAGER

Has a clear picture of the future

Anticipates changes in the market

Works toward clear, long-term goals

Lives day to day without planning

Reacts to changes in the market

Has only short-term objectives

BUILDING A TEAM

Producing a marketing strategy from scratch can be daunting, especially if you are not a marketing specialist. Pull together a marketing strategy team from a range of departments to assist with drawing up future plans. Involve people whose function touches on marketing, and those whose job involves considerable customer contact. Before embarking on your marketing strategy, establish common ground by agreeing on definitions and purpose. Build team unity, perhaps by organizing a day out of the office at a pleasant venue to discuss shared marketing issues and concerns. Show that you recognize the contribution each team member can offer. Establish your authority as team leader by chairing meetings and overseeing follow-up activity.

▲ BEING AN EFFECTIVE MARKETING MANAGER

A successful marketing manager is strategic in outlook, ensuring maximum returns on marketing spending and boosting profits. A nonstrategic manager has no clear, long-term strategic objective in mind.

85 Choose team members for their range of skills.

External consultant is able to offer impartial advice

USING A ▶ FACILITATOR

Consider bringing in an external facilitator or a marketing expert to work with the team and to keep you focused.

ANALYZING YOUR SITUATION

Planning your future marketing strategy is much more effective if you begin by examining the present. Study all aspects of your organization: your products and services, your customers, your market, and your competitors. Look closely at the marketing activity you currently undertake as well as the reasoning behind it. Ask yourself why you adopt certain working practices. Are there strong reasons for undertaking marketing activity in the way you do, or is it merely force of habit? What are your marketing successes? What about your failures? Examine your position in the marketplace and see how you compare with your competitors. Build up a realistic picture of your organization as it is today. Now you are ready to look to tomorrow.

PLANNING YOUR APPROACH

Work out how long you will need to develop the strategy, bearing in mind all the stages involved. Ensure that everyone on your team can dedicate the necessary time to the task. Map out a process for producing the strategy. This may comprise weekly team meetings, with individual tasking/follow-up work in between. Set a deadline for the completion of the strategy to keep the momentum going. Agree on dates in advance for all meetings and enter them into engagement calendars to ensure that there is little excuse for non-attendance. Keep notes of meetings and principal decisions and circulate these to team members.

CREATING A STRATEGY

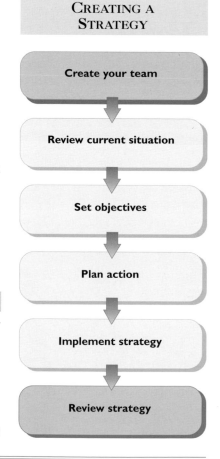

Create your team

Review current situation

Set objectives

Plan action

Implement strategy

Review strategy

QUESTIONS TO ASK YOURSELF

Q Is there anyone else I should really have on the team?

Q How long should I allow for the planning process?

Q Will we need to report to anyone higher up the ladder, such as the chief executive?

Q Would it be helpful to engage an external marketing expert to help guide the planning process?

PERFORMING A SWOT ANALYSIS

The acronym SWOT stands for Strengths, Weaknesses, Opportunities, and Threats. Analysis of these four factors provides information on how to shape your marketing strategy. Devise objectives aimed at strengthening weak areas, exploiting strengths, seizing opportunities, and anticipating threats. To help your analysis, list your strengths, then ask the following questions:

- Do you use your strengths to full advantage? Could you do more to capitalize on them?
- Are there current or future opportunities you could exploit? Are new markets emerging or are there existing, untapped customer groups?
- What threats do your competitors pose? What threats exist in the wider marketplace?
- What lets you down? What are you not good at? What do your competitors do better?

86 Set a deadline for the completion of your strategy.

87 SWOT analyze competitors to see how you compare.

▼ STEPPING STONES TO MARKETING SUCCESS

All marketing strategies comprise three main stages: first, determine what you want to achieve; next, adopt the right approach or method to achieve that aim; finally, measure performance to gauge the level of success

| **Aim** | **Act** | **Assess** |

INVOLVING ▶ COLLEAGUES

Ellie was in charge of sales for a small firm making sofa beds. Although not trained in marketing, she was also given overall responsibility for the company's marketing activity. She discovered the benefits of involving colleagues in major marketing initiatives.

CASE STUDY

Without consulting her colleagues, Ellie decided to launch a website to attract new business. It was an enormous success, with 40 orders received on the first day. Unfortunately, these were from different parts of the country, which posed distribution problems (the company's orders had previously come from local retailers, making deliveries quick and simple). Given that the production department already

had an order of 500 sofa beds for a new hotel, they were unable to meet all the delivery dates, and the new customers were disappointed. This embarrassing situation made Ellie realize that she had to include members of the production and dispatch departments in the planning of any future promotional activity so that they could share important information about busy periods, existing commitments, and distribution problems with her.

SETTING OBJECTIVES

Astrategy is a plan of action devised to meet certain objectives. Draw up your objectives carefully, because your entire marketing strategy will be structured around them, and ensure that they are measurable so that you can evaluate their success.

88 Take time to plan your marketing objectives carefully.

89 Set objectives that are challenging yet achievable.

PLANNING OBJECTIVES

Analyze current position

⬇

Specify ideal and modify to incorporate reality

⬇

Define measurable short- and long-term objectives

⬇

Seek advice or views of colleagues

⬇

Modify and finalize objectives

TAKING STOCK

Objectives are goals that are drawn up to take your organization from its current position to where you would like it to be in the future. Short-term objectives can be staging posts on the way toward fulfilling long-term goals. Analyze your situation and then ask: "what if we do nothing?" Will products become out of date? Will your customers remain loyal to a company stuck in a time warp? Will your competitors grow more powerful? Spend time asking "what if?" to help you realize the effects of not keeping up with customer needs and competitors' activities. It can serve to spur action.

CREATING A VISION

Ask yourself where, in an ideal world, you would like your organization to be in five years' time. What position would you like to attain in the marketplace? Would you like to achieve significant growth in your customer base and profitability? Would you like to be the brand leader? Paint a picture of the perfect scenario. Now bring a little reality to bear. Think about likely economic, legal, technological, social, and political changes. Will they pose opportunities or threats? Modify the ideal situation to take account of the realities of the market. What is achievable if you work really hard at it? Keep a record of your ideas.

DEVISING OBJECTIVES

The framework for your objectives has already been created in your vision of the future. Now take each of your goals for the future and translate it into an objective. Remember that an objective simply states what you want to achieve, not how you will achieve it. Each one should have both a quantity and a timeframe. These will help you to tighten the focus of your objective and to measure success. Some objectives will be achievable in the near future: these are your short-term goals. Others will be longer term. Organize objectives into short- and long-term so that you can manage the workload that goes with turning goals into reality. Phrase them so that they are clear and unambiguous.

▼ **MAKING OBJECTIVES MEASURABLE**

Underneath your vision, list your objectives, then quantify each one and set out a date or timescale within which the objective will be achieved. This enables you to evaluate progress and measure success far more effectively.

Future vision

To be the premier player in our field

Objectives	Quantity	Timeframe
To increase our customer base	By 25 percent	Within 12 months
To widen our product range	With the introduction of two new lines	By the end of January
To raise our customer profile	So that consumer awareness of the organization and products is boosted by 20 percent	Nine months into the profile-raising campaign

90 Set at least one objective that can be achieved imminently.

91 Discuss objectives with colleagues to ensure their support.

GAINING AGREEMENT

Once you have devised a set of objectives around which to build your marketing strategy, seek agreement for them from across the organization. Marketing is a discipline that cuts through many departmental boundaries. Marketing activity will have a knock-on effect in various parts of the operation so, for it to be effective, you will need the support of colleagues. Ensure they understand the need for these objectives and the impact they may have on their work. Listen to any objections they may have and assess their validity. It is better to spend time discussing objectives at this stage, so that they can be modified where necessary before you invest considerable effort in devising ways of achieving your goals.

ACHIEVING YOUR GOALS

Having established your objectives, now work out how you are going to attain your ultimate goal. Investigate constraints, such as time and money, and then create a timetable of activity to give you a working marketing plan.

92 Encourage full participation at brainstorming sessions.

93 Try brainstorming away from the workplace; it may be more effective.

DEVISING SOLUTIONS ▼
Discuss each suggestion put forward during a brainstorming session. If an idea seems unworkable at first, encourage the team to think of innovative solutions rather than to discard it without consideration.

BRAINSTORMING IDEAS
Coming up with ideas for achieving your objectives is a creative process. The best technique for freeing creativity is brainstorming. Display an objective on an overhead, screen, or flipchart. Next, ask your strategy team to suggest ideas for helping achieve that objective. Write all ideas on a flipchart. Do not comment on, assess, discuss, or evaluate ideas at this stage. Simply record all suggestions. Aim to attract as many ideas as possible and encourage all group members to participate.

Team member suggests sending written product briefing to all customers each month

Colleague questions whether idea would be affordable in terms of time and money

Team member suggests email briefing would be both easy and cheap

Manager agrees that modified idea is good and agrees to implement it

SETTING BUDGETS

Look at your marketing ideas and work out the cost of each. Remember that marketing involves meeting customer need at a profit. To be justified, marketing activity should have a positive impact on the balance sheet. Examine not only the cost but also the benefit. An advertising campaign may cost a lot of money, but if it reaps profits amounting to several times its cost, it is cheap. Avoid setting an overall marketing budget to start with. Instead, work out costs and outcomes, decide what is justified, then calculate the budget.

94 Determine costs and outcomes before setting a budget.

▼ SETTING OUT A PLAN
Some marketing ideas will require little time or money to implement. Others will be costly and/or complicated. List your ideas and give them a high, medium, or low priority. Then assign start and completion dates. Consider implementing low priority ideas immediately if they are quick, cheap, and easy.

TIMETABLING ACTIVITIES

Prioritize activities and then organize them into a logical order. Put a date alongside each activity. When assigning dates, consider the importance of timing. Some ideas are best undertaken when there is an obvious marketing link. For example, if you manufacture pumpkin pies, aim to tie in your promotion with a significant or high profile event, such as Thanksgiving Day. When timetabling, bear in mind the impact that your marketing activities will have on internal resources. Avoid time-intensive activities during periods of high staff absence, such as during the summer vacation period. Remember that this timetable is your working marketing plan.

MARKETING PLAN

ACTIVITY	PRIORITY	START DATE	COMPLETION DATE
Organize lunch for top ten customers	Medium		by end February
Produce new brochure	High	mid-January	end March
Update mailing list ready for new brochure	High		end March
Mail new brochure	High	early April	

EFFECTING THE STRATEGY

*P*roducing a marketing strategy is a
means to an end; results will come
from implementing it. Assign tasks to staff,
provide any support they need, then review
progress, measure performance, and
periodically revise objectives.

95 Ask for regular
progress reports,
specifying which
facts you need.

96 Make sure that
staff inform you
of implementation
delays and
difficulties.

ASSIGNING ACTIVITIES

Some organizations invest considerable effort in
developing a strategy, but enthusiasm and energy
wane when it comes to implementation. Ensure
that your marketing strategy is put into action,
not left to gather dust on a shelf. Assign each task
or activity due for implementation within the next
12 months to a named person. Check that anyone
given responsibility for an activity has the time,
knowledge, expertise, budget, and authority to
complete the task. Give clear instructions on what
is expected and by when. If necessary, ask for
regular progress reports,
so that you are assured
everything is running
according to plan.

◀ **REVIEWING
PROGRESS**
*The general marketing forum
might be open to a large
number of staff. In addition to
this you will need a smaller
review group. This might
comprise the original
marketing strategy team. Meet
at least quarterly, possibly
more often. The purpose of this
group is to compare progress
against planned activity.*

ACTIONING THE PLAN

Make sure you allow staff to get on with their marketing tasks, but, equally, make sure you do not neglect them. Create a forum for those involved in the creation and implementation of the strategy so that problems and difficulties can be discussed. Work together to devise solutions. Build a supportive atmosphere, rewarding those who are staying on course and encouraging those who are not. Although staff may be involved in implementing only a small part of the strategy, an inclusive forum will enable them to see the bigger picture. Use the forum to receive and discuss progress reports. By sharing these with staff, you will help them to see the benefits of the marketing activity and strengthen their commitment to implementing a successful strategy.

QUESTIONS TO ASK YOURSELF

Q Have profits increased since the strategy was implemented?

Q Have we seen an increase in our customer base?

Q Have we attracted a greater number of orders, or larger individual orders?

Q Has the number of product/service enquiries risen?

Q Has awareness of our organization and its products or services increased?

▼ REVISING OBJECTIVES

The world is not static. Things within your organization or within your market are likely to change over time. If they do, you might need to redefine your objectives. Review objectives semiannually or annually to check that you are still on track.

97 After delegating a task, try to avoid interfering unless there is a risk that objectives will not be met.

YES	CHECK OBJECTIVES	NO
Continue implementation	Are your objectives still relevant?	Revise objectives
Consider adding new objectives	Have you achieved any of your objectives yet?	Continue implementation
Devise new objectives	Have new issues arisen that require new objectives?	Continue implementation

GAINING SUPPORT

Marketing has a vital role to play in every organization, but its contribution is not always recognized. As part of your strategy, build support within the workplace. Break down departmental barriers and help create a marketing organization.

98 Explain how marketing can support colleagues in their work.

99 Make colleagues aware of marketing successes.

100 Cultivate the support of all your colleagues.

WINNING ALLIES

Marketing managers often complain that their departments are always blamed when things go wrong and are never credited when they go well. It can be difficult for staff on the frontline of the business to see the relevance of marketing. Win the support, understanding, commitment, and collaboration of your nonmarketing colleagues, including the chairperson and chief executive. Tell them of your organization's marketing successes. Show them what effective marketing can achieve, and use hard data to demonstrate its benefits.

BECOMING A MARKETING ORGANIZATION

If staff across the organization can see the relevance and benefits of marketing, their cooperation will follow naturally. They may offer sales leads, provide constructive feedback on marketing materials, or come up with workable ideas for improving customer service. Involve all staff in marketing activities. Ask for ideas and show that you value their contribution. In addition to telling them about your work, become acquainted with their work, too.

▼ **SHARING SUCCESSES**
Explain to colleagues how marketing techniques can be used to support them in their work. Involve relevant staff from other departments in marketing planning. Give them a stake in its success.

SHARING INFORMATION

Keep colleagues informed of any marketing activity. Staff sometimes grumble that they are the last people to hear about what the marketing department is doing; the first they may know about a new ad is when customers or friends tell them. When this happens, staff feel stupid, embarrassed, or ill-informed. Use memos and emails to brief colleagues. Let them feel that they have insider knowledge. Tell staff the day before a new press ad appears or a new radio ad is broadcast. Tip them off that a direct mail campaign is about to get underway. Obviously you will not wish to publicize commercially sensitive information, but there is no harm in keeping staff up to date and involved.

▲ SUPPORTING OTHER DEPARTMENTS
Find out what colleagues in different departments do from day to day and see if your marketing skills can help them provide a better service to customers.

POINTS TO REMEMBER

- Cross-organization support is required for effective marketing.
- The marketing department cannot operate in a vacuum.
- Colleagues should not be given an opportunity to question your value and contribution.

101 Be prepared to justify your existence in a positive way.

HANDLING SKEPTICISM

It is not unusual for employees to criticize other departments within their organization, and marketing often attracts more than its fair share of adverse comment. If people outside of the marketing department are heard complaining that "we do not know what marketing finds to do all day," or "marketing does not understand the realities of our work," you are working in a compartmentalized organization. If this is the case, do all that you can to cultivate the support and respect of colleagues in other departments. In a true marketing organization, all members of staff are able to see the direct benefit of marketing and are fully aware of how the marketing team contributes to its overall success.

ASSESSING YOUR MARKETING ABILITY

A good understanding of basic marketing theory, combined with experience of techniques, will ensure your ability to implement an effective marketing program. This questionnaire will test your approach to marketing. Answer the questions as honestly as you can. If your answer is "never," mark Option 1, and so on. Add your scores together, and refer to the Analysis at the end of the questionnaire.

OPTIONS
1 Never
2 Occasionally
3 Frequently
4 Always

1 I research customer need before developing new products and services.

| 1 | 2 | 3 | 4 |

2 I obtain customer information and use it to influence decisions.

| 1 | 2 | 3 | 4 |

3 I consider customer "buying points" when promoting products.

| 1 | 2 | 3 | 4 |

4 I take action to make sure that every customer is a satisfied customer.

| 1 | 2 | 3 | 4 |

5 I ensure that orders are processed swiftly as well as accurately.

| 1 | 2 | 3 | 4 |

6 I set standards to ensure effective customer care.

| 1 | 2 | 3 | 4 |

7 I measure performance against the standards of customer care.

1 2 3 4

8 I take the complaints of customers very seriously.

1 2 3 4

9 I monitor the number of customer complaints that we receive.

1 2 3 4

10 I try to see if there is anything I can learn from a customer's complaint.

1 2 3 4

11 I find reasons to keep in touch with customers.

1 2 3 4

12 I try to turn onetime customers into regular ones.

1 2 3 4

13 I keep a record of key customer contacts.

1 2 3 4

14 I ask customers whether they will recommend us.

1 2 3 4

15 I show customers that their business is valued.

1 2 3 4

16 I try to find out why we have lost a customer.

1 2 3 4

17 I attempt to win back lost customers.

1   2   3   4

18 I am on the lookout for new customers.

1   2   3   4

19 I try to nurture customer loyalty.

1   2   3   4

20 I seek customer comment and feedback.

1   2   3   4

21 I listen to what customers say.

1   2   3   4

22 I pay attention to the little details that make all the difference.

1   2   3   4

23 I try to add value to our products and services.

1   2   3   4

24 I emphasize benefits, not features.

1   2   3   4

25 I use public relations techniques to boost marketing effectiveness.

1   2   3   4

26 I draw up a pricing strategy for every new product marketed.

1   2   3   4

27 I set objectives for publicity campaigns.

1 2 3 4

28 I carefully target mailshots.

1 2 3 4

29 I am careful to select the right envelope for a direct mail campaign.

1 2 3 4

30 I test mailshots to find the most successful combination.

1 2 3 4

31 I measure the overall effectiveness of a publicity campaign.

1 2 3 4

32 I keep nonmarketing colleagues informed of key marketing activities.

1 2 3 4

ANALYSIS

Now that you have completed the self-assessment, add up your total score and check your performance. Whatever level of success you have achieved, there is always room for improvement. Identify your weakest areas, then refer to the relevant sections of this book, where you will find practical advice and tips to help you establish and hone your marketing skills.

32–64: You need to take a more organized, planned, methodical, and measured approach to improve your effectiveness.

65–95: Some of your marketing activity is a success, but you need to develop your skills to become wholly effective.

96–128: You have adopted a thoroughly professional, strategic approach to marketing and are running successful marketing campaigns. Keep up the good work to stay ahead of the competition.

UNDERSTANDING IT

INTRODUCTION

Nowadays, information technology permeates virtually every aspect of modern business, to the extent that its effective use can easily mean the difference between success and failure. Managers in every field, from human resources to marketing, must understand the implications and quickly learn how to benefit from the new industrial revolution. Understanding IT will help you to break through the jargon and mystique that often surrounds the subject and face up to the challenge of IT. Practical advice helps you to deal with the business issues, gives you the confidence to use and manage IT, and shows you how you to profit from the Internet revolution. There is further assistance in the form of 101 concise tips, and a self-assessment exercise allows you to evaluate your IT skills.

FACING THE CHALLENGE OF IT

To be successful in today's fast-changing, highly competitive business world, it is vital that an organization uses IT effectively. Ensure that you and your staff fully accept the need to learn.

UNDERSTANDING IT

The effective use of IT is one of the biggest challenges facing most organizations today. Understanding the role IT plays and how to make the best use of IT systems is an essential requirement for any organization seeking competitive advantage.

1 Help your staff to understand the importance of IT to business success.

CULTURAL DIFFERENCES

American military, research, and commercial organizations led the development of information technology, but today its use has spread worldwide. The US still leads in the production of IT tools, but European countries, India, and others are carving out their own technology niches.

WHAT IS IT?

IT stands for information technology and, in its widest sense, refers to any technology controlled by a microprocessor (or computer chip). For example, microprocessors are used to control the delivery of essential services such as water, electricity, and telecommunications. They are also a crucial part of most types of manufacturing and distribution processes. However, most managers' involvement with IT is limited to two types of computer systems: those that store and manipulate data, and those that provide fast and efficient communication between people and businesses.

<table>
<tr><td>**2**</td><td>Look for new technologies that make work easier.</td></tr>
</table>

| **2** | Look for new technologies that make work easier. |

| **3** | Focus on how IT can empower you and your business. |

BENEFITING FROM IT

There is no organization that can afford to ignore the empowering technology of the modern world. Today's IT systems can help a business to be more responsive, efficient, and flexible in the face of continuous and rapid change. Properly used, information technology will allow your company to streamline its processes and focus on the core skills and abilities that differentiate it from its competitors in the marketplace. Failure to embrace the opportunities that are offered by IT today is likely to result in business failure.

MAKING THE MOST OF IT

Using the power of modern IT systems to best advantage is a strategic skill that has become an essential requirement if an organization is to keep ahead of its competitors. IT fulfills many functions in an organization, including automated process and systems; but for managers the key role is as an enabling technology. Managers must select and use IT systems to communicate more efficiently, to simplify business processes, and to acquire, analyze, and manage the data on which their business depends.

| **4** | Find out all the ways in which your organization currently uses IT. |

▼ USING IT EFFECTIVELY
Making effective use of the power of IT offers important benefits at both a personal and an organizational level.

PERSONAL ASPECTS | BUSINESS ASPECTS

IT can help me work smarter, not harder

IT can get me closer to my customers

IT allows me to work away from the office

IT can help me to reduce costs

IT keeps me informed, even on the move

IT can make my business more flexible

HARNESSING THE POWER OF IT

To gain maximum benefit from the use of IT, an organization must ensure that systems are truly effective in meeting its needs. Decision-makers must create efficient ownership of technology, and should focus on using IT to gain competitive advantage.

> **5** Pick systems for their ability to deliver competitive advantage.

DEPENDING ON IT ▲

Many organizations – for example, financial markets – rely totally on efficient IT systems in order to conduct business.

CREATING EFFECTIVE SYSTEMS

IT is a business tool that can radically improve the way you manage your business and communicate with your key audiences. If systems are to deliver real benefits, they must be:

- Transparent to the user: users do not need to know how systems work; the requirement is simply that they perform as and when needed.
- Fast and easy to use: users should find systems simple to use, and must be able to complete tasks quickly without having to wait any significant time for the system to respond.
- Flexible: changing needs require systems that are capable of being adapted quickly.

HIGHLIGHTING NEEDS

Organizations need to be responsive to changing markets; they must act quickly to develop new products and satisfy customer expectations. To help create competitive advantage, IT systems must be focused on real business needs. Give departmental users the power to identify their specific needs and then request IT solutions, rather than allowing an IT department to impose technology-led systems.

> **6** Design technology to fit the business needs, not the other way around.

DECIDING WHO MANAGES THE IT RESOURCE

An important consideration when selecting new systems or changing to new technologies is who will manage the resource. All systems must be maintained and monitored so that failures and downtime are kept to an absolute minimum. If a new technology is being introduced, make sure that your IT staff understand it fully and are capable of managing it. If in any doubt, arrange for IT staff to have training, or contract with the supplier for external support services.

TAKING OWNERSHIP

Given that the effective use of IT is a strategically important corporate skill, the issue of who controls IT is absolutely critical. In the past, the IT function often reported to a chief financial officer, who may not have fully understood the technology. Today, it is vital to have an IT-literate person on the board, as well as in each department, of your organization. The senior person focuses the use of IT on the organization's current and future needs, while the departmental champions promote its efficient use.

7 For speed and flexibility, keep IT systems simple.

8 Learn about IT and promote its use in your team.

BOARD
IT-literate board member champions IT

◀ CHAMPIONING IT
An IT-literate board member ensures IT serves strategic business needs. In addition, each department has an IT-literate member of staff who promotes effective IT and liaises with the IT department.

DEPARTMENT	IT DEPARTMENT	DEPARTMENT
Managers and IT champions are responsible for IT in their department	Liaises with other departments and with internal or external support staff	Managers and IT champions are responsible for IT in their department

FOCUSING ON THE HUMAN ELEMENT

While great effort is put into developing better, faster, and more complex IT systems, the human element is often ignored. If the full value of IT is to be realized, you must ensure that users feel in control of the technology and are positive about its use.

9 Value human knowledge and creativity more than IT systems.

10 Aim to be positive about technology and learn to use it.

11 Remember, people are the best guide to information within a business.

TAKING CONTROL

It is very common for people to fear technology when they do not feel in control of it. This is especially true when the technology is obviously complicated and involves the use of jargon that alienates the uninitiated. In contrast to other complex technologies, such as television or the telephone system, IT systems are still prone to failures and are not yet transparent to users. The user must learn a new language and significant new skills to get the best from IT. You and your staff will feel in control only when you make an effort to learn about the technology.

BEING POSITIVE

It is important for your career as a manager that you understand the business implications of IT and learn how to use common systems. Start by eliminating negative attitudes to technology and focus on its benefits. After all, this technology is not going away; indeed, it will increasingly have impact on every aspect of your life. Make a decision to learn how to use IT and seek out colleagues who can help you. Jargon is often a barrier to learning, so ask them to avoid its use, or explain key terms.

QUESTIONS TO ASK YOURSELF

Q Have I made sufficient effort to learn about technology and the IT systems I use at work?

Q Am I being positive enough about the use and value of IT in my organization?

Q Do I understand the technology enough to feel in control of the systems I use?

HOW PEOPLE ADD ▼ VALUE TO INFORMATION

Data becomes information only when it is interpreted and put in context by an analyst. A decision-maker uses information to plan actions and inform staff.

DATA
Computers collect and store data such as sales figures or customer details

ANALYST

INFORMATION
Information is created by a person who can interpret the data and put it in context

DECISION-MAKER

KNOWLEDGE
Business knowledge is derived from information by decision-makers with a broad overview

INFORMED STAFF

ACTION
Following decision-maker's instructions, informed staff take action

CREATING AN INFORMATION CULTURE

The lifeblood of any organization is information, and IT systems are often created to manage, store, and distribute it. However, many of these systems fail to achieve their objectives. A common reason for this is the tendency to focus on technological capabilities rather than how people actually work with information. This usually creates a rigid, computer-centered view, rather than a flexible, human-centered, and often disordered one, which reflects the way people actually use and share information. Equally common is the assumption that people will naturally share information if they have the technology to do so. In fact, when information means power, people are unlikely to share key information unless the culture of the company encourages them to do so. So it is important to create an information culture before using IT to assist in its management.

12 Ensure people learn good inter-personal skills before relying on IT-based communication tools.

DO'S AND DON'TS

☑ Do be prepared to acknowledge that you don't understand your colleagues' IT jargon.

☑ Do consider how people naturally use and share information.

☑ Do create incentives to encourage the sharing of information.

☒ Don't use jargon when explaining IT to new computer users.

☒ Don't expect people to share valuable information if the culture is competitive.

☒ Don't try to use IT to solve problems that are people-based.

KEEPING UP WITH CHANGE

A common complaint concerns the difficulty of keeping up with changes in IT systems, which seem to be developing at breakneck speed. Managers must learn to recognize and respond to IT developments that are relevant to their organization.

13 Accept that change is inevitable and look for ways to use it to advantage.

THINGS TO DO

1. Focus on technologies that offer demonstrable benefit.

2. Be prepared to allocate time to stay in touch with new developments.

3. Develop contacts with colleagues who are better than you in the use of IT tools.

4. Explain your key needs to the IT department.

ACCEPTING CHANGE

Change in the business environment is caused by technological developments and the increasing globalization of markets, but it is in the use of IT that the speed of change is most apparent. Even IT experts complain that it is difficult to keep up to date with changes in technology, so it is perfectly understandable that most managers feel that keeping up is beyond their skills, or that they do not have time. However, it is extremely important to be aware of changes that may influence your business or job. The pace of change will not slow down in the near future, and those unwilling or unable to adapt quickly could find themselves out of business while more flexible competitors succeed.

BEING SELECTIVE

Don't try to keep up with all changes. Instead, be selective and concentrate on learning about new tools or technologies that can make important tasks easier, save you time, or help cut business costs or increase profits. Look for IT systems that are of strategic or operational importance to your business. Increasingly, these will include Internet ecommerce systems (for buying and selling on the Internet), or an intranet (a private website) for internal information management. Identify the key areas and concentrate on their development.

14 Harness useful changes faster than your competitors.

15 Help your team focus on changes that are significant.

MONITORING NEW DEVELOPMENTS

The only way to stay in touch with fast-changing technology is to allocate a small amount of time, on a regular basis, to monitor the developments in those areas that are important to you. The best sources of information are the Internet, specialized magazines, reports on technology in general media, and colleagues who are IT-literate and use similar technology. If your organization has an IT department, ask it to keep you informed of important changes. Show interest in, and ask questions about, technology that is important to you. If you use commercial software, visit the maker's website regularly to get details of bugs, upgrades, and usage tips. Many software suppliers publish Internet mailing lists through which you can receive regular product information.

16 Use the Internet as your main research tool.

QUESTIONS TO ASK YOURSELF

Q Are the hardware or software tools I use up to date or have they been superseded?

Q Are there features in other tools that would make me or my business more efficient?

Q Has the latest software been fully tested by others so that I can be sure there are no major problems?

One team member is responsible for reading specialized magazines

IT champion updates team on relevant developments

Departmental manager keeps focus on business issues and needs

KEEPING UP WITH ▲ NEW DEVELOPMENTS
Hold regular meetings with your staff to share information on new hardware or software that might have implications for your organization's performance.

17 Keep an eye on Internet-led changes, since these will have the most impact on your business.

LOOKING AT IT ON THE DESKTOP

A wide perspective on IT is essential if managers are to pick solutions that match the needs of their organization and staff. Gain a full understanding of common hardware and software tools.

FINDING THE RIGHT TOOLS

Selecting the most appropriate technology and systems for your particular needs is a vital first step in making the best use of IT. These decisions can have long-term implications, so you should involve system-users and IT staff in the selection process.

18 Learn about the technologies that are leading current IT developments.

POINTS TO REMEMBER

- IT systems have gone through many developments. Many of the old systems are still in use and must be allowed for when adding new systems or technologies.

- Sharing data between old systems and modern, Internet-based ones can be difficult, time-consuming, and expensive.

- Doing business electronically requires IT systems that are compatible (or work) with the standards used on the Internet.

CHOOSING APPROPRIATE TECHNOLOGY

IT systems have changed considerably in just a few years, with the result that many organizations have a mixture of old (legacy) systems and newer technology. Today's IT systems are being driven by Internet technology as most organizations rush to exploit the medium and to run intranets (private websites) on their internal networks. If you need to select new systems, look for ones that will work with "open" (published) Internet standards to give maximum flexibility. They must also be able to communicate with any legacy systems you have.

EXPLAINING BASIC JARGON

KEY TERM	DEFINITION
Bit	The smallest unit of information that a computer can process.
Byte	One character (a number, letter, or symbol). Made up of eight bits.
CD-ROM	Removable compact disc (CD) for read-only memory (ROM).
Chip	The computer's microprocessor, which controls its functions.
DVD	Removable digital versatile disc (DVD), which is superseding CDs.
Hard disc	The computer's permanent data storage device. Also called the hard drive.
Hardware	The physical, visible components of a computer system.
Operating System	Software that controls a computer's overall operation.
RAM	Random Access Memory: impermanent working storage within a computer.
Software	Electronic instructions for the computer, which run on hardware.

ASSESSING TOOLS

The starting point for assessing new IT tools must always be the business requirement, not any aspect of technology. First, clearly define the tasks that the tools must perform, then examine the potential solutions that are available. Benchmark your competitors, if possible, to find the systems they have chosen, and draw up a shortlist for further consideration. Do not rely on technical specifications or the promises of sales people.

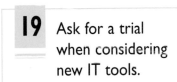

19 Ask for a trial when considering new IT tools.

▼ **CHOOSING CAREFULLY**
Take time to make a considered judgment when selecting a new system. It may have to last for some years. Involve users and focus on business benefits.

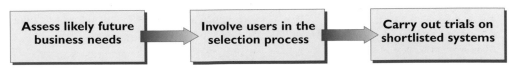

Assess likely future business needs → Involve users in the selection process → Carry out trials on shortlisted systems

IDENTIFYING THE COMPONENTS

It is not necessary to understand how a computer works to make effective use of it, but you will achieve better results when working with IT systems if you have a good understanding of the roles of the various hardware devices and software programs.

20 Add more RAM to speed performance when using large programs or files.

UNDERSTANDING YOUR COMPUTER

The chips and circuitry that are the heart of a computer reside in the computer case. Input and output devices (known as peripherals) are connected to this by cables or infrared devices. When the computer is working with data, it stores it in its active, primary storage—called Random Access Memory (RAM). Adding more RAM is an effective, easy way to boost your computer's performance. A magnetic hard disc in the computer case provides permanent storage. Modern hard discs store several gigabytes (GB) of data. Extra storage is provided by removable media such as CD-ROMs.

HARDWARE COMPONENTS ▶
Many types of input and output devices can be connected to allow you to input data and retrieve it in a usable form.

A printer is a commonly used output device

PRINTER

A modem allows you to connect to the Internet

MODEM

Monitors are available in various sizes

MONITOR

COMPUTER

The microprocessor and RAM are housed in the computer's case

KEYBOARD

MOUSE AND PAD

Data can be written to external storage discs

Various types of cable are used to connect hardware

CD BURNER

CABLES

UNDERSTANDING HARDWARE

The term hardware refers to all the physical parts of your computer, the network it is connected to, and any peripherals (attached devices). Although computer hardware is often technologically outdated within a year or so of purchase, most organizations find it can handle the tasks required of it for up to a decade. Equally, since standard business software rarely requires the speed and power of the latest computers on the market, you will find it is not normally necessary to buy the fastest computers available.

QUESTIONS TO ASK YOURSELF

Q How old is my computer hardware, and is it obsolete?

Q Am I kept waiting while my computer performs processing tasks?

Q Can I add more RAM to speed up my computer?

Q Does my software perform all the tasks I need?

Q Do I need new hardware to run the software I need?

21 Choose leading suppliers for your equipment needs.

22 Have at least 32MB of RAM to suit the memory needs of modern programs.

UNDERSTANDING SOFTWARE

The term software refers to the invisible parts of a computer system that provide the functionality and flexibility to perform useful work. System software, usually called the operating system (OS), controls the computer (and all communication with attached devices), provides the user interface (what is visible on screen), and acts as an intermediary for application software. Applications are software programs designed for specific tasks, such as accounting or word processing. A huge number of applications exist to cater for virtually any need.

ESTABLISHING PRIORITIES

Ideally, you should first select the application software best suited to the particular needs of your organization, and then choose hardware and an operating system that meet the requirements of those software packages. However, unless you are installing computer hardware for the first time, or are ready to upgrade existing equipment, you will have to pick from applications that will run on the hardware you have installed.

23 Remember that you do not need the latest, powerful computer chips to run most business software.

SELECTING HARDWARE

*C*hoosing hardware can seem confusing because of the complicated technical specifications that are often quoted. In fact, it is not difficult, even for nontechnical managers, to select suitable computers, monitors, and basic input devices.

24 Remember that "Wintel" PCs and Macs can share the same network.

25 Ensure that you take maintenance costs into account.

POINTS TO REMEMBER

- Stability and reliability are most important for business use.
- Powerful computers are needed for multimedia applications such as website design, graphic design, and video or audio editing.
- Less power is needed for most business desktop computers than home ones designed for games and multimedia applications.
- Modern, "multisync" monitors allow you to adjust screen resolution according to the need.

CHOOSING COMPUTERS

In many business situations the decisions about computer selection and purchase are made by IT staff, but in smaller organizations the task may fall to nontechnical managers. Most modern personal computers will be fast enough for common business applications, so you should focus on issues such as ease of use, ownership cost (on-going costs, including dealing with problems and breakdowns), and reliability. The standard business desktop PC has an Intel processor and one of the Windows operating systems (often called a Wintel machine), but Apple Macintosh computers (Macs) are a worthy alternative, as are PCs running the Linux OS. Macs have a strong reputation as fast and user-friendly, with a low total cost of ownership, and are often chosen for creative and multimedia work.

Check that the supplier can provide the aftersales service you require.

Make a list of the features you need, and compare potential products against your checklist

MAKING THE DECISION ▶
Use a checklist to assess the merits of possible products, then discuss your specific requirements with the suppliers.

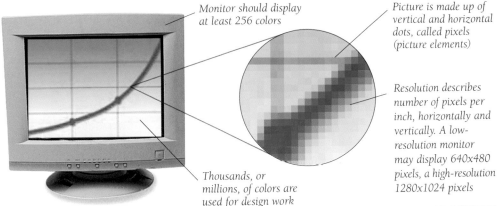

Monitor should display at least 256 colors

Picture is made up of vertical and horizontal dots, called pixels (picture elements)

Resolution describes number of pixels per inch, horizontally and vertically. A low-resolution monitor may display 640x480 pixels, a high-resolution 1280x1024 pixels

Thousands, or millions, of colors are used for design work

DECIDING ON A MONITOR

A standard monitor has a CRT (cathode-ray tube), like a TV set. Size is measured diagonally across the picture tube but the visible area is slightly smaller. A 15-inch screen is standard for most business applications, but a 17- or 21-inch screen is better for large spreadsheets or graphics work. LCD (liquid crystal display) screens are used on laptops, and may well become the norm for desktop use.

▲ CHOOSING RESOLUTION

A high resolution shows more information on screen because the images are smaller than on a low-resolution display.

26 Pick a large, high-resolution monitor for design work.

Most keyboards have a standard layout

Mouse pad used under mouse

Drawing tablet and pen useful for precise graphic or technical work

INPUTTING TOOLS ▲

Various designs of keyboards, mice, and drawing tablets are available. Choose ones that are well made and comfortable to use for long periods.

CHOOSING A KEYBOARD AND MOUSE

The keyboard and mouse are the primary means of entering information and controlling the computer. Keyboards vary in quality and feel, so try out different makes before making your choice. Some have a shaped wrist support that can increase comfort when typing, and help reduce wrist and finger strain. The mouse is used to control a pointer that selects and moves objects on the screen. It is usually connected to the keyboard by a thin cable, but cordless types are available. Mice are made in different shapes and sizes, and have one, two, or three buttons.

PUTTING INFORMATION IN

Input devices are used to communicate with the computer and to transfer information into it so that the data can be processed. The keyboard is the most commonly used input device, but there are many others available to suit the type of data you need to capture. For instance, a bar-code reader transfers data from a printed bar code into a stock system, and a voice input system allows you to use speech to control the computer.

27 For fast scanning of small amounts of data, use a handheld scanner.

COMMON INPUT DEVICES

HARDWARE	WHAT IS IT? HOW IS IT USED?
 BAR-CODE READER	A bar-code reader is needed to scan the black-and-white bars that are used to store product details, and to transfer the data into a computer. Typical uses are point-of-sale applications, distribution control, and the tracking of supplies and products.
DIGITAL CAMERA 	The latest digital stills and video cameras are very effective and can be plugged directly into a computer. This makes it possible to edit the images on-screen and quickly incorporate them into a brochure, catalogue, or presentation.
MICROPHONE	Modern desktop computers now allow the use of speech recognition to control the computer. In addition, text can be dictated directly into a word-processing program. This is extremely useful, especially for inexperienced typists.
NETWORK CONNECTION	A network connection gives access to information stored on other computers or storage devices on the network. If the network is also connected to the Internet, users can access and input information from innumerable sources worldwide.
 SCANNER	A scanner is a useful office tool used to capture an image of a document or graphic that can then be manipulated and stored in the computer. An optical character recognition program (OCR) is used to convert scanned text into an editable form.

GETTING INFORMATION OUT

Output devices are used to convert digital computer information into other forms, or to transfer information to other equipment or storage media. A monitor is an output device that allows you to view and interact with text and images displayed on its screen. Other devices include printers, plotters for large graphics or technical drawings, and audio speakers. Connection to a network allows data to be shared with others.

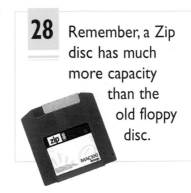

28 Remember, a Zip disc has much more capacity than the old floppy disc.

COMMON OUTPUT DEVICES

HARDWARE	WHAT IS IT? HOW IS IT USED?
STORAGE MEDIA	Removable storage media range from floppy discs storing 1.4MB (megabytes) to CD-ROM and DVD discs with capacities of 650MB or up to 9GB (gigabytes). These allow easy storage or distribution of video or multimedia information.
FAX MODEM 	Faxing a document directly from your computer is far more efficient than printing it out and sending it from a fax machine. This is achieved simply by connecting your computer to a fax modem, either directly or via a network.
 INKJET PRINTER	Inkjet printers are not as fast as laser printers and their print quality is slightly lower, but they can produce good results in full color at a much lower cost than a laser printer. They are ideal for users who require low-cost, color-printed output.
LASER PRINTER	A laser printer is the standard choice for an office because it provides high-speed printing with high-quality output. A laser printer can be connected directly to the user's computer or, more commonly, to a network so that it can be shared.
 VIDEO TAPE	Both audio and video can be edited on computer and then output to a variety of media including tape, CD-ROM, and DVD discs. Audio/video presentations can be run from the computer using speakers and projection equipment.

USING NETWORKS

Networks are the arteries of modern business and are vital for sharing information and communication both inside and outside the organization. A network system must be selected to suit the number of users and to provide fast file-sharing.

29 Select a network that will run quickly, even when sharing large files.

30 Use a laptop for working on the move, and connect to the office network to share files.

SHARING INFORMATION

Information stored on a computer that is not connected to a network can be shared only by printing it out or by copying it to a removable disk. A network solves this problem, and allows a group of computers to share files and have access to other devices, such as printers and scanners, that are also connected to the network. Networks must transfer files at sufficient speed to prevent delays in working. When all the computers are in the same department or building, the network is called a Local Area Network (LAN).

KEEPING THINGS SIMPLE

The simplest form of network is a peer-to-peer arrangement, which provides a low-cost way of connecting a small number of computers (usually fewer than 10) in the same office. Each user's files are stored on his or her own computer, but anyone on the network can be given access to those files. Because the files are all stored on individual computers, they can be difficult to manage efficiently, but a peer-to-peer network does mean that if one computer fails, the others on the network are still usable. Since any standard desktop system can manage file-transfer tasks, a peer-to-peer network does not require a more powerful, special network-operating system.

THINGS TO DO

1. Decide on the number of users who need to be connected to the network.

2. Consider the size of files that you need to transfer: large multimedia files need higher network capacity than text files.

3. Decide whether a peer-to-peer or client/server network is more appropriate for your needs.

INTERNET CONNECTION

PRINTER

CLIENT

CLIENT

CLIENT

SERVER

A COMMON ▲ CLIENT/SERVER NETWORK

A client/server network links all users with a powerful central server and with input or output devices connected to the network.

31 Consider installing two servers to avoid network loss if one fails.

32 Use passwords to control user access to the server, its files, and folders.

SERVICING THE LARGER ORGANIZATION

An organization that has more than about 10 computers requires a more sophisticated network if it is to share information effectively. The most common type is called a client/server system, in which users' computers (clients) are connected to a central, more powerful computer called a server. All data files are stored on the server, which usually has extra-large hard discs and a powerful server-operating system. Because all the files are stored centrally, they can be organized easily, protected against viruses, and backed up regularly (by being saved to another storage device) to prevent loss of valuable data. The server also controls communications, managing the performance of the network and controlling users' access to the Internet or to fax facilities. If the server fails, however, all users will be affected.

HARNESSING INTERNET STANDARDS

Early networks used several different, and often incompatible, systems to transfer information; but the growth of the Internet has transformed network systems. By using software and hardware tools that conform to Internet standards, you achieve compatibility with the Internet and the ability to build an intranet (a private, internal website). This gives you an efficient, low-cost method of sharing your information internally and across the Internet.

33 Use network systems compatible with the Internet.

34 Create an intranet for easy sharing of information.

35 Plan a network to cope with the demands of users for fast, reliable data sharing.

MOVING OUTSIDE YOUR NETWORK

The usefulness of a network can be extended considerably, especially if it is based on Internet standards. A LAN can be connected to other LANs within the organization, even in other cities or countries, by creating a Wide Area Network (WAN) using dedicated telephone lines. Or you can ask your Internet Service Provider (ISP) to set up a Virtual Private Network (VPN), on which information is encrypted for privacy before being sent across the Internet. An Internet connection also provides you with access to global email, the Web, and other resources.

◀ **SETTING UP A SIMPLE NETWORK**
This case study shows that setting up a simple network need not be complicated or require a lot of technical knowledge. The job can be done quickly and cost-effectively, yet it can also deliver real benefits to staff, the organization, and clients.

CASE STUDY
Fiona, director of a small PR agency, was asked to organize the networking of computers in a regional office. The office had eight unconnected computers, requiring staff to use floppy discs to exchange files. Staff were now asking for the ability to share files and to have email. Fiona started by employing a consultant to advise on networking issues and decided to include the requirement to give staff access to the Internet, initially for email only. Together with the consultant, Fiona reviewed the performance of the existing computers and decided to upgrade the four oldest. A simple peer-to-peer network was quickly installed, with an Internet connection and an email server. Fiona provided good training and monitored results. Productivity increased and clients were pleased at being able to deal with the company by email.

PREDICTING FUTURE DEVELOPMENTS

Today's client/server systems are powerful but require the use of personal computers that are costly to maintain and hard to keep updated. Modern, fast networks based on Internet standards offer an alternative, lower-cost solution. Simple network computers (NCs) are linked to a very powerful server using a high-speed network. The NCs do not need a powerful processor or any internal hard discs for data storage, so they are cheap to build and maintain. They use a programming language called Java or a simple version of Windows, which enables them to control application programs based on a server. Because all computing activity takes place on the server, it is easy to control, but it needs a powerful server and a fast network.

Key
- Server
- Terminals

Fast network links powerful server to simple computers

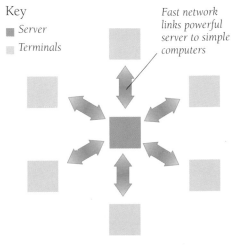

▲ NETWORK COMPUTERS
Network computers offer the potential for a low-cost, easily maintained system, but they remove users' "ownership" of processing power and personal data storage.

POINTS TO REMEMBER

- Copper cable is commonly used for network cabling.

- Fiber-optic cable, which is now increasingly cost-effective, offers far higher data transfer speeds.

- The most common system for transferring data across a network is called Ethernet and gives speeds of up to 10 megabits per second (Mbps).

- A system called Fast Ethernet gives speeds of up to 100 Mbps.

- Speeds of up to 1000 Mbps – needed for multimedia and video conferencing – are provided by systems such as New Ethernet.

ENSURING RELIABILITY

Large networks are quite complicated and require specialized skills to set up and manage them. A network administrator is usually responsible for ensuring the system runs efficiently. Speed and reliability are key factors. A slow network reduces efficiency, and any failure can bring work to a complete halt. Get a specialist to check your network if it does not give 99 percent reliability, or if it slows significantly under heavy traffic.

36 Explore the potential benefits of using the Java language to run network applications from a server.

FOCUSING ON SOFTWARE

As a manager you must be able to use a selection of software programs, many of which have become standard management productivity tools. You should be familiar with common programs, know how to select software, and understand your staff's needs.

37 Let others be the first to experiment with new software on the market.

38 Choose widely used software for best compatibility when sharing data.

CHOOSING SOFTWARE

In large organizations, decisions about software may be made by an IT department; in others, you will have some freedom to choose software that suits your needs. Always take time to select software carefully: it is often expensive and takes time to learn, so choosing inappropriately can be an expensive mistake. If software is chosen by others and you feel you need new tools, research possible alternatives, then make your case.

COMMON SOFTWARE TOOLS

TYPE OF SOFTWARE	KEY POINTS
OPERATING SYSTEM Software that controls the computer, all inputs and outputs, and the user interface.	Modern operating systems such as Windows, Linux, and MacOS use an icon-based, graphical user interface (GUI) to simplify working. Computers running different operating systems can communicate on a network.
APPLICATION SOFTWARE Accounting, desktop publishing, and graphic-design tools are examples of specific application programs.	Many managers have particular job requirements that demand expertise in specialized tools. Pick industry-leading programs, learn to use them well, and install any important upgrades to stay compatible with other users.
PRODUCTIVITY SOFTWARE Application software for standard office tasks such as word processing is often called productivity software.	Pick productivity software that allows you to use information from one program in another application. Thus, data from a spreadsheet can be inserted easily into a word-processor document, database, or presentation.

PINPOINTING MANAGEMENT SOFTWARE

The software you use at work will depend on the nature of your job and the type of organization, but most managers regularly use office productivity software. With the growth of the Internet, email and Web-browsing software are also commonly used. In addition, you may use powerful business-management software written for your specific industry, or specialist application software such as graphic, multimedia, or design tools. Thorough training in all specialized software is essential if you are to get the best use out of it.

39 Remember, 80 percent of users need only 20 percent of the features offered by most programs.

SELECTING SOFTWARE

Check what software others use and ask for their opinion

List the key features you require

Make a short list of possible products

Evaluate by trial, from reviews, or with expert advice

MICROSOFT WORD ▼
Microsoft Word is the most commonly used word-processing software. With it, you can set up standard templates for letters, faxes, and memos.

Space for address on headed notepaper

Text can be formatted in bold or italics

Text can be set in columns

Bullet points separate key items

Ms. Jones
The Company Inc.
I The Street
ZIP code

Today's date

Dear Ms. Jones
Subject of letter
Further to our telephone conversation,
I would like to confirm our order for:

• Item no. I
• Item no. 2
• Item no. 3

• Item no. 4
• item no. 5
• Item no. 6

I look forward to hearing from you.

Yours sincerely

Signature
Name

USING A WORD PROCESSOR

Word processing is the most common software requirement for managers. In most cases, the needs are quite simple: to write and format a letter or report, for instance. Today's word processors have, however, almost the same features as professional desktop-publishing software and are far more feature-packed and complicated than most people require. Focus on fully learning only the features you use most often. Ignore those you rarely need. Important skills include formatting a document, saving a format as a template that can be re-used, and applying fonts and styles (such as bold and italics) to text.

USING A SPREADSHEET

A spreadsheet program is potentially the most useful and powerful tool at a manager's disposal. A spreadsheet is a simple grid of cells arranged in rows and columns. Each cell can hold text, a number, or a formula, and users can create their own layout, define relationships between data, and devise formulas for calculations. You can also present the data in chart, table, or graph form. Spreadsheets are far less structured than most software but offer a very flexible tool for working with numbers and formulas. They are ideal for financial work or any other numerical calculation such as building sales forecasts or identifying cost or profit scenarios to answer "what if?" questions. The latest spreadsheets allow you to publish data on a Web or intranet site and share your data with your customers and suppliers.

POINTS TO REMEMBER

- Spreadsheet programs may seem daunting to learn, but they are important and powerful tools for analyzing data.
- More time will be spent mastering this software than most others.
- A wide range of graphical presentation styles is offered by modern spreadsheet programs, allowing complex information to be clearly presented.
- To save time formatting a spreadsheet, a template should be set up for calculations that are used regularly.

VERSATILE SPREADSHEETS ▼
Learning to use a spreadsheet effectively enables you to organize, analyze, and present data – such as year-end results – in ways that suit your needs.

40 Make it a priority to learn how to use a spreadsheet.

Quarter	01	02	03	04	Total
Seasonal adjustment	0.9	1.1	0.8	1.2	
Number units sold	5,644	6,898	5,017	7,525	25,084
Sales revenue	214,467	262,126	190,637	285,956	953,186
Cost of sales	124,165	151,757	110,369	165,553	551,844
Gross margin	90,302	110,369	80,268	120,403	401,342
Sales costs	8,000	8,000	9,000	9,000	34,000
Advertising	10,000	10,000	10,000	10,000	40,000
Overheads	25,736	31,455	22,876	34,315	114,382
Total costs	43,736	49,455	41,876	53,315	188,382
Gross profit	46,566	60,914	38,392	67,088	212,960
Profit margin	22%	23%	20%	23%	22%

Create headings and rows, then enter data and formulas into cells

When a variable is changed, results can be calculated automatically

The most popular spreadsheets include Microsoft Excel and Lotus 1-2-3

Most spreadsheets can present data in charts, tables, or graphical form

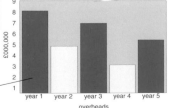

000,0003

9
8
7
6
5
4
3
2
1

year 1   year 2   year 3   year 4   year 5
overheads

First Name	Last Name	Address	ZIP Code	Telephone
James	Talbot	15 Moonshill Road	80303	303-123-4567
Jonathon	Dean	306 Hastings Drive	08077	609-891-2345
Joshua	Brown	Ash Lane	29708	803-678-9123

A record is a collection of items of information about one person or thing

A field is one element of the record: in this case, the client's last name

A table consists of a number of records. One or more tables make a database

ELEMENTS OF A DATABASE ▲

A database consists of one or more tables, each of which is made up of fields and records. By performing a search of the database, you can quickly locate information of specific interest – for instance, all clients living in a particular town.

WORKING WITH DATABASES

A spreadsheet is a useful tool for organizing lists of data, but when you need to manage large amounts of information, a database program is far more powerful. A database can be built to manage a mailing list, customer and supplier information, product details, employee payroll information, or any other information that requires collating, managing, and analyzing. In today's business environment, which focuses on information and knowledge management, databases are essential. Simple, "flat-file" databases give access only to the data stored in that database, but a "relational" database allows you to define relationships between two or more databases. This gives you a powerful tool for finding, sorting, and analyzing information stored in different databases.

41 Increase availability of data by linking several databases.

42 Create standard reports for the information you need regularly.

THINGS TO DO

1. Consider how you wish to use and present the data once the database is in use.

2. Plan your database on paper before building it on screen.

3. List all the fields you want to include in the database.

4. Identify any necessary relationships between separate databases.

43 Unless you have specialized needs, choose a ready-made program rather than a custom one.

MAKING A PRESENTATION

*P*resentation software can make the task
of producing a presentation relatively
quick and easy, and it offers new ways of
distributing information. Practice is needed
to master the software, however, and some
design skills are required for best results.

44 Take notice of the ways others create presentations and learn from them.

THINGS TO DO

1. Be clear about the type and frequency of presentations you need to produce.

2. Discuss your needs with colleagues and get advice on software and techniques.

3. Allow plenty of time to learn new software.

4. Practice with the software before you need to use it.

5. Use specialized designers for important or complex, interactive presentations.

CHOOSING THE RIGHT PRESENTATION PACKAGE

Before you pick a software program to use, you must consider the type of presentations you plan to produce. A simple presentation may require only paper handouts and overhead projection transparencies, but a major event could call for video, audio, animation, and transition effects. Think about whether you want to produce 35mm slides or display the presentation from a laptop computer. You may need to create an interactive presentation for use on a website or DVD disc. Microsoft Powerpoint is a popular business presentation package; other, specialized programs, such as Macromedia Director, offer greater power and more flexibility, but demand greater expertise to exploit their features.

QUESTIONS TO ASK YOURSELF

Q Am I the right person to be producing these presentations?

Q Will I need to create presentations on a regular basis?

Q What kind of presentations will I need to produce?

Q How will I deliver the presentations – do I need to publish on the Web?

Q Is there a software program available in my organization?

Q Can I learn to use the program or do I need a specialist?

45 Distribute interactive presentations on CD-ROM, by email, or on a website.

CREATING A GOOD PRESENTATION

Just because a software program provides many features, it does not mean you should use them all. This is very true of presentation software, which typically gives you the option of selecting from a wide range of styles, effects, and transitions. Unless you are a professional designer, the best advice is to keep it simple:

- Use a clear layout that does not distract from the content of your presentation.
- Use graphics, video, and audio for impact, but do not overuse animated effects and transitions.

46 Minimize text by making use of bullet points.

47 Choose graphics to help communicate your message in a clear way.

MAKING ▶ AN IMPACT
Remember that simplicity and clarity are likely to have greatest impact. Avoid messy or confusing effects that distract the audience.

POINTS TO REMEMBER

- All graphics and text should be prepared before the building of the presentation is started.
- Audience handouts should be produced to enhance an on-screen presentation.
- Alternative means of delivering an electronic presentation should be arranged in case of problems.
- Interactive material can be used effectively on your website to inform and entertain customers.

AVOIDING PROBLEMS

Remember that complex and important presentations require significant time and skill to create, and entail the possibility of things going wrong. Avoid getting carried away by the abilities of the technology and focus on the importance of the audience. Ensure that the content, style, and sophistication of the presentation are appropriate to the messages you are trying to relay. Allow plenty of time to build the presentation, and make time for a practice run at the location, using the same equipment that you will use on the day.

MANAGING EMAIL

E mail provides a cheap, fast, and efficient means of sending electronic messages around the office or around the world. The ease of sending messages can cause problems, so you and your staff must learn when and how best to use email.

48 If you send a very urgent email, use the telephone to warn the recipient.

49 Pick up your email when you are on the move by using the latest mobile phone technology.

RUNNING EMAIL

An email program lets you create, receive, store, and manage your messages. Popular programs include Microsoft Outlook, Qualcomm Eudora Pro, and Netscape Communicator. The best way to run email in an organization is to use a network server to manage internal email and control a permanent, or dial-up, Internet connection. If you have a permanent or regular, periodic connection, email will arrive automatically at each computer on the network. Otherwise, it is kept at the ISP until you dial in and collect it.

HOW EMAIL WORKS ▼
Email is sent to your Internet Service Provider (ISP) and then, via Internet mail servers, to the recipient's ISP.

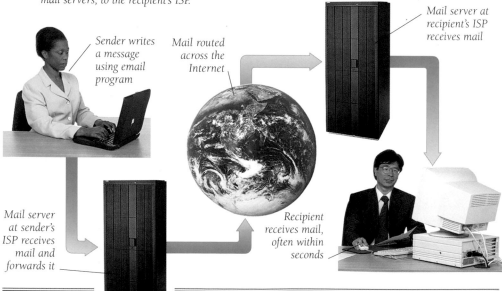

Sender writes a message using email program

Mail routed across the Internet

Mail server at recipient's ISP receives mail

Mail server at sender's ISP receives mail and forwards it

Recipient receives mail, often within seconds

Using Email Efficiently

Today, email is an increasingly important tool, but if used poorly it can be a time-waster and a cause of irritation. It is vital to ensure that you and your staff thoroughly learn how to use your email program.

- Use a modern email program for maximum compatibility with other email users.
- Learn how to add file attachments to messages.
- Organize your messages into folders, and regularly delete or archive old messages.
- Take as much care composing an email as you would a letter.

Points to Remember

- Your organization should have an email use policy – make sure you know and follow its instructions.
- The assumption should never be made that a message has been read – some people do not check their mailboxes regularly.
- If an email you sent is returned to you (called "bouncing") it is likely you addressed it incorrectly.
- Email is not a secure form of communication. A message may be read by someone other than the intended recipient.
- An encryption program should be used to keep important email messages secure, but discuss this with your IT staff first.

Do's and Don'ts

- ✔ Do deal with incoming emails quickly and file important messages.
- ✔ Do delete "junk" mail unread or use a filter in your program to discard it automatically.
- ✔ Do learn to use reply and forward features in your email program.
- ✔ Do keep messages and any attachments as small as possible.

- ✘ DON'T WRITE IN CAPITALS. It is called "shouting" and can cause offense.
- ✘ Don't automatically include all recipients of an original message in your reply.
- ✘ Don't use rude or profane language.
- ✘ Don't use your business email address for personal messages.

50 Use your email address book feature to organize contact details and create groups of contacts.

Avoiding Problems

Most of the problems users have with email stem from misunderstanding or misuse. Many organizations implement email systems without sufficient training for staff and without considering the implications of this latest form of written communication. Because email is quick and easy to write, it can be used indiscriminately. Tell staff to check before sending an email that it is really necessary and that there is not a more appropriate way to communicate. They should write clearly and concisely, and take trouble to ensure that spelling, grammar, and punctuation are correct. Remember that laws such as those dealing with libel and contract issues apply to email as much as other written forms. A great deal of damage can be done by a carelessly written message or a sensitive note sent to the wrong recipient.

USING THE WEB

The World Wide Web is just one part of the Internet, but its rich graphical presentation has made it the most popular and fastest-growing area. The Web is an increasingly important business resource, so learning how to explore and use it is vital.

51 Upgrade your browser to make use of the latest Web features.

CULTURAL DIFFERENCES

The Internet is a global medium that in many ways transcends conventional, national, and cultural boundaries. Because it was American organizations and individuals that first took up use of the Internet, English is the principal language, but as usage spreads and cultural variety increases, we can expect to see an increase in sites in all other languages.

STARTING ON THE WEB

The Web uses a programming language called HyperText Markup Language (HTML) and a transmission standard called HyperText Transfer Protocol (HTTP). HTML allows the publication of "pages" containing text, graphics, video, and audio files. It also allows any element on a page to be linked to any other page on the Web. A website consists of a collection of pages published by an individual or organization. It is stored on a Web server connected to the Internet. Using a Web browser program on your computer, you connect to the Internet and request a page on the Web, which is then delivered by the server that holds it.

52 Pick the browser that feels the most intuitive to use.

EXPLORING A WORLD ▶ OF INFORMATION
The Web is an invaluable resource for fast research into new suppliers, including services such as corporate training, client entertainment, and overseas travel.

USING A BROWSER

The HTML language is constantly evolving as new features are added to improve the Web's ability to display multimedia (text, graphics, audio, and video) content, and to enhance the presentation of information. Web browsers are updated frequently, so make sure you use the latest upgrade for your chosen browser. Microsoft Internet Explorer and Netscape Navigator are the two most popular browsers, and both are free to download from the Web. Browsers are easy to use, and offer features that can save time while "surfing" (exploring websites). Use the "Favorites" or "Bookmarks" feature to save addresses of favorite Web pages, and the "History" feature to find sites you visited recently.

BEING SECURITY AWARE

Contrary to popular perception, security for online financial transactions is high, and potentially safer than most traditional means of paying by credit card. There are, however, real security issues to consider:

- Encode sensitive email information by using an encryption program.
- Be aware that a Web server can track your movements and can identify certain information about you.
- Financial transactions should be carried out on an encrypted, secure server. Most browsers show a padlock in the status bar to indicate when a secure connection exists.

---

http:// tells the browser to look for a hypertext document

Most, but not all, Web addresses have www. as the next part of the address

Dots (.) separate the elements of the Web address

The final part loosely indicates the type of organization

http://www.dk.com

There are no spaces in a Web address

dk.com is the domain name of the organization that owns this site

"com" is used for a company, "org" for a non-profit organization, and "edu" for an educational institution

---

▲ A WEB ADDRESS

In order for a Web browser to find a single page among the millions on the Web, each page is given a unique address

> **53** To speed up page downloading, turn off graphic loading.

UNDERSTANDING WEB ADDRESSES

Every Web page has a unique address called a Uniform Resource Locator (URL), which describes the location of the server where it is stored. For instance, www.dk.com is the address for the home (starting) page of Dorling Kindersley's website. In fact, though Web addresses start with http://, a modern browser does not need you to type this.

PICKING OTHER SOFTWARE

In addition to the main software tools that most managers encounter, there are many others that you may need, or choose to use. Make sure that your basic business needs are met before considering other programs that can help you to be more efficient.

54 Wait to buy new software for 3–6 months after it is first released.

55 Always ensure that your data is backed up on a frequent basis.

PICKING USEFUL TOOLS

If your computer is maintained by IT staff you should discuss software options with them, and avoid installing programs without their knowledge. Otherwise, do some research, ask colleagues for their advice, and test out trial versions before buying programs. Use the Internet to research software and download trial copies.

ADDITIONAL BUSINESS SOFTWARE TOOLS

SOFTWARE	BENEFITS
DATA BACKUP	Crucial for peace of mind, backup software runs on a network or individual PCs to make copies of your data.
COMPRESSION TOOLS	These compress and decompress files for transmission over the Internet or to increase disk storage capacity.
PC & NETWORK MONITORING	PC and network analysis tools monitor PC and network performance, and are used to spot and solve problems.
SECURITY SYSTEMS	Security programs can control access to data on PCs, or to resources on a network, an intranet, or the Internet.
VOICE RECOGNITION & SPEECH	These useful business tools allow you to control the computer by voice and enable it to speak to you.
GRAPHICS PRODUCTION	Graphic tools allow you to produce literature, multimedia programs, and presentations quickly and cost effectively.

USING BUSINESS MANAGEMENT SYSTEMS

Business management systems are designed to integrate many or all of the main organizational functions (such as accounting, manufacturing, sales, supply ordering, and distribution) within a single system that is used to run and manage the entire business. These systems are usually designed for specific industry needs, and they use powerful databases to store and manipulate the corporate data. They are often very expensive to implement, and users must be involved in their design if they are to be successful. Users must also be given sufficient training in how to use the system.

GETTING IT RIGHT ▶

Implementing or upgrading business management software can have a major impact. Managed properly, it can deliver significant productivity improvements.

56 Involve users when planning important computer systems.

CASE STUDY

The board of a medium-sized manufacturing company decided to upgrade the computer systems that managed their transaction processing. The existing systems did not communicate with one another, so information from the sales system had to be reentered into the accounting and distribution systems. The re-keying of data at least three times for each order caused delays, errors, and costs. The systems were incompatible with emerging Internet standards. The decision makers decided to implement a full business-management system and insisted that it be able to share information across the corporate intranet and the Internet. Sales staff were able to enter orders from their laptops while with customers, and the system then managed the sales data through each stage of the business process.

POINTS TO REMEMBER

- Successfully implementing a business management system can be one of the hardest challenges facing an organization.
- Ample time must be allowed for planning and consultation.
- The business process must be reviewed from start to finish, with the help of those who operate it, and any improvements made, before it is computerized.

SELECTING CUSTOM SOLUTIONS

Some business management systems are available "off the-shelf," but the wide variety of different business models means that many organizations have to pay developers to modify a "standard" system to suit their individual needs. If a system has to be modified considerably, it will greatly increase the costs and complexity of the project. There is also an increased risk of major cost or time overruns, or even outright failure. Beware of completely custom projects, where a new system is developed from scratch, as these are notoriously difficult to manage. In all cases, have a clear and detailed contract with your supplier.

MANAGING IT

The importance of IT brings with it new requirements for managers. As well as being an able user of IT, you must be ready to manage the impact of technology on your staff.

PREPARING STAFF FOR IT

The most common reason for the failure of IT projects to deliver their potential benefits is lack of attention paid to the people who must work with the technology. It is essential to encourage staff to adopt IT, seek training, and use good working practices.

57 Maximize the benefits of IT by encouraging your team to embrace it.

QUESTIONS TO ASK YOURSELF

Q Do I take the importance of IT seriously enough?

Q Do I involve my team in decisions about IT systems?

Q Have I ensured that all my staff have been fully trained in the software they use?

Q Have my staff been trained in health and safety issues?

Q Do we have guidelines for the use of email and the Web?

EMPOWERING YOUR TEAM

People who are asked to use new technology are often reluctant to do so. This can surprise the designers of new systems, who tend to focus on technology rather than the people who will use the systems. Avoid problems by involving your team in all decisions about any IT system that affects them. Encourage users to think about ways in which IT can help with their work. Discuss IT developments with your staff, and empower them to suggest ways of improving performance. Lead by example, and point out that IT proficiency offers personal, as well as professional, benefits.

BEING AWARE OF HEALTH AND SAFETY ISSUES

Working at a computer for long periods of time can lead to some discomfort or health problems if attention is not paid to posture, workspace arrangement, and taking regular breaks. It is important to:

- Arrange your desk and chair so that you can sit comfortably and have enough space for a keyboard and mouse.
- Use an adjustable chair that gives firm support to your lower back.
- Position the monitor so that the top of the screen is at eye level.
- Adjust the distance of the screen from your eyes for personal comfort.
- Make sure that the screen is positioned to minimize glare or reflections.
- Use an adjustable monitor on a tilting stand so that you can easily adjust its position.
- Take frequent breaks, stand up and stretch, or walk around to ease tired muscles.
- Relax eye muscles by looking up from the screen regularly. Look into the distance, and blink often.

▼ CORRECT POSTURE

Adopt a good posture when working at a keyboard to avoid muscle and eye strain. Position the mouse within easy reach.

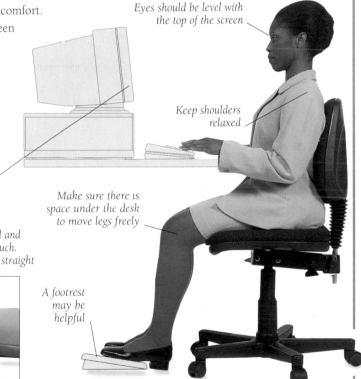

Eyes should be level with the top of the screen

Keep shoulders relaxed

Monitor should not reflect lights or windows

Make sure there is space under the desk to move legs freely

A footrest may be helpful

Relax hand and use light touch. Keep wrist straight

Breaking Down Resistance

An investment in technology can be largely wasted if users are not given sufficient training to use it effectively and to be proficient with new software. A common mistake is to assume that people are eager to learn new skills; but users may feel threatened by new technology or fail to see any personal benefits in training. Be sure to explain the reasons for using new technology, and create a business culture that encourages staff to increase their IT skills.

▼ TRAINING COURSES

Learning in a group situation with a good trainer can be an effective way to master new programs, especially if the course can be tailored to any specific needs that your staff may have.

Explain the benefits of taking training	→	Offer incentives to become proficient	→	Give good training and monitor results

HELPING YOUR TEAM LEARN ▲

Managers frequently make the assumption that staff will readily take up training when it is provided. This is often not the case, and you may need to win them over to the idea.

DO'S AND DON'TS

✔ Do listen to users and ask them to define their training needs.

✔ Do make proficiency in using IT systems part of regular staff assessment.

✔ Do assess training providers carefully before selecting training courses.

✘ Don't arrange training before discussing needs with staff.

✘ Don't schedule training courses without checking users' availability.

✘ Don't assume that an off-the-shelf course will be suitable for all your staff equally.

58 For best results from a training course, keep each session short.

59 Encourage proficient staff to learn how to help the less skilled.

PICKING A TRAINING METHOD

METHODS	PROS	CONS
LEARNING BY USING	This can be the quickest method for staff experienced in similar programs.	This can be slow and very difficult for inexperienced or reluctant computer users.
USING THE MANUAL	A good manual will help experienced computer users solve problems as they learn.	Many manuals are poorly written and confuse inexperienced users.
SPECIALIZED BOOKS	Many books dealing with specialized programs are much better than the manual.	Many are very large, seem daunting, and can confuse novices more than they help.
TRAINING COURSES	Organized training courses with good teachers are often a good way to learn quickly.	These may be expensive, and require staff to be away from the office for several days.
IN-HOUSE TRAINING	This can provide flexible learning for small groups, with lessons based on their need.	This is more expensive than out-of-house training courses and needs more organization.
ONLINE AND CD-BASED	The best programs are very flexible and are effective for self-motivated learners.	This requires multimedia PCs. Users need to put time and effort into solo learning.

ORGANIZING TRAINING

Many users have very specific requirements from their software, and only rarely need to understand all the features of a package. Focus training for most users on the parts of the package they need to use all the time, and have just one or two team members trained in the features that are used less frequently. If possible, arrange training in-house rather than at a training establishment, and ask the trainer to tailor the course to suit your requirements. After initial training, make further courses available as needed, and ensure that users know how to get help if they encounter problems.

THINGS TO DO

1. Discuss training with users.
2. Research the options for training, and ask others for referrals and references.
3. Sit in on a similar course before picking a trainer.
4. Make sure that users have all the details of the training course well in advance.

HELPING YOUR STAFF AVOID PROBLEMS

In order to help your staff avoid problems you should publish guidelines for using IT resources, especially email and the Web. Encourage staff to keep up to date with IT and provide ways for them to do so. Inform staff if their use of IT resources is monitored.

60 To minimize time spent on email, teach staff how to use the software.

POINTS TO REMEMBER

- Staff must be given full training in the use of your email system.
- Balance the cost and time implications of monitoring staff with the need to minimize time-wasting and maintain productivity.
- Staff must be told that emails can be used as evidence in libel, contract, or other legal disputes.
- Staff may be overwhelmed by email unless taught to organize it.

SETTING WEB USE POLICY

When staff are first given access to the Web it is normal for individuals to spend quite some time exploring sites and learning about the Web. This is to be encouraged, but guidelines should set parameters to prevent time-wasting online, and to prohibit visits to inappropriate sites. You will probably wish to limit the downloading of software to a network administrator, to reduce the risk from viruses. You should also use server software to bar entry to inappropriate sites, and to monitor, and log, use of the Web by your staff.

SETTING EMAIL POLICY

Far too many companies implement the use of email without providing appropriate guidelines. An organization should have clear rules for using email, and should ensure that all staff receive full training in using it efficiently. Guidelines should specify that all email belongs to the organization, that staff use can be monitored, and that all saved emails are archived as part of the organization's record keeping. The legal status of email should be explained, and guidance should be given on what is considered acceptable personal use.

61 Ask staff to keep personal email use to a minimum.

62 Learn how to use filtering tools in email software.

KEEPING STAFF AWARE

The rapid developments taking place in IT will have significant business impact. If opportunities are to be identified, it is important to encourage your key staff to keep up with the speed of change. Suggest they focus on technologies that are important to your business, and on new developments in the software you use. A regular check should also be kept on wider developments, especially those offering faster network speed and wireless communication.

63 Encourage staff to have a computer and Internet connection at home, to help them learn.

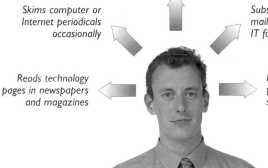

Talks to IT-literate staff regularly and shows interest in the subject

Skims computer or Internet periodicals occasionally

Subscribes to Internet mailing lists covering IT for managers

Reads technology pages in newspapers and magazines

Has a computer for home use and surfs the Web

◀ **KEEPING UP**
Remember that it is important for your career to understand the benefits to be obtained from technology both for your staff and for your business. Develop your own preferred strategies for keeping up with developments, and encourage your staff to work on the same principles.

MONITORING YOUR STAFF

The technology that helps your staff to communicate easily and quickly also makes it possible to monitor their use of the technology. Monitoring staff to the extent allowed by the latest systems has ethical and practical implications and should not be done without staff being informed. Remember that monitoring without a clear purpose is pointless, takes human and network resources, and could easily lower morale.

DO'S AND DON'TS

☑ Do help staff to keep up to date with new developments in IT.

☑ Do have guidelines for using computers, network resources, and the Internet.

☑ Do discuss use of monitoring with staff and draw up agreed guidelines.

☒ Don't expect staff to want to learn to use new technology.

☒ Don't be impatient with staff who take time to learn to use new technology.

☒ Don't forget to create a forum for staff to discuss technology and make suggestions.

REVIEWING THE BUSINESS PROCESS

An organization's business process often evolves over time, to suit changes in the company or its marketplace. It is essential to review the process and make it as efficient as possible before implementing IT solutions to support it.

64 Start by assuming that there is a better way of doing things.

65 Listen to your customers and your staff to find new opportunities.

POINTS TO REMEMBER

- A process is not necessarily effective just because "it has always been done this way."

- A business process is liable to become static and inflexible, while business needs can change rapidly.

- IT issues must not be considered until the best scenario for the business process has been devised.

- Top-performing competitors should be benchmarked.

ANALYZING THE ▶ SITUATION
Try looking at your organization with a fresh eye, and consider every part of your business process to find ways to improve it.

ANALYZING THE CURRENT SITUATION

In today's fast-changing world, it is not unusual to find that parts of your business process have become unnecessary or inefficient since they were first implemented. Many organizations are now choosing to outsource parts of the process as they redefine their core business skills. Before implementing any major IT solution, always start by reevaluating your current business process. Check that the business strategy has not changed since the existing process was created.

Considers whether business needs have changed

Benchmarks competitors to test for new alternatives

REDEFINING THE BUSINESS PROCESS

Once you have analyzed the current situation, you should create a "wish list" that describes your ideal business process. Make sure you have a good IT strategist in your team to advise on the capabilities of technology, but do not consider specific IT tools at this stage. Give users a "blue skies" scenario to find their ideal process. Involve suppliers and customers, if possible, in order to develop the most effective business process.

66 Look outside your own industry for good ideas your business can use.

THE BEST ▶ WAY FORWARD

Reviewing business strategy and core processes is time-consuming but necessary when significant IT expenditure is considered.

CASE STUDY

A leading car distributor needed to update its aging transaction processing system. First, however, decision-makers decided to conduct a full review of the marketplace and the existing business process.

They reviewed the long-term strategy, and then asked staff working in the core process for ideas to make the process more efficient. Customers and suppliers were involved in the review, and a wish list of needs was drawn up. Ideas on how to use IT to improve the process were put forward, but the process re-design was not limited by planning for specific software.

The company looked outside its industry and identified the Internet as being of increasing importance, so it decided to require Internet compatibility for all software. Finally, potential suppliers were briefed on requirements, and a successful bidder was selected.

PLANNING AN IT SOLUTION

Agree the business process with management and users

⬇

List all requirements for an IT system to handle the process

⬇

Work with IT staff to evaluate potential solutions

⬇

Ensure users accept chosen system and give full training

DESIGNING A SOLUTION

Once you have redefined your strategy, examined your existing process, and decided on changes that may be needed, you are ready to discuss specific IT solutions with potential suppliers. Using the analysis of your ideal process, produce a specification describing the results that a new system must be able to deliver. Do not specify how the software should deliver the results; leave suppliers free to suggest alternative approaches that you may not have considered. Remember to specify the existing systems with which a new one must communicate, and insist that new software be Internet-compatible, to allow you to share information easily with others.

PLANNING RESOURCES

In order to plan the resources you will require in the future, you have to imagine how your organization will need to work in an increasingly Internet-dominated world. You must focus on creating a seamless process that is targeted at meeting customers' needs.

67 Use improved productivity as your key test for new resources.

68 Plan on doing more and more business online.

LOOKING AHEAD ▼

When planning IT resources, you need to examine the current position, take note of staff suggestions, and then look ahead, always focusing on working effectively with suppliers and customers.

LOOKING TO THE FUTURE

The pace of change in information technology is now so rapid that planning the resources you will need, even for the next year or two, can be very difficult. Although it is impossible to predict the future fully, you should spend some time trying to imagine your business in two or three years' time, and consider how you wish to be doing business in the future. Focus on how many people you expect to be using your IT systems, and what kind of services your customers require. Pay special attention to conducting business via the Internet.

Aims for efficient sharing of customer and supplier information

Works toward sharing databases internally, and with suppliers and customers

Listens to users' suggestions or requests for better tools

Ensures systems and tools work with online suppliers and customers

Establishes how up-to-date current systems and tools are

Checks systems are as effective as those of competitors

IDENTIFYING YOUR NEEDS

Start by asking your customers and suppliers for comments on the process of doing business with you and look for ways in which IT can improve the customer and supplier relationships. Work with your staff to identify the pros and cons of existing systems. If possible, research how your main competitors are using IT to improve their performance, and look at other industries for new ideas. Look for software tools that can deliver the results you want, then decide on hardware needs.

QUESTIONS TO ASK YOURSELF

Q Have I taken the time to look at my business from my customers' point of view?

Q Do I accept the need to turn my organization into an online business for future success?

Q Have I taken into account the views of my staff, and allowed for their different needs?

POINTS TO REMEMBER

● For most organizations, adopting the Internet as a major business tool should not be thought of as an option – it is essential.

● A fast internal network and a fast and reliable Internet connection must be considered as absolutely vital to future plans.

● Considerable growth in network traffic should be allowed for when your network needs are being planned.

MOVING TO E-BUSINESS

The development of the Internet has changed business forever. Organizations that were quick to realize the commercial implications have focused on developing IT systems compatible with Internet standards, so as to ensure effective use of the medium. Many businesses are adapting to e-commerce (the process of selling goods and services online) but this is only a part of the transformation into an e-business, in which all the organization's processes and systems are integrated to provide seamless and transparent service.

ALLOWING FOR VARIETY

Remember that different groups of staff will have vastly different information and computing needs. Some will only require reliable network access to databases with simple, effective tools for data input. Others may need powerful computers, and graphic or design software, together with a high capacity network to allow for fast transfer of very large files. Marketeers and after-sales staff will require quick access to customer and product databases and analytical tools. Most staff will benefit from a good intranet through which they can easily access the company's information pool.

69 Look at other industries for their view of the future.

70 Build flexibility into your systems to allow for changing needs.

Working with IT Staff

The relationship between IT staff and the rest of the organization is an important element in using technology successfully. IT services must be focused on delivering real business benefit, and IT users should be encouraged to assess the service they receive.

71 Pick staff for IT services who can communicate well with users.

72 Devise a questionnaire so that users can assess the quality of their IT service.

Assessing the IT Service

IT staff are too often seen as a separate part of an organization and are sometimes considered to be difficult to communicate with. A good IT service understands business issues and provides strategic IT advice at senior level. It delivers high-quality systems, training, and support services to users, and communicates effectively. Evaluate IT staff by consulting non-IT staff on the quality of service, and by comparing costs with external suppliers.

Assessing Your IT Service

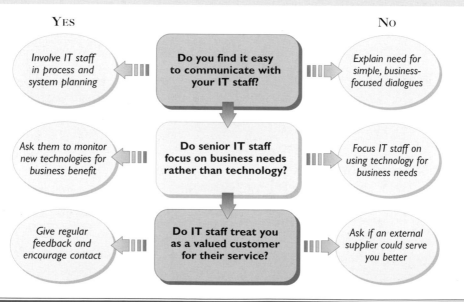

YES		NO
Involve IT staff in process and system planning	**Do you find it easy to communicate with your IT staff?**	Explain need for simple, business-focused dialogues
Ask them to monitor new technologies for business benefit	**Do senior IT staff focus on business needs rather than technology?**	Focus IT staff on using technology for business needs
Give regular feedback and encourage contact	**Do IT staff treat you as a valued customer for their service?**	Ask if an external supplier could serve you better

FOCUSING ON BUSINESS REQUIREMENTS

If an organization is to get the best out of IT, it must involve senior IT staff in business decision-making and focus them on using technology not for its own sake but to deliver specific business benefits. An organization should have a senior person who is sufficiently knowledgeable in IT, as well as the business strategy, to be able to advise at board level on the implications of emerging technologies. IT staff should work closely with managers and users in all departments to ensure that the IT function is fully integrated into the organization's operations. The staff who provide support services to users, manage systems, and organize training must have good communication skills in order to provide top-quality assistance.

THINGS TO DO

1. Examine the quality of the IT service you receive.
2. Involve your team in assessing IT performance.
3. Seek to build better relationships with IT specialists.
4. Explain the business needs behind requests you make for IT services.
5. Involve IT staff in business project teams.
6. Give feedback to IT staff.

BUILDING RELATIONSHIPS

It is quite common for staff to feel intimidated by IT experts and to find it difficult to ask for help or advice. Look for ways to bring together IT staff and users of the technology. Use formal and informal situations to develop links and build relationships. Arrange sessions to explain the importance of IT to users, and the needs of the business to IT staff.

A GOOD WORKING RELATIONSHIP ▲

The effective use of IT is now so important for commercial success that it is essential to build good working relationships between IT staff and other parts of the organization.

73 Motivate IT staff to focus on the real needs.

741

WORKING WITH CONSULTANTS

Consultants are an important part of many IT projects, since they provide skills and experience not available in-house. Costs can be high, however, so it is vital that you understand when to employ them and how to manage the working relationship.

74 Always define specific objectives when employing consultants.

APPOINTING A CONSULTANT

Define the project in detail and set firm objectives and deadlines

Consider building a project team with staff and external consultants

Shortlist potential consultants and invite written proposals

Set up a steering group of senior staff to oversee complex projects

Review references. Look for required expertise and good communication skills

Invite a shortlist to do a presentation to the steering group

Finally, consider cost, and focus on paying for results, not time spent

Negotiate fixed-price contracts where possible

WHEN TO USE A CONSULTANT

There are several situations in which you should consider employing consultants. At the strategic level, an independent and objective viewpoint can be very useful, even if you have a good understanding of the value of IT. At the operational level, a consultant may offer specific skills or experience not available in-house. The implementation phase of a new project is often one for which specialized skills are needed for a limited time, and the use of consultants is usually more appropriate than employing extra in-house staff.

75 Try to ensure the transfer of useful skills to your staff.

SELECTING A CONSULTANT

Before starting the selection process make sure you have clearly defined the project, its objectives, the timeline, and the results expected from consultants. If the project affects more than one part of your organization, form a steering group to oversee the project. Members should be drawn from senior managers representing the departments affected by the project. Prepare a consultancy brief and research a shortlist of suitable consultants. Invite a small number to make a presentation to the steering group and review references.

▼ MEETING THE CONSULTANT
When choosing a consultant, check technical, personal, and communication details before considering price.

---

76 . Make sure that consultants are able to be productive by providing any information they need on time.

DO'S AND DON'TS

✔ Do use a project team approach that brings together in-house staff and consultants.

✔ Do define the roles and responsibilities of consultants and in-house staff.

✔ Do use a steering group of senior managers to guide and monitor the project to its conclusion.

✘ Don't employ consultants on open-ended contracts without agreed aims and objectives.

✘ Don't relinquish control once you have appointed consultants.

✘ Don't use consultants for tasks that can be done by in-house staff more cost-effectively

MANAGING THE RELATIONSHIP

A project manager should be appointed to take control of the assignment and manage the relationships with consultants on a day-to-day basis. For long projects, in particular, aim to develop good relationships between key team members and encourage informal contact. Hold regular review sessions with members of the project team and refer to the objectives and key deadlines to keep the project on track. Quickly resolve any difficulties between your in-house staff and consultants, and do not allow minor problems to escalate into serious friction.

OUTSOURCING IT

*T*oday, *outsourcing part or all of an organization's IT function is becoming increasingly popular. It can be a sensible approach if it delivers high-quality services at lower cost than in-house resources, but it requires careful assessment and management.*

> **77** Consider letting your own IT department bid for contracts.

POINTS TO REMEMBER

- A business activity might be of strategic importance, but the IT function that supports it need not be, and could be outsourced.
- Vital flexibility will be lost if you pick a single supplier or agree long-term contracts.
- Consideration should be given to outsourcing the whole function, rather than the IT systems (for example, the payroll function).
- Your flexibility will be increased by competition for contracts between suppliers, including your IT department.

CONSIDERING THE BENEFITS AND THE RISKS

Outsourcing can be an attractive option because, in theory, it gives access to market-leading skills and technology while delivering savings on the IT budget. One problem, however, is that if outsourcing is not handled correctly, it may limit your organization's flexibility and control over its direction. In order to decide if outsourcing is of benefit, you should look at each of your IT systems in turn and consider whether cost savings could be achieved without restricting flexibility. Decide whether a system is of strategic value to your business (few are), of business-critical importance, or of a basic service nature.

NEGOTIATING CONTRACTS

When selecting potential outsourcing partners, and negotiating contracts, it is very important to avoid handing over too much power to one supplier. If you are planning to outsource several systems, draw up a shortlist of potential suppliers and seek individual bids for each service. If you do not have experience in outsourcing contracts, appoint a consultant and an IT contract lawyer to assist you. Examine each bid carefully and look for the "hidden extras" with which suppliers aim to earn extra profit from you.

> **78** Agree only to short contracts, with strict performance targets and penalty clauses.

ANALYZING THE DECISION PROCESS

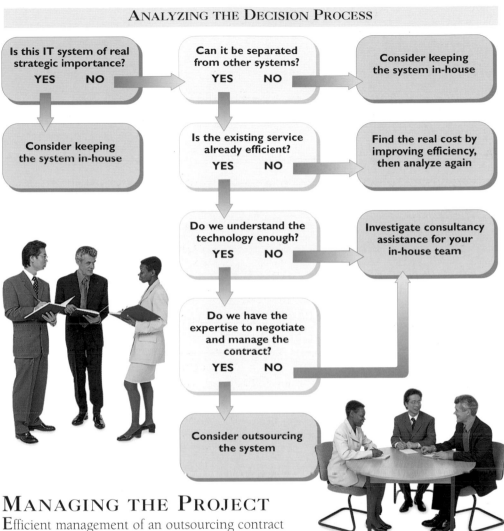

Is this IT system of real strategic importance?
YES   NO

Can it be separated from other systems?
YES   NO

Consider keeping the system in-house

Consider keeping the system in-house

Is the existing service already efficient?
YES   NO

Find the real cost by improving efficiency, then analyze again

Do we understand the technology enough?
YES   NO

Investigate consultancy assistance for your in-house team

Do we have the expertise to negotiate and manage the contract?
YES   NO

Consider outsourcing the system

MANAGING THE PROJECT

Efficient management of an outsourcing contract is often a full-time job for one or more staff members. Pick these staff with care. Ideally, they will have been involved in the selection process, since they will need an intimate knowledge of the contract and your organization's requirements. They also need good interpersonal and communication skills because they must act as the link between internal system users and your suppliers.

79 Provide sufficient staff and resources to manage the contract effectively.

PROFITING FROM THE INTERNET

The Internet is the most significant business development since the Industrial Revolution. Managers must assimilate the huge changes it is creating if their businesses are to succeed.

A BUSINESS REVOLUTION

The Internet is enabling and driving unique opportunities and new markets. Yet for many organizations it also poses a real threat. You must quickly learn how to use the Internet more effectively than your competitors if you are to stay ahead.

80 Make it a priority to learn how to use the Internet for business.

81 Think about a global market for your products.

82 Use the Internet to reach niche markets and build relationships.

REALIZING THE POTENTIAL

The Internet is at least as significant as the invention of the printing press, the telephone, or the television. It has already brought immense change to the business world. Some companies will benefit from the changes, but many will not. Those who cannot react fast enough to competition and changing markets will find their existence seriously threatened by the Internet. Make it a priority to learn how to use the Internet for your business. Concentrate on ways to use the Internet for research, speeding business with your suppliers, and getting closer to your customers.

Useful Parts of the Internet

Part	Use
EMAIL	Email is an essential tool for most businesses because it is the most efficient way of sending messages very quickly and cheaply. Documents or graphics can be attached to an email message, saving courier or postal service charges.
WORLD WIDE WEB	Another essential tool, the Web offers access to a world of information that can help organizations reduce their costs and develop individual relationships with their customers. The Web is also a vital business research tool.
NEWSGROUPS	Newsgroups can be very useful for conducting customer research or for keeping up to date with industry news. Newsgroup users post messages for others to read and respond to. Most email programs also read newsgroups.
MAILING LISTS	Mailing lists covering thousands of specialized topics are available by email. Many websites offer their users regular updates of information by email. Subscribe to mailing lists to research into products, customers, and IT.
CHAT ROOMS	Internet chat rooms allow people to congregate and "chat." Text typed on one keyboard can be seen on other users' screens. While public chat rooms have little business value, private ones can usefully be set up for meetings.
FTP (FILE TRANSFER PROTOCOL)	FTP allows files to be transferred to and from servers on the Internet, whatever type of computer you use. Modern Web browsers incorporate FTP ability. Much information and even software is freely available from FTP servers.
GOPHER	Gopher is another part of the Internet dedicated to finding information. It existed before (and has been largely eclipsed by) the World Wide Web, but it can be useful for finding specialized information not available on the Web.

CUTTING COSTS

The Internet is creating a ferociously competitive marketplace in many industries. Managers can use this to help cut their operating costs. Use the Web to cut the costs of communications and travel, and to get the best possible deals from suppliers.

---

83 Remember that the Internet puts power in the customer's hands.

POINTS TO REMEMBER

- The quality of Internet telephony was much poorer than the telephone system, but it is improving and is much cheaper.

- If you use a Wide Area Network with excess capacity, consider re-routing some of your internal phone calls and faxes across it.

- The Internet is in its early development period, but as bandwidth increases expect to use it for online conferences.

- Save costs by allowing staff to work at home with online access to the organization's intranet.

REDUCING YOUR COMMUNICATION COSTS

The Internet can be used to help cut business communication costs. Use email rather than faxes, mail, or couriers to send documents; and, if a large number of international faxes must still be sent, investigate Internet services that transmit faxes at lower cost than the telephone system. If you have a fast Wide Area Network connecting remote offices, explore online video-conferencing systems that can be effective enough to reduce the need for face-to-face meetings. Use your website and intranet to post answers to all those questions regularly asked by customers, suppliers, and staff, to save them from having to ask employees.

◀ **VIDEO-CONFERENCING ONLINE TO CUT COSTS**
With a fast network, you can save on travel costs by video-conferencing online with colleagues working at home or elsewhere in the country.

---

84 Use the Internet to get quotes from a wide range of potential suppliers.

REDUCING TRAVEL COSTS

The travel industry has been quick to exploit the Internet. It enables companies to offer last-minute deals and reduce the number of airline seats and hotel beds left empty, while providing excellent prices to customers. Use web travel sites to plan business travel, compare prices, and make sure you get the best discounts and frequent-flyer deals. Find the best deals quickly by using websites that compare prices across a number of airlines, hotels, car rental, and travel companies. Many of the best sites offer mailing-list services that inform you of last-minute deals.

THINGS TO DO

1. Research travel-related websites to find ones that are relevant to you.
2. Subscribe to mailing lists to stay informed.
3. Use travel-center sites that compare prices to find the best deals available.
4. Check deals and book online with your favorite airlines and hotels.

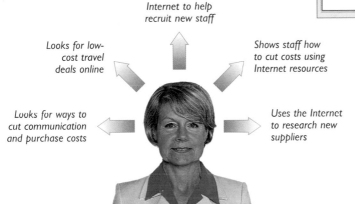

Uses the Internet to help recruit new staff

Looks for low-cost travel deals online

Shows staff how to cut costs using Internet resources

Looks for ways to cut communication and purchase costs

Uses the Internet to research new suppliers

◀ **LOOKING FOR SAVINGS**

As a manager, you should explore ways in which you can use the Web to make savings in cost areas that are significant to your organization, whatever its type and size. Your staff, too, must be educated in the potential savings.

CUTTING YOUR PURCHASE COSTS

The extraordinary growth in the Internet means that in many industries it is now possible to compare specifications, support services, and prices offered by a large number of suppliers. Indeed, there are websites that specialize in specific industries, putting you in touch with those suppliers that best match your needs. Whatever your requirements, use the Internet as a powerful research tool to reduce purchase costs.

85 Cut recruitment costs, and increase your reach, by recruiting via the Internet.

GETTING CLOSER TO THE CUSTOMER

The Internet allows you to reach a worldwide customer audience, whatever the size of your organization in the real world. Use it to get closer to your customers and provide a genuinely better service than that offered by your competitors.

86	Give customers choices in how they do business with you.

SHORTENING THE SUPPLY CHAIN

For organizations that operate through a supply chain, the Internet offers the opportunity to shorten the chain and get much closer to the customers. This increases flexibility, helps increase profits, and allows the company to research, develop, and introduce new products more quickly. Beware, however, of forgetting your existing supply chain. The Internet model is an additional chain, not a replacement. Find ways to use the Internet to support existing trade partners and help them get closer to your customers in order to provide a better service.

MANUFACTURER

Purchases made via traditional supply chain

Purchases made online through Internet reseller

WHOLESALER

INTERNET RESELLER

Purchases made online direct from manufacturer

RETAILER

◄ **LETTING THE CUSTOMER CHOOSE**
Use the Internet to give customers the best possible service, whether the product is bought online or in offline stores.

CUSTOMERS

IMPROVING CUSTOMER SERVICE

Because the Internet provides instant access to many competing suppliers, thereby ensuring that customers can always compare prices, it encourages ferocious price competition. In order to compete, organizations are increasingly focusing on customer service to differentiate themselves from competitors. Look for ways to engage with your customers, and design a website that provides quick and easy access to product information and after-sales help. Look at your organization from the outside in, and try to demolish all barriers to communication.

▼ REACHING CUSTOMERS

This case study shows the benefits of designing your website so that it gives your customers easy access to the information for which they are searching. It is important that it also provides good after-sales support service.

CASE STUDY

A leading electrical and electronic goods manufacturer decided to use its website to provide better customer service than that of its competitors, who focused on using the Web for sales material but gave few extra services. After consulting with its real-world supply chain, the company decided to create a Web presence that would provide customers with the information they needed and help existing retailers by directing customers to them.

The resulting website helps customers find the product they need (and is even able to customize some products) and then gives them the choice of purchasing online or being directed to the nearest or most convenient retailer. The extensive customer-support features include discussion groups, mailing lists, and live, text-based contact with support staff.

---

87 Monitor the ways in which your competitors deal with customers.

88 Encourage and facilitate customer contact online or with human staff.

UNDERSTANDING THE PITFALLS

Although many organizations talk about customer service, and claim to be committed to it, the perception of many customers is the opposite. Do not underestimate the power of the Internet audience to damage your reputation if you fail to perform. There is very little loyalty on the Web; customers can move to your competitor with the click of a mouse. Constantly monitor the way customers use your website to find ways to improve it. Make sure that the site is not a barrier to communication. Too many sites give no real-world contact details and seek to prevent contact with human staff, rather than encouraging communication in any way the customer chooses.

BUILDING THE SUPPLIER RELATIONSHIP

*C*lose cooperation with each organization in your supply chain is essential if you are to minimize costs and maximize your flexibility. Take advantage of Internet technologies to share information and build closer relationships with suppliers.

89 Post specifications on your intranet and let suppliers bid for contracts.

90 Give your staff an incentive to share information.

91 Seek users' input when building an intranet.

IMPROVING YOUR PURCHASING ABILITY

Fast communication between all members of a supply chain has become vital to minimize time-to-market, stock holdings, and just-in-time production. Electronic Data Interchange (EDI) was developed to facilitate fast transfer of repetitive business data. EDI used to be sent over expensive, private networks with many system incompatibility problems. Today, the Internet offers lower costs and more flexibility, enabling information to be easily shared with partners.

ASSESSING SUPPLIERS' READINESS FOR E-BUSINESS

It is important to identify which suppliers are ready and able to conduct business with you electronically. Ask your suppliers pertinent questions, focusing on their ability to share data using the Internet or a private intranet.

Do you have an intranet to enable easy sharing of data?

How much of your business with customers like us is conducted electronically?

Can we track our orders by accessing your extranet?

Can we access your stock database online and in real time to check stock levels?

USING AN INTRANET AND EXTRANET

An intranet is an internal website to which access is restricted to chosen audiences. Many companies use an intranet to share information within their organization. By using low-cost and flexible Internet technology, an intranet can also replace paper-based information. The value of an intranet can be extended by giving access to suppliers and, in some cases, important customers. This system is often referred to as an extranet. Create an extranet to share important information quickly with your partners and to allow them online, real-time access to selected data.

▼ INTERNAL WEBSITES

Building an intranet can be quick, easy, and cost-effective. You should delegate to individual departments some of the reponsibilities for creating and updating information.

Access your intranet on the office network, or via the Internet when traveling.

POINTS TO REMEMBER

- To benefit your customers, you and your suppliers should be able to share information quickly.

- Smaller organizations who have not used EDI before will need encouragement to explore the benefits of fast and accurate data-sharing via your extranet.

- Business-to-business transactions are expected to form the largest share of electronic commerce.

- Many large organizations are requiring companies to conduct business electronically before they can quote for contracts.

HELPING YOUR SUPPLY CHAIN

The development of EDI allowed large organizations to form electronic links with their most important suppliers and customers. The cost and complexity of EDI meant, however, that many smaller organizations could not take part in the information-sharing. Now, any size of organization can benefit from shared information by using Internet technologies. Aim to share as much information as possible with your business partners to ensure short production and delivery times, and to minimize costs or quality problems. Work with all partners in the supply chain to add value, reduce costs, and improve flexibility.

Researching on the Web

The Internet provides rapid access to free or low-cost information that can give you commercial advantage if you learn how to use it better or faster than your competitors. Find out how to use search engines, and to conduct research effectively.

92 Remember, the Internet is a gold mine, but you have to do the mining.

93 Learn how the major search engines work.

94 Try searching newsgroups as well as the Web.

Using Search Engines

All search engines offer a simple search facility to help you locate information. Very often, however, a simple search returns too many results. Use the advanced search option to enter more key words, and to use powerful "Boolean-logic" searches that reduce the quantity and improve the quality of results. To do this, pick two or three leading search engines and study their search help files.

Speeding Research

The Internet is an enormous global resource of information on every subject imaginable, but it is also very unstructured. Finding the information you want, while avoiding a deluge of useless material, can be a challenge unless you learn how to search the Internet efficiently. To help solve this problem, Internet search engines create databases or catalogs of Web pages. Use these as your starting point. No one search engine is sufficient. Even the best cover less than half of Web content, so pick a few of the leading ones to use regularly.

Do's and Don'ts

✔ Do get to know how to use the top two or three leading search engines.

✔ Do explore the instructions for using advanced search features.

✔ Do think of several appropriate key words before starting your search.

✔ Do focus on finding information you need, and ignore the rest.

✘ Don't expect to get full coverage from just one or two search engines.

✘ Don't restrict yourself by using only the simple search function of a search engine.

✘ Don't search using very general words or phrases that will find too many results.

✘ Don't allow yourself to be sidetracked by irrelevant information.

GETTING CUSTOMER FEEDBACK

Customer feedback can be very valuable if it can be obtained quickly and cheaply, and then acted on efficiently. The unique communication power of the Internet provides an ideal means for conducting customer research and processing results. Build communication with your audience and encourage customer feedback using your website, email, mailing lists, and forums or discussion groups. Consider using online customer focus groups to test new product ideas, and to help refine your marketing strategies.

95 Assume that your competitors are researching your online activities.

▼ **KEEPING IN TOUCH WITH YOUR CUSTOMERS**
Customer focus is vital when operating on the Web. Aim to be the best in your industry at seeking customer feedback and acting on knowledge you receive. Try to reward each customer for their input.

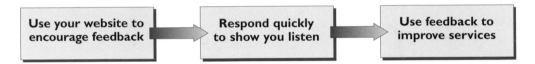

Use your website to encourage feedback → **Respond quickly to show you listen** → **Use feedback to improve services**

FINDING OUT ABOUT YOUR COMPETITORS

If your competitors have an Internet presence, you can use it to track their activities and even to predict their actions. Analyze their websites to see how they present themselves online, whether they sell products from their site, and how they handle customer relations. Use search engines to find pages on their site that may not have links from public areas but are accessible if you find their address. Look for ways they collect customer data and any password-protected areas for business customers or suppliers. Be aware, however, that many websites deposit "cookies" (small text files) in your browser to identify you and track your movements on the site. Do not accept these if you are viewing the site from your network, as your competitor may recognize your address and be able to monitor you researching their site.

POINTS TO REMEMBER

● The sophistication of your competitors' websites can indicate how committed they are to Internet commerce.

● Strange characters in an URL suggest you are being closely tracked around the site.

● Knowing which sites link to your competitors' is useful knowledge that will help you to compete online.

96 To improve your browsing privacy, set your browser to reject cookies.

MARKETING ON THE INTERNET

The Internet has become a vital business tool because it has the power to reach an enormous audience while giving you the ability to talk directly to individuals. Learning how to market your brand on the Internet is already essential for survival.

PUTTING YOUR BRAND ON THE WEB

Whether you have a real-world presence, or exist solely as an online organization, your brand is your most valuable asset. In the online world, where customers cannot see or touch your products, it is your brand values that create confidence and encourage customers to do business with you. The virtual world is so vast, though, that however well-known your brand is in the real world, it is easy to get lost in the commercial noise online. Fortunately, the Internet allows you to target your audiences closely and concentrate your efforts on niche markets. Work hard to identify the niche markets for your brand and use your online presence to contribute to your audience. Always aim to give added-value to online customers as no other method will build repeat business and loyalty.

97 Think of the Web as a very large number of small communities.

98 Remember that small competitors can be big online.

▼ TAPPING INTO NICHE MARKETS

A great strength of the Web is the ability it gives you to reach small interest groups and do business with them cost-effectively. Develop long-term relationships by giving added-value service.

CASE STUDY

The butcher in a small Texas town understood that the Internet was an opportunity to increase his business.

He realized that he should target Web users interested in food, who would pay extra for high-quality, home-grown meat products.

Knowing that he needed to offer something very special to gain attention and draw repeat visits, he developed a website which offers mouth-watering recipes that change with the seasons. The site was created with a Texas theme, and stressed the qualities of local, speciality meats, with features on the local environment.

The website was designed to enable customers to order quickly online and pay by credit card through a secure server. Next-day delivery was guaranteed within the US.

Tapping the strengths of the Internet, the service created a valuable niche market.

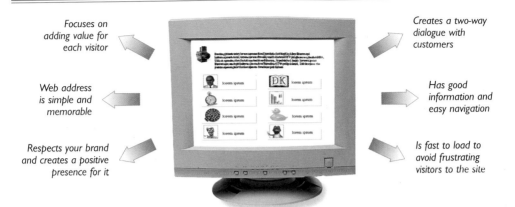

Focuses on adding value for each visitor

Web address is simple and memorable

Respects your brand and creates a positive presence for it

Creates a two-way dialogue with customers

Has good information and easy navigation

Is fast to load to avoid frustrating visitors to the site

PROMOTING YOUR PRESENCE

Promote your Internet presence in the real world at least as much as you do online. Integrate online activities into all your offline promotions and seek to grab your audience's attention in both the real and online worlds. Even purely online brands, with no physical main street presence, must use extensive marketing and promotion in other media if they are to become known and trusted. Online, place "click-through" ads on sites that attract large numbers from your target audience. These send visitors direct to your site.

▲ CREATING AN EFFECTIVE WEBSITE

To do your brand justice, your website should have an effective address, be quick to load and simple to navigate, and must give every visitor good value.

99 Test online ads by alternating different ones on selected websites.

POINTS TO REMEMBER

- Websites should not be designed like brochures if visitors are to be encouraged to return often.
- Ads can be used on other popular sites to attract visitors. Effectiveness should be tracked.
- New ways to use conventional direct marketing methods online should be actively sought.
- Always monitor your main competitors' online marketing and compare it with your own.

LAUNCHING INTO DIRECT MARKETING ONLINE

Direct marketing works extremely well online because the Internet facilitates one-to-one contact. Conventional loyalty and retention campaigns are effective and important to keep customers. Direct marketing on the Internet has the major advantage of allowing an organization to track results easily and get fast feedback when testing new marketing campaigns. To collect good-quality information you need visitors to part with personal details. Provide real incentives to encourage participants.

LAUNCHING E-COMMERCE

*S*etting up shop to sell on the Internet is a low-cost and quick process compared to opening premises in the real world. This means, however, that barriers to entry are low. In order to stay ahead of others, you must learn how to benefit from e-commerce.

100 Watch others' e-commerce efforts closely to learn what works.

SETTING UP SHOP

Your website is your storefront on the Internet, and its design must reflect the fact that you have something to sell online. Early websites were little more than electronic brochures, but an e-commerce site requires careful attention to structure, design, and content issues if it is to be successful. When planning to open an e-commerce site, remember that you must offer convenience, savings, and added-value if you are to attract and keep online shoppers. Crucially, you must also be able to fulfill orders quickly. This requires an efficient "back-end" operation to cope with the level of orders.

101 Use the savings made from selling online to reduce your prices.

Company appoints consultant to advise on e-commerce

Employee aware of potential of e-commerce puts proposal to manager

Manager fails to take up suggestion

CULTURAL DIFFERENCES

English is the dominant language of the Internet, but it is important to remember that the audience is global. If you plan to sell online to an international audience, you should take the trouble to have versions of your site in all the major languages. Also ensure that you take account of national taxes and import duties when you sell across national frontiers.

TAKING PAYMENTS ONLINE

Taking online payments is simple to arrange. Many ISPs offer the use of "shopping cart" software and a secure server, and you can set up an online business account. For credit card payments, choose between real time or batch authorization. If you sell downloadable software or information online, real-time card-checking is important, but batch checking is cheaper.

Company appoints designer to create effective website

A year later, manager reports a sharp rise in online profits and discusses expansion of the business

A year later, manager realizes his business is not keeping up with competitors

POINTS TO REMEMBER

- An e-commerce site must be designed to be quick and simple for customers to use.
- An online business account can usually be set up quickly.
- Customer use of your website should be monitored carefully.
- Your site should be developed in response to customer feedback, which you must actively seek.

TARGETING YOUR AUDIENCE

Ensure your website is designed to be fast and easy for visitors to use. Do not use large graphics that result in slow downloads, or your customers will go elsewhere. If you are selling a product from the site, make the fact clear to visitors, and include prominent pointers to your sales catalog on each page. Provide good information on products, and make sure that the site is designed to ask for, and close, the sale.

ASSESSING YOUR IT SKILLS

Remember that the skills required for managing IT take time and effort to develop, but it is essential to learn them. Evaluate your performance by responding to the following statements, marking the option closest to your experience. Be as honest as you can: if your answer is "never," circle option 1; if it is "always," circle option 4, and so on. Add your scores together, and refer to the Analysis to see how you scored. Use your answers to identify which skills or attitudes need development or improvement.

OPTIONS
1 Never
2 Occasionally
3 Frequently
4 Always

1 I think about the importance of IT to my work or my career.

| 1 | 2 | 3 | 4 |

2 I spend time talking to IT staff about the systems in my organization.

| 1 | 2 | 3 | 4 |

3 I look for ways to use IT to help me work smarter and to save me time.

| 1 | 2 | 3 | 4 |

4 I help my team understand the importance of IT to our business.

| 1 | 2 | 3 | 4 |

5 I feel in control of the hardware and software I use regularly.

| 1 | 2 | 3 | 4 |

6 I understand most of the jargon used by IT staff or my colleagues.

| 1 | 2 | 3 | 4 |

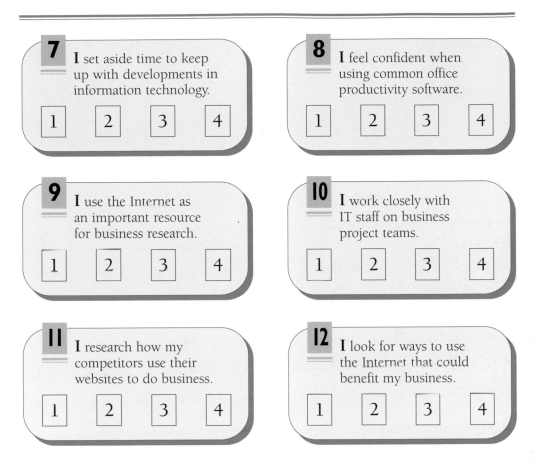

7 I set aside time to keep up with developments in information technology.

1   2   3   4

8 I feel confident when using common office productivity software.

1   2   3   4

9 I use the Internet as an important resource for business research.

1   2   3   4

10 I work closely with IT staff on business project teams.

1   2   3   4

11 I research how my competitors use their websites to do business.

1   2   3   4

12 I look for ways to use the Internet that could benefit my business.

1   2   3   4

ANALYSIS

Now you have completed the self assessment, add up the total score and check your performance by referring to the corresponding evaluation below. Whatever level of success you achieved in managing IT, remember that technology moves on rapidly, and make an effort to keep in touch with developments. Identify your weakest areas, and refer to the relevant sections in this book for guidance.

12–24: You need to work on developing your skills if you are to be able to use IT to benefit you and your organization.

25–36: You have a sound grasp of many IT issues: review your weaker areas to improve your expertise.

37–48: Your understanding of IT and its importance to your business is good: focus on keeping up to date.

MOVING TO E-BUSINESS

INTRODUCTION

The fast-changing digital world demands a new approach to the way we structure our businesses and interact with our customers. Managers must be ready to embrace new technologies and redefine strategies so that their organizations are able to adapt to the continuing rate of change. Moving to E-Business will show you how to integrate your systems, and those of your business partners, so that you can offer the best products and services to your customers. Practical advice, including 101 concise tips, will help you put e-business into practice, and a self-assessment test at the end of the book allows you to evaluate your readiness for the challenge. As you embrace e-business practices within your organization, this book will be an invaluable source of reference and advice.

PREPARING FOR E-BUSINESS

The benefits of e-business have led to fundamental changes in the way business is organized and conducted. Prepare your organization to face the challenge and build a foundation for e-business.

DEFINING E-BUSINESS

The business world is continually being transformed by information technology (IT). Understand the implications of e-business, learn to see the possibilities new technologies bring to business strategies, and challenge existing strategic assumptions.

> **1** View the change to e-business as a necessity, not an option.

AN E-BUSINESS STRUCTURE

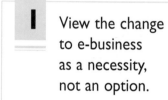

INTEGRATED NETWORKS
Data shared across organization

MULTIPLE SALES CHANNELS
Service channels are integrated

CUSTOMER VALUE
Consistent customer satisfaction

WHAT IS E-BUSINESS?

E-business stands for electronic business. It describes an organization that exploits the full potential of information technology (IT) to streamline its operations, with the aim of delivering the best possible value to the customer. E-business is not the same as e-commerce (electronic commerce); it is an extension of it. Crucially, e-business emphasizes the need to provide the same efficiency and value to the customer across all sales channels, not just online transactions via a website. Rethink your structure and begin to integrate all your systems into a cohesive whole.

LOOKING AT STRATEGIES

E-business relies on the development of new business strategies based on networks. The world has become increasingly interconnected via digital computer and telecommunication networks. These offer fast, flexible, and cost-effective ways of doing business. Seek to find new opportunities ahead of your competitors and devise new business strategies that take advantage of this changing world.

CHALLENGING OLD ASSUMPTIONS

Past business models were developed in a world where a person or organization communicated oneway with many others at the same time, for example, through television advertising. The customer relationship devolved, at best, to the sales teams and, at worst, to distributors, agents, and independent retailers. Now that global networks have the ability to carry high volumes of data, you can move your emphasis to target audiences directly via interactive media.

2 Challenge your existing business assumptions.

3 Identify ways to effectively use new technology.

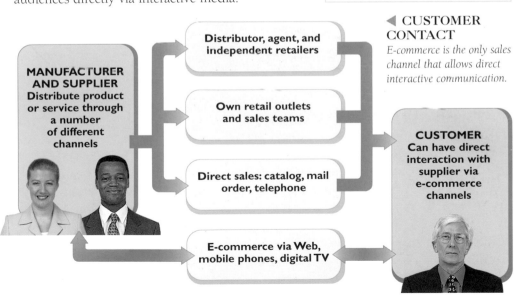

◀ CUSTOMER CONTACT
E-commerce is the only sales channel that allows direct interactive communication.

MANUFACTURER AND SUPPLIER
Distribute product or service through a number of different channels

Distributor, agent, and independent retailers

Own retail outlets and sales teams

Direct sales: catalog, mail order, telephone

E-commerce via Web, mobile phones, digital TV

CUSTOMER
Can have direct interaction with supplier via e-commerce channels

UNDERSTANDING E-BUSINESS

A ny organization wanting to survive in the newly interconnected business world must embrace e-business. Prepare to compete and learn to be forward-thinking so that your business stays ahead of competitors and retains existing customers.

4 Work at changing fear of the future into excitement at new opportunities.

COMPETING TO SUCCEED

The pace of business change has increased dramatically. Ensure that your organization has a clear vision of the digital future. Educate your team members to identify changes in markets due to the developing digital economy. Accept that the current changes are only the start of a business revolution that is likely to be as significant as the invention of the telephone.

Research and understand new technologies

Browse internet to pinpoint new markets

◀ **KEEPING AHEAD**
Study advances in e-business and technology so that you are in a position to embrace the future.

TAKING NEW COMPETITORS SERIOUSLY

Do not allow yourself to become complacent about the size of your organization. In the change to e-business, new entrants often have an advantage over larger, more inflexible competitors. They have the freedom to implement new, integrated IT systems designed for e-business. Work fast to identify and build on your organization's strengths and eliminate its weaknesses. Work to prevent faster competitors from overtaking you.

POINTS TO REMEMBER

- New competitors often have flat and lean structures and are able to adapt swiftly and efficiently to change.

- New businesses can design their processes from scratch to suit digital markets.

- It is important to stay receptive to new challenges and be willing to step into the unknown.

RETAINING CUSTOMERS

E-business is about harnessing IT systems and fast networks to focus your efforts on identifying and satisfying your customers' needs and wants. Never before have customers had so much choice of products, services, and suppliers. This choice can be exercised through digital networks that offer instant access to information for comparative decision making and purchasing. Your competitors may come from anywhere in the world. The message is clear. Put your customers first so that they remain your customers.

5 Remember that organizations of all sizes can cost-effectively sell products anywhere in the world.

CULTURAL DIFFERENCES

Because e-business developed first in the US alongside the growth in the internet, the language and culture of e-commerce and e-business has been dominated by the use of English and Western commercial values. As e-business becomes ever more pervasive, consider delivering your electronic communication in different languages and cultural styles to hone your approach to markets or suppliers in other countries.

RECOGNIZING OPPORTUNITIES AND THREATS

OPPORTUNITIES	THREATS
Building closer relationships with your customers.	Losing your customers to new entrants or faster moving competitors offering more efficient services.
Cutting costs caused by inefficient supply, service, and sales.	Finding your markets disappear completely, for example, because of changing technologies.
Receiving direct customer feedback and communication.	Finding internal inertia or politics prevent you making the necessary changes demanded by your customer.
Recognizing a new market niche out of changing customer demands.	Making wrong decisions about new technology and increasing costs.
Reacting faster and being more responsive than your competitors.	Being paralyzed by an inability to understand changes and by being scared of making wrong decisions.

MOVING TOWARD E-BUSINESS

Converting to e-business is a complex process. It requires the conversion of existing processes and IT systems to suit new business strategies. Understand the changing value of knowledge and learn about the technology that supports e-business.

6 Identify the stage you have reached on the route to e-business.

7 Provide customers and suppliers with real-time data.

8 Aim to move and share information effectively.

HOW DID E-BUSINESS DEVELOP?

The rise of the internet quickly gave birth to e-commerce, as suppliers and customers realized the cost and time benefits of online transactions. Greater efficiencies were also gained when online systems were applied throughout an organization's supply chain. Having an electronic storefront on the web, linked and constantly updated (real-time) to back-office information systems, led to the real challenge of e-business – providing audiences with up-to-date data through every sales channel.

VALUING KNOWLEDGE

With the increasing lack of differentiation in features, quality, or price of products and services, the ability to move and share information can be more valuable than the product itself. Recognize that, in the digital world, the ease with which information can be shared has radically changed the start-to-finish process (or value chain) that creates products and services. A niche has arisen for information intermediaries, or "infomediaries."

▲ **SHARING INFORMATION**
Digital technologies provide the crucial ability to quickly share real-time and accurate information, such as in the fast pace of this air traffic control tower.

HARNESSING TECHNOLOGY

The revolution in changing markets is technology driven. New telecommunication and IT networks and applications offer the ability for truly interactive, global communication. Work hard to maintain understanding of the changing technologies so that you are able to make strategic decisions for a technology-led world. Make it a fundamental part of your strategy to increase your organization's knowledge of relevant technology through recruitment and continuous training.

QUESTIONS TO ASK YOURSELF

Q Do I work to keep up-to-date with new technology, so that I can form effective strategies?

Q Do I rely on IT experts, rather than learning about new and developing technologies myself?

Q Do I have staff with the appropriate awareness of new and future technologies?

TYPICAL ROUTE TO E-BUSINESS

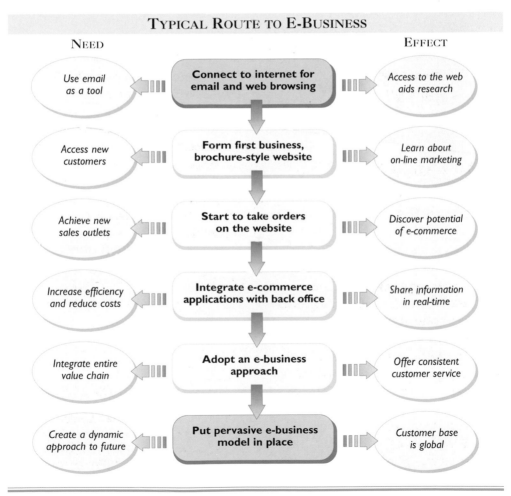

NEED

EFFECT

Use email as a tool ⟸ **Connect to internet for email and web browsing** ⟹ Access to the web aids research

Access new customers ⟸ **Form first business, brochure-style website** ⟹ Learn about on-line marketing

Achieve new sales outlets ⟸ **Start to take orders on the website** ⟹ Discover potential of e-commerce

Increase efficiency and reduce costs ⟸ **Integrate e-commerce applications with back office** ⟹ Share information in real-time

Integrate entire value chain ⟸ **Adopt an e-business approach** ⟹ Offer consistent customer service

Create a dynamic approach to future ⟸ **Put pervasive e-business model in place** ⟹ Customer base is global

DEVELOPING AN E-BUSINESS STRATEGY

In a digital economy, you must be ready for a future of continual change. Reexamine your vision for the future, work closely with your staff, suppliers, and partners to implement change, and learn to view your organization from the customer's perspective.

> **9** Be prepared to question accepted business practices and methods.

> **10** Consider that the markets for your products or services are potentially global.

REDEFINING YOUR VISION

Look at new and future potential and redefine your business vision. In the global business environment, barriers to trade and the movement of capital are rapidly disintegrating due to digital technologies. Recognize that markets can increasingly be reached electronically, without significant cost or access barriers. Understand that you have more freedom to explore new opportunities, but so do your competitors.

WORKING INCLUSIVELY

The need to share and collaborate in defining future strategy is one of the first steps in moving to e-business. Involve your staff, suppliers, partners, and customers in redefining the vision for the future and your subsequent business strategy. Rethink your attitude to sharing information, and work with your colleagues to identify the types of information that should be shared so that your working relationships are more efficient.

> **11** Think of new ways to work with your partners.

▼ IDENTIFYING CHANGE
To successfully identify and implement change, aim to involve staff, partners, and customers by educating, enthusing, and empowering them to be actively involved.

Educate ➤ **Enthuse** ➤ **Empower**

BECOME YOUR OWN CUSTOMER

The focus of e-business must always be on the customer. The technology and the business structure follow on from, and are defined by, your vision of the value you intend to provide to your customers. Start by analyzing existing and future customers' needs and desires. Use your knowledge of your market to consider how customers' expectations will change in the future. This exercise can tell you more about your business than many far more costly initiatives.

FOCUSING ON CUSTOMER NEEDS ▼

Take a hard look at your organization from a customer's perspective. Services that keep the customer satisfied will ultimately benefit your organization.

DEVELOPING A STRATEGY

> **Focus on your customers and define them into groups**

> **Identify the needs and desires of each group**

> **Define the best process to deliver value to the customer**

> **Examine your existing structure to identify necessary changes**

CUSTOMER BENEFITS

> Receives prompt and helpful service

> Develops confidence in organization

> Specific needs are satisfied and met

BUSINESS BENEFITS

> Attracts customers from competitors

> Maintains customer loyalty

> Increases market share

DO'S AND DON'TS

✔ Do implement procedures for sharing information.

✔ Do encourage your staff and colleagues to put customers first.

✘ Don't hold "strategic" information back from staff.

✘ Don't encourage hierarchical attitudes in your organization.

12 Take every opportunity to study competitors' strategies.

BUILDING A FOUNDATION FOR E-BUSINESS

Your e-business should be built on the solid foundation of fast, flexible, and integrated systems and good business relationships. Share your vision with your team, develop strategic partnerships, and make important decisions about technology.

13 Make sure your entire management team shares the same vision.

14 Empower teams to promote e-business developments.

EMPOWERING A TEAM ▼
Create an e-business team that is focused on identifying and solving e-business development issues and on championing your organization's transformation efforts.

SHARING THE VISION

Your staff can become so involved in the day-to-day running of existing processes that little time is left to focus on the more far-reaching changes that are required for e-business. However, developing an e-business strategy is a complex procedure, so it is essential that the entire management team and its staff understand and accept the strategic vision. Share the e-business strategy broadly within your organization and empower your staff to contribute to the process of change.

Customer service manager offers input

Managing director chairs meeting

IT manager offers technical viewpoint

Sales manager presents sales perspective

Business manager collates ideas

IN-HOUSE

- Human resources
- Product design and development
- Customer services
- Sales and telesales
- Brand and product marketing

OUT-OF-HOUSE

Accounting and payroll

Information Technology

Manufacturing

Warehousing and distribution

CUSTOMER

BUILDING PARTNERSHIPS

It is important to realize that you cannot be good at everything. The use of outsourcing has grown steadily as organizations, driven by a need to lower costs, have moved cost centers to outside specialists. Electronic business communities (EBCs) bring together skilled partners who collaborate to deliver excellent products and services to a global market. Develop the ability to enter and leave flexible partnerships when changing market conditions require it.

◀ CREATING PARTNERSHIPS
Successful organizations focus on their core competencies. They outsource other functions that are not cost-effective to retain in-house, to skilled and trusted out-of-house specialists.

MAKING DECISIONS ABOUT TECHNOLOGY

IT is no longer a primary enabler to business, it is now a major driver of change. Understand how technology will radically affect the whole foundation of your business. As soon as one organization in your value chain moves to an e-business model, all partners must follow or risk being replaced by a competitor that is better prepared. Recruit the internal and external resources you need to help your decision-making and to bring expertise to any areas in which your organization does not excel.

THINGS TO DO

1. Identify the core competencies on which you plan to concentrate.
2. Be ready to make decisions about technology.
3. Consult internal and external experts to define the areas of your system that need overhauling.
4. Make time to learn about e-business technologies.

MAKING CULTURAL CHANGES

The changes required by e-business do not stop at the strategic or structural levels but invariably involve the need to transform the culture of your organization. Recognize the value of retaining quality staff and provide ongoing training and incentives.

> **15** Help staff to understand the possibilities the digital future offers.

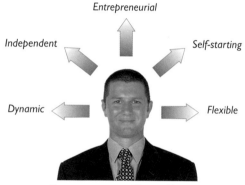

Entrepreneurial

Independent

Self-starting

Dynamic

Flexible

QUALITIES OF GOOD STAFF

FOCUSING ON PEOPLE

If your organization is to cope with continual change, you will require staff who are ready to act as entrepreneurs, take risks, and act on their own initiative. You and your staff must be flexible and able to react quickly to identify new opportunities. Ensure that your team is in a position to align strategy, technology, and processes to deliver superb customer value. Recruit staff who can fulfill these needs.

EDUCATING YOUR STAFF

Give your staff the opportunity to gain the skills necessary to manage in an e-business environment. Offer in-house training opportunities for staff so that they are in a position to undertake the changes to e-business. Look for a partner organization that can provide ongoing technology intelligence and practical training to support your staff. Check their credentials and make sure they understand your market and can focus on changes that will impact on your organization.

▼ TRAINING STAFF
Educate your staff about the impact of e-business and digital markets and equip them with the necessary technical skills.

IT consultant gives employee one-on-one training

PROVIDING INCENTIVES

Make finding and retaining high-quality staff one of your highest priorities. E-business has created a major skill shortage in both technical and managerial positions. Technology experts have to cope with fast developments while managers struggle to translate technology-led marketplaces into moneymaking business strategies. Offer your staff incentives and make sure they feel they have a valuable role to play within your organization.

 16 Show commitment to your staff, keep them well-informed, and reward their feedback and ideas.

CULTURAL DIFFERENCES

The use of incentives to retain and motivate staff varies across countries and industries. In the US, large rewards for success are standard, while in Japan employees are expected to be fully committed without extra incentives. In Europe, the UK is closer to the US model than most countries, but the situation is moving toward more performance-based rewards.

CONSIDERING STAFF INCENTIVES

REWARD	ADVANTAGE
STOCK OPTIONS Gift of shares or the option to buy stocks.	Staff have a material reason to aim for the organization's success and are result focused.
PERFORMANCE-RELATED BONUSES One-time payments related to performance.	Staff have an incentive to produce excellent results and work efficiently.
TRAINING Continual opportunities to learn new skills.	Staff will be more highly skilled and better able to handle the challenges of fast change.
FLEXIBLE WORKING CONDITIONS Working at home options and flexitime.	Staff feel trusted, and the organization can retain staff that they might otherwise lose.
CAREER DEVELOPMENT The chance to move up the managerial ladder.	Staff are motivated to do well, knowing that good results will lead to promotion.
SALARY INCREASES A structure of basic pay increases.	Staff know that the improvement of their skills is reflected in their pay.

FOCUSING ON CUSTOMERS

The golden rule of e-business is that the customer is king. Focus on your customers and understand their needs so that you can put the appropriate customer service processes in place.

CARING ABOUT CUSTOMERS

Your aim is to provide exceptional service for your customer. Understand that customers have immense choice and seek to create systems that allow one-on-one relationships, putting quality of service ahead of the expectation of making a sale.

17 Focus all your efforts on creating the best customer experience.

THINGS TO DO

1. Keep an eye on new competitors.
2. Establish a way of monitoring existing and new competitors.
3. Identify your customers' needs and wishes.
4. Give customers access to the information they need.

UNDERSTANDING CUSTOMERS' CHOICE

In the days when your customers shopped exclusively on main street, or purchased by telephone or mail order, their opportunity for direct comparison of price or features was limited. The internet allows individual or business customers to make comparisons easily and complete their purchases from their own home or office. Many websites now exist solely for the purpose of enabling comparison shopping. Understand that power rests with the customer and put their needs at the center of your business.

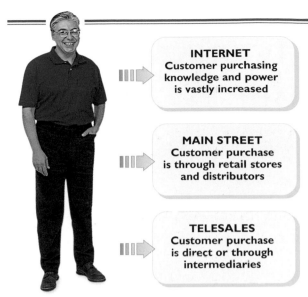

INTERNET
Customer purchasing knowledge and power is vastly increased

MAIN STREET
Customer purchase is through retail stores and distributors

TELESALES
Customer purchase is direct or through intermediaries

◀ **UNDERSTANDING CUSTOMER CHOICE**

The internet has given customers access to comparative information on products and services on a global scale, far greater than that offered by retail, mail order, or telesale outlets. You have increased access to customers, but so do your competitors.

18 Put maximum effort into retaining valuable customers.

BUILDING A ONE-ON-ONE CUSTOMER RELATIONSHIP

In a situation where customers have so much choice and where many products and services cannot be differentiated on price or quality, caring for the customer has become the key point of differentiation. Avoid thinking of your customers as one or several broad groups. Focus on creating better customer relationships by tailoring customer communication according to the needs of each individual customer.

POINTS TO REMEMBER

● Customers expect a personal level of service.

● Customers should be treated on the basis of their own needs.

● It can cost up to ten times as much to gain a new customer as it can to retain an existing one.

● A one-size-fits-all approach to customer relationships does not work.

19 Ensure you and your staff are always in service mode before and after a potential sale.

MOVING THE SERVICE AHEAD OF THE SALE

Customer service traditionally begins after a sale. Start providing service from the moment of first customer contact. Eliminate the distinction between sales and service and focus on providing continuing, exceptional service. Attract customers by delivering excellent product information before the sale, and retain customers by building loyalty through after-sales service. Anticipate their needs by offering related products and services.

DELIVERING CUSTOMER NEEDS

Global competition has changed customers' expectations and the development of digital technologies has changed their experiences. Learn about the behavior of your e-customers and respect their concerns about privacy and security.

20 Provide your customers with a faster service than your competitors.

21 Remember that time is money, integrate your processes to gain maximum efficiency.

FOCUSING ON DEMANDS

Customers increasingly demand fast service, quality goods or services, and competitive prices. Integrate your processes of search, selection, ordering, and fulfillment to deliver the speed and efficiency that customers demand. The ability to check availability at time of order and make accurate fulfillment promises, together with an efficient packing and delivery system, is crucial to providing fast and excellent service.

BEING SENSITIVE

The development of e-commerce has increased the demand on individuals to release their personal details. Many organizations design their websites to gather data about potential customers as soon as they enter a site through mechanisms such as online forms. Be careful how you present these requests for information. Avoid upsetting potential customers by demanding too much information, especially if there are no apparent benefits to them. Answer potential concerns with a clear and easily accessible policy statement on your use of customer data and ensure this is consistent across all your customer service channels.

CULTURAL DIFFERENCES

Attitudes to privacy tend to vary between cultures, and laws governing date protection vary considerably between different countries. Be aware that you will potentially be dealing with customers in different legal systems, and with different cultural expectations, and adjust your actions accordingly.

BEING SECURITY AWARE

A major issue in the development of e-commerce has been the question of online security. Customers want the speed and flexibility of electronic transactions, but they also want to know that their data cannot be accessed by third parties. A failure of your data security could lose you customers very quickly. Seek to reassure your customers and implement the best security measures available.

Consultant outlines security issues

22 Make your privacy and security policies clear.

23 Screen your own security systems for problems.

▲ IMPLEMENTING SECURITY ISSUES

The human element is usually the weakest link in an organization's security system, but it is commonly ignored. Use an external consultant to brief staff on security procedures.

GIVING THE CUSTOMER ASSURANCES ABOUT SECURITY

Many individuals are understandably concerned about maintaining their privacy and security. Give customers the opportunity to decide whether you can share their data with third parties and give clear statements about your security safeguards.

66 *It is as safe to give banking details online as it is to give details to a store employee or over the telephone.* 99

66 *We will refund any loss you may suffer resulting from any lapse in our security or our duty of care to you.* 99

66 *We have a responsibility to protect our customers in the event of a security breach.* 99

66 *We will never release your details to another organization or person unless you give us permission.* 99

Adding Customer Value

The key aspect to e-business design is the need to redefine processes in terms of the value they offer the customer. Integrate your services so that your customer is in control, and ensure you deliver a consistently satisfying and individual experience.

24 Assess the total experience you deliver to your customers.

Ensuring Good Customer Service

Most organizations focus on the price or quality of their products or services, but this is not sufficient when customers judge you on the total experience of doing business with you. Offer an excellent product or service, but also ensure that the experience of purchasing from you is the best that the customer can receive. Work to eliminate time-consuming, error-prone, or unsatisfactory customer service. Always consider the total experience and manage expectations by promising only what you are certain you can deliver.

◀ **MONITORING CUSTOMER SERVICE**
Put procedures in place to check that customer requirements are being met. Here, an electronic device records receipt of delivery, and sends confirmation to the customer database instantaneously.

DO'S AND DON'TS

✔ Do use customer self-service where possible.

✔ Do remember that competitors' products are easily available to your customers.

✔ Do always aim for higher standards.

✘ Don't give unrealistic delivery times.

✘ Don't allow any of your customer contact points to deliver unsatisfactory service.

✘ Don't rely on customer loyalty.

25 Take note and keep a careful eye on the products and services offered by your rivals.

TREATING CUSTOMERS AS INDIVIDUALS

Consumers regularly complain that they are made to feel unimportant and irrelevant by many businesses. Customers want to be treated as individuals and to be offered services personalized to their specific needs. Learn enough about your customers to be able to treat them as individuals. Build a detailed picture of each customer and ensure that this information can be accessed by all areas of your organization that come into contact with the customer. Tailor each customer interaction to the individual's needs.

26 Ask yourself how well you know your customers' individual needs.

▼ **SHARING INFORMATION**
All areas of your organization that come into contact with the customer must operate from a single customer database. Store a record of every contact with the customer, made through whatever channel.

Customer record is set up on first contact

NAME Anne Grant	REFERENCE 25 0124 005
ADDRESS 29 Hawthorne Road, Boulder, CO 80303	
CONTACT 313-449-2251	

Customer is assigned reference number to gain quick access to information

Each subsequent contact is entered on same log

17.02.00 - Customer contacted sales office to inquire about the possibility of purchasing book by mail order.
18.02.00 - Customer called to inquire about website address and methods of payments acceptable.
21.02.00 - Customer ordered three books online.
22.02.00 - Customer's order delivered.

All customer comments are recorded

INTEGRATING SERVICES

Effective e-business design requires you to identify all the processes within your organization that the customer comes into contact with and to use technology to integrate them for the benefit of your customers. This technology must be able to customize the sales and service experience for each individual customer. Extend integration beyond your own organization and share customer data with your supply-chain partners. Then you can achieve the level of service that is demanded by your time-hungry customers.

THINGS TO DO

1. Tailor selling opportunities according to the profile of each individual customer.

2. Build customer loyalty by creating a unique, personalized relationship.

3. Examine ways of integrating supply-chain partners.

SIMPLIFYING SERVICE

Be proficient at delivering a consistent quality experience irrespective of how the customer approaches your organization. Make it as simple as possible for the customer to get information, make a purchase, check delivery details, or get after-sales advice through all potential sales and service channels. Integrate all your service channels so that there is no perceptible difference between them in the eyes of your customers.

27 Take customer complaints seriously and act on them to improve your service.

28 Deliver fast, accurate, and helpful service.

ENSURING CONSISTENCY

Customers are quickly alienated when their details, complaints, or service history are not available to the representative dealing with them. Customers do not see why there should be a difference between the service they receive from you on the web, in your retail locations, or over the telephone. Replace fragmented service with a reliable and consistent approach. Make sure your customers do not have to explain problems repeatedly to different people within your organization.

29 Test the service your competitors offer customers.

POINTS TO REMEMBER

● All staff who have customer contact should have easy access to the central customer database.

● Customer service must be consistent and reliable across every channel of communication.

● Your competitors will be working to gain your customers.

SHARING INFORMATION ▶

In this example, a customer asks a store employee if he can provide a product she has seen on the internet. His response will determine customer satisfaction.

Product is not available in retail outlet

Customer asks sales representative for a product advertised on website

GIVING THE CUSTOMER CONTROL

Frustrated by poor service, customers who value their time have embraced the opportunity for self-service that is offered by e-commerce. The ability to find information and order products or services on a 24-hour basis without having to deal with sales personnel has driven the take-up of e-commerce and has changed the face of entire industries. Implement self-service and benefit from lower costs, and fewer errors caused by multiple points of data reentry.

30 Make customer contact points a top concern.

31 Benefit from the consumer taking control.

Satisfied customer receives product within 24 hours

Sales assistant obtains product details and processes order

Customer tracks delivery details of product from internet at home

Sales assistant does not have access to web database

Customer leaves dissatisfied

BUILDING ON E-COMMERCE EXPERIENCES

The emergence of e-commerce has been the catalyst for IT solutions designed to enable the online, digital economy. Learn the lessons of e-commerce and use internet technology throughout your organization to give customers consistent service.

32 Review all your IT systems to ensure they work with e-commerce systems.

THINGS TO DO

1. Monitor the levels of speed and service through all your sales channels.
2. Critically assess your ability to deliver consistent customer experience.
3. Build business processes on sound and adaptable technological systems.

33 Recognize how the digital world affects customers.

34 Ensure your staff understand the full business picture.

LEARNING FROM E-COMMERCE

E-commerce has shown organizations the digital future. It has opened up a vision of an instant, global means of sharing information and has conclusively demonstrated that the customer must be the focus of e-business. Customers have demonstrated through their use of e-commerce that they judge organizations on the complete experience. They expect businesses to continually improve price, and to provide fast, accurate, personalized, and convenient service.

DO'S AND DON'TS

✔ Do ensure that every aspect of your business is focused on the customer.

✔ Do extend the technology of e-commerce throughout your organization.

✔ Do remember that customers will move to another supplier if they are not satisfied.

✘ Don't allow your traditional outlets to retain nonintegrated technology systems.

✘ Don't concentrate on your internet outlets to the detriment of your other outlets.

✘ Don't develop IT systems in isolation from your key business goals.

INTEGRATING DATA

The web has seen the development of real-time systems in direct interaction with the customer, which deliver tremendous customer value. These systems are now essential tools in managing the customer experience whatever the channel used to interact with your organization. Make sure your organization has effective on-line customer and product databases, while your stores, call centers, and field sales force can also access and benefit from the new and fully integrated systems.

35 Work from one customer database across all channels.

36 Constantly review the effectiveness of your IT systems.

POINTS TO REMEMBER

- You should judge performance on how well you deliver the entire customer experience.
- You should aim to continually improve integration in all areas of your business.
- It is not enough to have effective online databases if the rest of your organization is not effectively integrated.

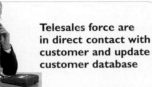

Telesales force are in direct contact with customer and update customer database

Website is continually monitored and database updated

Store employee has easy access to organizational and customer databases

An e-business organization presents a fully integrated front to customers and creates satisfaction and loyalty

Field staff can access product, customization, and delivery details, and place orders online

▲ INTEGRATING SYSTEMS

Customers expect your business to present a united front and provide consistent service, whether face-to-face, via the web, by telephone, or through field staff.

DEVELOPING YOUR E-BUSINESS

Moving to e-business requires radical changes to business strategy, processes, and culture. Lead the practical development of e-business, and work to put integrated systems in place.

MANAGING CHANGE

The transformation to e-business requires your staff to face some new challenges. Sell the need to change, provide effective systems, implement ongoing training, and motivate staff with good incentives to create a forward-thinking team.

37 Prioritize the changes required throughout your organization.

▲ BRAINSTORMING
Consider using external e-business visionaries to educate and enthuse staff through brainstorming sessions.

FACING THE CHALLENGE

The business world is undergoing continuous, rapid change. Darwin said that it is not the strong or intelligent who survive, but those who are the most responsive to change. Rediscover the entrepreneurial spirit and be prepared to destroy old ways of doing things in order to create new, dynamic alternatives. Expect to adjust the business model and operating strategies and processes constantly in response to changes in markets and in customers' needs. Develop new ways of thinking in this dynamic environment, so that new ways of behaving can follow.

PRIORITIZING CHANGE

Every organization has particular strengths and weaknesses. It may not be possible to excel in all areas, but it is possible to outshine your competitors in narrowly focused areas that please your customers. Refine your focus according to your strengths and your customers' desires before prioritizing change. Focus on one of three qualities according to your market niche, your core competencies, and your customer interests:

- Deliver superb and accurate customer service.
- Deliver high-quality products or services.
- Offer irresistible and continual innovation.

Now prioritize change in the way that will best help you improve performance in your focus area.

38 Recognize your strengths and focus your energies on them.

39 Make sure you and your staff share the goals of your organization.

FOCUSING ON PRIORITIES FOR CHANGE

PRIORITY	BUSINESS ISSUES	FOCUS FOR CHANGE
SERVICE ● Personalized ● Proactive ● Flexible	● Instant access needed for accurate customer details. ● Flexible response systems needed to fight off competition. ● Concentrate on the customer value proposition.	● Streamline customer-contact channels. ● Build cross-functional customer-related processes. ● Ensure suitable technology infrastructure.
PROCESS ● Efficient ● Low in cost ● Fast	● Efficient allocation of materials and resources. ● Share fast and accurate data with suppliers. ● Monitor processes to improve service and lower costs.	● Streamline internal information flows. ● Build an end-to-end process structure. ● Remove barriers between you and your suppliers.
INNOVATION ● Predict trends ● Listen to customers ● Create new products	● Manage continuous change and accept risks. ● Manage mergers and acquisitions for growth. ● Encourage entrepreneurship and forward thinking.	● Create a robust and scaleable network infrastructure. ● Organize processes around your networks. ● Integrate with suppliers and partners.

SELLING CHANGE

Few people like change, yet the transition to e-business requires enormous and continuing change both in the way we operate and the way we think about business. Help staff to comprehend fully the scale of the global business changes now taking place and show them the implications for your business and your industry. Lead change from the top and ensure staff feel directly involved in the decision process and the implementation of the transformation of the business.

DIRECTOR

Management works closely with senior directors

Director champions the implementation of e-business

Views and input from partners and external consultants are considered

MANAGER

Manager supports staff in embracing e-business concepts

Frontline staff give their ideas and feedback

LEADING CHANGE ▶
Act as an evangelist for new business strategies and show that organizational change is being led from the top, while continuing to accept input from all levels.

STAFF

POINTS TO REMEMBER

- Technology is the creator of change and the main enabler of the e-business concept.
- Understanding technology is no longer the preserve of the IT professional alone.
- All your staff must understand the concepts behind e-business systems and technologies.
- If your staff can see how technology reduces repetitive procedures, they are more likely to embrace change positively.
- Proficient staff should help other staff learn new technical skills.

EMBRACING TECHNOLOGY

An e-business must be built on technology that streamlines and integrates processes. The target is the flow of information and ways to add value to it. Focus on your customer and partner relationships and become more responsive to the continuing need for change. Recognize that the implementation of technology for e-business is so entwined with business strategy and organizational structure, and so difficult to execute, that it should be embraced by all your staff, not just IT staff.

40 Recognize that your staff are your most valuable asset.

QUESTIONS TO ASK YOURSELF

Q Have I sold the need for business transformation effectively to my staff?

Q Have I offered the necessary ongoing training opportunities?

Q Do my staff have the necessary support to implement changes to e-business?

Q Do I keep my staff informed about new procedures?

PROVIDING TRAINING

It is necessary to maintain the momentum for change after you have initially built up enthusiasm for it. If you want entrepreneurial and dynamic staff, support them with the necessary training. Implement a thorough, effective, and ongoing program to get you and your staff ready and able to make the changes you need. Instigate training for yourself and fellow managers to understand the business implications of e-business so you can work together to shape new strategies. Train operational staff to learn to use new technologies, since they will be using the systems on a day-to-day basis.

▼ UNDERSTANDING TECHNOLOGY
Reassure your staff about new technologies. Train them and yourself to understand and learn about new systems so that you are all in a position to evaluate the possibilities and implications for new business models and strategies.

Reassure ▷ **Train** ▷ **Evaluate**

BENEFITING STAFF

Explanations and training are essential to help your staff prepare for change, but you must also show staff how e-business can directly benefit them. Change your remuneration strategy to make your key staff partners in change. Concentrate on using networked applications to make work less repetitive, and to provide staff with online learning resources.

BENEFITS FOR STAFF ▷
Consider providing internet access for staff who do not have this facility at home so that they can discover the benefits of using technology in their personal lives.

PLANNING FOR E-BUSINESS

The traditional methods for planning for the future have become outdated in an e-business environment. Adopt a dynamic, continuous approach to planning and utilize constant feedback so that you can quickly adapt plans as business conditions change.

41 Ensure that planners work very closely with implementers.

42 Be prepared to discard developing projects quickly, if the direction of change shifts.

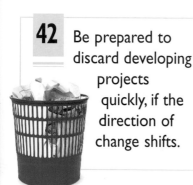

PLANNING ANALYTICALLY

Traditional businesses often use an analytically based planning approach to determine likely outcomes and to develop appropriate strategies. This process relies on analyzing historic data that may already be out-of-date. It can lead to problems in execution such as a lack of clear targets or a failure to use feedback to modify strategies. Be aware that this approach is unlikely to deliver useful results in a fast-changing business environment.

PLANNING PRAGMATICALLY

A pragmatic approach to planning is often taken by large organizations. This relies on operational staff finding solutions to meet new, urgent needs. However, the communication of frontline staff's knowledge of imminent change to decision-makers is often too slow within hierarchical structures. This leads to projects being implemented to meet current needs, rather than thought out in terms of future strategies. If you are serious about e-business, adopt a more dynamic approach to planning.

43 Be prepared for a multitude of possible future developments and ensure you can respond quickly.

FORECASTING

In a stable business environment, forecasts can be developed by measuring past performances. However, in a rapidly changing and uncertain e-business world, past performance may bear little relation to future opportunities. In this situation, aim to create rather than predict the future. Define your desired outcome, then work backward to identify the steps you need to take to achieve your goal.

USING CONTINUOUS DYNAMIC PLANNING

A continuous approach to planning allows you to make constant modifications based on feedback. This helps remove the problems that frequently arise from the gap between planning and implementation. Set trigger points that initiate planned action when external factors meet a determined measure. Focus your centralized planning on aligning business processes with strategy and implementing a network infrastructure. Leave application selection in the hands of the frontline departments who will be using them.

44 Rely on feedback to plan effective strategies.

45 Continue to plan effectively even in a volatile business environment.

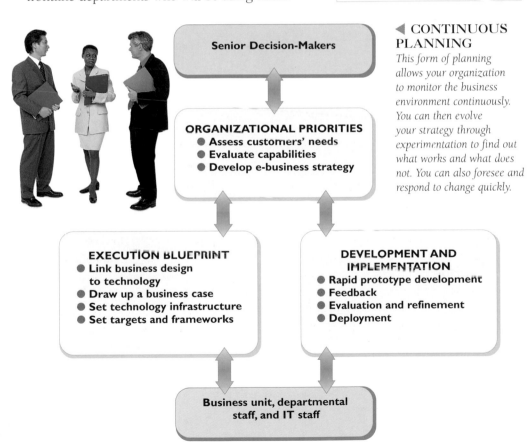

◀ **CONTINUOUS PLANNING**
This form of planning allows your organization to monitor the business environment continuously. You can then evolve your strategy through experimentation to find out what works and what does not. You can also foresee and respond to change quickly.

Senior Decision-Makers

ORGANIZATIONAL PRIORITIES
● Assess customers' needs
● Evaluate capabilities
● Develop e-business strategy

EXECUTION BLUEPRINT
● Link business design to technology
● Draw up a business case
● Set technology infrastructure
● Set targets and frameworks

DEVELOPMENT AND IMPLEMENTATION
● Rapid prototype development
● Feedback
● Evaluation and refinement
● Deployment

Business unit, departmental staff, and IT staff

Transforming an Existing Business

You need to make the transition to e-business before new, flexible competitors move quickly into your markets. Work with your staff to identify your customers' future needs, create an e-business strategy, and realign processes.

46 Stay in touch with present needs, while also planning for the future.

Building Your Team

To plan an e-business transformation, you will require a cross-functional team that must include top-level executives. Your team should not be so large that it prevents quick decision-making, but should include a mix of key operational and IT staff. Remember that the day-to-day business must continue to be run effectively while change is being planned. Employ good quality assistants who can focus on running the business efficiently while you concentrate on delivering future success.

47 Employ external specialists to give the team guidance.

Forming an E-Business Team

People	Role
Senior Management Chief executives and directors.	Top management must actively focus on and lead the move to e-business.
IT Staff Senior IT managers and IT planners.	Senior IT staff can advise on enabling technologies that meet your business needs.
Business Managers Representatives from units impacted by change.	Senior business managers work with IT managers to manage the teams and identify IT solutions.
Partners Business and IT representatives of your organization's partners.	Key partners are involved to ensure integration with their processes and technologies.
Consultants Specialists in areas in which in-house skills are insufficient.	External specialists strengthen your team's skills. Do not allow them to run your project.

IDENTIFYING ROUTES

The input of your team is integral to transforming a business. Work together to form a strategy that explains what you plan to do and define what you intend to offer your customers. This is the starting point for your e-business design, which shows how you are going to evolve. Your e-business design identifies what internal or external processes you need and how they should be integrated.

48 Actively encourage suggestions from all your staff.

▼ **LISTENING TO STAFF**
Listen to your frontline staff, since they are in a position to identify beneficial routes or possible obstacles to change.

Sales manager explains her team's ideas and feedback

IT manager advises on technology issues

QUESTIONS TO ASK YOURSELF

Q Do I know who my customers are and what their specific needs are?

Q How are my customers' priorities changing and how may they change in the future?

Q Where will new competitors for my customers come from?

Q Which is my best customer group and what do they value most in our service?

Q Have I anticipated possible future needs of existing or potential customers?

FOCUSING ON CUSTOMERS

Take the customer's needs as the starting point. Gather detailed knowledge about your customers and all trends that indicate how they and their needs are changing. Use any existing customer databases you may have – including customer questionnaires, focus groups, and consumer research – to help understand your customers and how you can deliver them measurable benefits.

49 Identify the specific future needs of your customers and focus on those you are best able to satisfy.

UNDERSTANDING EXISTING PROCESSES

Before you can identify the steps to an e-business structure, ensure you have a clear understanding of how your existing processes work. Rather than trying to examine all the processes at once, pick those that most directly affect the value you intend to offer the customer. If superb customer service is the factor you will focus on, concentrate on identifying how all the processes that deal directly with the customer currently interact.

QUESTIONS TO ASK YOURSELF

Q What are we best at and what are we worst at?

Q How can we improve our current processes?

Q Is our use of technology led by IT or by business units?

Q What new capabilities do we need to be able to deliver value to our future customers?

50 Make sure you understand your target customers.

51 Look outside your industry for new, dynamic ideas.

SIMPLIFYING PROCESSES

Plan new ways of operating to simplify and speed up your business processes before turning your attention to the technology that will be needed to implement your new design. Remember that the e-business design process starts by focusing on customers and then works backward to find the simplest, fastest, or most cost-effective process needed to deliver customer value. Integrate functions to achieve a seamless, end-to-end process. Consider outsourcing parts of your business if this will aid an effective solution.

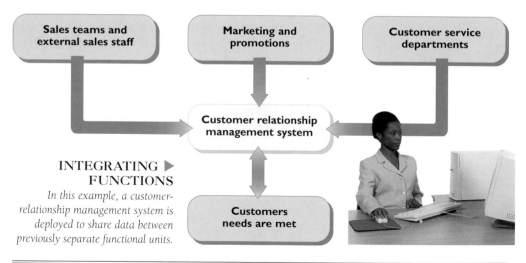

Sales teams and external sales staff

Marketing and promotions

Customer service departments

Customer relationship management system

Customers needs are met

INTEGRATING ▶ FUNCTIONS
In this example, a customer-relationship management system is deployed to share data between previously separate functional units.

IDENTIFYING TECHNOLOGY

With a new business design in place, consider which technology applications will best suit your requirements. Critically examine your existing use of technology and identify your strengths and weaknesses in this area relative to your proposed e-business strategy. Develop a technology blueprint to define the tools that will be used, how they will be integrated, and what costs and timescales will be involved. Aim for an infrastructure of open standards and internet-enabled technologies.

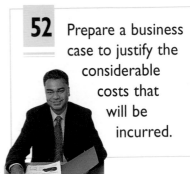

52 Prepare a business case to justify the considerable costs that will be incurred.

PRIORITIZING DEVELOPMENT

Many large-scale technology projects take more than a year to plan, plus another year or more to implement. Large projects with long lead times are increasingly risky in times of rapid change because, if business needs change, the initiative may lose its relevance or importance before it can be implemented. Work with a technology supplier who can adapt to your needs. If a single initiative cannot be broken down into stages that can be implemented within the timescale, find an alternative approach.

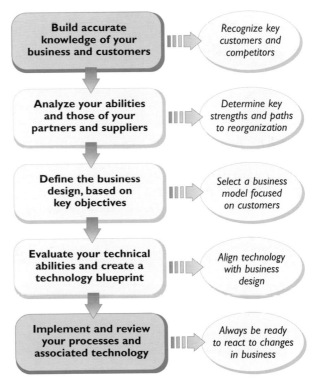

Build accurate knowledge of your business and customers → Recognize key customers and competitors

Analyze your abilities and those of your partners and suppliers → Determine key strengths and paths to reorganization

Define the business design, based on key objectives → Select a business model focused on customers

Evaluate your technical abilities and create a technology blueprint → Align technology with business design

Implement and review your processes and associated technology → Always be ready to react to changes in business

53 Look at the technology used by your competitors.

▲ FORMING AN E-BUSINESS DESIGN
Set targets that are quickly achievable. Plan your development in steps that can be achieved within a 3–6 month timescale. Aim to take small steps so that results and benefits can be quickly demonstrated to the organization and enjoyed by your customers.

Understanding Back-Office Systems

*T*he adoption of integrated back-office systems, or Enterprise Resource Planning (ERP) applications, is driven by the need to make businesses more efficient. Understand their importance and match system design to your e-business strategy.

54 View back-office systems as an essential foundation of your business.

55 Seek ways to integrate different functions into a single back-office application.

Using ERP Systems

Many organizations operate on disparate systems that cannot deliver real-time information and which are unable to communicate easily, if at all, with other IT systems in the organization. The growth of back-office systems, or Enterprise Resource Planning (ERP) systems, has come from the need to eliminate problems caused by multiple and disconnected software applications.

Common Elements of an ERP Application

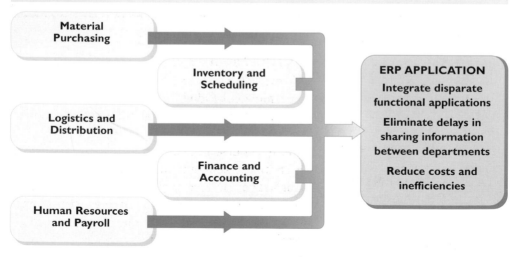

Material Purchasing

Inventory and Scheduling

Logistics and Distribution

Finance and Accounting

Human Resources and Payroll

ERP APPLICATION

Integrate disparate functional applications

Eliminate delays in sharing information between departments

Reduce costs and inefficiencies

CREATING A FOUNDATION FOR E-BUSINESS

The move to e-business requires ERP systems to be integrated into other systems so that your entire value chain is streamlined. Make your ERP system the foundation for your e-business structure. Ensure seamless communication between ERP systems and other essential applications, such as customer relationship management and supply chain management systems. Recognize the benefits of systems using internet standards, so that information can be shared easily between partners and suppliers.

56 Expect systems implementation to be complex.

57 Implement back-office systems that are fully internet-enabled.

INTERNET COMPATIBLE SOFTWARE

Since an ERP system must act as the foundation for an e-business structure it is important that it can communicate seamlessly with other IT systems in the organization. Today's ERP systems make use of internet standards to ensure that they are widely compatible with other systems, and to allow information to be shared and accessed easily. This need has resulted in a move toward Java-based software (a platform-independent programming language) that works in a standard web browser. This means that users can gain access to their ERP system and corporate data from any networked computer with a normal web browser.

POINTS TO REMEMBER

- You should select an ERP solution that matches your business strategy.

- You may encounter internal resistance when you plan changes to existing systems.

- Systems using internet standards can communicate easily and share information effectively.

- The streamlining of processes should be led by your strategic needs, not your ERP system.

MATCHING ERP NEEDS WITH STRATEGY

Before picking an ERP system you must first determine what kind of organization you are planning to be in the digital future. Only choose an ERP system after you have created your e-business design. Business process re-engineering is an inevitable requirement when an ERP system is installed. However, try to avoid adapting your processes to fit the ERP software. Concentrate on the processes you need to streamline in order to reach your strategic e-business targets.

INTEGRATING IT SOLUTIONS

M*any organizations have inherited IT systems that are incompatible with their newer systems. Examine your systems to understand how they developed and where information bottlenecks and barriers exist, and then begin to plan integration processes.*

58 Identify how many incompatible systems your organization uses.

59 Seek out any bottlenecks of information.

60 Think about how your network may need to extend.

HOW SYSTEMS DEVELOPED

Computer hardware and software programs, or applications, were developed to meet functional requirements, such as payroll, but these systems were typically unable to share data. Networks developed to connect systems with users but were often unable to connect to separate networks. The advent of the internet brought a set of open standards (protocols), for communicating, storing, sharing, and transporting data, which finally created the opportunity to share information with any system or anyone, anytime, and anywhere.

FINDING BOTTLENECKS

The secret to success in the digital business is to use internet-aware networks and applications to eliminate information bottlenecks. Avoid a mix of old and new nonintegrated systems, which tend to form islands of information within your organization. In this situation, information may be transferred between nonintegrated systems by means of batch transfer of files at set times across a network, but this means that information is not available in real-time. Accept that the free flow of information is a key part of your IT architecture.

QUESTIONS TO ASK YOURSELF

Q Do any departments have to transfer files to each other, or to suppliers, by disk?

Q Do any departments have to reenter data manually?

Q Is everyone within the organization able to share real-time information?

Q Are there adaptable IT systems in place?

REMOVING BARRIERS

The goal is to streamline the end-to-end business process. Many organizations are faced with a mixture of systems and isolated, functionally based departments or business divisions. Recognize that replacing inherited systems is always difficult and expensive, and may be impractical. Some systems can be retained and adapted. Consider adopting integrating software, or "middleware," to transfer data between old and new systems.

STREAMLINING NETWORKS ▼
Identify and eliminate systems that are not integratable within your organization. Adapt systems that can be effectively integrated, and invest in the technology that will allow integration.

THINGS TO DO

1. Ask staff to identify information blockages.

2. Identify the limitations of your existing systems.

3. Eliminate redundant systems that cannot be integrated into a new business structure.

4. Identify the costs and time implications of integration.

Identify	→	Adapt	→	Integrate

▲ BUILDING AN E-BUSINESS STRUCTURE
The network services are the foundation of your e-business. Databases and applications rely on this, and create a path to your audiences and customers.

DEVISING A STRUCTURE

E-business architecture can be thought of as an interdependent layer of services. The network services are the infrastructure that forms the basis for various services such as file transfer, email, and databases. These facilitate the business applications that form the next layer. The top layer comprises the interfaces used to communicate with your audiences, such as a public website, an extranet for partners, and retail outlets. These gateways collect information from the business services in the layer below and present them to audiences in an appropriate form.

61 Use customer interfaces to identify and collect data and relay feedback to business services.

CREATING A NETWORK

Since e-business is built on the concept of networks, it is essential that your network is fast, robust, scalable, secure, and fully internet-enabled. Your network must also have sufficient capacity for future increases in traffic. Ensure that your network can be expanded as and when required without adding complexity, reducing flexibility, or disturbing any other part of the infrastructure. In the digital environment, your organization needs to work on internet time, which means being available 24 hours a day. Remember that any network downtime is unacceptable.

62 Ensure your systems are stable and will not fail.

63 Select an application service provider partner with care.

BUILD, BUY, OR RENT?

A key issue for organizations moving to e-business is the decision to build, buy, or rent IT systems. Self-built systems can be expensive and difficult to improve. Building simple middleware applications to integrate old systems, may, however, be justified. Off-the-shelf systems should be internet-aware and compatible with open standards. Consider leasing applications from application service providers (ASPs). The applications reside at the ASP to which you connect via a secure internet connection. This may allow you to outsource your technology needs, reduce costs, and retain flexibility.

MOVING OUTSIDE THE ENTERPRISE

Integrating systems within your organization is not enough – successful businesses must share their information seamlessly with partners and suppliers throughout the value chain. This requirement adds to the importance of adopting internet standards, open systems, and a limited set of widely used enabling technologies. Ensure your systems can communicate easily with those of partners and suppliers. Retain the flexibility needed to change the organizations you work with according to changing business requirements.

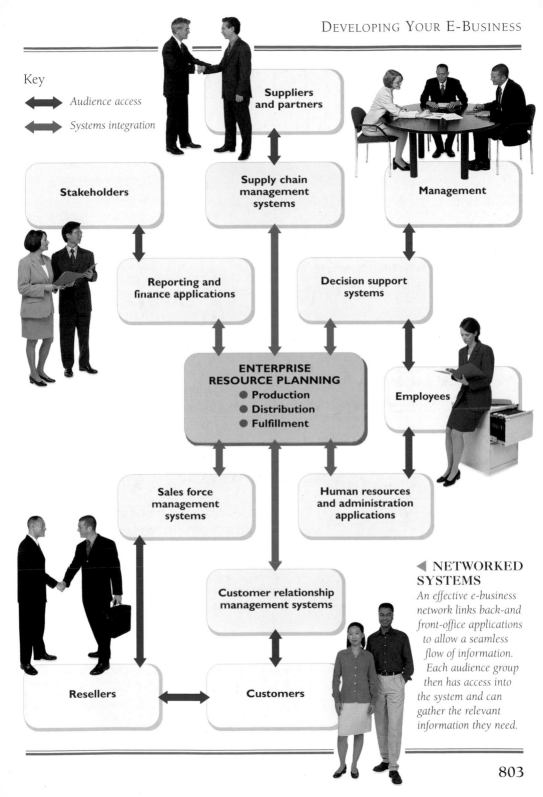

Key

Audience access

Systems integration

Suppliers and partners

Stakeholders

Supply chain management systems

Management

Reporting and finance applications

Decision support systems

ENTERPRISE RESOURCE PLANNING
- Production
- Distribution
- Fulfillment

Employees

Sales force management systems

Human resources and administration applications

◀ **NETWORKED SYSTEMS**

Customer relationship management systems

Resellers

Customers

An effective e-business network links back-and front-office applications to allow a seamless flow of information. Each audience group then has access into the system and can gather the relevant information they need.

803

USING CUSTOMER – MANAGEMENT SYSTEMS

T*here has been a rapid growth in technological solutions for customer relationship management (CRM). Understand the forces driving CRM systems and develop a suitable strategy that will ensure consistent service across multiple contact channels.*

64 Design your infrastructure to be accessible to your business partners.

65 Remember that a 5% increase in customer retention can increase profits by over 75%.

WHY USE CRM?

As customers increasingly focus on the quality of service they receive, an effective customer relationship management (CRM) strategy is essential for improving customer retention. CRM systems use a single source of customer data to feed one or more applications designed to support tasks such as ordering, sales, customer service, and marketing. Increasingly, they also enable the customer to select self-service through a website.

DEVELOPING CRM

Effective customer relationships are important for every e-business, but their degree of importance will vary depending on your organization's strategic focus. If delivering superb service is your goal, then a powerful CRM system will be more essential than if your focus is on constant innovation. Once you have decided to embark on a CRM system, use your e-business design to identify the customer contact functions that are critical to your business. Remember that the introduction of a CRM system will inevitably require internal reorganization. Constantly communicate with the staff involved with the reorganization.

QUESTIONS TO ASK YOURSELF

Q Have I determined how the CRM system will help us achieve our strategic goals?

Q Have I evaluated the merits of different CRM systems and considered the benefits of a custom-built system?

Q Have I compared CRM systems from a variety of vendors to decide which is best?

Q Have I identified a list of our functional requirements for a CRM system?

Being Consistent

Whichever CRM system you choose, make sure that it will enhance the customer's experience of your organization, irrespective of which channel is used. It is not sufficient to have a CRM system linked to your website if your call centers cannot access the same database. The customer may be impressed by your service on the internet, but will be quickly disillusioned if he or she does not receive the same standard of service from your store. Customers often research products through one channel before initiating a transaction through another. Ensure your CRM system is capable of seamlessly integrating information. Make use of digital contact technologies, such as WAP phones, iTV, and Kiosks to interact with your customers.

66 Consider only internet-based CRM systems.

Points to Remember

● Each service channel must have immediate access to customer history and contact data.

● Digital contact devices offer new ways of accessing customers.

● Your sales personnel should determine the appropriate approach for each individual.

Acquire → Improve → Retain

67 Provide strong leadership and overcome internal resistance when introducing a new CRM system.

▲ STAGES OF A CUSTOMER LIFECYCLE
A CRM system must support all three stages of a customer lifecycle – acquiring a customer, improving the relationship, and retaining their loyal business.

Explaining New Contact Technologies

Key Term	Definition
WAP Phone	WAP (wireless application protocol) mobile phones allow users to connect to the internet, receive email, and browse WAP-enabled sites.
iTV	Digital, interactive television marries broadcast television and the internet, allowing advertisers to exploit the best of both media.
Kiosk	Kiosks are easy to use, often touch-screen, computers sited at point-of-sale or inquiry locations to give customers a self-service option.

USING SALES FORCE MANAGEMENT

The needs of e-business are driving the introduction of sales force management (SFM) systems. Assess the needs for a sales force management system and set definable goals before creating an appropriate process and its supporting technology.

68 Look for opportunities to coordinate sales teamwork.

69 Cut down on reentry of data, since it takes time and can introduce mistakes.

DEFINING SALES FORCE MANAGEMENT

Sales force management (SFM) is the integration of the often-separated functions involved in moving from a customer's initial inquiry to order taking. This process typically includes pricing and quoting, confirmation of availability, or allocating commission payments. Introduce applications to integrate the separate functions into an end-to-end process, which seamlessly connect to CRM and ERP systems for maximum performance.

COORDINATING SALES

The aim of sales force management is to streamline the sales process in order to increase sales force effectiveness and meet customer requirements. For example, your external sales staff may be operating in a number of different countries and cultures, but must tailor products to meet local requirements. Ensure information is readily accessible to your sales staff, wherever they are.

ACCESSING AND INPUTTING ▶
Give your sales staff the ability to access and input information from contact devices such as laptops and WAP phones, so that they can service customers' needs, even when they are traveling.

CASE STUDY

A major supplier of networking components was quick to adopt e-business strategies and solutions. As part of their move to e-business, the organization implemented a sales force management system online, to eliminate typical manual processes that were both inefficient and error prone. Implemented in phases, the system comprised a suite of networked commerce agents, which enabled resellers to configure, price, route, and submit electronic orders directly online. They started small by deploying an order-status agent, and then added pieces to the commerce suite. This suite was expanded to include a pricing and configuration agent, order placement, and invoice agents. As a result of developing the system, the organization cut the error rate for order processing from 20% to 2%.

◀ **GAINING EFFICIENCIES**

In this case study, a leading organization was quick to see the advantages of streamlining its sales processes. The benefits of increased efficiencies were quickly seen after an online sales force management system was implemented.

CREATING SFM SYSTEMS

The proliferation of channels available to the customers, the rise in self-service, and the increase in product customization means that the sales process is highly complex and often fragmented. First integrate this process by identifying every step required in the sales process for each important customer group. Look at the process from your customers' viewpoints and check that it meets their needs. Form a cross-functional team drawn from all departments involved in the process. Now identify those steps that are responsible for delays or inaccuracies in acquiring and processing an order.

FINDING AN SFM SOLUTION

DEFINE
Outline an end-to-end process that streamlines sales activity

Aim to work off centralized databases

DESIGN
Eliminate unnecessary steps and allow a free flow of information

Provide access to data via a web browser interface

IDENTIFY
Find technology solutions that give sales teams access to data

Include tools such as online product customization

IMPLEMENT
Integrate individual functions into a streamlined process

Link seamlessly to back-office ERP systems

USING OUTSOURCING SUCCESSFULLY

The rapid growth in outsourcing has occurred because organizations are struggling to cope with the demands on their skills. Identify core competencies, create new partnerships to deliver needed skills, and learn to manage these vital relationships.

70 Increase flexibility by working with more than one outsourcer.

71 Look at every part of your business in your evaluation.

ANALYZING STRENGTHS

The first step to identifying whether outsourcing is viable for your organization is to identify your core skills. Focus on your competitive edge and define what differentiates you from competitors. Look at those areas where others may be able to do the job better, faster, or cheaper than you. Even if you are a manufacturing business, your manufacturing skills may be less important than your brand management abilities. You could increase efficiency by outsourcing manufacturing and focusing on managing your brand.

OUTSOURCING SKILLS ▼
Many organizations outsource key functions, such as accounting and IT services, once they have determined that these functions are not a core skill and can be done more efficiently by out-of-house specialists.

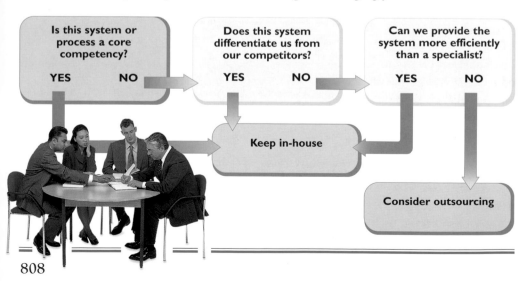

Is this system or process a core competency?

YES   NO

Does this system differentiate us from our competitors?

YES   NO

Can we provide the system more efficiently than a specialist?

YES   NO

Keep in-house

Consider outsourcing

CREATING SUCCESSFUL PARTNERSHIPS

Once you have decided which, if any, functions can be outsourced, select an organization with whom you can develop a close partnership. Select organizations whose competencies can enhance your business and whose systems can be integrated with your own with minimum disruption. Your partners must be integrated so tightly with your organization that they become indistinguishable to your internal or external audiences. Define the commercial relationship and tailor rewards to the accurate delivery of services.

73 Provide sufficient staff and resources to effectively manage the outsourcing relationship.

72 Create competition for your contract between rivals.

THINGS TO DO

1. Set performance targets and make rewards dependent on performance.

2. Negotiate short-term contracts, rather than long-term ones.

3. Retain flexibility to allow a change of partners when circumstances dictate.

MANAGING OUTSOURCING

The success or failure of outsourcing will depend on the degree to which your organizations can learn to think and act as one. Achieving this ideal requires active relationship management. Pick managing staff who have good communication skills because they will act as the crucial link between internal system users and your suppliers. Ensure staff are trained in managing external relationships before implementing the changeover and carefully monitor performance and feedback.

▼ MEETING REGULARLY
Regular meetings with outsourcers should take place to ensure projects are progressing well. Build a management team with good interpersonal skills.

Sales manager outlines customer perspective

Outsourcing manager explains issues

STARTING A NEW E-BUSINESS

In many ways, the start-up e-business has an easier task than the existing business that has to transform old methods. Take advantage of recent rapid changes, clearly focus on customer value, identify your core skills, and choose beneficial business partners.

74 Fully research your target customers before starting a new venture.

75 Benefit from a clean slate and the ability to design systems from new.

STARTING FROM NEW ▼
The internet allows a new organization to quickly research existing offerings, plan a unique strategy, and then implement it.

RESPONDING TO CHANGE

The rapid change to a digital environment is causing problems for many existing businesses; but, for new organizations, it offers enormous opportunity. Your start-up organization has the ability to design effective systems without the hindrance of inherited systems. Define a value proposition for your potential customers, unhindered by current customer perceptions or complicated commercial relationships with partners.

Research ➡ **Plan** ➡ **Implement**

RESEARCHING ONLINE

The internet is the perfect tool for rapidly conducting wide-ranging research into the market of your chosen value proposition, and gaining insight into your existing competitors. Use the web to explore details of your competitors' offerings and pricing, and use newsgroups and other discussion forums to identify the wishes of potential customers.

76 Focus on delivering exceptional customer service within your chosen niche market.

FOCUSING ON A NICHE VALUE PROPOSITION

If an opportunity exists within any industry to significantly add value for customers, then there is a niche that a new e-business can fill. Your aim is to create an e-business design that offers an enhanced value proposition to your target audience and which consistently delivers, or exceeds, customers' expectations. Carefully tailor your offering to the niche you have identified rather than adopting a wide focus in the hope of attracting a larger audience. Before settling on the niche you will attack, make sure you answer all the searching questions you raise.

QUESTIONS TO ASK YOURSELF

Q Who are my target customers and how well do I know them?

Q How do I get and retain customer loyalty?

Q Who are my existing and possible future competitors?

Q How will my product or service reach the customer?

Q What are our core competencies?

Q How will technology continue to change the marketplace?

DIFFERENT TYPES OF ONLINE VALUE PROPOSITION

BUSINESS MODEL	VALUE PROPOSITION FOR CUSTOMER
INFOMEDIARY	Provides a one-stop shop for all the information required in a specific area by a customer. Offers ease of use, quick results, and cost savings.
TRANSACTION INTERMEDIARY	Provides a unified process for finding, comparing, selecting, and purchasing products or services online. Offers speed and cost savings.
CATEGORY LEADER	Becomes a market leader by identifying a new value proposition and constantly innovating the customer experience. Offers the best total customer experience.
COMMUNITY CENTER	Creates a topic-specific meeting place online where members can interact to share ideas and information. Offers ease of contact and community membership.
INDUSTRY PORTAL	Provides a single, easy-to-use facility for organizations within a specific industry to conduct business-to-business trading. Offers time and cost savings and access to new suppliers.

IDENTIFYING YOUR AIMS

Early dot-com businesses worked on the principle of rapid growth, financed by early investors, and aimed at building a large customer base. This was used to justify high valuations that would enable the business to move rapidly to an initial public offering. Some valuations could not be justified and markets now have more realistic expectations. Before embarking on your e-business design, clarify your business aims. Are you building a business for the long-term or is this venture one that you expect to sell in a short time?

77 Make sure you know who your competitors are.

78 Carefully assess potential threats to your proposed business model.

BUILDING A BUSINESS COMMUNITY

As a start-up, it is very likely that you will not have all of the skills needed within your organization. Decide on the core competencies you need in-house, then look for organizations that you can partner with to acquire the skills, functions, and infrastructure that you require. Research electronic business communities (EBCs), which bring outsourcing partners together in a flexible arrangement that can be altered relatively easily as your needs change.

OFFERING ▶ NEW VALUE

This case study shows that even market-leading organizations in very established and low-margin industries can be vulnerable to attack from a small start-up business that successfully identifies and delivers an innovative value proposition.

CASE STUDY

A start-up organization, built on e-business principles, took on real-world market leaders in the bookselling world by identifying and aggressively pursuing a new customer value proposition. A powerful ingredient in the new organization's ability to rattle the market leaders was the recognition that it could use technology to add new value to the book buying public's shopping experience. The organization innovated the book browsing, selection, and buying experience and carefully managed its customers' expectations to achieve new levels of customer satisfaction. It focused on its core competencies and built an electronic supplier community to enable it to take on the heavyweight market leaders. In doing so, it raised customer expectations to a new level that its competitors had to struggle to meet.

RAISING PROFILES

A small organization can have a big presence in the virtual world without the cost of overhead. However, one of the biggest challenges you face is the ability to attract sufficient potential customers to your website. Promoting yourself online may go largely unnoticed. Recognize that real-world advertising will probably be a very significant part of your start-up budget. Seek unpaid advertising through editorial coverage and use your EBC partners' presence in their own markets to extend the reach of your promotions.

▲ ADVERTISING PRESENCE
Real-world advertising, such as sponsorship, will help increase customer awareness of your presence. Look for innovative ways of advertising your presence.

79 Extend your market presence in the real world.

80 Allocate resources to promotion in the real world.

OPERATING IN THE REAL WORLD

Most new e-businesses operate exclusively in the online world, since this offers lower costs and easy access to customers. However, a physical presence can extend your reach. Consider creating a real-world presence by partnering with a retail organization. A store-within-a-store scenario could offer a low-cost entry in key geographic locations and give you an edge over your competitors. Make sure your customer interface in the real world is linked to the same data as your on-line operation.

BRINGING IN A WEB CONSULTANT

Your public website and private intranet site will be crucial elements in your new business design. Unless you have excellent web development skills in-house you will need to work with a consultant or supplier to design and build your sites. Take the time to carefully research a suitable supplier. Make sure that the brief you supply is comprehensive and look at previous examples of their work to ensure that they are capable of creating the type of web presence you need.

LOOKING AT E-MARKETING

Marketers must adapt the techniques they use for broadcast messages, via television, to narrowcast communication, such as via the web. Understand how you can use e-media marketing techniques and look for opportunities for new promotions.

81 Use on-line sponsorship to reach potential customer groups.

THE FOUR PS

Product – spot emerging trends to offer continuous innovation

Price – innovation or added value can justify premium price

Place – customers are targeted through multiple channels

Promotion – shift to focus on a one-on-one approach

REAPPLYING MARKETING

The classic elements of marketing, the four Ps – product, price, place, and promotion – still apply to e-marketing, but they must be reexamined within the context of the new digital environment. In a world where it is increasingly difficult to differentiate products by price, identify how you are adding new value for the customer. Segment your customer base to effectively use the unique targeting abilities offered by e-media.

82 Use a mix of online and offline promotion, but ensure they both use consistent images and messages.

MARKETING THE BRAND

The value of a strong and trusted brand image is crucial to differentiate you from your competitors and encourage customer loyalty. Brands that are already leaders in the physical world have an advantage provided that they can successfully translate their brand values to the online world. If your brand exists solely online, create awareness among your target audience, and portray messages that reflect your brand values.

POINTS TO REMEMBER

- The online medium is more suited to target marketing, rather than mass marketing.
- Test advertising banners on web-sites that attract large numbers of your target customers.
- You should consider developing demographic and psychographic profiles of your targets.

GETTING AHEAD

The interactive and focused nature of digital media means that direct marketing techniques are ideal for one-on-one marketing online. Conduct direct marketing campaigns online and benefit from the ability to measure, in close to real time, the effects of changes to copy, placement, and other variables. Test and refine targeted offerings to key audience groups.

83 Use your website to build customer email lists for use in direct marketing campaigns.

BENEFITTING FROM ONLINE PROMOTIONS

MEDIA	ACTIONS TO TAKE
WEBSITE	Study leading websites for lessons on design and presentation. Keep loading times low and tailor the presentation to support users with older browsers. Analyze the use of your site constantly.
EMAIL	Encourage customers to register with you in order to receive news and updates via email. Only send emails to customers who have chosen to receive them. Use emails for direct marketing.
ONLINE ADVERTISING	Segment your audience, then pick sites that attract your potential customers. Constantly test and refine all aspects of your ads including copy, size, media property, position, and offering.
ONLINE SPONSORSHIP	Use sponsorship to build relationships with key target audiences. Sponsor sites that attract your targets. Reinforce leads generated by sponsorship with advertising and direct marketing.
COMMUNITIES	Identify online communities whose interest area attracts your target customers. Do not alienate users by an overtly commercial approach. Be open when dealing with queries about your products.
MOBILE PHONES	Send customers news and updates via digital mobile phones with the ability to connect to web-based data. Ensure the content is tailored to small display screens.
INTERACTIVE TV	Allow users access to web-based data and email via digital, interactive TV. Using click-through links from programs to suppliers' websites, reach customers via their lifestyle interests.

GETTING CLOSER TO SUPPLIERS

The opportunity to improve the supply chain is an important benefit of e-business. Drive supply chain transformation and gain savings, greater flexibility, and enhanced customer value.

UNDERSTANDING E-SUPPLY

Supply chains vary considerably depending on the size and type of business; but, whatever the setup, streamlined processes offer the best benefits to the end customer. Understand your supply chain and learn how to transform it for e-business.

84 Identify the steps your products take before they reach your customers.

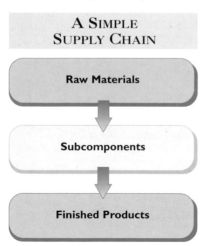

A SIMPLE SUPPLY CHAIN

Raw Materials

Subcomponents

Finished Products

DESCRIBING THE SUPPLY CHAIN

An organization's supply chain is the system that produces the finished products needed to service customers. It invariably consists of several interdependent relationships with suppliers and partners that assist in the sourcing, manufacturing, storage, and distribution of products or services. The supply chain is responsible for adding value to physical goods by taking raw materials and manufacturing, assembling, and distributing them as a finished product. Remember that the chain must also facilitate the flow of information.

FOCUSING ON REQUIREMENTS

Many organizations have concentrated solely on reducing costs in their supply chains. In your e-business, focus on your customers' needs. Deliver what your customer wants, when they want it, and where they want it. Be able to fulfill their demands rapidly and cost-effectively. Aim to improve responsiveness and shorten order cycle times. Ensure you have the support of your supply-chain partners in your aims.

ASSESSING YOUR SUPPLIERS

The increase in outsourcing and the development of tightly integrated electronic business communities (EBCs) are being driven by the urgent need to streamline and integrate all the elements of a supply chain. Suppliers vary from those already using e-business systems, to those for whom integrating IT systems is still a remote ideal. Define the ways in which your partners' systems should integrate with yours and shortlist only suppliers who have the will and the technical abilities to meet your needs.

Suppliers

Manufacturers

Warehousing

Distributors → **Resellers**

CUSTOMER

◀ SUPPLY CHAIN ELEMENTS

The elements of the supply chain are frequently separate entities that cooperate to transform raw materials or components into finished products for distribution to your customer. Along with moving materials and products, the supply chain must also be adept at moving information.

DO'S AND DON'TS

✔ Do recognize that you need the support of your suppliers.

✔ Do work to bind your supply chain together.

✔ Do ensure information flows between all your suppliers and partners.

✘ Don't underestimate the importance of an integrated supply chain.

✘ Don't neglect any one element of your supply chain.

✘ Don't stop monitoring supply chain processes.

85 Look for the bottlenecks in your supply chain and ensure information moves efficiently.

INTEGRATING THE SUPPLY CHAIN

*O*rganizations can no longer work in isolation and must examine their supply chains for opportunities for integration. Understand the benefits of supply chain management and re-engineer your supply chain to remove barriers to information.

86 Understand that information is as important an asset as inventory.

87 Good relationships with partners lead to a better chance of retaining customers and reducing costs.

MANAGING SUPPLY

Each typical key activity within a supply chain is often handled by separate organizations. The purpose of supply chain management (SCM) is the coordination of the flow of information, money, and materials between all the organizations in the chain. Consider adopting internet-enabled SCM to achieve efficient relationships with your partners, reduce costs, and, more importantly, provide competitive advantage in the battle to win and retain customers. Recognize that it is competition between business communities rather than between individual organizations that is changing the face of many industries.

◀ **OPERATIONAL EXCELLENCE**

In this example, a computer business used supply chain management to integrate suppliers into a flexible supply chain that quickly delivered high-quality, customized products at reasonable prices.

CASE STUDY

A computer business identified its best customer value proposition as building top-quality but inexpensive computers and delivering them quickly to the end customer. This required the organization to focus on delivering operational excellence through the creation of an end-to-end process that integrated demand from the sales chain with a flexible supply chain. The organization became one of the leaders in developing SCM solutions to enable it to offer customers a fast and efficient build-to-order service. It recognized that a key supply-chain requirement was the ability to respond quickly to continual changes in customer demand. The web-based customer interface became crucial for delivering real-time demand data, while allowing customers to customize orders online, and check their order status through to final delivery.

REMOVING BARRIERS

Aim to eliminate any barriers to information in your supply chain. This requires optimization of the whole, end-to-end process rather than optimizing processes within a single organization. Until recently, it was almost impossible for an organization to gather sufficient information to synchronize their entire supply chain, so the chain often carried expenses such as incorrect inventory levels. Implement internet-enabled SCM systems to eliminate information barriers between you and your supply chain partners.

88 Ask yourself if your supply chain causes poor customer service and look for SCM solutions.

INTEGRATED SUPPLY CHAIN
Suppliers, manufacturers, warehousing, distributors, and resellers use an internet-enabled SCM database

CUSTOMER
benefits from efficient results and is more likely to reward you with business

▲ FULLY INTEGRATED
Use internet-enabled SCM to eliminate interorganizational barriers, share data, and streamline entire processes.

POINTS TO REMEMBER

- If your supply chain is not integrated, it can lead to poor levels of customer service and nonoptimal inventory levels.
- An SCM system must be integrated with ERP systems.
- ERP systems are a useful research database for SCM planners.

PLANNING AND IMPLEMENTING SCM

Planning and execution are the two key elements of SCM. They are often poorly related in businesses that do not have integrated SCM. Undertake these elements collaboratively with supply chain partners. Your SCM system should eliminate the gap between planning and execution for all your partners, and allow for continual adjustments to your processes using real-time data from the chain.

ELEMENTS OF A SCM SYSTEM

PLANNING	DATA	EXECUTION
● Demand Forecasting	Information must	● Product Management
● Fulfillment	be available in	● Warehousing
● Transportation	real time to all	● Replenishment
● Manufacturing	partners and suppliers	● Distribution
● Scheduling	in the supply chain	● Reverse Logistics

ENSURING FULFILLMENT

Efficient fulfillment means delivering your promises on time. Work with your supply chain partners to give accurate fulfillment promises. Allow customers access to delivery status and keep them fully informed throughout the fulfillment process.

89 Make fulfillment a primary goal of your integrated supply chain.

90 Set fulfillment targets and then track performance.

91 Always aim to exceed customer expectations.

ACHIEVING PROMISES

Few things are guaranteed to upset customers more than a failure to deliver goods or services at the promised time or date. The ability to give accurate promises at the time of order is critical to efficient fulfillment, yet it can only be achieved if you have access to accurate, real-time information. Make sure that your SCM system allows you to constantly and accurately update demand forecasts and calculate accurate delivery promises. Ensure that the promises you make have a safety margin for any problems that may occur.

KEEPING CUSTOMERS INFORMED

Customers should be able to access details of their order, check its status, and confirm delivery through whatever point of contact with your organization – store, website, call center, or kiosk – that they prefer to use. This means that you must be able to give customers access to information that may be held by other organizations in your supply chain.

Customer checks delivery details on internet

GIVING CUSTOMERS ACCESS ▶

Ensure your website links data from all your supply chain partners and allows your customers to gain access easily to order details.

THINGS TO DO

1. Align your supply chain partners with your strategy.

2. Ensure supply chain partners are focused on customers.

3. Train team members in interpersonal skills and business issues needed for collaborative partnerships.

WORKING WITH PARTNERS

Aim to work collaboratively with your suppliers and partners. Think and act as one extended enterprise focused on efficiently delivering a specific form of customer value. This requires new ways of thinking and excellent business, communication, and interpersonal skills. Work to create a project team, led by a senior executive, to manage supply chain reorganization and integration. This team, together with their equivalents from your partners, will be responsible for integrating the entire supply chain.

MANAGING RELATIONSHIPS WITH PARTNERS

MANAGER
Be responsible for ensuring that your team, partners, and suppliers are working toward the same aims and that information is shared and free-flowing at all levels.

TEAM MEMBERS
Train your team members to be responsible for liaising with partners to reorganize and automate the supply chain.

PARTNERS
Treat your partners as an equal part of your business team. Work together to avoid any conflict of interests.

SUPPLIERS
Encourage communication and avoid behaving like the "customer." Accept suppliers as an extension of your business.

92 Use email to confirm order and delivery details to customers.

DO'S AND DON'TS

✔ Do give convenient delivery time options to customers.

✔ Do allow for delays when ensuring that promises can be met.

✘ Don't direct customers to a separate website for delivery details.

✘ Don't make website access time-consuming or complicated.

IMPLEMENTING SCM SYSTEMS

Supply chain management (SCM) implementation is critical to the success of your e-business. Work with your partners to define issues, identify solutions for streamlining processes, make a business case for change, and manage the transformation.

> **93** Only consider SCM applications that are fully internet-enabled.

POINTS TO REMEMBER

- You should understand your organization's strategy and e-business design before embarking on a SCM planning process.
- Your e-business design should describe how your supply chain must service customers.
- You should seek suppliers who are ready to adopt e-business practices and technology.

GETTING STARTED

Aim to merge functions inside your organization and across the supply chain to achieve greater efficiencies. Inherited supply chain applications may not have been designed to work with other systems. Consider whether to replace all inherited systems at once or take a step-by-step approach. Remember that no single organization or decision-maker owns or even fully comprehends the entire interorganizational process that is to be streamlined.

DEFINING YOUR SUPPLY CHAIN PROCESSES

Structure your supply chain processes to reflect your e-business strategy and business design. Your e-business design defines the competencies you intend to keep in-house, and the services you plan to outsource. If you outsource a key element, such as manufacturing, so that you can concentrate on sales and marketing, your supply chain requirements will change markedly.

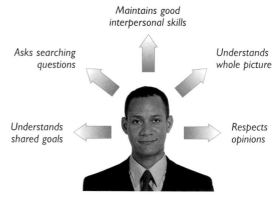

Maintains good interpersonal skills

Asks searching questions

Understands whole picture

Understands shared goals

Respects opinions

▲ **MANAGING INTEGRATION**
A good manager has the qualities needed to lead change positively and is able to work constructively with partners and suppliers to identify the issues that need addressing.

CREATING AN SCM SOLUTION

> **Create an SCM project team and work closely with partners**

⬇

> **Communicate with and educate your team and partners**

⬇

> **Clarify SCM goals and audit the supply chain**

⬇

> **Identify technology options and prepare your business case**

⬇

> **Implement your ideas and new processes**

⬇

> **Use feedback to monitor results and refine future actions**

95 Examine the complete supply chain process to find areas for cost-savings.

STREAMLINING PROCESSES

The goal of your SCM plan is to achieve a process that links all parts of the supply chain and allows all parties access to the information they need in as close to real time as possible. Audit your supply chain to identify where nonessential activities take place. For instance, do you really need to swap purchase orders constantly with your suppliers? Can you share the data directly between each other's SCM or ERP systems?

94 Find examples of activities that are duplicated, repetitive, or redundant, and eliminate them.

QUESTIONS TO ASK YOURSELF

Q Have I identified areas where data is rekeyed unnecessarily?

Q Have I identified barriers to information?

Q Have I identified where costs could be reduced?

Q Have I understood why some SCM systems have not been successful?

Q Do I understand why SCM execution must be carefully managed?

Q Have I clarified the potential rewards of implementing SCM?

MAKING THE CASE

Construct a clear business case to justify the often substantial investment in technology. Address both the strategic and bottom-line benefits that your solution will deliver. There are case studies on the internet from leading organizations that were early adopters of internet-enabled SCM. Many demonstrate excellent return on investment and improved customer service, and some demonstrate the possible pitfalls to be avoided.

COMMUNICATING WELL

Integrating the supply chain is a considerable undertaking that requires close and cooperative working by all partners if it is to be successful. Supply chain reorganization will affect departmental and business unit divisions in all the partner organizations. Problems can occur if there is a lack of individual understanding or commitment to change. Communicate constantly with all parties impacted by the change. Expect to invest considerable resources in educating your staff, suppliers, and partners on the reasons for, and techniques of, optimizing business processes.

96 Plan for ongoing training initiatives to take place.

97 Monitor new processes and continually assess performance.

METHODS OF COMMUNICATING

Ensuring good communication between all parts of your supply chain can be difficult, especially if your partners and suppliers are on the other side of the world. Use your organization's extranet as a key means of ensuring constantly updated information. Create a separate section on your extranet to allow team members to share ideas or issues that need resolving, and use regular email updates to keep everyone abreast of developments. Online video-conferencing is a useful way of bringing participants together without the need to travel to meetings.

CASE STUDY

A start-up organization in the fulfillment market built a systems infrastructure that was entirely internet-based. As a business-to-business supplier, it decided to manage all its communications through its extranet. The organization distributed order and inventory information, customer data, and shipping details via the internet to its partners and customers, and also conducted fund transfers electronically. Because the organization did business via the internet, its physical location was irrelevant to its customers and partners. This meant the organization could reduce overhead by locating in a low-cost area, without the risk of alienating customers. It ran the technology on which it relied through an outsourcing arrangement with a technology provider, who supplied full systems support remotely via the internet.

◀ INTERNET-ENABLED

The global nature of the internet, and its increasing speed and capacity, has had a huge effect on the choices open to businesses. Even key members of the supply chain, such as this specialist fulfillment organization, can be tightly integrated within your internal processes without needing to be located close to your business.

CHOOSING TECHNOLOGY

Ensure you, your partners, and your suppliers have the fundamental network and supporting technologies in place before you implement an SCM system. If these elements are in place, choose between an off-the-shelf (OTS) SCM system or a collection of smaller, tightly integrated applications. Increasingly, organizations are using smaller, web-enabled applications working off shared databases to address issues such as fulfillment.

USING FEEDBACK

It is easy to become so focused on supply chain realignment that you forget its purpose. Always keep in mind that supply chain changes are driven by the goal of delivering customer satisfaction. They are defined by the value proposition your e-business strategy has selected, and their success is measured by the extent that they have delivered value to the customer. Your customers are the best source of SCM performance data so make sure you have the ability to collect and analyze their responses. Always be ready to adjust processes in response to feedback and changing environments.

THINGS TO DO

1. Use your website to monitor customer responses and feedback.

2. Ensure your CRM and SFM systems can relay feedback on process efficiencies.

3. Use feedback constructively to adapt systems and processes where necessary.

RESPONDING TO CUSTOMER FEEDBACK

Actively seek customer feedback and recognize that it is a key ingredient in refining the performance of your supply chain. Your customer will feel valued if they know their views are listened to and acted upon. Use phrases such as these to welcome and react to feedback:

Hearing your comments about our performance helps us to improve the service we give you.

Please let us know if any part of our product or service fails to meet your highest expectations.

How can we change our performance to ensure that your needs are met successfully in the future?

How can we best resolve your complaint to ensure that you receive complete satisfaction?

SAVING MONEY
WITH E-PROCUREMENT

Procurement refers to the process of acquiring the goods and services that keep an organization functioning, such as office equipment or travel. Adopt web-based applications to provide a new approach to procurement and reap the benefits.

98 Recognize the cost savings available from automating procurement.

99 Give staff access to procurement online.

100 Integrate your procurement and back-office systems.

DEFINING PROCUREMENT

The terms procurement and purchasing are often used as if they are interchangeable, but purchasing is only one part of procurement. Purchasing covers the buying part of the process, but procurement also includes selection, authorization, and delivery. Paper-based procurement requires a series of forms and authorization, which take employees time to fill, chase, and process. Adopt e-procurement and give staff less paperwork and more time.

PUTTING EMPLOYEES IN CONTROL

Put procurement online on your corporate intranet, and give your staff the benefits of self-service. Use web-based procurement applications so that employees can access authorized suppliers' catalogs from within their own intranet. If you retain control of supplier approval and online catalogs, then you can ensure corporate purchasing standards are followed.

Employee accesses online catalog

▲ **AUTOMATING APPROVAL**
Make sure that the ordering system allows staff to check availability and delivery details online and that it automates approval and purchase order systems.

IMPLEMENTING E-PROCUREMENT

Make sure your purchasing team is empowered to manage the e-procurement implementation to ensure that employee controls are retained in the automated system. Install workflow systems that automate approval and authorization tasks according to each employee's level of authority. Online systems allow you to give each employee a purchasing profile that controls the goods and quantities they are authorized to purchase.

> **IOI** Focus procurement systems on reducing order-cycle times and organizational overhead.

BENEFITS OF E-PROCUREMENT

Automate repetitive and time-wasting tasks

↓

Employees have access to suppliers' catalogs online

↓

Purchasing staff have time to negotiate better deals

↓

Employees and organization benefit from efficiencies

REAPING THE BENEFITS OF E-PROCUREMENT

BENEFICIARIES	BENEFITS
ORGANIZATION	Significant cost savings are made from greater efficiency in the processes of procurement and the resulting greater employee productivity.
EMPLOYEES	Employees benefit from a reduction in repetitive tasks and increased time to focus on real business issues. They have convenient, simplified choices to make.
PROCUREMENT SPECIALISTS	They receive better purchasing information and are in a strong position to make good deals with e-procurement suppliers. They are able to manage supply more efficiently.
SUPPLIERS	They benefit from a loyal partnership with your organization and more efficient ordering systems. They therefore maintain an advantage over their competitors.

Assessing Your E-Business Skills

*E*valuate your readiness for e-business by responding to the following statements, marking the option closest to your experience. Be as honest as you can: if your answer is "never," circle Option 1; if it is "always," circle Option 4, and so on. Add your scores together and refer to the Analysis to see how you scored. Use your answers to identify areas of e-business that you should focus on for improvement.

Options
1 Never
2 Occasionally
3 Frequently
4 Always

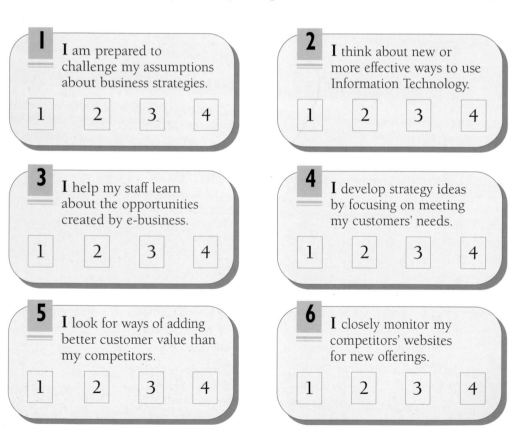

1 I am prepared to challenge my assumptions about business strategies.

1   2   3   4

2 I think about new or more effective ways to use Information Technology.

1   2   3   4

3 I help my staff learn about the opportunities created by e-business.

1   2   3   4

4 I develop strategy ideas by focusing on meeting my customers' needs.

1   2   3   4

5 I look for ways of adding better customer value than my competitors.

1   2   3   4

6 I closely monitor my competitors' websites for new offerings.

1   2   3   4

7 I encourage my staff to suggest and implement process improvements.

1 2 3 4

8 I utilize a dynamic planning method for e-business developments.

1 2 3 4

9 I make sure that my staff receive regular training to help cope with changes.

1 2 3 4

10 I look for ways to integrate separate functions into an end-to-end process.

1 2 3 4

11 I focus on ensuring that we know and fulfill our customers' expectations.

1 2 3 4

12 I look for ways to make our supplier relationships more effective and less costly.

1 2 3 4

ANALYSIS

Now you have completed the self-assessment, add up your total score and check your performance by referring to the corresponding evaluation. Whatever your level of e-business skills, remember that technology and the resulting business opportunities move on rapidly, and you must make an effort to keep in touch with new developments. Identify your weakest areas, and refer to the relevant sections in this book for guidance and advice.

12–24: Your e-business skills are quite limited: work on developing them if you are to benefit yourself and your organization.
25–36: You have a sound grasp of many e-business issues: review your weaker areas to improve those skills.
37–48: Your understanding of e-business is good: focus on continually keeping up-to-date.

INDEX

E

U

ACKNOWLEDGMENTS

PUBLISHER'S ACKNOWLEDGMENTS

Dorling Kindersley would like to thank the following for their help and participation in producing this book:

Editorial Corinne Asghar, Alison Bolus, Michael Downey, Richard Hammond, Kate Hayward, Amanda Lebentz, Nicola Munro, Sean O'Connor, Daphne Richardson, Jane Simmonds, David Tombesi-Walton, Sylvia Tombesi-Walton, Mark Wallace; **Design** Helen Bracey, Arthur Brown, Pauline Clarke, Sarah Cowley, Emma Forge, Jamie Hanson, Caroline Marklew, Sharon Moore, Nigel Morris, Tish Mills, Laura Watson; **DTP assistance** Rob Campbell, Jason Little; **Indexer** Sue Lightfoot; **Proofreading** Polly Boyd, John Sturges; **Photography** Steve Gorton, Paul Mattock, Gary Ombler, Richard Parsons; Matthew Ward. **Photography assistance** Silvia Bucher, Nici Harper, Andy Komorowski; **Picture research** Anna Grapes, Franziska Marking, Jamie Robinson, Andy Sansom, Andrea Stadler; **Picture library assistance** Sue Hadley, Rachel Hilford, Denise O'Brien, Melanie Simmonds.

Models Tracey Allanson, Roger André, Phil Argent, Clare Borg, Angela Cameron, Anne Chapman, Kuo Kang Chen, Brent Clark, Jane Cooke, Russell Cosh, Roberto Costa, Felicity Crow, Sander deGroot, Patrick Dobbs, Miles Elliot, Carol Evans, Vosjava Fahkro, Jeanie Fraser, Mark Fraser, John Gillard, Ben Glickman, Lucy Kelly, Emma Harris, Kate Hayward, Nigel Hill, Richard Hill, Gill Hooton, Cornell John, Aziz Khan, Janey Madlani, Zahid Malik, Maggie Mant, Frankie Mayers, Sotiris Meliomis, Sophie Millett, Roger Mundy, Karen Murray, Chantal Newall, Mutsumi Niwa, Mary Jane Robinson, Kiran Shah, Lois Sharland, Lynne Staff, Kaz Takabatake, Suki Tan, Peter Taylor, Anastasia Vengeroua, Dominica Warburton, Michael Weinkove, Ann Winterborn, Roberta Woodhouse, Gilbert Wu, Wendy Yun.

Makeup Nicky Clarke, Evelynne, Debbie Finlow, Jane Hope-Kavanagh, Janice Tee.

Special thanks to the following for their help:

Ron and Chris at Clark Davis & Co. Ltd for stationery and furniture supplies; Pam Bennett and the staff at Jones Bootmakers, Covent Garden, for the loan of footwear; Alan Pfaff and the staff at Moss Bros, Covent Garden, for the loan of the men's suits; David Bailey for his help and time; Graham Preston and the staff at Staverton for their time and space, Tony Ash at Geiger Brickel (Office Furniture) and Carron Williams at Bally (Shoes).

Suppliers Apple Computer UK Ltd, Austin Reed, Bally, Cadogan and James, Church & Co., Clark Davis & Co. Ltd, Compaq, David Clulow Opticians, Elonex, Escada, Filofax, Gateway 2000, Gieves and Hawkes, Geiger Brickel, Marc Holman, Jones Bootmakers, Moss Bros, Mucci Bags, Positive (Computing), Staverton, Viper Microsystems.

PICTURE CREDITS

Key: *b* bottom, *c* center, *l* left, *r* right, *t* top

Ace Photo Agency: 638*bl*; ©1995-2000 **Agfa-Gevaert Group:** 712; Alan Thornton 666*cb*; **Allsport** John Cameron/APL/AllsportUSA 26; Clive Mason 813*tr*; ©2000 **Apple Computer Inc:** 735*tr*; **BT Archives/Pictures:** 715*tc*; **Colorific** M Hardwick 412; **Compaq Computer Corp:** 715*c*; **Corbis UK Ltd:** 657*br*; R W Jones 764; **Elizabeth Whiting Associates** 24; **Empics Ltd:** Steve Lipofsky 261*tr*; Tony Marshall 230*tr*; ©2000 **Iomega Corporation:** 713*tr*; **NASA** 120*b*; **Pictor International:** 628, 635*bl*, 689*tr*; **Powerstock/ZEFA** 30, 33, John Lawrence 49; 311, 315 *tr*, Index 335 *br*, 346 *bl*; Raoul Minsart 288; 391, 424, 426; 587, 621; 732, 741; **Robert Harding Picture Library:** 791*br*; **Science Photo Library:** George Bernard 709*b*; **Sporting Pictures (UK) Ltd** 272*bl*; **The Stock Market** Philip Wallick 513; Jon Feingersh 601; **Superstock Ltd:** 220; 456; 523*t*, 536; 663*bl*, 676*cr*; **Telegraph Colour Library** Bavaria Bildagentur 476; 492; 576; 686*bl*; B&M Productions 36; Benelux Press 127*tr*, 162, Larry Bray 123*l*, Rob Brimson 271*br*; Paul Campbell 369; Jim Cummings 696; 806*br*; FPG/M Malyszko 349 *bl*; Elke Hebber 211; Terry McCormick 206; Ryanstock 84, 303,.384; Ed Taylor 152; 222*bl*; **Tony Stone Images** Bruce Ayres 53, John Blaustein 77, Donovan Reese 16; Walter Hodges 174, 196, Antonio Mo 190, Stephen Peters 154, Walter Hodges 245*tr*; Ken Fisher 356, Stephen Peters 363 *tl*; Stewart Cohen 568, Peter Correz 575; Dan Bosler 748; Paul Kenward 726; Robert Mort 700; 770*br*, Christopher Bissell 788*bl*; **UPS:** 656*bl*; 782*cl*

AUTHORS

Moi Ali has worked in marketing for over 15 years and runs her own public relations and marketing company, specializing in clients with limited budgets – in particular small businesses and charities. She is a regular contributor to marketing and PR journals and is the author of a number of books.

Stephen Brookson qualified as a chartered accountant with KPMG and went on to work for Ernst & Young before setting up his own management and training consultancy. He has presented seminars and training events in many countries, and is the author of *Mastering Financial Management*.

Andy Bruce is the founder of SofTools Limited – a specialized business research and consulting company. Following completion of a largely academic MBA program, he has spent the past eight years helping a variety of organizations manage major projects and cope with change in the real world – more information on tools and techniques can be found at www.SofTools.net.

Dr. John Eaton PhD is a founder and director of Coaching Solutions, an innovative company offering executive coaching and training programs in coaching skills to blue-chip concerns throughout the UK. He contributes regularly to such journals as *Theory and Psychology*, *Organisations and People*, and *Changes and Training Journal*. He is also, with Roy Johnson, the author of *Business Applications of NLP: 30 Activities for Training*.

Robert Heller is a leading authority in the world of management consulting and was the founding editor of Britain's top management magazine, *Management Today*. He is much in demand as a conference speaker in Europe, North and South America, and the Far East. As editorial director of Haymarket Publishing Group, Robert Heller supervised the launch of several highly successful magazines such as *Campaign*, *Computing*, and *Accountancy Age*. His many acclaimed – and worldwide best-selling – books include *The Naked Manager*, *Culture Shock*, *The Age of the Common Millionaire*, *The Way to Win* (with Will Carling), *The Complete Guide to Modern Management*, and *In Search of European Excellence*. Robert Heller has also written a number of earlier books in the Dorling Kindersley *Essential Managers* series

Roy Johnson MBA is a founder and director of Coaching Solutions and is also director of Pace – an award-winning management and sales training company with a wide variety of medium- to large-sized clients. He is the author of *40 Activities for Training in NLP* and co-author of *Business Applications of NLP: 30 Activities for Training*. He and John Eaton have recently launched their new on-line coaching skills training service at www.coachskills.com

Ken Langdon has a background in sales and marketing in the computer industry. As an independent consultant he has lectured on strategic thinking and planning in the US, Europe, and Australasia. He has helped companies, big and small, to review their strategies at board level and widely at team level. Companies for whom he has provided strategic guidance include computer majors such as Hewlett Packard, and utilities companies, such as a European electricity supplier.

Steve Sleight is an author and independent consultant with a background in writing, broadcasting, and communications. He has advised several prominent international companies on communications strategies as well as the use of IT and digital, interactive media to enhance their projects. Most recently, he has been developing an e-business approach to information publishing and he is now concentrating on producing digital, multimedia content that can be presented and delivered in traditional or new media forms. He writes on business subjects as well as on his real, all-consuming passion, sailing. He is the author of *Essential Managers: Information Technology* as well as the DK *Complete Sailing Manual*.